# Principles
# of Sociology

# Principles of Sociology

## Canadian Perspectives

Edited by
Lorne Tepperman / James Curtis

OXFORD
UNIVERSITY PRESS

# OXFORD
## UNIVERSITY PRESS

70 Wynford Drive, Don Mills, Ontario M3C 1J9
www.oup.com/ca

Oxford University Press is a department of the University of Oxford.
It furthers the University's objective of excellence in research, scholarship,
and education by publishing worldwide in

Oxford   New York

Auckland   Cape Town   Dar es Salaam   Hong Kong   Karachi
Kuala Lumpur   Madrid   Melbourne   Mexico City   Nairobi
New Delhi   Shanghai   Taipei   Toronto

With offices in

Argentina   Austria   Brazil   Chile   Czech Republic   France   Greece
Guatemala   Hungary   Italy   Japan   Poland   Portugal   Singapore
South Korea   Switzerland   Thailand   Turkey   Ukraine   Vietnam

Oxford is a trade mark of Oxford University Press
in the UK and in certain other countries

Published in Canada
by Oxford University Press

Copyright © Oxford University Press Canada 2006

The moral rights of the author have been asserted

Database right Oxford University Press (maker)

First published 2006

Statistics Canada information is used with the permission of Statistics Canada. Users are forbidden
to copy the data and redisseminate them, in an original or modified form, for commercial purposes,
without the expressed permission of Statistics Canada. Information on the availability of the wide
range of data from Statistics Canada can be obtained from Statistics Canada's Regional Offices, its
World Wide Web site at http://www.statcan.ca, and its toll-free access number 1-800-263-1136.

**Library and Archives Canada Cataloguing in Publication Data**

Principles of sociology : Canadian perspectives / edited by Lorne Tepperman and James Curtis.

Includes bibliographical references and index.

ISBN-13: 978-0-19-542348-8
ISBN-10: 0-19-542348-8

1. Sociology—Textbooks. 2. Canada—Social conditions—1991– —Textbooks.
I. Curtis, James E., 1943–  II. Tepperman, Lorne, 1943–

HM586.P75 2006          301          C2005-906439-0

Cover design: Brett J. Miller
Cover image: Take Two/© stockbyte

1 2 3 4 - 09 08 07 06
This book is printed on permanent (acid-free) paper ∞.
Printed in Canada

# Contents

# Detailed Contents

# Preface

For twenty years, I have been writing and editing textbooks introducing students to sociology. The present book is a brief version of a longer book that, itself, was the fourth edition of a book, originally titled *The Social World*, that I starting working on in 1984.

The first edition was published in 1986 by McGraw-Hill Ryerson and co-edited by Lorne Tepperman and Jack Richardson (who gave the book its name). It provided an up-to-date picture of Canadian society and sociology in the late twentieth century. Our goal was to provide a high-quality Canadian textbook, written by Canadian experts in the important subfields of sociology, for students at Canadian colleges and universities. In short, we wanted to teach Canadians about Canada and about sociology, and, in that way, make a modest contribution to both Canadian society and Canadian sociology.

A lot has happened since 1984, in every area of life. Just think about a few of those changes. For example, most readers of the present book had not yet been born. Televisions were in every home in 1984, but VCRs, CD players, DVD players, and computers were not. Try to imagine a world without e-mail, the Internet, or PlayStation! Health problems and health possibilities were different then. AIDS was scarcely registering on people's consciousness. SARS hadn't crippled the country and the Ebola virus wasn't part of everyday culture. There was little or no concern about germ warfare, West Nile, the avian flu, or anti-biotic resistant superbugs. Genetic engineering was still a dream (or a nightmare) and no one had yet mapped the human gene. What we now call the 'new reproductive technology' scarcely existed.

Twenty years ago, the Soviet Union, Yugoslavia, and the Berlin Wall still existed. Communism was a functioning political system in many societies. The Cold War persisted, as did a balance of power between the United States and the USSR. Novels and movies about communist espionage were popular. Islam had scarcely registered on Westerners' attention span. Japan and the rest of East Asia were just starting to infiltrate our consciousness.

We feared different things twenty years ago. For example, overpopulation was a greater world concern as fertility rates were high and still rising in many "developing" countries. Ecology and pollution were new and growing concerns, but there was little concern with homelessness. People knew the Canadian population was aging, but there was little concern about mandatory retirement or how the economy would support the retired elderly population. Fears of war were muted and fears of terrorism were virtually non-existent, at least in North America.

In 1984 tattooing and body piercing were rare and considered bizarre. Homosexuality was hidden. Marriage and divorce were common but cohabitation was relatively rare and not socially acceptable among middle-aged middle-class people. Most people shunned childbirth and parenting outside of marriage. Women were slowly gaining equality with men, as they still are, but many more men than now expressed ridicule at the idea of gender equality, which they characterized as mere bra burning or bitchiness.

Quebec separatism was a much bigger cultural concern in 1984 than it is today. Now, globalization is the main focus of concern. Canada was multicultural in those days, but less multicultural than it is now. The large-scale immigrations from Asia, Africa, South America, and the West Indies had yet to reach a peak. Since 1984, international trade has also grown dramatically and globalization has more completely assimilated Canada into a worldwide trading network dominated by the United States. Contending for influence in this new global economy are a growing European Economic Community and various aggressive new economies, many of them in Asia—Japan, China, Taiwan, and Singapore, among others.

Other important things have happened since I first began working on *The Social World* and its descendants, *Sociology: A Canadian Perspective* and *Principles of Sociology: Canadian Perspectives*. Jack Richardson, who worked on the first two editions of the book, passed away in 2002. Jim Curtis, who worked on the last two editions of the book and helped design the present book, passed away in May of 2005. Both Jim and Jack are sorely missed. Both were outstanding scholars and wonderful people; what's more, both Jim and Jack believed in the power of knowledge—especially sociological knowledge—to improve the world.

On behalf of Jim and Jack, I hope this book continues to provide an up-to-date picture of Canadian society and Canadian sociology at the beginning of the twenty-first century. What has not changed is our commitment to providing the best, most reader-friendly presentation of social facts and theories. Our publisher, Oxford University Press of Canada, has helped us do so, and we are grateful for this help. Acquisitions Editor Lisa Meschino has guided and encouraged us. It has been a great pleasure working with Lisa on this project, as on other projects over the past two years. I also want to thank editor Stephanie Fysh. It is Stephanie who, with preliminary advice from Jim and I, refashioned the textbook that you now hold. Stephanie is one of the best editors I have worked with in decades of writing books; her assistance has always been supportive, enlightening, and provocative. I also want to thank Phyllis Wilson and Jessica Coffey for having a final read through the manuscript and otherwise taking care of the backstage practical matters at Oxford—making sure that all the pieces come together when and where they should. And thanks to those talented people who took the photos and painted the pictures that appear in this great-looking book.

Our main thanks are extended to the authors of chapters in most recent version of *Sociology: A Canadian Perspective*, whose work formed the basis of this streamlined version. Without their work, this book would not exist. They put up with our (seemingly endless) demands and cavils, and somehow we all got from A to B without any homicides or other untoward emotional displays. It has been a great privilege working with this distinguished group of top Canadian scholars from all over the country. Thank you, authors.

In closing, I dedicate this book to my two friends and colleagues, Jack Richardson and Jim Curtis, who helped to build earlier versions of this book and, in countless other ways, enriched our lives. Sociology misses you and so do I. However, your own hope for this book—that it might contribute to Canadian sociology and the education of young Canadian scholars—remains alive. I hope the readers of this book will agree.

Lorne Tepperman, University of Toronto

## From the Publisher

In preparing *Principles of Sociology: Canadian Perspectives*, the general editors, chapter authors, and publisher have from the start kept in mind one paramount goal: to produce the most authoritative, comprehensive, yet accessible and interesting introduction to sociology available for Canadian students. In streamlining the material for this publication, a number of the chapters from the previous edition of *Sociology: A Canadian Perspective* have been combined to provide a tighter, more concise editorial focus. Bruce Arai, Joseph M. Bryant, James Curtis, and Lorne Tepperman, all previous chapter authors, graciously allowed us the editorial free reign to merge their ideas and perspectives together to create a more theoretical introduction to the text as a whole.

Because the roles and identities we maintain as individuals so closely relate to the groups and organizations that we participate in on a daily basis, the work of Cheryl Albas and Dan Albas on roles merged seamlessly with the work by Jack Richardson and Lorne Tepperman on organizations.

In a similar vein, Frank Trovato's earlier chapter on population, William Michelson's work on cities and urbanization, and G. Keith Warriner's writing about the environment have been tightened into a solid and well-supported discussion on the role of the Canadian society in the global context. And finally, thanks are extended to Peter R. Sinclair, John Veugelers, and Randle Hart, for allowing us to merge their work on politics and political movements (Sinclair) and social movements (Veugelers and Hart) into a thorough and detailed study of the Canadian political structure and its affect on Canadian sociology. Additionally, we have welcomed a new contributor—Augie Fleras—to the collection, with his chapter about mass media communication.

Among the features of the text designed to enhance usefulness and interest for students and instructors alike:

**Top Canadian contributors**. Sociology is a global discipline, but one to which sociologists working in and studying Canada have made unique contributions. Not merely an adaptation of an American book, this textbook was conceived and written from the ground up as a Canadian perspective on this fascinating field. Experts in their particular sub-disciplines examine not only the key concepts and terminology of sociology as an academic subject, but also use those concepts to shed light on the nature of Canadian society and Canada's place in the world.

**Global perspective**. Although this is a book written by and for Canadians, the editors and authors never forget that Canada is but one small part of a vast, diverse, and endlessly fascinating social world. Along with Canadian data, examples, and illustrations, a wealth of information about how humans live and interact with the world around is presented in every chapter.

**Theoretical balance**. The very mention of the term "theory" seems to make first-year undergraduates uneasy, but the overriding goal in *Principles of Sociology: Canadian Perspectives* has been not only to make the theories that underpin the discipline comprehensible, but to show how they inform one's understanding of the data that sociologists gather— and how the choice of which theoretical perspective to employ can yield new and surprising insights.

**Aids to student learning**. A textbook must fulfill a double duty: while meeting instructors expectations for accuracy, currency, and comprehensiveness, it must also speak to the needs and interests of today's students, providing them with an accessible introduction to a body of knowledge. To that end, numerous features to promote student learning are incorporated throughout the book, including:

• *Learning Objectives* at the start of each chapter, which provide a concise overview of the key concepts to be covered.
• *Theme Boxes* illustrating important points and providing examples of how sociological research sheds light on the 'real world'. These theme boxes have been divided into four categories: *Sociology in Action*, to show how sociological research can help us better understand the everyday world; *Open for Discussion*, to focus understanding of core concepts through contemporary social issues and debates; *Global Issues*, to show the various opinions and discussions held by sociologists on matters of global importance; and *Human Diversity*, to show students how the unavoidable and overwhelming level of human diversity impacts issues at local, national, and global levels.

**Global Issues**
Changing Views of Men

While most of the research and writing on changing relations between the sexes has focused on women, in the last two decades there has been a flurry of publications that look at emerging patterns for men. Analysis of advertising offers just one example of this trend.

In her examination of the representation of males in advertising, Judith Posner (1987) found that the new male is smaller, has a less pronounced jaw, and is more likely to smile. He is also more likely to be found undressing or partially dressed, and he appears more vulnerable. Yet Posner concludes that this does not reflect a move toward equality, but rather demonstrates "the increasing commercialization of sexuality" for both men and women (1987: 188).

In another analysis of advertising, Andrew Wernick argues that as women have moved into the labour force, men have become more involved in private consumption; this change has been reflected in "a steady drive to incorporate male clothing into fashion, and mounting efforts to sell men all manner of personal-care products, from toothpaste and bath oil to hair dye and make-up" (1987: 279). Wernick suggests that men are being subjected to the same kind of "intense consumerization as women and are no longer defined as breadwinners" (279). More recently, however, Varda Burstyn (1999) has argued that both advertising in sports and the practice of sport promotes what she calls "hypermasculinity."

**Human Diversity**
Who Are the Deviants?

In 1969, the sociologist J.L. Simmons (1969) reported the results of a small study in which he asked 180 respondents to list people and things they regarded as deviant." His respondents varied by gender, age, and other socio-demographic characteristics.

The list of people and behaviours nominated was extensive, with more than 250 items. Many of the categories suggested by respondents were expected, including (in the language of the day) homosexuals, prostitutes, drug addicts, radicals, and criminals.

However, the list also included liars, career women, reckless drivers, atheists, Christians, the

retired, card players, bearded men, artists, pacifists, priests, girls who wear makeup, divorcées, perverts, smart-aleck students, know-it-all professors, modern people, and Americans.

It might be interesting to conduct a small follow-up survey to see what sort of list that question might generate (among your classmates, for example). As well, it worth speculating what such a list teaches us about everyday understandings of deviance and what the list generated by Simmons might reveal about the historical period during which it was made.

**Sociology in Action**
"Emotional Labour": Is Marx's Concept of Alienation Relevant Today?

Arlie Hochschild has appropriated Marx's concept of alienation, making it more relevant today by applying it to service employees. Hochschild re-examines alienation by comparing Marx's vignette of a factory worker's arm pressing a lever all day and thereby becoming alienated from her tools of production, her smiles.

In her analysis of flight attendants, Hochschild refers to "emotional labor," meaning "the management of feeling to create a publicly observable facial and bodily display" (1983: 7). One of the pillars of Hochschild's argument is that a flight attendant's smile is appropriated or alienated from the individual flight attendant, through airline advertising that stresses smiling flight attendants. Hochschild describes the smile as the emotional tool used by flight attendants to complete their jobs. Not smiling is not "okay." In Hochschild's words, "emotional labor

is sold for a wage and therefore has *exchange value*" (1983: 7). Flight attendants, like Marx's factory workers, do not own the means of production and so the seller/labourer does not reap the profits.

Hochschild's concept of emotional labour is a mutation and extension of the concept of alienation. Hochschild is concerned with the psychological consequences of emotional labour and the alienation of emotions. She argues that the alienated labour cannot be utterly faked, which leaves flight attendants not as actresses, but as the "givers" in a non-reciprocal relationship with customers. In short, they feel emotionally drained. Hochschild's work may be of particular concern in future because evidence suggests that the service industry will continue to be a key industry while manufacturing will continue to decrease in wealthier nations.

**Open for Discussion**
Do the Media Contribute to Disordered Eating Among Young Adolescent and Pre-adolescent Girls?

Most women in fashion magazines, movies, and television are pencil-thin. Indeed, the media create an impression that thinness is highly valued in Western society. Viewers of all ages use these images as points of comparison when evaluating their own body image. No wonder body dissatisfaction is universal. Kevin Thompson and Leslie Heinberg (1999) connect exposure to unrealistically thin images in magazines and television with body dissatisfaction and disordered eating among girls and women. Their solution is to counter these extreme images: "The media itself

is one potential vehicle for communicating productive, accurate, and deglamorized messages about eating and shape-related disorders" (339).

What do you think about this issue? Are girls susceptible to images of ultra-thin models? Are girls more susceptible than young boys? In what other ways besides the mass media is thinness reinforced? How do we reconcile media images with reports of increased numbers of obese children and youth? Does the solution lie, as these authors suggest, in changing the images in the media, or is it a larger and more complex problem?

• *Graphs and Tables* assist students in understanding the essential quantitative data that is increasingly important to the study of sociology, and allows trends and patterns to be seen in a way that written text does not.
• *Annotated Recommended Readings*, listed at the end of each chapter, point the students toward useful sources for further research and study.
• *Annotated Recommended Web Sites* direct readers to additional resources, with useful commentary that will assists students as they navigate through the tremendous volume of information available online.
• *Questions for Critical Thought* at the end of each chapter draw out key issues and to encourage readers to draw their own conclusions about sociological issues.
• A *Glossary* located at the end of the book defines important terms, which have been highlighted in **bold** throughout the textbook.

**Contemporary design**. Much as society and sociology have changed over the past twenty years, so too has textbook design. We have striven for a look that is contemporary yet clear and clean, a design that reflects the vibrancy and excitement of sociology today without sacrificing content or authoritativeness. The use of colour and novel design elements is a necessary acknowledgment to the changes wrought by new media and how readers expect information to be packaged and presented. At the same time we remain well aware that this is indeed a printed book, with both the limitations and the very real and enduring strengths that are a product of the print's long history as the pre-eminent method of codifying and transmitting knowledge.

**Supplements**. Today's texts are no longer volumes that stand on their own, but instead are the central element of a complete learning and teaching package. *Principles of Sociology: Canadian Perspectives* is no exception. The book is supported by an outstanding array of ancillary materials for both students and instructors.

## For The Instructor

**Instructor's manual**. The instructor's manual, available from the online companion Web site (http://www.oup.com/ca/he/companion/teppermanprinciples), includes comprehensive outlines of the text's various parts and chapters, additional questions for encouraging class discussion, and suggestions on how to use videos to enhance your classes. Extra material for use in lectures, including Lorne L. Dawson's previously published chapter on religion, is also available.

**Test bank**. A comprehensive collection of multiple choice, true/false, short answer, and essay questions, and suggested answers, are available on the companion web site.

**PowerPoint® slides**. Hundreds of slides are available for classroom use to adopters of the text. The slides incorporate the figures and tables from the textbook, summarize key points from each chapter, and

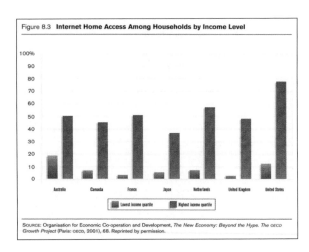

Figure 8.3 **Internet Home Access Among Households by Income Level**

SOURCE: Organisation for Economic Co-operation and Development, *The New Economy: Beyond the Hype. The OECD Growth Project* (Paris: OECD, 2001), 68. Reprinted by permission.

allow for each user to download and edit the slides in order to customize individual lectures.

Instructors should contact their Oxford University Press sales representative for details on these supplements and for login and password information.

## Student Supplements

**Companion Web site**. Visit http://www.oup.com/ca/he/companion/teppermanprinciples for details about the accompanying Web site. Available resources include annotated links to other useful resources and automatically graded study questions. Students will not require login or password information to access this material.

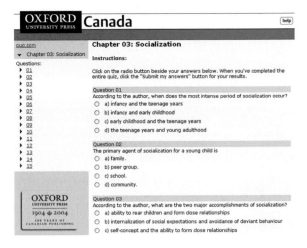

This book is dedicated to a friend and leading Canadian sociologist, James (Jim) Curtis, who passed away on 27 May 2005. Jim was convinced that good sociology could improve our society. His desire to teach another generation of sociologists lives on in this book.

# part one

>  >  >

## Introduction:
## The Sociological Approach

# 1

Bruce Arai, Joseph M. Bryant,
James Curtis, and Lorne Tepperman

> > >

# Sociology: Its Purposes, Theories, and Research Approaches

© PhotoDisc, Inc.

## ☐ Learning Objectives

In this chapter, you will:

- learn about the purposes of sociology and the types of questions sociologists attempt to understand and answer
- examine the difference in perspective between macrosociology and microsociology
- consider the difference between sociology and other academic fields that also study human behaviour
- explore the meanings of the two basic phenomena studied by sociology—social structure and culture—and how the two relate to each other
- learn about the development of sociology, its major founders (Karl Marx, Émile Durkheim, and Max Weber), and their main ideas and contributions
- see the basic elements of four major approaches in sociology: functionalist, conflict, symbolic interactionist, and feminist
- review the basic research techniques in sociology
- consider the role of sociology in creating social and cultural change

# Introduction

Why does someone become a sociologist? There are many answers to this question, but some of them can be summarized with the expression, "It is a wonder that everyone doesn't want to become a sociologist." We say this because all people experience peculiar facts of social life that affect their opportunities, and they try to understand them. This is where sociology begins for most people. When people proceed from here, there is even more motivation to do sociology. What can be more fascinating, more empowering, and more personal than to begin to understand the society that shapes our lives? For these reasons, sociology is an inherently attractive area of study, and many people do study it.

Maybe as a child you noticed that

- Parents sometimes treat their sons differently from their daughters.
- Teachers often treat pretty little girls better than plain-looking ones.
- Adults treat well-dressed children better than poorly dressed children.
- Movies typically portray people with "accents" as strange or ridiculous.

If you noticed these things, you may have wondered why they happen. They may even have affected you, as a daughter or son, a plain-looking or attractive person, a poorly dressed or well-dressed person, or a person with or without an "accent." You may have felt ashamed, angry, or pleased, depending on whether you identified with the favourably treated or the unfavourably treated category of people.

All sociologists, sometime or another, got hooked on trying to better understand their own lives and the lives of people around them. They also came to understand that common sense gave them only incomplete explanations about what happened to people, about people's behaviour, and about the society in which they live. They were not satisfied with the incomplete explanation and wanted to know more.

For many people, and for much of what we do, common-sense understanding is just fine. Still, for anyone who *really* wants to understand how society works, it is not good enough. You may already realize that there are many questions common sense cannot answer adequately. For example,

- Why are some people so different from you, and why are some so similar?
- Why do apparently similar people lead such different lives?

- How is it possible for different people to get along?
- Why do we treat some people as if they are more "different" than others?
- Why do we often treat "different" people much worse than others?
- What do people do to escape from being treated badly?
- Why do some aspects of society change very quickly and others hardly at all?
- What can citizens do to make Canadian society a more equitable place?
- What can young people do to make their elders think differently?
- Can we bring about social change by changing the laws of the country?

Sociologists try to answer these questions by studying societies methodically. They want to understand how societies change and how people's lives change with them. Social changes, inequalities, and conflicts captivate sociologists because such issues—war and peace, wealth and poverty, environmental destruction and technological innovation, for example—are very important for people's lives. However, sociologists always see two sides to these issues: a macro side and a micro side. They know that "personal problems" are very similar across many individuals. They know that many of our personal problems are the private side of public issues. As such, we need to deal with them collectively and, often, politically—with full awareness that we share these problems and their solution with others.

However, solving problems entails clear thinking and careful research. Consequently, sociologists have developed concepts, theories, and research methods that help them investigate the social world more effectively. Our goal as sociologists is to be able to explain social life, critique social inequities, and work towards effecting social change. In this book, you will learn how sociologists go about these tasks, and some of what sociologists have found out about the social world.

Our starting point in this chapter is a formal definition of *sociology*, comparisons of sociology with other related fields of study, and a discussion of sociology's most basic subject matter.

# A Definition of Sociology

Scholars have defined **sociology** in many ways, but most practising sociologists think of their discipline as the systematic study of social behaviour in human societies. Humans are intensely social beings and spend most of their time interacting with other humans. That is why sociologists study the social units people create when they join with others. As we will see in the following chapters, these units range from small groups—comprising as few as two people—to large corporations and even whole societies (see Chapter 4, on social organization). Sociologists are interested in learning about how group membership affects individual behaviour and, reciprocally, how individuals change the groups of which they are members. In most social life, at least in Canadian society, there is a visible tug-of-war between these two forces: the group and the individual.

It is impossible for any sociologist, however, to study all social issues or to become an expert in all the subareas of sociology. As a result, most sociologists specialize in either macrosociology or microsociology—two related but distinct approaches to studying the social world—and choose problems for study from within these realms.

**Macrosociology** is the study of large social organizations (for example, the Roman Catholic Church, universities, corporations, or government bureaucracies) and large social categories (for example, ethnic minorities, the elderly, or college students). Sociologists who specialize in the macrosociological approach focus on the complex social patterns that people form over long periods (see many examples in Part III of this volume, on social institutions).

On the other hand, **microsociology** focuses on the typical processes and patterns of face-to-face interaction in small groups. A microsociologist might study a marriage, a clique, a business meeting, an argument between friends, or a first date. In short, he or she would study the common, everyday interactions and negotiations that together produce lasting, secure patterns (see many examples in Chapters 3 and 4, on socialization and social organization).

The difference in names—*macro* versus *micro*—refers to the difference in size of the social units of interest. Macrosociologists study large social units—organizations, societies, or even empires—over long periods of time: years, centuries, or millennia. Microsociologists study small social units over short periods of time—for example, what happens during a conversation, a party, a classroom lecture, or a love affair. As in nature, large things tend to move (and change) slowly and small things move more quickly. As a result, macrosociologists are likely to stress how slowly things change and how amazingly persistent a social pattern is as it plays itself out in one gener-

ation after another. An example is the way society tends to be controlled by its elite groups, decade after decade. The connection between business elites and political elites is amazingly persistent. By contrast, microsociologists are likely to stress how quickly things change and how very elusive is that thing we call "social life." In their eyes, any social unit is constantly being created and reconceived by the members of society. An example is the way one's friendship group changes pretty much yearly, if not more rapidly, as one moves through the school system or the world of work. Some people remain our close friends over years, but many are close friends for only a short while.

Combining macro and micro approaches improves our understanding of the social world. Consider a common social phenomenon: the domestic division of labour—who does what chores around the home. From the micro perspective, who does what is constantly open to negotiation, a result of personal characteristics, the history of the couple, and other unique factors. From a macro perspective, different households tend to have pretty similar divisions of labour, despite differences in personal history. This suggests that the answer lies in a society's history, culture, and economy. It is far from accidental that, across millions of households, men enjoy the advantage of a better salary and more social power, both in a great many workplaces and at home.

While these approaches are different, they are also connected. After all, both macro- and microsociologists are studying the same people in the same society. All of us are leading somewhat unique lives within a common social context, faced by common problems. The question is, how can sociologists bring these elements together? The great American sociologist C. Wright Mills (1959) gave the answer when he introduced the notion of the **sociological imagination** as something that enables us to relate personal biographies—the lives of millions of ordinary people like ourselves—to the broad sweep of human history. The sociological imagination is what we need to understand how societies control and change their members and, at the same time, to understand how societies are constantly changed by the actions of their members.

All of this is the subject matter of sociology. We may choose to focus on problems of microsociology or macrosociology because of our personal interest, but a proper or full understanding of most problems will require that we consider elements of both. The two approaches are closely connected.

# Sociology Goes Beyond and Corrects Common Sense

Accomplishing the tasks of sociology requires systematic research, not merely **common-sense knowledge**. Some students studying the subject for the first time think that sociology is nothing more than common sense. After all, so many of the principles sociologists discover about everyday life seem familiar; we know these principles already because we live with them all the time. Yet, for all that familiarity, few people are able to guess correctly how a marriage, a friendship, a business partnership, or a political campaign will turn out. Our experience gives us "rules of thumb"—guidelines for accomplishing everyday life. They often even become folk wisdom, for example, "If you lead a good life you will be rewarded in the next life" or "Anyone can get whatever success they try hard for." However, sociologists would not consider these to be scientific statements, even if they make sense to us and seem true. Most of the time, scientific research finds they are not true; in fact, they're usually false. They're false because they are rooted not in careful research but in wishful thinking.

One of the problems with common-sense explanations of social life is that they are often based on a *voluntaristic* view of life. This point of view suggests that people live as they want to and get the lives they want. Supposedly, people with good ideas, attitudes, and values get good lives, while people with bad ideas, attitudes, and values get bad lives. This view implies that what you make of your life is up to you and that people who lead bad lives probably deserve to.

Yet most sociologists would deny that. Consider the following facts; they all pose a problem for the so-called voluntaristic approach:

- certain kinds of people (such as people who are poor) get sick more often and die at younger ages than other kinds of people.
- certain kinds of people (such as job applicants who are black) are less likely to get hired for jobs than other kinds of people.
- certain kinds of people (such as young women) are more likely than other kinds of people to be presented semi-nude in the **mass media**, or in sexually provocative poses.

Is it really true that poor people *want* to die younger? Or that black job seekers *want* to be unemployed? Or that young women are mainly worth knowing as sex objects? Would their lives improve overnight if only they adopted the right attitudes and values, as the common-sense argument seems to suggest? Or do social forces push these people into certain kinds of lives, putting harm in their way and limiting their choices, despite their deepest wishes to the contrary?

This last question of choice—of free will—is at the heart of sociology. It raises additional questions—for example, why do some people get more choices and better chances than others? Why do some people keep getting a bad deal? And, given these unpleasant facts of life, and despite plenty of personal experiences to the contrary, why do so many people believe in the "common-sense" ideas of free will and happy endings?

By the time you finish reading this book, you will have the beginnings of an answer to all these questions. For now, take it as given that because of their voluntaristic bias and untested character, common-sense explanations are more likely to be wrong than right. Sociology—both macro and micro—is about seeing beyond such popular beliefs. That is why sociologists take a systematic and studied approach to

Sociologist C. Wright Mills said that the sociological imagination is the ability to see connections between large and small, fast-changing and slow-changing, portions of our social world. The sociological imagination is what enables us to relate personal biography to the broad sweep of human history.
(Photo © Megan Mueller)

understanding everyday life. When we do, we often find the unexpected.

## The Example of Job Searches

To get a better idea of sociology's approach, consider a debate about how people find jobs. Common sense might tell you to talk to close friends and relatives to get a job. They have the greatest motivation to help you. However, sociological research shows that this common-sense approach can be misleading.

Imagine you are searching for a full-time job, a good one if possible—something related to what you studied at college, with good pay, good working conditions, and prospects for advancement. Now, imagine that you can search in any of three ways:

- *Strategy 1.* You can ask your best friend for information, help, or advice.
- *Strategy 2.* You can randomly pick a name out of the telephone book, phone that person, and ask him or her for information, help, or advice.
- *Strategy 3.* You can work your request for information, help, or advice into a conversation with an acquaintance at school or work; you are on a first-name basis with this acquaintance, but you don't consider him or her a close friend.

Common sense would tell you to avoid Strategy 2, the random phone call. That strategy is unlikely to land you a job, though it has one thing in its favour: you are likely to reach someone you have never talked to before. In 10 random telephone calls, you are likely to reach very different kinds of people. Random calling maximizes the variety and range of information you might possibly receive. However, the people you reach in this way are not likely to be useful. They have no motive for helping you find a good job. After all, they don't even know you.

Common sense says Strategy 1 is more promising. Your best friend, like your mother, father, brother, and sister (and perhaps a few other relatives), is motivated to help you: he or she likes you. However, if you think about it, you will realize we tend to choose friends who are like us. Because of this similarity, our close friends, though motivated, are not very helpful. They tend to form cliques. In cliques, our best friends—and their best friends—know the same things, which are often things that we already know. The information reaching our best friends is not very different from the information already reaching us. So while close friends are motivated to help us, they can't help us much if we need varied or obscure information.

That leaves Strategy 3, the use of acquaintances. We all have dozens, if not hundreds, of people we know on a first-name basis. They are people with whom we have casual conversations from time to time. Some of them know each other; they may even be kin, friends, neighbours, or acquaintances of each other. A great many of our acquaintances, however, do not know each other. Thus, the information reaching a dozen of our acquaintances is quite varied—not as varied as the information reaching a dozen randomly selected people, but much more varied than the information reaching our dozen closest friends and relatives.

At the same time, because we know our acquaintances and they know us, we are willing to ask them for information or advice and they are likely to be willing to provide it. What's more, our experience with these acquaintances gives us some basis for evaluating the quality of the information they are providing. So we might very well tell an acquaintance we are looking for a job, and listen for suggestions about where to look.

In our society, we like to believe that people who are talented and work hard will—somehow—get the best jobs, and that the best jobs will—somehow—find the best employees. There is supposedly a job market with an "invisible hand" operating. People who get bad jobs, by this reasoning, probably deserve bad jobs. They lack the qualifications, or even the skills of self-presentation that are important when interviewing for a job. Likewise, jobs that fail to find good candidates probably also deserve to fail. They haven't advertised effectively or presented candidates with a positive corporate image or an attractive employee package.

Yet research finds little merit in this commonsensical analysis. In a systematic study of managers in Boston, sociologist Mark Granovetter (1974, 1982) learned that a significant number of the managers he studied had found their jobs through an acquaintance—what Granovetter called a *weak tie* (to distinguish it from a close friend or relative, which would be a *strong tie*). In fact, managers found the *best* jobs in that way.

Why do weak ties pay off in this way? Granovetter argues that acquaintances provide the best combination of awareness, or information quantity, and evaluation, or information quality. Networks of acquaintances are large, and the information that flows through them is much more varied than that through networks of friends or relatives. Yet networks of acquaintances provide more reliable information than you can obtain from a random selection of names, or even (which is similar) from the job applications and résumés of hundreds of strangers.

## How Sociology Differs from Other Academic Fields

Sociology is just one of several fields of study designed to help describe and explain human behaviour; others include journalism, history, philosophy, and psychology. How does sociology differ from these other endeavours? Canadian sociologist Kenneth Westhues (1982) has compared sociology's approach with those of the other fields. He emphasizes that journalism and history describe real events, as does sociology. However, journalism and history only sometimes base their descriptions on a **theory** or interpretation, and then it is often an implicit theory. Sociology is different. It strives to make its theories explicit in order to test them. Telling a story is important for sociologists, but less so than the explanation on which the story is based. Sociology may be good preparation for doing history or journalism, but it differs from these disciplines.

Sociology also differs from philosophy. Both are *analytical*—that is, concerned with testing and refining theory. However, sociology is resolutely *empirical*, or concerned with gathering evidence and doing studies, while philosophy is not. Philosophy has greater concern with the internal logic of its arguments. Sociological theories must stand up logically, but they must also stand up to evidence in a way philosophical theories need not. Sociologists, no matter how logical the theory may be, will not accept a sociological theory whose predictions are not supported by evidence gathered in a sound way.

Finally, sociology differs from psychology, which is also analytical, empirical, and interpretive. The difference here lies in the subject matter. Psychologists study the behaviour of individual humans (or, sometimes, animals), and generally under experimental conditions. Sociology's subject matter is social relationships or groups observed in society. The family, the educational system, the media, the way work is organized, and the total society are the matters of inquiry. Sociology and psychology come close together in a field called *social psychology*, but this field is defined differently by sociologists and by psychologists. Studies conducted by sociologists in this field are more likely to focus on the effects of group living upon the views or behaviours of individuals, while psychologists are more likely to be concerned with particular individuals and how they respond under certain experimental conditions.

One way of characterizing sociology and saying what makes it unique has been put forward by Earl Babbie (1988). He states that we can describe sociology in terms of 10 basic or fundamental ideas not shared by other fields:

1. Society has an existence of its own.
2. Society can be studied scientifically.
3. Society creates itself.
4. Cultures vary over time and place.
5. Individual identity is a product of society.
6. Social structure must satisfy survival requirements.
7. Institutions are inherently conservative.
8. Societies constrain and transform.
9. Multiple paradigms or fundamental models of reality are needed.
10. Sociology is an idea whose time has come.

As we will see in this chapter and those that follow, these are many of the most basic ideas or assumptions of sociology. However, some sociologists would disagree about whether other ideas are just as important.

## Social Structure and Culture are the Central Topics of Sociology

**Concepts** are the keys to understanding any field. Faced with needing to learn a new subject, the experienced learner knows how to practise "'ceptsmanship"—the mastery of key concepts, names, and debates. Concepts are the tools we use to capture central ideas in a field. They are like the *x*'s and *y*'s in algebra. In any field, all the debates and "laws" are built around the relations between concepts. So by understanding the basic concepts of sociology, you can start to understand what sociologists are concerned about and how they think. Of all the concepts sociologists use, none are more important than social structure and culture, so we will begin the discussion with them.

### *Social Structure*

By **social structure**, sociologists mean any enduring, predictable pattern of social behaviour and social relationships among people in society. **Social relationships** are any relations in which people's actions have consequences for others. People are bound together by these relationships.

As an example, consider the operation of the economic marketplace, in which people compete for incomes, profits, savings, and other financial benefits. Typically, markets—which are social structures—produce wide social inequalities. The less regulated a market, the more unequal the economic outcome will be. Governments—which are also social structures—work to counterbalance this effect by regulating markets (for example, by legislating rules about minimum wages) and by redistributing income (for example, through taxation and transfer payments, such as unemployment insurance or social welfare). In this way, governments reduce inequality and increase equality.

A **social institution**—for example, a government or a market—is one kind of large social structure, made up of many social relationships. Typically, people use institutions to solve common problems faced by society, as schools do in educating students, as hospitals do in attending to people's health, or as economic organizations do in producing and distributing goods. Within a social institution, people join together in social relationships, as (for example) teacher and student, doctor and patient, or producer and consumer.

**Roles** are actual patterns of interaction with others. Thus, to act like a doctor is to give a role performance. **Role expectations** are shared ideas about how people—any people—will likely carry out the duties attached to a particular social position, whatever the personal characteristics of those people. We have particular expectations about how a doctor will behave towards a patient, how a parent will behave towards a child, and how a teacher will behave towards a student. On the other hand, **statuses** are socially defined positions that specify the rights and responsibilities associated with a particular role—a doctor, patient, parent, child, teacher, student, and so on. Moreover, statuses also specify *reporting relationships*—people with whom others will likely interact. Statuses are relational in this way: each one calls for interaction to take place with other statuses.

Each of us participates in social life in terms of the statuses and roles we have adopted or have been assigned. However, we are all individuals, and we experience and act out our roles and statuses in our own particular ways. Despite this, behaviour is still largely predictable. Moreover, social roles and relationships do not just exist: we enact them through interaction and negotiation. By **social interaction**, we mean the processes by which social actors—people trying to meet each other's expectations—relate to each other, especially in face-to-face encounters. It includes many forms of communication, such as words, body language, attentiveness (or inattentiveness), and what some sociologists have called "face-work." By **negotiation**, we mean all of the ways people try to make sense of one another, and to one another.

**Societies** (and international organizations among societies) are the largest collections of social relationships. Canadian society is made up of all the families, clubs, groups, corporations, and so on in which its members participate. Seeing the boundaries of a given society is sometimes difficult because many social relationships span international borders, like the one between Canada and the United States. Indeed, some writers have wondered whether Canada and the United States, which are certainly distinct nation-states because they have different governments, should be viewed as distinct societies. Others have wondered whether the two have distinct economies. These questions come up, of course, because of the close ties of economic trade and ownership and the frequent flows of communication and of people (as travellers and migrants) between the two societies.

Yet the idea of "Canadian society" still is meaningful to sociologists because the social relationships of Canadians with other Canadians indeed differ from the bonds of Canadians with Americans (and vice versa). We need only consider the strong shared attachments that Canadians and Americans have to different national **symbols**—the one national anthem versus the other anthem, the one national flag versus the other, the Canadian Parliament versus the US Congress, Canada's "mechanical arm" in the US space shuttle versus the US space program—to know that we are speaking of two societies here. Most Canadians share in the strong positive sentiments that the idea of Canadian society elicits; few Americans would do so.

## Culture

This discussion of symbols, their meaning, and their importance, brings us to the issue of **culture**. One cannot do an adequate sociological study without considering culture because culture creates social structures and social structures sustain culture. Let us explain.

A classic definition of *culture* by social anthropologist Edward Tylor is as follows: culture is "that complex whole which includes knowledge, belief, art, morals, law, custom and any other capabilities and habits acquired . . . as a member of society" (1871: 1). Thus, culture includes all manner of ideas shared by society members. Culture includes meanings that people learn from others. It includes **beliefs**, some of which are descriptive (for example, ideas about what "is" or "was" or "will be"), while others are normative (ideas about what "should be" or "ought to be"). It also includes **values**, that is, general criteria for judging people's behaviours. It involves **ideologies**, which are emotionally charged sets of beliefs that explain and justify how society is organized or should be organized. Culture also contains **norms**—rules, regulations, laws, and informal understandings.

Culture and society are closely linked. They are different sides of the same coin of social reality. Society, as we said above, is made up of sets of social relationships. Culture consists of the ideas developed in social relationships and fostered, taught, and learned through social relationships. Culture also helps determine how social relationships take place because these relationships are guided by shared norms, values, and beliefs.

Because people share culture, social relationships and society are made possible. For one thing, people can act predictably with each other when they share culture. Consider the automobile traffic on Canada's streets and roads. Drivers know what to expect of other drivers, as well as from pedestrians, on the basis of commonly understood rules of the road. We can make reasonably accurate predictions about other drivers' behaviours on the basis of what others should do according to the rules. Indeed, we routinely stake our lives on these understandings. And the social relationships of traffic run more or less according to plan, day in and day out. Imagine travelling in an automobile across one of our cities if we did not share such understandings!

We can take this conception of shared culture too far, though. Some parts of a culture are exclusive to some members of the society: some aspects of culture are learned and known by most of us, but other cultural items are shared by only a few. In addition to the rules of traffic, most of us know the meanings of such concepts as "money" (such as what a dollar will buy today), "work," "family," and "education." Very few of us, however, are privy to the information shared in the federal cabinet or in the boardrooms of major corporations. Only some of us know much about classical music, jazz, or bluegrass; and very few know how to fly a jet plane, perform a heart transplant, or build a house. In other words, much of the culture that has been accumulated within a society resides within **subcultures**.

These subcultures share some of the common culture with others, but not all of it. Without some shared culture, though, there can be no society because we would no longer have the social relationships that are needed for society to exist. And without social relationships and society, there can be no culture.

## Social Structure and Culture Influence People in Groups

Social structure and culture both limit and change people's behaviours. First, they both cause different kinds of people to act in similar ways in the same social situation. They shape people's actions in a way that the situation dictates and, in that sense, limit their actions. Given the same situation—for example, a church, a classroom, a theatre, or a bus queue—people with very different histories, attitudes, and lifestyles will all behave similarly.

Second, social structure and culture both cause the same people to act differently in different social situations. In that way, they are change-producing. So, for example, people in authority—police officers, bank presidents, judges, and schoolteachers—who may behave carefully and even stiffly while on duty, cut loose when they are among friends or at a party. Then they are likely to make as much noise and tell as many dumb jokes as your friends do in the same situation. Social situations change us—even the stiffest of us—in similar ways.

The social forces that limit and change us are both outside and inside us. During childhood, we learn the norms, values, and beliefs that are part of our culture, and we internalize them—take them inside ourselves. We will consider in Chapter 3 how this occurs through the process of **socialization**. In Chapter 5, on deviance, we will see how external social sanctions are also brought to bear to limit and change people's behaviour.

Note that our description of the consequences of social structure and culture is precisely opposite to the assumptions that underlie genetics, biology, and personality psychology. According to sociology, people's behaviours vary in relation to the social structural context and subculture in which they find themselves. According to genetics, biology, and personality psychology, people do not vary much from one situation to another—a view that is hard to defend in the light of observable reality.

Consider the sociological approach to problem gambling—a topic gaining ever more public attention and concern. Problem gambling is a kind of addiction—like an addiction to drugs or alcohol—and as such it is intensely personal. Yet sociological research shows that the risk of problem gambling varies from one social group to another. Young men run the highest risk. Certain ethnic groups run a higher than average risk, for reasons that are not yet fully understood. People who live near casinos run a higher than average risk, for reasons that are not as hard to understand. This tells us that personal behaviour is subject to social and cultural influences. We learn how to behave—even how to misbehave—in social situations, and practise our knowledge in other social situations. As a result, to a large degree our behaviour can be predicted by looking at the characteristics of particular situations.

The reason we behave predictably in social situations is because otherwise, social interaction becomes impossible. No one knows what to say or do. Social life rests on a certain predictability, especially when strangers are interacting with other strangers. This is obvious in many settings. Consider the university or college classroom. There, surrounded by 50, 100, or even 500 students, the professor cannot deal with students in a personalized, intimate manner. He or she must act according to the students' (and institution's) expectations—specifically, to act "professionally," in a serious, concerned, and knowledgeable manner. The students, in return, must also act "professionally," or else the classroom interaction breaks down. Both teacher and student start wondering what to say and do next.

We learn to value stable relationships. Often, we don't know how to change them. Sometimes the people who hold power in our society have a strong commitment to and interest in maintaining these relationships and oppose changing them. People with the most to gain urge us to meet other people's expectations. We will discuss all the reasons for this throughout the course of this book.

Researchers have found that what we learn about one social relationship—for example, the teacher–student relationship—can help us understand other, quite different social relationships. The similarities and differences between relationships fascinate those who study sociology. The structures they form when fitted together also fascinate sociologists, who love to study the relationship between small structures and large structures—their similarities, differences, and interconnections. And they love to apply insights and concepts developed in studying one social situation to understanding a different situation. For an example of this, see the discussion in Chapter 4 of small groups and large organizations.

This willingness to generalize is one of sociology's most distinctive features. In the end, sociology is the study of all social structures and cultures—from two-

position (or dyadic) relationships, such as doctors and patients or marriages, to business enterprises or political campaigns, all the way up to total societies and global empires.

# The Development of Sociology

We typically credit three individuals with founding sociology as a scientific discipline: Karl Marx, Émile Durkheim, and Max Weber.

### *Marxism*

Karl Marx is widely known as the intellectual founder of modern communism, a philosopher whose ideas inspired political movements, revolutions, and social reforms that did much to shape the world we live in today. Besides being a revolutionary, Marx was a thinker of profound originality, whose contributions to the study of history and the workings of the capitalist system are still important.

Marx's sociology is founded on what is called a *materialist* conception of history. Human affairs, he insisted, are not driven principally by political values or religious beliefs (as had been maintained in various *idealist* philosophies), but by material factors, above all

Karl Marx (1818–83), German-born social theorist and political activist. (Marx/Engels Image Library)

by an ongoing need to produce the necessities of life: food, shelter, clothing. Human existence is possible only through collective labour, and the survival of any group or community depends on this co-ordinated practical activity. How communities produce will thus determine how their societies are organized, what kinds of human beings they become, and how they express and define themselves culturally. Marx's materialism does not discount the importance of ideas and values (what he called *social consciousness*), but those ideal factors must be explained in connection with their origins and functions in productive practices.

**Marxism**'s core concept is the **mode of production**, which refers to the arrangements humans establish in the collective task of extracting from nature the essentials of life. Each mode of production in history is organized by the specific forces or means used and by the legal-political relations directing their use.

The *productive forces* consist chiefly of three components: the tools and instruments used in the work process (that is, all invented technologies, from the stone axe to the microchip); the patterns of social labour (from handicraft to assembly-line processes); and the available natural resources. The *relations of production* are essentially proprietary; they specify the rights of ownership and control of the productive forces. Differences in who possesses what result in a division of **classes**, usually featuring a dominant or ruling class that owns the land, the animals, the factories, the machines, and so on, and various dispossessed

classes that are compelled to labour and produce for the benefit of their oppressors.

According to Marx, the mode of production forms the organizing foundation, or *base*, of any particular society, the other institutions of which—government, law, religion, art—make up its *superstructure*. "The mode of production of material life," Marx insisted in 1859, "determines the general character of the social, political, and intellectual processes of life" (1956: 51). How communities are governed, how family life is ordered, what kinds of values and ideas people hold—all such superstructural phenomena are conditioned by the economic structure of the society in question.

Marx identified several modes of production in world history, each characterized by a particular level of development in productive forces and by corresponding legal-political relations (see Figure 1.1). Once communities pass beyond the egalitarian primitive-communal phase, conditions of hereditary inequality enter into their arrangements. Property rights, social privileges, and coercive powers are claimed and exercised by certain groups at the expense of others. Marx and his colleague, Friedrich Engels, announced this thesis on the famous opening page of *The Communist Manifesto*, published in 1848:

> The history of all hitherto existing society is the history of class struggles. Freeman and slave, patrician and plebeian, lord and serf, guildmaster and journeyman, in a word, oppressor and

Figure 1.1 **Major Modes of Production in Historical Sequence, Identifying Social Organization, Economic System, and Class Structure**[a]

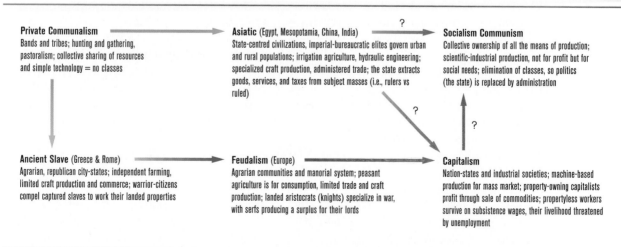

[a]? symbolizes possible or predicted historical pathways.

oppressed, stood in constant opposition to one another, carried on an uninterrupted, now hidden, now open fight, a fight that each time ended either in a revolutionary reconstitution of society at large, or in the common ruin of the contending classes. ([1848] 1948: 1)

**Exploitation** is thus the defining relationship between classes. The owners of property extract from the primary producers a *surplus*—a disproportionate share of the material wealth that frees the dominant classes from the burden of producing for themselves. This appropriation enables them to exercise leadership and control in war, politics, art, and religion. Just how the exploiting classes extract that surplus varies with the mode of production. In the agriculturally based Asiatic, ancient, and feudal modes, the subject masses, slaves, and serfs were forced to toil for their masters, and they delivered specified quantities of produce and labour services. But under **capitalism**, Marx notes, the exploitation is less direct and is partially concealed by the complex intricacies of industrial production: here the workers create *surplus value* (rather than merely a *surplus*), by receiving less in the form of wages than the exchange value of the commodities they produce—a monetary differential that enables capitalists to garner profits through sales in the market.

The dominance of the ruling classes is based on their ownership of the means of material production, but this also enables them to control the means of mental production. As Marx noted in 1845, "the ideas of the ruling class are, in every age, the ruling ideas: i.e., the class that is the dominant material force in society is at the same time its dominant intellectual force" (1956: 78).

What are these ruling ideas? They are **ideologies**—systems of norms, values, and beliefs that legitimize or justify the supremacy of the ruling classes and that rationalize the subordination of the labouring classes. Such ideologies typically sanctify the established social order by invoking nature, divine approval, or the alleged superior merits of the privileged. By controlling the media of cultural expression, the dominant classes are able to represent reality in terms beneficial to themselves and to impress subordinates with displays of achievement in the arts and in fields of higher learning. As a result, oppressed classes tend to partially internalize and defer to the ruling ideologies of their oppressors, a situation Marx termed **false consciousness**. Political resistance is possible only when subordinate classes reject those ideologies and forge instead *class consciousness*, an

awareness of their exploited status and of their common interests in overthrowing an unjust system.

Revolutionary political developments occur in conjunction with changes in the productive base, as new technologies and working arrangements begin to destabilize the established hierarchies. Marx believed that just such a situation was arising within capitalism. The tremendous productive capacities of modern science and industry are able to solve the historic problem of scarcity—of universally satisfying basic human material needs. But so long as the private property system maintains vast disparities in the distribution of wealth and resources, there will be luxury for the few and continued misery for the many.

Marx, principally in his three volumes of *Capital* (*Das Kapital*, [1867] 1967), traced the boom–recession cycle of capitalist economies to this structural inequality: millions are hungry and homeless around the globe not because the means to feed and house them are lacking, but because they cannot be fed and housed within the limits set by the private-profit motive—hence the paradox of massive layoffs and unemployment despite the public need for expanded production. Marx argued that this "contradiction" would intensify over time, and that the working class would organize politically and overthrow the capitalist system, whether by armed revolution or through the ballot box. Private ownership of the **means of production** would be abolished and production redirected to serve "the social needs of all" rather than "the private interests of the few." Under socialism/communism, classes would disappear, the state would "wither away" (in Marx's famous phrase of 1875), and human beings would at last be free to develop their full humanity and creative potential.

Marx's sociology shines a powerful light on the complex dynamics of world history, but his vision of a future society free from want and oppression now seems hopelessly utopian. Yet even if it is, he nonetheless gave social science a necessary critical edge. As Marx memorably commented in 1845, "philosophers have only interpreted the world in various ways; what matters is to change it" (1956: 69).

### Max Weber's Historical Sociology

For sheer breadth and depth of learning, the German sociologist Max Weber has few peers. His writings—though left incomplete at the time of his death in 1920—contain nothing less than a sociology of world history. At the core of Weber's research lay one overriding question: how and why did capitalism originate in Western Europe in the sixteenth and seventeenth centuries, rather than in the advanced civilizations of China, India, or the Muslim world? Weber was following in Marx's tracks, respectful of his predecessor's insights but convinced that additional understanding was needed to explain developments and histories so complex and of such great consequence.

The best introduction to Weber's project is his early and most famous work, *The Protestant Ethic and the Spirit of Capitalism*, published in 1904. As the title indicates, Weber was investigating a connection between two cultural developments: a new religious ethos and changing economic values. The rise of capitalism, Weber argues, could not be explained solely in terms of technological advances and class conflict. Social life must always be viewed in terms of multiple causes—economic, political, military, religious, and so on—whose influence changes over time and place. He acknowledged that the origins of modern capitalism lay primarily in certain economic innovations: the introduction of machines, the harnessing of new sources of energy, the technological displacement of peasants from the land, rationalized accounting, and the factory system. He rightfully held, however, that a comprehensive explanation must also incorporate non-economic factors.

Weber ([1904] 1958) argued that the Protestant Reformation, by introducing religious values that affirmed worldly activity, contributed significantly to the consolidation of the new economic order. This was not, he stressed, the intention of the leading reformers, Martin Luther (1483–1546) and John Calvin (1509–64). These "protestors" were spiritual men, distressed by what they saw as the corruption of Christianity by the Church's seemingly limitless appetite for wealth and power. In breaking with Roman Catholic tradition, however, the reformers were forced to create new standards of religiosity.

Central to the Protestant view was the idea that individuals must reach God directly, through their own personal faith and holiness—and not through the sacraments administered by the Church. No bishop or priest could control the means of salvation by assigning penances and selling indulgences to free people from their sins. God's revealed word must therefore be made available to all, and so the Latin Bible was translated into English, French, German, and other vernacular (everyday) languages, thereby breaking the Church's monopoly over scripture.

With personal faith now holding the key to salvation, the early Lutherans, Calvinists, and Puritans came

Max Weber (1864–1920), celebrated German scholar and one of the founders of modern sociology. (The Granger Collection, New York)

to view disciplined work as a "calling," a form of religious devotion to God. Diligent and dutiful in the labours God had assigned, these Protestants did not believe in building ornate churches filled with gold and fine art, in adorning themselves in luxurious clothing, or in dining on rich foods in houses of splendour. Against these worldly vanities, they practised *asceticism*, a frugal lifestyle of sober, methodical piety.

As Weber observed, this new "**Protestant ethic**," while religious in inspiration, provided a powerful stimulus for and legitimation of economic pursuits. Not only was work redefined as a spiritual vocation, but savings and investment were encouraged, as the faithful shunned all conspicuous consumption. Success in business came to be seen as a sign of election—an indication that one was predestined for heaven. What greater support could an emerging economic system obtain, Weber asked, than religious sanctification? The relationship between Protestantism and capitalism was not one of simple cause and effect, but one of *elective affinity*, a situation in which originally distinct but compatible lines of development intersect to produce an intensified synthesis or fusing.

Like Marx, Weber believed that societies are organized in terms of **power**—what he called *relations of domination* ([1908] 1978). Unlike Marx, he did not believe that economic inequalities were always and everywhere of primary influence. Weber insisted that power is derived from multiple sources, ideological as well as material. Through the control of diverse social and natural resources, some groups and strata are able to establish positions of authority and privilege.

Weber held that class, status, and party were the principal channels along which power flows. *Class inequalities* derive from the differential ownership of property, and also from the market opportunities that follow from differences in labour-skill levels. *Status inequalities* derive from styles of life, most strongly in association with ethnic, racial, or religious identities. As for **party**, this refers to the formation of organizations that recruit individuals in order to gain political power, whether through armed violence or electoral victories. Control over economic, cultural, military, and political resources thus leads to different forms of domination. Living in a military dictatorship or in a religious one is quite different from living in a society dominated by class inequalities or one organized on a discriminatory ethnic basis.

Weber's concern with political forms of domination is illustrated most clearly in his analysis of bureaucracy. A **bureaucracy** is an organization featuring a hierarchical, pyramidal chain of authority, with specialized offices of jurisdiction. Duties are based on written regulations and filed information (reports, data). The bureaucrat is a functionary: he or she operates by implementing the rules and by processing individuals and cases as "types" and "categories." Depersonalization is thus the very hallmark of bureaucratic procedure. In terms of administrative efficiency, however, and as an instrument of control, bureaucracy is unrivalled, and so it spreads wherever social life grows in scale and complexity—in economics, politics, warfare, education, religion, science, medicine.

The fate of the modern world, Weber feared, was one of increasing bureaucratization, a trend he saw relentlessly erecting "a prison-house of future bondage," an "iron cage" that would reduce the human experience to forced regimentation. Marx's humanistic expectations for socialism were utopian, Weber argued, for socializing the means of production would lead to a totalitarian state, a situation in which the "administrators" would reign unchecked by any competing powers. As the Nazi and communist dictatorships of the twentieth century tragically confirm, Weber's fears were well founded. The fact that we now share our lives with that most efficient of processing and monitoring machines—the computer—only confirms the continuing relevance of Weber's concerns about the prospects for freedom in a bureaucratized world.

## Durkheim and the Functionalist Tradition

No figure in the history of sociology contributed more to its professional development than Émile Durkheim. He was among the first to offer university courses in sociology, and in 1898 he founded one of its most influential journals, *L'Année sociologique*. It was this French scholar's self-appointed mission to legitimize the science of sociology at a time when it was barely acknowledged in academic circles.

Durkheim insisted that social reality is unique and that the focus of sociology is distinct from the subject matter of other academic disciplines. In *The Rules of Sociological Method*, published in 1895, Durkheim attempts to define the scope of sociology and to provide a manual for proper scientific procedure. Rejecting all reductionist approaches, Durkheim stresses that social reality is an emergent, objective order that transcends the level of acting individuals. Each of us enters into, and thereafter confronts, a ready-made world of institutions, customs, moral traditions—a society within which we are socialized and constituted as social beings. Social facts are thus to be studied as things, as collective arrangements and ideas external to and coercive of the individuals functioning within a community. For Durkheim, the primacy

Émile Durkheim (1858–1916), French academic and influential pioneer in sociological theory and method. (Bettmann/CORBIS)

of society is central: it surpasses each individual in time and space, and imposes on each person "ways of acting and thinking which it has consecrated with its prestige" ([1895] 1964: 102).

What each individual thinks and values is informed by the **collective consciousness**, a system of shared symbols, beliefs, and sentiments. The binding force and complexity of this consciousness will vary with the organization of the society in question. In simple societies, with only a rudimentary division of labour, the collective consciousness will be powerful and uniform; in complex societies, it will be more diffuse and internally diverse.

How a community reacts to crime and deviance, Durkheim ([1893] 1964) observes, reveals what kind of collective consciousness is at work. In undifferentiated societies, there is *repressive law*, which imposes harsh and violent punishments upon even minor infractions, because deviance of any sort scandalizes the homogeneous community and offends against the rigid moral order that preserves it. In complex societies, in contrast, there is *restitutive law*, a system of fines and sanctions that seeks to restore order whenever it breaks down and that tolerates a wider divergence of personal opinion and conduct, in recognition of the greater diversity within the society.

Durkheim's famous study *Suicide*, published in 1897, best exemplifies his theoretical perspective. The topic would appear to pose a major challenge for sociological analysis, for is not self-murder a private act, with the individual as both willing victim and perpetrator? Through a careful scrutiny of suicide statistics, however, Durkheim proves that social factors operate even here, at the very moment when an individual is contemplating the voluntary termination of his or her existence.

Contrary to the claims of various biological and psychological theories, Durkheim ([1897] 1951) found that suicide rates do not vary directly with racial and ethnic factors, or with insanity and alcoholism; nor is contagion, or "copy-cat" practices, much in evidence. What the statistics do reveal is that suicidal tendencies are strongly influenced by social relationships—specifically, by the degree of solidarity and *normative integration* that can be found in an individual's life situation. That is, individuals are prone to suicidal acts in inverse proportion to the strength of their social ties (to kin, friends, community) and to their adherence to the collective consciousness.

In modern societies, individuals tend to be more autonomous and independent, left on their own to succeed or fail, while also being less committed and less bound to traditional norms and values. This situation, Durkheim argues, is conducive to two characteristic modern forms of self-murder: *egoistic suicide*, which arises from the stresses of excessive individualism, a loss of group cohesion and solidarity, and *anomic suicide*, which arises from moral confusion or anarchy, an absence of binding norms and values. More rarely, where social bonds are exceedingly strong, instances of *altruistic suicide* occur (as in the sacrificial efforts by parents to save their children, or by soldiers to save their comrades and country). And where the cultural norms are too binding and restrictive, instances of *fatalistic suicide* are found (as among slaves, or prisoners condemned to long terms of incarceration). As Durkheim's classification tellingly reveals, suicide is a highly personal act, but it occurs as a result of social forces, which variously shield or support us in our in times of difficulty or leave us exposed to loneliness, uncertainty, and despair.

Durkheim's last major work, *The Elementary Forms of Religious Life*, published in 1912, provides a brilliant synthesis of his sociological vision. In this influential study, Durkheim seeks to explain the social origins and functions of religious belief—one of the main components of the collective consciousness. He begins by defining *religion* as "a unified system of beliefs and practices regarding things that are sacred" ([1912] 1995: 44). The *sacred*, in this definition, involves symbols, images, objects, and rites that invoke feelings of reverence and awe; it forms a special realm set apart from the profane world of everyday objects and affairs. All religions, Durkheim argues, are ultimately founded on this distinction between the sacred and the profane, and so the sociological task is to explain how and why a sense of the sacred arises.

Examining the ethnographic records about the earliest forms of human society—the Aboriginal clans and tribes of Australia and North America—Durkheim notes that each clan or tribe offers veneration to a totemic object that also symbolized the community itself. In the totem's spirit, the worshippers acknowledge the existence of a superior, superhuman force. This feeling of dependence and attachment is real, Durkheim insists, not imaginary. Religious devotees are mistaken only in the true identity of the "sacred being" they worship: it is not a god or spirit, but the collective powers of the society in which they live and upon which they depend. Society is that greater force that transcends each individual, for as it compels obedience to its rules, it provides identity and security and so gives meaning and purpose to our lives.

Durkheim insists that religions are socially produced and communicated, and that people experience the sacred most dramatically during social gatherings, such as festivals and ceremonials. With celebrative dance and chanting, individuals are carried away in a group-induced ecstasy, a **collective effervescence** that expresses their membership in a power greater than themselves. Society, then, is the true "god"—the basis for our existence and the moral force that imparts to us our values and ideals.

As societies change, Durkheim reasons, so will human representations of the divine, for each deity is really only a symbolic totem of how the group conceives of itself. Religions thus provide an essential stabilizing force in social life, for while "their apparent function is to strengthen the bonds attaching the believer to his god, they at the same time really strengthen the bonds attaching the individual to the society of which he is a member, since the god is only a figurative expression of the society" ([1912] 1995: 226).

Durkheim's intellectual legacy remains highly influential. In France, his ideas provided the basis for the theoretical perspective known as *structuralism*. Though many-sided and supported by diverse thinkers, such as the anthropologist Claude Lévi-Strauss and the philosopher Michel Foucault, this perspective follows Durkheim in giving priority to the social arrangements that shape and constrain action and that confine human thought and imagination to what is "thinkable" within structurally determined *mentalités sociales*.

Durkheim's ideas were no less central in the development of the English and American tradition known as *functionalism*, which flourished in the social sciences from the 1920s through the 1960s. The initial elaboration of functionalist analysis came with early anthropological field research, as contact with other cultures soon yielded a major discovery. However "strange" local customs might appear to European eyes, closer examination typically revealed what is called their *adaptive utility*: of the customs and institutions that exist in social life, most appear to contribute to *system maintenance*.

# Four Sociological Paradigms

Today there are four major theoretical approaches to the study of society and social behaviour, and two of them were developed from the works of Durkheim, Marx, and Weber. **Structural functionalism** and the **conflict theory** emphasize research at the macro level—the whole society or its major institutions—although these perspectives are sometimes applied to social behaviour in small groups too. **Symbolic interactionism** features microanalysis of small groups and interpersonal interaction. **Feminism** is rooted in macrosociological analysis, but it also has been effectively applied to research on small groups and interpersonal interaction.

These four approaches have also been called *sociological perspectives* or **paradigms**. A *perspective* or *paradigm* is a general way of seeing the world. It embodies broad assumptions about the nature of society and social behaviour. It suggests which questions to ask in research and how to interpret the answers obtained from research. You will see these approaches applied repeatedly to different subjects in the various chapters of this textbook.

## *Structural Functionalism*

The structural functionalist perspective is based on Émile Durkheim's work. It views society as a set of interconnected elements that operate together in equilibrium to maintain the overall stability and efficiency of the society as a whole. For example, the individual social institutions—families, the economy, government, education, and others—are each said to make a vital contribution to the functioning of the larger society. Families operate to reproduce and nurture members of society; the economy regulates the production, distribution, and consumption of goods and services; government controls conflict between groups and contributes to the sharing of values and norms; and education socializes young people, teaching them things they will need to know for adult life.

Robert Merton (1957), a key figure in the development of this perspective, argued that social institutions perform both manifest and latent functions. *Manifest functions* are outcomes that are intended and easily recognized; *latent functions* are unintended and hidden from participants. Education, for example, is manifestly responsible for providing students with the knowledge, skills, and cultural values that will help them to operate effectively in society. Both the school system and its participants formally recognize these functions. At a latent level, however, education also functions as an institutional "babysitter" for young children and teenagers not yet ready to work full-time or to roam the streets independently while their parents are at work, and as a "matchmaker" where older high school and university students socialize with potential future lovers or marriage partners. These functions, though important to society and accomplished with equal success, are considered latent because they are not the intended consequences envisioned by designers of the educational system, nor are they acknowledged in any official way by school administrators, students, or parents.

Structural functionalists argue that because society is a system of interrelated parts, changes in one part of society always produce changes—unintended—in another part. Society is always reacting and readjusting to new inputs, even when people do not intend the changes that occur. This fact is important for both sociology and social planning. Unless we are aware of the likely consequences of a planned change—the latent and the manifest functions—we are likely to end up with changes we did not want. One sociologist (Sieber, 1981) has coined the term *fatal remedies* to describe attempts at social planning that fail to think through the consequences. In the end, they may do more (unintended) harm than they do (intended) good. At the least, they produce new, unforeseen problems. This is because any society is an extremely complex, unpredictable social system.

Functionalists argue that sometimes there is a failure of institutions to fulfill their functions, particularly during times of rapid change. They believe that sudden and major social change sometimes disrupts traditional values and common ways of doing things. For example, during the phases of industrialization and urbanization in Western Europe and North America in the late nineteenth and early twentieth centuries, crime, poverty, unsanitary living conditions, environmental pollution, and other forms of social disorganization increased sharply. Durkheim ([1893] 1964, [1897] 1964, [1912] 1965) introduced the term *anomie*, or normlessness, as a name for this condition in which social norms are weak and different values are in conflict with one another. As traditional forms of guidance break down, social control declines and people bond less with one another; they become more likely to commit non-conforming, deviant acts (crime, drug use, and so on). The general solution to this situation, according to the functionalist perspective, is to strengthen social norms and slow the pace of social change.

The functionalist emphasis on the interconnectedness of society has been useful in highlighting how one part of the society influences other parts. For example, recent changes to the family, such as the rise in divorces and in single parenting, have important consequences for work and education, particularly with respect to time constraints among those juggling the dual—and conflicting—roles of employee and parent.

Functionalists would emphasize the unexpected consequences of easier divorce laws and more births to unwed mothers. Ever more Canadian children are experiencing parental separation by ever younger ages (see Figure 1.2); this experience is particularly common among children whose parents were cohabiting, not legally married. The resulting lone parenthood, in turn, increases the likelihood of financial hardship, emotional stress, and worse parenting. These in turn can hinder the children's mental and physical health and can result in worse school outcomes.

Functionalists also assume that people in the society largely agree on *values*—the valued goals that individuals believe they should pursue—and on the way the society and its institutions operate. Thus, functionalists would expect there to be considerable consensus on family values, the best type of political system to live under, the best form of economy, and so on, and within Canadian society the dominant value preferences would reflect the types of institutions that do exist.

In summary, the basic principles of the structural functionalist perspective are these:

1. Society is a system of interrelated parts, a social system, with each part contributing to the whole.

Figure 1.2 **Children Born to a Lone Parent or Who Have Experienced Parental Separation by Age and Year of Birth, Canada**

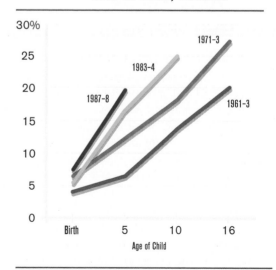

SOURCE: Adapted from Statistics Canada, *Social Trends in Canada* Seminar, Catalogue 10H0052, April 2002.

2. A social system tends to be stable, in equilibrium; when it changes, it changes gradually, especially if the change is for the better.
3. A society cannot remain stable unless there is considerable sharing of values and norms among people.
4. Societies persist through time because their parts, such as institutions, serve the survival needs of the whole.

### Conflict Theory

Conflict theory has its roots in the basic division between the "haves" and the "have-nots" of society. Conflict theorists take exception to the structural functionalist assumption of consensus in values among members of society and to the limited attention given to power struggles and competing interests within the population. The conflict perspective instead views society as largely a collection of disparate groups struggling over a limited supply of resources and power. Some have more resources and power than others, and this helps the haves to dominate and coerce the have-nots.

Conflict theory has its origins particularly in the works of Karl Marx. Marx believed that as societies shift from an agricultural to an industrial economy, the predominant social concerns of the people shift from survival to earning a living wage. Marxists also contend that labourers in a capitalist system experience a feeling of **alienation** from the processes and products of their labour since these processes and products are highly fragmented and specialized. They have narrow job functions and are therefore powerless to control or change the conditions of their work.

Besides exploiting their workers, boardroom executives—the post-industrial successors to the factory owners of the industrial era—sometimes maximize profits through the perpetration of corporate violence: actual and potential harm caused to workers, consumers, and the public for the sake of the company's efficiency or success. Examples of this include failing to remedy unsafe working conditions, exposing employees to hazardous materials, knowingly marketing dangerous or inferior products, and releasing industrial pollution into the environment.

Two main criticisms of the Marxian conflict theory approach are that, historically, communist societies founded on Marxism have failed either to prosper or to eliminate inequality and that the approach overemphasizes the importance of one type of inequality—class inequality—at the expense of other types of inequality and social injustice. Non-Marxist conflict theories argue that there are several forms of inequality. While they recognize the value people place on differences in income and class, proponents of this perspective believe that other divergent interests and characteristics can also lead to conflict and oppression. Thus, conflict theorists have noted that women and men have competing interests that cause social conflict and social problems too. Others cite the conflicting interests of various ethnic groups, for example, Aboriginal and non-Aboriginal groups in Canada or blacks and whites in North America. Still other dimensions of social conflict involve, for example, heterosexuals and homosexuals, the young and the old, liberals and conservatives, urbanites and rural-dwellers, and environmentalists and industrialists.

Conflict theorists do not consider conflict a destructive force. Instead, they believe it focuses attention on social problems and brings people together to solve these problems. Sociologists working within this perspective would emphasize that conflict has been central to the women's movement, the civil rights movement, and trade unionism, among other social movements. Conflict is more common than consensus, and conflict can serve as the vehicle of positive social change, conflict theorists say.

This outlook on social life also focuses attention away from shared values and towards ideologies. An *ideology*, as we have said, is a coherent set of interrelated beliefs about the nature of the world and of people. It guides a person's interpretation of and reaction to external events. *Dominant ideology* is the ideology of the dominant group, justifying its power and wealth. The rest of us do not rebel because we have accepted the dominant ideology. We teach young people this ideology in the schools, churches, and media; we hear it repeated throughout life. Ideas included in the dominant ideology of this society are "people are poor because they are lazy; they could get ahead more if they were not so lazy" and "women who get less pay than men for the same job don't want to be paid at a similar rate to men." Sociological research has shown that these forms of "common sense" are patently false.

The work of Max Weber also inspired sociologists who follow the conflict approach. Weber argued that conflict arises as much over values, status, and a sense of personal honour as over economic status. From Weber's point of view, even modern corporations with no identifiable owner experience conflict. The bureaucratic managers of the corporation come to think of themselves as a **status group** and act to further their own group interests. That is why, Weberian theorists argue, conflict can be found in *any* large society, not only in capitalist societies.

A key modern proponent of conflict theory today is Jürgen Habermas. In his critical analysis of Western institutions and rationality, Habermas stresses the humanist side of Marx's work as a critic and examines tensions between theory and practice in philosophy. Bridging the connections between sociology and philosophy, Habermas's major work, *The Theory of Communicative Action* (1984), addresses not only philosophies of agency and rationality, but also the theories of sociologists such as Max Weber, George Herbert Mead, Émile Durkheim, and Talcott Parsons.

We can summarize the basic assumptions of the conflict perspective as follows:

1. Societies are always changing.
2. Conflict and power differentials are always present in society as groups pursue their interests.
3. Conflict is a major contributor to social change.

### Symbolic Interactionism

Whereas the structural functionalist and conflict perspectives focus on large elements of society such as social institutions and major demographic groups, symbolic interactionists focus on the opposite end of the sociological spectrum: on small groups and interpersonal interactions.

Symbolic interactionism sees society as a product of face-to-face interaction between people using symbols. In simple terms, a **symbol** is something that meaningfully represents something else. It can be a written or spoken word, a gesture, or a sign (such as a raised fist). Thus, the language that humans share and use in their interaction is a system of symbols and their understood meanings. *Interaction* refers to how two or more people respond to one another. Most interaction between human beings is symbolic, in the sense that it depends on words and actions that have meanings beyond themselves. A frown, a kiss, and a smile all have meanings that we learn, share, and change through interaction. Some acts even have hidden meanings and double meanings.

One of the outstanding works in this tradition is *The Social Construction of Reality*, by Peter Berger and Thomas Luckmann (1966). These authors claim that the job of sociology is to understand "the reality of everyday life"—how it is experienced, co-ordinated, and organized. They point out that the everyday world is an *intersubjective* world, meaning that we must

all work to find communicative meeting places for common or shared understanding. They also emphasize that the everyday world is "taken for granted," and it is the job of the sociologist to make us aware of the socially constructed nature of the world.

Symbolic interactionism focuses on the processes by which people interpret and respond to the actions of others. It studies the way social structures, as patterns of behaviour, arise out of these processes. When naming the approach "symbolic interactionism" in 1937, Herbert Blumer described the basic elements of the paradigm in terms of three propositions: (1) "human beings act toward things on the basis of the meanings that things have for them"; (2) these meanings "arise out of social interaction"; and (3) social action results from a "fitting together of individual lines of action" (1937: 172). This perspective was strongly promoted by Blumer, but it also has roots in the work of a group of scholars centred at the University of Chicago in the early twentieth century, among them George Herbert Mead, W.I. Thomas, and Robert Park.

One forerunner of the interactionist approach was German sociologist Georg Simmel ([1943] 1997), who investigated the effects of urbanization on group relations at the community level. He found the urban lifestyle to be relentless and ultimately alienating, with city dwellers numbing their emotional contacts with others in order to cope with the excessive stimulation that city life offered. The fragmentation of urban life leads to a reduction in shared experience, Simmel argued. Within such a framework of distinctive, isolated, and isolating experiences, urban people must work out their social lives.

The symbolic interactionist sees society as the product of interaction between people in their everyday social relationships. In these relationships, the culture of the larger society is adapted to daily life, and sometimes new ways of doing things are developed. Culture is fluid rather than static; it is always open to revision. It is especially situated in specific relationships and occasions for interpersonal interaction. Thus, society and its social relationships are always changing, always being reconstructed by people (Blumer, 1937).

One of the types of shared meanings emphasized in the symbolic interactionist approach is "the definition of the situation." This definition guides the course of interaction in social relationships. A *definition of the situation* is a person's understanding of the package of norms governing and regulating a social situation, such as a classroom, a hockey game, or an office. It includes norms defining the appropriate reasons for people's participation in the situation and the goals one may properly pursue within it. It also spells out how these goals may be achieved, as well as regulating the relationships among the various participants. Because definitions are also shared, they permit people to co-ordinate their actions in pursuing their goals. Seen this way, a definition of a situation is a source of meaning for participants because it permits them to make sense of the situation (Thomas and Thomas, 1926).

Definitions of the situation emerge out of interpersonal negotiations. Negotiations may be formal and explicit (for example, when a contract is drafted between a union and an employer). However, most agreements are less dramatic and tangible, as people informally and tacitly communicate with each other about the situations in which they find themselves. **Communication** is verbal, but it may also consist of gestures, body language, and people's attire.

One way people communicate involves the impressions they create, sometimes intentionally and other times unintentionally, when they first encounter each other. Wearing a clerical collar, highly polished shoes, or jeans, having one's hair in a bun, or introducing oneself as "doctor"—all have consequences for how people regard one another. **Impression management** and first impressions foster understandings about the meaning people attach to their relationships, their goals, and what actions are acceptable and unacceptable to them. People have many motives governing how they present themselves and the kinds of interpretations they invite. They may or may not be conscious of these motives, and they may or may not be sensitive to the cues they convey to others. Symbolic interactionists also study these social processes.

Society is fluid and dynamic, according to interactionists, but this does not mean a lack of controls on people's behaviour except for the whims of the people involved. Situations physically and socially constrain what can reasonably be done in them and therefore limit the kinds of effectively available definitions. It is difficult to play ice hockey, for example, without ice. Likewise, what we do in the classroom is surely constrained by the facts of organizational life outside the classroom. Sexual harassment policies, for instance, remind those who are forgetful that the larger community has a continuing interest in what transpires within the classroom as well as the workplace.

A definition of the situation constrains interaction, but it is not rigid. Relationships between fellow workers or between customers and clerks sometimes turn into romantic relationships, which is to say that the relationships have been redefined. Symbolic interactionists are therefore interested in the tactics used to redefine and reconstruct relationships. Seduction, for example, refers to a class of interpersonal manoeuvres that bring about a redefinition of the relationship between a man and a woman. The possibility of such redefinitions underscores the fact that people are actively involved in exploiting and modifying the social situation and are not merely its puppets. The interactionist studies such redefinitions of the situation and how they came about.

The structural functionalist and conflict perspectives do not necessarily contradict the symbolic interactionist approach, or vice versa. For one thing, the meanings studied by symbolic interactionists are not at all unique or original to a particular relationship. Much of it has its origins in the larger society and is reworked for the immediate requirements of a particular relationship. We can also easily imagine interpersonal negotiations being studied by sociologists working within the structural functionalist and conflict perspectives, even though this would not be a priority for them. Structural functionalists might analyze what is functional in such negotiations, while conflict theorists might consider the different forms of conflict in such negotiations. The structural functionalist and conflict viewpoints emphasize, though, that important shared meanings exist beyond those found in small groups. In addition, these meanings are seen as less transitory and localized than the symbolic interactionist view might lead us to expect.

In relation to the central sociological questions we raised earlier, symbolic interactionists are enormously interested in the *social construction* of differences and inequalities. They would hold that understanding perceptions of difference and similarity, inferiority and superiority, is central to the sociological enterprise. Likewise, they would say that similar people lead different lives because they have been socially construed as different, thus as deserving different opportunities. Why we treat some people as if they are more "different" than others and why we treat "different" people much worse than others are important questions in the symbolic interactionist's library, starting with the classic statement of this problem by Erving Goffman, in *Stigma* (1964).

Summarizing, basic principles of the symbolic interaction perspective include:

1. People are, above all else, symbol users; they acquire these symbols and their shared meaning through social interaction with others.

2. People respond to others and to others' actions based on their understandings of meaning in the particular situation—their definition of the situation.

3. Society and the social groups within it are processes whereby people have constructed meanings and have negotiated social interaction.

### The Feminist Perspective

A fourth paradigm that is ever more influential in sociology is the feminist perspective. It can be traced back two centuries, to work in philosophy by Mary Wollstonecraft, in *A Vindication of the Rights of Woman* ([1792] 1986).

Since the nineteenth century, there have been at least two waves of feminist activity and research. The first wave of feminism occurred from the middle of the nineteenth century through the early twentieth century. It culminated in women's gaining the right to vote in many Western countries. Then two strands of feminism emerged: one concerned with the objective of gaining equal rights with men in the public sphere, the other with gaining recognition of women's difference from men and improving their position in the private sphere of the family. This second wave, or re-emergence, of feminism crystallized in the 1960s. It saw the development of the modern women's movement, which has greatly influenced sociology. Modern feminism has focused research on the oppression that women commonly experience. In addition, recent feminist scholarship has emphasized the diversity of women's experience as members of different countries, classes, and racial and ethnic groups.

One widely accepted distinction is that between *radical feminism* and *materialist* (*socialist* or *Marxist*) *feminism*. Radical feminism—perhaps the dominant form of feminism in the United States—is characterized by a belief that **patriarchy** is the main and universal cause of women's oppression, owing to the superior power of men over women. This view has promoted the notion that women must organize separately from men to protect their own interests and foster a distinct women's culture. Materialist feminism—which is equally important in Canada and dominant outside North America—traces its roots to Marxism and, like Marxism, views gender relations in a historical, economic context. It sees social class relations as determining the conditions women experience within capitalism. This approach calls for women to organize alongside men of the same social class to solve the problems women are suffering.

The two main types of feminism have in common a belief that the domination of women is a result not of **biological determinism**, but of socio-economic and ideological factors. Though they differ in thinking about how equality can be achieved, both types are committed to eliminating the continued social inequality of women. Feminists view most, if not all, gender differences as socially constructed, and all gender inequalities as socially constructed. For feminists, patriarchy is the cultural mechanism that translates differences of biology into differences of social condition and opportunity.

Feminism emphasizes that women and men have different experiences in the same social interaction. For example, men and women typically have different views about divorce because the experience of divorce is different for men and women. For men, it means a brief reduction in the standard of living, if any reduction at all, and a huge reduction in parenting responsibilities. For women, it typically means a dramatic, long-term loss in income and standard of living. Poverty is common among single mothers and their children. Divorce also means an increase in

Canadian society is made up of all the families, clubs, groups, corporations, and so on in which its members participate. Seeing the boundaries between the Canadian and American societies is sometimes difficult. But Canadians have different national symbols; we have a different culture. (© W.P. Wittman Limited)

parental responsibilities for women, since mothers most often retain custody of the children. For all these reasons, divorce has a different meaning for women than it does for men. Similarly, sex, love, marriage, housework, child care, and leisure time all have different meanings for men and women, as we will see in later chapters.

To be a woman in our society is to act out a role that others have defined, feminists emphasize. The "feminine" role tends to be a subservient one, in which women are sometimes degraded or victimized. Along with children, women are comparatively powerless and in danger of their lives (men far more often kill women and children than women and children kill men, for example). Thus, women's acceptance of the female role is far more costly, even more dangerous, than men's acceptance of the male role.

Feminism is also a form of political activism, with an emancipatory goal. If gender relations always reflect the larger pattern of male-dominated social relations in a society, then changing gender relations requires changing those social relations as well. In this respect, feminism is one of the *new social movements*, which include the anti-war, youth, civil rights, and anti-racism movements that in the last several decades have reshaped modern politics. Like these other movements, feminism has appealed to the social identity—the personal life experience—of its supporters. More than that, by arguing that "the personal is political," feminism opened up new domains of social life—sexuality, housework, child-rearing, and so on—to political debate and legislation. It also forces us all to examine the roots of our being as gendered subjects—that is, how we get to be, and to think of ourselves as, men or women, mothers or fathers. Thus, in a century, feminism has moved dramatically from demanding an equal access to social positions defined and dominated by men to demanding that we re-examine the organization of roles, identities, even knowledge about reality in a gendered society.

We can summarize essential characteristics of the feminist approach as follows (see Sydie, 1987):

1. All personal life has a political dimension.
2. The public and private spheres of life are both gendered (that is, unequal for men and women).
3. Patriarchy, or male control, is present in society.
4. Because of routinely different experiences and differences in power, women's and men's perceptions of reality differ.

## Using the Four Sociological Perspectives

As we have seen, there are many differences between the four major approaches to research in sociology. Moreover, there is no simple relationship between the four main perspectives and the two broad levels of analysis—macrosociology and microsociology. True, symbolic interactionism specializes in micro analysis, functionalism and conflict theory in macro analysis. The feminist approach calls for work at both levels, although it is especially rooted in understandings about macro-level processes that are underpinnings for the greater power of males. All four perspectives have something to contribute at both levels of analysis.

These four perspectives will keep reappearing in the chapters that follow. Sometimes the authors are explicit about their use of one or more of the theoretical perspectives; other times the matter is more implicit as the authors draw from studies conducted within each research tradition. Throughout this book, we will see that each of the four perspectives provides explanations for many of the same aspects of the social world. However, they lead us to look at different dimensions of the problem under study. The answers offered by these different perspectives to questions on a particular subject of inquiry are complementary.

# Sociology's Research Techniques

Sociology is not merely made up of various theories and concepts. It also employs varied research techniques in learning about the social world, some of which are shared with other social sciences. The most common research approaches will be described in this section.

## Experiments

A popular image is that the primary method scientists use to conduct research is the experiment. However, even in the natural sciences, experiments are often the exception rather than the rule. A great deal of biology, astronomy, and other sciences is not done—and, in many cases, cannot be done—experimentally. Nevertheless, the image persists, and has traditionally been the standard against which science of all types, natural or social, has been measured.

The main advantage of experiments is that (1) they provide a controlled environment in which it is possible to (2) manipulate specific factors in an attempt to determine their effect on an outcome. Experiments can show the effects of one variable on another variable quite convincingly because of these two features.

However, sociologists can only occasionally use experiments, for two reasons. First, we cannot manipulate many of the variables we are interested in, for either practical or ethical reasons. Sociologists are often interested in the effects of variables like gender, ethnicity, and social class on other variables like educational outcomes, earnings, or health status. But it is neither ethical nor practical to alter people's ethnicity or gender just so we can observe what happens to their educational outcomes. Nor can we simply move a person from an upper-class home into a lower-class home (or vice versa) just so we can find out what effect this might have on his or her eventual choice of career.

Second, one of the enduring criticisms of experiments is that it is not always clear that what happens under the controlled conditions of an experiment will also happen when we try to apply our findings to the "real world" (that is, external validity). For instance, many of the experiments in medical research are done first on rats and other animals, and it is always a question whether or not what happens to rats will also happen to humans. Similarly, in social-scientific research, it is never clear that what we observe in a controlled social experiment will also happen to people in their daily lives. Yet what happens in the real world is of most interest to sociologists. So the findings from a social experiment are often not interesting for us until it can be shown that the results are relevant in the real world as well.

### Surveys

Surveys are the most widely used technique in social-scientific research. Sociologists, economists, political scientists, psychologists, and others use them regularly (Gray and Guppy, 2003). They are an excellent way to gather data on large populations that cannot be studied effectively in a face-to-face manner. The goals of almost all social-scientific surveys are to produce detailed data that will allow researchers to describe the characteristics of the group under study, to test theories about that group, and to generalize results beyond just those people who responded to the survey.

You have probably participated in a survey or opinion poll before, although perhaps not in one used for social-scientific research. Many polls done by political parties or polling organizations generalize from a small sample of people to find out the politi-

cal preferences of voters. Consequently, polling organizations put a great deal of effort into constructing and administering their polls properly. The one disadvantage of many of these polls is that they are often very focused on time-sensitive issues or candidates, so they are only useful for a limited range of social-scientific research topics. However, studies of voting behaviour and other political processes have profited immensely from public opinion polls.

But many "surveys" are done for purposes other than social-scientific research, and most of these will not produce data that are amenable to social science research. Designing and administering a good survey is much more difficult than it seems, but respondents rarely see all of the work that goes into producing a good survey. This may partly explain why surveys seem easy to create, and it may also contribute to the proliferation of pseudo-surveys in many different forms.

A great deal of marketing and customer satisfaction research does not meet the standards of a social-scientific survey, despite the fact that generalizable results remain an important goal. That is, companies do this research only to find out what their customers and potential customers want and do not want to see in their products and services. But if their results apply only to the specific people who answered the survey and not to their customers and potential customers more generally, then they have very limited value. The usual problem in these surveys is that not enough attention is paid to the selection of the people to whom the survey will be sent or administered or to ensuring that enough of the surveys are actually returned. Both of these factors jeopardize the generalizability of the results.

Typically, a customer satisfaction survey will be sent to a selection of customers, perhaps all customers during the past year, in the hope that some of these customers will send it back. But the keys to being able to generalize the results of a survey are that the sample be chosen using a randomized selection procedure and that enough people return the completed survey to ensure that there are no important differences between people who did and did not return it. Unless the company chooses its sample randomly, the results will apply only to those who actually answered the survey.

Moreover, it is not unusual for a company to send a survey to all of its customers and to get only 20 per cent of them back. Why did so many people not return it, and are these people different from those who did return it? Some people probably moved and did not get it, but others probably did not return it because they were unhappy with the service or product they received. To improve a product or service, you need this "negative" information as much as or more than the positive information from the people who did respond.

You have probably also seen TV shows that ask you to register your opinion about something covered in the show by phone or Web site. You may have also seen people in shopping malls asking passersby for their opinions, or come across a survey on an Internet site, or read a mail-in questionnaire in a magazine. Sometimes the results of these questionnaires are released with outrageous claims, like "46 per cent of Canadians think X." The problem with many of these questionnaires is that respondents are chosen based on convenience and luck rather than at random. After all, the respondents to these questionnaires have to watch the TV show, read the magazine, or be in the mall, and these groups of people are not necessarily representative of the larger population. Indeed, one of the main purposes of TV and radio shows, magazines and newspapers, and shopping malls is to appeal to specific, and often unique, parts of the population. So clearly the results of any of these polls are not generalizable to larger populations.

To alleviate some of the confusion around surveys and pseudo-surveys, and also to remove the derogatory connotation of the latter category, it is useful to distinguish between surveys and questionnaires. The pseudo-surveys mentioned above can be classified as questionnaires, but not as surveys. A *questionnaire* is any set of questions administered to a group of people. A *survey*, on the other hand, is a properly designed set of questions that is systematically administered to a randomly chosen sample from a population. In other words, all surveys are questionnaires, but not all questionnaires meet the standards of being a survey. What sets a survey apart are the design of the questions, the goal of collecting data rather than manipulating people, the method of administration, and how the sample is chosen.

## *Field Research*

In surveys, the primary aim is to collect quantitative or numerical data that can be generalized to a larger population. In contrast, field researchers are concerned about collecting qualitative or non-numerical data that may or may not be generalized to a larger population. In field research, the aim is to collect rich, nuanced data by going into the "field" to observe and talk to people directly. Researchers will often spend time getting to know their subjects in order to be able to capture their world view. Some of the classic sociological field studies, such as William Whyte's *Street Corner Society* (1943) and Elliot Liebow's *Tell Them Who I Am* (1993), are vivid portrayals of what life is like for certain groups of people—in the former case, the members of a lower-class urban community, and in the latter case, homeless women.

Field research can involve several separate techniques. These include participant observation or ethnography, in-depth interviewing, and documentary analysis. In many studies, more than one of these techniques is used.

## Ethnographic or Participant Observation Research

In *ethnographic* or *participant observation research*, the researcher participates in the daily activities of his or her research subjects, usually for an extended period of time. This may include accompanying them on their daily activities (such as following police officers on patrol), interviews and discussions about their lives, and occasionally even living with them. During these activities, researchers take field notes (or recordings) either during or after an episode in the field.

A good example of participant observation is Rebecca Tardy's research (2000) of how mothers interact with each other in a "moms and tots" play group. Tardy participated in the group in a small community in the southern United States over a 14-week period. Her purpose was to construct ideas about what a good mother is, and to determine how closely the women in the group matched that ideal. As is typical of participant observation research, Tardy did not have a rigid research design that she followed strictly over the time she was in the field. Rather, her main interest was in the women's conversations about health care and how they used these conversations to define, alter, and reconstruct ideas about "good mothers." She did not direct the women's conversations or ask them to focus their talk on particular issues. Instead, she simply participated in the play group and allowed the conversations to occur naturally. She found that women's understandings of good mothers centred on a few very particular health issues and on a heightened concern for their babies.

Tardy's research is interesting for several reasons, but two are particularly relevant to her use of participant observation. First, her use of Erving Goffman's dramaturgical theoretical approach (in which the metaphors of the theatre are used to understand social life) made participant observation a particularly appropriate method (Goffman, 1959). It allowed her to observe interactions as they occurred and to relate these data directly to some of Goffman's points about how people present themselves differently when they are in more public interactions (frontstage) from when they are in more private interactions (backstage).

Second, by focusing on naturally occurring conversations, Tardy was able to show how cultural ideals about concepts such as "motherhood" and "good mothers" are embedded in and recreated by seemingly mundane discussions among mothers. In other words, ideals about good mothers do not just appear out of nowhere and exert pressure on people through "norms" or "society." Instead, ideals about good mothers get defined, interpreted, and reconstructed by actual people in actual interactions.

### In-depth Interviews

In-depth interviews are another popular field research technique and are often used in conjunction with participant observation. In-depth interviews are extensive interviews that are often tape-recorded and later transcribed into text. In some cases, these interviews are highly structured and neither the researchers nor the respondents are permitted to deviate from a specific set of questions. At the other extreme, unstructured interviews may seem like ordinary conversations in which researchers and respondents simply explore topics as they arise. In many cases, researchers use semi-structured in-depth interviews that ask all respondents a basic set of questions but also allow participants to explore other topics and issues. Striking the right balance between structured and unstructured questions can pose problems for sociologists, as can asking the right questions.

Like Tardy, Elizabeth Murphy (2000) investigated the connections between health-care conversations and ideals about good mothers. Obviously, field research techniques can be used to investigate many more issues than motherhood, but Murphy's and Tardy's studies provide a nice illustration of how different field methods can be used to study the same topic. Murphy used theories about how people understand and respond to risks as the basis of her research on breast-feeding and motherhood. She interviewed 36 British mothers six times each, from one month before the birth of their babies to two years after birth. Each interview was semi-structured. In Murphy's sample, 31 women breast-fed their babies initially, but only six were still breast-feeding four months after birth. This is interesting in light of current medical advice about the importance of exclusively breast-feeding infants for at least four months.

Did the women in this study who stopped breast-feeding before four months think of themselves as bad mothers? Or were they able to set aside this medical advice and still think of themselves as good mothers? Murphy found that almost all of the women who had stopped breast-feeding recognized formula feeding as inferior, but none of them perceived this as a threat to their status as good mothers. Rather, they were able to justify their decisions because other people were at least partly—and, in many cases, primarily—responsible for the switch to formula feeding. The interviews revealed that some women encountered health-care workers who were unsupportive of breast-feeding or who did not diagnose medical or mechanical problems that prevented breast-feeding. Other women had babies who were either unco-operative or could not do it because of "incompetence" (Murphy, 2000: 317).

One of the strengths of Murphy's research is the flexibility of her semi-structured interview technique. By directing the women to discuss their breast-feeding decisions and then following their leads, Murphy was able to gain a much deeper understanding of these choices. Had she not imposed some structure on the interviews, it is possible that the women might not have talked about their breast-feeding choices at all. Instead, her research presents us with a better understanding of how women can reconcile individual decisions to stop breast-feeding with seemingly contradictory ideals about "good motherhood."

### Conducting Field Research

The elaborate procedures needed to choose a sample for a survey are not necessary for selecting the research site and the sample in field research. Strictly following a randomization protocol is only necessary if statistical analysis and generalization are the goal of the research. Field research is done to gain greater understanding through the collection of detailed data, not through generalization. Nevertheless, it is important to choose both the research site and the subjects or informants carefully.

The first criterion in choosing a site for field research is obviously the topic of study. A field study of lawyers or police officers will likely take place at the offices and squad rooms of the respective groups. Choosing which offices and squad rooms to study depends on many factors, including which ones will be the most useful for the purposes of the research. But there is also a practical element in much field research. That is, the actual choice of research site can come down to which law offices or squad rooms will grant access. This is not a criticism of field research but a recognition of the realities facing scholars doing this kind of research.

Once the site has been chosen, the issues of whom to talk to, what types of data to record, and how long to stay in the field become important. Some things can be planned in advance, but many things are often decided during the course of the field research. The selection of key informants—those people who will be most valuable in the course of the study—cannot always be made beforehand. Similarly, figuring out what to write down in field notes, whom to quote, and which observations to record cannot always be determined until after the research has begun.

Deciding when to leave the field is almost always determined during the course of the research. Most researchers stay in the field until they get a sense that they are not gaining much new information. In many cases, researchers decide to leave the field when they find that the data they are getting from new informants merely repeats what they have learned from previous informants. This is often taken as a sign that the researcher has reached a deep enough level of understanding to be confident that he or she will not learn much from further time in the field.

This flexibility during the course of the study is one of the great advantages of field research over survey research. Mistakes in research design and the pursuit of new and unexpected opportunities are possible in field research but are not usually possible in quantitative survey research. Once a survey has been designed, pre-tested, and administered to a sample, it is impractical to recall the survey to make changes. This is one of the reasons why pre-testing is so important in surveys.

### *Existing Data and Documentation*

In both surveys and field research, sociologists collect new, original data. However, a great deal of sociological research is also done with data that already exist. Several different types of existing data lend themselves to different modes of analysis. Some of the major types of existing data are official statistics and surveys done by other researchers; books, magazines, newspapers, and other media; case files and records; and historical documents.

In some field studies, researchers will have access not only to people, but also to documents. This is more common when studying formal organizations like police forces or law firms, but can also be true when studying churches, political groups, and even families. These documents (case records, files, posters, diaries, even photos) can be analyzed to provide a more complete picture of the group under study.

### Secondary Data Analysis

The analysis of official statistics and existing surveys (also known as *secondary data analysis*) has grown immensely with the development of computers and statistical software packages. It is now one of the most common forms of research reported in the major sociological journals, such as the *American Journal of Sociology* and the *American Sociological Review*. Statistical analyses of existing surveys can also be found in almost every issue of the *Canadian Journal of Sociology* and the *Canadian Review of Sociology and Anthropology* for at least the past 10 years.

Quantitative data are often presented in tables like Table 1.1. Tables can be designed in many different ways, and the type of information presented in a table will determine the types of comparisons that can be made. In Table 1.1, on marital status in Canada, comparisons can be made within or across the values of marital status (for example, how many people are married versus single), by sex, and across five different years.

As an example, we can see that the number of divorced males has increased by over 93,000 between 1997 and 2001 (641,734 − 547,914 = 93,820) and the number of divorced females has risen by over 125,000 (868,037 − 742,671 = 125,366), while the numbers of married men and women have increased by 87,500 and 106,136 respectively. However, the table does not tell us anything about why these numbers may have changed, nor can we make any comparisons with the number of married and divorced people in other countries.

In Table 1.2, though, comparisons between countries are possible. Some of these results may seem surprising, depending on your impressions of high school graduation rates here in Canada versus other countries. Many media portrayals of the US school system would suggest that it is inferior to the Canadian system, yet the United States has a higher graduation rate than Canada.

However, this table also reveals some of the problems that may be present in tables, especially those presenting data from different countries. First, the school systems vary widely between countries, and despite careful efforts by the Organization for Economic Co-operation and Development (OECD)

Table 1.1 **Population by Marital Status and Sex, Canada, 1998–2002**

| | 1998 | 1999 | 2000 | 2001 | 2002 |
|---|---|---|---|---|---|
| *Total* | | | | | |
| Both sexes | 30,248,412 | 30,499,323 | 30,770,834 | 31,110,565 | 31,413,990 |
| Male | 14,978,787 | 15,107,404 | 15,236,964 | 15,405,773 | 15,552,644 |
| Female | 15,269,625 | 15,401,919 | 15,543,870 | 15,704,792 | 15,861,346 |
| | | | | | |
| *Single* | | | | | |
| Both sexes | 12,797,263 | 12,911,946 | 13,031,272 | 13,175,106 | 13,304,129 |
| Male | 6,849,478 | 6,912,620 | 6,979,618 | 7,059,481 | 7,131,973 |
| Female | 5,947,785 | 5,999,326 | 6,051,654 | 6,115,625 | 6,172,156 |
| | | | | | |
| *Married*[a] | | | | | |
| Both sexes | 12,979,263 | 12,911,946 | 13,031,272 | 13,175,106 | 13,304,129 |
| Male | 7,299,132 | 7,337,226 | 7,381,266 | 7,431,522 | 7,476,537 |
| Female | 7,331,041 | 7,374,567 | 7,425,428 | 7,482,244 | 7,541,593 |
| | | | | | |
| *Widowed* | | | | | |
| Both sexes | 1,489,388 | 1,503,843 | 1,518,633 | 1,534,232 | 1,550,367 |
| Male | 263,490 | 269,220 | 274,910 | 280,748 | 286,940 |
| Female | 1,225,898 | 1,234,623 | 1,243,723 | 1,253,484 | 1,263,427 |
| | | | | | |
| *Divorced* | | | | | |
| Both sexes | 1,331,588 | 1,381,741 | 1,434,235 | 1,487,461 | 1,541,364 |
| Male | 566,687 | 588,338 | 611,170 | 634,022 | 657,194 |
| Female | 764,901 | 793,403 | 823,065 | 853,439 | 884,170 |

[a] Includes persons legally married, legally married and separated, and living in common-law unions.
SOURCE: Adapted from Statistics Canada, CANSIM database <http://cansim2.statcan.ca>, Table 051–0010.

to standardize the data, all of these numbers should be treated with caution. That is, many of these numbers could change significantly depending on how graduates are counted, and especially on how each country reports its data to the OECD. Second, data may simply not be available, as in the case of Slovakia in Table 1.2.

Personal computers, statistical software packages, and the ready availability of many national and international data sets have made secondary data analysis possible for almost every social scientist. The advantages of secondary analyses are that the coverage of the data is broad and that the hard work involved in constructing and administering a survey has already been done, usually by an agency with far more expertise and resources than most individual researchers. The disadvantages are that the data collected are often not precise enough to test the specific ideas that researchers are interested in and that the learning curve associated with mastering the techniques to analyze the data properly is potentially steep.

## Historical Research and Content Analysis

The analysis of historical documents, print and other media, and records and case materials can be done by several methods. The two most common forms of analysis are probably historical research and content analysis. *Historical sociology* relies on historical research into all kinds of historical documents, from organizational records, old newspapers, and magazines to speeches and sermons, letters and diaries, and even interviews with people who participated in the events of interest. In *content analysis*, documents such as newspapers, magazines, TV shows, and case records are subjected to careful sampling and analysis procedures to reveal patterns.

One of the major issues facing historical sociologists is that someone or some organization has created the records used in their analyses, but the potential biases and reasons for recording the information in the documents are not always clear. Further, over time some documents get lost or destroyed, so the histori-

Table 1.2 **Percentage of 25- to 64-Year-Olds Graduating from Upper Secondary (High School) Programs, by Country, 1998**

| | Percentage Graduating from Upper Secondary |
|---|---|
| Canada | 79.7 |
| Mexico | 21.2 |
| United States | 86.5 |
| Japan | 79.9 |
| Korea | 65.4 |
| Australia | 56.0 |
| New Zealand | 72.7 |
| Belgium | 56.7 |
| Czech Republic | 85.3 |
| Denmark | 78.4 |
| Finland | 68.3 |
| France | 60.7 |
| Germany | 83.8 |
| Hungary | 63.3 |
| Italy | 41.0 |
| The Netherlands | 64.3 |
| Norway | 83.0 |
| Poland | 54.3 |
| Portugal | 20.1 |
| Spain | 32.9 |
| Slovakia | – |
| Sweden | 76.1 |
| Turkey | 17.7 |
| United Kingdom | 60.2 |
| OECD Mean | 61.2 |

SOURCE: Organisation for Economic Co-operation and Development (OECD), <http://www.oecd.org/pdf/M00019000/M00019568.pdf>, accessed 30 June 2003. Reprinted by permission.

cal sociologist must be aware that the existing documents may not give a complete picture of the events or time period under study. Why have certain documents survived while others have not? Also, is there any significance to the ordering or cataloguing of the documents? These and other issues must be dealt with continually in historical research.

Content analysis can be done in a number of ways, but it usually involves taking a sample of relevant documents and then subjecting these documents to a rigorous procedure of identifying and classifying particular features, words, or images. For instance, in studying political posters, content analysis could be used to determine whether the posters from particular parties put more emphasis on the positive aspects of their own party or the negative aspects of other parties. These results could then be used to better

understand styles of political campaigning in a particular country or time period. In *manifest content analysis*, words, phrases, or images are counted to provide a sense of the importance of different ideas in the documents. In *latent content analysis*, researchers focus less on specific word or phrase counts and more on the themes that are implicit in the documents.

### Selecting a Research Method

To summarize, sociologists use all of the methods described here to collect data on particular research problems, and they use theories to help them understand or solve these problems. Any of these methods can be used to investigate problems from any of the theoretical perspectives encountered in this text, although some methods are almost never used in some perspectives. For instance, symbolic interactionists rarely if ever use quantitative surveys, while most conflict theorists prefer surveys to participant observation.

So how do you know which method to use with which theory or theoretical perspective? A complete answer to this question is beyond the scope of this chapter, but the general rule in sociology has been that you let the problem determine the method. For example, if you want to find out something about the national divorce rate and how divorced people differ from those who remain married, then you need a method, like a survey, that will give you data from people all over the country. But if you want to find out how nurses manage the many pressures of their jobs, then participant observation is an appropriate method.

As with any rule of thumb, though, there are exceptions. And as Sheldon Goldenberg (1992) and others have argued, letting the problem determine the method is not as straightforward as it seems. The main reason for this is that sociologists often become much more comfortable using one technique or another. They may then frame their research questions in ways that allow them to use those familiar techniques. In other words, many researchers "load the dice," and the methods they are comfortable with tend to determine the questions they investigate.

# Sociology and Social Change

### Sociologists Value Particular Forms of Change

Not all sociologists attempt to achieve social change through their research, but most sociologists place a high value on improving the lives of human beings.

Whatever theoretical perspective or research technique a sociologist uses in his or her research, improvements in people's lives and in society as a whole are what he or she hopes will result from the research, even if the application of the research is left for others to do. And most research that leads to better understanding of how society operates can be useful for improving social life in some way. Research on some topics, such as social problems, is, of course, more directly useful for the betterment of people's lives than other research.

Sociology is, for the most part, an engaged, progressive, and optimistic discipline founded on the notion that people can improve society through research and the application of research-based knowledge. Consistent with this, we find that much of the research that sociologists do is guided by one or more of these seven value preferences (Alvarez, 2000):

• Life over death
• Health over sickness
• Knowing over not knowing
• Co-operation over conflict
• Freedom of movement over physical restraint
• Self-determination over direction by others
• Freedom of expression over restraint of communication

In this sense, sociology may be said to be a "moral enterprise," and a humanistic one. Sociologists value the outcomes listed above and pursue these outcomes. As a result, much research in sociology criticizes the existing social order. Much of the sociological literature shows a desire to change society, protect the vulnerable, and redress injustices.

Researchers are concerned with combatting myths, ideologies, and stereotypes—for example, about women, visible minorities, poor people, the elderly, or youth—that perpetuate harmful conditions for vulnerable peoples. A related concern is the frequently observed tendency for "public issues" to be turned into "private troubles." The public and public officials wrongly see a social problem as the personal responsibility of the sufferers, who are blamed for having these problems.

Consider as an example research on depressive disorders, which are a major public health problem today. The general public and health practitioners see depressive disorders as personal problems of individuals. However, depression occurs frequently and produces severe suffering for the people affected and their families, leading to higher risks of death, disability, and secondary illness. For various reasons, including the aging of the population and the extended life expectancy of people suffering from chronic physical disorders, the frequency of depressive disorders has been increasing and will increase in years to come. Sociologists have emphasized how ideological thinking about these disorders, which blames the victims, should be questioned, and they have made clear the social nature of these disorders to policy-makers and the public (Sartorius, 2001).

Like many other sociologists today, and just like two centuries ago when sociology began, we assume that the purpose of sociology is to use knowledge to improve social life. Thus, one of the goals of a book like this is to aid our understanding of how people's lives may be improved by better understanding how society and culture operate.

## The Individual, Organizations, and Social Change

C. Wright Mills's (1959) point in describing the sociological imagination in the way he did was that knowledge can be power—if individuals or groups choose to act upon it. That is, when we know what is going on in society and then act accordingly and in our best interests, we stand some chance of maximizing our opportunities. Under individual-level solutions, we can act to "work the system" to our specific benefit.

A good example of this is our earlier discussion of how people find jobs. Armed with the results of sociological analysis of what types of job searches turn out to be most successful, you can better maximize your chances of finding a good job, being careful to draw on both strong and weak ties as sources of information, not de-emphasizing the latter. As a second example, if you learn that some sections of the workforce are shrinking while others are expanding, you can consider preparing yourself for a job you would like in one of the expanding sectors. We all have choices of this type to make. Your power to choose means that while society and culture may constrain your options, they do not entirely determine your life. What you choose to do at certain points in life can make a difference. Opportunities can be exploited or squandered, difficulties overcome or compounded. The trick is to know what is occurring and how to help your chances. Information and understanding can lead us to individual solutions for personal problems, as we will see repeatedly in the remaining chapters.

You can also consider getting involved in groups or organizations—there are political parties and interest groups of all sorts. Some of them will have

## 1.1

# Global Issues
## The Health Challenges of Climate Change

*Pollution Probe released a report in October 2001, with Health Canada looking into the impact of climate change on the health of people in the Toronto and Niagara regions. Here is an edited excerpt.*

The impact of the health effects of climate change will be determined, in large part, by how well the health infrastructure is able to cope.

Until recently, the prevailing view of many experts was that both Canada and the United States are well protected against adverse health outcomes due to a strong public health-care system (especially in Canada), a high standard of living, and high levels of public awareness.

Evidence emerging from climate change and human health research suggests that this may be an optimistic view for a number of reasons.

First, changes in the frequency, intensity and severity of extreme weather events may pose a greater challenge than small changes in mean temperatures. This may be especially true for vulnerable groups, whose health is already being affected by current climate conditions.

Extreme weather events—such as the Saguenay-Chicoutimi flood in 1996 and the 1998 ice storm in Ontario and Quebec—clearly demonstrated the vulnerability of municipal infrastructures in Canada to climate stresses, with harmful consequences for human health. Similarly, the illnesses and deaths due to a highly virulent strain of E. coli in Walkerton in spring, 2000, were triggered by weather conditions (drought followed by intense rainfall).

The Walkerton disaster has heightened public concern over the quality of our water and the ability of municipal infrastructure to deliver clean water. Ongoing health concerns over periodic heat waves, severe cold spells and, especially, intense smog episodes continue to attract the attention of politicians from all levels of government, as well as members of the health-care community.

Second, the health-care system has been able to cope relatively well with most climate stresses in the past. However, this is not a guarantee that the health of Canadians will be well protected in the future. In many regions of Canada, the health-care system is already becoming overburdened.

In Ontario, for example, there is growing concern that emergency hospital departments and home care services are in a state of crisis. Further, the vulnerability of Canadians may also be increasing. The population is getting older, and in some urban centres, such as the Greater Toronto Area and the city of Hamilton, the disparities between rich and poor are on the rise, with areas of poverty becoming increasingly marginalized from the more affluent suburban communities.

Consequently, the ability of the health infrastructure to respond effectively to climate change impacts, such as new and emerging diseases, and ensure the health of Canadians is by no means certain and, at the very least, demands closer attention.

In order to reduce the vulnerability of Canadians to the health effects resulting from climate change, it is necessary that decision-makers have a strategy for developing an effective adaptation action plan.

Such a plan requires a clear understanding of the health risks associated with current climate and climate change, the options that are available and the capacity of health infrastructure to adapt to future climate change impacts.

SOURCE: Excerpts from Part 1 – Introduction, *Towards an Adaptation Action Plan: Climate Change and Health in the Toronto-Niagara Region, Summary for Policy Makers,* by Q. Chiotti, K. Ogilvie Morgan, A. Maarouf, and M. Kelleher. Pollution Probe, 2002. Reprinted by permission of Pollution Probe. Available online <http://www.pollutionprobe.org/Reports/adaptation.pdf>

goals for social changes that you would like to see realized. Here, too, knowledge of your society and culture is needed to make good decisions about which groups and organizations are most appropriate to your interests. Your values and ideologies (which are socially derived) will also determine your choices of goals and organizations.

People acting in groups and organizations make history. The chapters that follow will demonstrate this many times through different examples. Consider, for example, the changes in health-care legislation, family law, and unemployment insurance and minimum-wage legislation that have been achieved by reform groups over the past several decades. Be warned, though, that this strategy of political action through groups and organizations can be a slow road. Moreover, many of your journeys may be unsuccessful. The analyses to come in other chapters will indicate, too, that dominant groups oppose certain solutions to improve people's lives because they are not particularly in their own interests. As Marx and Weber, along with other scholars, have emphasized, such dominant groups will have considerable organizational and ideological power.

However, political struggles can be won. There are many examples in Canada and the United States alone of successful protest movements by subordinate groups: the civil rights movement in the United States, the Quiet Revolution in Quebec, the women's movement in both countries, to name only three. Another important example is the success of the labour movement in Canada and the United States, fighting over many decades to secure better wages and job conditions for the working class. This textbook will refer to many instances of social change initiated by social organizations, including many examples initiated by government agencies. Such developments should give us heart concerning the possibilities of joint action to resolve societal problems. Many problems will be shown to be formidable in their social causes and social consequences, but there is room to effect social change if we work at it.

# Conclusion

Sociology is a good idea. It pays off in enlightening us, and it has worthy goals. It is the systematic study of how society and patterns of social behaviour within society are structured and change.

It is a broad field of study. This is evident in the four theoretical perspectives used to guide much sociological research. The breadth of the field of study is further evident in that sociology emphasizes both micro- and macro-level analyses and in the complex relationships between the two that Mills points out in his concept of the sociological imagination. Sociology also covers a broad subject matter—consider the subject matter of the following chapters, ranging across deviance, family, education, politics, the economy, health, and beyond. Sociologists pursue these topics using a wide range of research techniques.

Sociology allows people to move beyond a purely common-sense approach to better understanding social life. It allows them to use more powerful methods of investigation that reveal the multifaceted and elaborate ways that aspects of social life are interconnected. In the process, much common-sense knowledge is shown to be faulty. Sociology will help you see that things are not always what they seem.

Sociology emphasizes the relationships among individuals, social structure, and culture. Social structure and culture are shown to constrain greatly the behaviour of individuals, yet they are essential for the persistence of human life and society. In addition, social structure and culture are shown to be creations of humans through social interaction, and are, therefore, subject to future change by individuals acting in group settings. Strong constraints are placed on certain forms of social and cultural change, however, by the actions of powerful interest groups.

Sociology has obvious personal relevance, since it addresses everyday life issues. And, finally, sociology has an important goal overall: to contribute positively to the future of humanity.

## ☐ Questions for Critical Thought

1. Thinking about the roles that you have in your life (student, worker, mother, father, daughter, son, and so on), choose one role and examine your patterns of interaction from a macro and a micro perspective. How does this role influence your current behaviours? From what sources in society did you learn this role?
2. Marxists emphasize class inequalities and conflict, while functionalists emphasize order and consensus based on shared value systems. Which perspective offers a more realistic picture of Canadian society? State your reasons.
3. Which of the four sociological paradigms do you think best fits your own ideas about how society is arranged? Explain why this particular paradigm is most applicable and how you might use it in some of your own research.
4. Feminists maintain that our social worlds are fundamentally structured in terms of gender inequalities. Identify three key institutions that are based on such differentiation. Identify three patriarchal features in our culture.
5. Standardized testing for children in elementary and high school is becoming more common in Canada. Consider the manifest and latent functions of this type of testing. In addition, using a conflict perspective, consider who has the most to gain in the implementation of this testing.
6. If you wanted to find out more about the motivations of parents who send their children to a particular private school, what methods would be most appropriate? Justify your answer.
7. Sociological research can provide important information about how people can effectively deal with many situations in their daily life. Consider how we could make sociological research and information more accessible to the common person than is currently the case. In addition, could we increase the use of sociological knowledge by members of the general public?

## ☐ Recommended Readings

**Earl Babbie, *The Basics of Social Research*, 2nd edn (Toronto: Wadsworth Thomson Learning, 2002).**
Babbie's books are used in more research methods courses across North America than those of any other author. This one is a comprehensive treatment of research methods.

**Randall Collins and Michael Mayakowsky, *The Discovery of Society* (New York: Random House, 1989).**
A brilliant short history of the development of sociology, set against the backdrop of nineteenth- and twentieth-century social and political change.

**Anthony Giddens, *Central Problems in Social Theory: Action, Structure, and Contradiction in Social Analysis* (Berkeley: University of California Press, 1979).**
Giddens's book is perhaps the best place to start for getting a handle on contemporary debates, with much attention given to the necessity of integrating the agency and structure perspectives.

**Charles C. Lemert, *Social Things: An Introduction to the Sociological Life*, 2nd edn (Lanham, Md: Rowman & Littlefield, 2002).**
An easy-to-read book for introductory sociology students, this text examines how local and global forces influence individuals' lives, with particular attention paid to political and economic events and trends.

**C. Wright Mills, *The Sociological Imagination* (New York: Oxford University Press, 1967).**
This classic work in sociology is written from the conflict perspective. It emphasizes the close connection between personal troubles (private experience) and public issues (the wider social context). This is perhaps the best-known, most often quoted sociological work in the world.

## □ Recommended Web Sites

**Research Methods Resources on the www**
**www.slais.ubc.ca/resources/research_methods**
> This useful site lists both qualitative and quantitative methods resources, originally developed at the University of British Columbia library. Resources include on-line books, data, journals, and more.

**A Sociological Tour through Cyberspace**
**www.trinity.edu/~mkearl/**
> An excellent set of links to sociology resources on the Internet.

**SocioSite**
**www2.fmg.uva.nl/sociosite**
> Sociologists, dead and very much alive, with links to biographies, works, and research in sociology.

# part two >>>

# Major Social Processes

Chapter 1 emphasized that people's behaviours, and even their personal identities, are greatly influenced by two types of processes—culture and social structure. Both culture and social structure are always all around us, and they continually shape our behaviours and views. At the same time, culture and social structure are produced and maintained by individuals. In short, the sociological perspective points out that there are very close and dynamic relationships among individuals, culture, and social structure. Part Two focuses on the ways in which individuals, culture, and social structure mutually affect each other.

# 2

Shyon Baumann

> > >

# Culture and Culture Change

© Getty Images

## ☐ Learning Objectives

In this chapter, you will:

- see that *culture* has many meanings, and that we need to specify a particular cultural dimension when raising questions about culture

- observe that culture is ubiquitous: it is thoroughly a part of our lives, and we would not have societies without it

- learn that culture is powerful: it integrates members of society but can also cause great conflict

- learn that one of the quintessential elements of culture is its ability to carry meaning and facilitate communication

- see that change in culture is inevitable: it is within the nature of culture to evolve and to build on its own previous configurations

- find that the reasons and mechanisms behind culture change are various—some are social-structural, while sometimes cultural changes spur on other cultural changes

# Why Study Culture?

What do we mean by the word **culture**? And why do we want to know? To answer the second question briefly, we want to know because culture is an amazingly powerful social force that influences events as diverse as whom we marry and whether we go to war. Marriage and war are interesting examples—while they seem unrelated, they are similar insofar as they both involve the bonds between people, in one case bringing people closer together and in the other pushing them further apart.

Let us consider how culture is involved in each of these events. How we choose whom to marry is incredibly complicated, but in general people marry those with whom they share interests and experiences. Such shared ideas and preferences create a feeling of comfort and familiarity. If we like the same music and the same kind of movies, if we share a belief in the importance of family and the role of religion in our lives, if we share a notion of the different roles and responsibilities of men and women, if we support the same political ideals, then we feel more connected to each other. In all these ways, culture is influencing how we relate to others. Culture includes all these preferences and ideas and notions, and these are the things that allow us in our daily lives to feel connections to other people. Cultural similarities influence our decisions not only about getting married, but about all kinds of connections—with whom we become and stay friends, even with whom we work.

Just as we are often brought closer to other people, so, too, we often experience social divisions, some relatively minor and others quite significant. Like marriage, war is an enormously complicated phenomenon; it can result from a wide array of social, economic, and geopolitical factors. It is also clear that culture can play a role in creating or worsening the divisions between groups or societies that can lead to war. While a conflict of material interests is usually the basis of war, culture can play a large role in determining whether war is the ultimate outcome. If we differ in fundamental **beliefs** about such things as democracy and human rights, if we speak different languages and cannot easily communicate, if we cannot understand others' religious concepts and practices, if we do not share preferences for what we consider to be the normal and good ways to live our lives, then we feel less connected to each other. In all these ways, culture plays a role in dividing us from others, and it is only in the presence of such divisions, when we feel essentially different and disconnected from others, that we are able to pursue as drastic a course of action as war. In addition, culture plays a role in many more minor social divisions—the various social cleavages among **social groups** within the same society—that are not as significant as war.

Culture, then, is important because it is the key to understanding how we relate to each other; specifically, it is behind both what unites us and what divides us. Our cultural differences and similarities are continually coming into play, in our daily face-to-face interactions and on a global scale. To truly understand the dynamics of war and peace, love and hate, and more, we need to look at how culture facilitates or inhibits the bonds and the rifts between us.

The goals of this chapter are to review the many nuances to the meaning of *culture* and to explain how culture is implicated in many important social processes. To achieve this goal this chapter will first further specify what culture is through a clear conceptualization of culture's many dimensions. With the many connotations of *culture*, we need to pay heed to various aspects of it. In addition, this chapter will summarize how culture is used in sociological theorizing about society. It examines how culture fits into causal explanations about the way society works. In this chapter, we are also interested in a description of those realms of social life that are primarily cultural—the loci of culture. The nature of culture change is another focus of this chapter, and we will examine the reciprocal relationship between culture change and social change. Finally, we will discuss the insights of this chapter as they pertain to Canadian culture.

# What Is Culture?

Think of the many ways that you might use the word *culture* in casual conversation. You might use it to refer to the way an entire society lives, visible most clearly when it is foreign to you, as in "Thai culture." You might use *culture* to refer to the refined aesthetic productions that "highbrow" people enjoy. *Culture* takes on a still different meaning in a phrase such as "consumer culture," which focuses on a major pattern of people's behaviour and a set of economic institutions in contemporary society. Or you might use *culture* to refer to the practices and preferences of a subgroup of people (for example, "jock culture," "geek culture," or "skater culture") who are nonetheless part of the larger society, in whose culture they also participate.

Perhaps no term in the sociological vocabulary has as many meanings as *culture*. Although some of these meanings are closely related to each other, others are remarkably divergent. For a concept that has traditionally been viewed as central to much sociological analysis, this is a strange state of affairs and one that complicates any attempt to provide a succinct and definitive summary of the sociology of culture.

To begin defining *culture*, we can recognize that at its most expansive, culture can be conceived of as the sum total of human creation: everything that is a product of a human mind, no matter how small or large, how concrete or abstract, how individual or widely shared, constitutes an element of culture. Of course, for a concept to be useful, it must allow us to distinguish what it is referring to from what it is not referring to. The first clear distinction, then, is that between culture and the natural world as it exists apart from human interaction. For the purposes of sociological analysis, when we speak of *culture* we do not refer to the physical reality of our natural environment, the complex ecological system billions of years in the making. This first distinction, however, still leaves quite a lot under the rubric of culture—namely, all of social reality—and this begs for further clarification.

## Distinctive Elements of Culture

Defining *culture* as the sum total of the human-influenced and human-created environment, including anything and everything that is the product of a human mind, leaves us with a rather bloated notion of the term's meaning. This expansive definition rests on the notion that all of our thought processes are conditioned and shaped by the **social environment** into which we are socialized. Without this social environment, without this culture, we would have nothing to form our thoughts except for our natural instincts and desires. All human societies, however, develop a cultural way of life that can significantly shape the minds of individuals and allow them to develop into socialized members of that society. Insofar as this **socialization** process influences all that we do—if not directly then at least indirectly—we can plausibly call all of social life *cultural*.

Although *culture* can mean all of this, the concept is really only useful for helping us to make sociological arguments and draw sociological insights if we can limit it. In practice, we are usually interested in determining the relative influence or functioning of cultural factors in society compared to other, non-cultural factors. We therefore often employ various,

more restricted senses of the term and strive to set apart certain elements of social life as "cultural" from those elements that are not. To add to the complicated nature of defining *culture*, a certain amount of disagreement exists over which elements of social life are properly "cultural."

For the sake of giving initial form to the idea of culture as it is discussed here, we can create a list of specific things that are always or usually classified as "culture" in sociology. Languages, symbols, discourses, texts, knowledge, values, attitudes, beliefs, norms, world views, folkways, art, music, ideas, and ideologies are all "culture." In sociological analysis, these social phenomena are differentiated on the basis of inherent cultural qualities. To better understand why these things are "culture," we need to think about their characteristics.

We can do that by first examining how culture is different between places and at different times. Examining the nature of those changes is a first step in providing a full description of culture. Second, to better understand what makes the above list of cultural elements conceptually coherent, we need to examine how sociologists distinguish between the cultural and the non-cultural. We will review two major distinctions employed in the sociological literature to specify the elements of culture: the difference between culture and structure, and the difference between the symbolic and the non-symbolic.

## Culture in Place and Time

*Culture* is quite often used to refer to the entire social reality of particular social groups in comparison to other social groups. Perhaps the largest cultural groupings frequently in use differentiate between large regions of the globe—Western culture, for example, while encompassing tremendous variation, is seen as distinctive, in regard to its history and present reality, from Eastern and Near Eastern cultures. Such a distinction obscures the many similarities and historical continuities between these cultures and instead emphasizes how they differ. Nonetheless, it is a first step in limiting the concept of "culture" to a more helpful definition, namely the social environment, in its entirety, of people from within a circumscribed physical space.

It should be immediately clear that we often think of culture in more specific geographic terms than just Western or Eastern. We frequently think in national terms, with fairly strong ideas of what we mean by, for example, Japanese culture, Italian culture, or Mexican culture. These ideas exist in our minds as stereotypes or generalizations about the kind of lives inhabitants of these countries choose to lead. We might think of, among many other things, Japanese rituals of politeness and a preference for sushi, the sights and sounds of Italian opera and the speed of Vespa scooters, and small Mexican towns where elaborate, solemn Catholic ceremonies can give way to lively and colourful festivals. Likewise, you might have noticed when talking to people from other countries that they sometimes impose expectations on you based on stereotypes of Canada and Canadians: "Do you play hockey?" "Do you drive a snowmobile?"

Whatever the accuracy or generalizability (frequently low) of such stereotypes as images of the typical culture of these countries, their pervasiveness points to the reality that culture can vary systematically between nations, even if it is often in ways of which we are commonly unaware. There is good reason for this: nation-states have often coalesced around a common cultural foundation, or if one was not clearly defined from early on, they have tended to promote such a cultural foundation for the sake of national unity and cohesion.

Despite the definitional clarity that a notion of national culture offers, upon closer inspection we can see that, like the larger generalizations of "Western culture" or "Eastern culture," national cultures also entail a great deal of regional and local variation. For example, in a large country such as the United States, the culture of the politically liberal, highly urbanized, and economically successful Northeast can be contrasted with the culture of certain of the politically conservative and less affluent states in the South. Such a contrast points to the differences between the whole way of life of Northeasterners and Southerners; however, we need to be mindful that both share a culture that is more generally "American" and that they therefore share countless cultural features.

We can continue to limit our concept of culture spatially by pointing to the general social differences between various cities and even between parts of cities. The culture of downtown Toronto, for example, brings up notions of a lifestyle and a built environment that are business-oriented, cosmopolitan, and culturally rich. Toronto's **urbanism** is often cited for its impersonality and inward-lookingness, and contrasts with the particular habits, manners, and interaction styles of, for example, St John's, Newfoundland. Remember, though, that as with the differences in regions, such local cultural variations belie more similarities than differences.

Just as with the differences between regions, however, we must be careful not to overstate the precision with which we can delineate a concept of culture based on physical space. Cultural similarities are bound to exist between various *physical* spaces—no matter how narrowly we draw our boundaries—on account of shared *social* spaces. Just as we can identify culture as the human environment of specific geographic locations, so we can also identify culture as the human environment of groups who are similar socially despite being geographically disparate. Therefore, we can think of the culture of, for example, adolescent males as distinct from adolescent females or from adult males, no matter whether their geographic location is Vancouver or Halifax. (See also Table 2.1 on the cultural activities of adult Canadian males.) Acknowledging culture's social, not just physical, boundedness provides us with a second dimension for understanding and limiting the meaning of culture.

Age and gender, the social groupings in the above example, are just two of many social boundaries that can differentiate between cultures. Other social lines along which cultural features may fall include race and ethnicity, sexual orientation, religion, and many other ways that people see fit to distinguish themselves. Another social space with important cultural implications is that of social class. Stereotypes of distinct working- and upper-class cultures are at least as pervasive as national stereotypes. We have firm ideas about the typical speech, mannerisms, dress, culinary preferences, occupations, and leisure activities of the working class and the upper class.

At this point it is necessary to point out again that, just as the cultures of urban Ontario and rural Alberta share more similarities than differences, the cultures of different social groups within a society likewise share more similarities than differences. By enumerating how, for example, social classes in Canada differ, we neglect many ways in which they are similar: difference in accent is trivial to the overall nature of a language; a similar reliance on automobiles overshadows any consideration of whether those automobiles are foreign or domestic; and a propensity to vote for different political parties cannot diminish the tremendous importance of a shared faith in parliamentary democracy.

In addition, it is necessary to point out that the dimensions of physical and social space are relatively but not entirely independent. In some instances there is considerable overlap, when a social grouping exclusively or almost exclusively inhabits a physical space. Thus, if we were to study the culture of retirement

Table 2.1 **Participation in Cultural Activities, Canadians and Male Canadians, 1998**

| | Both Sexes | | Male | |
|---|---|---|---|---|
| | **Thousands** | **%** | **Thousands** | **%** |
| Read a newspaper | 19,851 | 81.8 | 9,915 | 83.1 |
| Read a magazine | 17,264 | 71.2 | 8,166 | 68.4 |
| Read a book | 14,881 | 61.3 | 6,478 | 54.3 |
| Use library services | 6,688 | 27.6 | 2,845 | 23.8 |
|     Borrow materials | 6,036 | 24.9 | 2,432 | 20.4 |
|     Use Internet | 583 | 2.4 | 296 | 2.5 |
|     Do research | 1,898 | 7.8 | 964 | 8.1 |
|     Attend a program | 277 | 1.1 | 81 | 0.7 |
|     Other | 107 | 0.4 | 49 | 0.4 |
| Go to a movie | 14,340 | 59.1 | 7,216 | 60.5 |
| Watch a video on VCR | 17,690 | 72.9 | 8,921 | 74.7 |
| Listen to cassettes, records, CDs | 18,625 | 76.8 | 9,166 | 76.8 |
| Use Internet | 7,171 | 29.6 | 4,117 | 34.5 |
|     Research | 5,412 | 22.3 | 3,248 | 27.2 |
|     Communicate | 5,478 | 22.6 | 3,081 | 25.8 |
|     Read a newspaper, magazine, book | 2,322 | 9.6 | 1,432 | 12.0 |
|     View video, film, TV, listen to music | 1,204 | 5.0 | 799 | 6.7 |
|     View art or museum collections | 1,011 | 4.2 | 611 | 5.1 |
|     Create artistic compositions, designs | 983 | 4.1 | 601 | 5.0 |
|     Electronic banking | 1,437 | 5.9 | 942 | 7.9 |
|     Download software, other | 2,714 | 11.2 | 1,864 | 15.6 |
| **Total population (15 and over)** | **24,260** | | **11,937** | |

SOURCE: Adapted fromStatistics Canada, "Participation in Cultural Activities by Sex, Canada," General Social Survey, 1998; available at <www40.statcan.ca/l01/est01/arts36a.htm>, accessed 15 May 2003.

communities, we would see that these are physical spaces populated mostly by a specific social group defined by age. The social boundedness of culture by age (the culture of an older generation) maps onto a physical boundedness of culture by residential location (the culture of a retirement community). Likewise, there is a great deal of overlap between the physical space of Anglican churches and the social space of Anglicans.

Notice that cases in which the physical and social spatial dimensions of culture intersect to the exclusion of other social groups are fairly narrowly circumscribed. For the most part, our social lives are messier, and different **subcultures** interact with each other all the time. Sometimes the young visit their grandparents in their retirement homes; quite frequently individuals of various social classes occupy the same classrooms, malls, arenas, and workspaces (although with different functions within those workspaces); segregation on the basis of race sometimes occurs residentially, though for the most part the common venues in which daily life is played out are racially integrated.

Finally, we can recognize that culture varies over time. The temporal dimension is an important qualifier because of the magnitude of differences that accumulate to produce cultures that are vastly different from what came before. In other words, culture evolves.

Leaving aside the precise mechanisms of cultural evolution for now, we can recognize that for the most part culture is never static. It is always developing new features and characteristics. Therefore, Western culture of today is remarkably different from 500 years ago and is in many ways quite different from even 10 years ago. The temporal dimension of culture is independent of its physical and social locations—culture changes over time in all countries and regions and for all social groupings. Norwegian culture today is different from what it was in 1900; French-Canadian culture, irrespective of actual geographic roots, has evolved over the century as well; and the culture of Canadians in their sixties has changed dramatically over time—the leisure and work options and the values and ideals of older Canadians bear little resemblance to what they were in earlier time periods. Many observers of culture argue that cultural changes are occurring more frequently in recent time periods: the rate of cultural change is increasing. When we turn to the specifics of cultural dynamics, we will learn more about the reasons behind this increase in the rate of change.

## Culture and Structure

While a description of culture's dependence on time and location shows us the changing nature of culture, we also need a clear idea of what "counts" as culture and what does not. To help us to draw this boundary, we can consider the distinction between *culture* and **structure**, two terms that have specific meanings within formal sociology. This distinction, as described by Philip Smith, sees culture primarily as the realm of the "ideal, the spiritual, and the non-material" and opposed to the "material, technological, and the social-structural" (2001: 3–4).

One might characterize the *ideal*, the *spiritual*, and the *non-material* as things that exist primarily in people's heads, limited to an essentially mental existence. This version of culture privileges the distinction between thoughts, emotions, beliefs, and the more abstract elements of organized social life, on the one hand, and the "concrete" elements of society that are literally embodied and enacted by actual things and people, on the other hand. Drawing the boundaries of culture in this fashion allows us to classify, for example, attitudes about gender roles and about the kinds of work appropriate for men and for women as "cultural." Such attitudes are shared modes of thinking, and to the extent that they are only mental constructs, they are properly cultural.

At the same time, a high degree of occupational segregation by gender, with some jobs (for example, elementary school teachers) primarily done by women and others (for example, elementary school principals) primarily done by men, is not cultural. Rather, this segregation is structural. It is an enduring pattern of social behaviour, existing primarily not at a mental level but at a level of lived experience. The idea that it is normal or proper for men to be principals and women to be elementary school teachers is a cultural value. The fact that this pattern exists in our society (however changing) is a structural property of our society.

We can find another example in the realm of **politics**. The widely held preference for representative democracy and a belief that it is a legitimate and necessary form of self-government in Canada represents a deep-rooted aspect of Canadian culture. This polit-

ical orientation is related in a significant way to many other beliefs about authority, individual rationality, and justice, and thus is an element of culture clearly tied to other important cultural elements. In contrast, representative democracy is not merely an idea—it is a practice that involves a tremendous amount of material resources and engenders long-standing patterns of social behaviour. Known in the sociological literature as **the state**, our democratic government is a structural dimension of social life. It is related in significant ways to many aspects of citizens' daily existence; it influences, among other things, our work lives, our consumption patterns, our health outcomes, and our educational outcomes, and thus is a material element of social life clearly tied to other important structural elements.

## Culture as Symbolic

*Culture* is frequently defined in sociology according to the role it plays in creating meaning. In this view, culture is the elements of social life that act as symbols and are subject to interpretation. These elements are produced in order to be received and understood by individuals who derive meaning—a personal understanding—through the reception process. Any element of society that has meaning for both its creator and its audience, even if there is a discrepancy between the intended and the perceived meanings, is part of the symbolic order. Culture, then, both is a product of **social interaction** and is the social force that enables social interaction because it allows people to communicate meanings to each other.

In contrast, culture is *not* those things that serve no communicative or expressive role. This is a fine distinction because meaning can often be found wherever we look hard enough, especially by those with a postmodern sensibility. However, it is important to limit culture to those things that are intended to be interpreted and to have meaning, even if the nature of those eventual interpretations might vary.

Going back to the political example demonstrating the difference between culture and structure, we can see the state as an instrumental **social institution** designed to achieve governance. It does not qualify as "culture" because it is not in itself a symbol: it does not exist to be received and understood as having a meaning. However, there is no shortage of politically oriented culture or of political symbols, existing in a wide array of forms. Political ideologies of the left, centre, and right, expressed in political discourses, in conversations, newspaper articles, and books, both fiction and non-fiction, are squarely in the realm of culture. The national anthem and the Canadian flag are both explicit political symbols. The neo-Gothic Parliament buildings in Ottawa, while serving as the venue for federal politics, also serve as a political symbol, not only through the "messages" associated with their stately, traditional, European appearance (they are not pagodas or pyramids), but also because they are widely known to conjure up an association with the federal government and so can represent the wider country. Their very image has gained interpretive currency and can be effectively used as a tool for communication.

The symbolic view of culture bears much similarity to the view that opposes culture to structure. In both views, the roles of ideas and mental states are important elements of culture. The two views do differ, however. Where the opposition between culture and structure emphasizes the distinction between the material and the non-material, the symbolic view of culture, with its focus on the expressive function of culture, recognizes that meaning is often conveyed through symbols that take material form. By combin-

The Centre Block of the Parliament buildings is immediately evocative of Canada. It is an effective symbol of the nation, and its image is both a part of and representative of Canadian national culture. (Photo © Library of Parliament/Bibliothèque du Parlement. Mone's Photography)

ing the insights of each perspective, we can recognize that culture is ideas, beliefs, emotions, and thoughts *and* their direct physical embodiments.

A few interesting features of this combination of insights are worth noting. First, the two views together provide a more comprehensive description of what constitutes culture than either does individually, but without being unduly or impracticably broad. Second, those topics that are clearly "culture" from both perspectives are generally closer to the core of the concerns of the sociology of culture. For example, language—non-material words spoken to convey meaning—is cultural subject *par excellence*. Third, the two perspectives show us that social phenomena can be viewed in multiple ways. It is possible that certain things can be analyzed as culture while they are simultaneously understood as being outside the realm of culture.

To take a technological example, the automobile can be analyzed on different levels. On one hand, automobiles are material objects that are instrumental in facilitating social needs. They are part of the structural side of social life, namely, our transportation system. On the other hand, automobiles are designed with an aesthetic dimension to them, and as such they are the embodiment of ideas about taste and style, which are cultural elements. They play a role in self-expression for many people. On a deeper level, attitudes towards automobile use and the kind of lifestyle that their use engenders are known as "car culture," and in this sense automobiles are implicated in the realm of culture in a second way.

## The Role of Culture in Social Theory

Now that we have a clear idea of what culture is, we can gain an understanding of how it has figured in the works of some of the major sociological theorists. In this section, we will outline how these thinkers have employed culture in their writings about the fundamental driving forces of society.

Above all else, theories explain things. The defining feature of a **theory** is that it tells why or how something is the way it is. *Social theory*, then, is explanations of social things—it tells us why certain aspects of society are the way they are. A great deal of social theory, it turns out, is strongly concerned with culture. This concern, however, appears in different forms: social theories are concerned with culture for a variety of reasons. Below we will review the place of culture in five major social theoretical perspectives.

## Orthodox Marxist and Neo-Marxist Theories

One of the most influential theoretical perspectives in sociology is **Marxism**. In developing his theory of society, Karl Marx was responding directly to previous philosophical arguments about the central role of ideas (squarely cultural) in determining the path of history and the nature of social reality. In such arguments, the general cultural environment worked at the level of ideas to shape people's thoughts and actions, and so was in principle the root cause behind events and social change. This "spontaneous unfolding" of the spirit or culture of a given time could explain the course of history (P. Smith, 2001: 13).

By contrast, in Marxism, social reality is seen as determined primarily by the prevailing **mode of production**, evolving through history from agrarian societies to slave ownership to feudalism and then to industrial **capitalism**. This perspective posits that the best way to explain social facts—and all of history—is by recognizing that they are outcomes, direct or indirect, of the economic organization of society.

Societies shift from one mode of production to the next in a historical progression, with the current state being industrial capitalism. The economic organization of society forms the *base* upon which the rest of society, the superstructure, is founded. In a strict reading of Marxism, the *superstructure* responds to but does not cause changes in the base. Culture, in all its forms—ideas, beliefs, values, art, religion, and so on—is part of the superstructure and must be understood as essentially a product of the base.

In today's society, then, all aspects of our culture are shaped by the needs and dictates of industrial capitalism. One of the most important cultural productions of capitalism is the *dominant ideology*. This ideology is a system of thoughts, knowledge, and beliefs that serves to legitimate and to perpetuate capitalism. Our mental lives and our entire thought modes are shaped to minimize criticism of capitalism and to maximize participation in and support of capitalism.

Neo-Marxist perspectives do not adhere so strictly to the view that culture is entirely dependent on society's mode of production. While they borrow extensively from Marx's insights, they also modify these insights, and in so doing they provide a significantly different view of culture. These perspectives share with Marxism a focus on the role of culture in maintaining and supporting capitalism, but they differ from Marxism insofar as they seek to explain culture as more than simply the reflection of the underlying economic base.

Neo-Marxists recognize that culture can be shaped by specific groups and individuals who seek to achieve certain social outcomes. For example, Antonio Gramsci (1992) argued in the 1920s and 1930s that intellectuals within spheres such as politics, religion, the mass media, and education provide knowledge, values, advice, and direction to the general population that perpetuate the status quo and suppress revolutionary tendencies. To take another example, members of the Frankfurt School, who began writing in the 1920s, identified pro-capitalist functions in much of popular culture, which promotes capitalist ideals and stifles critical, independent thinking. The groups responsible for the creation and promotion of popular culture within the entertainment industry are themselves significant members of the **bourgeoisie**. In the view of the Frankfurt School, the entertainment industry is of great use to the capitalist order through the cultural products it creates.

It is important to note that neo-Marxists make a fundamental advance in their view of culture insofar as they see it as more than simply an artifact of the economic base. Culture, they argue, can also help to determine other facets of social reality—not merely reflective of other things in society, it also helps to shape society. A significant continuity between Marxist and neo-Marxist views of culture is that culture is implicated in the essentially conflictual nature of society. Culture, in a sense, supports dominant groups in their efforts to maintain their dominance.

## Cultural Functionalism

A contrasting approach to understanding culture can be found in work based on the theoretical insights of Émile Durkheim. In contrast to the conflictual emphasis of the Marxists and neo-Marxists, the views of culture based on Durkheim's insights focus on its integrative ability. Rather than pointing to how culture can create social fissures, Durkheim ([1912] 1995) identified how culture can create social stability and solidarity. In this view, rather than dividing us, culture unites us.

Culture, in terms of norms, values, attitudes, and beliefs, is not reflective of the economic mode of production. Instead, these cultural elements are generated according to the needs of society by its form as a more or less complex system. Culture rises up out of a particular society's **social structure** to produce a general consensus about the goals and nature of society. As such, for example, our values about the importance of education evolve in response to the changing needs of a modernizing society in which higher general levels of education allow for a more smoothly functioning society. In this sense, culture serves a necessary function: through common values and beliefs, society is able to remain coherent and all the different parts of society can effectively carry out their specific purpose.

Durkheim paid special attention to the role of religion as a motivating force in society that made possible the affirmation of collective sentiments and ideas. Religion, therefore, could play an important role in strengthening social bonds that could then strengthen and reinforce the fabric of society.

### Symbolic Interactionist and Dramaturgical Perspectives

A third important perspective treats culture as a product of individuals' interactions. In **symbolic interactionist** thought, culture plays the role of a vehicle for meaning (hence "symbolic") and is generated by individuals in face-to-face encounters (hence "interactionist"). Culture is the enacted signals and attitudes that people use to communicate as they go about their daily lives. Body language and the signals we send through it, however subconsciously, are a clear element of culture in this perspective. The decisions we make and carry out to reveal or to suppress certain pieces of information about ourselves are also culture.

Social interaction can be analyzed to reveal layers of meaning behind routine actions. It becomes evident that there is a communicative element in a great deal of our interactions although we are not always conscious of its presence or of the nature of the messages we send. The result of our interactions is (usually) the successful management of our relationships with others.

In terms of its view on culture, the symbolic interactionist approach contrasts with Marxist and functionalist approaches insofar as it attributes more responsibility to individuals as the active creators and implementers of culture. Rather than originating from an economic order or indirectly from the general social structure, culture is a product of creative individual agents who use it to manage their everyday tasks and routines.

One of the most influential theorists to write about the interactions of individuals was Erving Goffman. Goffman developed an analytical framework that analogizes social interaction to what goes on in a

theatre. For that reason, it is known as a *dramaturgical* perspective. In a theatre, there are actors with roles to play for an audience. Likewise, when we interact with people, we assume a role for the situation we find ourselves in and perform that role according to a well-known script that defines the boundaries of what is expected and acceptable for the role. We learn these rules of social behaviour through the ordinary process of **socialization**. We use these rules to create meaningful and effective interaction with others. When we are interacting with others and are in our roles, we are managing impressions and performing in a *frontstage* area. When we let down our guard and behave informally and in ways that would embarrass us in front of others, we are in the *backstage* area.

Culture plays a part in the dramaturgical perspective that is in one sense quite central: social order is constituted by the creation and use of meanings embodied in interaction. The sending and receiving of signals and messages is the key to understanding why society functions at all when there is so much potential for chaos. When you think about it, we are remarkably efficient at maintaining social order most of the time, and this achievement is made possible through shared meanings in face-to-face interactions.

This view of culture, however, is one that is perhaps less rich than that offered by the cultural functionalist perspective. Rather than playing a fundamental role in shaping individuals' very consciousness, as the functionalist perspective would argue, the dramaturgical perspective sees culture as just a tool for creative individuals to manipulate strategically. Rather than being fully subject to the influence of culture, culture is subject more to the influence of individuals.

### The Cultural Studies Tradition

Cultural studies is a field with roots in British literary scholarship and in sociology. Much of the work accomplished in this tradition builds on the work of Marxism and neo-Marxists. The specific insight that cultural studies borrows from neo-Marxists is that culture can be shaped and manipulated by dominant groups and employed to maintain hegemony, that is, the power to lead and control. Cultural studies practitioners agree that culture can function to maintain social divisions, keeping some groups dominant over others. Where they break from Marxists and early neo-Marxists is in the recognition that class conflict is only one of many sites of ideological dominance. As Philip Smith writes of cultural studies, "a move has gradually taken place away from Marxism toward an understanding of society as textured with multiple sources of inequality and fragmented local struggles" (2001: 152). Dominant groups can be defined not only by class position, but also by race, gender, geography, and sexual orientation.

In addition to a focus on the multiple forms of domination, cultural studies has provided a more sophisticated understanding of how meaning functions in society. One of the main figures in this tradition is Stuart Hall, who has produced some of the seminal concepts of cultural studies. As Hall (1980) explains, communication of meaning requires both **encoding** and **decoding**. By this he means that such things as an advertisement or a television show are created in such a way as to convey a particular perspective. The predominant beliefs of the creators are encoded into these cultural productions (or *texts*) in subtle and sometimes subconscious ways. A fresh, critically informed reading of such texts is required to see how they encode assumptions and messages about such things as gender and social class relations. Another significant insight of Hall's is that meaning does not simply exist as part of cultural creations, but instead is constructed by individuals through the process of receiving and interpreting culture. Meaning is created by people while they make sense of the culture they consume or take in.

As evidence, note how the very same cultural products may carry very different meanings for different individuals or for different groups. For example, a study of the meaning of Hollywood Westerns showed that the movies were interpreted quite differently by "Anglos" and by Native Americans: the films' messages about the frontier, Native–European relations, and the value of authority and independence were construed quite differently by the Anglo and the Native viewers (Shively, 1992). While those who create cultural products may intend them to convey a certain meaning, there is, nonetheless, opportunity for individuals to read or understand messages, texts, and symbols in oppositional or idiosyncratic ways. Thus, meanings are derived through a process influenced by the individuals' backgrounds and interpretive abilities.

## The "Production of Culture" Perspective

The "production of culture" perspective studies those aspects of culture created through explicit, intentional, and co-ordinated processes. There is, therefore, a focus on material culture, and studies taking this perspective focus on mass media, technology, art, and

other material symbol-producing realms such as science and law. The guiding insight of this perspective is that culture is a product of social action in much the same way as non-cultural products are. The implication of this view is that culture is best studied according to the same methods and analysis as are standard in other fields of sociology.

A key figure in the development of the "production of culture" perspective, Richard A. Peterson (1994), notes that this approach to understanding culture was developed to account for perceived shortcomings in the prevailing "mirror" or "reflection" view that posited that culture was somehow a manifestation of underlying social-structural needs or realities. This view, held by orthodox Marxists and by functionalists, is quite vague about the specific mechanisms through which culture is created. The metaphor of a mirror is descriptive of the content of culture—it represents the true nature or character of society—but is mute about culture's production.

Such a view would find that, for instance, the contours of Canadian national identity are visible through studying the literary output of Canadian authors. As a body of work, Canadian literature takes on the characteristics of and "reflects" the essence of Canadian society. Likewise, Baroque art forms are seen as expressions of society in the Baroque period, and modernist art is explained as an expression of societal sentiments and values in the early decades of the twentieth century.

By contrast, the "production of culture" perspective insists on specifying all the factors involved not only in cultural production per se, but also in how culture is "distributed, evaluated, taught, and preserved" (Peterson, 1994: 165). Through a thorough analysis of all these processes, we can better account for the specific content of culture. We need to examine the resources and constraints that specific actors were working with and that influenced the kind of art or other symbols that they created. In this way, the "production of culture" perspective provides us with the means of explaining the shape of culture.

## Conflict, Integration, Origin, and Autonomy

It is useful to compare these various perspectives according to their views on several key features of culture. Marxists and neo-Marxists are clear in their argument that culture is a tool of conflict in society, a view that contrasts with functionalists, who emphasize the integrative function of culture. Functionalists are interested in explaining social order, and they see culture as a key factor in creating social stability.

For symbolic interactionists, culture is primarily the means by which individuals create order out of potentially chaotic and unpredictable social situations, and so they support an integrative view of culture. The cultural studies tradition, building on the work of neo-Marxists, has an explicit focus on the many ways in which culture is implicated in various forms of domination and conflict in society.

The "production of culture" perspective has little to say about characterizing culture as integrative or as implicated in conflict. But while it has the least to say about that dimension of culture, it says the most about the origin of culture because it developed out of dissatisfaction with the views of Marxism and functionalism in this regard. While these older perspectives relied on a "reflection" metaphor to explain where culture comes from, the production perspective locates cultural origin in "purposive productive activity" (Peterson, 1994: 164). Cultural studies does not provide quite so articulate an account of cultural origin, but neither does it merely rely on vague notions of reflection. Instead, it sees culture as originating in the work of hegemonic leaders who create the texts, symbols, and discourses that embody particular ideologies. Symbolic interactionists also provide an explanation for the origin of culture: it is produced in the meanings that people create through social interaction at the micro level.

Finally, the various perspectives place different emphases on what we can call the "autonomy of culture." *Autonomy of culture* refers to the place for culture within causal explanations. Is culture primarily a dependent variable, something that deserves to be explained but does not warrant recognition as a fundamental cause of social outcomes? Or is culture autonomous—does culture merit a place at the core of sociological explanation, wherein it is the key to understanding the contours of social reality?

Marxism clearly denies the autonomy of culture by making it a reflection of the economic base of society. Functionalism views culture as far more autonomous: culture is, in and of itself, the predominant stabilizing force in society and can account for social order. Symbolic interactionists are less sympathetic to the autonomy of culture, preferring instead to privilege the role of spontaneous human creativity in understanding how social order is maintained; culture is more appropriately viewed as the product of action than as the motivator of action. The cultural studies tradition gives us a view of culture as enjoy-

ing a significant degree of autonomy; the crucial role of ideology in various forms of dominance portrays culture as primarily shaping the conflictual nature of social life. The "production of culture" perspective, to conclude this summary, is largely concerned with how myriad social processes create cultural products, and so finds little room for the autonomy of culture.

## Cultural Realms

The stage is now set to discuss some of the attributes of those realms of social life most commonly located at the core of the sociology of culture. Although we could discuss the cultural dimension of almost any area of society, we will limit our discussion to the realms of language and discourse, the mass media, religion, and art. Within each realm, we will highlight the insights that the sociology of culture can bring to bear.

### Language and Discourse

As mentioned above, language is a cultural subject par excellence. But before describing the interest of sociology in language more fully, we should distinguish it from the related concept of communication. *Language*, a system of words both written and spoken, is but one means of communication. **Communication** is the sharing of meaning, by which the thoughts of one person are made understandable to another. Communication can occur through a variety of signs and symbols, but we reserve a special place for the study of language because it is the primary means by which our communication takes place.

Languages are complicated systems of many symbols deployed according to a set of rules, and their use gives rise to a number of interesting social phenomena. It is argued, for instance, that the presence of language structures our very thoughts and consciousness, that without a vocabulary with which to label events (as is the case for infants) we cannot remember them. The character of social reality is tied to language insofar as we make sense of all our experiences in terms of the linguistic devices of and the logic made available through the language we speak.

As evidence of the consciousness-determining nature of language, we can point to examples of concepts and thoughts that exist in one language and are not entirely translatable to other languages, such as the German concepts of *Kultur* and *Geist*, or the French concepts of *ennui* and *savoir faire*. Speakers of a language are said to share a certain *mentalité* that differentiates their mindset and world view. Likewise, it has been argued that the advancement of science in the West was in part related to the structure of European languages that encourages linear, causal thought patterns.

**Discourse** is a linguistic phenomenon that refers to ideas, concepts, and vocabulary that recur in texts. A *text* can be broadly defined as any material or non-material communication act. Discourse is a habitual way of speaking about and understanding a topic or issue. Discourses abound in society. We encounter them constantly, but rarely do we explicitly recognize their features even when we are employing them ourselves. That is because it is natural for us to adopt a singular way of understanding an issue, and so a singular way of discussing or talking about an issue.

Take, for example, the issue of crime. In talking about crime, we might employ an *individualist discourse* that understands crime as the actions of a self-interested individual who is presented with options and makes certain choices. Crime in this discourse is conceived as something that one person does to one or more others, and it occurs in discrete instances.

This discourse of crime encourages an understanding of the psychological factors involved in criminal behaviour and leads to solutions that work at the level of the individual. An individualist solution might suggest that if we alter the attractiveness of the option of committing crime by making penalties harsher for those who are caught, the individual will, we hope, no longer choose to commit crime.

In contrast, a *collectivist discourse* of crime also exists. This discourse views crime as a social problem. Crime is conceived as a feature of society that can be more or less prevalent. The focus is on crime rates and on the social conditions that influence the likelihood that crime will be committed in society. This discourse encourages a view more sociological than psychological of the factors contributing to crime, focusing on the social level rather than the individual level. Just as the problem is conceived at the group level, so the ideas and terminology of a collectivist discourse promote a conception of solutions at the group level. For example, an effort to reduce crime might be based on information gained from a comparison of

 2.1

## Sociology in Action
Patients with AIDS

AIDS presented a serious challenge to established identities—and patterns of trust and control—in the treatment domain. A knowledge and treatment vacuum emerged as a result of a very public display of scientific uncertainty and institutional impotence in the face of this new crisis. Suddenly, old understanding about who was knowledgeable, who could and could not be trusted, and who should and should not be granted control, were open to contestation. For example, early on in the epidemic, the expertise of the "doctor" was in doubt. Not only did physicians *not* have the expertise to deal with this new challenge, some were patently unwilling to acquire it or even to act in the interests of their patients. Many early AIDS patients were abandoned, as discrimination, bigotry and fear led to some doctors "dumping" their patients.

PWAS ["persons with AIDS"] began to reject the identity of "patient" and the victimhood it implied. "Patients" (from the French "patienter," which means to wait, as in a physicians' wait-

ing room, and originally from the Latin, where it means "to suffer") would be "patient" and suffer in silence no longer. "*Silence = Death*," an expression made popular by the activist group ACT-UP, became the call to action for HIV/AIDS patients seeking to re-define themselves and their role within the domain. Community members stressed that they were neither "patients" nor "victims," but "people living with AIDS." . . .

The identity of PWAS, collectively, is thus very different from that of traditional patient groups. The notion of patients as passive, ignorant, requiring the medical expertise of an elite was successfully deconstructed and replaced with a notion of a patient group as empowered, informed and organized decision makers.

―――――

SOURCE: Steve Maguire, Nelson Phillips, and Cynthia Hardy, "When "Silence = Death", Keep Talking: Trust, Control and the Discursive Construction of Identity in the Canadian HIV/AIDS Treatment Domain," *Organization Studies*, 22, 2 (2001): 296. Reprinted by permission of Sage Publications Ltd.

low- and high-crime societies to determine how certain social differences influence crime rates.

As the example of discourses about crime shows, discourses have the potential for great influence. The promotion of certain discourses throughout society, by those with the power to do so, can have the effect of setting the public agenda for certain issues. A discourse of abortion as an issue of privacy, for example, portrays the central concern as autonomy. It privileges the discussion of government impingement on the right of women to control their own bodies. But an opposing discourse surrounding abortion privileges a discussion of the need to uphold the value of all human life, no matter how inchoate that life appears to be. In this discourse, the primary concern is the religiously based idea that human life is sacred and cannot be compromised.

Such discourses play a role in the social construction of the categories and definitions we use to understand and to analyze social life. In our daily lives, we constantly refer to these categories and definitions to make judgements about good and bad, right and wrong, desirable and undesirable, to distinguish between "us" and the "other," and to understand the very nature of things—Is abortion murder? Are movies an art form or entertainment? Is eating animals a question of morality? Is race about biological differences? Is crime an individual failing? For all these questions, our answers will be influenced by the way that predominant discourses shape and frame our notions of the core issues at play.

### Mass Media

The **mass media** are a powerful social force. They constitute a key realm of cultural production and distribution and can be seen to play a variety of social roles. The *mass media* are those technologically based methods and institutions that allow a single source to transmit a message to a mass audience. The mass media in Canada include print (newspapers, magazines, books, and journals), film, radio, television (broadcast, cable, and satellite), and the Internet. The Internet is a special case because although it can function as a mass medium, it is also much more: it is a *network* medium by virtue of its ability to allow multiple message sources. Every person on the Internet can potentially be a source of mass media content.

The mass media are a core cultural concern because of the nature of the content that they bring to the vast majority of people. That content can be categorized as *information* and *entertainment*.

Let us first consider the mass media as the primary source of news information in society. They are the means by which we find out about important political, economic, and social happenings. We rely on them for the information we need to understand our local, regional, national, and global contexts. In addition to information delivered as news per se on news programs and in newspapers, the mass media provide us with a wealth of other information about the world that we might never have access to through first-hand experience. Through the mass media, we can read about the modernization of industries in China, we can see what the skyline of Buenos Aires looks like, and we can hear about the best way to invest money in a sluggish economy. In short, the mass media bring a world of information to us, and their capacity to do so has greatly increased with the advent of the Internet, which allows us to access only the information we desire, when we desire it.

As the providers of so much information, the mass media have an enormous amount of influence on people's attitudes and behaviours, which are determined by the state of our knowledge. For example, some people will alter their eating habits based on information they learn from magazine articles about the dangers and benefits of certain foods. And some people will form an opinion about strengthening environmental protection regulations based on reports they see on television news programs. Because the mass media select a limited amount of information to present to audiences from a virtually infinite supply, they serve as informational gatekeepers (White, 1950). This gatekeeping function can account for much of their influence. However, just as important as what they present is the question of how they present media content. There is a connection here to the preceding discussion of discourses, because it is through the mass media that most discourses are disseminated to the general public.

The mass media are also the primary source for popular culture. While high culture is only rarely made available through the mass media, popular culture is everywhere. We will discuss the aesthetic dimension of culture in a later section, on art and aesthetics. Here we can outline how the popular culture productions brought to us by the mass media are linked to deep-seated social problems. This link is specified as the ability of the mass media to warp or corrupt our culture: television shows, movies, popular music, and so on. Some have argued, have a profoundly negative impact on our entire way of life.

An important criticism of mass media content finds fault with the materialistic values the mass media explicitly and implicitly advocate. By constantly connecting depictions of happiness and success to material wealth, the mass media have been a principal cause of the development of a consumer culture that focuses our attention and energies on gaining and spending money and away from spiritual, moral, ethical, and social issues. The mass media are also often blamed for a culture of violence: some would say they contribute to high levels of violence in society insofar as portrayals of violence incite violent acts and desensitize people to the presence of violence. At the same time, the mass media contribute to an unhelpful, unrealistic, and shallow understanding of and response to this violence. The list of social problems linked to how the mass media may distort and negatively influence our culture is long, including such serious issues as body consciousness and eating disorders, racism, and sexism, exacerbated through stereotypical and misleading depictions.

## Religion

Religion is a sociological subfield of its own, but it merits inclusion in a discussion of culture because it has had such a large impact on the development of values and social traditions in most countries, Canada included. The case for the importance of religion as a cultural force was strongly made by Durkheim ([1912] 1995), who saw religion as providing the basis for social solidarity. More generally, we often characterize Western countries as belonging to a Judeo-Christian tradition, a tradition that denotes a specific history and related social institutions and dominant values. A specifically religious mindset is not needed for people in Western society to be influenced by general Judeo-Christian values. Rather, these values permeate our culture and are seen in such things as predominant views of the role of authority, beliefs in the value of punishment and of rehabilitation, and attitudes towards work and leisure.

Perhaps the best-known thesis regarding the influence of religion on culture is Max Weber's argument in *The Protestant Ethic and the Spirit of Capitalism* ([1904] 1958). Weber argues that several specific aspects of Protestant (specifically Calvinist) doctrine encouraged the values and behaviour of economic rationalism, thereby promoting the rapid advancement of capitalism in Protestant societies. The accuracy of this argument has been questioned, but its importance for an understanding of the cultural role of religion remains.

## Art and Aesthetics

In common usage, *culture* is often synonymous with *art*, though for the reasons described in this chapter so far, there is good reason for distinguishing between the two. Art is best seen as one element, albeit a unique element, of our larger culture. The realm of art is, above all, an expressive area of social life. Whereas much of our behaviour is oriented towards the practical achievement of a useful goal, art stands out as an activity done for its own sake.

The essence of art is communication through aesthetic means. *The New Shorter Oxford English Dictionary* (1993) defines *aesthetics* as "a system of principles for the appreciation of the beautiful." Art, then, employs a set of rules or principles pertaining to our notions of what is beautiful. This makes art a special form of communication: it is those thoughts and emotions that we find difficult to communicate through ordinary language. Instead, it relies on the much more implicit and intuitive rules that people in general use to assess beauty.

Art is an inherently imprecise form of communication, in which particular works carry implicit messages that require a sense of appreciation for the aesthetic principles at play in order to be received. That is why we can read a novel and generate many different ideas about what the novel "is really about" or what the author "is really saying," just as we can for paintings, sculpture, plays, and so on. Moreover, we like to think of truly good art as the expression of artistic genius. Masterpieces, we believe, are the works of geniuses, special people whose ideas and forms of self-expression represent models for human creativity and thought. The very best of art, we believe, represents the very best of humanity, and so art occupies an honoured place in society.

As discussed above, we often distinguish between "popular culture" and "high culture." This distinction points to the existence of a *cultural hierarchy*, in which certain forms of culture are granted greater legitimacy and prestige. Oil painting is higher on the hierarchy than filmmaking, which in turn is higher than television. It is important to recognize that such status distinctions are themselves cultural productions. That is, our categories of "high" and "low" are socially constructed. These categorizations represent more than just real differences in the characteristics of cultural productions. They also reflect differences in the social contexts in which high and popular culture are produced, distributed, and received.

Take, for example, Italian opera. We have a clear notion of opera as a high art. The dominant discourse of art portrays art as the product of artistic minds and as inherently special—something about art allows us to recognize it when we see it. So long as we are informed about the value of art, we will never confuse Italian opera with popular culture. This discourse neglects the reality that our definitions of "high" and "popular" reflect an entire social process involved in bringing art to audiences. Our ideas about Italian opera as high art are based partially on an array of cues, such as its high cost, the status of its audiences, the physically distinct and opulent venues in which it is performed, its non-profit status (we like to oppose art to commerce), and intellectual analyses of Italian opera to explain why it is great art.

This approach to art highlights several of art's sociologically significant features. First, as explained by the "production of culture" perspective, art does not just spring out of a **collective consciousness**, or even out of an individual's consciousness. Instead, art is a collective activity that requires collaboration between many actors in an art world (Becker, 1982). This collective activity helps to determine how legitimate or prestigious artistic genres are.

Second, the socially constructed nature of distinctions between high and low in art also points to the significance of art in helping to determine the contours of social stratification. This link is rooted in the notion of **cultural capital**: the knowledge, preferences, and tastes that people have concerning art and aesthetics. Having high cultural capital means sharing the knowledge, preferences, and tastes that are common among those of high status in society (see Figure 2.1 on the size of this group). The link between cultural capital and stratification is based on the power of high cultural capital to provide access to informal interpersonal connections that can influence our occupational and economic prospects. Sharing similar artistic tastes and consumption patterns with those in economically privileged positions provides us with access to networks and opportunities not open to those who do not have the necessary aesthetic preferences and expertise. In sociological terms, our cultural capital can increase our economic capital. (This is an interesting inversion of the Marxist logic whereby the cultural realm is determining, or influencing, the economic realm.)

Figure 2.1 **Attendance Rates of Canadians over 15 for Cultural Activities, 1998**

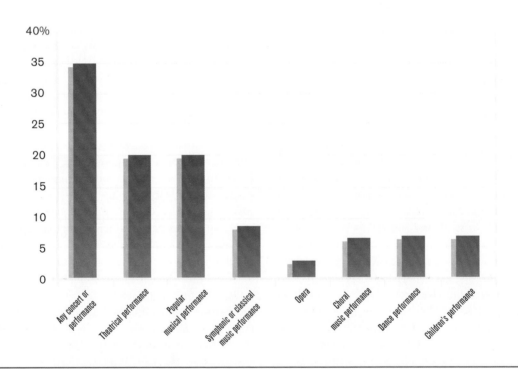

SOURCE: Data derived from Statistics Canada, "Performing Arts Attendance," based on General Social Survey, 1998; available at <www.statcan.ca/english/Pgdb/arts08a.htm>, accessed 16 May 2003.

Third, and perhaps even more significant, is the role that artistic consumption plays in creating social groupings in society. The enjoyment of aesthetic products is deeply related to our conceptions of our own identities, of who we really are, and of the kind of people with whom we wish to be associated. In this way, our tastes are profoundly implicated in how our lives are structured. We've already seen how artistic tastes can interact with our class position, but just as important, tastes can also be a way of expressing racial, gender, regional, and age-based identities.

Take the example of youth culture. Although this term refers to many aspects of how young people live their lives, one important way that adolescents and young adults set themselves apart is through the music they listen to, the publications they read, the television shows and channels they watch, the films they see, and, increasingly, the Web sites they visit

and create. Knowledge of and participation in this particular set of aesthetic preferences allows young people to experience group belonging. Through aesthetics, they can distinguish themselves from prior generations.

## Cultural Dynamics

We have already seen that culture changes over time, but we have yet to fully consider any specific mechanisms of cultural change. We can take various perspectives to understand why and how culture changes over time. First, we can view changes in culture as responses to particular social-structural changes. Second, we can also view changes in culture as responses to other cultural developments, a view that emphasizes the weblike, interconnected nature of culture.

Sometimes art is employed to achieve ideological ends. This painting by Franklin Carmichael, a member of the Group of Seven, depicts the landscape of the Canadian north. The Group sought to express their nationalistic sentiments through paintings of scenes that were uniquely Canadian. (Franklin Carmichael [1890–1945] *Northern Tundra* 1931. Oil on canvas. 77.4 x 92.5 cm. Gift of Col. R.S. McLaughlin. McMichael Canadian Collection. 1968.7.14)

### Economic, Technological, and Cultural Change

At the most basic level, all of culture can be seen as human adaptation and ingenuity to better control and survive in the physical environment. Beyond that most basic level, but in keeping with the premise that culture allows us to deal with our surroundings, it also gives us the means to function effectively in our social environment, in our dealings with other people. Changes in that social environment, then, encourage and enable corresponding cultural changes.

The discussion of Marxism earlier in this chapter reviewed the case for the economic foundation of culture. In Marxism, culture is a reflection of the underlying economic basis of society. But it is not necessary to adopt Marxists' assumptions of culture as merely a reflection of economics to see that important economic changes are capable of provoking specific changes in culture. An example of such a change is the liberalization of attitudes towards women and work. In the mid to late nineteenth century and the first half of the twentieth century, most people in Western societies believed that women, especially married women, should not to work outside the home but rather should fulfill their roles as mothers and housewives. While the reasons for the more recent change in this attitude are many, one important reason is economic. Maintenance of a middle-class standard of living increasingly required a second income. Changing attitudes about women and work, in this view, were an adaptive response to a changing economic reality.

Over the same period, rising levels of affluence made it possible for teenagers to possess a certain amount of disposable income. The development of youth culture, while deriving from various causes, was facilitated by the economic changes that created consumers out of young people and thereby encouraged cultural producers to target and cater to youth. The continued growth in spending power of teenagers has also allowed them to become the primary demographic target of Hollywood film studios. Because young people see films in theatres more often than do older groups, a great deal of film production is tailored to their tastes and expectations. This dynamic is representative of the more general dependence of the content of cultural industries on economic conditions.

Technological change can also be viewed as the source of a great deal of the change in our culture. Perhaps the clearest and most significant technological influence on culture has been the development of the mass media. The printing press, invented by Johannes Gutenberg in 1452, has been credited with transforming European culture in diverse ways. For example, the printing press allowed many people to own Bibles, a precondition for the Protestant Revolution. The invention of the telegraph, which vastly hastened the speed with which information could travel over great distances, has been cited as changing our attitudes concerning the pace of life and punctuality, and even our very definitions of the proportions of space and time.

Television is arguably one of the most powerful technologies ever invented. It has wrought profound cultural changes. First, a specific form of cultural content has developed for the purposes of the medium, shaping our tastes for and expectations of dramatic entertainment, but also, and more fundamentally, influencing our perceptions of social reality and of the nature of the world outside our daily lives. Second, this technology has brought a major leisure activity into our homes, promoting the growth of television culture, in which we spend our free time in a one-way relationship with a screen rather than interacting with others or engaging in community-based activities.

It would be impossible to enumerate all the ways in which technology has created cultural change. To take an example of a broad cultural pattern, the very idea of "nightlife" and all its attendant activities is predicated on the existence of artificial light. Much more narrowly, the technological innovation of the electrification of musical instruments has influenced tastes in musical styles. Suffice it to say that technological change frequently has the potential to create cultural reverberations, sometimes of limited significance and other times life-transforming.

In addition, it is important to recognize that the influence of technological, economic, and other (for example, demographic) changes on the shape of culture is in no way a denial of the transformative power of culture. The relationship, to be sure, is reciprocal. Cultural changes can at times influence these very same structural features of society.

### Change for the Sake of Change

Despite the strength of the relationship between culture and social structure, culture also has internal dynamics that can account for cultural change. In this view, cultural change is inevitable because culture, as representative of individual and collective self-expression, is inherently progressive, evolutionary, volatile, and unstable: it is the nature of culture to evolve.

The validity of this view is perhaps best exemplified by the phenomenon of fashion. Fashion is change for the sake of change in the realm of aesthetics. In the realm of economics it is change for the sake of continued sales and profits. Ongoing change is built into the very idea of fashion. Moreover, fashion is not just the styles of clothes that are popular, although that is one of its most visible manifestations. Rather, elements of fashion can be found in many areas of social life.

Consider, for instance, how vocabulary choices acknowledge that some words are "in" while others are "out." To express approval, one might have heard adjectives in the past such as *swell*, *groovy*, or *mod*, words that sound dated now despite the fact that the need to express approval has not gone away. New, more fashionable words do the job today. Consider also how changes in furniture and interior design occur gradually but consistently enough to evoke associations with particular decades. Few of these changes are linked to changes in function or technological innovations. Finally, consider how fashion operates to change the popularity of first names (Lieberson, 2000). The Ethels, Mildreds, and Eunices of yesterday are the Emilys, Hannahs, and Madisons of today (see Table 2.2). The function of naming remains constant, while the aesthetic element of naming reveals continuous modification. The kinds of aesthetic modifications made today depend on the nature of the aesthetic modifications of the past.

Although aesthetic changes do not serve any practical or functional purposes, they may still be related to a social purpose: they satisfy needs for self-expression. In this sense, the aesthetic dimension of life is symbolic—we communicate to others and articulate (however obliquely) for ourselves certain thoughts, values, identities, and senses of group affiliation. Change in aesthetics results from shifts in the meanings or understandings commonly attributed to certain aesthetic elements, such that they no longer connote what they used to.

To see how this is so, consider Georg Simmel's theory of fashion (1957). This argument has become

**Table 2.2  Top 20 Names for Baby Girls Born in Illinois by Race, 1989, 1940, and 1920**

| 1989 | | 1940 | | 1920 | |
|---|---|---|---|---|---|
| **Shared by Blacks and Whites** | | **Shared by Blacks and Whites** | | **Shared by Blacks and Whites** | |
| Ashley | Jessica | Barbara | Joyce | Alice | Helen |
| Brittany | Michelle | Beverly | Margaret | Anna | Margaret |
| Christina | Nicole | Carol | Mary | Catherine | Marie |
| | | Dorothy | Patricia | Dorothy | Mary |
| | | Joan | Sandra | Elizabeth | Mildred |
| | | | Shirley | Evelyn | Ruth |
| | | | | Frances | Virginia |
| **White Only** | **Black Only** | **White Only** | **Black Only** | **White Only** | **Black Only** |
| Amanda | Alicia | Carolyn | Betty | Betty | Ethel |
| Caitlin | Amber | Donna | Brenda | Eleanor | Gladys |
| Catherine | Ariel | Janet | Dolores | Florence | Lillian |
| Elizabeth | Bianca | Judith | Gloria | Lorraine | Louise |
| Emily | Candace | Karen | Gwendolyn | Marion | Lucille |
| Jennifer | Crystal | Linda | Helen | Marjorie | Thelma |
| Kelly | Danielle | Marilyn | Jacqueline | | |
| Lauren | Dominique | Nancy | Loretta | | |
| Megan | Ebony | Sharon | Yvonne | | |
| Rachel | Erica | | | | |
| Rebecca | Jasmine | | | | |
| Samantha | Kiara | | | | |
| Sarah | Latoya | | | | |
| Stephanie | Tiffany | | | | |

SOURCE: Stanley Lieberson, *A Matter of Taste: How Names, Fashions, and Culture Change* (New Haven, CT: Yale University Press, 2000), 204. Reprinted by permission of Yale University Press.

known as the *trickle-down model*. In this model, fashion is triggered by the status concerns of high-status groups who seek to distinguish themselves by adopting a new fashion. Those elements of fashion that they adopt then come to imply high status on account of their association with a high-status group—that is the symbolism of the fashion. Lower-status groups then adopt this fashion for themselves to share in the high status, but in doing so they change the meaning of the fashion: it no longer expresses what it used to. High-status groups thus no longer find the fashion appealing or useful, and so they adopt a new fashion. Although this model cannot in fact explain much of the fashion world, which often appropriates the symbols of lower-status groups, it is nonetheless a clear illustration of how culture can evolve according to an internal set of principles that do not reflect social-structural change.

## Canadian Culture

The concepts and arguments reviewed in this chapter can help us to understand the current state of Canadian culture, along with some of the more contentious issues facing Canadian society. Because of its unique history, Canadian culture is unlike any other national culture, with a unique set of challenges and a unique set of opportunities.

### Distinct Societies

One of the defining features of Canadian culture is its basis in "two founding peoples," French and English. The term *peoples* refers, of course, not only to the actual members of the French and English colonies, but also to their respective ways of life—their cultures. How different or similar are the cultures of French and English Canada? On a global scale, they are quite similar to one another in com-

parison with, for example, Pakistani or Indonesian culture. However, there are still important ways in which they differ. Most obvious is the linguistic basis for the distinction (see Table 2.3). As discussed earlier, language is a core component of culture, with significant implications for social life. The ability to communicate with verbal and written language is a key element to social bonding. Without this form of communication, opportunities for social interaction are limited. Differences in other cultural traditions exist as well, ranging from cuisine and leisure activities to political values and views on marriage and family.

The challenge for Canada has been and continues to be the need to forge a unified Canadian culture that respects the unique characteristics of both traditions. To this end, we employ a policy of official bilingualism and we foster cultural events and new traditions that embrace both French and English cultural elements. The great concern over the success of this endeavour has been with us for decades. The movement for sovereignty within Quebec is to a large extent based on the belief that the health of French-Canadian culture, and especially the vigour of the French language in Quebec, can only be adequately maintained and nurtured separate from a wider Canadian culture. The challenge for our country is to capitalize on the potential for Canadian culture to unite us rather than to divide us.

### Multiculturalism

The conception of two founding peoples can be seen as primarily a legal construct rather than an accurate historical depiction. In reality, there have always been more than two cultural traditions in Canada. The Aboriginal cultures of **First Nations** and Inuit peoples were, of course, present before the idea of a Canadian society or culture was ever proposed.

Table 2.3   **Population by Language Spoken Most Often at Home, Canada, 1991, 1996, and 2001**

|  | 1991 | 1996 | 2001 |
|---|---|---|---|
| English | 18,440,535 (68.3%) | 19,294,835 (67.6%) | 20,011,535 (67.5%) |
| French | 6,288,425 (23.3%) | 6,448,615 (22.6%) | 6,531,375 (22.0%) |
| Non-official language | 2,265,075 (8.4%) | 2,784,645 (9.8%) | 3,096,110 (10.5%) |

SOURCE: Adapted from Statistics Canada, *Profile of Languages in Canada: English, French and Many Others* (Ottawa: Statistics Canada, 2002); available at <www12.statcan.ca/english/census01/products/analytic/companion/lang/contents.cfm#nine>, accessed 17 May 2003.

More recently, increased immigration from a large number of countries and the formation of an equally large number of ethnic communities in Canada have added to the number of cultural traditions we have to work with (see Figure 2.2 on Canada's increasing linguistic diversity). As a society, we have adopted a stance of official **multiculturalism**, although the merits of this position engender a good deal of debate. We should distinguish between multiculturalism as a fact of contemporary Canadian society—there are ethnic subcultures that are thriving—and multiculturalism as a policy: the tolerance and encouragement of the maintenance of the national cultures that immigrants bring with them from their countries of origin.

Proponents of multiculturalism point to its helpfulness in easing the transition of new immigrants into Canadian society. This happens through the fostering of ethnic communities that can provide social support. In addition, proponents argue that multiculturalism policy is properly respectful to all Canadians and enriches the wider Canadian culture. Detractors, on the other hand, argue that this policy only makes it more difficult to create a unifying Canadian culture. Moreover, they question the wisdom of a policy that encourages, to however small a degree, self-segregation rather than facilitating the full cultural integration of immigrants into Canadian life. Again, just as with the question of two founding peoples, the challenge here is to balance the potential of culture for unifying us with our desire to maintain certain cultural partitions.

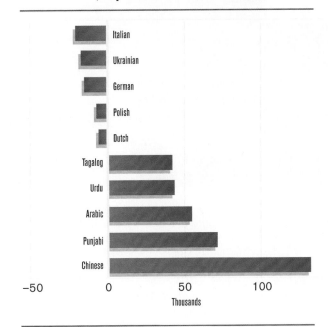

Figure 2.2 **Allophone Groups[a] That Increased or Decreased the Most from 1996 to 2001, Canada (Population in Thousands)**

[a] Groups of people who possess the same non-official language as their mother tongue.
SOURCE: Adapted from Statistics Canada, *Profile of Languages in Canada: English, French and Many Others* (Ottawa: Statistics Canada, 2002); available at <www12.statcan.ca/english/census01/products/analytic/companion/lang/contents.cfm#nine>, accessed 17 May 2003.

2.2

# Human Diversity

Canadians Bilingual? How About Centilingual?

The image of a bilingual Canada is becoming less accurate because Canadians speak more than 100 languages, a report from Statistics Canada says.

The report, released on Tuesday, is based on data from the 2001 national census. It says Canadians reported 100 different mother tongues—the first language they learned and still understood at the time of the census.

Most Canadians, nine out of 10, said they speak either English or French at home, but more than five million people, a sixth of the population, said they learned another language first.

The number of those people grew by 12.5 per cent since 1996, far eclipsing the general population growth rate of four per cent.

After French and English, Chinese was the third most common mother tongue.

———

SOURCE: "Canadians Bilingual? How About Centilingual?" CBC News Online, 10 Dec. 2002; available at <www.cbc.ca/stories/2002/12/10/statscan_021210>, accessed 17 May 2003.

The smaller Canadian market makes it difficult for Canadian cultural industries to compete with their US counterparts, who can generate vast profits from the American market. Nonetheless, there are occasional inversions of the usual patterns, whereby Canadian artists find success in the United States, such as the rock band Sum 41. While certainly welcome, these successes tend to draw attention away from the fact that Canadians consume vastly more American culture than Americans do Canadian culture. © Tim Mosenfelder/Corbis/Magmaphoto.com

### *Globalization and American Cultural Imperialism*

**Globalization** typically refers to the fact that goods, services, information, and labour, now more than ever, can easily flow between distant countries. Of particular concern for us is the cultural influence that globalization brings. There are various implications of globalization for Canadian culture. Technological advances in mass media have made possible easy and abundant access to the sights and sounds of geographically distant locales. Through media representations we can be made aware of cultural elements from across the globe, and the potential exists to incorporate these elements into Canadian culture. In a sense, one effect of globalization is the internationalization of national cultures as they are increasingly exposed to one another. The mass media, then, are the main channels of the cultural diffusion occurring through the mutual influence of many national cultures.

Globalization, however, can bring with it many difficult cultural challenges. Chief among these challenges is the need to manage the global export of American popular culture. Popular culture, in the form of films, television shows, music, and Web sites, is one of the largest American exports, reaching every corner of the globe. The sheer volume of American cultural export has led to the term *cultural imperialism*, describing the scope of the global dominance of American culture.

The reaction to this state of affairs in Canada has been one of alarm, and a concerted effort has been mounted to maintain the integrity of Canadian culture. The importation of American cultural products is seen as dangerous to Canadian culture because the many pre-existing similarities with American culture threaten to overwhelm the differences by which we recognize our culture as distinct and, for us, preferable. To promote Canadian cultural production, the federal government has for several decades enacted policies that require Canadian broadcasters to make a sizable proportion of their content of Canadian origin. In addition, a variety of government programs subsidize Canadian film, television, music, and book production.

This policy of Canadian cultural protectionism has clearly succeeded in some regards. Scores of Canadian artists have gained a level of success that would have been unlikely if left to compete on the unequal playing field with American artists who are promoted by vast media conglomerates. Yet despite these successes, and despite the strict requirements of Canadian content regulations, Canadians consume tremendous amounts of American popular culture. There is no question that the continuing distinctiveness of Canadian culture and identity is threatened by the extensive consumption of American cultural products. There is an unfortunate contradiction between Canadians' preference for their own national norms, values, attitudes, and beliefs, on the one hand, and their preference for American popular culture, on the other.

## Conclusion

*Culture* is undoubtedly one of the most difficult sociological terms to pin down—it has many meanings—but through careful analysis sociology can bring those multiple meanings into focus and can explain why we have them. Many different social phenomena can be called "cultural." We need to understand what those various phenomena have in common to cause them all to be considered "culture." Culture is always evolving and is intimately tied to other social changes and to other cultural changes. Finally, we need to be aware of the role of culture in social life because it is the key to under-standing some of the most important events in our society and in the world today. Culture is implicated in the social dynamics both of conflict and of people coming together, and for that reason as well as others, it is an essential subject for sociological analysis.

## ☐ Questions for Critical Thought

1. What is Canadian culture, and what are its most important or distinctive facets?
2. What subcultures are you a member of? What are the characteristics of those subcultures, and how did you enter them?
3. How much do you know about other cultures and how did you learn about them? How do you know if your impressions are accurate?
4. Where does culture come from? How could you begin to research such a question? What dimensions of culture are particularly amenable to such a research question?
5. What role do art and music play in your life? Do your friends like the same art and music that you like? Do these art forms bring you together?
6. Who gets to decide what is good literature, painting, films, television, or music, and on what bases? Should you listen to experts on these matters, or can you decide for yourself?
7. How would you go about measuring cultural change? Moreover, how would you try to explain such change?
8. Is cultural change beneficial to society? Is it conceivable to have no changes in our culture?

## ☐ Recommended Readings

Jeffrey Alexander and Steven Seidman, eds, *Culture and Society: Contemporary Debates* (New York: Cambridge University Press, 1990).
  This book touches on many of the central issues in the sociology of culture and deals with fundamental issues concerning culture in social theory.

Peter Berger and Thomas Luckmann, *The Social Construction of Reality: A Treatise in the Sociology of Knowledge* (Garden City, NY: Doubleday-Anchor, 1966).
  This is a seminal work in the sociology of culture, laying the groundwork for social constructionist thought.

Gary Alan Fine, *Gifted Tongues: High School Debate and Adolescent Culture* (Princeton, NJ: Princeton University Press, 2001).
  Fine employs an analysis of many key cultural sociological concepts to illuminate a particular subculture.

Nelson Phillips and Cynthia Hardy, *Discourse Analysis: Investigating Processes of Social Construction* (Thousand Oaks, Calif.: Sage, 2002).
  This short book provides a concise and insightful review of the theory and research in sociology and related fields on the role of discourse in social life.

Lyn Spillman, ed., *Cultural Sociology* (Malden, Mass.: Blackwell, 2002).
  Spillman provides an entertaining overview of many excellent empirical studies in the sociology of culture as well as many intriguing theoretical works.

☐ **Recommended Web Sites**

**Culture & Tradition**

**www.ucs.mun.ca/~culture/**

The bilingual journal *Culture and Tradition* focuses on Canadian folklore and folk culture, both French and English.

**Culture/Online**

**www.ncf.edu/culture/**

This is the site of the American Sociological Association's Section on the Sociology of Culture. Here you can find links and news about new work done in the field.

**Poetics**

**www.elsevier.com/wps/product/cws_home/505592**

The electronic version of the journal *Poetics: Journal of Empirical Research on Culture, Media and the Arts* is here.

**UNESCO**

**www.unesco.org**

The United Nations Educational, Scientific and Cultural Organization deals with, among others, issues of cultural diversity and preservation.

# 3

Sue Wilson

# Socialization

© W.P. Wittman Limited

## ☐ Learning Objectives

In this chapter, you will:

- gain an understanding of the process of socialization
- understand and develop the capacity to apply basic concepts in the study of socialization
- reflect on personal experiences growing up in terms of socialization
- think about ways the hidden curriculum in educational institutions reproduces inequalities of gender, class, and race
- think critically about how the mass media both shape and reinforce social values
- learn about the National Longitudinal Survey of Children and Youth as a resource for studying Canadian children

## Introduction

Peter Berger (Berger and Berger, 1975) defined **socialization** as the process by which people learn to become members of society. For every individual, this process starts at birth and continues throughout life.

The most intense period of socialization is infancy and early childhood. Almost from the moment of birth, children begin to learn the basics of **social interaction**; they learn to recognize and respond socially to parents and other important people in their lives. In the process of interacting with parents, siblings, and other caregivers, children typically acquire the necessary cognitive and emotional skills to get along in their society. Moreover, as they adjust to daily routines, they learn to conform to adult expectations about a wide range of behaviour: where and when to sleep and eat, what to wear and play with, what is funny and what is serious, and so on. At the same time, children develop an individual **identity**, a self-concept.

Language is an important aspect of socialization. As children learn to understand words and later to use

Socialization is a life-long process. Almost from birth, children begin to learn the basics of social interaction. They adjust to daily routines and they learn to conform to adult expectations about a wide range of behaviour. (Photo © Megan Mueller)

them, they simultaneously learn to categorize their experience. Children also begin at an early age to evaluate their own behaviour and that of others. Indeed, one of the first words many children say is No!

In time, children learn to identify social **roles**—first the roles of family members, and later, as their experience broadens, those of others with whom they interact. They begin to identify consistent patterns in how they should act around relatives, teachers, doctors, religious leaders. They also develop an understanding of status differences, and the ways in which roles interact with **race**, **class**, and **gender** to create a complex social structure. When children respond appropriately, conforming to social expectations, they are said to have internalized behavioural **norms**.

Socialization patterns vary with class, ethnicity, family structure, gender, and birth order. The way people are socialized is therefore affected by whether they grow up in Vancouver or Moncton; whether they speak English or Cantonese at home; whether they worship at a church, a synagogue, or a mosque; whether they grow up in a single-parent or a two-parent household; and whether their parents are strict or lenient in their discipline, among many other factors. Despite such differences, the research cited throughout this chapter reveals certain interesting patterns in socialization practices and outcomes. According to Eleanor Maccoby, for example, as a result of socialization, most people acquire a package of attitudes, skills, and behaviours that enable them to "(a) avoid deviant behaviour; (b) contribute, through work, to the economic support of self and family; (c) form and sustain close relationships with others; and (d) be able to rear children in turn" (1992: 1006).

Parents (or parent substitutes) control much of the early learning environment of their children. But children are not simply passive receptors in the processes of socialization. Because of individual differences, some children thrive on routine; others resent it. Some grow up wanting to be like their parents; others react against parental models. Even within the same family, children will experience socialization differently.

Socialization, then, occurs in the process of social interaction. The two major accomplishments of socialization are the development of a self-concept and the internalization of social expectations. This chapter will examine some of the processes by which the complex learning that is socialization occurs and will discuss a number of theories of socialization. As you will see, families, schools, peer groups, and the media all play a part in socializing children. Moreover, adolescent socialization is a process that prepares young people for adult family and employment responsibilities. The chapter closes with a brief look at future directions in socialization.

# Forms of Socialization

Socialization is complex and multi-dimensional. In many ways, "socialization" is an umbrella concept: it takes in all social contacts and continues from birth to death. This section will consider the various forms of socialization experienced throughout life.

### Primary Socialization

The most intense learning, **primary socialization**, occurs from birth through adolescence. The family is the most important agent of primary socialization. This socialization is both intentional and unintentional, imposed and reciprocal. Parents socialize their children intentionally in countless ways as they teach them how and what to eat, what to wear, what to play with, what is funny, what is sad, how to address and treat others, which behaviours are rewarded and which punished, and so on. At the same time, unintentional socialization takes place as children learn about power and authority; gender, age, class, and ethnic differences; love, affection, and intimacy. Furthermore, the family's status in the community will affect the responses of others to the child, as well as where and with whom the child will play or go to school.

Although it is not entirely a "top-down" process, primary socialization is largely imposed, because children have less power and are less competent than adults. Yet, although the relationship is far from equal, there will be some elements of reciprocity in parent–child interactions. On the other hand, the relative power of parents will not guarantee socialization outcomes: children do not simply absorb life lessons from their parents.

### Secondary Socialization

**Secondary socialization** is an ongoing process of "recalibrating" throughout the life cycle as people anticipate and adjust to new experiences and new situations. In changing jobs, marrying, having children, coping with life crises, and so on, people are continually being socialized.

In many ways, socialization is a reciprocal process: children learn from their parents, but parents also

Family is the most important agent of primary socialization. Parents socialize their children in a wide variety of ways. They teach them how and what to eat, what to play with, what is funny. (© Fotosearch)

learn from their children. Thus, as children learn social interaction from their parents, parents learn how to parent. Reciprocal socialization is not confined to parents and children. Students learn from teachers, teachers from students. Family members, friends, and co-workers also socialize one another. In learning related to digital media, children are typically far more sophisticated than their parents and teachers. Much of this high-tech learning will involve children teaching adults.

Adult socialization differs from childhood socialization because it is based on accumulated learning and previous experience. Frances Waksler likens the difference between primary and secondary socialization to the difference between being born into a religion and converting from one religion to another: "In the latter process, one has both more choice (e.g., the very choice of converting or abandoning the endeavour) and more limits (e.g., the difficulty or even impossibility of coming to believe something that one had previously thought unbelievable)" (1991: 14).

### Anticipatory Socialization

In most situations, previous experience provides the capacity to imagine new experiences, so people become adept at **anticipatory socialization**. People mentally prepare themselves for future roles and responsibilities by means of anticipatory socialization, which Robert K. Merton defined as "the acquisition of values and orientations found in statuses and groups in which one is not yet engaged but which one is likely to enter" (1968: 438–9). Many college and university students, for instance, are engaged in anticipatory socialization as they acquire necessary academic skills and credentials for their future occupations.

The effectiveness of anticipatory socialization will depend on the degree of ambiguity of a new situation, as well as on its similarity to previous experience. According to Diane Bush and Roberta Simmons, "if the individual is prepared ahead of time for a new role, in the sense of understanding the norms associated with the role, having the necessary skills to carry it out, and becoming aware of expectations and rewards attached to the role . . . he or she will move into the new role easily and effectively" (1981: 147). This sums up very well the assumption underlying the concept of anticipatory socialization.

Many vehicles exist to ease the process of anticipatory socialization. Familiar examples include high school and university initiation, new employee orientation programs, parenting courses, and pre-retirement courses.

### Resocialization

Most people would not be able to anticipate successfully what it would be like to join the Armed Forces or a religious cult, to experience the sudden death of a loved one, or to be fired. When people encounter such situations, they must learn new rules. When new situations are so unique that people cannot rely on their previous experience to anticipate how to act, they may encounter a period of **resocialization**.

Some institutions, such as prisons and psychiatric hospitals, are specifically designed to resocialize "deviants." Timothy Seiber and Andrew Gordon (1981) introduced the idea of *socializing organizations* as a way of understanding socialization. Socializing organizations include total institutions such as prisons, as well as schools, job-training programs, counselling centres, and voluntary associations. These organizations are formally mandated to bring about some change in their members, but often the explicitly stated aims are less important than the latent messages they impart. In the words of Seiber and Gordon, "as recruits participate in the organization they learn its social and speech etiquettes, modes of self-presentation, rituals, routines, symbolic codes of deference, and other patterns of social relations" (1981: 7).

# Theories of Socialization

The questions sociologists ask, and often the methods they use, depend on which theoretical perspective they adopt. Some sociologists take **social structure** as their point of departure; others begin with individual interaction. Alan Dawe calls these two approaches, respectively, the *sociology of social system* and the *sociology of social action*: "One views action as the derivative of system whilst the other views system as the derivative of action" (1970: 214).

These two contrasting views of socialization are the focus of this section. The sociology of social system—"action as the derivative of system"—is best represented by the functionalism of Talcott Parsons (1955), who was interested in how individuals internalize social norms and become conforming members of society. **Symbolic interactionism**, by contrast, explains how individual self-concepts develop in the process of social interaction.

### The Functionalist Perspective

Sociologists who take the functionalist perspective, such as Talcott Parsons, describe socialization as a process of internalizing socially approved norms and behavioural expectations. People who grow up in a particular culture internalize a similar set of norms and values. The more widespread their acceptance, the more smoothly the group will function. Sociologists refer to a smooth outcome as *social integration*.

According to functionalist thinking, conformity is the consequence of internalizing behavioural expectations. This sounds very deterministic—as if norms necessarily make individuals conform. Indeed, the functionalist emphasis on individual conformity to group norms amounts, as Dennis Wrong (1961) put it, to "an oversocialized view" of humankind. To say that people are socialized does not imply that they have been completely moulded by the norms and values of their culture.

### The Feminist Critique

Sexist socialization practices were one of the first targets of **feminist** critiques of sociology, in the 1970s. Feminists were highly critical of Parsonian analysis because of the implication that differences between men and women could be understood as differences in socialization. In the first place, to describe inequities as the result of socialization avoided the issue of the structural barriers faced by women. Second, the socialization approach begged the question of change: how could parents socialized in traditional ways adopt non-sexist child-rearing practices? Therefore, feminists typically do not use socialization to explain gender differences, viewing them instead as consequences of systemic inequalities.

Gender socialization will be discussed in more detail later in this chapter. An extensive literature documents differential socialization practices, both implicit and explicit, and the ways these contribute to establishing gender differences in adolescents and adults.

## The Symbolic Interactionist Perspective

The symbolic interactionist approach, in contrast to the functionalist perspective, assumes that individuals actively participate in their own socialization. George H. Mead and Charles H. Cooley, two American sociologists who were active around the beginning of the twentieth century, were key influences in developing the symbolic interactionist perspective. Perhaps more than any other theorists, these two men influenced how most sociologists understand socialization.

Both Cooley and Mead were interested in the way individuals develop a sense of **self**, and in the importance of family interaction in this process. Cooley believed that children's instinctive capacity for self-development matures through interactions in *primary groups*, which he defined as "characterized by intimate face-to-face association and cooperation" ([1909] 1962: 23).

Adults communicate their attitudes and values to their children primarily through language, and children develop a self-concept on this basis. In other words, people begin to see themselves as they imagine others see them. This feeling—"I feel about me the way I think you think of me"— Cooley called the **looking-glass self**. The looking-glass self has three elements, according to Cooley: "the imagination of our appearance to the other person; the imagination of his judgment of that appearance; and some sort of self-feeling, such as pride or mortification" (1902: 184). The reaction of others, then, is important in determining how people feel about themselves.

Mead (1934) was also interested in the development of self-concept, which he considered to have two components: the Me, the socially defined self that

has internalized society's norms and values, and the I, the spontaneous, creative self. The I is what makes every person different from others. The Me induces people to conform to behavioural expectations.

Mead emphasized the importance of children's imaginative play in early socialization, believing that, through play, children become sensitive to the responses of others. He believed that people learn symbolically, by taking roles, to present themselves in different social situations. This process consists of four stages. At first, children's behaviour is a combination of instinctive behaviour and imitation. This Mead called the *pre-play stage*. Later, when children pretend to be a parent, teacher, doctor, and the like, they are in effect role-playing. Mead called this the *play stage*, in which children learn to assume the roles of others and to objectify that experience by seeing themselves from the point of view of others. In the next stage, the *game stage*, children learn to handle several roles at once, to anticipate the behaviour of others and the expectations others have of them. Finally, children learn to internalize general social expectations by imagining how any number of others will act and react. At this **generalized other** stage, a child has a sense of self and can react in a socially approved way.

Marlene Mackie (1987) regards the pre-play stage as lasting until the age of about two, the play stage as extending from two until the entry to school, and the game stage as continuing until puberty. Judy Dunn (1986), however, argues that children have an early and sophisticated sense of the emotional states of family members, and respond appropriately. On the basis of her study of British families, Dunn asserts that by two years of age, children have developed "powers to anticipate the feelings and intentions of other family members" and "powers to recognize and transgress social rules and to understand that jokes about such transgressions can be shared with other people" (1986: 112). Nonetheless, because social meanings are based on assumptions concerning the understanding and intentions of others, these meanings are always more or less ambiguous and subject to ongoing interpretation and reinterpretation.

## Psychological Theories of Socialization

Sociologists owe a considerable debt to psychological theories of development, including the psychoanalytic theories of Sigmund Freud (1856–1939). According to Freud ([1938] 1973), the emotional development of children can be measured as a progression through five stages: oral, anal, phallic, latent, and genital.

The *oral stage* occurs in the first year when children experience positive sensations through suckling. At this stage, too, children begin to explore the world by putting objects in their mouths. The *anal stage* focuses on toilet training and is the child's first experience with self-control (Collier, Minton, and Reynolds, 1991). Gender differences in development begin at the phallic stage, when children become aware of sex differences. This is followed by a latent period during which a child's sex drive is dormant before being awakened in adolescence.

Phase theories of development that focus on particular life tasks accomplished at specific stages in the life cycle inevitably build on Freud's work. Erik Erikson (1982), for instance, identified eight stages, or "turning points," from infancy to old age. Each stage involves a conflict whose resolution creates a specific human capacity. For example, in the first phase, infants resolve the conflict between trust and mistrust, developing hope in the process. In the final stage, old age, the conflict is between integrity and despair, and people develop wisdom from the resolution of this conflict.

Another way Freud influenced the thinking of social psychologists was through his theory of personality development ([1923] 1974). Indeed, awareness of the three components of personality (the id, the ego, and the superego) has seeped into popular culture and become part of everyday parlance. For Freud, the ego mediates between the id—our basic instincts—and the superego—internalized values. The insight for sociologists is that both the ego and the superego develop socially—in other words, in the process of socialization: "One of Freud's central theses is that society forces people to suppress basic human impulses such as sex and aggression, so that they must find expression in indirect and often distorted ways" (Collier, Minton, and Reynolds, 1991: 105).

Behavioural theories, by contrast, describe socialization as a process of learning through identification or reinforcement. Reinforcement, typically by parents, encourages some behaviours and discourages others. Albert Bandura (1973), whose work on children's imitation of violence has been very influential, developed his social learning theory based on observations of children imitating parents and other models. While we have all seen children imitating parents, and may have family stories that centre on such imitative behaviour, it is hard to explain all learning in terms of this model.

There are, then, two views of socialization: action as derivative of system, and system as derivative of action. Those who focus on ways individuals *internalize* social norms and values fall into the first group. This perspective was the focus of early feminist critique of socialization theories. Mead and Cooley, in contrast, focus on ways individuals are active participants in socialization—that infants are born with the capacity for self-development. Students interested in understanding more about this topic are encouraged to read the original work of Freud, Mead, Cooley, and Erikson.

# Agents of Socialization

**Agents of socialization** are those social institutions in children's environments that have the greatest effect on their socialization. The principal agents of socialization are the family, friendship or peer groups, the education system, the media, religious institutions, and the neighbourhood or community. The socializing effect of these agents varies over time, and is different for different children.

For most children, the family is the most important agent of socialization. Although children today spend fewer of their preschool years in the exclusive care of a family member, children still learn basic life skills and develop their values and beliefs in the course of family interaction. The other important agents of socialization to be discussed here are schools (including daycare centres and preschool), friendship or peer groups, and the media. Parents and schools have legally defined responsibility for socializing children; peer groups do not.

## The Family

Most children today have early and extensive experience of the world around them. Nevertheless, the family is still the most impressive agent of socialization. In families, children learn how to relate to other people, express intimacy, and resolve conflict. Parents play a major part in the lifelong social adjustment of their children. To cite Maccoby, "successful socialization of children involves not only bringing about their outward conformity to parental directives, but also enabling them to become self-regulating, and motivating them so that they become willing to cooperate with parental socialization efforts" (1992: 171).

How do parents encourage their children to internalize social norms and values and to behave in socially appropriate ways? On the surface, it might seem that parental control of scarce resources would be sufficient inducement. However, asserting parental power is only effective in the short term. Longer-term effects are achieved when children have a say in setting the standards with which they are expected to comply (Maccoby, 1992). The parenting style that seems to be most effective in developing high self-esteem and encouraging self-regulating skills is a combination of warmth and discipline. Diana Baumrind (1971) called this style *authoritative parenting*. Authoritative parents are affectionate, but clear in their expectations for pro-social, responsible behaviour. An authoritative parenting style is balanced between the two extremes of authoritarian and permissive parenting.

The family is the child's window to the world. A child's experience of the world will be framed by his or her family's social class, religion, ethnicity, and so on.

Families today are also far more varied structurally than families in the past. More children are born to single women, live in single-parent households, or enter reconstituted families. What effect do these outcomes have on socialization? Do socialization practices differ by type of family? Many researchers have considered these questions. Sociologists Elizabeth Thomson, Sara McLanahan,

and Roberta Curtin, for instance, argue that "the most consistent findings from studies of family structure and socialization are that single parents exert weaker controls and make fewer demands on children than married parents" (1992: 368). The researchers wondered why this was so. Was it because one parent can exert only half as much control as two, or because single mothers have not been socialized to display traditional paternal control behaviours? They concluded that socialization differences are determined primarily by the structural conditions of being a single parent, not by gender. In other words, the primary reason for the greater leniency of single parents is their lack of time.

Does parenting style matter? According to the National Longitudinal Survey of Children and Youth, it does indeed. Sarah Landy and Kwok Kwan Tam (1996) looked at the effect of parenting style on children who were also at risk because of family characteristics. Four styles were identified: ineffective, aversive, consistent, and positive. *Ineffective parents* are often annoyed with their children and prone to telling the child he or she is bad, or not as good as others. *Aversive parents* raise their voices when children misbehave and use physical punishment. *Consistent parents* discipline the same way for the same behaviour. *Positive parents* praise their children and play and laugh

---

**3.1**

# Sociology in Action
## The National Longitudinal Survey of Children and Youth

The National Longitudinal Survey of Children and Youth (NLSCY) was initiated in 1994. Its purpose is to follow Canadian children by interviewing them every other year until 2018. The initial national sample comprised 22,500 individuals aged newborn to adult.

Information is gathered about the children and their families from the "person most knowledgeable"—usually the child's mother. Teachers and school principals also contribute information about school performance. Children aged 10 and 11 are asked about their experiences with friends, family, and school.

The study was designed to support the analysis of child and youth characteristics over time and to allow for the investigation of the

impact of social and physical environments on outcome measures such as sociability and success in school.

Longitudinal studies such as this one allow researchers to identify factors in a child's environment that affect later life abilities, capacities, health, and well-being. The NLSCY includes key development indicators such as family composition, employment, economic well-being, parenting styles, and community resources. Some of the research cited in this chapter is taken from this survey. To find out more about the survey, go to the study Web site: <www.hrdc-drhc.gc.ca/sp-ps/arb-dgra/nlscy-elnej/home.shtml>.

together. Risk factors that might negatively affect physical or mental development include family dysfunction, low social support, and low income. Fewer than 4 per cent of the children in the survey were significantly at risk, and these children had four or more risk factors. The authors found that parenting practices had a greater impact on outcomes than risk factors. Indeed, positive parenting practices significantly contribute to child outcomes and protect children who are at risk: "Children in at-risk situations who enjoyed positive parenting practices achieved [outcome] scores within the average range for children in Canada" (Landy and Tam, 1996: 109). The parenting style that most strongly predicts delinquent behaviour in children aged 8 to 11 is the ineffective style, followed by aversive and inconsistent styles (Stevenson, 1999). (See also Table 3.1.)

Children gradually move beyond their experience of the family. As they become involved in groups in the neighbourhood—other families, play groups, school classes, church groups, and the like—they gain social experience, deal with conflicting demands, and become increasingly sophisticated social actors. Nevertheless, at the base of this experience of the world is their initial experience of family, which acts as a benchmark throughout life.

## Mass Media

The **mass media**, including newspapers, magazines, television, radio, films, and the Internet, are more than sources of entertainment or information. They are influential agents of socialization. The mass media are instrumental in transmitting and reinforcing certain values, social behaviours, and definitions of social reality. By focusing on some groups and not others or by stereotyping social characteristics, the media provide important lessons about power and influence. In this way, the media contribute to racial and sexual stereotypes. The impact is circular. Media representations are indicative of "who counts" in our society, and in turn provide lessons in who counts.

One of the first targets of feminist critique was the mass media, for contributing to the stereotyping of men and women. One would expect to find less stereotyping now than in the past because of this criticism and because women have made economic and political gains in the last four decades. It is therefore surprising to discover that television commercials continue to reflect a gender imbalance. Robert Bartsch and colleagues (2000) replicated two earlier studies of stereotyping in television commercials and found that most voice-overs continue to be male, and men are still more likely to appear in all commercials except those advertising domestic products. The authors did find some movement, however. The proportion of male voice-overs dropped from approximately 90 per cent to approximately 70 per cent, and the proportion of women advertising non-domestic products increased (2000: 739–40).

What about advertisements in non-Western media? In India, magazines, not electronic media, are the primary vehicle for advertising. Mallika Das (2000) studied changes in portrayals of men and women in Indian

Table 3.1 **Poor Parenting Practices**

| Parenting Style Used | Children with Conduct Disorder | |
| --- | --- | --- |
| | **Frequency** | **%** |
| Ineffective | Rarely | 4 |
| | Sometimes | 24 |
| | Very often | 63 |
| Aversive | Rarely | 7 |
| | Sometimes | 22 |
| | Very often | 40 |
| Consistent | Rarely | 38 |
| | Sometimes | 24 |
| | very often | 16 |
| Positive | Rarely | 27 |
| | Sometimes | 19 |
| | Very Often | 14 |

SOURCE: Adapted from Kathryn Stevenson, "Family Characteristics of Problem Kids," *Canadian Social Trends* (Winter 1999), Catalogue 11-008, 4.

3.2

# Human Diversity
## More Immigrant Children Enjoy Good Mental Health Than Canadian Children

Children in recent immigrant families have better mental health than Canadian children according to a study conducted by Beiser, Hou, Hyman, and Tousignant (1999) using the National Longitudinal Survey of Children and Youth. Canadian children are more likely to have severe symptoms of hyperactivity, emotional, or conduct disorders when compared to the children of new immigrants.

This is an interesting finding in that a higher proportion of immigrant families are poor, and poverty is an important risk factor for children. In addition, both children and parents in immigrant families suffer from the stress of relocation. The authors of the study suggest the following explanation:

> Unemployment and poverty are initial conditions of adversity in a new land—the promise of a better life sustains immigrant families. For poor Canadian families, poverty tends to be part of a negative spiral of family dysfunction, single-parent family structure, alcohol abuse and parental mental illness—all of which affect parenting practices as well as the mental health of children. The context of poverty modifies the effect that it has on the mental health of immigrant and Canadian children, resulting in different rates of well-being.

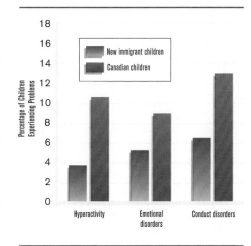

Figure 3.1 **Mental Health Outcomes in New Immigrant Children and Canadian Children**

SOURCE: Morton Beiser, Feng Hou, Ilian Hyman, and Michel Tousignant, "Immigrant Mental Health," Human Resources Development Canada, *Applied Research Bulletin* (Fall 1999), 21.

SOURCE: Exerpts from 'Immigrant Mental Health' by M. Beiser et al, *Applied Research Bulletin*, Human Resources Development Canada, Fall 1999. Catalogue MP32-27. Reproduced with the permission of the Minister of Public Works and Government Services Canada, 2005.

magazine advertisements in 1987, 1990, and 1994. Interestingly, the results showed that the 1990 ads portrayed women in less traditional situations than the earlier or later ads. At the same time, men were portrayed in more traditional ways in 1990 than before or after. In North American media, men and women are most typically shown in athletic roles in advertisements. This is far less evident in India. On the other hand, Indian women are less likely to be portrayed as sex objects than women in British media. Das writes, "In India the trend seems to be to portray women less often as housewives or concerned with looks, but not more often in non-traditional, career-oriented, or authority

figure roles" (2000: 713). Das suggests that this may reflect the patriarchal values of Indian society.

Concern about media violence has been of long standing. Today, this concern focuses on violence and pornography in digital media; 20 years ago it was television, particularly music videos; but movies, comics, and magazines have all been considered potentially dangerous sources of influence, especially for young people. In the 1950s, Frederic Wertham published his book *Seduction of the Innocent* (1954) to protest violence in comic books, proposing that the increased popularity of comic books was related to the rise of violence in the United States. Those concerned about media violence feel that the negative effects of the media are self-evident, that the sheer amount of violence speaks for itself. They are concerned that children will imitate what they see on television or on the Internet. A second, more subtle, more pervasive problem is the media's role in creating definitions of social reality. For example, we may tolerate high levels of violence because we have come to think that "that's the way life is."

Media effects have been studied by psychologists in laboratory experiments. Under laboratory conditions, subjects display more aggressive behaviour than control groups when exposed to television portrayals of violence (see Bandura, 1973). It is not clear, however, whether the kinds of imitative behaviour that occur in the laboratory also occur in normal social interaction. Experiments may confidently conclude that the response (aggressive behaviour) was triggered by the stimulus (violent media portrayals) but not that it will also occur outside the lab (Singer and Singer, 2000). In natural settings, the difficulty lies in controlling extraneous variables. In other words, how can we be sure that the behaviour we observed was, in fact, triggered by the media and not by something else?

Television accounts for the third largest block of time in our lives, after work or school and sleep. It is interesting that the number of hours Canadians spend watching conventional television has decreased over

the past two decades. Canadians watched television for an average of 21.5 hours a week in the fall of 2000. The average ranged between 23 and 24 hours a week during the 1980s. Young men (aged 18–24) spent the least amount of time watching television— only 13.2 hours a week. Women watched an average of 5 more hours of television than men, although for both sexes, viewing time increased with age (Statistics Canada, 2001d).

Television is the primary medium accessible to children and is a potent agent of socialization. While we might worry about the amount of television children watch and about the way television contributes to a sedentary lifestyle, the amount of time children spend watching television has, like adult viewing, decreased. According to Statistics Canada figures, adolescents watch an average of 14.1 hours a week and children watch 15.5 hours. Part of the decline is due to the increased use of VCRs and DVDs. However, the main reason for the change in television behaviour has been pay-TV and specialty service. Almost 84 per cent of Canadians had access to cable or satellite services in 2000 (Statistics Canada, 2001d; see also Figure 3.2).

In 1997, Statistics Canada began to collect data about Internet use. The 2000 General Social Survey, with over 25,000 respondents, provides an interesting picture of Internet use in Canada. In this survey, use

Figure 3.2 **Average Hours per Week of Television Viewing for Children and Teens in 2002, by Province**

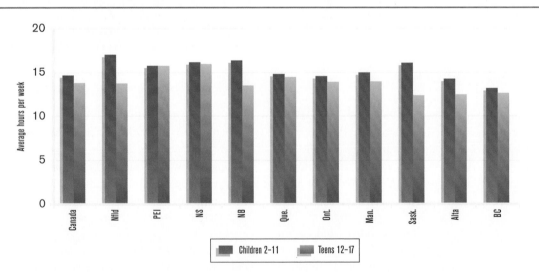

SOURCE: Data from Statistics Canada, "Average hours per week of television viewing, 2002" based on CANSIM data. Available at <http://www.statcan.ca/english/Pgdb/arts23.htm>, accessed 29 December 2004.

was defined as at least once in the past year. As we might predict, Internet use is related to age, income, and education. Only 30 per cent of low-income Canadians (with a household income of below $20,000) said that they used the Internet in the previous year, compared to 81 per cent of those with household income over $80,000. The education gap is even more dramatic. Only 13 per cent of adults over 20 with low education (less than a high school diploma) used the Internet, compared to 79 per cent of those with university degrees (Statistics Canada, 2001c: 3).

In his book *Growing Up Digital*, Don Tapscott (1998) refers to what demographers have called the *baby-boom echo generation* (born between 1977 and 1997) as the *Net generation*. The media sometimes call this group *screenagers*. While their parents, the baby-boom generation, were shaped by television, which influenced their values, their political beliefs, and how they spent their leisure time, the Net generation is immersed in digital media, with perhaps more far-reaching effects—digital media, after all, can be an educational tool in a way that television was never able to be. The Net generation also use the Internet to communicate with friends and to establish and maintain community. Young people, according to Tapscott, have become bored with the unidirectional medium of television, preferring the engagement required by digital technology. Indeed, they watch far less television than their parents did when they were young. Young people are also sophisticated users of the new technology, far surpassing their parents or their teachers.

Two aspects of shifting media use are worth noting. The first is that media use is increasingly a solitary activity. Today there are more televisions and fewer people per household. In other words, more people are watching television alone. We also watch more videos and go to fewer movies. Again, going to the movies is usually a social activity; video viewing may not be. Typically, entertainment and communication on the Internet are solitary. The second point concerns what Tapscott (1998) calls the *digital divide*: the class and educational difference in digital media use. This has created a system of information haves and have-nots. The digital divide occurs within societies like Canada and the United States, and it occurs between societies where dramatic differences in access distinguish the developing and the developed world.

The Statistics Canada General Social Survey of 2000 asked Canadians about their Internet use. Of the 3,300 young people (aged 15–24) among the respondents, 56 per cent were connected to the Internet at home. Almost half of these young people used the Internet every day. Frequent users also access the Internet at school and at work. Nevertheless, those with home access indicated far more hours of use than those without home access. Men use the Internet for more hours per week than women. E-mail is the most popular Internet activity for young Canadians (Rotermann, 1999: 5–6; see also Figure 3.3). Internet use for 15- to 24-year-olds is lower in Quebec than in the rest of Canada. This is presumably because much of the content of the Internet is in English only, a factor that affects usage worldwide.

### The Peer Group

Patricia Ramsey writes, "For both children and adults, friends enhance our pleasure, mitigate our anxieties and broaden our realm of experience" (1991: 3). The family is the first reference group for most people, that is, the group with which children compare their behaviour, ideas, and values. But starting at an early age, the peer group also becomes very important. Because so many parents are now in the labour force, more children are spending more time with children of the same age, and at a younger age. Peer groups have therefore gained increasing recognition as important socializing agents for even very young children. The success of children's peer relationships is linked to their later psychological development and to school success. It has also been suggested that children with poor peer relationships may experience job-related and marital problems in later life (Ramsey, 1991).

Play groups provide important opportunities for children to learn to relate to others and increase their social skills. By interacting with their peers in play groups, children develop a frame of reference not based on adult authority. Gerald Handel asserts that "it is in these peer groups that a child learns to function more independently, to acquire and test skills and beliefs that earn him a place among people of the same generation, to develop new outlooks that reflect youthful interests rather than adult ones" (1988: 17).

The peer group assumes great influence in adolescence. In developmental terms, the task of adolescents is to begin to establish emotional, social, and economic independence. By the age of 13 or 14, adolescents typically spend most of their leisure time with peers. In an international survey, Klaus Hurrelmann found, for example, that Western adolescents report spending more time talking to peers than on any other single activity—and are happiest doing just this (1989: 16).

Figure 3.3  **Young People's Use of the Internet (Ages 15–24)**

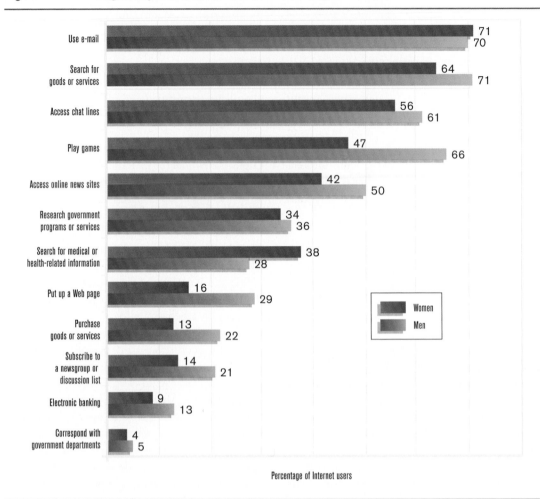

| | Women | Men |
|---|---|---|
| Use e-mail | 71 | 70 |
| Search for goods or services | 64 | 71 |
| Access chat lines | 56 | 61 |
| Play games | 47 | 66 |
| Access online news sites | 42 | 50 |
| Research government programs or services | 34 | 36 |
| Search for medical or health-related information | 38 | 28 |
| Put up a Web page | 16 | 29 |
| Purchase goods or services | 13 | 22 |
| Subscribe to a newsgroup or discussion list | 14 | 21 |
| Electronic banking | 9 | 13 |
| Correspond with government departments | 4 | 5 |

Percentage of Internet users

SOURCE: Adapted from Michelle Rotermann, "Wired Young Canadians," *Canadian Social Trends* Catalogue 11-008 (Winter 2001), 6.

Adolescence is commonly depicted as period of testing limits. It is not a surprise that more adolescents are killed in accidents than die from health-related problems. If we were to rely on the mass media, we might be persuaded that youth violence is increasing in this "age of Columbine." Certainly there have been a few spectacular incidents of adolescent violence in Canada and in the United States. On the other hand, official statistics suggest that the incidence of violent crime is declining and that only a small proportion of young people are involved in physical violence. When Canadian sociologist Reginald Bibby surveyed Canadian young people, he found that many were fearful of encountering violence: 22 per cent of young people did not feel safe in school—a smaller proportion than found in comparable US studies (2001: 84, 88). (See also Table 3.2.)

Why do some adolescents resort to physical violence and others don't? The National Longitudinal Survey of Children and Youth (NLSCY) provides some interesting information about aggressive behaviour among Canadian pre-adolescents. Indeed, children become less, not more, violent as they become older. The age at which children are most likely to hit, bite, or kick was 27 to 29 months (Tremblay et al., 1996: 129), suggesting that most Canadian children "benefit from the socializing impact of their families and other socialization agencies" (Tremblay et al., 1996: 130). Children who are physically aggressive are also often hyperactive and suffer inattention problems.

Table 3.2 **Teens' Concern About Violence by Region, Community Size, and Birthplace (Percentages)**

| | School Violence a Very Serious Problem | Close Friend Attacked at School | Not Safe at School | Not Safe at Home | Close Friend Physically Abused at Home |
|---|---|---|---|---|---|
| Nationally | 50 | 32 | 22 | 7 | 31 |
| British Columbia | 51 | 30 | 19 | 7 | 30 |
| Prairies | 49 | 32 | 17 | 5 | 30 |
| Ontario | 53 | 32 | 22 | 7 | 32 |
| Quebec | 43 | 33 | 27 | 7 | 33 |
| Atlantic | 54 | 30 | 21 | 8 | 27 |
| North | 53 | 34 | 19 | 2 | 31 |
| Cities, towns | | | | | |
| <30,000 | 53 | 29 | 21 | 8 | 33 |
| 30,000–99,999 | 56 | 36 | 28 | 7 | 31 |
| 100,000–399,999 | 51 | 32 | 21 | 7 | 34 |
| >400,000 | 44 | 35 | 21 | 5 | 32 |
| Rural | | | | | |
| Non-farm | 52 | 32 | 18 | 7 | 27 |
| Farm | 50 | 24 | 19 | 6 | 25 |
| Born in Canada | 50 | 31 | 21 | 7 | 32 |
| Born outside Canada | 47 | 35 | 26 | 6 | 28 |

SOURCE: Reginald W. Bibby, *Canada's Teens* (Toronto: Stoddart, 2001), 84.

They also have lower self-esteem, tend to exhibit high levels of indirect aggression and high emotional disorder, and tend not to help other children (Tremblay et al., 1996: 132).

Families have an important impact on the aggressive behaviour of pre-adolescents. Boys and girls who have siblings with behavioural problems are more likely to be aggressive themselves. They are also more likely to live in families with high levels of parent–child conflict and sibling conflict. Aggressive children have poor peer relationships and are more likely to be victimized by other aggressors (see Table 3.3). Will these young people outgrow their adolescent behaviour? Richard Tremblay and colleagues (1996) suggest that because the aggression stems from family interaction problems, this appears unlikely. Without support, these children are more likely to continue aggressive behaviour into adulthood. It is, however, important to keep in mind that these children represent a small proportion of all Canadian children. Most children are not inappropriately aggressive. In addition, they are, as Bibby (2001) points out, highly resilient. In the face of family problems and economic and educational disadvantage, Canadian adolescents are optimistic about the future.

Although much is made of the idea of adolescent rebellion, parental and adolescent values generally are quite similar. Because parents want their children to be well liked and want good relationships with them, they tend to be supportive of their children's activi-

Peer play groups provide important opportunities for children to learn and relate to others and increase their social skills. Peer groups have gained increasing recognition as important socializing agents even for very young children. (Photo © Megan Mueller)

Table 3.3 **Prevalence of Bullying and Victimization in Canada (Percentages)**

| | Parent's Report | | Children's Self-Report[a] | |
|---|---|---|---|---|
| | **Boys** | **Girls** | **Boys** | **Girls** |
| Ages 4–6 | | | | |
| Bullying | 14.4 | 9.4 | – | – |
| Victimization | 4.9 | 4.4 | – | – |
| Ages 7–9 | | | | |
| Bullying | 14.8 | 7.9 | – | – |
| Victimization | 4.0 | 7.4 | – | – |
| Ages 10–11 | | | | |
| Bullying | 13.0 | 9.2 | 17.2 | 8.7 |
| Victimization | 8.6 | 9.1 | 13.6 | 8.1 |

[a] Self-report data were not collected in the 4–6 and 7–9 age groups.
SOURCE: Wendy Craig, Ray Peters, and Roman Konarski, "Bully and Victim: Child's Play or Unhealthy Schoolyard Behaviour?" *Applied Research Bulletin* (Fall 1999), 17. Catalogue MP32-27. Reproduced with the permission of the Minister of Public Works and Government Services Canada, 2005.

ties. Peer-group influence is tempered by parental influence because parents control scarce and valued resources, including their approval. Certainly some adolescents rebel, but for most young people learning to be independent adults, adolescence is not a particularly turbulent time. In fact, research suggests that the majority of teenagers experience adolescence positively. Daniel Offer's 1988 study of 6,000 adolescents in 10 countries (Australia, Bangladesh, Hungary, Israel, Italy, Japan, Taiwan, Turkey, the United States, and West Germany) revealed surprising similarities in the experience of growing up. Most adolescents

(about 80 per cent in each country) were well adjusted and confident, enjoyed life, had a positive self-image, and liked their parents (Offer et al., 1988). They had positive expectations about the future and felt emotionally able to cope with it.

### School

Schools do more than instruct students in the three R's; they also provide an important environment for the transmission of social values. Next to the family, the school is probably the most important locus of childhood and adolescent socialization, because it is central to a young person's social life and acts as a filter for future occupational choice. A key component here seems to be the effect of positive reactions by parents and teachers on a child's self-concept. Doris Entwisle and Leslie Hayduck (1988) report that parent and teacher reactions to Grade 3 children had a significant effect on achievement almost a decade later. As they explain, children in the early grades are building their "academic self-images." During transitions, children depend on significant others for support: "getting off to a good start gives them a competitive advantage from then on" (Entwisle and Hayduck, 1988: 158).

Self-concepts are particularly fragile when adolescents are in middle school (senior public or junior high). David Kinney (1993) reports that older adolescents remember this as a difficult time. Students universally recall a rigid social structure dominated by a popular (and powerful) group. Unpopular adolescents remember being ridiculed, shunned, and ignored by

Next to the family, school is probably the most important locus of childhood and adolescent socialization because it is central to a young person's social life and acts as a filter for future occupational choice. (© Getty Images)

their popular classmates. Fortunately, the impact of popularity is short-lived. In high school, student culture is more open and more diverse. There are far more reference groups with which to identify, and the social structure is less hierarchical (Kinney, 1993).

As children mature, they increase their experiences and contacts. However, these events and associations will not be random. Rather, they are largely compatible with earlier experience. It is therefore unlikely that the school environment will promote values different from those already learned by a child. For example, middle-class children will attend school with other middle-class children, who for the most part will value school achievement.

Yet much of what is learned in school is implicit, sometimes referred to as the **hidden curriculum**. The hidden curriculum comprises unspoken rules and practices such as the acclaim given by students and teachers alike to academic versus athletic endeavours; the behaviours that are punished versus those that are excused; the age, sex, race, and ethnic structure of the administration, the teaching staff, and the student body; and the similarity or difference between a student's friends' and his or her family's expectations for the student's success. The greater the

disjunction between the behaviours reinforced at school and those reinforced by the family or the peer group, the smaller the likelihood that the student will see success in school as relevant.

Parental involvement, including helping children with homework, encouraging them to study, having contact with the school and teachers, and attending events at the school, has a positive effect on children's academic performance. This relationship holds for younger as well as older students.

Many immigrant parents in particular have high expectations for their children regarding education. As shown in Table 3.4, the majority are actively involved in their children's education and want their children to go to university. Canadian-born children of Canadian-born parents are much less likely to want to choose their children's career or to expect their children to go to university. They are, however, among the most likely parents to help their children with school. Lilia Salazar and colleagues (2001) studied the family socialization processes used by Filipino-Canadian parents living in Winnipeg to motivate their children in school. The children, who were in Grades 7 through 12, completed a self-report questionnaire about parenting styles, parent involve-

Table 3.4  **Parental Expectations About Education and Career (% of Teens Agreeing)**

| | Caribbean[a] | Chinese[a] | East European[a] | Latin American[a] | South Asian[a] | Canadian[b] | All |
|---|---|---|---|---|---|---|---|
| My parent(s) want to choose a career for me | 15 | 26 | 17 | 19 | 26 | 8 | 19 |
| My parent(s) expect me to go to university | 69 | 89 | 70 | 68 | 77 | 45 | 70 |
| My parent(s) think high marks in school are important | 92 | 87 | 91 | 81 | 90 | 75 | 84 |
| I feel a lot of pressure from my parent(s) to do well in school | 50 | 55 | 49 | 52 | 60 | 45 | 52 |
| If I have problems at school, my parent(s) are ready to help me | 76 | 64 | 71 | 81 | 78 | 80 | 73 |

[a] Children not born in Canada or whose parents were not born in Canada.
[b] Children born in Canada to Canadian-born parents.
SOURCE: Barbara Helm and Wendy Warren, "Cultural Heritage and Family Life," *Transition Magazine* (Ottawa: The Vanier Institute of the Family, Sept. 1998), 7. Reprinted by permission of The Vanier Institute of the Family.

ment, the importance of family reputation, attribution of success, and student involvement. The results suggest that student involvement in school was promoted by parental involvement (as perceived by their adolescents) and authoritative (not authoritarian) parenting. Authoritative parents encourage psychological autonomy and exert firm behavioural guidelines. Authoritarian parents, in contrast, are strict, demand obedience, and are emotionally distant. Adolescents indicated that they felt obliged to do well in school to maintain their family's reputation. Those students who were concerned about family reputation were inclined to believe that effort and interest, not academic ability, were the basis of student success. That these findings corresponded very closely to findings of a study done of Filipino immigrants in San Francisco suggests that, indeed, the emphasis on family reputation as a mediating factor in school success may be characteristic of Filipino adolescent immigrants.

In schools throughout the world, adolescents are "sorted" during secondary schooling. High school grades and course selection will determine whether a student attends a post-secondary institution or enters the labour force upon graduation. One of the most important variables influencing which of these paths is taken is gender.

## Socialization Outcomes

This section will look at the effects of gender, race, and class on socialization practices. It will also examine how children learn to make gender, race, and class distinctions and to understand their implications. For children, adolescents, and adults alike, gender identity and perceptions of socio-economic status are fundamental aspects of the development of self-concept. Gender and class infuse social interaction as children develop physically, cognitively, and emotionally and as they anticipate adult family and economic roles.

### The Social Reproduction of Gender

Individuals develop an understanding of gender through a complex interweaving of individual and environmental factors, predispositions, and expectations. In the course of gender socialization, children are exposed to many models of behaviour and gain a sense of masculinity or femininity from a variety of sources. Furthermore, individuals receive inconsistent messages even from the same sources.

How much of what we are is determined by socialization, and how much is inborn? This question is often referred to as the *"nature versus nurture" debate*. The assumption that nature dominates is called **biological determinism**. The opposite of biological determinism is what is described as "an oversocialized view" of human nature (Wrong, 1961) that implies that people are largely moulded by their socialization experiences.

In the past, people believed that behavioural differences were largely genetically determined, that people were born with certain aptitudes and dispositions—including a predisposition to good or evil. This assumption of inherent characteristics was taken to apply to differences between races as well as between men and women. This line of reasoning is now regarded as fallacious. It is one thing to suppose that nature helps explain individual differences, quite another to say the same thing about group differences. Nevertheless, the question of nature versus nurture remains a focus of continuing research, with much attention given to differences between females and males. Are sex distinctions in adults better explained in terms of biological differences or in terms of differential socialization?

Gender differences have been the subject of thousands of studies. Much of the research has focused on the behaviour of infants and young children. Reviews of this body of work, including an early review by Eleanor Maccoby and Carole Jacklin (1974) of 1,400 studies, find few behaviours that consistently differentiate males and females. In many cases, studies investigating similar behaviours have had contradictory results. For instance, consistent gender differences have been reported in aggression and in a preference for certain toys. In fact, most studies have found that the actual distinctions between boys and girls are minor. Most children are not aggressive, and they spend most of their time playing with toys that are not gender-related. Furthermore, since boys are handled more roughly from birth onward, some sex-related differences are predictable in behaviours such as level of activity or aggressiveness; however, these differences may have more to do with socialization practices than with biology. Most adult behaviours do not have clear antecedents in early childhood. The important differences between adults—status distinctions, for example—are unrelated to the differences typically found in children.

Some researchers argue that gender differences develop because of parental reaction to innate differences (see Ruble and Martin, 1998). That is, girls become more verbally skilled because they are more receptive to verbal interactions, while boys become more physically aggressive because they respond more positively to aggressive play. Others argue that parents reinforce behaviour in a way that is consistent with their own expectations and stereotypes. Parents have different expectations of their infant boys and girls in language, cognitive, and social development (see Ruble and Martin, 1998). This may or may not also extend to motor development. E.R. Mondschein, K.E. Adolph, and C.S. Tamis-LeMonda (2000) measured mothers' expectations regarding crawling and compared this to crawling ability. Mothers of boys had higher expectations of their sons than did mothers of daughters regarding crawling. Although the infant boys and girls in the study did not differ in motor abilities, mothers expected them to differ. This difference in expectation has significant implications for later motor development and risk-taking.

Very young children show sex-stereotyped toy preferences and sex-stereotyped activities. Research evidence seems to favour a socialization explanation. Television ads, catalogue layouts, toy packaging, and the organization of toy departments all seem to collude to steer the toy purchaser in the direction of stereotyped choices. It is no surprise that toys and other aspects of the physical environment of very young children are differentiated according to gender. Andrée Pomerleau and colleagues (1990) found that boys under the age of two tended to be given sports equipment, tools, and large and small vehicles, while girls were presented with dolls, fictional characters, child's furniture, and other toys for manipulation. They also observed the traditional pink/blue differences in the room decoration of the children in their sample.

Socialization is, to a large extent, based on nuance and subtlety. By the age of two, children are perceptive readers of their **social environment**. They observe patterns of interaction in the home, including the gender-relatedness of household tasks. Even in homes where both parents are gainfully employed, women take greater responsibility for housework and child care than men. Socialization to such divisions of labour presumably affects the family and occupational choices of young people. Children grow up with gendered names, toys, clothes, games, and room decorations. By the time they get to school, **gender stereotypes** are well established. The structure and practices of education, then, reinforce rather than challenge these earlier perceptions.

As argued earlier in the chapter, the media are a significant source of gender stereotyping. Studies of

media content continue to find that women are underrepresented, stereotyped, and trivialized. Susan Losh-Hesselbart (1987) made the interesting discovery that those who watch a lot of television show more rigidity in gender stereotyping than occasional viewers. It is hardly surprising, then, that one of the women's movement's first targets among traditional socialization practices was the gender stereotyping in children's books and television programming. These criticisms have met with some success. A study of children's picture books by Carole Kortenhaus and Jack Demarest found that newer books show a greater representation of female characters: "Prior to 1970, children's literature contained almost four times as many boys as girls in titles, more than twice as many boys in central roles, almost twice as many boys in pictures, and nearly four times as many male animals as female animals" (1993: 225). After 1970, there were more female characters in all categories—but still not an equal number. Kortenhaus and Demarest also noted that activities depicted in books were strongly stereotyped by sex, with males dominating in instrumental behaviours and females in passive, dependent roles. Again, however, they found some improvement over time.

Childhood experiences have lifelong implications. Patricia Coats and Steven Overman (1992) compared childhood play and other early socialization experiences of women in traditional and non-traditional professions. They found that women in non-traditional fields had received different forms of parental encouragement than women in traditional professions. Women in non-traditional (business) professions participated in more competitive activities as children and continued to seek competitive recreational activities as adults. The members of this group also had more male companions when they were children. Interestingly, the fathers of all the professional women encouraged their daughters' competitiveness. Mothers of women who entered non-traditional professions echoed that encouragement, whereas mothers of women who entered traditional professions encouraged more traditional values.

Data from a US intergenerational panel study of parents and children provide an opportunity to see the effect of childhood socialization practices regarding household division of labour on the next generation (Cunningham, 2001). Women in this sample were interviewed first in 1962 and again in 1977, and their 18-year-old daughters were interviewed in 1980. Indeed, the mothers' attitudes during their children's early years had a strong influence on the children's ideal division of household labour at 18. The

3.3

# Open for Discussion
## Do the Media Contribute to Disordered Eating Among Young Adolescent and Pre-adolescent Girls?

Most women in fashion magazines, movies, and television are pencil-thin. Indeed, the media create an impression that thinness is highly valued in Western society. Viewers of all ages use these images as points of comparison when evaluating their own body image. No wonder body dissatisfaction is universal. Kevin Thompson and Leslie Heinberg (1999) connect exposure to unrealistically thin images in magazines and television with body dissatisfaction and disordered eating among girls and women. Their solution is to counter these extreme images: "The media itself is one potential vehicle for communicating productive, accurate, and deglamorized messages about eating and shape-related disorders" (339).

What do you think about this issue? Are girls susceptible to images of ultra-thin models? Are girls more susceptible than young boys? In what other ways besides the mass media is thinness reinforced? How do we reconcile media images with reports of increased numbers of obese children and youth? Does the solution lie, as these authors suggest, in changing the images in the media, or is it a larger and more complex problem?

family division of labour also had an important impact: adolescent women whose fathers had shared housework were more apt to support men's participation in stereotypically female household tasks.

Gender stereotypes continue to frame our understanding of the social behaviour of males and females from infancy to old age. Minor behavioural and attitudinal differences in childhood are reinforced through adolescence and become pronounced in adults. However subtly, people react to boys and girls, men and women, differently, and in the process encourage different behavioural responses. The differential reactions may be quite unintentional. Parents tend to say they have similar expectations for their children with regard to dependency, aggression, school achievement, and so forth, although fathers are typically more concerned than mothers about gender-typed behaviour in their children.

The gender stereotyping of occupational choices has important implications for a young person's future. Occupational stereotypes frame educational, occupational, and interpersonal choices, especially for women, and are the basis of discriminatory practices in education and the workplace. Nonetheless, significant changes certainly have occurred in the family and occupational responsibilities of both women and men during the past three decades. These changes indicate that behaviour can be modified, even for those whose primary socialization was highly traditional.

## The Social Reproduction of Race and Class

*Racial socialization* refers to all of the ways parents shape children's learning about race and race relations (Hughes and Johnson, 2001). Racial socialization is an important component of child-rearing among ethnic and racial-minority families. It appears that efforts to instill racial pride are successful. Generally, children whose parents have emphasized racial pride have higher self-esteem and greater knowledge of their ethnic or racial group (see Marshall, 1995).

Racial socialization, like gender and class socialization, is an iterative process. Children are not simply sponges. Their reactions and needs interact with their parents' own experiences of being socialized and with their parents' experiences in the world to determine parental racial socialization strategies.

D. Hughes and D. Johnson (2001) used reports of 94 dyads of African-American parents and Grade 3, 4, and 5 children to see if socialization practices were influenced by whether or not children had experienced racial **discrimination**. Most parents reported that they talked to their children about their own and other ethnic groups, and most talked to their children about the possibility that the child might experience discrimination. Only about one-fifth of parents reported that they had cautioned or warned their children about other racial or ethnic groups. Hughes and Johnson refer to this strategy as "promotion of mistrust." Not surprisingly, promotion of mistrust was related to parents' reports that their children had received unfair treatment from adults as well as to children's reports of unfair treatment from peers. Interestingly, parental promotion of mistrust was not related to their own experiences of discrimination.

How does racial socialization work when parents and children are of different races? Tracy Robinson (2001) studied this issue by analyzing interviews of white mothers of mixed race (white–Maori) children in New Zealand. These mothers described the importance of exposing their children to both white (*Pakeha*) and Maori culture and their frustration in the face of the discrimination their children experienced. One woman discussed tearfully the difficulty her child encountered in finding an apartment. Her daughter had phenotypical characteristics (brown skin, dark hair, and brown eyes). One day the daughter said, "Mum, you come along with me so that I can get the apartment" (Robinson, 2001: 180).

Another important context of socialization is socio-economic class. The kinds of work adults perform and the coping strategies they employ to make sense of their work have fundamental implications for the socialization of their children. As in gender socialization, children begin at a very young age to absorb the implications of class in society. They learn early "who counts" and where they fit into the social hierarchy.

Child-rearing practices and socialization contexts change over time and reflect cultural, ethnic, and class differences. Melvin Kohn was a pioneer in researching the relationship between social class and socialization values and practices. His research has important implications for understanding cross-cultural variations as well. Kohn argues that attitudes to child-rearing vary by social class because of important class differences in occupational experiences. According to Kohn (1977), the key variables are closeness of supervision, routinization, and the substantive complexity of work. Blue-collar workers are more closely supervised, perform more routine tasks, and work primarily with physical objects rather than with people or ideas. Parents who hold these kinds of jobs emphasize conformity, neatness, and orderliness. Typically, middle-class parents are more permissive and place greater emphasis on self-reliance. White-collar parents focus on behavioural intentions, blue-collar parents on consequences. Attitude studies done in the United States support these findings. Duane Alwin (1990) observes that, typically, the middle and upper classes emphasize self-direction, while working-class families emphasize obedience and conformity to tradition or authority.

Alwin (1990) argues that there was a general shift in North American parental values over the five decades leading up to his study. Whereas parents used to want their children to be obedient and conforming, they were now more inclined to want to instill a sense of independence or autonomy. He looked at five studies measuring parental socialization values from the 1920s through the 1980s. Public opinion surveys done in Detroit in 1958, 1971, and 1983 revealed some interesting differences (Alwin, 1984). Parents were asked the following question:

> If you had to choose, which thing would you pick as the most important for a child to learn to prepare him for life?
> (a) to obey
> (b) to be well-liked or popular
> (c) to think for himself
> (d) to work hard
> (e) to help others when they need help (Alwin, 1984: 365)

Respondents were asked to rank their top four choices. Alwin found that "to think for himself" was the most preferred quality and that the number of parents citing it as most important increased over time. "To be well-liked or popular" was the least preferred and became even less important over time. Obedience also decreased in importance, while hard work increased. The number of parents who valued the quality of helpfulness remained stable. In other Western countries, too, there seems to be a similar parental concern for developing independence in children (Alwin, 1990).

What accounts for this shift in focus? Alwin feels it results partly from increased education, partly from increased secularization. Predictably, increased education is associated with the valuation of autonomy and with a decrease in the value of conformity. Parental preference for obedience is linked to levels of church attendance, which have declined over recent decades. Finally, it is interesting that some evidence exists that the youngest cohorts are slightly more inclined towards conformity and obedience than older cohorts. Nevertheless, parental values are only one part of the equation. Myriad factors combine to influence children's behaviour. The fact that parents claim to value self-reliant behaviour does not necessarily imply that children will respond accordingly.

## *The Social Reproduction of Adult Family and Work Roles*

Childhood, adolescence, and adulthood are social constructs that broadly define periods of social, psychological, and biological development. They are generally, but not absolutely, determined by age. Because life-cycle stages do not follow a predictable or orderly track, there is no specific point at which an adolescent is declared to be an adult, for example. Some young people will have assumed adult roles of marriage, parenthood, or economic independence before their eighteenth birthday. Others remain in school and financially dependent on parents well into their twenties. Still others return to the parental home after divorce or job loss. Some of these adult children will have children themselves, thus creating a temporary three-generation household. During the past quarter-century, the transition from adolescence to adulthood has been altered by such trends as increased schooling and a rise in the age at first marriage. Now, young adults enjoy a period of independent living before marriage. Two or three decades ago, this period of independence was shorter, as both men and women typically married in their early twenties. Ceremonies such as graduation or marriage may therefore be more appropriate than age as signals of the transition to adulthood.

José Machado Pais (2000) has argued that the transition to adulthood takes longer now than in the past. One of the reasons for this is uncertainty about future education, work, and family roles. The transitional process from youth to adulthood is affected by past socialization experiences and by expectations about the future. To the extent that the future appears uncertain, the transition to adulthood is stalled. Leaving school, starting a job, or making a commitment to a relationship does not necessarily signal permanent departure or the assumption of adult responsibilities.

A second characteristic of the transition to adulthood today is that it is reversible. Education, employment, relationships, and living arrangements all are more transitory than they were in the past; young people may return to school, or again live with parents at the end of a romantic or employment relationship. Pais (2000) calls this reversibility the "yo-yo-ization" of the transition to adulthood. Parents of youth in transition are also affected by this pattern because of the societal dominance of youth culture. Parents adopt aspects of youth culture in an effort to forestall aging.

One of the greatest challenges of adolescence is preparation for adult family and work responsibilities. Dating is one of the vehicles for this learning. Even though dating is much less formal than it was in the past, it still helps develop social and communication skills and contributes to the development of self-esteem. In our culture, dating provides opportunities for anticipatory socialization for future cohabitation or marriage.

Adolescents are also required to make decisions about educational options that will affect their future opportunities in the labour force. While not irreversible, decisions such as quitting school or selecting math and science rather than languages and history will open some doors and close others.

Not all of the socialization children receive for adult roles is positive. For instance, violent or abusive adults have internalized this inappropriate response to stress or frustration through socialization. In the area of family violence, researchers have just begun to clarify the links between experiences in childhood and adult behaviour. Judith Seltzer and Debra Kalmuss predicted that people who have experienced violence in their homes as children "may incorporate abuse into the behavioural repertoires they bring to intimate relationships that they establish in adulthood" (1988: 475). Their findings support this prediction: "Early childhood exposure to family violence has a substantially greater effect on spouse abuse than does . . . exposure to recent stressful experiences or chronic economic strain" (1988: 487). Furthermore, observing parents' marital aggression has more of an effect on children than being hit by a parent.

However, the relationship is not absolute. Some adults have violent marriages even though they did not grow up in violent homes. Moreover, not all children growing up in such homes become abusive adults. Extra-familial socialization agents, including peer groups, dating partners, and the media, explain the discrepancies (Seltzer and Kalmuss, 1988).

### Socialization for Parenthood

Do adolescent boys and girls anticipate parenthood differently? A New Zealand study by Barbara Calvert and Warren Stanton (1992) found considerable evidence to support the conclusion that adolescent males and females were equally committed to becoming parents. Among the respondents, 89 per cent answered "Yes" to the question, "Would you like to have children of your own?" When asked whether they would want to adopt if they were unable to have children, 83 per cent of the girls and 72 per cent of the boys answered in the affirmative (Calvert and Stanton, 1992: 317). Both boys and girls wanted to have their first child when they were in their mid-twenties, and both genders listed "fond of children" as an important quality in a spouse. All the young people in the study expected to combine family and employment responsibilities, although the majority thought that, ideally, one parent should stay home with young children. Interestingly, 82 per cent of the boys and 85 per cent of the girls said it did not matter whether the mother or the father was the care-giving parent (Calvert and Stanton, 1992: 319). Other responses indicated that both girls and boys expected both parents to nurture and perform child-care tasks.

The major gender difference between these teenagers was not in attitudes, but in experience; the boys had considerably less exposure to young children and less experience in caregiving. As Calvert and Stanton suggest, this difference could result in a definition of women as more expert and thus could promote a gendered division of labour when the adolescents form families of their own. The study also found strong evidence to suggest that children will be strongly influenced by the child-rearing practices to which they were exposed when growing up: "Most respondents expected to do pretty much as their parents had done" (Calvert and Stanton, 1992: 325).

Studies of new parents find that many are ill-prepared for the time and energy demands of caring for a newborn. Not surprisingly, Renee Steffensmeier (1982) found that anticipatory socialization had a significant effect on the transition to parenthood. The more previous experience new parents had, or the better they were prepared by training for the experience of parenting, the more satisfying they found it. Jay Belsky (1985) found that women were more likely than men to experience a disjunction between their expectations and their experiences regarding childbirth and, consequently, to report less satisfaction. Since women hold the greatest responsibility for infant care, this is hardly surprising. While the household division of labour tends to become more traditional following birth, the mothers in Belsky's sample were more involved in infant care relative to the fathers than either the mothers or the fathers had anticipated, and this was a major source of dissatisfaction.

While most men marry, and while attitude surveys indicate that men give high priority to family life, early socialization does little to prepare them to be fathers. To some extent, low involvement by fathers is a self-fulfilling prophecy. Men have very little preparation for the care of infants or young children, and they are likely to feel awkward; they therefore experience failure in their attempts to help. Alice Rossi's investigations of interactions between fathers and infants suggest that men "tend to avoid high involvement in infant care because infants do not respond to their repertoire of skills and men have difficulty acquiring the skills needed to comfort the infant" (1984: 8). She sees a solution in teaching fathers about parenting and so encouraging their participation. Rossi assumes that men are not more active parents because they have not been socialized to anticipate this role.

In recent years, it has become more the rule than the exception for fathers to attend prenatal classes, to assist during labour, and to be present during the birth of their child. Other trends, such as high divorce rates, have brought about an increase in the number of "weekend fathers"—divorced men who have periodic responsibility for their children. Such parenting experiences seem to pave the way for increased male involvement in child care.

However, no amount of compensatory socialization will alter the structural barriers to equal involvement in child care and other domestic tasks. Primary caregiving fathers in a study in Australia had made a decision to be involved in child-rearing and household tasks, although only half the sample defined housework and child care as their primary tasks (Grbich, 1992). In Australia, the role of caregiver is not considered appropriate for men. The fathers all recognized that parenting and housework have low status, and one-third of them were uncomfortable with their role for this reason. Some of the fathers mentioned that they received verbal put-downs from neighbours, shopkeepers, and others. They reported a number of subtle tactics used to marginalize them, including sexual labelling, avoidance, ostracism, active confrontation, lowered expectations of their performance or capabilities, and non-payment of child allowances (Grbich, 1992). Clearly, it will take much more than changes in individual behaviour to change the structures of sexual inequality.

## Socialization for Employment

Frederic Jablin (1984) describes three stages of socialization to employment. The first is the period of *anticipatory socialization*. Prospective employees form expectations about the job on the basis of their education, training, and previous employment. The second stage is the *encounter phase*, during which the employees "learn the ropes"—what the organization and its members consider to be normal patterns of behaviour. If anticipatory socialization experiences have created an accurate sense of the work environment, the encounter phase will be a relatively smooth transition. From the organization's point of view, effective socialization of new employees is a key to organizational stability. Most organizations therefore formalize the encounter phase through orientation of new employees. The final *metamorphosis stage* continues throughout each employee's career in the particular organization.

Professional schools are important socializing agents for adults. Medical schools in particular have been studied in this regard. What students learn during their years in medical school goes well beyond the acquisition of technical skills: they are learning to behave like doctors. Some researchers, however, feel that the similarities in attitudes and values among medical school graduates have more to do with selective recruitment of middle- and upper-class students than with any training they receive. In their panel study of Canadian medical students, Neena Chappell and Nina Colwill (1981) found that students recruited to medical schools shared certain attitudes at the outset. Interestingly, these viewpoints seemed unrelated to either social class or gender. Although the researchers do not discuss their findings in terms of anticipatory socialization, it seems that a medical student's orientation to the profession begins long before he or she enters medical school.

Much adult socialization is self-initiated. Some is formal, such as the training provided in professional schools or work-related courses; some is informal. Increasingly, formal training is available in areas previously left to the family, the schools, or other agents of socialization, or in areas for which socialization was once taken for granted. Thus, prospective parents can take prenatal and, later, parenting courses, while people anticipating retirement can sign up for courses in retirement planning. When adults join such organizations as Weight Watchers or Parents Without Partners, they do so because they seek the social support these groups provide. During transition periods this support is most needed.

## Future Directions

It is not new to suggest that family life has undergone major changes over the past few decades. Marriage rates have declined, while divorce rates have increased.

More couples live together instead of marrying, and more children are born to single mothers. As social policy catches up to social attitudes, we are beginning to give legal recognition to same-sex marriages. More children live independently, too many of them on the street. At the same time, work demands and economic insecurities create stressful situations for many families. In the past decade, increased concern has been expressed for the plight of children worldwide, much of it arising from a concern about family instability and change. Thus, in the future, we might expect more research to focus on understanding the dynamics of early childhood development and socialization in order to provide the kind of support to families that will optimize their positive development.

Sociology has been criticized for not paying sufficient heed to children, but this inattention is likely to change in the future. In an aging society such as that of Canada (and Western nations generally), with well below replacement birth rates, children will become an increasingly valued resource. An important goal for the future, then, is to create a central place in the discipline of sociology for children. This place should be based on a deeper understanding of the role of children, not just as recipients of adult socialization practices, but as active agents in the lifelong socialization of the people with whom they interact.

## Conclusion

Sociologists view socialization as a lifelong process influenced by all of an individual's social interactions. The two main accomplishments of socialization are the development of a self-concept and the internalization of social expectations.

Sociologists who take the functionalist perspective have tended to describe socialization as being imposed on individuals. By contrast, symbolic interactionists such as Cooley and Mead have helped to shed light on the active engagement of individuals in their own socialization.

All socialization takes place in a social context. For most people, the enduring and intimate nature of family relations makes socialization in the family the most pervasive and consequential experience of childhood. Parent–child interactions are differentiated by class, race, and ethnicity and are framed by the relationships between the family and the community. They are further affected by family size, birth order, family structure, and household composition. Patterns of influence are extremely complex, and become more so as children increase their contacts to include friends, neighbours, and schoolmates. The messages people receive from others are inconsistent and sometimes contradictory, and all people draw their own conclusions from these competing influences.

Individual life chances are also strongly influenced by structural variables, the most important of which are gender and social class. Gender and social class have considerable influence on socialization and on the development of self-concept throughout life. The socialization of children and adolescents anticipates their adult work and family responsibilities. The competencies people develop in the course of primary socialization enable them to anticipate, prepare for, and deal with the ups and downs of adulthood.

## ☐ Questions for Critical Thought

1. Far too many children grow up in the face of societal conflict. When so many children are socialized in this way, is there a realistic hope for peace?
2. What are the implications of the research finding that few characteristics consistently differentiate very young females and males?
3. Why do gender stereotypes persist in the media despite the women's movement, the rise in female labour force participation, and other signs of structural change?
4. Talk to your parents and other family members about what they considered to be important values in your early development. What differences do you anticipate in raising your own children?
5. Ask students who have come to your university or college from another country to describe the resocialization they experienced in making the transition.
6. Can you link early socialization experiences to your decision to attend a post-secondary institution? To the courses you have chosen to focus on? To your anticipated career?
7. Are children's cartoons too violent? Watch a variety of cartoons and document the type and frequency of violent action. What about video games? Are these more or less violent than cartoons?
8. What, if anything, can be done to protect children from exposure to inappropriate content on the Internet?

## ☐ Recommended Readings

**Reginald Bibby, *Canada's Teens: Today, Yesterday and Tomorrow* (Toronto: Stoddart, 2001).**
Canadian sociologist Reginald Bibby has written a number of books based on his analysis of national surveys. This book documents attitudes and experiences of Canadian teenagers regarding violence, sex, and drugs and compares current patterns to past trends.

**Mary Pipher, *Reviving Ophelia: Saving the Selves of Adolescent Girls* (New York: Ballantine, 1994).**
This book, written by a clinical psychologist, examines the roots of young adolescent women's angst. Pipher addresses young girls' feelings of low self-esteem and the high incidence of depression, suicide, and eating disorders among adolescent girls.

**William Pollack, *Real Boys: Rescuing Our Sons from the Myths of Boyhood* (New York: Henry Holt, 1998).**
This book is in many ways a companion to Reviving Ophelia; it, too, is written by a clinical psychologist. Pollack documents the "silent crisis" affecting young boys in the United States. Stereotypical expectations of manliness are as damaging to young boys as are stereotypically feminine expectations to young girls.

**Statistics Canada, *Growing Up in Canada* (Ottawa: Human Resources Development Canada and Statistics Canada, 1996).**
This first volume of research from the National Longitudinal Survey of Children and Youth (NLSCY) includes an overview of the first published findings, as well as chapters on parenting, school performance, and aggression in children.

Marvin B. Sussman, Suzanne K. Steinmetz, and Gary W. Peterson, eds, *Handbook of Marriage and the Family*, 2nd edn (New York: Plenum Press, 1999).

> An excellent and comprehensive resource for students of marriage and the family, this book looks at parent and child socialization, adolescent socialization, and the development of gender roles, among other topics.

## ☐ Recommended Web Sites

### Canadian Research Policy Networks
**www.cprn.org**

> The family network at this site is dedicated to advancing public debate on policy issues that have an impact on Canadian families and on their living circumstances. Its research ranges from public values about children and families to broader concerns of social cohesion within communities and society as a whole.

### Growing Up Digital
**www.growingupdigital.com**

> This Web site is a companion to Don Tapsott's book *The Net Generation*, about those children and youth who have grown up surrounded by digital media. This, according to Tapscott, makes them a force for change. The Web site includes summaries of the main themes of the book and links to discussion groups related to this topic.

### Statistics Canada
**www.statcan.ca**

> The Statistics Canada Web site is a fundamental tool for all students of sociology. It provides links to volumes of current information about all aspects of Canadian economic and cultural life. Here you will find current data on demographic trends, labour force patterns, consumption, media use, and more.

### Vanier Institute of the Family
**www.vifamily.ca**

> The vision of the Vanier Institute of the Family is to make families as important to the life of Canadian society as they are to the lives of individual Canadians. The Institute advocates on behalf of Canada's 8.4 million families because it believes that families are the keystone of society. This Web site is designed to help build public understanding of important issues and trends critical to the well-being and healthy functioning of Canadian families.

# 4

Cheryl Albas, Dan Albas,
R. Jack Richardson,
and Lorne Tepperman

# Social Organization

© W.P. Wittman Limited

## Learning Objectives

In this chapter, you will:

- learn what *roles* and *identities* are and how they relate to each other
- learn to interpret roles and identities from different theoretical perspectives
- see how roles and identities constrain us and shape us
- distinguish types of groups and organizations
- understand the characteristics of a bureaucracy
- identify the discrepancies between the model or ideal bureaucracy and the real-world bureaucracy
- read about the significance of the Hawthorne studies
- learn about recent changes in the structure of organizations

## Introduction

This chapter is about some basic elements of society—roles, identities, groups, and organizations. These are the most fundamental aspects of **social structure**, the subject matter of sociology.

This chapter argues that sociologists view roles and identities as the main ways in which social structure constrains and changes us. Roles and identities are just one part of the social structure that we enact and internalize. Just as they form the basic elements of social structure, they are also the basic elements of who we are and how we lead our lives. Roles and identities are, therefore, the meeting point of social structure, culture, and personality. You cannot understand social life unless you understand roles and identities, the building blocks of social structure.

## The Social Nature of Identity and Role

Prior to birth, humans may have life, but it is not social: before birth, humans have neither status nor identity. Identities and roles are things we acquire over the course of our lives as we interact with others. **Identities** are the names we give ourselves (female, male; child, adolescent, adult; friend; athlete; "nice person") or who we announce ourselves to be in word, manner, and appearance that enables others to respond to or place us (Stone, 1981).

Our first placement by others is at the moment of birth, when we are introduced to the expectant audience with the words "It's a girl" or "It's a boy." As children learn the meaning of this placement, they usually identify with it and begin to present (or "announce") themselves accordingly. Throughout a lifetime of establishing identities, we act parts in the game of life by playing out organized scripts in the form of normative expectations, called **roles**, that are attached to social positions, or **statuses**. These roles include gender roles, age roles, occupational roles, and a multiplicity of others.

As agreed-to expectations for behaviour, roles help to smooth interaction in society. We don't realize just how dependent we are on role expectations to co-ordinate our acts with others until those expectations are violated. Similarly, to play roles, we need to know the identities of others as well as our own. As we will see, roles and identities are complementary and intertwined. The roles we play give us a sense of what and where we are relative to others with whom we interact. This allows us to act in ways that are both coher-

*"Let's play you're a guest, and I'll think of ways of trying to get rid of you."*

ent and purposeful. Every role we play has an identity waiting. When role expectations are breached, it is as if trust is betrayed, and we feel bewildered and insecure. It leads us to question who we—and others in the situation—really are.

Consider an example of how roles and identities work. The American sociologist Harold Garfinkel (1997) believed that we could best understand the constraints of social structure by breaking the hidden rules. To do this, he instructed his university students to return to their homes and behave in ways that breached the normal expectations of their family lives, by acting as if they were boarders and their parents were the landlords. Students were to be extremely polite, addressing their parents formally as "Mr" and "Mrs" and speaking only when spoken to.

The result: approximately 80 per cent of students who actually went through the experiment reported that their parents were stupefied, shocked, and embarrassed. Many worried that their children had "lost their minds"—that the pressures of school, work, and everyday life had "gotten to them." Others thought their children were being mean, inconsiderate, and impolite. In short, they couldn't make sense of this deviant, rule-breaking behaviour.

How can we understand these strange, disturbed reactions to deviance? As was noted in Chapter 1, sociology is a discipline with a variety of perspectives. Also called *theoretical frames of reference* or **paradigms**, these perspectives vary from theorist to theorist and from time to time. A number of different problems can be analyzed within the same paradigm, and any one problem can be analyzed from the standpoint of more than one paradigm. All discussion of problems involves concepts—their definitions, the ways they relate to each other, and the logical sense these relationships make for solving problems or answering questions that arise—in effect constructing theory.

# Role

## The Structural-Functional Approach to Role

The structural-functional approach generally stresses the part played by factors that exist independent of individuals and that constrain individuals to act, think, or feel in particular ways. In this perspective, the roles of actors in "real life" are described as expected behaviour corresponding to their positions in the "real world," positions that, in turn, are termed *statuses*.

In this view, individuals are evaluated in terms of how successfully they enact roles and are then accorded varying levels of esteem. Thus, "actors" earn high esteem if their performances are praiseworthy and low esteem if they are not. The term *status* is also used to describe society's ranking of tasks relative to each other, which, in turn, determines a corresponding amount of prestige for the individual involved. For example, in Canada, high-status occupations such as law or medicine bestow high levels of prestige on doctors and lawyers.

Émile Durkheim's initial orientation to the concepts of role and status was elaborated and systematized by the anthropologist Ralph Linton (1936). In this view, status is a position with specific rights and duties, which, in turn, confer reciprocal rights and duties on actors who occupy other, interacting statuses. For example, in the case of students and teachers, teachers have the right to expect that students come to classes, are attentive during class, join class discussions, and study conscientiously: these are student duties. Sometimes students, consciously or otherwise, breech these duties and exhibit what could be called 'Garfinkleing behaviour'.

However, such breakdowns are remarkably rare. Sociologist Talcott Parsons (1949), perhaps the best-

known structural-functionalist theorist, explains this by emphasizing that society is filled with common values that are the source of stability and social order; this is Durkheim's concept of *exteriority* ([1893] 1964). It is only when **socialization** is imperfect or inadequate that people break the rules. Then others reinforce conformity by public sanctions, such as shame—Durkheim's ([1893] 1964) concept of constraint.

One of Parsons's students, sociologist Robert K. Merton (1957), makes more explicit this structural aspect of society in general, and of roles in particular. In fact, the problem is that we all play so many different roles and, therefore, take on many different rights and responsibilities. Merton terms the specific collections of statuses we occupy *status sets*, and the collections of roles in one specific single status (which Linton did not identify), a *role set*, "that complement of role-relationships in which persons are involved by virtue of occupying a particular social status" (Merton, 1957: 110). The many statuses and roles that individuals occupy and play in their lifetimes follow recognizable patterns that Merton terms *status sequences*.

These concepts of role sets, status sets, and status sequences underlie the recognition of order and structure in society as structural functionalists view it. More specifically, for example, a physician's status set may include the collection of statuses of a spouse, a parent, an administrator, and a soccer coach as well as a medical specialist. For each status in this status set, the physician has a number of roles to play, every role requires considerable expertise, tact, and discretion for its performance. This collection of roles is termed a *role set*.

For example, a physician's role in a hospital or medical office involves interaction with a variety of other roles—nurses, paramedics, janitorial staff, clerks, medical colleagues, and patients—each interaction demanding different role behaviour. Consequently, physicians interact differently with each other than they do with other members of the medical team or with patients. Whereas physicians must routinely request that patients remove clothes so that their bodies can be examined, the same request to a ward clerk or nurse would be completely out of role.

A good synonym for Merton's concept of status sequence is *career*. An individual progresses from high school student to university student to medical intern to medical resident to qualified physician. Each phase of the sequence carries with it specific rights, duties, and associated prestige—generally, medical students do not have the right to carve up patients' bodies without supervision until they become fully fledged surgeons, at which time the carving process will be termed "surgery" and the knife will be designated a "scalpel."

## Role Strain

When roles compete and even conflict with each other, they produce *role strain* for actors. Strain above a critical level results in distress that we may describe simply as "stress." William Goode, Merton's student and a structuralist in the Mertonian tradition, states, "Role strain—difficulty in meeting given role demands . . . is normal. In general, the individual's total role obligations are over-demanding" (1960: 485). Role strain may undermine the tendency to order and interfere with people's ability to play their roles as expected.

The major sources of strain that constantly challenge the established order include *inadequate socialization*, when people simply do not know the appropriate rules of behaviour. Consider this real-life example: Almost three decades ago, a northern trapper came to the "big city," and his son took him to a relatively posh restaurant for dinner. On the way home, the father admonished his son, saying, "You're pretty careless with your money. You left some on the table but I took care of it." His socialization had taught him nothing about the convention of tipping. Both parties in this interaction then experienced a degree of strain—the father because of his unfamiliarity with the restaurant setting, the son because he was now responsible for **resocializing** his father, who was originally his mentor.

In a similar vein, high school students are used to being closely mentored and monitored. However, they face problems of inadequate socialization when they arrive at a 'loose' institutional context of a university, where they frequently find themselves unrecognized by instructors who rely heavily on course outlines that specify broad topics to be covered and due dates for exams and assignments. Given the impersonality of it all, many students feel as if their instructors don't care how they are doing until the time comes to assign a final grade based on highly weighted, infrequent exams and a major term paper. In the context of this loose structure, many students fail to keep up and fall by the wayside.

*Role conflict* occurs when individuals must play two or more roles that make incompatible demands—conformity to one role necessarily means violation of the other. For example, an athlete who becomes the coach of the team and is required to select members for the next year will experience role conflict when choices must be made whether to select outstanding new players or buddies and friends from the previous year.

*Role competition*, which can also cause strain, exists for almost everyone on a regular basis because our many and varied roles compete continually for our energy and our time. Students might plan to spend a night in with their books when friends call and ask them to go out. As long as there is enough time before the exam to study and catch up with work, they think they can do both. However, the night before the exam, they face role overload and must prioritize their roles as student and as friend and decide which role to honour.

The same principle applies to workers—especially, in our society, women, who are trying to balance multiple tasks, such as paid work, parenting, elder care, and household work. They, too, are faced with choices between competing tasks and competing loyalties. They experience role overload when they run out of time or energy and must choose to honour the demands of one role at the expense of others. Some women in a study by Hochschild spoke longingly of sleep "the way a hungry person talks about food" (Hochschild and Machung, 1989: 9).

Merton (1957) identifies some social mechanisms that help to articulate role sets and status sets more clearly, thus reducing strain. For example, people can appeal to hierarchies already established in society that distinguish between roles and order them in terms of institutional priority. In our society, the student role is valued and given high priority, so families and workplaces often give special concessions to students, allowing them more study time.

Another way to reduce role strain is to abide by the socially recognized power differences between roles. In schools, for example, principals, who must mediate altercations between teachers and students, are almost always expected to support and defend teachers unless teachers' behaviour breaches the legal code for that role (for example, through sexual misconduct). Few principals who fail to publicly support their teachers survive in their role for very long. At the same time, the underlying authority structure of society is publicly confirmed and reinforced.

Role strain is reduced when roles can be compartmentalized. Thus, families may separate and isolate the affectionate parent role from the affectionate spouse role and compartmentalize them into separate spaces in the home by installing locks on "master," parental bedrooms.

Finally, role strain can be reduced by providing opportunities for relinquishing a role. When parental roles become overwhelming, some workplaces allow employees to take time off. Likewise, it is increasingly the case that when life circumstances become generally overwhelming, employees may be granted some form of stress leave or offered compensation if they completely relinquish the role.

In performing their multiple roles, actors must learn what the roles really are about, what they involve for themselves and others, the strains inherent in the roles, and, finally, the societal mechanisms that can lessen some of those strains. Few of us in modern life have learned to play all our roles as smoothly and effortlessly as we should.

## The Interactional Approach to Role

### Mead and Turner

The concept of *role* in sociology was first borrowed from the world of the theatre to describe the behaviour of actors playing parts in the drama of life. However, roles in the theatre and the roles actors play in everyday life are not the same. From the interactional perspective, in everyday life, actors' roles are not completely set pieces: there is opportunity for mutual and reciprocal action and reaction to what other actors say and do. Thus the "script," or role, is really a dynamic, constantly changing drama. George Herbert Mead (1934), the first social scientist explicitly to use the concept of role, refers to this ongoing drama as *role-taking*.

Mead's outstanding contributions to role theory (1934) incorporate the concepts of significant **symbols** (language), role-taking, mind, self, and society. The concepts are linked together theoretically. First, intelligent human interaction rests on mutual understanding of the current symbols of meaning in society. Second, during interaction our (that is, our ego's) response to others' (called by Mead *alters*) behaviour towards us is based on role-taking, that is, our interpretation of their behaviour. Third, a further aspect of role-taking is the impression of self provided by the other's reaction to us (to our self). Fourth, when we have a distinct sense of **self**, we can name and recognize relevant objects in the environment and make decisions about the appropriate reaction to them. We make these decisions in the process of an internal conversation with self—the process Mead terms a **mind**.

Mead postulates that, as humans, we are universally vulnerable and our only hope for survival rests on our co-operation with others. In new and problematic situations, we use ingenuity to develop new ways of co-operating.

Meadian theory has been considerably refined and extended by Ralph Turner (1962), who regards the more structuralist approach put forth by Linton and Merton as being far too rigid and static. According to Turner, "The actor is not the occupant of a status for which there is a neat set of rules—a culture or set of norms—but a person who must act in the perspective supplied in part by his relationship to others whose reactions reflect roles that he must identify" (1962: 23). In effect, Turner shifts the focus from role-playing to the reciprocal joint processes of role-taking and **role-making**.

In role-making, we "devise" performances on the basis of an imputed other role. In turn, role-taking is the gestalt (the organized whole that is more than the sum of its parts) that we impute to be the role the other appears to be devising. As we might expect, in this process of self-presentation (role-making) and the imputation of the projected role (role-taking), there is the possibility of considerable inaccuracy and attempts to reinterpret the imputations involved. Turner refers to this process as "shifting axes," that is, continually testing the validity of our presumptions. Actors involved in role-making attempt to create a gestalt for each other so that they can more effectively take on a particular role. To this end, they use the symbolism involved in things such as clothing, gestures, eye contact, and tone of voice to communicate clearly with each other.

A former student illustrated the role-making/role-taking process involving a relationship between herself and a male friend, a relationship that, to this point (as she inferred from role-taking), had been on a casual level. She assumed it was a non-romantic relationship and that he was a friend (this is the gestalt implied by his actions towards her to that point). Then one evening, as they walked to a movie theatre, the axis shifted and the friend appeared to transform his role of friend into a role of lover. Instead of just walking side by side, he suddenly placed his hand on her upper hip. This unexpected action presented her with a problem of how to interpret his role: he was clearly role-making, and she was attempting to accept a change in her role but was uncertain at first as to how to proceed. Then she looked for cues to help her interpret the situation accurately. She glanced at him, he looked embarrassed and glanced away quickly, and when he finally did speak it was in a hoarse croak; she then noted with surprise that he was better dressed than usual; and, contrary to their custom of "going Dutch," he paid for her ticket to the movie. Confirmation of the transformation of the relationship into a romantic one occurred when the movie began and he reached for her hand to hold.

Turner's approach to the concept of role is interactive and symbolic; it involves mutual testing of the images projected by symbols. Because of the tentativeness of meanings, interaction is always highly fluid.

### The Conflict Approach to Role

W. Peter Archibald (1976, 1978) deals with the micro aspects of role from a conflict perspective and focuses on Marx's concept of alienation from others (Marx, 1964). Archibald emphasizes that status and power differences affect not only the roles we play, but also how we feel about those roles, how we play them, and how we feel about ourselves. According to Archibald, alienation from others is characterized by four features: (1) we feel indifference or separation; (2) when we approach others, it is for narrow egoistic purposes; (3) when we interact with more powerful others, we feel more controlled than in control; and (4) when we relate to others of different status, it is with feelings of dissatisfaction and even hostility. Archibald develops these four features in generalizations that can also be considered aspects of the symbolic interactionist paradigm as it is elaborated by Erving Goffman in his chapter "Nature of Deference and Demeanor" in *Interaction Ritual* (1967).

In the case of indifference or separation, Archibald (1976) notes that people of different classes, statuses, and power groups tend to avoid each other. In the work setting, for example, management tends to have separate maintenance facilities, such as entrances, elevators, washrooms, and cafeterias. Similar principles apply in a macrosociology realm. For example, in her historical study of urban transformation, Lyn Lofland indicates that zoning ordinances emerged in the nineteenth century as a "result of a desire on the part of the upper and middle classes to separate themselves from the 'dangerous classes'" (1973: 74). Developers took these sentiments to heart and did their best, creating district after district of similarly valued homes and "protecting" those values through covenants and "gentlemen's agreements."

Archibald (1976) argues that the two classes avoid each other because each feels threatened by the other. The position of the privileged depends on continued deference from the underprivileged. But such compliance is not always assured, and when it is not forthcoming it signals a loss of face and questions one's superiority. In addition, revealing slips in the presence of subordinates give evidence that one is not a superior person. People in lower positions feel even more threatened by those in higher positions.

Studies (see, for example, Cohen and Davis, 1973) demonstrate that performing in front of high-status audiences is more anxiety-producing (as measured by the Palmar Sweat Index) than performing before an audience of peers. Interacting with, or at least within hearing distance of, bosses may result in giving out information that can be used against one. Consequently, avoidance is a useful strategy in dealing with enemies and rivals. As Goffman states, "The surest way for a person to prevent threats to his face is to avoid contacts in which these threats are likely to occur" (1967: 15). Archibald concludes that "avoidance as a self-protective strategy is . . . a very plausible explanation for the 'detachment generalization'" (1976: 822).

Archibald maintains that higher-class, higher-status, and higher-power individuals are more likely than lower-class, lower-status, and lower-power ones to initiate activity and influence others. This point about the control–purposiveness generalization is further illustrated by experiments showing that those who drive expensive, high-status cars are more likely to honk at low-status cars in front of them (Diekman et al., 1996).

## Identity

*Identity* is the way in which people define themselves and, in turn, are defined by others. Hewitt (2000) classifies several aspects of identity. **Situated identity** focuses on identity as it emerges through and affects face-to-face interaction with others. *Social identity* is based on identification with groups (for example, family, ethnic, and occupational groups) and significant social categories (for example, age and gender). These, in turn, define us in terms of our similarities with some groups and our differences from other groups. *Personal identity* consists of factors that make us unique from others (including physical characteristics such as height, weight, and looks) as well as aspects of our past based on how other people have reacted to us and typed us. Personal identity and social identity are parts of our *biographical identity* and, as such, provide continuity as we step into and out of various situated identities. Identities are established by how we present ourselves and by others' placement of us. If one or both are compromised or less than complete, the result is identity trouble.

### *Classical Theorists on Identity: Cooley and Mead*

Charles Horton Cooley (1902) is best known for formulating the concept of the **looking-glass self** to describe how identity is formed. In effect, our identity is what we think others think of us. This reflected (hence, 'looking glass') self emerges as we imagine how we appear to others, and then how we imagine others judge that appearance. Finally, a self-feeling, such as pride or mortification, emerges. Not surprisingly, according to Cooley ([1909] 1962), this self-

**4.1**

# Open for Discussion
## Philip Zimbardo's Stanford Prison Experiment

Commonly held stereotypes portray prisons as pathological places because of the personalities of the prisoners (low impulse control, problematic character structure, sociopathologies) and guards (surly, sadistic, megalomaniac). However, psychologist Philip Zimbardo and colleagues (1972) thought otherwise and suspected that social roles were the major factors in determining prisoner–guard interactions.

To test their hypothesis, they set up a mock prison and advertised in a local newspaper for subjects to participate in a two-week experiment on prison life in return for modest remuneration. All of the more than 75 male applications were subjected to a rigorous screening process to ensure that they were mature, emotionally stable, and "normal." From this original group, 21 college students from middle-class homes were selected to participate in the experiment. Approximately half of the subjects (11) were randomly assigned to the status of prison guard, the remainder (10) to the status of prisoner. Guards were issued khaki uniforms, billy clubs, whistles, and handcuffs. Prisoners were dressed in smocks resembling hospital gowns and in nylon stocking caps.

Initially, subjects approached their role-playing in a light-hearted fashion, but it did not take long before they began to fall into stereotypical behaviour characteristic of their roles. The guards became increasingly callous and began to demonstrate inventiveness in the application of arbitrary power (Zimbardo, 1972). They refused prisoners permission to go to the toilet and forced them to do tedious and useless work (such as moving cartons back and forth, and picking thorns out of blankets that had been dragged through thorn bushes). Guards issued commands to prisoners to do push-ups and occasionally stepped on their backs in the process. They also forced prisoners to do humiliating tasks such as scrubbing toilets with bare hands.

As early as the second day, the prisoners began to rebel, and the guards responded with increased force and threats of violence. In turn (given the reciprocal nature of roles), prisoners became increasingly passive and began to "adopt and accept the guards' negative attitude towards them. . . . The typical prisoner syndrome was one of passivity, dependence, depression, helplessness, and self-depreciation" (Haney, Banks, and Zimbardo, 1973: 79).

The result was that prisoners began to develop serious pathologies. One prisoner developed a psychosomatic skin rash over his whole body, and others developed symptoms of severe depression and acute anxiety. The experiment had to be aborted after six days. As Zimbardo states,

At the end of only six days we had to close down our mock prison because what we saw was frightening. It was no longer apparent to most of the subjects (or to us) where reality ended and their roles began. The majority had indeed become prisoners or guards. . . . There were dramatic changes in virtually every aspect of their behavior, thinking, and feeling. . . . We saw some (guards) treat others as if they were despicable animals, taking pleasure in cruelty. While other boys (prisoners) became servile, dehumanized robots who thought only of escape, of their own individual survival, and of their mounting hatred for guards. (Zimbardo, 1972: 5)

image is reflected most strongly in primary, intimate face-to-face groups such as play groups, family, or even work groups.

Mead extended Cooley's ideas by emphasizing the cognitive skills acquired through role play and through learning the rules of games. Mead's best-known distinctions in the area of self-development are the definitions of the *play stage* and the *game stage* (1934). In the play stage, children "play at" being, for example, a mother or father and speak to themselves as the mother or father might. Consequently, they assume for themselves the identity of the label applied by parents. The development of identity, particularly biographical identity, is the result of a series of impulses to act and the resultant actual responses to those impulses. Mead terms the spontaneous motivations of the individual the "I" aspect of the self and the deliberate chosen behaviour the "Me" aspect of self. Over time, the chosen behaviour characteristic of an individual comes to characterize that individual's self.

## Contemporary Theorists on Identity: Blumer, Stone, Goffman

The structural view of interaction, as we have seen, emphasizes the relative stability and permanence of the social world. Symbolic interactionism, on the other hand, views social life as a process, involving continual interaction out of which emerge new situations and new interaction within them, producing, in turn, different identities and coping strategies. These situated coping strategies and identities rest on and are recognized by symbols, for example, the uniform identifying a police officer or the vestments identifying a priest. Herbert Blumer (1969) named this mode of thinking (that is, interaction as an exchange of meanings through symbols), which had been initiated by Cooley and Mead, *symbolic interactionism*, and is considered its predominant exponent.

In this ongoing process, Gregory Stone (1981) recognizes two aspects to identity: *identification of*, when placement coincides with announcement, and

**4.2**

# Sociology in Action
## Seymour Lieberman's Workplace Study

Seymour Lieberman (1956) studied the attitudes (that is, orientations toward a person, group, or social process) of 2,354 rank-and-file workers in an appliance factory toward unions and management. He demonstrated, as did Peter Archibald (1976) later, the Marxian hypothesis concerning the effect of status on attitudes and the resulting attitude of mutual hostility between upper and lower classes in society.

After the initial survey was completed, the usual workplace processes continued; 23 men were promoted to the rank of foreman and 35 people were elected by their work groups as shop stewards. After 15 months, promoted foremen and shop stewards whose attitudes had originally been recorded in the first survey were retested and the results compared with their answers on the first survey. The results of the second test showed an increase in pro-management attitudes on the part of the promoted foremen and an increase in the pro-union attitudes on the part of the shop stew-

ards. However, the increase in the pro-management attitudes of foremen was greater than the increase in pro-union attitudes of the shop stewards. Lieberman says that these differences should have been predicted because the move from rank-and-file labourer to foreman is greater than that of worker to shop steward.

After two more years, business conditions for the company changed and fewer foremen were needed in the plant, so eight of them were demoted to their former positions. Lieberman then conducted a third survey to compare the attitudes of foremen who were demoted with those who retained their positions. The results indicated that individuals who were demoted now had much stronger pro-union than pro-management attitudes—a clear reversal compared to the situation when they were at the level of foreman. In effect, all of the test results in Lieberman's study support Archibald's (Marxian) theories of inter-class, particularly Industrial World, attitudes.

*identification with*, when a comfortable compatibility exists between the person who does the announcing and the one who does the placement. An identification of the other is necessary before role-taking can occur, and this, in turn, makes possible an identification with the other.

Erving Goffman is perhaps the most lucid and imaginative exponent of identity analysis (though he does not label it as such); significantly for this discussion, his analysis also involves the concept of role. Goffman places the concept of role squarely back on the stage, thus suggesting its structural aspect while also explicitly indicating an interactionist orientation. In the case of the structuralist aspect of self-presentation, Goffman (1959) uses the theatrical analogies of "frontstage" and "backstage" to distinguish the two zones of open and explicit role-making in the frontstage from the hidden role-making in the backstage. Front adds "dramatic realization" to performances because it helps performers convey everything they wish to convey on any given occasion.

Goffman's treatment of presentation of self and the establishment of identity involves the concepts of role, status, and prestige presented by actors and recognized by an audience. In the process of self-presentation, we engage in **impression management** using the two basic strategies of self-revelation and concealment.

## Identity Troubles: Embarrassment

Embarrassment occurs when an announced identity is not supported or is even distorted, resulting in unsatisfactory placement (Gross and Stone, 1981). Typical instances of embarrassment resulting from dissonance between announcement and placement are a result of bodily accidents, which cause embarrassment because they project a less than fully mature persona, or possibly a careless one.

Another cause of embarrassment is insufficient support for identity announcement, for example, when someone announces that lunch is his or her treat, only to then realize he or she has forgotten to bring enough money. Yet a third source of embarrassment is *mistaken identity placement*, in which a person may adequately document an identity but fail to have others place it because of distraction or inadequate attention. Mismanagement of superfluous identities is a fourth cause of embarrassment.

In most encounters, there are more activities (roles) and identities than are necessary for ensuing transactions. For example, at parties people eat and drink (subordinate role) while they converse (dominant role). The subordinate roles and identities must be managed so that they remain in the background and don't interfere with what people have come together to do—their dominant roles. A misalignment of these subordinate and dominant roles and identities can result in embarrassment. This occurs when subordinate roles and identities impose themselves on dominant ones. Imagine engaging in small talk at a cocktail party only to accidentally splash a prominent guest with wine. The subordinate role becomes the focus of attention. Embarrassment also occurs when reserve identities inappropriately surface on the dominant identity (Gross and Stone, 1981). If a student's cellphone rings during a lecture, a reserve identity (friend) imposes itself on the dominant identity (student).

We also experience embarrassment when a *relict identity*—an element of our biographical identity we no longer wish to announce, such as an unfortuante nickname—resurfaces (Gross and Stone, 1981).

## Disclaimers and Accounts

Two related defence strategies to save face are disclaimers and accounts. *Disclaimers* are excuses that come before the act for which face-saving is expected to become necessary. *Accounts* are excuses and justifications that follow embarrassing acts. According to Stone (1981), both disclaimers and accounts can be verbal, in what he terms the *universe of discourse*, or they can be non-verbal mannerisms, in the *universe of appearance*. In the past, almost all research in this area of identity has focused on verbal disclaimers and accounts in the universe of discourse.

*Verbal disclaimers*—excuses that come before a potentially problematic act that may damage our identity—come in a multitude of forms. Verbal disclaimers, especially hedging, are rampant just before exams, when students offer many excuses why others should not expect too much from them. Actors can also use accounts to negotiate a more positive identity for themselves after a disruptive interaction. For example, two students who persist in talking to each other during lectures, even after being negatively sanctioned, might accuse the professor of picking on them, attempting to switch their identity from troublemaker to innocent victim.

Non-verbal forms of disclaimers and accounts are termed *motive mannerisms*; these occur within a universe of appearance (Stone, 1981) when talk is difficult or out of the question. An account "face-saving" mannerism can be seen in a story told by a student of one of the authors, who, at a high school social, emerged from the bathroom unaware that she had caught the end of the toilet paper in her skirt and was trailing it behind her. When she realized what was happening, she had the presence of mind to gather up the toilet paper behind her and wrap it around herself while dancing in perfect step with the music. She received a loud round of applause and managed to salvage heroism from embarrassment.

Disclaimer mannerisms (that is, excuses) prior to the problematic act can be seen regularly in traffic when a driver cuts in front of another vehicle and the offender then waves to the other driver, implying that the latter has generously allowed the privilege. It is possible that in this process ruffled feathers are smoothed and chances of road rage are decreased.

### Identity Management: Protective Practices

Protective practices are to some extent altruistic and show consideration of the other. They also function to protect the user as well as the communal assembly in which these practices are used because gaffes by a single person disrupt the interactional tone and thereby embarrass the entire group. Protective practices provide the user with some degree of self-protection because everyone is always vulnerable and considerate people are more likely to have consideration directed to them than are people who are thoughtless and unsympathetic. As Goffman (1959) notes, actors form a moral pact to support each other's fostered impressions of themselves.

Protective practices include studious inattention to small lapses in appropriate behaviour of others. For example, we might pretend not to notice a quiet burp emitted by the person next to us. Goffman (1959) refers to this face-saving device as *studied non-observance*. Studied non-observance can also be active: imagine a professor entering a large lecture theatre with his zipper down; a considerate student might prevent his embarrassment by going around the professor, back to the blackboard so that the professor's back is to the class, to let the professor know.

## Where Role and Identity Come Together

Three concepts that demonstrate strikingly how role and identity overlap are role distance, role embracement, and role exit. *Role distance* (Goffman, 1961b) designates the behaviour of actors who play roles in such a way as to announce identities that will have others place them at a distance from the identities they are seemingly announcing. *Role embracement* occurs when actors attempt to convey by their role-making actions the specific and correct self-images by which they wish others to identity them.

Role embracement represents the polar opposite of role distance; it can be observed when boys reach the age of 11 or 12 years. By this point, maleness "has become a real responsibility. . . . It is necessary to stay away or exert creative acts of distance" from childhood (Goffman, 1961b: 108). Boys accomplish role distance by treating the wooden horse on a merry-go-round as if it were a racehorse, or by pretending that they are stunt riders or comedians, jumping from horse to horse, all the while making faces at friends and passers-by. The purpose of these acts, of course, is to display distance from the role of a merry-go-round rider.

A contemporary example of role distance is practised by teenagers who no longer wish to be viewed as children and instead want to establish an identity of independence and maturity, and do so in part by insisting that parents drop them off around the corner from their destination.

*Role exit*, as distinct from role embracement, is the disengagement from a role central to one's self-identity (Ebaugh, 1988). This usually brings with it a continuing identity "hangover" from the past, which influences the playing of a new role. Helen Ebaugh, a former nun, used her own case as an example and also interviewed 69 other former nuns as well as another 116 "exes," including transsexuals, police officers, convicts, doctors, divorced people, and air traffic controllers. Drawing on Robert Prus (1987), she formulates a generic social process involved in becoming an "ex."

First, there are feelings of frustration, unhappiness, uncertainty, and burnout, which Ebaugh terms *first doubts*. This uncertainty on the part of people about to exit a role leads to what she terms *unconscious cueing*, whereby they begin to change the image they project to others. For example, nuns in this early phase of becoming an "ex" begin to let their hair grow. Consequently, their announcement leads to a tacit placement, which accordingly encourages or discourages the contemplated move.

Second, depending on whether there has been encouragement or discouragement in the first phase, role alternatives are considered and weighed, and a new role identity is tentatively decided upon. In this process, the person inevitably chooses and begins to identify with a new reference group, which will help to consolidate and confirm the new identity. For example, transsexuals, who identify with the opposite sex, cross-dress and take on new mannerisms before (often) undergoing sex-change surgery (Ebaugh, 1988). Role exit occurs after this anticipatory socialization in and by the contemplated new reference group, and finally the new reference group and the new membership group become one.

A fourth and final stage involves accommodating the new identity to the old one. This process is always problematic because the old identity constantly intrudes on the new one. Ebaugh cites examples of former police officers who find it difficult to interact affably with people they knew in their previous lives to be involved in shady activities.

Role exit is a predominant characteristic of modern society. In the past, people generally lived their entire lives in one community, gender, occupation, marriage, and religion. In today's society, these statuses and their accompanying roles are taken on and shed with increasing frequency.

## Groups and Organizations

What ties these changeable roles and identities together into stable, predictable sets of behaviours? The answer is, groups and organizations. We are linked together in groups by interpersonal bonds of sentiment and exchange. Beyond that, we are linked together in organizations by rules and the allocation of resources. As we shall see, it is impossible to understand the functioning of groups and organizations without understanding the roles and identities that make them up. Equally, it is impossible to understand our face-to-face interactions—our enactment of roles and identities—without understanding the group and organizational contexts within which they take place. We begin this section by discussing different sets or ways of organizing people; they include networks, groups, and cliques. We start small and build up to bureaucracies, because the two sizes of organization—large and small—are more similar than you might think.

First, all bureaucracies contain networks, groups, and cliques. These small, informal organizations actually accomplish much of the work of large, formal bureaucracies. Under some circumstances, they also subvert the plans and efforts of these bureaucracies. Second, many of the same organizational principles that shape small groups, cliques, and communities also shape large, formal organizations. Processes of leadership, commitment, control, and exchange shape all organizations, whatever their size. That means that what you already know about families, classrooms, and clubs can be applied—with some ingenuity—to things you know less about, like bureaucracies, societies, and empires.

Large organizations of the kind we see today are still relatively new to human history, and in some ways they are a major human accomplishment. Yet somehow this great ambition has gone wrong. The paradox of large organizations is that they are so effective and yet so dangerous. Large organizations are as likely to frustrate and disappoint as they are to satisfy our wishes. Moreover, they sometimes control us, rather than our controlling them. Next we trace the development of organizational theory from its crude beginnings at the turn of the twentieth century. In general, this development reflects the growth of sociological knowledge about human groups. The chapter ends with an examination of the ways that large organizations actually work, compared with how they are supposed to work.

## Sets of People

Imagine five sets of 20 people each. Call them *categories*, *networks*, *communities*, *groups*, and *organizations*. Sociologists will study these five sets differently, because they are organized differently and have different effects on their members.

### Categories

Imagine, first, that these 20 people are a mere aggregate or collection of people who are unconnected with one another—say, a random sample of Canadian 19-year-olds—but fall into the same category: they are the same age. This *aggregate*, or sample, of teenagers is of interest to sociologists if they represent the attitudes and behaviours of 19-year-olds across the country. Knowing these attitudes and behaviours may help us predict the future behaviour or explain the current behaviour of 19-year-olds. It will be of particular interest to market researchers who want to sell products to 19-year-olds and to political pollsters who want to shape their voting preferences. However, for the most part, sociologists will not be interested in such an aggregate of people. Since they are unconnected, people in categories possess no social structure of interest, and it is **social structure**—the invisible feature of social life that controls and transforms our behaviour—that is mainly of interest to sociologists.

There is no social structure to study in an aggregate or set of 20 unconnected teenagers. The same will be true of any category of people—people who live in Toronto, drive snowmobiles, eat yogourt, read *Sports Illustrated* magazine, go to church every week, or whatever. Categories, though interesting to market researchers, are relatively uninteresting to sociologists.

There is one major exception to this rule: categories become sociologically interesting when societies dramatize (or socially construct) meanings for the boundaries between one category and another. No such meaningful boundaries exist for 19-year-olds, compared with 18- and 20-year-olds. However, important cultural boundaries exist between the categories named "male" and "female," "young" and "old," and, in some societies, "white" and "black." As a result, these categories assume social importance. They assume importance only when the categorical differences are dramatized, the boundaries are enforced, and categorical differences give rise to social and cultural differentiation—for example, in the form of communities or **social movements**.

### Networks

Sets of people who are more interesting are organized in what sociologists call *networks*, or **social networks**. Imagine the same 20 people all connected to one another, whether directly or indirectly. By *direct connections*, we mean links of kinship, friendship, and acquaintanceship or otherwise among all 20, each connected to the other. In a set of 20 people, there can be [20(19)]/2 = 190 such pairwise connections—obviously, a lot of interesting relationships and combinations of relationships to study.

*Indirect connections* are also of interest to sociologists. In fact, some sociologists—such as Mark Granovetter (1974), whose work on job seeking was discussed in Chapter 1—believe that *weakly tied* networks, based largely on indirect links, may be even more useful than *strongly tied* or completely connected networks. Information, social support, and other valuable resources all flow through incompletely connected, or weakly tied, networks. Likewise, rumours, diseases, innovations, and job information all spread geographically through (indirectly linked) networks of weak ties. This is because weakly tied networks have a huge outreach. They connect very large numbers of weakly tied people (for example, acquaintances) at a few removes, unlike tightly connected networks, which tend to circulate the same information or resources repeatedly through the same set of people (for example, close friends).

The pairwise connections (which sociologists call *dyadic relationships*) that make up social networks are based on regular patterns of social exchange. In stable dyadic relationships, people give each other things they want and need. So long as these relationships satisfy their needs, people stay in these relationships. People usually act in their own best interests—when they are aware of these interests. They are rational and sensible, and they maintain **social relationships** that are useful to them. Accordingly, people enter, leave, and stay in the social networks in which their valued dyadic relations are embedded. Over time, as people enter and leave relationships, networks change in size and composition. This, in turn, affects the resources flowing to other members of the network.

As you can see from this glimpse, social networks are important and interesting. There is a huge and growing sociological literature on social networks. However, much of social life is not well understood in terms of networks. That is because networks lack several key characteristics. First, people in networks lack a sense of collective identity, such as a community would possess. Second, people in networks lack a complete awareness of their membership and its characteristics, such as a group would possess. Third, people in networks lack a collective goal, such as an organization would possess.

### Communities

Sets of people with a common sense of identity are typically called **communities**, and there is a long history of community studies in sociology. Imagine for the sake of consistency that we are thinking of a community of only 20 people—say, a commune of like-minded people living together.

These are likely to be people drawn together by common sentiments; or they may be people who have grown up together and share strong, unusual values. The nineteenth-century German sociologist Ferdinand Tönnies ([1887] 1957) took great pains to distinguish the foundations of community life, or what he called *Gemeinschaft*, from the foundations of non-community life, which he called *Gesellschaft*. Tönnies also associated community life with rural areas and non-community life with urban areas. At least since medieval times, the city has represented in the popular mind a place distinct from both rural communities and from the natural environment.

*Gemeinschaft* refers to the typical characteristics of rural and small-town life. These characteristics include a stable, homogeneous group of residents with a strong attachment to one particular place. Residents of the community interact around similar qualities and lead similar lives. Not only are their lives similar, they are also linked by intimate, enduring relationships of kinship, friendship, neighbouring, and (often) working together. Because rural people share so much, it is not surprising they also share similar moral values, and moral custodians such as the church, school, and local upper classes protect these values. In terms of social structure, the *Gemeinschaft* is marked by dense or highly connected networks, centralized and controlling elites, and multiple social ties.

By contrast, the ties among people in a city take the form of a *Gesellschaft*. This includes a fluid, heterogeneous group of residents with a weak sense of place. According to Tönnies ([1887] 1957), the residents have different personal histories and impersonal, brief relationships. They interact around similar interests, not similar characteristics or histories. There are few shared moral values and few moral custodians to enforce a common moral code. In terms of social structure, city networks are less connected, less centralized, less cliquish, and less redundant. In short, there is less cohesion and less control in the *Gesellschaft*.

The question that several generations of sociologists have debated since Tönnies is whether *Gesellschaft*—or city life—represents a loss of community or a new kind of community. Most sociologists in the first half of the twentieth century believed the former: they saw city life as disorganized and lacking in the cultural and social benefits of community. However, in the second half of that century, sociologists came around to another view. They demonstrated that people are not isolated and atomized in large cities. Rather, the majority form small communities based on residential proximity and social similarity, or on friendship and support networks among geographically dispersed people.

Communities, whether urban or rural, real or virtual, are important because people are conscious of their membership in them. They want the community to survive and may make large personal sacrifices to see that it does.

## Groups

In some cases, groups can be like small communities: highly engrossing and very demanding of loyalty. In other cases, groups are much less so. What all groups have in common is an awareness of membership. In addition, members are all connected with one another (directly or indirectly) and, to varying degrees, communicate, interact, and conduct exchanges with one another. To continue our example, a 20-student classroom would be one kind of group. It is more highly connected than a 20-person category, more self-aware than a 20-person network, but shows less solidarity (based on common values) than a 20-person community.

Since Charles Horton Cooley ([1909] 1962) in the early twentieth century, sociologists have distinguished between primary groups and secondary groups. *Primary groups* are small and marked by regular face-to-face interaction; an example is a family household. Cliques (which we will discuss shortly) and work groups also fall into this category of primary group. *Secondary groups* are larger, and many members may not interact with one another on a regular basis. However, even in secondary groups there is a clear membership, at least some members interact, and there is an identifiable normative system and some shared sense of collective existence (as in a community).

Typically, groups are less engrossing than communities. However, they have organizational structures and do what social structures are expected to do: namely, control and transform their members. All groups, even small groups, have clearly defined familiar roles: for example, husband–wife, parent–child, or brother–sister in families, leader–follower in cliques, or teacher–student–teacher's pet in classrooms. These roles, as we have seen, carry interactional expectations, and people are identified (and identify themselves) with the roles they play. Even in small groups, behaviours become scripted. Robert Bales, in the 1950s, found that in the discussion groups he studied, three roles—task leader, emotional leader, and joker—regularly emerged. Bales (1950) concluded that groups seem to "need" these roles in order to survive.

Informal work groups emerge within large formal organizations. Within these work groups, informal leadership roles and group norms emerge. These control and transform the behaviour of group members, sometimes to the consternation of the people who manage the formal organization. This discovery is one of sociology's most important contributions to the study of organizations.

Secondary groups, though less strongly integrated than primary groups, are no less important. We spend most of our waking hours as members of secondary groups, interacting, communicating, and exchanging resources with other people. Secondary groups are also the staging area for much social learning. They bind people together in relatively stable patterns of social interaction. Formal organizations, discussed below, are subtypes of secondary groups, and bureaucracies are subtypes of formal organizations.

### Organizations

As just noted, **organizations** are secondary groups with a collective goal or purpose. An organization can be a giant multinational corporation, such as General Motors, or a small corner variety store; a political party or a government; a church, a school, a sports club, or a search party. Given the endless variety of organizational forms, and the millions of specific examples, what do all organizations have in common?

One important distinction to make concerning organizations is between **spontaneous** and **formal organizations**. Both types fit the general definition of an organization, yet the two are different in important ways. A *spontaneous organization* is one that arises quickly to meet a single goal and then disbands when the goal is achieved or thought to be beyond reach or when the organization is absorbed by a formal organization. A clique, though informal, is not a spontaneous organization. Perhaps the most commonly cited examples of spontaneous organizations are bucket brigades and search parties. Each has a single goal—keeping a barn from burning down or finding a lost child. Each arises spontaneously, and its leaders emerge informally, without planning. Each has a crude division of labour—for example, filling buckets, passing them along, emptying them on the fire. Nevertheless, each is much more likely than an unco-ordinated mob to achieve its goals. Compare the chance that a mob, running off in one direction, has of finding a lost child with that of a group conducting a co-ordinated search pattern. Spontaneous organizations disband as quickly as they form. The bucket brigade will scatter when it achieves its goal of putting out the fire or the barn has burned down or the fire department arrives on the scene.

Organizations with loosely related goals that are relatively unstructured, with little differentiation between their members, are considered **informal organizations**. One familiar example of informal organization is the clique. Cliques seem very different from the formal organizations, yet, paradoxically, they share some common features. Moreover, as we will discover, cliques and other informal organizations can usually be found nested within formal organizations, doing much of the work.

## Cliques

Cliques satisfy human needs for interaction and support. Lloyd Siegel and Arthur Zitrin (1978), for example, in a classic study of New York male-to-female transsexuals on public welfare, found that all the people they were studying lived with one or more transsexual friends. Moreover, a transsexual community had apparently come into existence, creating its own **subculture**. A citywide informal network provided transsexuals with information concerning particular needs, and reportedly worked to create a feminine environment and appearance for clique members. The community, made up of multiple cliques, was stable, cohesive, and supportive. Transsexual friends often accompanied clients to welfare centre interviews and provided other practical assistance. The authors conclude that this subcultural community helped transsexual men to foster their illusion of being female, often without their having to undergo surgery.

The second thing we learn when we study cliques and communities is that they tend to produce new roles, rules, and cultural values. An example is the supposedly anarchic world of "bohemians." *Bohemians* are people who, for artistic or other reasons, have rejected the middle-class lifestyle. Paradoxically, once freed from middle-class conventions, they create their own conventions. In a classic study of bohemians, Patricia Nathe (1978) writes that although "Bohemia" is a classless society, there are distinct circles of membership: at the core are the true career artists and intellectuals; then their disciples, known as *pseudo-* or *professional bohemians*; then the weekend or part-time bohemians; then the entrepreneurs who profit from the bohemian scene; and in the "outer circle," the voyeurs, relatives, reporters, detectives, and groupies. These various "types" interact in cliques regularly, filling recognizable roles and playing out scripts based on the romance of art, poverty, self-expression, and identification with other socially vulnerable groups.

These two aspects of clique and community formation—the provision of social support and the production of new rules and roles—are familiar to us from our own experience of cliques at school. Everyone reading this book has, by now, suffered the savagery of school life—especially the cruelty of cliques. William Golding's classic novel *Lord of the Flies*, first published in 1954, has schoolboys tormenting, killing, and then eating the weakest on a desert island. This is a mere exaggeration of children's behaviour in schoolyards. Some might imagine that the cruelty the boys display in Golding's novel is a result of unvarnished human nature—Hobbes's state of nature ([1651] 1968), perhaps. In fact, their cruelty grows out of the operation of a hierarchical society controlled by a ruthless leader. Children's social structures can be just as cruel as nature, Golding tells us.

Cliques, though often supportive, offer an excellent example of structured cruelty, and they can be found everywhere. No one escapes childhood without becoming a member of a clique or feeling isolated because of exclusion from one. Though seemingly without goals, cliques have an unstated "mission" or purpose: to raise the status of clique members at the expense of non-members. Though lacking an organizational chart or stated division of labour, school cliques have a clear hierarchy of influence and popularity, with the leader on top surrounded by his or her favourites. In this sense, then, a clique is a group of people working together and co-ordinated by communication and leadership to achieve a common goal or goals.

### Defining the Term Clique

Dictionaries variously define *clique* as "a small exclusive set," a "faction," a "gang," a "noisy set." This meaning comes from the French *cliquer*, meaning "to click," or "to make a noise." People in cliques—especially the most popular ones—make a lot of noise, pumping themselves up and ridiculing others.

To come closer to our current sociological meaning, we would define *clique* as a group of tightly interconnected people—a friendship circle whose members are all connected to one another, and to the outside world, in similar ways. Usually, clique members

feel strong positive sentiments or liking for one another and contempt for outsiders. They spend more time with one another than with non-clique members, share their knowledge with one another, and think and behave similarly. They tend to ignore or exclude outsiders—people not like themselves, and not friends of their friends.

In short, *cliques* are groups characterized by friendship, similarity, interaction, exclusion, and the flow of valuable resources: information, support, and opinions, among others. In these respects, cliques are mini-communities, like mini-states. Like states, they accumulate power and resources. They receive, censor, and direct information flow. Like states, cliques remain distinct; resources (such as information) flow readily within the clique and less readily outside its borders. Cliques accumulate and redirect information. They also distort information, generate it, and send it out as gossip and rumour. Cliques, like other organizations, create and concentrate information flow. Because they generate and control the flow of information effectively, cliques are stable structures (on this, see Carley, 1989, 1991). They survive largely through what psychologist Irving Janis (1982) called *groupthink*.

### Cliques in School Settings

Cliques form in every area of life, even within bureaucracies and other formal organizations. However, cliques are most familiar to us from our childhood school experience. In school settings, cliques typically have a well-defined membership. Clique members are typically similar to one another in background and behaviour (Ennett and Bauman, 1996). Cliques typically have rituals that exclude outsiders and integrate insiders. Cliques also have a leader, who is the most popular member of the clique and who dominates the other members. Usually, the leader defines the group boundaries, invents group rituals, and chooses the membership.

Cliques are not only organizations: they are communities and miniature societies, just as Golding suggested. In cliques, children first learn the rules and expectations of society outside their family home. Through games and play with clique members, children internalize the beliefs, values, and attitudes of their group. By these means, children also come to form judgements of themselves. For example, they learn what it means to be "good-looking," "sexy," and "popular," to be chosen or passed over. Children's activities, their friendships, and their feelings about

Cliques teach young people the dynamic of power, manipulation, and conformity. They create a hierarchical social organization of students, with top-ranking, middle-ranking, and bottom-ranking groups. Ranking the clique strongly affects children's social experiences at school. Membership in a low-ranking clique can be humiliating or painfully isolating. (Photo © Harry Cutting Photography www.harrycutting.com)

themselves are tied up with their involvement in the cliques that organize their social landscape (Crockett, Losoff, and Peterson, 1984).

### How Cliques Form

Cliques form when people meet others like themselves. The social structuring of activity itself—for example, the age grading of activities such as education, entertainment, or work—increases the likelihood that people will meet others like themselves (Feld, 1982). In addition, since class or ethnicity often segregates neighbourhoods, and since children usually attend neighbourhood schools, they are likely to meet other children of the same class and ethnic background. The more homogeneous the people they meet, the more children will form relationships with others who are similar. It is, first of all, this structuring of acquaintanceships that leads to the creation of cliques.

However, an element of choice is also involved. Cliques carefully screen people for membership. Once formed, cliques maintain themselves by continuing to ensure that members remain similar. Cliques evolve as individuals enter and leave the group. Those

at the clique's centre—the leaders—are most influential in the recruitment process. They use their power, based on their popularity, to decide which potential members are acceptable and which are not.

Cliques control their members by defining appropriate and acceptable behaviours. Leaders are particularly skilled in exercising control. They often do so by building up the clique members and then cutting them down (Adler and Adler, 1995). One technique is to draw new members into an elite inner circle, allowing them to enjoy brief popularity, then humbling them by turning the group against them. Leaders also take advantage of quarrels to divide and conquer the membership. They degrade and make fun of those who are lower in the hierarchy or outside the group. All of these tactics allow leaders to build up their own power and authority. Such rites of degradation also foster clique solidarity by clarifying the norms for acceptance and rejection.

The cohesion of a clique is based mainly on loyalty to the leader and loyalty to the group. This loyalty, in turn, is based as much on exclusion as it is on inclusion. First, group members hive themselves off from non-members. Lack of contact with outsiders permits members to believe that outsiders are different and less socially desirable than themselves. As well, clique members use gossip to reinforce their ignorance of outsiders and maintain social distance from them, and to ridicule and spread nasty rumours about outsiders. Finally, they may pick on or harass outsiders. Doing so instills fear, forcing outsiders to accept their inferior status and discouraging them from rallying together to challenge the power hierarchy.

Cliques and the rituals of inclusion and exclusion on which they rely are more than mere children's games. They are small-scale models of how organizations state, teach, and enforce rules; as such, they provide a lesson in social control. Cliques remind us that every inclusive action is, at the same time, an exclusive action. Organizations, like cliques, can have unstated but real shared goals, unwritten but compelling norms, undocumented but powerful hierarchies, and effective but unplanned divisions of labour.

## Bureaucracies

### Formal Organizations

Organizations are *formal* if they are deliberately planned and organized. This planning may occur at the outset, when people found a new university, for instance. Or it may occur gradually, as happens when the people who form a bucket brigade find that enough fires are starting that they would do better to organize themselves into a volunteer fire department.

Within formal organizations, communication and leadership are provided through consciously developed and formalized statuses and roles. Often formal organizations have multiple goals, and they usually have a long lifespan. The Roman Catholic Church is a formal organization that has lasted nearly 2,000 years. Besides this, formal organizations normally have access to far greater resources and more complex technologies than spontaneous organizations.

As a result, we can define a *formal organization* as a deliberately planned social group in which people, resources, and technologies are consciously co-ordinated through formalized roles, statuses, and relationships to achieve a division of labour intended to attain a specific set of objectives. This is very similar to the general definition of organizations. A formal organization will have an overarching set of goals formulated by its leaders and more or less accepted by its members. But we cannot assume that these are the only goals of the membership. Workers, professionals, and managers will all have their own occupational goals as well.

A huge literature, containing many lively debates, addresses the question of why some organizations are more successful and powerful than others. The most common explanations cite the degree to which an organization fills a social need (either real or successfully promoted by the organization itself), controls or has access to needed resources and technologies, tailors its goals to match the goals of its members, and adapts to or causes changes in its environment. The main form of the large, powerful, and long-lived formal organization of the twentieth century is the **bureaucracy**.

"Bureaucracy" is a negative word for most people. It calls to mind images of red tape, an overemphasis on rules and regulations, inefficiency, and unwieldy government organizations moving at a tortoise-like pace. To sociologists, however, a bureaucracy is merely a particular type of formal organization that thrives in both the public and the private sector, in capitalist and socialist societies alike. The very fact that bureaucracy is the main organizational form taken by competitive corporations shows that it can be very efficient.

### The Emergence of the Bureaucratic Form of Organization

In a bureaucracy, the *superordinate*, or boss, personally owns none of the resources. All resources belong to the organization. Further, all resources are meant to flow from superior to inferior on the basis of authority or office-holding alone—not on the basis of personal attachment. In turn, office-holding is (ideally) based on expertise and effectiveness alone.

In bureaucracies, people move through positions, or offices, in the organization, based on their merit. The resources remain attached to *offices*; they do not follow the individual movers. Moreover, elaborate written rules govern many (if not all) of the relationships in the organization. Organization charts are constructed to show the (ideal) chains of responsibility, authority, and communication between superiors, subordinates, and equals.

It was obvious to Max Weber ([1908] 1978)—the first sociologist to study bureaucracies—that this form of organization held enormous advantages over earlier organizational forms, such as *clientelism*, in which clients are tied to their boss or patron by personal loyalty. First, bureaucratic organization holds the potential for rational planning. In bureaucracies, goals are stated explicitly, strategies are planned and communicated, the most capable people are hired and trained, resources are mobilized, effectiveness is evaluated, and organizational improvements are implemented. How very different this makes IBM or the University of Toronto—both bureaucracies—from the Italian Mafia or the court of Louis XIV—both patron–client organizations.

Bureaucracy in its modern form arose under three important historical conditions: European nation-building, capitalism, and industrialization. Nation-building—and by extension imperial conquest and colonization—created the need for effective tax collection and military capability. Kings cannot run countries, or wars, without taxes. They cannot raise taxes without the help of honest and hard-working tax collectors who are loyal to the king. An honest and effective military is needed to beat down the local aristocrats, and also to fight the armies of other countries.

Capitalism imposed similar demands. Under **capitalism**—a system devoted to the pursuit of maximum profits—people quickly discover that some forms of social and economic organization yield higher rates of profit on investment than others. The rationality of bureaucratic organization is well suited to the rationality associated with a pursuit of profits. The bureaucratic structure can grow as large as necessary, through a proliferation of roles, yet remain highly controlled from the top. This is less possible, if possible at all, in clientelist systems based on personal loyalty. The legal concept of "limited liability" allows a bureaucracy to manage investment and profits impersonally, in a way that protects both the owners and the workers. This impersonality also makes bureaucracy quite different from clientelist systems.

Finally, industrialization also favoured the rise of bureaucracies. Bureaucracies are good at controlling large workforces—even highly educated and differentiated workforces. As the size of an organization grows, its degree of differentiation typically increases. Related problems of co-ordination and control—formalization, decentralization, and supervision—must be solved (Marsden, Cook, and Kalleberg, 1996). Often reorganization is called for, especially if the number of personnel grows rapidly (Raadschelders, 1997).

On a broader scale, Weber ([1908] 1978) traced the rise of bureaucracy, capitalism, and the modern state to the **rationalization** of human activity. Indeed, rationalization is central to Weber's general conception of history. For Weber, *rationalization* refers to the movement away from mystical and religious interpretations of the world to the development of human thought and belief based on a methodical accumulation of evidence. Also associated with rationalization is the rise of impersonal authority based on the universal application of a codified set of rules and laws.

The value system associated with rationalization prizes efficient, effective administration in government and in the production of goods and services. In Weber's view, these values spurred the growth of bureaucracy, because bureaucracies organize human activity in a logical, impersonal, and efficient manner. Or so he thought.

## The Characteristics of Bureaucracy

Weber first analyzed the particular features of the bureaucratic form of organization. In his study of the major organizations of his day, Weber ([1922] 1958) identified six essential characteristics of bureaucracy:

- a division of labour,
- a hierarchy of positions,
- a formal system of rules,
- a separation of the person from the office,
- hiring and promotion based on technical merit, and
- the protection of careers.

In earlier eras, workers generally handcrafted specific articles from start to finish to produce society's goods. Gradually, this type of production process gave way to specialization and the *division of labour*. Adam Smith noted the overwhelming productive superiority of specialization as long ago as 1776 (Smith, [1776] 1976). A specialized division of labour became the foundation of modern industry and bureaucratization. An automotive assembly line is perhaps the typical modern example of such a division of labour. An assembly-line worker may perform one highly specialized operation every 36 seconds of the working day (Garson, 1972).

As on an assembly line, every member of a bureaucracy performs specified and differentiated duties. The bureaucracy itself provides the facilities and resources for carrying out these duties. Workers work with equipment they do not own; in other words, they are separated from the **means of production**. Moreover, administrators administer what they do not own. The goals of this combination—task specialization based on technical competence plus the centralized provision of resources—are increased efficiency and productivity.

We can visualize the structure of an organization as a pyramid, with authority centralized at the top. Authority filters down towards the base through a well-defined *hierarchy of command*. Thus, the structure explicitly identifies both the range and the limits of authority for people in each position. Within this hierarchy, each person is responsible *to* a specific person one level up the pyramid and *for* a specific group of people one level down.

The organizational chart of any large corporation is shaped roughly like a Christmas tree, in that the number of workers increases (and the division of labour becomes more specialized) as you move towards the base of the hierarchy. Together with the other characteristics of bureaucracy, this feature serves to increase efficiency: all communications flow upward to control central from large numbers of workers "at ground level." However, formal communication within a bureaucracy can be extremely awkward. What if a Halifax, Nova Scotia, sales representative wishes to discuss a special order with a craft worker in the Moncton, New Brunswick, plant? Does the sales rep really have to communicate through intermediaries, all the way up and down the structure, until he reaches the craft worker in Moncton? No. In real life, people work to avoid such unwieldy communication channels, often forming informal communication networks.

Bureaucracies operate according to *written rules*. The rules permit a bureaucracy to formalize and classify the countless circumstances it routinely confronts. For each situation, decision-makers can find or develop a rule that provides for an objective and impersonal response. The rules therefore guarantee impersonal, predictable responses to specific situations. This impersonality and objectivity in turn helps the organization to achieve its goals.

In a bureaucracy, each person is an *office-holder in a hierarchy*. The duties, functions, and authority of this office are all explicitly defined. That is, the rights and responsibilities of a Level 3 supervisor are all spelled out, in relation to a Level 4 supervisor (her superior) or Level 2 supervisor (her subordinate). The relationships between positions in a bureaucracy are, therefore, impersonal relationships between roles, not personal relationships between people. This separation of person and office means that people are replaceable functionaries in the organization: people come and

go, but the organization remains intact. It also means that personal feelings towards other office-holders must be subordinated to the impersonal demands of the office. Equally, relationships are confined to the official duties of office-holders and ideally do not invade their private lives.

A properly functioning bureaucracy *hires on the basis of impersonal criteria* such as technical competence, not on the basis of ascribed, inborn characteristics such as gender, race, or ethnicity. Likewise, technical competence is the basis for promotion or, sometimes, for seniority. People are neither discriminated against nor favoured because of such personal criteria as their personalities or their kinship with someone at the top of the hierarchy.

The final characteristic of bureaucracies is that people's *careers are protected* within them. People can look forward to long careers in a bureaucracy because they are not subject to arbitrary dismissal for personal reasons. So long as they follow the rules attached to their office or position, they are secure in their jobs. Generally speaking, their income will continue to arrive at the end of each month.

Compare these characteristics with the cliques considered earlier. In a bureaucracy, we find a much more detailed division of labour and a much longer hierarchy of positions than one finds in the typical clique. The system of rules in a bureaucracy is formal, or written, unlike the informal rules in a clique. A bureaucracy separates the person from the office, whereas there are no offices in a clique, only distinct individuals. Hiring and promotion in a bureaucracy are based on technical merit; in a clique, they are based on popularity, friendship with the leader, toughness, or attractiveness. Finally, a bureaucracy provides people with secure, often lifelong careers; as we have seen, clique memberships may be brief and insecure.

## Merton's Bureaucratic Personality

Robert Merton's analysis of bureaucracy (1957) focused on the pressure placed on bureaucrats to act in ways that serve to weaken the organization. Merton compared bureaucrats to overtrained athletes. Bureaucracies place immense pressure on their members to conform. This pressure, combined with intensive training, overemphasizes members' knowledge of the bureaucracy's rules. This, in turn, makes it easy for bureaucrats to act habitually in routine ways. In Merton's words, they follow rules in a methodical, prudent, and disciplined way. Inevitably, the routines become similar to blinkers on a horse, keeping bureaucrats from recognizing new situations in which the old rules are inappropriate. Thus, Merton argued, bureaucrats develop a "trained incapacity" for dealing with new situations.

In addition, the routine application of rules requires that all situations must somehow be classifiable by objective criteria so that they may be made to fit the appropriate pigeonhole. The result is that bureaucrats cannot see their clients as people with unique wants and needs, only as impersonal categories. This viewpoint is harmful to the organization since it causes bureaucrats to fail to meet the unique needs of individual clients. The result may be efficient but not effective, seemingly productive but unsatisfying and inhumane.

## Informal Organizations in Bureaucracies: The Hawthorne Studies

Although bureaucracy is intended to be an impersonal form of organization, actual people fill the bureaucratic roles. As human beings, workers resist becoming faceless cogs in the bureaucratic machine (replaceable cogs, at that). Consequently, they develop complex personal and informal networks that function within the formal organization. Collectively, these networks constitute the informal organization—bureaucracy's human face. Within formal organizations, we find informal organizations, even cliques of the kind discussed earlier in this chapter.

Informal networks among people who interact on the job serve many purposes. First and foremost, they humanize the organization. They also provide support and protection to workers at the lower levels of the hierarchy, serve as active channels of information (the grapevine), and become mechanisms for exchanging favours and exerting influence. They provide people with a sense of community, a sense of inclusion. They also direct the flow of information, enforce moral standards, and exclude people they consider inferior. All of these informal processes affect the operation of formal organizations. Paradoxically, informal networks within formal organizations—though similar to cliques in many ways—can serve to liberate people from the limitations of formal organization and, occasionally, allow them to protest and subvert their working conditions. They also confer human meaning on otherwise impersonal settings, as we see from the classic Hawthorne studies.

The Hawthorne studies were conducted between 1927 and 1932 at the Western Electric plant at Hawthorne, Illinois, under the direction of Elton Mayo. Mayo held the view that workers were non-rational, emotional beings. His studies provided a massive database that social scientists are still using to test a wide variety of hypotheses. They also spawned a huge literature, of which the account by George Homans (1951) is probably the most readable. The Hawthorne studies first revealed the importance of the informal organization in formal organizations.

Early conclusions drawn from the Hawthorne studies provided the foundation of the human relations school. One of the first conclusions became known as the **Hawthorne effect**. This proposition holds that when people know they are subjects of an important experiment and receive a large amount of special attention, they tend to behave the way they think the researchers expect them to. The Hawthorne effect has influenced the design of social-psychological experiments ever since, as researchers try to control for this distortion.

Other conclusions drawn from the studies dealt with the social aspects of work: the relationships among the members of the informal group, the norms developed by the informal group, and types of supervision. The relationships among the women in Phase II of the research were happy and supportive— and associated with higher productivity—while those among the men in Phase IV were not. This finding led human relations theorists to conclude that happy group relationships may even increase productivity. The Hawthorne studies also found that group relationships can limit productivity, particularly in the absence of rigid, formal supervision.

Decades later, further analyses of the Hawthorne studies by Perrow (1972) and others modified the original conclusions. In fact, they produced a very different idea of informal groups. Starting from the premise that people will respond rationally to the constraints placed on them by organizations, Perrow and other researchers investigated the objective conditions surrounding the original Hawthorne studies. They found that the Hawthorne plant, like most others, had a long history of raising the productivity standard once workers had consistently attained a certain level. As a result, workers had achieved an increasingly fast pace to maintain their incomes. It is entirely logical, then, that workers would try to keep a balance between productivity and earnings, protecting their jobs by not producing too much. This

## Sociology in Action
### "Emotional Labour": Is Marx's Concept of Alienation Relevant Today?

Arlie Hochschild has appropriated Marx's concept of alienation, making it more relevant today by applying it to service employees. Hochschild re-examines alienation by comparing Marx's vignette of a factory worker's arm pressing a lever all day and thereby becoming a machine with a flight attendant's alienation from her tools of production, her smiles.

In her analysis of flight attendants, Hochschild refers to "emotional labor," meaning "the management of feeling to create a publicly observable facial and bodily display" (1983: 7). One of the pillars of Hochschild's argument is that a flight attendant's smile is appropriated or alienated from the individual flight attendant, through airline advertising that stresses smiling flight attendants. Hochschild describes the smile as the emotional tool used by flight attendants to complete their jobs. Not smiling is not "okay." In Hochschild's words, "emotional labor

is sold for a wage and therefore has *exchange value*" (1983: 7). Flight attendants, like Marx's factory workers, do not own the means of production and so the seller/labourer does not reap the profits.

Hochschild's concept of emotional labour is a mutation and extension of the concept of alienation. Hochschild is concerned with the psychological consequences of emotional labour and the alienation of emotions. She argues that the alienated labour cannot be utterly faked, which leaves flight attendants not as actresses, but as the "givers" in a non-reciprocal relationship with customers. In short, they feel emotionally drained. Hochschild's work may be of particular concern in future because evidence suggests that the service industry will continue to be a key industry while manufacturing will continue to decrease in wealthier nations.

analysis forces organizational theorists to reject the early human relations idea of non-rational workers and group norms.

This later research has led to the conclusion that informal organization can either help the formal organization to attain its goals or hinder it; this will depend largely on the quality of the relationship between the workers and their managers. Frequently cited examples of hindrance are the British coal industry and Canada Post, both of which have a long history of bitter labour–management conflict.

## How Bureaucracies Actually Work

Weber's concept of bureaucracy, as we have seen, is a useful model for the study of this complex form of organization. It calls our attention to central features of bureaucracy. But it is a simplification, an idealization. It is like the notion of a perfect vacuum in

physics, or of a feather falling through space without meeting any wind resistance. Such images are good for starting to think theoretically, but they are not the real world. In the real world, bureaucracies have flaws, and sociologists since Weber have spent a great deal of time discussing these flaws.

### Actual Flows of Information

Ideally, every member of a bureaucratic organization is knowingly enmeshed in a network of reporting relationships. In graphic form, a bureaucracy is a Christmas-tree-shaped structure that repeatedly branches out as you go from top to bottom. Thus, at the bottom of the hierarchy a great many people (1) carry out orders from above and (2) report work-related information up the tree to their superiors. At the top of the hierarchy, a few people (1) issue orders to their subordinates, (2) process information received from below, and (3) maintain linkages between the organization and its (political, economic, and social) environment. Also at the top, information is shared between the heads of planning, manufacturing, shipping, public relations, and other sectors of the organization.

In practice, organizations do not work this way, as sociologists since Weber have pointed out. They could not afford to work this way, and human beings aren't constructed to work this way. Thus, alongside the ideal or formal structure—which prescribes how a bureaucracy *ought* to work—there is an actual or informal structure, which is how it *really* works.

In theory, a failure to report information up the hierarchy would never occur. In practice, it occurs all the time. That is because workplaces are politically "contested terrains" (Edwards, 1979), and controlling the flow of information from below is a means of changing the balance of power between superiors and subordinates. And, as the French sociologist Michel Crozier (1959) showed, bureaucracies work differently in different societies. This is because people raised in different cultures have different ideas about inequality, deference, openness, and secrecy. For example, people raised in France or Russia will be much more alert to the inequality of bureaucratic relations and the power of information control to equalize relations than workers raised in the United States. They will therefore behave differently, and as a result bureaucracies will work differently in these countries.

Bureaucracies also appear to work differently for men and women, as has already been noted. When playing a managerial role, women adopt a collaborative, relational approach derived from qualities used in familial relations, whereas men emphasize purely economic considerations. Women's managerial styles emphasize the establishment of good employer–employee relations and the sharing of information and power (Occhionero, 1996).

In practice, workers everywhere form friendships and acquaintanceships. As a result, they casually share work information. Much of the information that flows within an organization is shared orally, not in writing, to introduce civility and negotiation between work teams (Grosjean and Lacoste, 1998). In many cases, workers use information purposefully to help one another. In a few cases, they may even leak information for personal gain or to subvert their boss or the organization as a whole.

Thus, within organizations based ideally on strangers relating to other strangers on the basis of written rules, we find workers forming what amount

to secret organizations or subcommunities that obey their own rules. Political actors below the top level cannot employ routine channels or resources to negotiate in the idealized manner. There is a "politics from below" that includes all the actions that defy, oppose, or sidestep the rules or roles of the organization (Brower and Abolafia, 1997).

The basis of this informal organization is trust, which relies on friendship, acquaintanceship, and gossip about third parties to strengthen existing ties (Burt and Knez, 1996). In the end, the same materials that build cliques build the informal, often hidden infrastructure of bureaucracies.

As in cliques, trust in bureaucracies is built gradually, maintained continuously, and easily destroyed (Lewicki and Bunker, 1996). When trust is violated, the result is often revenge or another disruptive response—confrontation, withdrawal, or feuding, for example (Bies and Tripp, 1996). Trust is easier to generate within organizations than across organizations, since it is *within* organizations that managers, serving as third parties, can monitor and enforce reciprocity. The result is that organizational boundaries work effectively to restrict intellectual diffusion (Zucker et al., 1996). Within organizations, the flow of information is harder to contain.

Often team structures are purposely created to cut across the bureaucratic hierarchy, enabling workers to co-operate in the solution of a cross-branch problem. This is done with the recognition that requiring all information to flow to the top and then across is a slow and ponderous way of solving problems. Thus, increasingly, organizations have adopted horizontal, as well as vertical, reporting relationships. In many instances, this has improved organizational learning and given the organization a competitive advantage (West and Meyer, 1997).

Such temporary, cross-cutting groups rely on what is called *swift trust*. In these temporary systems, a premium is placed on making do with whatever information is available and in which swift judgements of trust are mandatory. Generally, trust develops most rapidly when (1) there is a smaller labour pool and more vulnerability among workers; (2) interaction is based on roles, not personalities; (3) behaviour is consistent and **role expectations** are clear; (4) available information allows a faster reduction in uncertainty; and (5) the level of interdependence is moderate, not high or low (Meyerson, Weick, and Kramer, 1996).

New information technology also makes it easier for horizontal groupings to form, since distant employees can easily exchange information through a large organizational computer network (Constant, Sproull, and Kiesler, 1996). New cultures emerge when computers, linked together to form intra-organizational networks, create a virtual organization parallel to but independent of the traditional bureaucratic hierarchical organization (Allcorn, 1997). As well, telecommuting, or teleworking, now occupies an important place in the world of information work, posing new problems (Di Martino, 1996). It may reduce costs by externalizing or delocalizing work, but we are far from knowing how it will affect work organization and productivity (Carre and Craipeau, 1996). For example, the increased use of computer-mediated communication appears to increase user satisfaction in task-oriented organizational cultures and to decrease user satisfaction in person-oriented organizational cultures (Kanungo, 1998).

### Organizational Cultures and Flexibility

In temporary or other horizontal groupings, a worker reports to more than one superior, which may create conflicts or inconsistent demands. In some cases, it becomes unclear where a worker's main duties lie and, therefore, how that person's work should be evaluated and rewarded. This means that greater flexibility and co-operation must be sought from the workers as well as built into the organizational structure itself.

Organizations require increasingly more flexibility from workers, which is possible only if those workers receive continuing education and training and participate in planning (de la Torre, 1997). Yet worker motivation, recruitment, and training all pose problems for bureaucracies. The motivational problem is greatest in organizations where professional expertise and judgement are most required, as in universities, law firms, and technology-development firms. There we find the greatest attention given to matters of organizational culture and career development. It is only by giving these workers considerable autonomy and rewards for strong identification with the firm that the most able workers can be induced to join, stay, and carry out their duties in conformity with organizational goals. Along with this comes a need for thorough organizational **socialization**, which begins at the stage of recruitment and interviewing and is never completed (Edwards, 1979).

Some organizational cultures are more effective than others in creating a high level of worker commitment and high rates of employee retention, and societies vary in their use of one or another kind of organizational culture. For example, in Japan, Korea, and China, there is more receptivity to a collective (or group) culture than we find in North America. (See also Table 4.1.)

Some organizations manipulate organizational culture to appear to tackle the perceived shortcomings of bureaucracy and empower the workers. They espouse open management, teamwork, continuous improvement, and partnership between customers and suppliers without replacing bureaucratic principles of standardization, differentiation, and control through a single chain of command. In the end, senior management has merely used these techniques to restructure management roles, justifying increased corporate control and intensifying work.

However, people usually form stronger attachments to other people than they do to "the organization" as an abstract entity. Thus, patterns of clientelism develop even within bureaucracies. In the end, bureaucracies are organizations in which two principles—rule-based rationality and person-based clientelism—contend for dominance, with neither being able to win decisively at the expense of the other.

### The Problem of Rationality

Bureaucracies are thought to be rational in the ways they make and execute plans. They are indeed more rational—in a limited sense—than patron–client relations. This is because, over the long term, by making impersonal decisions and rewarding excellence, they are more able to pursue long-term organizational goals with huge amounts of wealth and power.

Yet, the sheer size of large bureaucracies and their long-term outlook introduce certain types of irrationality that, in the end, may undermine the organization. A concern with the mere survival of the organization may undermine shorter-term concerns with the quality of decisions, products, and services the organization is providing to its customers. The much-hated "red tape"—or administrative delay—by bureaucracies persists not because of inadequate technology or personnel, but because it serves positive (as well as negative) functions for the organization (Pandey and Bretschneider, 1997). The bureaucratic demand to eliminate subjectivity and individuality actually undermines the productivity of institutions. By creating boundaries between the institution and outside influences, the institution loses touch with

Table 4.1   **A Diversity of Organization Styles: Aboriginal and Mainstream**

*In the article that this chart originally accompanies, Don Newhouse, Don McCaskill, and Ian Chapman argue that the differences in organization outlined here are important for Aboriginal people to maintain their cultural identities as distinct from mainstream North American culture.*

| Aboriginal | North American Mainstream |
|---|---|
| *Group orientation.* The interests and functioning of the group are more important than those of the individual. | *Individual.* The interests and functioning of the individual are paramount over the group. |
| *Consensual.* The organization respects employees and expects them to contribute to decisions in an equitable process. | *Majority rules.* Decisions are generally made by voting in which the majority wins the right to choose the course of action. |
| *Group duties.* Roles are not specialized, and the organization relies on peer support, team work, task delegation. | *Specialized duties.* Each person is expected to have a well defined job with a set of well defined duties. |
| *Holistic employee development.* The organization is concerned with all aspects of the employee's life, both inside and outside the organization. | *Organization employee development.* The organization is concerned only with those aspects of the employee which directly have a bearing upon the ability to do the assigned task. |
| *Elder involvement.* Elders are included formally and informally in the organization as advisers and teachers. | *No elder involvement.* Employees retire at the age of 65 and expertise and knowledge is lost to the organization. |

SOURCE: Don Newhouse, Don McCaskill, and Ian Chapman, "Management in Contemporary Aboriginal Organizations," *Canadian Journal of Native Studies*, 11 (1991): 341; available at <www.brandonu.ca/library/cjns/11.2/McCaskill.pdf>, accessed 22 May 2003. Reprinted by permission.

the individuals who are both the subjects and the objects of their efforts (Imershein and Estes, 1996).

Managerial tools such as corporate statements, corporate culture, performance appraisal, and reward systems are means for the **social construction** of homogeneity. Managers value obedience because it indicates a willingness to adopt and internalize dominant ideas, values, rationality, and, more generally, normative systems (Filion, 1998).

In bureaucratic organizations, the presumption of knowledge, heavy reliance on official records and procedures, and the predominance of routine all cushion "papereality"—a world of symbols—from other forms of representation. This inhibits both forgetting and learning (Dery, 1998). Another result is the creation of a *bureaucratic personality*, which substitutes proceduralism at the expense of any moral impulse or ethical concern with outcomes (Ten Bos, 1997). Anonymity and distance from decision-making make moral indifference likely, if not inevitable. Rule-making and record-keeping proliferate, particularly in private organizations. Some evidence suggests that

more alienated and more pessimistic managers make more rules (Bozeman and Rainey, 1998).

*Rule by offices* undermines personal responsibility for decisions the organization may take. No member of the bureaucracy is asked, or obliged, to take responsibility for collective decisions. As a result, so-called collective decisions—typically taken by the top executives—are liable to be foolish, harmful, or even criminal. Corporate and government entities are unique in that their deviant behaviour may be caused by systemic patterns in their organizations rather than only by individual malfeasance. However, once deviant behaviour has occurred, they are well positioned to evade responsibility. Managers may often refuse responsibility, by hiding behind organizational structures or by adopting the view that they were merely following orders. The deviant behaviour of big business and big government occurs because of limited information, the establishment of norms and rewards that encourage deviant outcomes, or the implementation of actions by organizational elites.

Managerial elites usually initiate and subsequently institutionalize such deviance into organizational culture. It will normally continue unchecked until it is challenged from inside or outside the organizations. Organizations themselves are rarely penalized for deviant behaviour (Ermann and Lundman, 1996).

As a legal person, the corporation is able to employ many more resources than can individuals seeking redress for their injuries by the corporation. The result may be fraudulent practices, dangerous commercial products, or even, as in Nazi Germany, death camps.

The administrative bureaucracies that carried out the extermination of the Jews progressed through several steps, ending in incarceration in concentration camps, starvation, and eventual annihilation. Once the machinery had been put into place, it was not con-

fined to Jews but spread to treatment of other groups, including Gypsies, asocial individuals, and Polish prisoners of war. Certainly, the managers responsible for this program experienced psychological repulsion. However, most managers rationalized their behaviour in terms of their duty in the bureaucratic system and the supposedly evil nature of the Jewish race (Hilberg, 1996).

### Relations with the Outside World

Ideally, the bureaucratic organization relates to the outside world as though it is looking through one-way glass. The outside world, composed of competitors, customers, and other bystanders, cannot see into the organization. However, the organization can see

---

**4.4**

**Global Issues**

Rational Means Can Lead to Irrational Ends

At the turn of the century, German sociologist Max Weber called attention to the dominant process underlying Western culture—rationalization. In Weber's view, the economic revolution and the Industrial Revolution combined to produce the Protestant Ethic and the Spirit of Capitalism. The driving force underlying both was rationalism—a quest for and the implementation of the most rational means for goal achievement. In order for capitalism and industrialization to reach their goals, a system of production and organization would emerge based on the principles of efficiency, predictability, calculability and control. The emergent result of this driving force is the bureaucracy.

While Weber certainly recognized the importance and the positive potentialities of rationalization, he also recognized its dangerous potential to erode individual liberties and to dehumanize. Weber feared the long-range consequences of a process which focused exclusively on means–end rationality to the exclusion of any concern with the human element of social organization. He expressed these fears in his concept of the "Iron Cage of

Rationality," i.e., a process so rational that (a) it is irrational and (b) [it] creates an inevitable cage from which there is no escape.

Contemporary sociologist George Ritzer (The McDonaldization of Society, 1996) has extended Weber's analysis to virtually every segment of modern society (the fast food industry, education, health care, child care, recreation and the work place). In a particularly penetrating analysis, Ritzer applies this analysis to the Holocaust. Drawing upon Weber and Holocaust scholar Zigmunt Bauman (Modernity and the Holocaust, 1989) Ritzer argues that the Holocaust displays all the characteristics of rationality: efficiency, predictability, calculability, control and the ultimate dehumanization of its victims by treating death as a unit of production.

The experiences of the Einsatzgruppen and the mobile gas vans served as the impetus for the Nazis to seek a more rational and efficient killing process.

SOURCE: Ben S. Austin, "The Camps," *The Holocaust/ Shoah Page* (n.d.); available at <www.mtsu.edu/ ~baustin/holocamp.html>, accessed 22 May 2003.

out as well as it needs to. In principle, the main contact between the organization and the outside world is by means of its top executive, who, in full possession of organizational intelligence, can act publicly in the organization's interests.

The separation of decision-making authority from front-line experience is also likely to create an "us versus them" point of view within the organization. As customers criticize the organization for unresponsiveness to their concerns, the organization takes a stance of embattled resistance to change. Union-based protest and organized citizen or customer protest movements put pressure on the bureaucracy. The result may be *groupthink*, a resistance within the organization to taking criticism seriously, considering a wide variety of options, or conceding the need for change. Nowhere is this organizational strategy more starkly depicted than in what Erving Goffman (1961a) has called *total institutions*.

### Total Institutions

As Goffman (1961a) pointed out, mental hospitals, convents, prisons, and military installations have a lot in common as organizations. True, they have different institutional goals and provide different services to society; they also employ different kinds of experts and oversee different kinds of "customers." However, what they have in common organizationally far outweighs these differences.

First, they all have total control over their "customers"—whether mental patients, nuns, convicts, or soldiers-in-training. Twenty-four hours a day, seven days a week, they are able to watch and, if desired, control behaviour within the institution. Though they can see their customer pool perfectly, none of them—whether as psychiatrists or nurses, priests or mothers superior, guards or officers—can be watched unknowingly or unwillingly. Thus, their relationships in the flow of information are highly unequal.

Total institutions offer an extreme example of the bureaucratic organization and the bureaucratized society. They are founded on principles of efficiency and procedural rigidity that are potentially in conflict with the values to which public organizations are expected to assign priority: particularly, democratic participation by employees and by those affected by organization practice (Davis, 1996).

What Goffman tells us about mental institutions and prisons reminds us of what we have heard about life in **totalitarian** societies like Nazi Germany and Soviet Russia. Under both Nazism and communism,

governance is further complicated by the competition between two bureaucratic hierarchies: the government (based on expertise) and the party (based on loyalty). (For details on East Germany, see Bafoil, 1996, 1998; on China, see Zang, 1998.) Moreover, in practice, both are dominated by a patrimonial ruler, making neither a true bureaucracy (Maslovski, 1996).

In fact, totalitarian societies are not only like total institutions, they also make liberal use of total institutions to punish, brainwash, and **resocialize** uncooperative citizens. Thus, as Weber warned, modern bureaucratic society is an "iron cage" in which we are all trapped by aspirations to career, efficiency, and progress ([1904] 1958: 181). Bureaucracy has an enormous potential for enslavement, exploitation, and cruelty. It also has an enormous potential for promoting human progress through economic development and scientific discovery, high-quality mass education, and the delivery of humane social services to the needy. It is to gain the second that we have risked the first. The jury remains out as to whether, in the twentieth century, the gain justified the cost.

## Conclusion

The concepts of role and identity can be viewed and analyzed from a variety of theoretical perspectives: structural functionalism, interactionist theory, and conflict theory. Role and identity are complex, far-reaching, and yet related entities.

Role is related to identity in that role involves a script of action, and that identity is a result of actions and how they are categorized, judged, and evaluated by others. Every role has an accompanying identity, and playing the role shapes both action and actor. We usually become that which we play at. Identity troubles, as manifested in episodes of embarrassment, make continued role performance difficult, if not impossible, raising the question of embarrassment management, which involves strategies such as avoidance.

The study of roles and identities stands at the intersection of society, culture, and personality. As such, it is inevitably connected with socialization—the process by which infants become socially competent—and with the formation and maintenance of communities. The process is social because it is through interaction with others and in response to social pressures that people acquire the culture—the language, perspective, and skills, the likes and dislikes, the cluster of norms, values, and beliefs—that characterizes the group to which they belong.

As we have noted, wherever you turn these days, you see particularly visible groups—organizations. Large organizations are daunting: they have their own impersonal cultures, they bring together large numbers of strangers, and they devise special ways of maintaining social control. However, it is unclear whether small, tightly connected organizations, such as cliques, are any better than large, tightly connected organizations, such as bureaucracies.

This chapter has reviewed a variety of different "sets" of people. These included categories, networks, communities, groups, cliques, and organizations. Sets of people with a common sense of identity are typically called *communities*, and there is a long history of community studies in sociology. Communities, whether urban or rural, real or virtual, are important because people are conscious of their membership and make personal investments in remaining members. Formal organizations combine many of the features of networks, groups, cliques, and communities.

The main form of the large, powerful, and long-lived formal organization of the twentieth century is the *bureaucracy*. The goals of bureaucracy—task specialization based on technical competence plus the centralized provision of resources—are increased efficiency and productivity.

Finally, this chapter considered *total institutions*. As Goffman pointed out, mental hospitals, convents, prisons, and military installations have a lot in common as organizations. These are all organizations that have total control over their "customers"—whether mental patients, nuns, convicts, or soldiers-in-training. Myths and ideologies are propagated to justify the differences between rulers and ruled. Total institutions offer an extreme example of the bureaucratic organization and the bureaucratized society.

## □ Questions for Critical Thought

1. What are the differences between workers and management? How are these differences expressed in roles?
2. What is the difference between the interactionist view of role and the structuralist view of role?
3. How is identity related to role?
4. What is the difference between "identification of" and "identification with"? Can you illustrate this from your own life?
5. Given the goal of fair treatment for all, argue that bureaucracy in the real world is better or worse than a spontaneous organization at achieving this goal.
6. Total institutions have an utterly different environment from the norm in which to socialize inmates. Do some research: do prisons teach inmates how to live "inside," or resocialize them to obey the rules of the outside world? Identify a few key procedures or values and argue your perspective.
7. Consider your own interactions with organizations, either at work or at school or in a community group. How does the goal of the organization—whether financial profit or helping the homeless—affect the organizational style employed?
8. Are some styles of decision-making more legitimate than others within a democracy? Rank different types of decision-making, such as consensus, majority rule, and incremental decision-making by bureaucrats, and explain your ranking of them.

## □ Recommended Readings

Holly Arrow, Joseph E. McGrath, and Jennifer L. Berdahl, *Small Groups as Complex Systems: Formation, Coordination, Development and Adaptation* (Thousand Oaks, Calif.: Sage, 2000).
   This text takes a micro approach. It adheres to the interactionist view while examining the impact of cliques and teams within workplace environments.

Paul du Gay, *In Praise of Bureaucracy: Weber, Organizations, Ethics* (Thousand Oaks, Calif.: Sage, 2000).
> Weber is a starting point for many sociologists' studies of organizations. This text focuses on the moral and ethical aspects of bureaucracy and examines Weber's contributions to these concerns.

Helen Ebaugh, *Becoming an Ex: The Process of Role Exit* (Chicago: University of Chicago Press, 1988).
> Ebaugh details how people disengage from social roles that previously were central to their self-identity.

Neil Garston, ed., *Bureaucracy: Three Paradigms* (Boston: Kluwer Academic Publishers, 1993).
> This collection looks at bureaucracies, how they work, and their effects on society. Readers of this text may find Part 2, which examines a range of organization styles in bureaucracies, of particular interest.

Erving Goffman, "Role Distance," in *Encounters: Two Studies in the Sociology of Interaction* (Indianapolis: Bobbs-Merrill, 1961), 85–152.
> Goffman describes how people use distancing techniques (here, role distance) when they do not wish others to identify them with a "self" implied in a particular role, especially if the role in question is considered beneath them.

Daniel A. Silverman, *Queen Victoria's Baggage: The Legacy of Building Dysfunctional Organizations* (Lanham, Md: University Press of America, 1999).
> This book offers a cross-cultural analysis of what the author calls "dysfunctional" organizations. Silverman focuses on the classroom as a site for examining different cultural concepts of discipline.

Robert Westwood and Stephen Linstead, eds, *The Language of Organization* (London: Sage, 2001).
> Taking a micro approach, the articles in this collection focus on language as a form of social control. The volume looks specifically at the kinds of words we use to describe organizations generally, the day-to-day interactions within organizations, and the components of organizations.

Kath Woodward, *Understanding Identity* (London: Arnold, 2003).
> This work explores personal and collective identities by drawing on experiences that highlight the importance of ethnicity and race, gender, and place in the production of meanings about who we are.

## ☐ Recommended Web Sites

Ellen Balka
www.sfu.ca/~ebalka/index.html
> Professor Balka's research includes cross-cultural examinations of organizations that assume a more collectivist model. Check out her publications on participatory design, including "Political Frameworks for System Design: Participatory Design in Non-profit Women's Organizations in Canada and the United States" (1995).

Erving Goffman: *The Presentation of Self in Everyday Life*
www.cfmc.com/adamb/writings/goffman.htm
> Adam Barnhart's article here elaborates on Goffman's influential book.

Social Networks and Social Capital
www.soc.duke.edu/~xioye/abstract.html
> This is a link to a conference, primarily of sociologists, concerning social networks and social capital. In some cases, both the abstracts and the full text of presented papers are available to read. Many of the papers are concerned with the uses to which groups put their social networks and social capital.

# 5

Vincent F. Sacco

# Deviance

© Digital Vision

## Learning Objectives

In this chapter, you will:

- learn to define deviance and social control as sociological concepts
- think critically about the images of deviance that we regularly encounter in the popular media
- learn to describe the major problems confronting researchers who study deviance
- identify the major questions that sociological theories of deviance and control are intended to answer
- compare and contrast various sociological explanations of deviant behaviour
- examine some of the social and demographic factors related to particular forms of deviant conduct
- learn how behaviours and people come to be categorized as deviant
- study how people who are labelled "deviant" cope with stigma

# Introduction

On a quiet, tree-lined street, two suburban teenagers sit in a kitchen and discuss how they will spend Friday night. They decide that one of them will try to get a fake ID to buy some beer for a party they are planning to attend. An older brother of one of the teenagers approaches the house. He picks the daily newspaper off the front step and glances at the front page with a prominent story about the mayor's resignation—it was discovered that the mayor had been giving untendered contracts to a construction firm owned by someone who made large contributions to her recent political campaign. The teenagers stop discussing their plans when the older brother, a student at the local university, enters. He instructs them to stay off the computer because he is waiting for a "very important" e-mail. What he doesn't tell them is that the e-mail is from a friend at another university who has promised to send a copy of an A+ essay, which the recipient plans to submit as his own work in a course he is failing.

Across town, in a gleaming corporate office, several key members of a clothing company meet to consider the bad press they have been getting since it was revealed that their clothing lines are made by children in sweatshops in less-developed countries. Rather than considering how they might improve employees' working conditions, they decide to launch a publicity blitz that denies the charges and calls into question the honesty and motivations of their accusers. One of the executives finds it difficult to concentrate on business because she is distracted by the situation at home. Her husband's occasional violent outbursts have become more frequent, and she worries that she and her children may be in some real danger.

What do all of these situations have in common? On the surface, it might seem that the answer is very little. However, some important common themes run through these examples. All relate to the central concerns of this chapter: the sociological nature of deviance and control. These situations raise questions about the nature of disvalued social action, why some people engage in it, and why others might react to it in particular ways.

This chapter will first talk about what the terms **deviance** and **social control** mean in sociology. Next, it will consider some of the major problems faced by researchers interested in investigating deviance and social control. Finally, it will focus on the three major theoretical questions that occupy the time and attention of sociologists who study deviance.

# What Is Deviance?

Any discussion of the sociology of deviance and social control must begin with some consideration of precisely what these terms mean. This is not a straightforward task. Formal sociological conceptualizations of deviance can be contrasted with more popular views. These more popular views define *deviance* by illustration, statistically, and in terms of a notion of harm.

When students are asked in a classroom to define *deviance*, a first response is typically to list types of people or types of behaviours that they think deserve the label. Most of us would have no trouble coming up with a long list of deviants, which could include (but would not be restricted to) criminals, child molesters, drug addicts, alcoholics, the mentally ill, members of religious cults, liars, and more. Of course, who makes the list and who does not is very much a function of who is doing the listing and when and where the listing is being done.

The major problem with these stand-alone lists is that they are incomplete. On their own, they tell us nothing about why some types of people and behaviour are (and why other types are not) included. In short, we are left in the dark regarding the nature of the definitional criteria being employed.

Statistical rarity suggests a more explicit way of thinking about the meaning of *deviance*. In this sense, deviant behaviour and deviant people are identifiable on the basis of their rarity. On the face of it, this makes a certain amount of sense. Many of the kinds of people we think of as deviant are, in a relative sense, statistically unusual.

A major problem with statistical definitions of deviance is illustrated by Figure 5.1. The areas between points $X_1$ and $X_2$ represent typical performance levels across some task. The shaded area on the far left represents that minority of cases that are statistically rare and that fall well below the average. On an examination, for instance, the people who fail very badly would be represented there. We might tend to think of such people as "deviants" in a conventional sense.

However, the shaded portion on the far right-hand side also suggests a statistically rare performance—but in the positive direction. On an examination, these people would be receiving very high A's. Statistical definitions thus obscure distinctions between people who exceed and people who fall short of expectations.

Another popular way of defining deviance is in terms of harm. In this sense, we equate deviant action

# Human Diversity
## Who Are the Deviants?

In 1969, the sociologist J.L. Simmons (1969) reported the results of a small study in which he asked 180 respondents to list people and things they regarded as "deviant." His respondents varied by gender, age, and other socio-demographic characteristics.

The list of people and behaviours nominated was extensive, with more than 250 items. Many of the categories suggested by respondents were expected, including (in the language of the day) homosexuals, prostitutes, drug addicts, radicals, and criminals.

However, the list also included liars, career women, reckless drivers, atheists, Christians, the retired, card players, bearded men, artists, pacifists, priests, girls who wear makeup, divorcées, perverts, smart-aleck students, know-it-all professors, modern people, and Americans.

It might be interesting to conduct a small follow-up survey to see what sort of list that question might generate (among your classmates, for example). As well, it worth speculating what such a list teaches us about everyday understandings of deviance and what the list generated by Simmons might reveal about the historical period during which it was made.

with action that produces destructive outcomes. Once again, many of those who would make most shortlists of deviants would also seem to be included by this definitional criterion. Murderers, thieves, liars, sexual abusers, and wife assaulters can all be said to be authors of real and tangible harm.

But any attempt to equate deviance with harm is also fraught with difficulties. First, while many of the people we treat as deviant in this society are the authors of harm, many others are not. The developmentally delayed, the mentally ill, gays and lesbians, and many others are often treated as deviant although it is difficult to document the harm they cause. In contrast, greedy corporate executives and unethical politicians are often able to manage quite effectively how others see them even though their actions may result in considerable damage to life and property. We tend to reserve the label of "deviant" in our society for other categories of people (Pearce and Snider, 1995; Simon and Hagan, 1999).

In many ways, harm is as much a matter of judgement and opinion as is deviance. There is considerable disagreement in our society about what is and what is not harmful and whom we do and do not need to fear (Glassner, 1999). Indeed, historical and anthropological evidence shows that judgements about harm change over time and from one culture to another.

## Deviance as a Sociological Concept

As sociologists, we are interested in trying to understand deviance as a product of **social interaction** and group structure. Simply put, we understand the study of deviance to be the study of people, behaviours, and conditions that are subject to social control. Conversely, we can define *social control* as the various and myriad ways in which members of **social groups** express their disapproval of people and behaviour. These include name-calling, ridicule, ostracism, incarceration, and even killing. The study of deviance is about ways of acting and ways of being

Figure 5.1  **The Normal Curve**

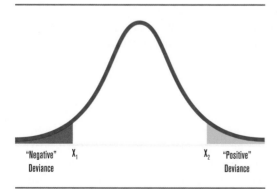

Statistical definitions of deviance make it difficult to distinguish "negative" deviance from "positive" deviance.

that, within particular social contexts and in particular historical periods, elicit moral condemnation.

When sociologists talk about deviance in this way, it sometimes creates confusion for those who are used to thinking about the subject in a more conventional manner. When a sociologist says, for instance, that homosexuality is an appropriate subject matter for the scholar interested in the study of deviance, the implication is not that the sociologist thinks of homosexuality as deviant. Rather, the point is that homosexuality is subject to various forms of social control in our society. As sociologists, we are interested in why those with the power to exert social control regard gays and lesbians in this way and what the consequences of such actions are (Herek, 2002).

In the study of deviance, it is important to distinguish between the *objective* and the *subjective* character of deviance (Loseke, 1999). The former refers to particular ways of thinking, acting, and being, the latter to the moral status accorded such thoughts, actions, and characteristics. It is important to keep this distinction in mind at all times. The "deviant" character of certain behaviours or world views or physical features is not implicit in those behaviours, world views, or physical features but is conferred upon them. Deviance thus requires both aspects of the phenomenon: there must be things (actions and so on) that can potentially be labelled as "deviant"; and deviant labels must exist and powerful others must be willing to use them.

Of course, as sociologists, we recognize the need to focus our attention on both sides of the deviance coin. We need to be alert to the fact that not everything that could be labelled "deviant" is labelled "deviant." The ability of some in society to use available resources to resist the efforts of others to consider them deviant is also of sociological interest.

## Researching Deviance

Sociologists who undertake empirical studies of deviance use all of the same methodological tools employed in other areas of the discipline. These include, for instance, experiments, surveys, content analyses, and field research. However, attempting to study the degree to which people might be engaging in behaviours that excite widespread disapproval can create some rather formidable problems. While the problems discussed in this section represent challenges to all forms of social research, they suggest special difficulties when the subject matter of the research is deviance.

### Secrecy

By its nature, deviant behaviour is often behaviour that people wish to keep secret. How, then, do sociologists undertake valid research in a way that does not intrude into the lives of those under study? Of course, there is no simple answer to this question.

Sometimes the researcher attempts to gain the confidence of the subjects by posing as one who shares their deviant status (Whyte, 1943). This involves some extremely hazardous ethical dilemmas. One much discussed case in this respect is an early study by sociologist Laud Humphreys. His book *Tearoom Trade* (1970) is a study of impersonal sexual encounters between homosexual men in public washrooms ("tearooms"). In order to familiarize himself with the social character of these sexual encounters, Humphreys presented himself to "tearoom" participants as someone who was willing to play the role of voyeur/lookout. This deception allowed him to observe the interaction between sexual partners in a way that did not arouse their suspicion. To compound the ethical problem, Humphreys recorded the licence plate numbers of the men who frequented the "tearoom" and was able to determine their addresses. After disguising his appearance, he went to their homes, under the guise of conducting a public health survey, in order to learn more about them. Needless to say, this provoked a firestorm of controversy. Generally, sociologists do not believe that such deception is ever excusable.

### Discovery of Reportable Behaviour

If research subjects confide in the researcher and reveal information about troublesome circumstances, does the researcher have an obligation to report that wrongdoing to authorities? The problem is brought about by the cross-pressures that the researcher experiences. On the one hand, the researcher has a professional obligation to respect the confidentiality of information that research subjects divulge. On the other hand, there is a social and moral obligation to protect the safety of the public or, even more, of the research subject.

Some of the complexities relating to reportability are illustrated by the case of Russel Ogden, who in 1994 was an MA student in the School of Criminology at Simon Fraser University in British Columbia. Ogden's study involved an investigation of the process of assisted suicide among terminally ill

HIV/AIDS patients. Shortly after he defended his thesis, he was summoned by a coroner's inquest, which asked him to reveal the sources of his information. Ogden refused, citing the pledge of confidentiality he had provided to his research subjects. He was subsequently charged with contempt of court, but, in spite of having little formal support from his university, he was able to win the case. The court later ruled that social science researchers have a qualified privilege to maintain confidentiality because such research contributes substantially to Canadian society (Palys, n.d.).

### Safety

Closely related to the problems of reportable behaviour are those related to the safety of respondents. In short, researchers should take no action that results in harm to those who participate in the research. While we tend to think only of physical harm in this respect, the injunction is much broader and includes emotional, mental, and economic harm.

Research could produce harmful outcomes in various ways. In the case of one major survey of female victims of male violence, for instance, there was a real concern on the part of researchers that calling women out of the blue and asking questions about violence in their lives could put them in danger if, for instance, a woman's abuser might be sitting next to her when she received the phone call (Johnson, 1996). As a result, it was necessary to take several special precautions, for instance, training interviewers to be sensitive to cues that the respondent might be under some immediate stress.

There is, as well, a more general sense in which research can put study subjects at risk. It is important to remember that, by definition, research into the disvalued nature of people and behaviour often involves research into the lives of the most vulnerable members of society. These could include the poor, the homeless, and others with whom society associates designations of deviance. The sociologist needs to remain aware that research findings can often be used against these vulnerable groups, especially when due care is not taken to qualify conclusions or to suggest appropriate interpretations of research evidence.

# The Sociology of Deviant Behaviour

We have defined *deviance* as ways of thinking, acting, and being that are subject to social control—in other words, as kinds of conditions and kinds of people that

are viewed by the members of a society as wrong, immoral, or disreputable. In so doing, we recognize that deviance has two distinct yet related dimensions: objective and subjective. *Objective* refers to the behaviour or condition itself, *subjective* to the placement of that condition in the system of moral stratification.

To choose a simple example, it is important that we not confuse the physical act of smoking marijuana with the designation of marijuana smoking as a deviant act. While each suggests a distinct realm of experience, each is an appropriate object of sociological attention. It is one thing to ask why people smoke marijuana, and it is quite another to ask why this is considered deviant conduct (in the law, for example). However, both types of questions are important and interesting.

We can identify several key problem areas that have been the focus of theoretical attention in the sociology of deviance. These include questions about (1) the causes and forms of deviant behaviour, (2) the content and character of moral definitions, and (3) the struggle over labels of deviance.

While sociologists are interested in a broad array of questions, questions about why deviants do what they do have always attracted the lion's share of attention. However, the "Why do they do it?" question contains a number of important (if unstated) assumptions. By implication, it assumes that most of us share a conformist view of the world and that the important thing to understand is why some deviant minority refuses to act the way that *we* act. The moral status of deviant behaviour is never called into question. In a sense, the "Why do they do it?" question proceeds from the assumptions that—by and large—society is a pretty stable and orderly place, that there is generally widespread agreement about what is right and what is wrong, and that we therefore need to understand what pushes or pulls some off the path the rest of us travel.

Quite obviously, most (but not all) of the theoretical thought in this respect reflects the influence of functionalist perspectives. Three major strands of thought can be identified—strain theory, cultural support theory, and control theory.

### Strain Theory

**Strain theory** derives from the writings of the famous American sociologist Robert Merton, who in 1938 published an influential paper entitled "Social Structure and Anomie." Merton sought to understand why, according to official statistics, so many types of non-conformity are much more pervasive among members of the lower social classes. Crime, delin-

- We tend to distinguish in our language between "drugs" and "alcohol" as though they are two different kinds of substances, but the nature of this difference isn't clear. The major distinction is really only a legal one—alcohol is not a prohibited substance, but marijuana and cocaine are. This invites a question: why is it legal to drink alcohol but illegal to smoke marijuana? Or, even more pointedly, why is it legal to smoke cigarettes but illegal to smoke marijuana? These distinctions do not derive from any logical assessment of the harm to self or others associated with consumption. Far more people die as a result of tobacco and alcohol use than as a result of the use of prohibited substances.
- We make distinctions between "religions" and "cults" as though these differences exist in nature. Some writers argue, however, that the world *cult* is typically used to describe a religion we do not approve of (Bromley and Shupe, 1981). Many of the contemporary mainstream religions (such as Roman Catholicism or Mormonism) have been accused in the past of doing what contemporary cults are

accused of doing (for example, brainwashing new members, exploiting believers, or covertly encouraging violence). Some critical writers maintain that our contemporary dislike of cults merely reflects the latest manifestation of long-standing religious intolerance.
- Women who are engaged in sex work (for example, prostitutes) have traditionally been the object of derision and ostracism (Brock, 1998; Larsen, 2000). The police, the courts, and the prisons have been directed toward the suppression of the prostitute. Interestingly, though, the societal attitude toward the seller of sexual services has always been much harsher than the attitude toward the buyer. This, too, defies logic.
- Especially after the events of 9/11, we have tended to use the words *terrorist* and *terrorism* as though their meanings were not problematic. Of course, terrorism, like any other deviant category, is socially constructed. Whom we see as a terrorist depends largely upon our political positions and national loyalties. One person's terrorist is another person's soldier of liberation.

quency, drug addiction, alcoholism, and other forms of deviance, Merton recognized, seem to emerge as more significant problems the further one moves down the socio-economic structure. As a sociologist, Merton was interested in trying to understand this issue in a way that made the structure of society—rather than the personalities of individuals—the central explanatory mechanism.

Merton argued that the answer could be found in the malintegration of the cultural and social structures of societies. In other words, the lack of fit between the cultural goals people are encouraged to seek and the means available to pursue these goals creates a kind of social strain, to which deviant behaviour is an adjustment. Merton's logic is elegant and compelling. In a society like the United States, there is little recognition of the role that class barriers play in social life. As a result, everyone is encouraged to pursue the goal of material success—and everyone is

judged a success or a failure in life based on his or her ability to become successful.

Merton knew, though, that many people near the bottom of the class hierarchy may not be able to achieve that overpowering goal of success because of their ethnic or regional or class origins. This, Merton said, is a type of socially induced strain to which people must adjust their behaviour, and often these adjustments take deviant forms. When people steal money or material goods, for instance, it can be said that they are attempting to use "illegitimate means" to achieve the trappings of success. When they take drugs (or become "societal dropouts"), they can be seen to have pulled out of the race for stratification outcomes. For Merton, these problems are most acute in the lower social classes because it is there that people are most likely to experience the disjuncture between the things they aspire to and things actually available to them (see Table 5.1).

Table 5.1    **Robert Merton's Paradigm of Deviant Behaviour**

Robert Merton argued that there are essentially five ways of adjusting to a social structure that encourages large numbers of people to seek objectives that are not actually available to them. Four of these adaptations represent types of deviance. Each type can be understood in reference to the goals and means of the culture.

| | Attitude to Goals | Attitude to Means | Explanation/Example |
|---|---|---|---|
| Conformity | accept | accept | Most people accept as legitimate the culturally approved ways of achieving those goals. In Merton's example, most strive for material success by working hard, trying to get a good education, etc. |
| Innovation | accept | reject | The bank robber, drug dealer, or white-collar thief seeks success, too, but rejects the conventional means for achieving that success. |
| Ritualism | reject | accept | Some people seem to simply be going through the motions of achieving desired social goals. In large organizations, we use the term *bureaucrat* to describe people who are fixated on procedures at the expense of outcomes. |
| Retreatism | reject | reject | Some people adjust to strain by "dropping out" of the system. Such dropping out could include losing oneself in a world of alcohol or illegal drugs or adopting some unconventional lifestyle. |
| Rebellion | reject/accept | reject/accept | Rebellion includes acts intended to replace the current cultural goals (and means) with new ones. In this category we might include the radical political activist or even the domestic terrorist. |

Later critics have pointed out several problems with Merton's arguments (Kornhauser, 1978; Vold, Bernard, and Snipes, 2002). For instance, Merton assumes that the distribution of crime and deviance found in official statistics is accurate, which it may not be. In a related way, the argument is not very successful in explaining acts of crime and deviance within middle- and upper-class populations.

Despite these limitations, the social-structural argument has had a great deal of influence on how sociologists think about the causes of deviant behaviour (Laufer and Adler, 1994). For example, sociologists Richard Cloward and Lloyd Ohlin (1960) expanded on Merton's ideas to explain lower-class gang delinquency. They agree with Merton that juvenile crime was prompted by the inability of lower-class youth to achieve the things their culture encouraged them to seek. However, they suggest a need to explain why different kinds of delinquent behaviour patterns emerge in different types of neighbourhoods.

For these researchers, delinquency patterns are like rare plants that require specialized conditions to flourish. Cloward and Ohlin identify three specific kinds of delinquent adaptations. The first, which they refer to as the *criminal pattern*, is characterized by instrumental delinquency activities, particularly delinquency for gain, in which those involved seek to generate illegal profits. We might think of drug selling or stealing and fencing stolen goods as examples of this kind of crime. The second, the *conflict pattern*, is characterized by the presence of "fighting gangs" who battle over turf and neighbourhood boundaries. The third, the *retreatist pattern*, is organized around the acquisition and use of hard drugs.

A more recent version of strain theory has been proposed by Robert Agnew (1985; Agnew and Broidy, 1997). Agnew theorizes that the inability to achieve the things we want in life is only one type of socially induced strain and proposes at least two others. A second source of strain involves an inability to avoid or escape some negative condition. For example, the youth who cannot avoid an abusive parent or a bully at school might turn to drugs, run away, or become aggressive with others as ways of coping with the strain that the situation creates. A third kind of strain results from conditions in which individuals lose something they value. Strain in this sense can result, for example, when a child is forced to move and thus to leave behind old friends, when a parent dies, or when a breakup with a boyfriend or girlfriend occurs.

Despite their differences, these arguments share certain features in common. First, they all take as their point of reference the need to explain why some individuals rather than others behave in ways that invite social sanction. Second, they share in common an explanatory logic that focuses on how the organization of our social relations creates problems that require solutions. In this sense, the causes of deviant behaviour are located in patterns of social life that are external to but impact upon individuals.

## Cultural Support Theory

A second explanation of deviant behaviour, **cultural support theory**, focuses on how patterns of cultural beliefs create and sustain such conduct (Cohen, 1966). According to arguments of this sort, people behave in ways that reflect the cultural values to which they have been exposed and that they have internalized. In this way, it can be said that you are attending university or college because you value education and learning. If conventional values support conventional behaviour, it should also follow that deviant values support deviant behaviour. The important task of such theories is to understand how the cultural meanings people associate with deviant conduct make that conduct more likely.

One of the earliest explicit statements of this position was provided by a sociologist associated with the University of Chicago, Edwin Sutherland (see Sutherland, 1947). Writing in the 1930s, Sutherland proposed that people become deviant because they have been exposed to learning experiences that make deviance more likely. In short, people end up deviant in the same way that they end up as Catholics, as stamp collectors, as saxophone players, or as French film fans—that is, as a result of exposure to influential learning experiences. People become deviant because they have learned in the context of interpersonal relationships how to become deviant.

But what does learning to be deviant actually involve? Most important, according to Sutherland, is the learning of what he called the "specific direction of drives, motives, attitudes and rationalizations" (1947: 7). In other words, we must learn to think about deviant conduct as acceptable to ourselves. Why do we not kill people who make us angry? It can't be because we don't know how (most of us do) or even, in many cases, because we fear getting caught. Most commonly, we refrain from murderous violence because we have come to define such action as morally repugnant, that is, as unacceptable to our-

selves. For Sutherland, this learning to accept or to value criminal or deviant action in a very real sense made such action possible.

Sutherland's cultural insights help us to understand how people come to value actions the rest of the society might despise. But other writers in this tradition have shown that the culture of deviant action is even more complicated. The complication concerns the fact that we live in a society that seems simultaneously to condemn and to support deviant behaviour. Is it possible, at the same time, to believe in and break important social rules? Most of us think, for example, that stealing is wrong, and we have learned to be wary of thieves. However, most of us have also stolen something of value (perhaps at work, perhaps from a corner store or a family member). This is possible because we have learned to define these deviant situations as ones to which the rules really do not apply. When we steal at work, for instance, we might not really see this as theft. We tell ourselves (and others) that we are underpaid and deserve whatever fringe benefits we can get or that our employers actually expect people to steal and build it into their budgets. The broader culture, from this perspective, both condemns deviance and makes available for learning the techniques to neutralize the laws that prohibit deviant action (Coleman, 1987; Matza and Sykes, 1957).

Like strain arguments, cultural arguments have been influential in the sociological study of deviant behaviour. Some critics have charged, however, that arguments using culture to explain deviance are ultimately tautological (Maxim and Whitehead, 1998). In other words, these arguments employ a kind of circular reasoning. Cultural theories tell us that deviant beliefs and values are the source of deviant conduct. Yet how do we ever really know what people's beliefs and values are? Usually, we observe how people behave and, on the basis of their behaviour, infer that they hold certain values. Is it appropriate, then, to use the values we have inferred from observations of behaviour to explain that behaviour? If we observe people stealing and then infer that they have acquired values supportive of stealing, and that these values explain the stealing, we have gone in a very large circle and have really explained nothing at all.

## Control Theory

The logic of the strain and cultural support theories contrasts quite sharply with the logic of a third type of view known as **control theory**. Advocates of control theory argue that most types of deviant behaviour do not really require a particularly sophisticated form of explanation. People lie, cheat, steal, take illicit drugs, or engage in sexual excess when and if they are free to do so. Lying and cheating can be the most expeditious and efficient ways of getting what we want in life. Experimenting with drugs and sexual promiscuity can be more fun than working or studying. The important question we need to ask, according to control theorists, isn't "Why do some people break rules the rest of us abide by?" Rather, "Why don't more us engage in forbidden behaviour?" For control theorists, deviant behaviour occurs when it is allowed to occur. Thus, we expect to find deviance when the social controls intended to prevent or check it are weak or broken. Seen in this way, deviance is not a special kind of behaviour that requires a special kind of motivation. Rather, it is behaviour resulting from the absence of pressures that would normally check or contain it.

This is a venerable idea in sociology—it can be traced back to the writing of Émile Durkheim ([1897] 1951). In his classic study of suicide, Durkheim sought to explain why some groups in society experience higher suicide rates than others and why suicide rates vary over time. Catholics, he found, have lower suicide rates than Protestants, and married people have lower rates than single people. As well, suicide rates increase in times of economic boom and economic depression. Durkheim suggested that the crucial variable might be social regulation (or what we might call *social control*). Social regulation forces people to take others into account and discourages excessively individualistic behaviours. So Catholicism—with its mandatory church attendance and practices such as confession—might suggest more social regulation than various strands of Protestantism. Married life implies more external regulation (in terms of obligations, duties, and so on) than single life. Periods of both boom and depression throw large numbers of people out of the customary social grooves in which they have been living their lives and disconnect them from social regulations. In short, suicide is more likely when people are left to their own resources.

In more recent times, sociologist Travis Hirschi (1969) has been the most influential social control theorist. Like many other sociologists interested in the study of deviant behaviour, Hirschi focused on the study of juvenile crime. In an influential book published in 1969, Hirschi attempted to use social control logic to explain the conduct of youthful offenders. For Hirschi, the problem of juvenile crime could be understood in reference to the concept of the bond to conventional society. Each of us, to a greater or lesser degree, has a bond or connection to the world of conventional others. In the case of youth, the world of conventional others is the world represented by their parents, teachers, and members of the legitimate adult community. Hirschi reasoned that if youthful bonds to conventional others are strong, youths need to take these others into account when they act; if the bonds are weak, however, they are free to act in ways that reflect much more narrow self-interest. Much of what we call crime and deviance, Hirschi reasoned, is evidence of this self-interested behaviour.

More recently, in collaboration with Michael Gottfredson (Gottfredson and Hirschi, 1990), Hirschi has proposed a general theory of crime and deviance that has been the object of a great deal of attention. Gottfredson and Hirschi argue that crimes of all types tend to be committed by people who are impulsive, short-sighted, non-verbal risk-takers. The underlying social-psychological characteristic of such people, they maintain, is low self-control. Further, individuals who have low self-control not only are more likely to commit crime, they are also more likely to engage in a wide range of deviant practices, including drinking, smoking, and activities that result in getting into accidents (Junger, van der Heijden, and Keane, 2001; Nakhaie, Silverman, and LaGrange, 2000). For Gottfredson and Hirschi, the problem of low self-control originates in inadequate child-rearing that fails to discourage delinquent outcomes.

Social control theories remain influential, but they have been criticized for their assumption that motivation is essentially irrelevant to the study of crime and deviance (Bohm, 1997). As well, some writers argue that while these ideas make a certain amount of sense when we are talking about crime and deviance among the more marginalized segments of society, they do not do a very good job of explaining why those members of society whose bonds to the conventional world seem strongest also engage in prohibited acts (Deutschmann, 1998).

## The Transactional Character of Deviance

Despite their sociological character, the strain, cultural support, and social control arguments tend to focus our attention on the individual. People, according to these theories, commit deviant acts because they respond to strain, because they are exposed to learning environments that support deviance, or because they are free from social constraints. Other writers, however, encourage us to understand deviant behaviour as an interactional product. From this perspective, we understand deviant behaviour as a joint or collective, rather than individual, outcome.

Murder provides an interesting case in point (see Figure 5.2 for homicide rates in Canada). When most of us seek to explain murder, we tend to focus on the murderous acts of the individual. As sociologists, for instance, we might try to understand how people who commit acts of lethal violence do so in response to social strain (Messner and Rosenfeld, 1997) or as a result of an affiliation with a culture of violence (Wolfgang and Ferracuti, 1967). Alternatively, though, we might try to understand how murder results from particular kinds of interactions.

David Luckenbill (1977), for example, has attempted to show how murder can in many cases be understood as a **situated transaction**. This means that murder is seen not as an individual act, but rather as an interaction sequence in which the participants (the eventual murderer, the eventual victim, and, perhaps, an audience) interact in a common physical territory. Based on a study of 70 homicides in the state of California, Luckenbill concludes that many murders move through six common stages:

* *Stage 1.* The transaction starts when the person who will end up the victim does something that the person who ends up the offender could define as an insult or as an offence to "face." This could be quite trivial. The victim might call the offender a liar, refuse to share a cigarette, or make a sexually suggestive comment about the partner of the eventual offender.
* *Stage 2.* The offender defines what the victim has said or done as threatening or offensive.

Figure 5.2 **Provincial Variations in Rates of Homicide (Number of Homicides per 100,000 Population), 2003**

For reasons that are not entirely clear, the rate at which the situated transaction we refer to as *homicide* varies from province to province.

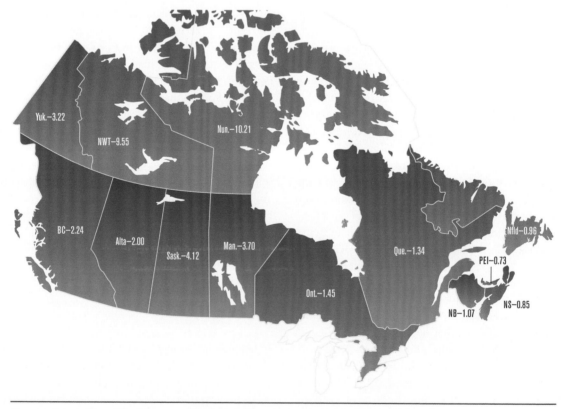

SOURCE: Adapted from Mia Dauvergne, "Homicide in Canada: 2001," *Juristat*, 22, no. 7 (2001): 3.

- *Stage 3.* The offender makes a countermove intended to respond and save face. This could involve a verbal response or a physical gesture.
- *Stage 4.* The victim responds in an aggressive manner. At this point, a working definition of the situation as one that will require a violent resolution seems to be emerging. The problems may be aggravated by the presence of onlookers who jeer the participants, offer to hold their jackets, or block a convenient exit.
- *Stage 5.* At this stage, a brief violent exchange occurs. It may involve a fatal blow, a thrust with a knife, or the pulling of a trigger. Typically it is over quickly.
- *Stage 6.* The battle, such as it was, is over and the offender either flees or remains at the scene.

Luckenbill's work shows us how murder can be understood as a social product. This does not imply an absence of guilt on the part of people who murder, and it is not offered as an excuse for killing. It does show that acts of deviance can be quite complex and can involve significant interactional dimensions.

# Making Sense of the "Facts" of Deviant Behaviour

Sociologists interested in the study of deviant behaviour have repeatedly demonstrated that deviant acts—especially the kinds of acts that seem to concern the average member of the society most—are not randomly distributed in the population. Instead, people with some kinds of social and demographic characteristics seem much more likely to be involved in such behaviour than others. The task for sociological explanations that focus on the deviant act is to explain these levels of differential involvement.

## Gender

It is well known that **gender** tends to correlate closely with a wide range of behaviours. This is no less true in the study of deviance than in the study of other areas in sociology. Males and females differ in terms of the amounts and the kinds of disapproved behaviours in which they engage.

Males, for instance, are more likely to be involved in a wide range of behaviours of which most members of Canadian society would say they disapprove. As illustrated by Table 5.2, males are much more likely to be involved in most types of criminal activity (crimes related to prostitution are one notable excep-

tion in this regard). The differential is greatest in the case of violence but is also very large in the case of other kinds of crime. While there has been some narrowing of the gender gap in recent years, crime remains very much a male-dominated activity (Hartnagel, 2000).

Males are also more likely to consume both legal and illegal drugs, including tobacco, alcohol, marijuana, and cocaine (Miethe and McCorkle, 1998). In addition, males are more likely to commit suicide, and when they do so, they are more likely to use guns or explosives (Thio, 1998). Overall rates of mental illness do not differ markedly between men and women, although there are significant variations by type. Women are more likely to be diagnosed as suffering from depression and anxiety, while men are more likely to experience problems relating to various forms of addiction and psychosis (Blackwell, 1992).

Several feminist writers have argued that there has been a marked tendency in the sociological literature to systematically ignore the deviant behaviour of women (Belknap, 1996; Boritch, 1997; Chesney-Lind, 1997). To be sure, most of what is written about crime and deviance concerns the behaviour of men, both as the deviants and as the police and other agents of social control. Moreover, many sociologists have assumed that female deviant behaviour could be explained by the same theoretical ideas and models used to make sense of male behaviour—a position with which many feminists do not agree (van Wormer and Bartollas, 2000).

The failure to be sufficiently attentive to the gendered nature of criminal and deviant behaviour has also been an empirical problem. Most research has dealt with the actions of men, either explicitly or implicitly. In the former case, sociologists tended, historically, not to be terribly interested in acts of crime or deviance that did not have a significant male

| Table 5.2 | **Adults Charged in Criminal Incidents, by Gender, 2001 (Percentages)** | |
|---|---|---|
| | **Males** | **Females** |
| Violence | 85 | 15 |
| Property | 78 | 22 |
| Other | 85 | 15 |
| **Total** | **83** | **17** |

SOURCE: Adapted from Statistics Canada, *Canadian Crime Statistics 2001* (Ottawa: Canadian Centre for Justice Statistics, 2002), 16–17.

dimension (Boritch, 1997). Through the work of feminist social critics researchers more recently have focused on problems that affect women more directly. These include, for instance, various forms of deviance that tend to victimize women, such as intimate violence and sexual harassment (Chasteen, 2001; Loseke, 1992; Rose, 1974).

### Age

Age, like gender, is strongly associated with many kinds of deviant behaviour (Tanner, 2001). Crime rates, for instance, tend to be greatest during the late teens and early adulthood, and to decline very sharply after that (Hirschi and Gottfredson, 1985). This pattern characterizes even violence in the home: young husbands (those under 30) are much more likely than older husbands to treat their wives violently (Johnson, 1996). Of course, this pattern does not hold for all kinds of crime. White-collar crimes (professional fraud, cheating on taxes, and so on) tend to occur somewhat later in the life cycle (Gottfredson and Hirschi, 1990).

Alcohol use and illicit drug use are also more heavily concentrated among young people (Tremblay, 1999). But while suicide rates among young people are a cause of considerable concern, such rates actually tend to be lower among younger Canadians (see Figure 5.3). And though it has traditionally been argued that older people in society are most likely to experience a variety of forms of mental illness (Gomme, 2002), recent research casts doubt on that generalization and suggests in some cases that the elderly may be the least likely members of society to suffer from various types of mental disorder. These more recent studies indicate that rates of some forms of mental illness (especially depression) have increased substantially among teenagers and young adults in the last few decades (Thio, 1998).

### Class and Ethnicity

As with gender and age, relationships between indicators of socio-economic disadvantage and various garden-variety forms of deviant behaviour are of considerable interest to sociologists. Many of the studies on this subject say that poorer people and people from minority groups are more likely to be involved in many forms of crime and delinquency, to use drugs and alcohol, and to develop various kinds of mental illness. Indeed, a great deal of sociological theorizing about the "causes" of deviant behaviour

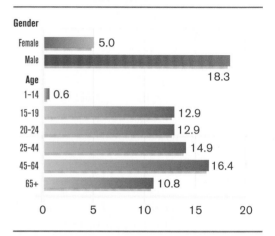

**Figure 5.3** **Suicide Rates by Gender and Age Group, 2002 (Rates per 100,000 Population)**

SOURCES: Adapted from Statistics Canada, *Canadian Vital Statistics*, Death Database, Table 102-0540 (2002); Statistics Canada, *Estimates of Population by Age and Sex for Canada, the Provinces and the Territories* (2002).

has taken as its central issue the need to explain why social and economic precariousness is related to deviant outcomes. This is very clear, for instance, in most versions of strain theory.

However, a consensus in the research literature does not really exist regarding how concepts such as poverty, economic inequality, ethnicity, or minority-group status should be measured for research purposes (Braithewaite, 1979; Hagan and Peterson, 1995; Wortley, 1999), and there is less consistency in research findings. While some studies seem to say that working-class youth are more likely to be delinquent, other studies tell us the opposite. As well, while minority-group status seems to be related to higher rates of crime in some cases, as with **First Nations** people, it seems to be related to lower rates of crime in others, as with Asian immigrants in British Columbia (Gordon and Nelson, 2000; LaPrairie, 2002).

Other interpretations of the significance of the relationship between social disadvantage and deviant behaviour point in the direction of a more general fault line that runs through the sociology of deviance. These other interpretations encourage us to ask different types of questions. Are poorer or minority people more likely to be deviant, or are they just more likely to get caught and labelled as "deviant"? Even more profoundly, do our definitions of what constitute crime and deviance themselves reflect class biases? Poor people, for instance, are less likely to commit many kinds of crimes, such as fraud and embezzlement. They are even less likely to manufacture faulty products, to engage in false advertising, to profit from political corruption, or to engage in various kinds of stock market swindles.

These observations suggest that while questions about who commits deviant acts and who does not are interesting and important, we need to move beyond them and to ask questions about the subjective character of deviance. Why are some ways of thinking, acting, and being more likely than others to excite indignation and disapproval, and why are some people more likely than others to become the objects of social control attention?

## The Sociology of Deviant Categories

As stated at the beginning of the chapter, the sociology of deviance is also the study of moral stratification. To call something or someone "deviant" is to articulate a judgement that that thing or person is disreputable. An important set of issues in the sociology of deviance relates to the creation of categories—some deviant and some not—in which people and actions are sorted (Loseke, 1999).

In the course of daily living, we tend to treat these distinctions as common sense. The deviant qualities of people and acts, we convince ourselves, reside within the people and acts themselves. However, judged from another standpoint, known as **social constructionism** (Miller and Holstein, 1993; Spector and Kitsuse, 1977), this logic is flawed. Acts and people are not inherently deviant but are defined as such by those in society with the power to do so.

Proceeding from this assumption, we are led to another set of questions. For example, how do we make the moral distinctions that we make? This perspective maintains that there is nothing self-evident or commonsensical about the deviant quality of people and their behaviour. Instead, the deviant quality assigned to people and behaviour is itself problematic and requires investigation.

Further, we need to recognize that the character of social condemnation is fluid and dynamic over time (Curra, 2000). It is easy to think of behaviours once widely viewed as deviant but that have come to be seen as much less deviant in recent years. "Living together," having a child outside of marriage, or being gay might only a few years ago have

been widely seen as grounds for social exclusion. While there is some resistance to these behaviours in the society at large (and a great of deal of resistance in some particular sectors of society), societal attitudes have moderated considerably.

At the same time, it is equally easy to think of many examples of ways of acting or being once widely tolerated but that now seem to draw considerable disapproval. One clear example is cigarette smoking (Troyer and Markle, 1983; Tuggle and Holmes, 1999). Only a few decades ago, cigarette smoking was widely approved of, even seen as glamorous. People smoked on elevators, in restaurants, and around children—even while attending sociology classes. That view of smoking contrasts sharply with the present-day view. Today, smokers are pariahs in many circles, and their habit is the object of scorn. Increasingly, they are the objects of a variety of forms of legal and extra-

The moral status of tobacco use has changed markedly over the years. Once considered largely harmless, even romantic, cigarette smoking is now viewed by many as highly deviant. (© Toronto Star)

legal control (Wagner, 1997). Other examples include drinking and driving (Gusfield, 1981), wife assault (Johnson, 1996), and sexual harassment (Rice, 1996).

### Deviance as a Claims-Making Process

What are the sources of the distinctions that the members of a society make between what is and what is not deviant? Social constructionist writers understand this to be a **claims-making** process (Best, 2001; Spector and Kitsuse, 1977). This refers to the process by which groups assert grievances about the troublesome character of people or their behaviour. Claims-making thus involves the promotion of a particular moral vision of social life. In a practical sense, we recognize claims-making in many different sorts of activities. It includes voting for "reform" candidates in a local election, a debate about some exotic sexual practice on a daytime talk show, a protest march to call for the police to do something about local crime, and the testimony provided by experts before a parliamentary committee. In short, claims-making is anything anybody does to propagate a view of who or what is deviant and what needs to be done about it (Loseke, 1999).

As a social process, claims-making is directed towards the achievement of three broad types of objectives:

1. *Publicizing the problematic character of the people with the behaviour in question.* Before they see people as troublesome, the members of a society generally need to be convinced of some tangible reason to regard those in question as troublesome. Claims-makers may endeavour to convince us that deviants are dangerous or irresponsible or that their behaviour is contagious (Best, 1999). In many cases, there is no objective basis to the claim, but this does not mean that it is not understood by many as a valid statement about the world.
2. *Shaping a particular view of the problem.* Deviants can be defined in many different ways, and it matters greatly whether we see people as troubled or as troublesome (Gusfield, 1989). Generally, claims-makers not only want to convince us that certain people are a problem, they also want to convince us that they are problems of a particular type. "Problem drinking," for instance, can be constructed in many different ways (Holmes and Antell, 2001). We might see it as a sin, which

implies a religious problem. We might see it as a crime, which implies a legal problem. Or we might see it as a sickness, which implies a medical problem. In all cases the behaviour in question remains the same, and in all cases it is seen as deviant. What changes is the kind of deviant the problem drinker is understood to be. These differing constructions have very different implications for how we deal with the deviant person.

3. *Building consensus around the new moral category.* Claims-makers endeavour to build widespread agreement about the correctness of a particular moral vision (Heimer, 2002). This is accomplished by winning the support of the media, officialdom, and the general public (Hilgartner and Bosk, 1988). As consensus is built, dissenting views become relegated to the margins of legitimate discourse. It is precisely the establishment of consensus and the marginalization of dissenting views that give the deviant categories in our society their common-sense character.

### Who Are Claims-Makers?

The movement to "deviantize" (Schur, 1979) people and behaviour originates in the perceptions (however narrowly shared at the outset) that something is troubling and needs correction. Howard Becker (1963) coined the term *moral entrepreneur* to describe those who "discover" and attempt to publicize deviant conditions. Becker says that moral entrepreneurs are crusading reformers who are disturbed by some evil they see in the world and who will not rest until something is done to correct it.

In the early stages, definitions of deviance are often promoted by those who have some direct connection to the problem. In the case of drinking and driving, for instance, claims-making to heavily criminalize this conduct originated with victim groups such as MADD (Mothers Against Drunk Driving), whose members had a powerful emotional stake in the issue (Reinarman, 1996). In contrast, many of those involved in the construction of deviance have no vested interest in or emotional connection to the problem or the outcome. Lawmakers, journalists, daytime talk show hosts, and the producers of television drama often play a significant role in the promotion of particular designations of deviance (Altheide, 1997; Hilgartner and Bosk, 1988). However, their social distance from the issue is often greater that that of victims' groups, and for many of them, the construction of deviance is just another day at the office.

## What Are Claims?

When social constructionists speak of *claims*, they are talking about the actual message content that conveys a moral vision of deviance and non-deviance. What do claims-makers say, for example, in interviews on television talk shows, in pamphlets, in newspaper editorials, and on picket signs to convey the message that something or someone deserves the appellation of "deviant"? The study of claims is the study of rhetorical communication, since such communications—by design or in effect—persuade audiences.

Successful claims-making rhetoric can demonstrate the gravity of a problem in several ways, including these:

- *Using compelling statistics.* Statistics are often used to impress upon consumers of the media the size of a problem and that the problem is getting worse over time (Best, 2001; Gilbert, 1997). Statistical estimates of a problem's dimensions that suggest that a large problem is getting worse legitimate concern and provide compelling evidence of the urgency of a problem.
- *Linking an emergent concern to problems already on the public agenda.* In this way, familiar moral language can be used to provide ready reference points for the emergent problem. For instance, because addiction is well recognized as a problem in North America, new problems are often described as "addictions." We use the term *addiction* in a very liberal way and speak of, for instance, "pornography addicts," "gambling addicts," and "Internet addiction" (Butters and Erickson, 2000).
- *Using emotionally compelling examples to typify the seriousness and character of the threat posed by the behaviour* (see Bromley and Shupe, 1981). For example, the killings at Columbine High School in Colorado are often used in a rhetorical way to exemplify the problem of school violence even though such incidents are extremely rare and most school crime in no way resembles this incident (Fox and Levin, 2001).

## Deviance Ownership

Claims-making is not just about seeing particular types of people or behaviour as problems, it is also about seeing them as particular *kinds* of problems (Gusfield, 1989). What is at stake is the "ownership" of the problem: how a problem is framed determines who will be responsible for responding to or dealing with the problem (Sasson, 1995). If problem drinking is understood as a legal problem, we might expect the courts and police to do something about it. If it is understood as a religious problem, then we look to the clergy for solutions. If it is understood as a medical problem, we turn to doctors and psychiatrists.

One dominant trend in the way we think about deviance solutions concerns *medicalization* (Conrad and Schneider, 1980; Green, 2000). Increasingly, we have come to think about a very wide range of behaviours as forms of medical disorder that require treatment rather than punishment (Dworkin, 2001). More and more, it seems, we use the language of sickness, health, and disease when talking about conditions as diverse as violence, gambling, obesity, drug use, underachievement, and rampant consumerism. It can be argued that this shift suggests a more benign approach to deviants, since it implies that individuals are not to blame for their behaviour; the stigma associated with deviant conduct is therefore reduced (Appleton, 1995). At the same time, it can be argued that medicalization encourages us to ignore structural contexts when we think about various kinds of deviance. In other words, medical models imply that these problems occur because individuals get "sick" and not because social-structural conditions make some kinds of behaviour more likely.

## Deviance and Social Conflict

Moral differentiation suggests processes of social conflict. Disagreement exists in society regarding who or what should be seen as disreputable (Hier, 2002). These conflicts are evident in the battle over abortion, the movement to legalize marijuana, and efforts to control cigarette smoking. In other cases, the conflict is less evident only because effective claims-making has resulted in consensus.

While sociology makes available to us a large number of versions of **conflict theory**, two broad types can be distinguished: conservative and radical (Williams and McShane, 1994). These theories suggest different ways of understanding the wider social dynamic of the claims-making process.

From the perspective of conservative conflict theory, social conflicts regarding the moral meaning of conduct emerge from diverse sources (Turk, 1976; Vold, 1958). As members of various ethnic, religious, professional, lifestyle, or cultural groups seek to pursue their social interests, they may come into conflict with other groups over scarce resources. In the context of such models, **power** is seen as relatively diffuse and thus not concentrated in any one sector of the society (Gusfield, 1963). Instead, various **status groups** come into conflict, often over specific issues.

From this perspective, the study of moral differentiation is the study of how some groups in society are able to influence systems of social control so as to allow them to compete more effectively in their struggle to achieve their goals.

There may be many ways in which the creation of new categories of deviance may facilitate the pursuit of social goals. Social control bureaucracies may find that the resources made available to them become more plentiful when they can identify new forms of danger that require control (Becker, 1963; Jenkins, 1994). Alternatively, new or struggling medical specialties can find their social status enhanced if the members of a society become convinced they are indispensable to the solution of some pressing social problem (Pfohl, 1977).

Often the struggle to define deviance reflects a much more evident cultural difference regarding what is or what is not moral. Contemporary debates over abortion, for instance, can be seen as debates about who will, in the end, get to call whom a "deviant." In a similar way, those whose cultural or religious beliefs lead them to oppose a movement for gay rights may think of gay people as deviants. At the same time, gays and lesbians (and others in society) may think of those who actively (or even violently) oppose the movement for gay rights as suffering from a psychological malady known as *homophobia*. Both examples suggest status struggles over whose moral vision shall prevail and, conversely, over who shall be thought of as deviant.

Deviance has both objective and subjective dimensions. It is one thing to ask why people smoke marijuana, another to ask why doing so is considered deviant. (CP/Phill Snel)

In contrast, radical conflict theory draws on the Marxian understanding of society (Spitzer, 1975). Thus, it views the economic organization of society as the key to understanding moral stratification. From this point of view, the **social construction** of deviance must be understood as reflecting the economic realities of capitalism and the class exploitation capitalism engenders.

It is important to note that, from a Marxian position, the internal logic of capitalism gives deviance both its objective and its subjective character. For example, capitalism requires a large pool of labour that can be exploited by keeping wages low. But this means there will always be more workers than jobs and that some people will of necessity be marginalized. These marginalized populations will have little stake in the system and will be at greater risk of criminal involvement and of being labelled as criminal.

## The Sociology of Deviant Stigma

A third key area of study in the sociology of deviance concerns how "deviants" are stigmatized and how stigma is managed (see, for example, Table 5.3). This body of research and theory focuses our attention on the social interaction between those who exercise social control and those who are thought of in society as disreputable. In this respect, questions about the application and consequences of deviant stigma tend to be more micro- than macrosociological.

### The Process of Labelling

People are seen as deviant because of what others believe they have done or what others believe them to be. The labels of "deviant" that are assigned to people are not benign. Rather, they are charged with a great deal of emotion. Such labels sort through the thousands of acts in which a person has engaged and indicate that the person's identity is best understood in terms of the act according to which the label is affixed (Erikson, 1966).

The assignment of stigma suggests what sociologists refer to as a **master status**. This means that the label of deviant overrides all other status considerations (Becker, 1963). To be known as a murderer, for example, is to possess a status characteristic that trumps any other status characteristics the person might have. Whatever else one might be (bright, interesting, poor, blond, left-handed), one is a murderer first.

## Table 5.3   **Types of Deviant Behaviour**

Howard Becker (1963) suggested that once we recognize that deviant stigma is separable from the deviant act, it is possible to recognize at least four types of deviants. These types are created by the contrast between what people actually do (breaking rules or keeping them) and what they are perceived as (deviant or not deviant).

|  |  | Behaviour | |
|  |  | Obedient | Rule-Breaking |
|---|---|---|---|
| Perception | Perceived as deviant | Falsely accused | Pure deviant |
|  | Not perceived as deviant | Conforming | Secret deviant |

Sociologists use the term **status degradation ceremony** to refer to the rituals during which the status of "deviant" is conferred (Garfinkel, 1956). These ceremonies, like other public ceremonies such as marriage or graduation, publicly and officially acknowledge a shift in social roles and the emergence of a new identity. Status degradation ceremonies, including incompetency hearings, psychiatric examinations, and courtroom trials, mark the movement from one social position to another as the individual at the centre of the ritual is officially declared deviant. While we have designed ceremonies to move people into the status of "deviant," we don't have comparable ceremonies to move them out of these statuses and back to "normality."

### Resistance to Labelling

Of course, many people do not submit willingly to the imposition of labels of deviance. The ability of some in society to confer the status of "deviant" on others reflects differentials in social power. When people have access to power resources, they are able to negotiate more effectively the status of "deviant" (Pfuhl and Henry, 1993). A high-priced legal team (like the O.J. Simpson "dream team") can effectively counter efforts by the state to impose the status of "deviant." Plea-bargain negotiations, as the name implies, suggest straightforward attempts to negotiate moral status.

People might use a range of other strategies to avoid or negotiate a label of deviance. One obvious method involves efforts to undermine social control efforts through evasion. Such statuses are negotiated most effectively, perhaps, by avoiding their assignment in the first place. "Successful" deviants learn to engage in prohibited conduct in ways that decrease the likelihood of getting caught (Becker, 1963).

Individuals also try to avoid or negotiate stigma through what Goffman (1959) calls *performance*. Many of us are quite explicitly aware of the dramatic roles we might perform if we are stopped by the police officer who suspects we have been speeding; the performance is intended to neutralize the efforts of the police to impose a deviant designation (Piliavin and Briar, 1964). Under some conditions, people use what are called *disclaimer mannerisms*. These are actions intended to signal to agents of social control that they are not the appropriate targets of deviant attribution.

### Deviant Careers and Deviant Identities

One important potential consequence of the labelling process is what is known as *deviancy amplification*: the ironic situation in which the attempt to control deviance makes deviance more likely (Lemert, 1951; Tannenbaum, 1938).

Efforts to describe how labelling processes result in more rather than less deviance usually distinguish between primary and secondary deviance (Lemert, 1951; McLorg and Taub, 1987). From time to time we all engage in *primary deviance*, and this has no real consequence for how we see ourselves or how other people see us. For instance, all of us might occasionally lie, cheat, drink too much, or engage in some other prohibited behaviour. *Secondary deviance*, in contrast, is marked by a life organized around the facts of deviance. Secondary deviance suggests emergence in a deviant role rather than ephemeral acts of deviance. It is one thing to steal on occasion; it is quite another to be a thief. While all of us might tell an occasional lie, most of us do not think of ourselves or are thought of by others as liars.

Some researchers have asked what turns primary deviance into secondary deviance. The answer is societal reaction. How agents of social control respond to

**5.3**

# Sociology in Action
## Disclaimer Mannerisms in University Examinations

Sociologists Daniel Albas and Cheryl Albas (1993) undertook a study of how students attempt to distance themselves from charges of academic dishonesty while writing examinations. Data of several sorts were collected, including interviews with students and observations of students writing exams. The authors note that people writing examinations are at high risk of stigmatization. Invigilators patrol the rooms on the lookout for suspicious behaviour. Too often, neither the professor (who may or may not be at the exam) nor graduate assistants have any direct knowledge of the individuals writing the exam. For these reasons, students take many steps to ensure that they will not be falsely accused of cheating.

The authors were able to define two major types of strategies: actions that students take and actions that they attempt to avoid taking.

Actions taken include the following:

- *Picayune overconformity with regulations.* This involves the demonstration of conformity with even the most minor examination rules. Students are careful, for instance, to hand in their papers before gathering up their possessions to leave. In this way, there can be no suspicion that anything untoward is occurring. A student who needs to blow his or her nose will be sure to wave the tissue around first so it is clear that it is nothing other than a tissue.

- *The expression of repression of creature releases.* Creature releases are those aspects of the self that steal through the facade of social control, including sneezes and yawns. A student who needs to use the bathroom during the exam might make very exaggerated gestures to impress upon invigilators the urgency of the situation.

- *Shows of innocence.* Students know, for instance, that a lack of activity might be read as indicative of a lack of preparation. So when they are not writing, they might be underlining or circling words or phrases on the exam sheet.

Actions avoided include these:

- *Control of eyes.* Students know that they are not supposed to have roving eyes, so they are careful where they look. One preferred strategy is to stare at the ceiling or the head of the person behind whom the student is sitting.

- *Control of notes.* Students might frisk themselves before they enter the exam room to ensure that they are not carrying anything with them that could get them into trouble.

- *Morality of place.* Students worry that where they sit can send a message about their trustworthiness. A student might be careful, therefore, not to sit next to a very good student or someone whom they believe is perceived as a potential cheater.

initial acts of deviance—through stereotypes, rejection, the degradation of status—can actually make future deviance more rather than less likely (Tannenbaum, 1938).

One of the key intervening mechanisms in this process, it is argued, is the transformation of the self. Consistent with social psychological theories (such as the one advanced by Charles Horton Cooley, 1902) of how the self emerges and is maintained, labelling theorists have argued that individuals who are consistently stigmatized may come to accept others' definition of their deviant identity. To the extent that indi-

viduals increasingly come to see themselves as others see them, they may become much more likely to behave in ways consistent with the label of "deviant." In a sense, individuals become committed to a life of deviance largely because others have expected them to. Deviance becomes a self-fulfilling prophecy (Tannenbaum, 1938).

## Conclusion

Our experience with deviance reflects the influence of the cultural context and the historical period in which we live. As times change, so do the categories of people and behaviour society finds troublesome. While gay and lesbian lifestyles were once viewed as highly deviant, today they are seen as less so. While drunk driving, wife assault, and cigarette smoking were once regarded as normal, they are now viewed as highly deviant. Deviance is thus a dynamic process, and the future will present further permutations and innovations. By way of example, we need only think about the large number of newly constructed forms of deviance that we already associate with computer usage, such as cyberporn, cyberstalking, and Internet addiction.

In the most general terms, the sociology of deviance is concerned with the study of the relationships between people who think, act, or appear in disvalued ways and those who seek to control them (Sacco, 1992). It seeks to understand the origins, the character, the consequences, and the broader social contexts of these relationships.

Deviance can be thought of as having two dimensions: the objective and the subjective. The objective aspect is the behaviour, condition, or cognitive style itself. The subjective aspect is the collective understanding of the behaviour, condition, or cognitive style as disreputable. A comprehensive sociology of deviance needs to consider both dimensions. Thus, we want to know why some people rather than others act in ways the society forbids, but we also want to know why some ways of acting rather than others are forbidden.

Correspondingly, it is possible to identify three major types of questions around which theory and research in the sociology of deviance are organized. First, how do we understand the social and cultural factors that make prohibited behaviour possible? Strain theory argues that people engage in deviant behaviour because it is often a form of problem-solving; cultural support theories focus on how people acquire definitions of deviant conduct that are supportive of such behaviour; control theories maintain that deviance results when the factors that would check or contain it are absent.

Second, what is and is not viewed as disreputable is not obvious, and we need to explain the prevailing system of moral stratification. Definitions of deviance emerge from a process of claims-making. The establishment of consensus around such definitions gives categories of deviance such a taken-for-granted quality.

## □ Questions for Critical Thought

1. What images of crime and deviance dominate coverage in the local media in your community? What sorts of images do they create of troubled and troublesome people?

2. Why do people cheat on university examinations? How might this question be answered by proponents of strain, cultural support, and control theories?

3. In your view, why are young males so much more likely than other groups in society to engage in a wide range of behaviours that many in society find troublesome?

4. What evidence do you see in your own social environment of the disvalued character of cigarette smoking and smokers?

5. Aside from the examples given in the text, can you suggest behaviours or conditions that have undergone a shift in moral status in the last few years? How would you account for these changes?

6. How might Marxian and Weberian conflict theorists differ in their interpretations of the legal and moral battle in our society regarding the use of "soft" illegal drugs, such as marijuana?

7. How might you explain to an interested layperson the difference between how sociologists and journalists view deviance?

8. In your opinion, does it make sense to speak of something called "positive deviance"? Why or why not?

## ☐ Recommended Readings

**Joel Best and David Luckenbill,** *Organizing Deviance* **(Englewood Cliffs, NJ: Prentice-Hall, 1982).**

> This book offers a systematic treatment of how deviance is organized. The authors discuss both the organization of deviants and the organization of deviant transactions.

**Deborah Brock,** *Making Work, Making Trouble: Prostitution as a Social Problem* **(Toronto: University of Toronto Press, 1998).**

> This study provides a comprehensive treatment of the social problem of prostitution in Canada. The author's analysis illustrates the value of a constructionist approach to the study of specific forms of social deviance.

**Barry Glassner,** *The Culture of Fear: Why Americans Are Afraid of the Wrong Things* **(New York: Basic Books, 1999).**

> An informed and highly readable discussion of why people fear what they fear. The author demonstrates a disjunction between the harms we perceive and the harms our social environments actually present to us.

**Erving Goffman,** *Stigma: Notes on the Management of Spoiled Identity* **(Englewood Cliffs, NJ: Prentice-Hall, 1963).**

> This is the classic discussion of how people who are defined as "deviants" by the society in which they live manage stigma. The book was formative in the development of the sociology of labels of deviance.

## ☐ Recommended Web Sites

**Canadian Sociology and Anthropology Association**
**http://www.csaa.ca/**

> This Web site contains the rules, regulations, and principles relating to the ethics of professional sociological research.

**Crimetheory.com**
**http://crimetheory.com**

> This site provides a comprehensive discussion of deviance and crime theory for educational and research purposes.

**Prostitution Issues**
**www.bayswan.org/student.html**

> This "student-friendly" page offers educational materials regarding prostitution. Of particular interest are the documents that redefine the moral character of such behaviour.

**Society for the Study of Social Problems**
**http://www.sssp1.org/**

> This is the main page for the Society for the Study of Social Problems (SSSP). The journal of this society, *Social Problems*, has played an important role in the development of the sociology of deviance.

# 6

Julie Ann McMullin

# Class and Status Inequality

© W.P. Wittman Limited

## ☐ Learning Objectives

In this chapter, you will:

- examine Marxist and Weberian conceptualizations of social class
- learn about the feminist critique of social class
- explore the relationship between social class and inequality in paid work, education, and health
- come to understand why class matters

# Introduction

In 1996, Kimberly Rogers left an abusive relationship in Toronto and returned to her home town, Sudbury, but she could not find work and applied for social assistance. In the fall of 1996, she registered in the correctional services workers program at Cambrian College. She later changed programs and continued her studies in the social services program, from which she graduated near the top of her class in the spring of 2000. By all accounts, she was a model student. To pay for her education, Rogers received student loans while receiving benefits under the general welfare program. This violated Ontario provincial law because the general welfare program does not permit recipients to receive student loans, nor does the Ontario Student Assistance Program (OSAP) permit its recipients to receive welfare.

In November 1999, OSAP uncovered the fact that Rogers had been receiving both OSAP loans and general welfare, and suspended her loan for the remainder of the academic year. She had to rely on two small grants obtained through the college to pay her tuition and books, and on charity for food. Because of her actions, she was also unable to benefit from the OSAP loan-forgiveness program and would have to repay the loan in its entirety (approximately $30,000) upon graduation. Ontario Works also began an investigation into her actions and, in September 2000, she was charged with welfare fraud.

In April 2001, Rogers pled guilty to the fraud charge. The judge sentenced her to six months' house arrest and required her to pay restitution to welfare for the amount of benefits she received while she was in college, approximately $13,000. Because of her conviction for welfare fraud, she was automatically suspended from receiving social assistance for a period of three months. A new regulation, which came into force on 1 April 2000, required that persons convicted of welfare fraud committed prior to 1 April 2000 be suspended for a three- or six-month period, and that persons convicted of welfare fraud committed after 1 April 2000 be subject to a lifetime ban.

Rogers was required to stay in her apartment at all times, except for attending medical and religious appointments and for a three-hour period on Wednesday mornings, during which time she could run errands and buy groceries. But she had no money to buy the necessities of life. Even after her lawyers succeeded in having the court lift the ban on her benefits, her monthly benefits were reduced to collect a portion of the amount owing under the restitution order. After rent was taken into account, she was left with about $18 per month to buy food.

On 9 August 2001, while under house arrest, Kimberly Rogers died. She was eight months pregnant. Sudbury was suffering through a second week of temperatures over 30 degrees Celsius and Rogers's top-floor apartment in an old house lacked air conditioning. Responding to her death, Rogers's lawyer stated that "she would have been better off if she had committed a violent crime and been sent to prison. . . . If sentenced to jail, she would have had the necessities of life, she would have had access to medications. If something had happened to her, it wouldn't have been two days before her body was found" (MacKinnon and Lacey, 2001: F1).

On 20 December 2002, after a three-month coroner's inquest, a coroner's jury determined that Rogers had committed suicide. The jury heard testimony from an expert witness in suicidology, who explained that the suspension from benefits, the house arrest, the effects of a criminal conviction—which would effectively act as a bar from employment in the social work field—had acted as a crushing weight on Rogers's spirit and played a decisive role in the decision to take her own life. At the conclusion of the inquest, the jury issued 14 recommendations, which it felt would prevent future deaths in similar circumstances. The recommendations included that the government remove the three-month, six-month, and lifetime bans for conviction of welfare fraud from the legislation and that it increase welfare rates to reflect the actual costs of shelter and basic needs. The government's response was a flat refusal (Income Security Advocacy Centre).

Activist groups use Kimberly Rogers's death as political leverage in their fight against poverty and inequality. These groups blame the policies of an ultra-conservative Ontario government for her death. Indeed, the election of Mike Harris and his neo-conservative government in 1995 led to a 21.6 per cent cut to welfare benefits, a radical dismantling of welfare services, the institution of the Ontario Works Act and the workfare program, massive cuts to social spending, and the deregulation of labour and other markets (Walkom, 1997). These social policy changes triggered massive protests. For instance, the Ontario Federation of Labour (OFL) sponsored Days of Action in most of Ontario's major cities, with participants from women's groups, unions, anti-poverty groups, and others (Munro, 1997). These were political strikes in which workers stayed "away from their jobs not to make a point during negotiations in their own workplaces or for their own contracts, but for the express purpose of making a point with an elected government" (Munro, 1997: 129). Clearly, this was not a government for the working-class people or those who were otherwise disadvantaged. As Kimberly Rogers's experiences demonstrate, this was a government whose policies helped the rich get richer and the poor get poorer.

Social class, a structural pillar of inequality in Canadian society, influenced Rogers's opportunities and experiences from the moment of her birth. It is not unusual, for instance, for people from working-class backgrounds to finish their education at the end of high school and to work at jobs such as bartending, as Rogers did; their opportunities for anything else are often severely restricted. That Rogers needed to rely on social assistance in the first place is also linked to her social class background.

The first part of this chapter deals with various conceptualizations of social class. The second part then considers the ways in which social class has been measured in the sociological literature and puts forth a working definition of *social class*. We will also examine the relationship between social class and social inequality. Although many of the topics just listed touch on issues of inequality, it is well beyond the scope of this chapter to discuss all of them. Instead, the focus will be on paid work, education, and health. Finally, we will conclude by briefly considering an ongoing debate in sociology: Does class matter?

# What Is Social Class?

First-year sociology students are often perplexed when they discover that they are not members of the middle class, as they had been led to believe, even though their family income was sufficient to afford them with the necessities of life and a university education. Unlike lay conceptions of social class that focus on income, sociologists define social class in relation to the paid work that people do. The general idea that people can be members of the working class without being aware that they are is a situation sometimes referred to as **false consciousness**. Members of the working class who are living in a state of false consciousness have not developed a revolutionary, collective sense of their plight in a capitalist world (Hunter, 1981: 47–8).

Debates about how best to conceptualize social class stem from the sociological traditions of Karl Marx and Max Weber, both of whom might arguably be considered **conflict theorists**. The next sections consider these debates and outline the key themes that emerge from conflict and feminist accounts of social class.

## Themes from Conflict Approaches to Social Class

Many of the debates about how to conceptualize social class stem from the work of Karl Marx and the subsequent critiques and elaborations of his views. Interestingly, although Marx discussed social class at length in his work, nowhere in his writings did he provide us with a succinct definition of what he meant by *social class*. Instead, scholars have had to piece together what they think he meant from the various contexts in which Marx uses the concept. A now-famous quotation from *The Communist Manifesto* is often used in such assessments. Marx and Friedrich Engels wrote:

> The history of all hitherto existing society is the history of class struggles. Freeman and slave, patrician and plebeian, lord and serf, guildmaster and journeyman, in a word, oppressor and oppressed. . . . Our epoch, the epoch of the bourgeoisie, possesses, however, this distinctive feature: It has simplified class antagonisms. Society as a whole is more and more splitting up into two great hostile camps, into two great classes directly facing each other—bourgeoisie and proletariat. ([1848] 1983: 203–4)

In these few lines, Marx emphasizes two issues that are central to his work on social class: first, he argues that society is characterized more by conflict than by harmony; second, he suggests that a distinctive feature of **capitalism** is the segregation of society into two central classes.

Few conflict theorists would disagree with Marx's view that society is characterized more by conflict than by harmony. Since the onset of industrial capitalism, workers and owners have fought over working conditions, pay, benefits, required hours of work, and so on (MacDowell and Radforth, 1992; Morton, 1998). Today, struggles continue over job security within the context of globalized economies and the rights of workers in developing countries.

The point on which scholars disagree is whether Marx's dichotomous conception of class is—or ever was—accurate. Some argue that these two basic class divisions still exist (Braverman, 1974), while others suggest that Marx's two-class conceptualization needs elaboration (Wright, 1997). Still others argue that

Marx's two categories represented a theoretical abstraction and that he was well aware of the presence of middling classes and of the historical complexities of class formation (Giddens, 1971). Although such debates are interesting, they are complex and, as yet, unresolved. Hence, rather than delving into debates about how many classes there currently are in Canada, it is more fruitful to discuss the themes central to Marxist conceptualizations of social class.

First, Marx and Marxists argue that class is a social relation. Marx believed that society is divided into social classes that are defined by their relationship to the principal **means of production** in society (Giddens, 1971; Zeitlin, 1990). *Relations of production* refers to the idea that individuals who engage in production processes have various rights and powers over the resources used in production processes (see Wright, 1999). Under capitalism, those who own the

means of the production (the **bourgeoisie**) exploit labourers (the **proletariat**), who have little choice but to sell their **labour power** to the bourgeoisie in order to survive. For Marx, class is not an economic relation but a social one. Hence, unequal access to the rights and powers associated with productive resources are class relations (Wright, 1999).

A second feature of Marxist accounts of class relations concerns who controls production processes (Poulantzas, 1975; Wright, 1997). *Control* refers to a specific form of authority. **Authority**, in turn, is connected to issues of **power**. More will be said on power as we move into a discussion of Weberian accounts of social class. For now, it is important to note that class relations reflect the amount of control that people have, over themselves and others, in doing the work that they do to achieve their means of subsistence. In other words, class relations reflect the rel-

Much inequality theory, from Marx to Weber, discusses the proletariat, or working class, but few people realize the devastating and long-lasting effects of such labour ghettoization. This working-class residence, close to Nova Scotia's defunct Sydney Steel Mill, captures the devastation. (CP/Andrew Vaughan)

ative amount of control that a person has over production processes.

Third, Marxists generally agree that **exploitation** is a central component of social class relations. According to Eric Olin Wright, class-based exploitation occurs if the following criteria are met:

1. *The inverse interdependence principle.* The material welfare of one group of people causally depends on the material deprivations of another.
2. *The exclusion principle.* The inverse interdependence in (1) depends on the exclusion of the exploited from access to certain productive resources, usually backed by property rights.
3. *The appropriation principle.* Exclusion generates material advantage to exploiters because it enables them to appropriate the labour effort of the exploited. (Wright, 1997: 10)

If the first of these two conditions are met, "non-exploitative economic oppression" (Wright, 1999: 11) occurs, but it is not technically a situation of class exploitation as such. Exploitation exists only when all three principles are operating simultaneously.

Note the relational component in each of these principles. Explicit in these statements is the idea that class exploitation involves **social interaction**. This interaction is structured by sets of productive social relations bind exploiters to the exploited (Wright, 1997). Class exploitation also highlights the presence of inherent conflict in class relations. Put simply, in a profit-driven capitalist system, owners want their workers to work longer and harder than the workers would freely choose to do. Hence, class conflict results, not simply over wage levels, but also over how much "work effort" is expected (Wright, 1997: 18).

In summary, Marxist accounts of social class focus on the relationships between those who appropriate the labour of others to make a profit and those who need to sell their labour power. Furthermore, class relations may be assessed through the concepts of exploitation and control. As we have noted, control is related to power. Hence, one similarity between Marxist and Weberian scholarship, as we shall see, is that both schools agree that power is a central dimension of class relations. Weberians, however, have a somewhat different understanding of power than do Marxists, and Weberians focus more on distribution than on exploitation in their assessment of social class.

For Weber, classes are groups of people who share a common class situation. In *Economy and Society*, Weber defines *class situation* as the:

typical chances of material provision, external position, and personal destiny in life which depend on the degree and nature of the power, or lack of power, to dispose of goods or qualifications for employment and the ways in which, within a given economic order, such goods or qualifications for employment can be utilised as a source of income or revenue. ([1908] 1978: 57)

For Weber, class situations are market situations, and "a class is simply an aggregate of people sharing common 'situations' in the market" (Grabb, 2002: 51–2).

Weber further argues that there are three types of classes: property classes, income classes, and social classes. A *property class* is one in which differences in property ownership determine class situations. An *income class* is one in which "the chances of utilising goods or services on the market determines the class situation" (Weber, [1908] 1978: 57). A *social class* is a combination of the class situations created by property and income, whereby mobility between the social classes is a typical occurrence within either an individual lifetime or over successive generations.

Weber identified four main social classes: (1) the working class as a whole; (2) the petite bourgeoisie; (3) propertyless intellectuals, technicians, commercial workers, and officials who may be socially different from one another depending on the cost of their training; and (4) classes privileged because of property or education. Although these social class distinctions are similar to those put forth by Marx (except with regard to the emphasis on education and the cost of training), Weber employs a different method in assigning groups of individuals to each class. For Weber, the emphasis is on the distribution of resources, whereas Marx is mainly concerned with the social relations of production.

Parties and status groups are other pillars of social power according to Weber. By **parties**, Weber means voluntary associations that organize for the collective pursuit of interests, such as political parties or lobbying groups. **Status** reflects an individual's position in society according to the relative prestige, esteem, or honour they are afforded (Clark, 1995; Turner, 1988). Samuel Clark (1995) argues that status varies along four dimensions: differentiation, criteria, ascription, and institutionalization. The meanings of these variables are summarized in Table 6.1.

Notably, Clark argues that status is a form of power—the "power to elicit respect" (Clark, 1995:

15). A **status group** comprises a number of individuals who share a common status situation. Status groups "are organized to maintain or expand their social privileges by a mechanism of social closure to protect existing monopolies of the privilege against outsiders, and by usurpation to expand the benefits by reference to proximate or superior status groups" (Turner, 1988: 8). Thus, although members of a particular class may not be aware of their common situation, members of a status group usually are (Giddens, 1971; Grabb, 2002). And although classes, status groups, and parties sometimes overlap, this is not always the case. In Weberian scholarship, each is analytically distinct and central to class analysis (Weber, [1908] 1978; see also Giddens, 1971; Grabb, 2002).

Weber's assessment of status groups and parties and the analytical importance that he attaches to these multiple bases of power point to the fundamental difference between his analysis of class and that of Marx. According to Weber, although status groups and parties are analytically distinct from classes, they are central to class analysis (Giddens, 1971; Grabb, 2002). For Weber ([1908] 1978), *status situations* are distinct but related to class situations; this term refers to the social status, prestige, and esteem that are associated with a social position. Unlike Marx, who believed that power is held by those who own the means of production, Weber felt that certain people in high-status groups derive power by virtue of their social position rather than through economic control.

The analytical importance that Weber attaches to the concept of power is evident in the preceding discussion. Unlike Marx, who believed that power relations are structural and cannot be separated from class relations, Weber defines **power** as "every possibility within a social relationship of imposing one's own will, even against opposition, without regard to the basis of this possibility" ([1908] 1978: 38).

He goes on to clarify this broad definition of *power* by introducing the concept of *domination*. Domination exists in social relationships in which one actor (or group of actors) comes to expect that his or her orders will be followed by others or a group of others (Weber, [1908] 1978). *Domination* is a specific power relation in which "regular patterns of inequality are established whereby the subordinate group (or individual) accepts that position in a sustained arrangement, obeying the commands of the dominant group (or individual)" (Grabb, 2002: 60). Weber states that although relations of domination are usually at work within associations or in cases in which an individual has an executive staff, other non-economic situations are also characteristic of relations of domination. One of the examples Weber mentions in this regard is that the head of the household exercises domination over the members of the household "even though he does not have an executive staff" ([1908] 1978: 39).

Three themes emerge from Weber's conceptualization of class that separate his work from that of Marx. The first is Weber's insistence that classes, class situations, parties, and status groups must all be considered if we are to understand the class structures of societies. The second is Weber's emphasis on and view of power. Marx felt that power was derived from an economic base and was largely structural. Weber, on the other hand, saw power as a multi-faceted concept that could be derived from many sources and has both structural and individual dimensions. Finally, unlike the social-relational approach to class in Marxist sociology, Weber focuses far more on distributional issues. For Weber, the ability of people to gain

**Table 6.1  Samuel Clark's Status Variables**

| | |
|---|---|
| Differentiation | The extent to which status is differentiated from other kinds of power, especially economic, cultural, political, and military power. |
| Criteria | What characteristics or possessions are accorded status (for example, wealth, erudition, military valour, athletic ability). |
| Ascription | Whether status is ascribed hereditarily. |
| Institutionalization | The extent to which stable norms and values regulate the distribution of status and the rights and duties associated with it. |

SOURCE: Samuel Clark, *State and Status: The Rise of the State and Aristocratic Power in Western Europe* (Montreal and Kingston: McGill-Queen's University Press, 1995), 17. Reprinted by permission.

access to scarce resources such as income and education is central to class analysis.

Drawing on Weberian scholarship, Canadian sociologist Edward Grabb's work on social inequality and social class is worth considering. According to Grabb, power is the "differential capacity to command resources, which gives rise to structured asymmetric relations of domination and subordination among social actors" (2002: 224–5). In an elaborate scheme of power, domination, and social inequality, Grabb suggests that three means of power—control of material resources, control of people, and control of ideas—correspond, respectively, primarily with economic structures, political structures, and ideological structures (see Figure 6.1). These structures of power are crossed by class and non-class bases of inequality that represent the "human content" of power relations.

Grabb defines *class* on the basis of ownership, education, and occupation. For Grabb, these factors represent a synthesis of the key concepts in class analysis. *Ownership* includes ownership of property but also material possessions and income. *Education* comprises credentials and knowledge. *Occupation* includes distinctions such as manual versus non-manual labour,

but also includes issues of skill. Grabb further suggests that, although classes should not be considered in static terms because they vary over time and space (that is, historically and in different regions and countries), there tend to be three main class categories in modern capitalist systems: an upper class, a heterogeneous central category, and a working class. Grabb defines the *working class* as those who do not own capital, who have no special skills or credentials, and who sell their labour to make a living. The *upper class* is made up mostly of capital owners, although individuals with significant political or ideological power fall into this category as well. The *middle class* is a diverse group that may or may not have limited ownership but that is mostly distinguishable from the working class on the basis of credentials.

According to Grabb, the means of power (economic, political, and ideological) are differentially distributed along class lines. Of course, people in the upper classes control the means of material production or the economic structure by virtue of their ownership of the means of production. Middle classes may have some economic power depending on whether their incomes are sufficient to purchase

Figure 6.1 **Edward Grabb's Theoretical Framework on Social Inequality**

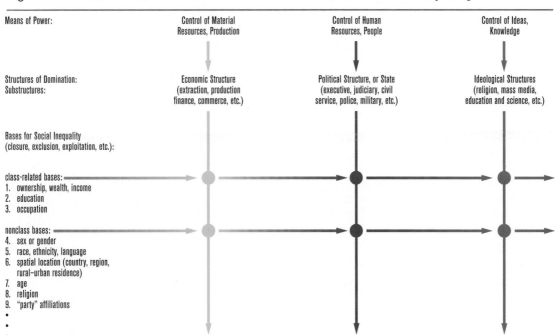

SOURCE: 'The Major Means of Power, Structures of Domination, and Bases for Social Inequality' from *Theories of Social Inequality*, Fourth Edition, by Edward Grabb. © 2002. Reprinted with permission of Nelson, a division of Thomson Learning: www.thomsonrights.com. Fax 800-730-2215.

desirable consumer goods and to the extent that their occupations confer a certain amount of authority or autonomy. And working classes tend not to have economic power at all. In Grabb's scheme, class also crosses political and ideological structures of power. Hence, those in the upper class, by virtue of their capital, high levels of education, and good occupations, tend to control political and ideological institutions such as the judiciary and educational systems. Those in the working class tend not to have ideological or political power, and those in the middle vary in the extent to which they hold such power, again on the basis of class-related factors.

Grabb's work holds a great deal of appeal to those who assume that Marxist conceptions of social class do not go far enough in explaining social inequality and that social inequality is, instead, a multi-faceted phenomenon. Why? Because the central focus in his framework is on power, not class. The inherent problem with theories of inequality that begin with issues of class is that other bases of inequality, such as gender, race, ethnicity, and age, carry less theoretical significance. Indeed, **feminist** scholarship has been critical of the literature on social class for this reason.

### Feminist Approaches to Social Class

Many theorists have worked to perfect the concept of social class. Researchers strive for a specific delineation of social class that corrects what they see as limitations in the classical work. But except among feminist sociologists and a few others (for example, Carroll, 1987; Cuneo, 1985), the exclusion of women and gender from class analysis has not traditionally been considered a theoretical limitation. Rather, if the social class of women is mentioned at all, it has been assessed using categories of analysis established to study men (Fox, 1989). Unwaged wives are assumed to take on their husband's social class, whereas women involved in the paid labour force are classed like men in what is assumed to be a gender-neutral class system (Acker, 1980, 1988, 1990; Fox, 1989).

Indeed, gender relations are intertwined with class relations in modern industrial capitalism. Particularly telling are the following research findings. (1) Housework and child care, which women are primarily responsible for, are important productive activities for capitalist production (Fox, ed., 1980). Hence, "ignoring gender relations in general, and household labour in particular, produces distorted analyses of 'the economy'" (Fox, 1989: 123). (2) Women are seg-

regated into low-paying jobs both across and within broad occupational classifications (Bielby and Baron, 1984; Fox and Fox, 1986, 1987). (3) This segregation cannot be explained by status-attainment variables (England, 1982; England et al., 1988). (4) The relations between men and women at work are often antagonistic (Cockburn, 1983; Milkman, 1987). And (5) the responsibilities that women have to their families are inextricably bound to their work lives: wives are more likely than husbands to work at home or to take time off of work to care for a sick child (Hochschild and Machung, 1989; Michelson, 1983), and their wages are influenced by the amount of time they spend engaged in household labour (Coverman, 1983; Shelton and Firestone, 1989).

Although this research demonstrates the prevalence of gender inequality within capitalism, feminists disagree over how these findings should be interpreted. Specifically, there is a theoretical debate among feminists over whether **patriarchy** (male dominance) and capitalism are two systems of oppression that serve to subordinate women (this is called *dual-systems theory*) or women's oppression can be best understood by theorizing about a single system of inequality that simultaneously considers gender and social class relations. Patriarchy, an essential concept in dual-systems theories (see Hartmann, 1981), is at the heart of the feminist debates over the appropriateness of single- and dual-systems approaches.

*Patriarchy* refers to "the system of practices, arrangements and social relations that ensure biological reproduction, child rearing, and the reproduction of gendered subjectivity" (Fox, 1988: 175). The term *patriarchy* has served a useful purpose in feminist theory because it gave women (although arguably only white, middle-class women) a political voice and also because it corrected some of the flaws of omission that were prevalent in social theory before the 1970s (that is, women were generally invisible; Acker, 1989). However, the concept of patriarchy is limiting in several respects.

Radical feminists conceptualize patriarchy as a "universal, trans-historical and trans-cultural phenomenon; women were everywhere oppressed by men in more or less the same ways" (Acker, 1989: 235). The tendency in this view is to reduce male oppression of women to biological essentialism, and it is limiting because it does not consider historical or contemporary variations in women's situations (Acker, 1989). In light of these problems, dual-systems theorists sought to describe a system of patriarchy linked to household production. The tendency in this approach was to view patriarchy as a system of domination that operates alongside and interacts with the political-economic system. The roots of patriarchy are thought to be located within the reproductive sphere of the family, whereas the roots of the political-economic system are located in the **mode of production** (Acker, 1989; Fox, 1989). Thus, although surprising given its Marxist roots, this perspective considers gender in a more Weberian manner, as one of several sources of inequality.

Recognizing these problems, some feminists have argued against using the concept of patriarchy (Acker, 1989; Fox, 1988). These researchers argue for a single-system approach whereby the oppression of women cannot be separated from issues of social class. This requires a reconceptualization of social class that adequately considers gendered processes as they structure the class system (Acker, 1988, 1990; Fox, 1989).

Taking issue with dual-systems theory, Joan Acker (1988), for instance, sets out to develop a single-system theory of social relations that places equal emphasis on gender and social class. According to Acker, this requires a reformulation of Marx's conception of class that is best done by taking the social relations of distribution as well as the social relations of production into account. Relations of distribution "are sequences of linked actions through which people share the necessities of survival" (Acker, 1988: 478). According to Acker, the fact that there has always been a sexual division of labour suggests that in all known societies, the relations of distribution are influenced by gender and take on a gendered meaning. Gendered relations of distribution in capitalist society are historically rooted and they are transformed (like the relations of production) as the means of production change.

Acker suggests that the wage, which is rooted in the relations of production, is the essential component of distribution in capitalist society. The wage has developed historically as a gendered phenomenon because women have always been paid less than men and because gendered job segregation is typical. Thus, "the wage and the work contexts within which it is earned are gendered in ways that re-create women's relative disadvantage" (Acker, 1988: 483).

Personal relations, marital relations, and state relations are the gendered processes through which distribution occurs. According to Acker, *personal relations of distribution* are held together by emotional bonds, usually between blood relatives, and depend on the wage. As a result of both the gender-based division of labour and the **ideology** of the family wage, gender organizes the personal relations of distribution. In its simplest form, this system requires that at least part of the male wage is distributed to women, who then redistribute it to the dependants in their families. The personal relations of distribution also often extend beyond the household. In instances where economic hardships are typical, women often maintain extensive kinship networks by means of which survival is ensured through the allocation of resources across households. Among the economically advantaged, gender-based personal relations of distribution also occur, helping to ensure the stability and reproduction of class.

*Marital relations* are the central component of distribution for married women who do not work for pay and thus depend on their husbands for their wage. According to Acker, unwaged housewives are connected to the production process through their husbands' wages. Although they share common standards of living with their husbands, they do not assume the same class because their situations, experiences, and activities are different. Unwaged wives have little control over their economic situation, although Acker suggests that this control likely varies by the men's and women's class.

*State relations of distribution* are the final type of distribution arrangement that Acker considers. The state relations of distribution are based in laws and governmental policies that have historically been developed in gendered ways. Policies and laws, established to alleviate the financial burden of the working class when the market fails, are based on gendered ideologies supporting the "male breadwinner/dependent housewife" ideal. This renders some groups of women—those who remain unmarried, single mothers, poor working women—particularly disadvantaged. Women are further disadvantaged by the gendered nature of entitlement regulations because many social security programs are based on the labour-force experiences of men.

For Acker, the culmination of these gendered relations structures social class. Conceptualizing class in this way allows unwaged persons to be included in the class structure. According to Acker, the aim of class analysis should not be to classify people into different categories; rather, class should be considered as "processes that produce contradiction, conflict, and different life experiences" (Acker, 1988: 496). Thus, to understand fully the "links between gender and class, divisions must be changed. One way to do this is to see class as rooted in relations of distribution (as well as in relations of production) that necessarily embed gender, both as ideology and material inequality" (Acker, 1988: 496).

Acker (2000) expands her analysis to include race and ethnic relations. She first argues that to understand fully how class is gendered and racialized, a rethinking of class is necessary. This rethinking, according to Acker, should be informed by a concept of class "anchored within a larger notion of the economic than is now used" (2000: 54). This idea corresponds with Acker's promotion of a conceptualization of class whereby class relations encompass relations of distribution and production. Second, class, gender, race, and ethnicity must be understood from the standpoints of many different people within these categories (see Smith, 1987). In other words, the experiences of men and women of different classes and of different racial and ethnic groups need to inform class analysis. Third, class is not simply an abstraction into which people can be placed. Rather, it is an "active accomplishment" (Acker, 2000: 53). Everything that people do and say is influenced by their class relations. Class is accomplished by people in interaction with one another. And fourth, class, race and ethnicity, and gender mutually constitute one another. That is, through structural processes and through processes of cultural representation and social interaction, race and ethnicity, class, and gender shape one another; they cannot be considered separately. Identity and meaning are not shaped simply by whether one is a man or black or middle class, but by the interacting influence of all three of these things (see also Glenn, 2000).

To summarize, a central problem in much of the traditional class analysis—and the key point of the feminist critique of social class—is that the study of class has focused far too much on the relations of production (Acker, 1988, 2000). Feminist scholars argue that class relations are social relations that extend beyond the arena of production and that Marxist approaches conceptualizing social class simply as a relation of production are too restrictive. This is true, in part, because traditional class analysis excludes far too many people who are not directly linked to production processes, such as homemakers and retired individuals. Notably, scholars have tried to reconcile this problem by attributing the social class of husbands to homemakers and by assigning a class to retired persons based on their pre-retirement status. However, these approaches are unsatisfactory because they do not capture important distributive and status differences between a housewife and her husband or between a retired autoworker and her employed counterpart (see Acker, 1988; Estes, 1999).

With these caveats in mind, the remainder of this chapter will nonetheless focus on social class as it has been traditionally defined and conceptualized. The difficulties associated with rethinking social class in light of gender, race, ethnic, and age relations are far too complex for an introductory chapter on social class and inequality. Readers should refer to the chapters on gender, ethnicity, and race for more detail about how these factors structure social inequality.

## Defining and Measuring Social Class

Researchers study social class using both quantitative and qualitative methods. Qualitative approaches to social class often draw on the insights of **symbolic interactionism** and emphasize issues of meaning, experience, and identity. Such assessments do not attempt to succinctly categorize people into various classes but are instead concerned with the meaning, identity, and experiences of one class in relation to another. Qualitative historical work, for instance, has examined processes of class formation (Comninel, 1987) and how class relations structure professionalization projects (Adams, 1998, 2000). Using observation or in-depth interviewing techniques, other studies have explored the meaning and experiences of class relations in workplaces (Gannagé, 1986; Reiter, 1996; Rinehart, Huxley, and Robertson, 1994) and in schools (Willis, 1977).

Quantitative work on social class tends to focus either on how class affects various outcomes of social inequality or on how the class structure has changed over time. Social class is defined differently depending on which of these particular focuses is at the heart of the research. In work on social inequality, for instance, proxies of social class (that is, such factors as income, education, and occupation that indirectly measure social class), derived from **structural functionalist** approaches to stratification, tend to be used.

Social stratification approaches to social class have been very influential, particularly in American sociology. Stratification approaches conceptualize inequality as a hierarchal order (Davis and Moore, 1945) in which individuals are grouped into strata on the basis of their socio-economic status (SES) as measured through indicators such as income, education, or occupation. As a result, inequality tends to be conceptualized at the level of individual difference rather than in relational terms or on the basis of class structures (Grabb, 2002; Tilly, 1998).

Traditionally, stratification approaches have assumed that the rank ordering of people into socially defined strata is a universal and functionally necessary dimension of society. In other words, an ordering of people according to their worth, variously defined, is required for the smooth functioning of society. Certain positions in society are more valued than others because of the high level of skill attached to them. Only a few people can attain the skills required to fulfill these positions, and such attainment requires significant time commitment for the appropriate training. People who invest the time in such training deserve higher-status positions in society and the resultant rewards attached to these positions. Furthermore, there is general agreement or consensus among the members of society that such stratification systems are acceptable (Davis and Moore, 1945).

Two underlying assumptions in stratification research set it apart from the Marxist and Weberian approaches to inequality. First is the tendency to overemphasize the extent to which society operates on the basis of consensus rather than conflict. Second, and related to the first, is the underemphasis in stratification research on issues of power and exploitation (see Grabb, 2002, for an extensive discussion of these issues).

The identification of problematic assumptions in stratification research has not, however, led to its demise. Instead, it remains influential in studies of inequality and informs much empirical research on the subject. Michael Grimes (1991) argues that many researchers apply stratification measures to the study of class inequality either because they remain committed to certain aspects of functionalist thought or because stratification measures are often used in large surveys. It is important to clarify that stratification researchers do not suggest that they are studying class; class researchers, although they sometimes do stratification research, make the distinction between the two (Grabb, 2002). The point that Grimes makes is nonetheless important, and stems, perhaps, from a more general observation that researchers whose primary interest lies outside of class and stratification analysis tend to convolute the two approaches. This propensity is most likely a result of the significant overlap between the various social factors examined in these approaches. For instance, occupation, defined in various ways, tends to be at the core of research on social class regardless of theoretical perspective. Further, there is a general concern in all conceptual frameworks about the distribution of scarce resources such as income, education, and skill. Hence, the tendency to use stratification measures as indicators of social class likely results from the continued use of traditional measurements in survey research and also

from the fact that the indicators of social class are quite similar, regardless of theoretical perspective.

There is little doubt that stratification measures tell us something about class-based inequality. However, these indicators cannot fully capture the extent to which social class matters in contemporary Canadian society. Instead, a relational understanding of social class is necessary. Such an understanding follows a long tradition in Marxist sociology that suggests that class is not merely an economic relation. Rather, social class manifests itself as people from various classes interact with one another in productive relations. Researchers who are concerned with the macro implications of the organization of the social relations of production operationalize social class using concepts central in Marxist and Weberian scholarship, such as power, exploitation, oppression, property ownership, and so on.

Eric Olin Wright's work is an example of how social class can be assessed quantitatively in this way. For the past 20 years, Wright and his colleagues have been developing a typology of social class that relies on measures of occupation, authority, skill, and the number of employees who work at a particular locale (see Figure 6.2). This latter classification category reflects the number of people who are under the authority of each particular class location. For example, managers tend to have many employees over whom they have authority and dominance, while non-managers have authority over no one. Owners are separated from employees in this scheme and are differentiated from one another only on the basis of how many employees they have. Hence, owners who have only a few employees are thought to be different from those who have many and from those who have none. Employees, on the other hand, are differentiated on the basis of number of other employees, skills, and authority. Expert managers have high levels of authority and skill and tend to supervise many employees. They stand in most stark contrast to non-skilled workers, who have no authority or skill and who supervise no employees.

In this typology, the cells do not represent classes as such, but rather refer to class locations within the capitalist class structure. The distinction here is a subtle but important one that allows Wright to cover all of his bases. Unlike an earlier version of this framework, in which he refers to the various groupings in this model as classes (Wright, 1985), in his more recent work Wright makes it clear that these cells represent class locations within an overriding framework of class relations. By doing this, Wright can stay true to a Marxist version of class relations in which

Figure 6.2 **Eric Olin Wright's Class Divisions**

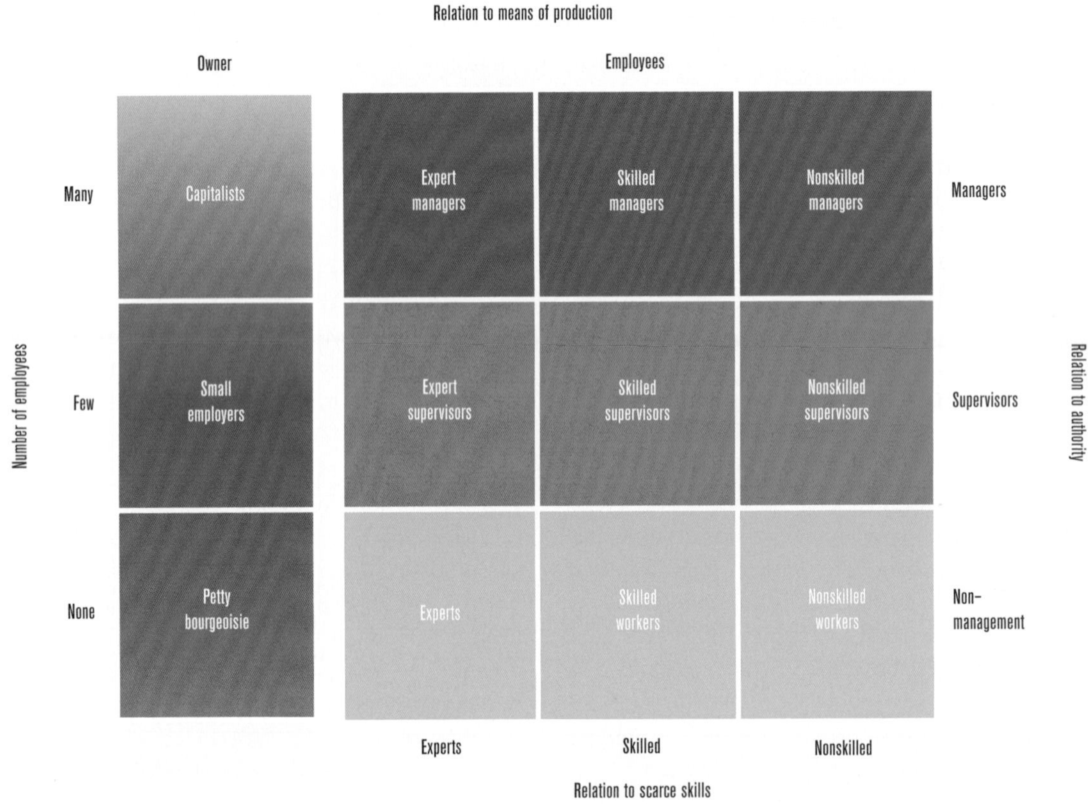

SOURCE: 'Relation to means of production' from *Class Counts: Comparative Studies in Class Analysis* by Erik Olin Wright (Cambridge: Cambridge University Press, 1997).

exploitation is at the core while at the same time identifying contradictory places within class relations that individuals occupy.

Class has thus been used in many ways in sociological thought. For the purpose of this chapter, stratification measures will be used to assess the relationship between social class and each of income, education, and health. To assess class structure, a modified, more parsimonious version of Wright's conceptualization, as it is put forth by Wallace Clement and John Myles (1994), will be used. Clement and Myles developed a four-class model in which the *capitalist-executive* class controls both the labour power of others and the means of production (see Table 6.2). The *old middle class*—the "petite bourgeoisie" in Marxist terminology—commands the means of production but not the labour power of others. The *new middle class* controls the labour power of others but not the means of production. And, finally, the *working class* commands

neither the labour power of others nor the means of production. The advantage of this approach to social class lies in its simplicity; it accurately reflects the "relations of ruling" in Canada while eliminating the unnecessary and often tedious class location distinctions inherent to Wright's approach.

## Social Class and Inequality

Social inequality reflects relatively long-lasting differences between individuals or groups of people that have substantial implications for individual lives, especially "for the rights or opportunities they exercise and the rewards or privileges they enjoy" (Grabb, 2002: 1–2; see also Pampel, 1998). So, for example, people who are a part of the working class earn less money, have less fulfilling jobs, do not have the same educational opportunities available to them, and have

Table 6.2 **Clement and Myles's Conceptualization of Social Class**

| Command Means of Production | Command Labour Power of Others | |
| --- | --- | --- |
| | **Yes** | **No** |
| Yes | Capitalist-executive | Old middle class |
| No | New middle class | Working class |

SOURCE: Wallace Clement and John Myles, *Relations of Ruling: Class and Gender in Postindustrial Societies* (Montreal: McGill-Queen's University Press, 1994), 16. Reprinted by permission.

worse health than do people from the middle and upper classes. The next sections consider the relationship between social class and each of paid work, education, and health.

## Paid Work, Income, and Poverty

Marx argued that as capitalism evolved, there would be an increasing polarization of workers into two central classes, the proletariat and the bourgeoisie. This polarization would involve at least three things: (1) a reduction in the proportion of small business owners and hence a shrinking of the old middle class; (2) increasing proportions of income going to the owners of large businesses and a reduction in the earnings of middle-class workers; and (3) continued deskilling of work and corresponding increases in the **alienation** of workers (Conley, 1999).

### Class Structure in Canada

According to Clement and Myles's definition of social class, a slight majority of employed Canadians in the early 1980s formed the working class (57.6 per cent), almost 25 per cent formed the new middle class, 11.3 per cent the old middle class, and 6.2 per cent the capitalist-executive class (1994: 19).

Since the early twentieth century, the proportion of Canada's class structure comprising small business owners has declined considerably (Clement and Myles, 1994). Between the 1930s and the early 1970s, for instance, the proportion of the workforce comprising small business owners declined from approximately 25 per cent to between 10 and 12 per cent (Conley, 1999: 24). Much of this decline occurred in the agricultural sector, where advances in farm technology made the business of small farming unprofitable (Clement and Myles, 1994; Conley, 1999). Nonetheless, for much of the twentieth century it

appeared as if Marx's prediction regarding the shrinking middle class was right.

Since the mid-1970s, however, this trend has reversed. Indeed, the most significant change in the class structure over the past 20 years in particular has been the increase in the proportion of the class structure represented by the old middle class. Clement and Myles report that the level of non-agricultural self-employment increased from 5.8 per cent in 1975 to 7.4 per cent in 1990 (1994: 42). When self-employed owners of incorporated businesses are included in this measure, the old middle class made up about 14 per cent of the total labour force in the early 1980s. By 1997, 17.8 per cent of the total labour force were self-employed in both incorporated and unincorporated businesses (Lin et al., 1999: 15). The majority of those who are self-employed either work on their own or hire fewer than three employees (Clement and Myles, 1994: 49; Hughes, 1999).

Reactions to recent increases in the proportion of employed Canadians who primarily constitute the old middle class have been mixed. On the one hand, some hail these changes as positive. According to this school of thought, small business owners are free of the control of large capitalist enterprises and as a result have more autonomy in their work. Their conditions of work are less alienating, and this is a positive development of post-industrial capitalism. Others have argued that, far from being a positive occurrence, the rise of small business owners is the result of workplace restructuring whereby workers lose their jobs and are forced to earn a living without some of the rewards (such as pensions and benefits) associated with employment in large companies (see Clement and Myles, 1994, for an overview of these opinions). This suggests that the conditions under which one becomes a small business owner are important considerations when discussing the social implications associated with higher proportions of workers in the "old" middle class.

Notably, the old middle class still includes a relatively small proportion of employed workers. Workers in the new middle class and the working class encompass the overwhelming majority in the Canadian class structure—82.5 per cent, according to Clement and Myles (1994: 19).

## Income and Poverty

There is a strong correlation between social class and income. Working-class jobs pay less than middle-class jobs, and owners of capital tend to have higher incomes than others (Krahn and Lowe, 1998). For instance, in 1995, average annual earnings in Canada for managers ($41,352), teachers ($35,330), and medical and health professionals ($34,410) were much higher than were the average annual earnings for clerical and service workers ($21,825 and $17,160, respectively; Krahn and Low, 1998: 96–7). These earnings stand in stark contrast to the incomes of the chief executive officers (CEOs) of large companies. In 1996, the CEOs of Canada's 100 largest corporations all earned over $700,000 (Krahn and Lowe, 1998). Notably, a strong correlation between social class and income does not mean it is a perfect correlation. Certain jobs, based on the definitions of social class found above, would be considered working-class jobs even though they command a relatively high wage. For example, assembly-line workers in any of the "big three" auto manufacturing plants are part of the working class, but because they are members of a relatively strong union they are paid a good wage and have good benefits.

Owners and executives of capital clearly have much higher incomes than do workers. The question that remains unanswered is whether there has been an increasing polarization of income over time. One way to address this issue is to divide Canadians into equal groups (typically either deciles or quintiles) on the basis of their income, calculate the proportion of the total income in Canada that each group accounts for, and then examine whether that proportion changed over time. In 1996, 44.5 per cent of all before-tax income was concentrated in the top quintile of the Canadian population, 24.7 per cent in the fourth quintile, 16.3 per cent in the third (middle) quintile, 10 per cent in the second quintile, and only 4.6 per cent in the lowest quintile. Between 1951 and 1996, there was a 2.9 per cent shift from the second and third quintiles to the two highest quintiles, while the proportion of income concentrated in the lowest

quintile remained relatively stable. Moreover, between 1981 and 1996, the second, third, and fourth quintiles lost 2.8 per cent of their before-tax income, a total of $14 billion, to the upper quintile (Urmetzer and Guppy, 1999: 59). These figures support the idea that there is increasing polarization of income in Canada.

The proportion of total before-tax income concentrated in the lowest quintile has remained relatively stable since 1951. These figures do not tell us, however, if this stability has been maintained largely through government transfers such as tax credits, social assistance, and unemployment insurance. Indeed, for low-income families, the proportion of their total income from labour market earnings has declined since the 1970s (Picot and Myles, 1995). Hence, income polarization is not as serious as it could be because government policies are in place to ensure more equitable income distributions in Canada (Ross, Shillington, and Lochhead, 1994). But how equitable is a system in which the lowest fifth of the population receives only 4.6 per cent of all before-tax income? And how equitable is a system in which the $14 billion gain made in the upper fifth during the 1980s and 1990s is equivalent to the amount of money it would take to eliminate poverty in Canada (Osberg, 1992)?

Poverty is a serious social problem in Canada. The National Council of Welfare reports that although poverty rates declined between 1998 and 1999, there were still more people living in poverty in 1999 than there were in 1989. Approximately 16 per cent of Canadians lived in poverty in 1999; poverty rates for families are about 12 per cent, and for unattached individuals they are around 39 per cent (National Council of Welfare, 2002: 4).

Poverty rates vary on the basis of gender, family status, age, immigrant and minority status, education, and labour-force attachment. For instance, in 1999, the poverty rate for single-parent mothers was 51.8 per cent—more than four times the poverty rate for all families (National Council of Welfare, 2002: 15). Unattached women under the age of 65 are more likely to live in poverty than are their male counterparts (42.3 per cent versus 33.2 per cent), as are unattached women who are aged 65 and over (48.5 per cent versus 31.9 per cent) (National Council of Welfare, 2002: 18–19). Children (18.7 per cent) and the elderly (17.7 per cent) are somewhat more likely to be poor than are all Canadians (16 per cent) (National Council of Welfare, 2002: 10–12).

6.1

# Human Diversity
Images of Child Poverty in Canada

Dirty, bare feet dangle over a licence plate in Prince Albert, Sask. A child plays with a lone tricycle on a cracked driveway in Winnipeg.

Those are images of some of the 1.3 million children in Canada who live in poverty, whose existence a group called PhotoSensitive is documenting in a cross-Canada exhibit.

The show was launched yesterday, in conjunction with a report on child poverty, released by Campaign 2000, that says nearly one in five children [was] living in poverty in 1999, compared with one in seven in 1989.

Campaign 2000 is a coalition of organizations formed to ensure that a 1989 House of Commons resolution to end child poverty by 2000 was implemented, a result still far from being realized, co-ordinator Laurel Rothman said.

"We are no closer [to ending child poverty]," she said. "In 1989, we were at one in seven children living in poverty. Now we're at almost one in five."

Ms Rothman said what is disturbing is that child poverty was prevalent even during the economic prosperity of the late 1990s.

"Governments have the option in the boom years of investing in children. Instead they took the strategy of cutting taxes, and in many cases, social services."

The report says that despite a strong economy between 1998 and 1999, the child-poverty rate dropped only slightly to 18.5 per cent from 19 per cent. And with the latest economic downturn, "those numbers are going to rocket up again," Ms Rothman said.

One positive number in the bulletin is the decrease in the depth of poverty, said Andrew Jackson, research director for the Canadian Council on Social Development, which compiled the data from several Statistics Canada studies.

Samantha naps in the attic apartment she shares with her mother and three brothers in Edmonton. They will be moving soon. (Chris Schwarz)

In 1999, poor families saw an improvement of more than $500 in their depth of poverty over the previous year (to $9,073 below the poverty line in 1999 from $9,597 in 1998), but the gap between the rich and the poor in Canada is still far too wide, Ms Rothman said.

The report makes several recommendations to government, including the development of a national housing strategy.

And the photographs by the 24 members of PhotoSensitive remind people of the "faces behind the numbers," Andrew Stawicki, photographer and founder of PhotoSensitive, said.

———

SOURCE: Allison Dunfield, "In 1989 We Were at One in Seven Children Living in Poverty. Now We're at Almost One in Five," *Globe and Mail* (27 Nov. 2001), A11. Reprinted with permission from *The Globe and Mail*.

Gainful employment significantly reduces poverty rates among both unattached individuals and families. Yet more than 40 per cent of families who were living in poverty in 1999 were headed by people who were employed. Compared to the total Canadian population (29.5 per cent), higher proportions of immigrant visible minorities (42.5 per cent) and Aboriginal people living off-reserve (49.4 per cent) lived in poverty for at least one year between 1993 and 1998. Finally, the poverty rate for single-parent mothers who worked full-time for the full year was still 19.7 per cent (National Council of Welfare, 2002: 6–7).

Poverty rates also vary from province to province. Newfoundland and Labrador has the highest poverty rate (20.7 per cent), followed closely by Quebec (19.5 per cent) and Manitoba (18.5 per cent). Ontario has the lowest poverty rate (13.5 per cent), followed by Prince Edward Island (14.7 per cent), New Brunswick (15.1 per cent), and Alberta (15.2 per cent) (National Council of Welfare, 2002: 42). Provincial variations in poverty rates are a result of regional differences in economic structures, provincial inconsistencies in government policies regarding social welfare transfers, and access to other social and economic resources (National Council of Welfare, 2002).

## Good Jobs/Bad Jobs

You will recall that Marx's third prediction with respect to the polarization of classes was that as capitalism developed, jobs would become increasingly deskilled and alienated. Indeed, skill and alienation are two characteristics of paid work that vary depending on social class. Generally, working-class jobs are characterized by low levels of skill required to do the job and by often corresponding high levels of alienation, whereas jobs held by those in the "new middle class" and the "old middle class" tend to require more skill and to be more intrinsically rewarding. That said, for Marx's prediction to be supported, we must see evidence that middle-class jobs have become increasingly deskilled.

In 1974, Harry Braverman published his classic book, *Labor and Monopoly Capitalism*. Taking issue with those who argued that rising white-collar employment was a positive effect of post-industrialism that resulted in an increasingly large middle class, Braverman convincingly argued that most white-collar jobs (such as clerical and retail jobs) should be considered working-class, not middle-class. White-collar jobs, Braverman argued, were increasingly being deskilled and organized according to **scientific management** techniques, thereby eliminating most of the control and

autonomy that workers may have had over their work. Advances in new technologies contributed to this process by giving managers sophisticated tools through which they can monitor their employees' work. For example, before the advent of computerized cash registers, cashiers needed to know how to make change. Now cash registers inform cashiers how much change they need to give a customer. Further, cash registers can now monitor the speed of keystrokes and the number of customers that a cashier serves per hour. Managers, in turn, use this information in employee job performance evaluations. Hence, new technology has been used both to deskill the work process and to monitor and control it.

One year before Braverman published his book, Daniel Bell published what was to become an influential text on post-industrial society. Unlike Braverman, who argued that occupations were becoming increasingly deskilled, Bell (1973) looked to the future and argued that knowledge, and hence skill, would become a highly valued commodity in post-industrial society. According to Bell, knowledge would be a basis of power much as the ownership of property had traditionally been, and knowledge workers would form a significant class (both in number and in power) in their own right. Bell argued that as the proportion of knowledge workers grew, the historical trend towards the polarization of society into two central classes, the bourgeoisie and the proletariat, would lose speed.

In the 30 years since Bell and Braverman published their books, debates have ensued over which thesis better explains the relationship between skill and class structure in post-industrial society. Although such debates are far from resolved, Clement and Myles are worth quoting at length on the issue. They note that the debate has unfolded as follows:

> We face either a postindustrial Nirvana of knowledge where everyone will be a brain surgeon, artist, or philosopher (Bell) or, alternatively, a post-industrial Hades where we shall be doomed to labour mindlessly in the service of capital (Braverman). When drawn in these terms, the historical debate is now no debate at all. Bell is the clear winner. Although much less than a knowledge revolution, the net result of the shift to services has been to increase the requirements for people to think on the job. (1994: 72)

In Canada, 42 per cent of jobs in the post-industrial service sector are skilled compared to only 26 per cent of those in the goods and distribution sector.

And 55 per cent of "new middle class" jobs are skilled, compared to only 23 per cent of working-class jobs (Clement and Myles, 1994: 76). Clement and Myles point out that the growth in the service sector has brought both skilled and unskilled jobs, but they underscore the fact that in Canada and the United States, unskilled service jobs are often entry jobs for new workers rather than serving as a basis for working-class formation. This—combined with the fact that these service jobs are now often exit jobs for older workers who have been displaced, discouraged, or restructured, or who have retired early—suggests that age may play a more significant role in labour market inequality in the years to come. Nonetheless, the point is that although the conditions of work in contemporary Canadian capitalism are far from ideal, the proletarianization of the labour force as predicted by Braverman has not occurred even though skilled jobs are concentrated in the new middle and executive classes (Clement and Myles, 1994).

In summary, considering debates about the deskilling of work in post-industrial capitalism, about whether the middle class is shrinking, and about the distribution of income and poverty, there is no consensus among sociologists about whether the class structure of Canadian society has become increasingly polarized. On the one hand, overall increases in the skill levels associated with many jobs and recent increases in the number of self-employed small business owners suggest that the polarization thesis is incorrect. On the other hand, huge inequities in the distribution of income in Canada cannot be ignored. Furthermore, regardless of where one comes down on the debate about overall class polarization, the fact is that compared to "middle-class" jobs, working-class jobs are characterized by low levels of income and other benefits, low levels of autonomy and control in the work process, poor working conditions, low levels of skill, and high levels of alienation. The combination of these things creates social disadvantage for members of the working class relative to members of the middle classes, which carries over to other social domains. Education and health are two areas of sociological study that stand out as sites of class-based inequality.

## Education

Many Canadians believe that education is a vehicle through which occupational and income advantages may be attained (Wotherspoon, 1998). Over the last 30 years, more education has come to be required to perform jobs that were done well without as much education in years past (for example, needing a high school degree to work at an auto manufacturing plant). But regardless of this "credential inflation" (Baer, 1999), strong correlations remain between education, occupation, and income in Canada (Hunter and Leiper, 1993).

Typically, highly educated people are employed in well-paid jobs (Little, 1995) that have relatively high degrees of autonomy and authority associated with them (Butlin and Oderkirk, 1996). Of course, we have all either heard about or met a taxi driver who holds a Ph.D., or a high school dropout who is the well-paid owner of a successful business. These examples illustrate that, just as with grammar, there are exceptions to the rules. Often, other extraneous factors account for these exceptions. For instance, in the case of the well-educated taxi driver, recent immigration status may affect his or her job prospects because of discriminatory hiring criteria (for example, a hiring requirement of Canadian education or work experience).

In light of the relationship between educational attainment and economic advantage, sociologists have long been concerned with the social determinants of educational attainment. Social class background, usually measured using SES indicators, is one such determinant. Two key measures of educational attainment are often considered in this regard: (1) whether young people complete high school and (2) whether they continue with post-secondary education.

On average, Canadians are among the most educated people in the world (Looker and Lowe, 2001). High school completion rates continued to increase throughout the 1990s such that only 12 per cent of 20-year-olds did not complete high school in 1999, as compared to 18 per cent in 1991 (Bowlby and McMullen, 2002). The more educated parents are, the more likely their children are to complete high school (Bowlby and McMullen, 2002). Figure 6.3 shows data for 18- to 20-year-olds from the Canadian 2000 Youth in Transition Survey. Here we see that the highest proportion of both high school graduates (34.7 per cent) and high school dropouts (45.2 per cent) have at least one parent who graduated from high school. However, among those who have at least one parent who has completed either a college or university program, the proportion of graduates is twice the proportion of dropouts (56.6 per cent versus 27.9 per cent). Among youth whose parents had not graduated from high school, the proportion of dropouts is three times the proportion of graduates (26.9 per cent versus 8.7 per cent). Furthermore, approximately 7 out of every 10 dropouts, compared to 4 out of 10 graduates,

Figure 6.3  **Highest Education Attainment of Parents or Guardians of Dropouts and Graduates**

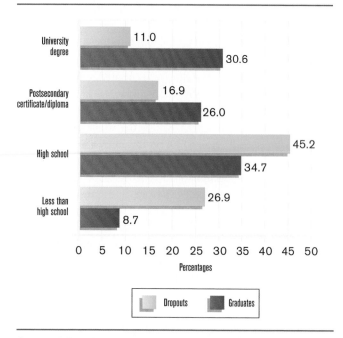

SOURCE: Adapted from Jeffrey Bowlby and Kathryn McMullen, *At a Crossroads: First Results for the 18–20-Year-Old Cohort of the Youth in Transition Survey 2002* (Ottawa: Statistics Canada, 2002), Catalogue 81-591, January 2002, 31.

had parents who did not complete high school (Bowlby and McMullen, 2002: 31).

Similarly, mothers' and fathers' occupations are correlated with whether youth graduate from or drop out of high school. Mothers of high school dropouts were more likely to be working in sales and service jobs or in primary, processing, manufacturing, and utilities jobs. Mothers of graduates were more likely to be working in social science, government, art, culture, health, and applied science jobs. Fathers of dropouts were more likely to be working in trades, transport, and equipment-operating jobs, whereas fathers of graduates were more likely to be working in management jobs (Bowlby and McMullen, 2002).

Approximately 65 per cent of high school graduates enter post-secondary educational institutions in Canada (Looker and Lowe, 2001: 4). Among youth, the higher parents' measures of SES, the higher their children's expectations regarding post-secondary educational attainment (Looker and Lowe, 2001). Plans to attend college or university are correlated with whether youth actually attend such institutions. Hence, educational attainment, including participa-

tion in college and university programs after high school completion, is also influenced by class background, regardless of how it is measured (Ali and Grabb, 1998; Wotherspoon, 1998). Several studies have shown that financial situation is listed by youth as a key barrier to pursuing post-secondary studies (Bowlby and McMullen, 2002; see Looker and Lowe, 2001, for an overview). Furthermore, youth from families in the highest SES quartile are much more likely to attend university than are those in the lowest SES quartile (Chippendale, 2002; Statistics Canada and CMEC, 2000).

The preceding findings demonstrate a clear relationship between parents' SES and children's educational attainment. A combination of economic, social, and cultural factors helps to explain the relationship between SES and educational attainment (Davies, 1999). In the first place, if parents are poorly educated and have low-paying jobs, families may not be able to afford to keep children in school. Poor families may need their children to drop out of high school and work to help with the family economy. In other situations, parents may not be able to help with the costs of post-secondary education, and the thought of excessive debt upon school completion may dissuade youth from continuing their studies. Notably, neither of these situations is likely to improve in the short term as rates of child poverty and the costs of post-secondary education continue to rise.

Besides economic factors, other social factors intersect with SES and social class to play a role in educational attainment. To the extent that children and youth of similar SES and social class backgrounds are segregated into schools based on community residence, they will develop social ties with other children and youth of similar backgrounds. Lack of exposure to middle- and upper-class children and their parents limits access to **social capital**, the resources that are available through our connections to others. In other words, working-class children and youth may not have access to the information gained through social capital that is required for them to succeed in their educational careers. For instance, whereas middle-class children can turn to their parents and friends to learn about the intricacies of the educational system, working-class children do not have those social resources available to them and may not know how to find answers to questions that would help them succeed within school environments.

Finally, **cultural capital** also plays a role in educational attainment. Cultural capital is derived mostly from education and reflects middle- and upper-class values, attitudes, and beliefs regarding various aspects of social life. If education and related activities such as reading, discussing politics, and learning about the world and music are valued within a family and by the individuals within it, high levels of educational attainment are more likely. Working-class families tend not to expose their children to these activities to the extent that middle- and upper-class families do. Hence, the value of education is often not as strongly held in working-class families as it is in middle-class families, and working-class children may not be as inclined to continue with their education as a result.

### Health

According to the World Health Organization (2003), *health* is broadly defined as "a state of complete physical, mental, and social well-being and not merely the absence of disease or infirmity," which suggests that multiple measures of health need to be examined to understand fully health and inequality. Income, status, and class advantages lead to better health outcomes within and across countries. Recent media and policy attention regarding the HIV/AIDS epidemics in developing countries suggests that developed countries need to pay more attention to the "have-nots" who live beyond our national borders. Indeed, mortality and morbidity rates tend to be higher in developing than in developed countries, and biotechnology researchers are in search of methods to reduce the health gap between rich and poor countries.

Among the many indicators of health, mortality is one of the most studied. There is a well-known and consistent relationship between SES and mortality. Individuals who have lower incomes and less education tend to have lower life expectancies than do individuals who have higher incomes and who are better educated (Mustard et al., 1997; Williams and Collins, 1995). Recent evidence suggests that the mortality gap between rich and poor is widening; this has been attributed to the more rapid gains for those with high SES relative to those with lower SES (Williams and Collins, 1995).

Recently, researchers have argued that beyond the simple relationship between SES and mortality, a socio-economic "gradient" also influences mortality. This *gradient effect* reflects the research finding that regions characterized by high levels of income inequality have higher death rates than do regions in which the income distribution is more equal. This suggests that the experience of disadvantage relative to others in a particular locale has an effect on mor-

tality rates that cannot be explained by SES alone (Kawachi et al., 1999).

*Morbidity* generally refers to the presence of illness or disease, chronic symptoms, and general malaise or sense of unwellness. Regardless of how it is measured, there is also a strong and consistent relationship between SES and morbidity such that those who are more disadvantaged experience higher levels of morbidity (Cairney, 1999; Humphries and van Doorslaer, 2000; Jette, Crawford, and Tennstedt, 1996; MacMillan et al., 1996; Mao, Ugnat, and White, 2000; Williams and Collins, 1995). Regional disparities regarding income and poverty have also been found to influence the experience of morbidity (Guernsey et al., 2000). Besides these differences in mortality and morbidity, individuals in lower SES groups suffer poorer mental health (measured either as the presence of mental illness or as more generalized distress) than do those in higher SES groups (Turner and Avison, forthcoming). Although there are debates about whether low SES causes poor mental health or whether poor mental health causes low SES, the correlation is strong.

What explains the strong and consistent relationship between SES and these various measures of health? People with lower levels of income and education and those employed in working-class occupations are more likely to experience malnutrition, disproportionately lack knowledge of health-care practices, and are more often exposed to dangerous working and living environments. All of these things negatively affect health status. As well, research has shown that SES is associated with access to health-care services even in countries such as Canada that have "universal" health-care systems (Newbold, 1998).

## Conclusion
### Does Class Matter?

For decades, sociologists have quibbled over the relevance of social class as a marker of inequality (Clark and Lipset, 1991; Nisbet, 1959; Pakulski and Waters, 1996). Some argue that because false consciousness is so widespread within contemporary capitalism, political distinctions between the middle class and the working class have become negligible. Others suggest that because some working-class jobs are well paid, distributive distinctions between the classes are becoming less significant. Still others purport that because most people self-identify as members of the middle class, not the working class, and because working conditions are better now than they were a century ago, class is losing its significance as a basis of inequality in Canada and other

Western industrialized nations (Pakulski and Waters, 1996). Indeed, Jan Pakulski and Malcolm Waters (1996) have proclaimed the "death" of class.

The claims in support of the "death of class" are true to a certain extent. Indeed, the fact that many students first discover their working-class backgrounds in their first year of university may add some support to the argument that class does not matter. As well, the conditions of and rewards for work have mostly improved over the last century. Social security systems are better now than they were during the rise of industrial capitalism in Canada, which has reduced the risk associated with working-class membership.

That said, it is also true that after students are given social class as an explanatory tool, they understand better the circumstances of their lives. Furthermore, if given a choice, most employees would choose to work in non-working-class occupations that are better paid, more autonomous, and less alienating; working-class parents are not able to provide their children with the same educational opportunities afforded to middle-class children; and unique health risks are associated with being a member of the working class. This information suggests that although the nature of class-based inequality has changed over time, class remains alive and well.

## □ Questions for Critical Thought

1. Some may argue that no one but Kimberly Rogers was to blame for her death. Others would argue that structural circumstances and social policy at least contributed to it. Compare and contrast these views. Which better explains Rogers's death?

2. Based on what you have learned in this and the preceding chapters, how many social classes are there in contemporary Canadian society? Which makes more sense today, a Weberian or a Marxist view of social class?

3. Discuss the feminist critique of social class. How can social class be reconceptualized so that the experiences of women are fully integrated into a theoretical framework of social class?

4. Why are sociologists concerned about the polarization of social classes? In other words, what are the social implications of a shrinking middle class and a swelling working class?

5. Under the conditions of contemporary capitalism, does small business ownership hold the same appeal as it did for Marx? In other words, assuming that alienation is reduced substantially or even eliminated for small business owners, are there other things that may matter more to one's overall well-being in contemporary capitalism? If so, why do so many Canadians dream of being self-employed?

6. Are there policies that could eliminate poverty? What might some of these policies be? Is the elimination of poverty a desirable social outcome?

7. Are there policies that could eliminate the relationship between social class and education? What might some of these policies be? Is educational equality a desirable social outcome?

8. Are there policies that could eliminate the relationship between social class and health? What might some of these policies be? Is health equality a desirable social outcome?

## ☐ Recommended Readings

**Joan Acker, "Class, Gender, and the Relations of Distribution,"** *Signs*, **13 (1988): 473–97.**

This seminal article tackles the complexities of integrating gender, class, patriarchy, and capitalism into a single system of inequality.

**James E. Curtis, Edward G. Grabb, and Neil L. Guppy, eds,** *Social Inequality in Canada: Patterns, Problems, and Policies* **(Scarborough, Ont.: Prentice-Hall Allyn and Bacon, 1999).**

This is an excellent source of information on various aspects of social inequality in Canada.

**Edward G. Grabb,** *Theories of Social Inequality*, **4th edn (Toronto: Harcourt, 2002).**

Grabb provides an excellent overview and analysis of classical and contemporary theories of social inequality.

**Desmond Morton,** *Working People: An Illustrated History of the Canadian Labour Movement*, **4th edn (Montreal and Kingston: McGill-Queen's University Press, 1998).**

This resource book explores the evolution of the labour movement in Canada from the late nineteenth century until the 1990s.

**Erik Olin Wright,** *Class Counts: Comparative Studies in Class Analysis* **(Cambridge: Cambridge University Press, 1997).**

This comprehensive book outlines Wright's ideas on social class.

## ☐ Recommended Web Sites

**Canadian Labour Congress (CLC)**

**www.clc-ctc.ca**

Labour-related publications, media releases, and the history of the CLC are among the many resources available on this site.

**Canadian Policy Research Networks**

**www.cprn.ca**

This is an excellent source of information regarding the relationship between social policy and social inequality.

**National Council on Welfare**

**www.ncwcnbes.net**

This site includes facts and reports on poverty in Canada and information about poverty myths.

# 7

Pat Armstrong

> > >

# Gender Relations

© Digital Vision

## ☐ Learning Objectives

In this chapter, you will:

- learn that biology alone does not account for differences between males and females

- see how ideologies, child-rearing practices, the division of labour by sex, the education system, and the media all influence the physiology, behaviour, and perceptions of both sexes

- examine the segregation by sex of the labour force, the political arena, and medical services

- consider why the life experiences of women are different from and more limited than those of men

- examine the issues of housework and caregiving

- consider the changing personal relationships between men and women

- take into account the effect of changing gender relations on men

# Introduction

"Is it a boy or a girl?" is the first question asked of new parents. Gender, as everyone knows, has profound implications for an individual's choices and possibilities throughout life.

All known cultures have distinguished between male and female. Furthermore, in all cultures the distinctions have provided the basis for divisions not only of labour, but also of most other activities. The distinctions made between genders and the particular gendered divisions of labour have varied enormously through time and across cultures, however, because such distinctions exist within a **social environment**. Their characteristics result more from social relations and social structures than from biologically determined differences.

This chapter examines gender distinctions and the relations between males and females in Canadian society. First, we discuss what is known about biological differences and their implications for behaviour and relationships. Next, we turn to the evidence of sex-specific patterns in behaviour, education, and occupations to evaluate existing explanations for these established patterns. Finally, we outline some strategies for altering these patterns and reshaping the relations between the sexes in Canada.

# Theories of the Sexes

From one perspective, clear biological distinctions exist between the sexes—men are suited to bring home the bacon, while women can produce babies and feed and nurture them—and these abilities determine what people can be when they grow up. Many sociologists, however, see clear lines to be drawn between distinctions that are biologically determined and those that are socially learned—between nature and nurture. Twenty years ago, Marlene Mackie explained that "sex is the biological dichotomy between females and males. It is determined at conception and is, for the most part, unalterable. Gender, on the other hand, is what is socially recognized as femininity and masculinity" (1983: 1). By differentiating **sex** and **gender**, sociologists sought to stress the **social construction** of distinctions between the sexes, but these terms raised their own problems. First, they implied that biological factors can be separated from social factors and that biological differences are firmly established. Second, they implied that biology is unchanging, that it endures outside of history and influence. Third, the distinction suggested that biology is irrelevant to an understanding of social distinctions between males and females.

Sociologists, in an effort to overcome these problems, have increasingly used only the term "gender". However, the growing popularity of the new genetics and biotechnology has once again encouraged an emphasis on biological differences between the sexes (Grant, 1998). The rest of this section will examine each of the problems in determining biological differences, explaining why it is not always easy to differentiate between sex and gender, biology and learning.

## *Separating the Boys from the Girls*

People throughout the ages have debated the biological differences between the sexes, and they continue to do so today despite extensive research. A 1993 CBC series based on the book *Brain Sex* (Moir and Jessel, 1989) stressed the **biological determinist** side. A more recent article in *Maclean's* magazine begins, "If there is a gene for murder, it is a safe bet it will be found first in someone who carries XY chromosomes. That is, a man. There may be no such gene. Many experts insist violence is learned, not inherited" (Wood and Kar, 2000: 5). Clearly the issue is far from settled (Blustain, 2000).

Most people would agree that hair length and high heels are socially created gender distinctions. Fewer would reach a consensus about which aspects of motherhood have biological links. Moreover, some would argue that women are "naturally" homemakers, men "naturally" breadwinners. Finally, while most would agree that women and men have different genitals, this difference alone cannot be used to divide all people into two categories. Indeed, the Olympic Committee considers visible genitals so unreliable in establishing sex that it rejects the distinction as a basis for determining who may compete in the women's games.

Science provides few definitive answers to many points in the debate over biological differences. There is little consensus in the vast research and literature on the topic. The lack of agreement reflects both the problems encountered in conducting the research and the more fundamental problem inherent in the assumption that nature and nurture can be isolated from one another.

Research into human biological differences linked to behaviour is difficult for several reasons. First, children begin learning at birth, or before, so we cannot be entirely certain that the behaviour even of newborns is innate. Second, while infants have a very limited repertoire for study, as they expand their activities they also increase their opportunities to learn. Moreover, the older the subjects, the more likely they are to respond in terms of their own values and expectations. In any event, there are severe restrictions on the kind and amount of experimentation permitted on humans, whatever their age. Third, even when genes or hormones or other biological factors are determined to be different for males and females, there is little basis for assuming that these differences translate into particular behaviours. Perhaps most important, researchers themselves cannot escape their own learning, which helps structure how they do research and interpret results as well as what they accept as evidence (Fausto-Sterling, 2000; Messing, 1998).

Research on other species encounters similar problems, even though fewer restrictions are placed on how it is conducted. Other animals, such as rodents and birds, learn just as humans do, and there is enormous variety in their behaviour. Males are not universally breadwinners or heroes, and in some species, mothers are so unnurturing as to eat their young. Frequently, researchers' values come into play here, too, guiding them to select from the evidence what best supports their own hypotheses (Blustain, 2000). While there are many things to be learned from studying other animals, we cannot be confident that anything we might argue as being innate in another species will be so in humans, for the simple reason that humans are qualitatively different from other species.

Such difficulties have led many observers to contend that the question "Nature or nurture?" cannot be answered, because it is the wrong question. Anne Fausto-Sterling has argued that it is impossible to determine which aspects of our behaviour are biologically determined, because "an individual's capacities emerge from a web of interactions between the biological being and the social environment. . . . Biology may in some manner condition behavior, but behavior in turn can alter one's physiology. Furthermore, any particular behavior may have many different causes" (1985: 8). This is why, as she has said more recently (Fausto-Sterling, 2000), even with the latest techniques, scientists still disagree about differences and their impact. These debates are not surprising because people do not exist outside their social environment, and what are often called "biological processes" are influenced by that environment.

Jogging or stress may delay a menstrual cycle; tight jeans or a radio carried too often below the waist may reduce sperm counts. The more often women run in marathons, the closer they come to matching the men; the more often men spend their days sitting in office chairs, the less muscular they become.

To argue that nature cannot easily be separated from nurture is not to argue that there are no biological components to people's behaviour or that there are no gender differences that can be related to biological factors. Rather, it is to assert that biological components have no predetermined meaning or value and that they are not unalterable.

### The Sexes: What's the Difference?

Researchers do agree on some sex differences. While both sexes have 23 pairs of chromosomes, in most females one pair is made up of two X chromosomes; in most males one pair consists of an X and a Y chromosome. The Y chromosome must be present for the embryonic sex glands to develop in a male direction. Furthermore, hormones must be present in both sexes for either males or females to reach sexual maturity. Although estrogens are often called "female" hormones and androgens "male" hormones, both sexes secrete both types of hormones—"what differs is the ratio of estrogen to androgen in the two sexes" (Rose, Kamin, and Lewontin, 1984: 151). Between them, the XX and XY chromosomes and the hormones are responsible for the different reproductive capacities of women (menstruation, gestation, and lactation) and men (semen production and impregnation).

At this point agreement ends. Debates rage over the implications of the differences in chromosomes, hormonal ratios, and reproductive capacities for male and female behaviour and possibilities (see, for example, Bancroft, 2002).

### The Genetic Perspective

Sociobiologists and others who are convinced that biology determines a wide range of behaviour attribute a powerful effect to the lone Y chromosome. Different researchers working from this perspective have argued that the genetic makeup of men makes them more intelligent than women, superior in visual-spatial abilities and mathematical skills, or more aggressive and dominant. It has also been suggested that women's double X chromosome creates a maternal instinct and makes females more intuitive, tricky, nurturant, and moral than men. For supporters of the genetic perspective, the hierarchical structure of society and the sexual division of labour are the natural and inevitable result of biological differences (Geary, 1998; Geary and Flinn, 2000).

They also cite genetics for the **double standard** in sexual practices. That is, men have a natural sexuality that results, in the words of David Barash, from the "biologically based need to inject their sperm into as many women as possible" (cited in Messing, 1987: 112). Some have concluded, on the basis of this viewpoint, that rape and violence against women have biological roots: the men cannot help themselves any more than women can stop being nurturant and deceitful. In the eyes of these theorists, women are destined to be mommies and men bosses. Moreover, women should expect to be dominated and sexually harassed.

Study after study has challenged these notions (Fausto-Sterling, 2000; Rose, Kamin, and Lewontin, 1984). Research in countries other than Canada reveals an astonishing variety in gender relations that seems to deny biological determinism. Margaret Lock (1998) found that the physical manifestations of menopause vary across cultures, R.A. Anderson and colleagues (1999) determined that testosterone replacement had a different impact on male sexuality in Hong Kong than it did in North America.

Within Canadian society considerable differences are evident in gender behaviour over the course of history. Elizabeth Mitchell examined Prairie households early in the twentieth century and concluded that "there is no question at all of inequality; the partners have several departments, equally important, and the husband is the first to admit how much he owes his wife, and to own that the burden falls on her heaviest" ([1915] 1981: 48). Mitchell also maintained that city life served to create inequalities and make women subordinate in ways we see today. In addition, **First Nations** families have a long tradition of female independence and of community participation in childrearing (Cassidy, Lord, and Mandell, 2001).

In sum, research has not revealed any simple dichotomy between the sexes or any direct link between genetics or hormones and the behaviour patterns commonly attributed to each sex. Sociobiology has not succeeded in demonstrating "that a genetically based human nature or genetically based sex differences exist" (Lowe, 1983: 13). The variability across cultures, the minor differences

---

**7.1**

## Global Issues
### Changing Views of Men

While most of the research and writing on changing relations between the sexes has focused on women, in the last two decades there has been a flurry of publications that look at emerging patterns for men. Analysis of advertising offers just one example of this trend.

In her examination of the representation of males in advertising, Judith Posner (1987) found that the new male is smaller, has a less pronounced jaw, and is more likely to smile. He is also more likely to be found undressing or partially dressed, and he appears more vulnerable. Yet Posner concludes that this does not reflect a move toward equality, but rather demonstrates "the increasing commercialization of sexuality" for both men and women (1987: 188).

In another analysis of advertising, Andrew Wernick argues that as women have moved into the labour force, men have become more involved in private consumption; this change has been reflected in "a steady drive to incorporate male clothing into fashion, and mounting efforts to sell men all manner of personal-care products, from toothpaste and bath oil to hair dye and make-up" (1987: 279). Wernick suggests that men are being subjected to the same kind of "intense consumerization as women and are no longer defined as breadwinners" (279). More recently, however, Varda Burstyn (1999) has argued that both advertising in sports and the practice of sport promotes what she calls "hypermasculinity."

between the sexes in any particular culture, and the variations in patterns within the sexes all challenge notions of simple genetic determinism.

### The Hormonal Perspective

Other researchers have looked to hormones as causal agents (Moir and Jessel, 1992). Supporters of this perspective argue that different levels of hormones affect the brain, resulting for males in higher intelligence, more ambition and drive, and more aggressive behaviour. The effect on women is seen as far more negative, inasmuch as menstruation and menopause are viewed as incapacitating them, making them unsuitable for many kinds of work.

Again, research provides very limited support for this viewpoint. Although the injection of hormones might influence a rodent brain in ways that encourage mating behaviour, in non-human primates it does not create the same results (Lowe, 1983). In the words of Fausto-Sterling, "the evidence that male hormones control aggression in humans and other primates ranges from weak to non-existent" (1985: 45). A survey of research has concluded that "there is no known causal relationship between sex hormone levels and other traits, such as intelligence, intuition, and creativity" (Richardson, 1988: 149). Indeed, Lynda Birke (1999) cites evidence that hormone production itself is influenced by the social environment.

### Reproductive Capacity

Some feminist theorists have looked to reproductive capacities, rather than to genes or hormones, to explain differences between the sexes. Mary O'Brien, for example, has argued that the very different parts women and men play in reproduction lead to different forms of consciousness and to men's efforts to control women: "Women's reproductive consciousness is a consciousness that the child is hers, but also a consciousness that she herself was born of a woman's labour, that labour confirms genetic coherence and species continuity. Male reproductive consciousness is splintered and discontinuous, and cannot be mediated within reproductive process" (1981: 59). In O'Brien's view, men experience reproduction mainly as alienation of their male seed, which in turn motivates them to seek control over both mother and child.

Theoretical arguments are much more difficult to examine through scientific research than those that attribute sex differences to genes or hormones. What is clear is that the effects of reproductive capacities, like those of genes or hormones, cannot be under-

stood outside the context of time and place. How women experience childbirth, for instance, is related to the available technology and medical care, nutrition, and social support. These factors can transform not only how women feel about giving birth, but also the very biology of the birth process. Women's reproductive capacity makes the consequences of sexual intercourse different for women and men, especially in the absence of safe, effective birth control (Armstrong and Armstrong, 1983a; Hamilton, 1978) and different for women from different racial and cultural groups (Cassidy, Lord, and Mandell, 2001). Moreover, the consequences are different today than in our grandmothers' time, not only because contemporary women have a better chance of avoiding childbirth, but also because they have a better chance of surviving it. The development of relatively effective birth control has made the implications of sexual intercourse more similar for both sexes and has thereby contributed to changes in sexual practices and in the double standard. In turn, these social changes have affected the workings of our bodies and the meaning of what are often called "biological processes."

The recent spread of HIV/AIDS provides another example of the complex relationship between biology and social environment. In making some men more vulnerable to the long-term consequences of their sexual activities, HIV/AIDS has altered the sexual practices of at least some men. Furthermore, at least today, the spread of AIDS can only be controlled by changes in **social relationships** and social practices, not through biological means.

In the end, we are left to conclude that biology cannot be separated from the social environment that influences both its meaning and its structure. Biology is not an independent variable. Moreover, "female" and "male" do not constitute "opposite" sexes. Women and men share both genes and hormones. They differ mainly in reproductive capacities, and the significance of these differences is structured primarily socially, rather than biologically. Furthermore, "human biology and behavior are anything but immutable. Stimulate the brain, and neurons branch out to form new connections. Arouse the senses, and hormonal levels change. Exercise the muscles, and the body becomes stronger and sleeker" (Hales, 2000: 9). As Judith Lorber and Susan Farrell point out, "it makes more sense to talk of genders, not simply gender, because being a woman and being a man change from one generation to the next and are different for different racial, ethnic, and religious groups, as well as for the members of different social classes" (1991: 1). This does not mean that biology is irrelevant. What it does mean is that sex differences cannot be attributed to biology alone.

# Growing Up Feminine or Masculine

When parents answer the question about the sex of their new child, they trigger a range of social responses that have very little to do with genes, hormones, or reproductive capacities. Sex distinctions are a central part of the content and structure of child-rearing practices in the home, and they are just as integral to the content and structure of **social institutions**, such as the formal education system and the **mass media**. The distinctions are reinforced by the dominant **ideology** manifested in all these social contexts. This is not to suggest that children and adults are mere passive recipients or transmitters of ideas and practices. Through interaction with their social and physical worlds, people alter them as well as their ideas about them. Nevertheless, child-rearing practices, educational systems, and dominant ideologies have a powerful influence on the pace and nature of social change, as well as on the distinctions made between males and females.

### The Influence of the Home

Once we know the sex of a child, we know what toys to bring, what clothes to buy, what colour to paint the baby's room, what stories to read, what games to play, how rough we can be, how much we should talk to the newborn, and what kind of name the child will have, although the specifics of what is considered appropriate within these categories varies with the culture (Mackie, 1996). In recent years, unisex clothes, toys, and hairstyles have become popular, and many parents are attempting to raise their children in what is termed a "non-sexist" manner. Despite some important changes, however, many differences based on sex still persist.

Parents tend to spend more time interacting with little girls, while they not only tend to leave boys alone more often, but also to punish them more often. Boys are more likely to have computers and to be shown how to operate them so they can play their adventure games. Girls tend to be more closely supervised, especially when they reach adolescence. Boys are seldom allowed to wear dresses and are taught rough, physical games such as football. Girls are seldom given footballs or guns to play with, but are taught how to play house and dress Barbie in ball gowns. Toughness, aggression, and emotional control are rewarded in boys and sanctioned in girls (Kilmarten, 1994). When tasks are assigned in the house, boys are told to take out the garbage and shovel the walk, girls to clean the toilet and wash the floor—though more boys are helping with the dishes and operating the microwave. As Jane Gaskell's research on Canadian adolescents shows, the division of household labour contributes to the shared view among young men and women that "young women will add work outside the home to their domestic work" (2001: 229).

These child-rearing practices help shape the physiology, behaviour, and perceptions of both sexes. Girls and boys learn different skills and develop in different ways. Playing with computers and construction equipment encourages males to develop visual–spatial and mathematical skills. Playing hockey encourages them to be aggressive and dominant. Shovelling snow and lugging garbage develop strength and foster muscle growth. At the same time, playing with dolls encourages girls to develop verbal and relational skills. The wearing of stacked heels discourages a range of physical activities, while cleaning toilets contributes little to muscle growth. Close supervision limits adventurousness and encourages passivity or trickery.

Inside and outside of the home, mothers are still considered the primary caregivers. (© Harry Cutting Photography www. harrycutting.com)

These differences in experience also lead females and males to view themselves and the other sex in particular ways. Research undertaken for the Royal Commission on the Status of Women found that children "were more certain about the meaning of masculinity and femininity when they thought in terms of potential jobs or relations than when they thought in terms of personality dispositions" (Lambert, 1971: 69). What they experience in the area of jobs is a division by sex in which the tasks assigned to females have less value, are less interesting, and have less potential than those done by men. What they experience in the area of relations is greater freedom, more choices, and more power for males than for females.

Such division along gender lines is most evident in the context of child care. Even though a majority of women now work in the labour force and men help more than they used to with the children, women still bear the primary responsibility for child care (Frederick, 1995; Ghalam, 2000; Sinclair and Felt, 1992). Some theorists (Chodorow, 1978; Pollack, 1998) have argued that this aspect of the division of labour has profound implications for the psyches of females and males. Given that women are child-rearers, females can continue to identify with their mothers and can feel comfortable with intimate or nurturant relations. Men, on the other hand, can find **identity** only by separating themselves from the caregiver. This painful separation helps create the urge to dominate women and to repress intimate or nurturant behaviour.

Although this explanation simplifies the complex and often contradictory process of gender development (Connell, 1995), it nevertheless draws our attention to the importance of the division of labour in forming gender distinctions in children. It also suggests the implications of these differences for the perceptions of males and females throughout life.

### The Influence of the Educational System

Even if parents try to raise their children in a social environment patterned on equal relations between the sexes, once children enter the educational system they are exposed to sex distinctions and relations in which women are subordinate. Schools often structure classes in ways that encourage girls to focus on courses leading to clerical jobs or other similar work associated with women (Gaskell, 1992; Gaskell and Willinsky, 1995). At the same time, they frequently structure sports in ways that help boys move in other directions and encourage them to be dominant. As former Olympic runner Bruce Kidd makes clear:

> by giving males exciting opportunities, preaching that the qualities they learn from them are "masculine," and preventing girls and women from learning in the same situations, sports confirm the prejudice that males are a breed apart. By encouraging us to spend our most creative and engrossing moments as children and our favorite forms of recreation as adults in the company of other males, they condition us to trust each other more than women. (1987: 255)

The very place of women in the educational system is also instructive for the young. Most principals are men. While most elementary school teachers are women, the higher the level, the greater the number of male teachers. Although university programs have long abandoned a quota on the number of women admitted, many less visible barriers remain in place. Women in post-secondary education are still concentrated in health, education, and the social sciences, while the number of women in science and technology remains low relative to their enrolment in other fields (Statistics Canada, 2000).

Various women's groups—some of them made up of teachers—have exposed and successfully attacked such practices. More women are now principals and greater numbers of men teach in elementary schools, though the latter trend may well be more a reflection of higher wages and scarce employment than of feminist action. When quotas on female enrolments were removed, women rushed to take places in faculties of law, medicine, and dentistry. Indeed, in some institutions women now constitute the majority of those enrolled in such traditionally male-dominated programs. Career counsellors discuss non-traditional job possibilities with students, and new courses introduce counsellors to more alternatives for women.

Research revealing the way girls were encouraged to see paid work as secondary to the "real" work as mothers has been used to bring about some changes within the classroom. Indeed, there are now concerns being raised that girls are doing much better in traditional male subjects, leaving the boys behind. However, there is evidence that there is still a **hidden curriculum** that silently encourages girls and boys in different directions (Bourne, McCoy, and Novogrodsky, 1997).

### The Influence of the Media

Gender divisions are reflected in and reinforced by the majority of books, magazines, videos games, music, television programs—in short, all the media. Research a decade ago showed that in television and film there were only half as many parts for women as there were for men (Armstrong, 1991). Women were much less likely than men to be portrayed as the initiators of adventures or as the rescuers in the action. They were more often evaluated primarily in terms of their youth, beauty, and ability to attract a man, while men were more often evaluated in terms of their skills, courage, and ability to capture women (Robinson and Salamon, 1987). The major preoccupation of women of any age in many programs and much music remains being attractive to a man.

The content of some textbooks and some television programs and films has changed. Women are now far more likely to be portrayed as employed outside the home in such fields as medicine or law and as taking the initiative in sexual relationships (changes that reflect a new reality). Nevertheless, in books, as in other media, men are still more powerful and more plentiful, and they are in the society as well. Pictures of gatherings of world leaders make this very clear.

### The Influence of Ideologies

Practices in the home, the educational system, and the media cannot be separated from the dominant ideologies in a society. Indeed, in many ways they constitute those ideologies. But ideologies are not static—they are constantly being transformed as experiences and interests change. Ideas that do not coincide with people's life experiences or that make little sense of people's lives are difficult to maintain.

Feminist sociologist Dorothy Smith makes it clear that women "have historically and in the present been excluded from the production of forms of thought, images, and symbols in which their experience and social relations are expressed and ordered" (1975: 353). She goes on to argue that women "have never controlled the material or social means to the making of a tradition among themselves or to acting as equals in the ongoing discourse of intellectuals" (353).

While many would argue that women have developed some specifically female ideologies, few would challenge the notion that men have been in a far better position than women to have their views of the world and its workings prevail. This has been the case even in the home, traditionally the woman's sphere, because it is men who have most often provided the primary monetary support. Moreover, the male view of the place of both men and women is likely to reaffirm the dominance of men, given their continuing superior place in the home, the educational system, and the media.

Although women do not control what Smith calls "the means of mental production" (1975: 355), they have nonetheless developed their own perspectives from their own life experiences. For instance, the traditional notion of women focusing exclusively on the home no longer makes sense in light of women's actual experiences. As women gain power in every social institution, their views are likely to become more visible and shared by men. Nevertheless, in 1995, while 41 per cent of women disagreed with the notion that what most women want is home and family, this was the case for only 34 per cent of men (Ghalam, 2000: 72).

Ideologies, child-rearing practices, the division of labour by sex, the education system, and the media all work together to shape infants into feminine and masculine adults. At the same time, children and adults of both sexes are shaping the practices and ideas of society in response to changes in their daily experiences and the structure of their lives.

## The Division of Labour by Sex

Gender divisions are still most obvious in the context of work. Men and women tend to do different work, in different places, for different wages. These differences in work not only create both limits and possibilities, but also help shape the ideas of members of each sex about themselves. In turn, work itself is shaped by the ideas people bring with them to the job, by employers' demands, and by people's responsibilities outside their paid labour.

### Paid Work

As with their clothing and hairstyles, women and men's paid work has become increasingly similar in recent years. Women have been moving into the labour force in greater numbers, so the gap between male and female participation rates has been narrowing. In 1976, 42 per cent of women and 73 per cent of men were counted as employed; women constituted just over one-third of the labour market. By 2003, the official employment rates were 57 per cent for women and 68 per cent for men, with women forming 46 per cent of the labour market (Statistics Canada, 2004: 6). These figures actually underestimate the number of women employed at some point during the year and hide significant variations by marital status, citizenship status, race, and culture (Statistics Canada, 2000).

Most of the increase in female labour-force participation is accounted for by the movement of married women into the labour market, largely in response to family economic need. Even married women with young children are keeping their paid jobs. In 2004, over two-thirds of women with preschool-aged children were in the labour force (Statistics Canada, 2004: 7). Edward Pryor points out that between 1971 and 1981 the income of wives "was the significant factor in preventing family income from declining in real dollars," although "by 1979–81, increases in wives' income were no longer able to offset the decline in husbands' average income" (1984: 102). By the end of the 1990s, wives' income accounted for nearly one-third of household income in dual-earner families (Statistics Canada, 2000: 140). Without wives' income, the number of families living in poverty would increase by three-quarters of a million and many more would suffer significant setbacks in lifestyle (Statistics Canada, 2000: 146).

Furthermore, a growing number of women have taken jobs traditionally done by men. According to Katherine Marshall, "during the 1971–1981 period, the proportional representation of women increased in all but 1 of the 34 professions identified as male-dominated" (1987: 8). The largest percentage increases were in management, law, veterinary work, and engineering, while the largest numerical increases were in management, pharmacy, law, post-secondary teaching, and medicine (Marshall, 1987). This invasion into male-dominated domains was not limited to the professions, but extended to construction, agriculture, mining, and forestry. A few women even acquired licences to operate their own fishing boats. The pace of the movement of women into these occupations has slowed since then, but women do still move into male-dominated fields.

As more women have entered the labour force and followed patterns similar to men's, more of them have joined unions. Indeed, women's unionization rate grew throughout the 1970s and 1980s, while that of men declined. However, the number of employees grew in the 1990s faster than the rate of unionization. By 2001, only 30 per cent of men and women belonged to unions (Statistics Canada, 2002d: 1).

Despite these widely publicized gains, most women have remained doing women's work at women's wages; few have had a choice about taking on paid employment. And many face additional barriers linked to their race, age, or geographical location (Das Gupta, 1996; Statistics Canada, 2000). In 2004,

one-quarter of all employed women still did clerical work, and women accounted for three-quarters of all clerical/administrative workers. Another one in three women did sales or service work (Statistics Canada, 2004: Table 11). Table 7.1 shows that while nearly 30 per cent of women have work in business, finance, and administrative occupations, only 6 per cent of women have managerial jobs. While women account for nearly 90 per cent of those in nursing, therapy, and other health-related jobs, they constitute just over 20 per cent of those in natural and applied sciences. In other words, over half of employed women are segregated into traditionally female clerical, sales, and service employment, as opposed to 26 per cent of men. Thus, although some women moved into traditional male areas, the labour force still remained highly segregated. According to the 1996 census, nearly two-thirds of employed women worked in the 40 jobs in which women accounted for 70 per cent or more of the workers. Men were significantly more dispersed and dominated more job categories—67 of them (Armstrong, 2000: 41, 43).

Not only do women and men do different jobs, they often do them in different places. Three-quarters of those employed in the goods-producing industries were male, while more than half of those working in community, business, and personal services were female (see Table 7.2). Women also are more likely than men to do paid work in their homes. If men do work out of their homes, they are far more likely than women to be their own bosses.

Women also have a greater tendency to work part-time or part of the year. As Table 7.3 indicates, women account for nearly 70 per cent of those employed part-time, a pattern that has changed little over the years. Although the proportion of women employed full-time in the labour force has increased over recent years, it is still the case that over one-quarter have only part-time paid work.

Shorter workweeks and fewer years of paid employment help account for women's lower wages. But this is only part of the story. In 1999, women's average wages were 64.1 per cent of men's—not much improvement over the decade (see Table 7.4). Even full-time wages for women averaged only 72 per cent of full-time wages for men (Akyeampong, 2001: 53).

Census data for 1996 indicate that 80 per cent of those in the 10 highest-paying occupations are male, while nearly three-quarters of those in the 10 lowest-paying occupations are female. Table 7.5 offers a graphic illustration of the wage gap in these top jobs.

## Table 7.1    Female Labour Force 15 Years and Over, by Occupation, 2001

| | Number of women | % female | % of total female labour force |
|---|---|---|---|
| Management occupations | 574,380 | 35.4 | 7.9 |
| Business, finance, and administrative occupations | 2,016,255 | 72.8 | 27.8 |
| Natural and applied sciences and related occupations | 215,620 | 21.5 | 3.0 |
| Health occupations | 642,745 | 79.1 | 8.8 |
| Occupations in social science, education, government service, and religion | 667,340 | 62.4 | 9.2 |
| Occupations in art, culture, recreation, and sport | 235,560 | 54.1 | 3.2 |
| Sales and service occupations | 2,238,510 | 58.7 | 30.1 |
| Trades, transport, and equipment operators and related occupations | 157,845 | 7.2 | 2.2 |
| Occupations unique to primary industry | 153,460 | 23.0 | 2.1 |
| Occupations unique to processing, manufacturing, and utilities | 363,720 | 30.5 | 5.0 |

Source: Adapted from Statistics Canada, "Experienced labour force 15 years and over by occupation and sex (2001 Census)," available at <http://www40.statcan/l01/cst01/labor45a.htm>, accessed on 16 January 2005.

## Table 7.2    Female Labour Force, by Industry, 2004

| | Number of women | % female | % of total female labour force |
|---|---|---|---|
| **Goods-producing sector** | **944.0** | **23.4** | **12.6** |
| Agriculture | 99.2 | 29.7 | 1.3 |
| Forestry, fishing, mining, oil, and gas | 48.3 | 16.2 | 0.6 |
| Utilities | 34.7 | 26.4 | 0.5 |
| Construction | 114.9 | 11.7 | 1.5 |
| Manufacturing | 646.9 | 28.3 | 8.6 |
| **Services-producing sector** | **6,545.5** | **54.6** | **87.4** |
| Trade | 1,210.4 | 48.4 | 16.2 |
| Transportation and warehousing | 195.9 | 24.5 | 2.6 |
| Finance, insurance, real estate, and leasing | 574.7 | 58.4 | 7.7 |
| Professional, scientific, and technical services | 431.8 | 42.2 | 5.8 |
| Business, building, and other support services | 294.0 | 46.8 | 3.9 |
| Educational services | 695.0 | 65.9 | 9.3 |
| Health care and social assistance | 1,427.8 | 81.6 | 19.1 |
| Information, culture, and recreation | 351.8 | 48.8 | 4.7 |
| Accommodation and food services | 608.9 | 60.2 | 8.1 |
| Other services | 360.0 | 51.7 | 4.8 |
| Public administration | 395.4 | 48.2 | 5.3 |

Source: Adapted from Statistics Canada, "Employment by industry and sex (2004)," available at <http://www40.statcan.ca/l01/cst01/labor10a.htm>, accessed 16 January 2005.

Although large numbers of women have moved into what is classified as managerial and professional work, they earn significantly less than the men in the same occupational categories. The largest wage gaps are in the male-dominated groups. Although unions have helped close the wage gap in some occupational groups, this is not the case for the primarily non-unionized occupations listed in Table 7.5.

One result of women's lower wages is less power, both within and outside the household. Another is their far greater economic dependence on marriage, to the extent that many women are only a man away from poverty: "In 1997, 2.8 million women, 19 per cent of the total female population, were living in low-income situations, compared with 16 per cent of the male population" (Statistics Canada, 2000: 137).

Table 7.3 **Full-Time and Part-Time Employment in Canada, 1997–2001**

| | 1997 | | 2001 | |
| --- | --- | --- | --- | --- |
| | % Female | % of All Females | % Female | % of All Females |
| **Full-time** | 39.7 | 70.6 | 41.1 | 72.9 |
| 15–24 years | 40.3 | 7.1 | 42.8 | 7.9 |
| 25–44 years | 40.9 | 42.1 | 41.9 | 40.5 |
| 45 years and over | 37.4 | 21.4 | 39.5 | 24.5 |
| **Part-time** | 69.9 | 29.4 | 69.1 | 27.1 |
| 15–24 years | 56.7 | 8.5 | 56.6 | 8.2 |
| 25–44 years | 80.4 | 13.0 | 79.7 | 10.9 |
| 45 years and over | 72.5 | 7.9 | 72.5 | 8.0 |

SOURCE: Adapted from Statistics Canada web site <http://www40.statcan.ca/l01/cst01/labor12.htm>, accessed 5 August 2003.

Table 7.4 **Average Earnings by Sex, 1993–2002 (Constant 2002 Dollars)**

| | Women ($) | Men ($) | Earnings Ratio (%) |
| --- | --- | --- | --- |
| 1993 | 22,300 | 34,700 | 64.1 |
| 1994 | 22,500 | 36,200 | 62.0 |
| 1995 | 23,000 | 35,400 | 64.8 |
| 1996 | 22,700 | 35,300 | 64.5 |
| 1997 | 22,900 | 36,200 | 63.3 |
| 1998 | 23,900 | 37,400 | 64.0 |
| 1999 | 24,200 | 37,800 | 64.0 |
| 2000 | 24,900 | 39,000 | 64.0 |
| 2001 | 25,100 | 39,100 | 64.1 |
| 2002 | 25,300 | 38,900 | 65.2 |

Source: Statistics Canada, "Average earnings by sex and work pattern," available at <http://www40.statcan.ca/l01/cst07/labor01a.htm>, accessed on 16 January 2005.

The difference is accounted for by senior women and lone-parent mothers. On the other hand, more women now can leave an unhappy marriage because they have a job that pays them enough to survive on their own.

The fact that men and women do different jobs for different wages means that they often have different life experiences and possibilities. Women are more likely than men to work in jobs that are dull, repetitive, and boring, with little opportunity for training or advancement (Armstrong and Armstrong, 1983b, 1993). As Figure 7.1 shows, women are more likely to be in employment that includes part-time work (less than 30 hours per week), second jobs, and self-employment. It is interesting to note that across the different age groups, close to 50 per cent of wives have such employment. This reflects an ongoing need for wives to supplement family income and, at the same time, fulfill all their family and household responsibilities.

Men and women also tend to face different health hazards in their paid work. Men are more likely to suffer visible physical injury, women to be exposed to cumulative, invisible hazards that are difficult to trace directly to employment. These tend to create effects such as nervousness, headache, and irritability that are often blamed on female physiology rather than on working conditions (Messing, 1998). Another hazard of the workplace that women are far more likely than men to face is **sexual harassment** (Duffy and Cohen, 2001). To quote Marlene Kadar, "sexual harassment is almost expected in job ghetto areas where women represent the service and clerical occupations. Here women are most vulnerable to a supervisor's or a co-worker's explicit or implicit demands" (1988: 337). In one important aspect, however, women's and men's jobs are very similar. While both girls and boys are likely to have female caregivers, both men and women are likely to have male bosses.

Table 7.5  **10 Highest-Paid Occupations, 2000**

| | Number of workers | % Women | Average earnings ($) | | | Earnings ratio (%) |
| --- | --- | --- | --- | --- | --- | --- |
| | | | Both sexes | Women | Men | |
| **Total – 10 highest-paying occupations** | 237,715 | 23.3 | | | | |
| Judges | 1,825 | 24.4 | 142,518 | 131,663 | 146,008 | 90.2 |
| Specialist physicians | 12,480 | 30.8 | 141,597 | 98,383 | 160,833 | 61.2 |
| Senior managers – financial, communications carriers, and other business services | 40,919 | 21.5 | 130,802 | 90,622 | 141,829 | 63.9 |
| General practitioners and family physicians | 22,040 | 30.8 | 122,463 | 96,958 | 133,789 | 72.5 |
| Dentists | 8,710 | 22.9 | 118,350 | 82,254 | 129,104 | 63.7 |
| Senior managers – goods production, utilities, transportation, and construction | 44,630 | 11.6 | 115,623 | 75,267 | 120,914 | 62.2 |
| Lawyers and Quebec notaries | 47,290 | 31.0 | 103,287 | 77,451 | 114,894 | 67.4 |
| Senior managers – trade, broadcasting, and other services, n.e.c. | 37,690 | 17.8 | 101,176 | 67,161 | 108,527 | 61.8 |
| Securities agents, investment dealers, and traders | 17,765 | 36.8 | 98,919 | 55,299 | 124,290 | 44.5 |
| Petroleum engineers | 4,370 | 10.0 | 96,703 | 61,057 | 100,633 | 60.7 |

Source: Pay Equity Task Force, Pay Equity: A New Approach to a Fundamental Right (Ottawa: Department of Justice, 2004); available at <http://canada.justice.gc.ca/en/payeqsal/index.html>, accessed 16 January 2005. Reproduced with the permission of the Minister of Public Works and Government Services Canada, 2005.

Research in both the United States (Hochschild and Machung, 1989) and Canada has shown that the structure of men's jobs can have a significant effect on family life and gender relations. For example, Meg Luxton's interviews in Flin Flon, Manitoba (1983),

Figure 7.1  **Age of Wives with Children, 2000, Percentage of Each Age Group with Non-traditional Employment**

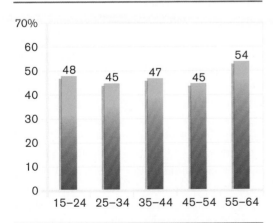

SOURCE: Roger Sauve, "Tracking the Links Between Jobs and Family Job, Family and Stress Among Husbands, Wives and Lone Parents 15–64 from 1990–2000," *Connections* (2002). Reprinted by permission.

show how shift work disrupts social life, making it very difficult for couples to participate together in regularly organized community activities. The frustrations the men interviewed felt over their mining jobs were often brought home and "taken out" on their wives; they were also reflected in disrupted sleep patterns. Luxton's more recent study of families in Hamilton, Ontario, shows such patterns continue (Luxton and Corman, 2001).

The structure of women's paid work likewise affects gender relations in the home. A study conducted in Toronto suggests that the entry of women into full-time work has profound consequences for relationships—one woman explained, "My husband works evenings, from 5 p.m. until 1:30 or 2 a.m. My work hours are from 7 a.m. until 4 p.m. We avoid child care expenses and it gives the kids enough time to spend with both parents" (Johnson, 1986: 18). Such arrangements may allow children to spend more time with their parents, but they don't leave the parents much time to spend with each other. In their study of Toronto women, Ann Duffy, Nancy Mandell, and Norene Pupo found that many women who had paid work "describe such burnout symptoms as chronic fatigue, depression, apathy, irritability and anxiety" (1989: 37). These symptoms are bound to affect the relationships of couples. A decade later, Bonnie Fox still found that "parenthood has meant increased differences between the lives of women and men with respect to responsibility, work and time," regardless of whether both had paid employment (2001c: 296).

On the positive side, as employment patterns grow more similar for both sexes, women and men can share their work experiences, which may serve to bring a couple closer together. Parenthood is also more shared. More research is necessary before we have a clear idea about how the conditions of women's and men's work are reflected in their relationships. More research is also necessary on how the work of women and men in different classes, racial and cultural groups, age groups, and locations affects gender relations.

### Unpaid Work

Unpaid work, like paid work, is segregated. Women not only do work different from that of men, they also do more work. As Figure 7.2 shows, regardless of the employment arrangement between the spouses, women do more housework than their husbands.

Study after study has shown that women and men do different kinds and amounts of labour in the home. Research conducted in the 1970s in Vancouver concluded that "most married women do the regular, necessary and time-consuming tasks in the household

Women entering the workforce have to face not only often unchallenging jobs and lower wages, but also the possibility of sexual harassment, whether explicit or implicit. (© Harry Cutting Photography www.harrycutting.com)

every day" (Meissner et al., 1975: 431) and that "when men's workload and regular housework are plotted against their own job hours . . . and compared with the data for women, men always work less than women" (429). On the basis of their Newfoundland research, Peter Sinclair and Lawrence Felt report that women's "routine housework declines somewhat as hours of employment increase. . . . It is hardly possible for men to reduce their participation" because they are already doing so little (1992: 67).

Luxton's research in Flin Flon, Manitoba (1983), indicates that when husbands do take over work in the home, they tend to do tasks with clearly defined boundaries or those that are the least boring or monotonous. On the basis of a study in Halifax, Nova Scotia, Susan Shaw (1988) suggests that this is why men tend to define cooking and home chores as leisure. Moreover, men's contribution does not seem to significantly reduce women's domestic workload. For example, men are helping more with the children, but the father frequently "plays with them and tells them stories and other nice things" while the mother performs most of the personal services and other tasks associated with child-rearing (Luxton, 1983: 37).

Even when women have paid jobs outside the home, they still do most of the domestic work. In his Toronto study, William Michelson found that wives do three times as much household work as their husbands: "In families where the wife has a part-time job, this ratio is approximately 5 to 1, and it increases to 6.7 to 1 when the wife is employed" (1985: 65). In other words, when wives take on paid work, they take on an additional job and get very little help from their husbands. Susan Clark and Andrew Harvey's Halifax research indicates that "at the present time it appears that the wife does most of the adapting; she reduces her household work and leisure hours quite significantly and is more likely than her husband to hold a part-time job" (1976: 64). Studies among unemployed men in Northern Ontario (Wilkinson, 1992) and among immigrant men in Toronto (Haddad and Lam, 1988) do indicate that some men increase their workload when they are unemployed or when their spouses take on paid work, but a clear division of both amounts and types of labour remains. There is little indication that things have changed significantly since this research was done. In 1996, two-thirds of those doing less than 5 hours a week of unpaid housework were men while over 80 per cent of those doing 60 or more hours were women (Statistics Canada, 2003b). And "women's share of unpaid work hours has remained quite stable since

7.2

# Sociology in Action
## More Work for Mother

More and more women are taking on paid work in addition to their domestic work. The most recent data indicate that the overwhelming majority of married women had paid work at some time during the year. This second job has important consequences for women and for their relations with men. Research conducted by Graham Lowe for the Canadian Advisory Council on the Status of Women (1989) concluded that 80 percent of women's illness can be attributed to the stress caused by their double day of paid and unpaid work. This stress may have an impact on relationships with men. When asked if her husband helped at home, one secretary replied:

Are you kidding? That's why I had a big fight with my husband last week because I was fed up. He was complaining about this and that and I turned around and gave it to him. I said, "I work seven hours a day. I come home, I make supper, I clean up." I said, "I do work before I leave in the morning. All weekend I'm working like crazy to get the house clean." I said, "You've got the nerve to tell me not to use the bathroom because you want to use it in the morning."

SOURCE: Pat Armstrong and Hugh Armstrong, *The Double Ghetto: Canadian Women and their Segregated Work* (Toronto: Oxford University Press, 2001), 207.

the early 1960s," in spite of their growing labour-force participation (Statistics Canada, 2000: 97).

Although women with relatively high-paying careers can afford to hire other women to do much of the domestic work, any remaining tasks are still divided by sex and done disproportionately by women. In her study of career women, Isabella Bassett reports that "close to half the career women polled say cleaning the house, grocery shopping, and doing the laundry are their responsibility, and over half say the same about cooking. This traditional division of labour applies also to the so-called 'male' jobs: two-thirds of career women say household repairs and maintenance are their husband's duties in their households" (1985: 144).

Women take primary responsibility for the sick, disabled, and elderly as well. As daughters, mothers, partners, friends, or volunteers, women are the overwhelming majority of unpaid primary caregivers and spend more time than men providing care. As Figure 7.3 shows, women are expected to take time off from work to take care of sick children or other child-related problems. This in turn greatly hinders women's ability to advance or be promoted in the workplace.

Women are also much more likely than men to do personal tasks such as bathing and toileting, while men are more likely to do household maintenance tasks (Frederick and Fast, 1999; Morris et al., 1999).

Figure 7.2 **Percentage of Spouse 15+ with Children Who Do 30 or More Hours of Unpaid Housework per Week by Labour-Force Status, 1996**

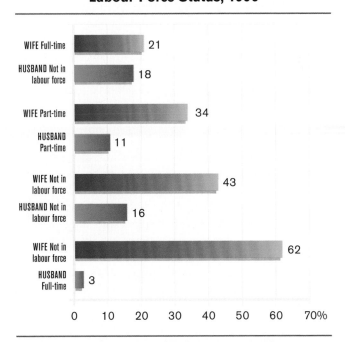

SOURCE: Roger Sauve, "Tracking the Links Between Jobs and Family Job, family and Stress Among Husbands, Wives and Lone Parents 15–64 from 1990–2000," *Connections* (2002). Reprinted by permission.

Figure 7.3    **Days Lost for Personal and Family Reasons Excluding Maternity**

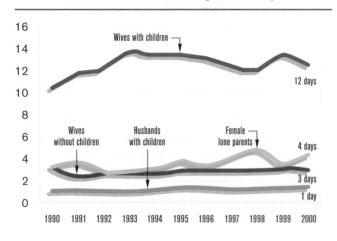

SOURCE: Roger Sauve, "Tracking the Links Between Jobs and Family Job, family and Stress Among Husbands, Wives and Lone Parents 15–64 from 1990–2000," *Connections* (2002). Reprinted by permission.

Moreover, women's caregiving workloads are increasing as governments across Canada reduce hospital and other institutional care (Armstrong et al., 2001). In situations in which women and men provide support to people outside the home, the former tend to do the regular and time-consuming chores such as housework and babysitting, while the latter help with yardwork and transportation. Similar divisions appear in volunteer work. Women work longer hours than men at volunteer jobs, and they are more likely than men to provide personal care. Men who do volunteer work are most likely to coach male teams or to raise and handle funds.

Like paid work, women's and men's unpaid work is often done in different places and under different conditions, resulting in different experiences. Again, women's domestic work tends to be boring and repetitious, as well as fraught with hidden health hazards and the real possibility of sexual harassment. Thus, "while differences in degree exist among social classes and ethnic groups, women and men in heterosexual partnerships continue to encounter essentially unequal experiences of married life" (Mandell, 2001: 204). We know less about equality in other kinds of partnerships, however.

## Community and Social Life

Relationships between men and women are characterized by change and the persistence of traditional patterns of behaviour—in brief, by ambiguity. The "dating game," politics, and medical services all provide examples of both emerging and lingering patterns in relations between the sexes.

### Dating and Sexual Relations

Women are now more likely to pay their own way and open their own doors, and they are even more likely to take the initiative in sexual activity (Wilson, 2001). Women are also, as far as we can tell from the research, more likely to engage in premarital or extramarital sex than they were in the past. However, young women are still more likely to justify having sexual relationships on the basis of love, while young men are far more likely to refer to physical grounds for sex.

The old double standard for female and male sexual behaviour has weakened significantly but not disappeared entirely with the advent of better contraceptives and new ideas about women's place. Research from 1998 suggests significant gender differences, particularly in relation to having only one partner and the importance of emotional involvement. Women are more likely than men to think it is important to be emotionally involved to have sex and to reject the idea of multiple partners (Meston, 1990). The persistence of the double standard may be related to the failure to develop completely effective and safe birth control techniques and to educate young people about their proper use. The spread of HIV/AIDS may serve to destroy the double standard, however. Both men and women are being educated about and encouraged to use condoms. Moreover, as pointed out earlier, AIDS has given men in particular cause for concern about the consequences of casual sex and therefore may make their sexual practices more similar to those of women, who have had to worry throughout history about the results of sexual contact. AIDS has also contributed to more public discussion of homosexual relationships.

Both the availability of contraception and women's participation in the labour force have given women greater choice about whether, when, and whom to marry. They also have more choice to enter lesbian relationships, although severe pressure against such relationships remains. Men now have greater choice as well because they do not have to assume the main financial burden of maintaining a household when they marry or have children. These changes may help to explain why more and more couples are living in conjugal relationships outside of marriage. Couples may live together without marriage because they want to see whether they are compatible, because they cannot marry for a variety of reasons, to save money, or because they reject the notion of marriage. Living together does not necessarily mean a rejection of marriage, however—many of these couples do marry eventually.

### Politics

Women have gained many legal and political rights since the turn of the century, including the right to vote and to be elected or appointed to political office. These rights have, in turn, helped to change laws related to equal opportunity for paid employment, to equal pay, and to property rights, to name but a few (Boyd, 1997; Brodie, 1996).

Women not only vote, they also run for office. The number of women who hold political office has grown enormously in recent decades, although women are still under-represented in Canadian politics. Canada's first female Prime Minister, Kim Campbell, held office for a short period in 1993 after being selected as leader of the Progressive Conservative Party, but in the ensuing election she and her party suffered a massive defeat. As of 2005, two women had served as provincial premiers, one by election, the other by assuming the leadership of her party. The active participation of women in politics has significantly altered relations within legislatures, regulatory bodies, and the courts, as well as altering legislation itself. Women's concerns and perspectives are more often taken into account.

In the political arena, too, the sexes frequently remain segregated. Although women have participated at all levels of government, the largest proportion of women is found in municipal politics, the lowest level of decision-making. Her study of municipal politics led Kathryn Kopinak to conclude that "women candidates and elected officials occupy positions of greater strength than men on several political dimensions," but also to suggest that this may be related to their smaller numbers at the higher levels (1988: 385). Little has changed in the intervening years. Furthermore, within municipal politics, women are segregated into traditional areas such as school boards, where they can oversee what is happening to the children. The balance of power is shifting, but the seats at the top are still reserved mainly for the men.

### Medical Services

Relations between the sexes in the area of medical services are also changing, albeit very slowly. Significant differences remain in the treatment of women as compared with men, reflecting old ideas about the relations between the sexes and about women's proper place. Most research still is done on male subjects and the results generalized to women; fewer studies are done on women, and even less research is done on differences among women (Manzer, 2001). Men are less likely than women to use health-care services (Health Reports, 2001); when they do, they are more likely to be treated as if they have a "real," biologically based medical problem. Ruth Cooperstock and Henry Lennard found that "women consistently receive twice the proportion of prescriptions for tranquilizers as do men" (1987: 314). Such prescriptions have been justified as a way of supporting social relationships, especially those based on sex. The prescription of tranquilizers to women is also "consistent with the culturally accepted view that it is the role of the wife to control the tensions created by a difficult marriage": Valium is used "as an aid in the maintenance of the nurturing, caring role" (Cooperstock and Lennard, 1987: 318).

Women's greater use of health services, which is related largely to their reproductive capacity, serves to reinforce the notion of dependency and the need for medical management. But as women move into the labour force and attain higher levels of education, traditional medical approaches are coming under attack—from men as well as women. Men now tend to be present not only at the births of their children, but also at prenatal classes. Such developments also influence relations between the sexes, often serving to bring women and men closer together as they share aspects of childbearing and other life experiences.

## Explanations for Inequality: Making Connections

There is at least one woman and one man in every occupational category. Some women are bosses; some women are sexual harassers. Some men stay at home and take responsibility for household chores and child care, while most never harass women or batter their wives. These facts reinforce the view that biology is not a major factor determining the division of labour by sex. Nonetheless, biology is far from irrelevant. The fact that women, not men, have babies does make a difference in society. Childbirth and child-rearing are separate from paid work. Because women bear children and because people have created a distinction between different kinds of work, women are to some extent limited from participating in the same way as men do in the labour force.

The differences are exaggerated by women's low wages and by the scarcity and high cost of child care. In addition, "licensed or regulated family daycare is still a rarity in Canada" (Baker, 2001b: 110). Good child care is not only difficult to find, it is also expensive. Daycare fees average almost half the average female wage. Consequently, the families most likely to enjoy access to such care still have "either an income high enough to pay for the service or an income low enough to qualify for subsidy" (Status of Women Canada, 1986: 72). For the many families who cannot afford or find daycare, it often makes economic sense for the woman to stay at home because she earns the lower wages. The young working-class Vancouver women interviewed by Gaskell (1992: 80) often said they would prefer working for pay to staying home with the children but saw little hope of having their male partners stay at home instead, given women's wages. Fewer women are dropping out of the labour force when they have children and more men provide care, but if anyone leaves the workforce to provide child care, it is almost always the female partner. As pointed out earlier, the same is true when elderly parents and disabled adult children require care. This type of work interruption can serve to boost men's earning potential and to reduce that of women—or at least be used as an excuse to do so.

Women's reproductive capacity and the social arrangements that turn this resource into a liability are not the only factors in the continuing division of labour by sex. The dominant ideology also plays a role. And this ideology is changing, especially for the younger generations. By 1995, the vast majority of women and men under the age of 24 thought paid work was important to personal happiness; however, over half of the men and women surveyed also thought growing children would suffer if both parents were employed (Ghalam, 2000: 70–1). Furthermore, many employers remain convinced that women are physically and mentally suited to some jobs and not others. Career women surveyed by Bassett (1985) cited sex discrimination as the most important factor contributing to their failure to win top jobs. Similarly, a Calgary study found that women in male-dominated professions had to work harder to establish authority, and it was assumed they had "greater split loyalties between work and home than their male peers" (Falkenberg, 1988: 77). A recent *Psychology Today* article reports that "women in male-dominated fields are so intimidated by their work environment that they tend to play down certain typically female traits" (2000: 18). For their part, many women have learned by example and experience that men and women do different work, and this notion has become part of their world view (Gaskell, 1992).

But economic need and the need of employers for employees can overturn ideology. Many married women move into the labour market because their families need the money, but during most of this century, single women have relied on paid work for personal economic survival. Women who are single parents depend either on wages or on welfare, given that the majority of women do not get support payments after separation but they do get the children (Galarneau and Sturrock, 1997). In addition, employers' need for people with the skills women have traditionally learned, as well as for cheap, often part-time, labour, has increased (see Table 7.3). Women have thus provided what Patricia Connelly (1978) described as a "reserve army"—a large number of workers who are available and who compete with others in their group for the jobs they can get.

Women's subordinate position in the labour market has reinforced their responsibility for domestic work. At the same time, women's domestic responsibilities have reinforced their subordinate position in the market. As women have gained both experience and income—at the same time suffering from the competing demands of paid and unpaid work—their ideas have changed. The resulting protests against male-dominated society and its ideology have changed both society and some of its dominant ideas.

Although large divergences remain, male and female life experiences have become more similar in recent years. Shared experiences open up new possibilities for more egalitarian relationships—though they may also create new areas of tension.

## Strategies for Change

Many women (and some men) have developed various strategies for change. Individual women have pushed men to do more domestic labour. They have entered the labour market, striven for interesting and well-paid jobs, and fought to end discrimination in the workplace. They have had the courage to publicize such previously hidden crimes as sexual harassment, wife abuse, and sexual assault, and to charge men—even their own husbands—with them.

Collectively, many women have worked—sometimes together with men—to create the conditions in which such individual efforts are possible and effective and to alter the structures that keep women subordinate. Women have succeeded in pressuring governments to pass laws recognizing women's equal contri-

**7.3**

## Open for Discussion
### The High Cost of an Interrupted Career

Statistics Canada data reveal that women who interrupt their careers in order to fulfill family responsibilities suffer in terms of pay and promotion. Meanwhile, being married can raise a man's income by 30 per cent. In 1997, married women earned only 68 per cent of married men's wages (Statistics Canada, 2000: 157). When this research was made public, it was suggested that it should be used to convince judges to award higher settlements to women when marriages end in divorce.

Yet career interruptions explain only part of the gap in pay and promotion. A Statistics Canada study concludes,

> Despite the addition of a rich variety of workplace variables, a substantial portion

of the gender wage gap remains baffling. After accounting for differences in worker characteristics, women's hourly wage rate is 83.9 per cent of the men's average. . . . Once differences in the characteristics of the workplace to which men and women belong are controlled for, women's average hourly wage rate is 86.9 per cent of men's average. . . . The inclusion of industry and occupation yield considerably larger adjusted gender pay differentials: women earn roughly 91.6 per cent of comparable men. (Drolet, 2001: 42)

In other words, various forms of discrimination combine to create these inequalities.

---

bution to marriage, mandating equal pay for work of equal value, providing maternity leave for employed women, and making legal offences of job discrimination, sexual harassment, and the sexual assault of wives by their own husbands. Women have succeeded in encouraging schools to develop new materials for classroom use that represent women doing more than domestic and secretarial work. Largely as a result of women's efforts, many of the practices (such as quotas) that prevented many women from entering such programs as law, medicine, and engineering have been ended. Women also have developed education programs to expand female skills and to provide information on birth control and self-protection. They have opened homes for battered women, rape crisis centres, and daycare centres. They have fought for affirmative action programs and for women's right to be heard in union affairs . . . and much more.

At the same time, men have started men's support groups and developed organizations intended to reduce violence against women. Increasing numbers of men are also seeking custody of their children and advocating equal rights for same-sex couples. They have actively worked to include the issues raised by the women's movement in classroom discussions and media presentations. More men are taking courses that teach them domestic skills, though few have enrolled in traditionally female university programs

such as nursing and domestic science. Some men have taken on their share of domestic work or opted to stay at home to care for the children.

Certain of these strategies have been successful in altering patterns and relations; many have not. Both men and women have resisted changes in gender relations (Cockburn, 1991; Faludi, 1991, 1999). Men in general and employers in particular have too much at stake to willingly alter the status quo. It cannot be denied, however, that relations between women and men have been fundamentally altered over the past few decades. Some men have learned the joys of child care, the skills involved in domestic work, the strengths of female managers, the value of egalitarian relationships, the relief of not being the sole breadwinner, the negative consequences of sexual harassment and unprotected sex. It can no longer be assumed that a girl will be a mother and homemaker, or a boy a breadwinner and hero. Nor can it be assumed that all families will consist of partners of different sexes living with their own biological children.

## Looking Ahead

Canadian society has been undergoing a fundamental economic restructuring that is bound to have a profound effect on gender relations. Jobs in resource-based industries, manufacturing, construction, and wholesale trade have disappeared, or at least become much less secure, in the face of free trade, new technologies, and new managerial strategies. Most of these jobs were held by men, and many were highly paid, unionized, full-time, and relatively permanent. Moreover, their existence was critical in making possible what is often called the "traditional" family, with mother at home and father in the workforce.

While jobs have become more precarious in the male-dominated areas, job growth has been in the service sector, where women dominate and where much of the work is part-time or short-term, insecure, and without union protection. Many service-sector jobs were created by the state, especially in health, social services, and education, where women dominate. But governments are now cutting back, and many of these jobs have disappeared or become precarious.

These developments have important consequences for both sexes. First of all, women and men are increasingly finding themselves in direct competition for work in all fields. Second, men's employment patterns are becoming more like women's as more men take part-time and short-term jobs in the sectors

in which women have traditionally worked and in which more women have full-time employment. A third result is that, with men less able to be breadwinners, there is even greater pressure on women to take paid work.

These changes in the labour market could lead to greater equality. Men's taking on of women's traditional paid work may develop more of the skills and personality traits relevant to family care; part-time workers may have more time to spend at home. As a result, domestic labour may become more equally shared as many women and men have more time to devote to household work. At the same time, women who become the family breadwinner may better understand the pressures men face; they may also acquire more power and more of the characteristics men develop as a consequence of their paid work.

The same changes could aggravate tensions between the sexes. Competition for scarce wage labour could lead to confrontations between men and women. Indeed, there has already been some backlash against employment and pay equity programs, as well as against public-sector jobs. Women's lower wages

The daily struggles of mothers to balance work and child care are further exacerbated by recent governmental reductions in hospital and institutional care. (© GettyImages/Photodisc)

mean that families dependent on a female breadwinner sink into poverty. Women are taking on more child care, elder care, and domestic work as a result of cutbacks in government services. Government restructuring of social programs is creating an equality deficit in many areas because many more women than men were dependent on such programs (Day and Brodsky, 1998). The decision of most provinces to close some institutions for those with disabilities means that more women provide home care for those previously institutionalized. At the same time, men who can no longer make a significant contribution to family economic support may leave because they are unable to face what many regard as their failure to act like men. Both tendencies—greater equality and greater tension—are evident today. Which one will prevail depends largely on the responses of men and women themselves.

## Conclusion

Relations between women and men have been characterized both by change and by lack of change in recent years. Although women have gained certain important rights, greater access to traditionally male-dominated institutions and jobs, and some protection from abuse, they still bear the primary load in domestic work, have lower wages than men, and face a double standard in many relationships. Put another way, although more men are helping with the housework and child care, learning to express their emotions, and treating women as equals, men still dominate in the most prestigious jobs in the labour force and seldom take on an equal share of caring work.

Biologically predetermined characteristics provide little explanation for these patterns, because there are few clearly established biological distinctions between the sexes and because biological factors are influenced to a high degree by the social and physical environments. Social structures and work relations provide much more useful explanations for change and lack of change in gender relations. These institutions and interactions are now undergoing significant changes themselves, changes that will have profound consequences for how men and women view one another. But these consequences are not predetermined. They will depend greatly on the decisions and actions taken by women and men, individually and collectively, to shape their own lives.

## □ Questions for Critical Thought

1. Why is it disturbing to some persons when they cannot readily determine a person's sex? Do you think this situation is a reasonable cause for such feelings?
2. Do you think it is possible to separate nature from nurture, biology from culture? Explain your reasoning.
3. Do similar clothes and hairstyles worn by males and females mean they will show similar kinds of behaviour?
4. Do we expect the same behaviour from a black man as from a white man, from a rich woman as from a poor woman? Why or why not?
5. Discuss the effect of HIV/AIDS on the double standard in sexual behaviour.
6. How do you explain women's continuing responsibility for domestic work when they take on full-time employment?
7. Select an article from a magazine directed at a female audience, and one from a magazine intended for a male audience. Compare the magazines with respect to the portrayal of women and men themselves and to the portrayal of the relations between the sexes.

## ☐ Recommended Readings

**Pat Armstrong and Hugh Armstrong,** *The Double Ghetto: Canadian Women and Their Segregated Work* **(Toronto: Oxford University Press, 2001).**
> Linking women's paid and unpaid work, this book examines different explanations for patterns in women's jobs.

**Meg Luxton and June Corman,** *Getting By in Hard Times: Gendered Labour at Home and on the Job* **(Toronto: University of Toronto Press, 2001).**
> Based on interviews with household members in Hamilton, Ontario, this book connects class and gender relations, family forms, labour markets, and the process of capital accumulation.

**Statistics Canada,** *Women in Canada 2000: A Gender-Based Statistical Report* **(Ottawa: Statistics Canada, 2000).**
> This compilation of data on the status, health, education, income, and family status of women is accompanied by useful, descriptive text. Important chapters include Aboriginal and immigrant women, visible minority women, and senior women.

**Stephen M. Whitehead and Frank J. Barrett, eds,** *The Masculinities Reader* **(Oxford: Blackwell, 2000).**
> The articles brought together in this text provide an overview of issues linked to being male in North American society.

## ☐ Recommended Web Sites

**Centres of Excellence for Women's Health**
**www.cewh-cesf.ca**
> This Web site offers access to a wide range of materials on women's health issues. Women's health is broadly defined to include factors that influence health as well as male/female differences in health.

**Status of Women Canada (SWC)**
**www.swc-cfc.gc.ca**
> SWC is the federal government department that promotes gender equality and the full participation of women in the economic, social, cultural, and political life of the country. SWC focuses its work in three areas: improving women's economic autonomy and well-being, eliminating systemic violence against women and children, and advancing women's human rights.

**Women Watch**
**www.un.org/womenwatch/**
> The United Nations Convention on the Elimination of Discrimination Against Women can be found on this site, along with routes to a variety of documents the United Nations produces on the current situation of women in the world.

# 8

Michael Rosenberg

# Ethnic and Race Relations

© W.P. Wittman Limited

## Learning Objectives

In this chapter, you will:

- become familiar with the sociological concepts of ethnicity and race and with some of the theories sociologists have developed to explain these phenomena

- come to understand the role of ethnic and racial groups in the evolution of Canadian society

- identify some of the major issues and concerns regarding immigration and the retention of ethnic identities in Canadian society

- examine the ways in which ethnicity and race can intersect with other social factors, such as gender and politics

- identify some fundamental patterns of relations among Canadians (bilingualism and multiculturalism) that are based on ethnic identity and diversity

- consider the differences between prejudice, discrimination, and racism, and the impact of each on Canadian society

## Introduction

In Canada, ethnic and racial diversity is a fact of life. Canada accepts more immigrants on a proportional basis than any other industrialized country, and the people who come to Canada are members of all of the major ethnic and racial groups to be found in the world. In the 2001 census, Canadians indicated more than 200 distinct ethnic origins, including such new groups (for Canada) as Kosovars, Azerbaijani, Nepali, Kashmiri, Yoruba, Ashanti, and Maya and Carib Indians (Statistics Canada, 2003a). Canadians, it would seem, value diversity and enjoy the blend of cultures, languages, and practices it promotes, especially in the large urban areas where most of the recent immigrants are to be found.

Canada has always been a culturally plural society. Founded as a political union of two **ethnic groups**, the British and the French, contemporary Canada owes its constitutional and political structure (as well as some of its problems) largely to the union of these two distinct groups. As a result, **ethnicity** and ethnic group relations hold a special place in Canadian society. Of course, pluralism does not necessarily mean that all groups are treated equally, nor that all have the opportunity to participate fully in the society, as the history of Canada's Native peoples makes clear. Still, Canadians have dealt with most of their group conflicts without violence, and those individuals who oppose ethnic or cultural diversity seem to be a minority among Canadians.

This acceptance of diversity does not seem to be true in many other parts of the world. Ethnic and racial differences, along with differences of religion, language, and national identity, are the bases for animosity, **discrimination**, and violence in many nations. Violence or institutionalized discrimination persists in the relations between Protestants and Catholics in Northern Ireland, between Hindus and Muslims in India, between indigenous peoples and the government in Mexico, between Romanians and Gypsies in Romania. Almost every day, we can read in

Pluralism does not necessarily mean that all groups are treated equally or that all have the opportunity to fully participate in society. The history of Canada's Aboriginal peoples illustrates this fact. This photograph, taken from a *Globe and Mail* special series called "Canada's Apartheid," illustrates an Inuit couple frustrated by their experiences of racism. (Fred Lum/*The Globe and Mail*). Reprinted with permission from *The Globe and Mail*.

newspapers of conflict somewhere in the world between tribal, cultural, or racial groups.

All of this global upsurge of ethnic identification and conflict has been somewhat surprising to most sociologists because for a long time social scientists had assumed that ethnicity would be of declining significance in any modern, industrial society. Industrialization itself, it was thought, would lead to the breakdown of racial and ethnic distinctions as new sources of solidarity—and of conflict—arose. Many Marxists, for example, argued that class differences supersede ethnic divisions and that in time all workers, regardless of race or ethnicity, would come to realize that they share the same interests in opposition to the interests of capitalists. Industrial theorists, too, had argued that ethnic differences would diminish with the spread of modernization. In this case, occupational, professional, or educational statuses were expected to replace ethnic identity in relations among individuals.

Neither of these seems to have happened. Indeed, some of the most violent and bitter ethnic conflicts are found in formerly communist countries, such as Russia, Yugoslavia, and Romania, where the previous Marxist governments worked hard for many years to eradicate ethnic differences. In addition, such highly industrialized nations as Britain, Germany, and France have been the scene for the rise of new racist movements, such as the National Front in France, the British National Party in Britain, and the Republican Party in Germany. Even in the United States, the most industrialized of all nations, racial prejudices persist as the most fundamental dividing line in the society (Smelser, Wilson, and Mitchell, 2001).

The rapid social, economic, cultural, and technological transformations found around the world, such as **globalization** and transnationalism, may make Canada's ethnic and racial diversity a model of what the whole world will be like in the near future. This evolving situation makes it urgent that we understand the nature of that diversity and the impact it has on all Canadians. How are our economy, our political system, and our lifestyles changed by immigration? How are the relations among citizens affected? Are all groups able to participate equally in the fundamental institutions of the country, or are some treated as second-class citizens? Do most Canadians wish to perpetuate diversity, or would they prefer the development of a new consensus among Canadians with respect to language, culture, values, and civic rights? Answering these questions has become a priority for many Canadian social scientists.

To discuss these issues in detail, we must explain what is meant by *ethnicity*, *ethnic groups*, and *ethnic group relations*.

# Defining Ethnicity and Race

It would be convenient to be able to give a clear and unambiguous definition of **ethnicity**. Unfortunately, it is not possible. Like many other sociological concepts, ethnicity is the subject of much disagreement. This is not surprising because ethnicity is a relational phenomenon emerging from the patterns of **social relationships** among and interactions between people and groups. It can take many forms and display many characteristics, nor does it play the same role in Indonesia, in Switzerland, and in Canada.

Nevertheless, ethnicity does possess some key features. In its broadest sense, *ethnicity* refers to sets of social relationships—particularly class, status, or power relationships—defined as being based on inherited biological differences. The noted German sociologist Max Weber ([1908] 1978) defined ethnicity as the sets of social distinctions by which groups differentiate themselves from one another on the basis of presumed biological ties. Members of such groups have a sense of themselves as a common "people" separate and distinct from others.

That this claim to form a "people" is biologically legitimated is of crucial importance. While sociologists and anthropologists often consider cultural distinctions to be just as intimately tied to ethnicity as is biology, cultural distinctiveness is not sufficient to characterize an ethnic group. If it were, then "intellectuals," for example, would constitute an ethnic group in many societies. This is not to say that intellectuals have never formed an ethnic group, but they have done so only after redefining common biological origin as the basis of their solidarity. This last point illustrates another crucial sociological feature of ethnicity: common biological origin need not be real—as long as it is believed to be real (Smith, 1988).

While most claims to ethnic distinctiveness may be biological, the **symbolic markers** used to differentiate groups rarely are biological, with the extremely important exception of racial distinctions. Instead, the indicators of ethnicity used as symbolic markers are usually cultural (De Vos and Romannuci-Ross, 1982; Geertz, 1973). In Canada, for instance, language is a particularly important symbolic marker for both francophones and anglophones. The preservation of the French language has been a source of pride for francophones, while the use of English was for a long time regarded as a sign of higher status by anglophones. Many other groups in Canada, too, consider language an important component of **identity**. Greek, Hungarian, Italian, Polish, and Ukrainian Canadians, for example, consider speaking their ethnic language, if only at home, extremely important for retaining their ethnic identity. Jeffrey Reitz (1980) has found evidence suggesting that they are right. Other symbolic markers are religion, attachment to a homeland, a sense of common history, festivals and ceremonies, traditions, even ethnic food or dress.

Racial distinctions are made according to supposed biological markers. In this case, sociologists use the term *race* rather than *ethnicity* when referring to a group. A *race* is a group that is defined on the basis of perceived physical differences such as skin colour.

Clearly, race and ethnicity are related concepts, and not too long ago it was common to treat ethnic groups as racially distinct. That is why, for instance, the British and French used to be referred to as the two "founding races" of Canada. The contemporary use of the term *race* differs from *ethnicity* in that racial groups are considered to be those whose perceived physical difference play a greater role than cultural differences as a symbolic marker in setting group boundaries. Blacks in Canada, for example, come from many cultural backgrounds. Some were born and raised in Canada, others in the United States; some come from Haiti, others from Jamaica, still others from Africa. To the degree that we treat them or they consider themselves all as a single group on the basis of skin colour alone, however, they constitute a racial group.

Keep in mind that the notion of distinct and definite biological races existing is largely a myth. Furthermore, sociologists are interested in the social, not the physical, significance of race. To sociologists, race is a symbolic marker by which individuals categorize themselves and others into different groups. Indeed, it is questionable whether the term *race* is still a useful one because its use may imply that it refers to real, rather than symbolic, distinctions (Mason, 1999). In Canada, the term *visible minority* has come to replace *race* in designating groups having a perceived physical difference from the white Europeans who make up the majority of Canada's population. Use of the newer term has the advantage of allowing us to avoid the negative emotional significance often attached to the term *race* and to regard groups that seem physically distinct primarily as ethnic groups.

People differ in their views regarding the degree to which their ethnicity plays an important role in their lives or in their identity. Ethnic groups defined largely by religion, such as Hutterites or Doukhabours, and groups whose physical or cultural traits make them conspicuous tend to see ethnicity as highly relevant. Such groups often come to form an *ethnic community*; that is, they develop a set of ethnic institutions based on common interests and identities. An ethnic community may try to close itself off as much as possible from the broader society. This is the case with the Hutterites, who form relatively isolated agricultural communities. Usually, however, an ethnic community is a *partial community*, organized around key institutions, such as an ethnic church, a school, or a political lobby group. However, even the family unit can serve as an institution in an ethnic community. A partial community is embedded in the broader society; most of its members work and live among people who do not belong to their ethnic group. Ethnic interests and identities, then, must compete with other interests and identities, such as those based on occupation, religion, gender, or status.

For some individuals, ethnicity has diminished to the point where it is a minor component of their identity, important only at ethnic festivals or family celebrations, when they cheer their homeland's sports victories or fear for it in time of war. Such people may not form an ethnic community in any sense useful to sociology, but we can still speak of them as an *ethnic group* to the degree that they are potentially capable of organizing and acting upon their ethnic interests or identity. An ethnic group, like an ethnic community, may have some central institutions, but these are unlikely to have been established by the group itself as specifically ethnic institutions. "National" churches, for example, may serve as a focus for group activity, as may ethnic stores, restaurants, or even travel agencies.

Finally, there are people for whom ethnicity is completely irrelevant. Such individuals may well be counted as part of an *ethnic category*, however. An ethnic category is a strictly objective measure of how many people have some particular ethnic origin, regardless of whether they identify with their ethnicity. An individual whose ancestors came from Ireland in the 1840s may consider himself or herself Canadian, or even Québécois(e), but may be counted among those of "Irish" ethnicity in census statistics.

## Theories of Ethnicity

While there are many theories of ethnicity, most tend to fall into two broad categories: pluralistic and remedial. We will now look at each of these in turn.

## Pluralistic Theories

*Pluralistic theories* see ethnic and racial differences among people as natural or inevitable. Their adherents maintain that there have always been and will always be ethnic distinctions between groups.

Many types of pluralistic theories exist. *Sociobiologists*, such as Pierre Van den Berghe (1987), see ethnic groups as based on genetically determined processes of kin selection and reproductive success. *Primordialists*, including John Stack Jr (1986), view ethnic differences as based on emotional ties to others with whom an individual identifies and shares a sense of kinship. American sociologists often link ethnicity to politics, and some argue that ethnic distinctions will exist as long as people form groups to compete for control over public institutions and political entitlements (Bell, 1975; Glazer and Moynihan, 1975).

Perhaps the most influential pluralistic theory is that of Fredrik Barth (1969), whose argument is that ethnic differences are a consequence of the patterns of **social interaction** that generate boundaries among people. By an *ethnic group boundary*, Barth means a "structuring of interaction" that divides people into groups (1969: 16). Ethnic boundaries make use of markers to indicate who is or is not a member of the ethnic group. Patterns of interaction will differ when an individual deals with fellow group members rather than non-members, says Barth, because membership "implies a sharing of criteria for evaluation and judgment . . . [and] the assumption that the two are fundamentally 'playing the same game'" (1969: 15). By contrast, identifying others as non-members "implies a recognition of limitations on shared understandings, differences in criteria for judgment of value and performance, and a restriction of interaction to sectors of assumed common understanding and mutual interest" (15).

Barth's approach has changed the way most sociologists—whether they are pluralists or not—think about ethnicity. Barth showed that an ethnic group cannot be examined in isolation because ethnic groups are always organized around patterns of interaction. As Barth himself put it, "to the extent that actors use ethnic identities to categorize themselves and others for purposes of interaction, they form ethnic groups in [an] organizational sense" (1969: 13–14). Ethnic groups are then seen as forms of social organization, and the issue of how and why ethnic groups are formed becomes an issue of how and why group boundaries are created and maintained.

This perspective is particularly useful because Barth does not assume that any particular set of ethnic group distinctions or ethnic institutions is natural. Instead, ethnicity can be understood only in a specific context, because it reflects the patterns of social relationships among the particular sets of people found in that context. Barth's approach is similar to what is known as the *emergent identity approach*, because it examines how and why the symbolic markers of ethnic identity evolve over time (Yancey, Ericksen, and Juliani, 1976).

## Remedial Theories

*Remedial theories* tend to treat ethnicity as a characteristic of a class or industrial society. While they largely discount the importance of ethnicity in modern societies, remedial theorists nevertheless try to explain how or why ethnicity may be of (temporary) relevance under certain conditions. They argue that ethnic differences are not inevitable but arise from class differences or cultural factors that inhibit economic rationality.

Remedial theories, like pluralistic theories, come in many varieties. *Class theories* tend to link ethnic or racial differences to differences centred on labour. According to the *split labour market theory* described by Edna Bonacich (1972), for example, employers take advantage of ethnic distinctions by paying some workers (who belong to a particular ethnic group) more and others (who belong to another group) less. The inequity is used to explain ethnic antagonisms, since higher-paid workers will attempt to exclude the lower paid. Conflict over access to and control over jobs therefore leads to racial or ethnic conflict.

The theory of *internal colonialism* also explains the relevance of ethnicity in terms of modern economy. As Susan Olzack describes this approach, "an internal colony exists to the extent that a richer and culturally dominant core dominates an ethnically identified periphery" (1983: 359). In this way, the core region is able to take advantage of the economic and political weakness of the peripheral region. The resources and raw materials of the peripheral region may be obtained at reduced cost, while workers in the peripheral area can be used as cheap labour. The result is resentment among the exploited "ethnics" that can lead to nationalist or separatist movements. This approach is little used by Canadian sociologists, since Canada as a whole can be viewed as peripheral to the United States. It has, however, been used by James

Frideres (1988) to account for the disadvantaged position of Native groups in Canada.

A particularly popular remedial approach in Canada looks at the role of **the state** in defining and promoting ethnic distinctions. Leo Panitch (1977) has suggested that the Canadian state played a particularly central role in the country's economic and social development. State policies such as official bilingualism and official **multiculturalism** have not only promoted ethnic distinctions, they have actually defined them. The federal government's policy has been to treat ethnic groups as primarily cultural groups, rather than as religious, national, political, or economic groups. Daiva Stasiulis (1980) has argued that this policy has caused many groups to redefine themselves and has also allowed the state to control ethnic group activities and to determine ethnic group leaders by how and to whom it disburses grants. Peter Li suggests that the policy allows for "managing race and ethnic relations within a state apparatus . . . through fiscal control of ethnic associations whereby the nature, duration, and amount of grants that ethnic associations receive fall in line with the officially defined priorities of multicultural programs" (1988: 132). Versions of this approach have been used by Terry Wotherspoon and Vic Satzewich (1993) to understand the relations between Native groups and the state, by Michael Rosenberg and Jack Jedwab (1992) to identify organizational differences between major ethnic groups in Montreal, and by Raymond Breton (1984, 1989) to examine the impact of state policy on ethnic identity and concerted group action.

A popular remedial approach in the United States is the theory of *symbolic ethnicity*—ethnicity that has become purely a matter of personal identification and that has little or no impact upon how people live their lives or relate to each other. Herbert Gans (1979) introduced the concept to resolve a seeming paradox in American social life: the resurgence of ethnicity in a society where people's lives have become increasingly alike. Third-, fourth-, or fifth-generation Italian, Polish, or Greek Americans have little that distinguishes them from one another, yet a so-called ethnic revival began in the United States in the late 1960s. In a sense, the phenomenon should not pose a paradox—as the real distinctions among people diminish, it is not surprising that those few distinctions that remain become more important, more central to group or personal identity. This can be seen in Quebec in the contemporary emphasis on the French language as the mark of a distinctive

Québécois identity while the other characteristics that once served as distinguishing marks of Quebec society, such as a rural lifestyle and a commitment to Catholic institutions, have all but disappeared.

Gans's assumption (underlying his use of the concept of symbolic ethnicity) seems to be that if ethnicity is merely symbolic, then it loses both its impact on everyday life and its ability to divide American society. In effect, ethnicity becomes purely a matter of personal sentiments. This theory is much less popular among Canadian sociologists because it neither reflects the corporate character of many ethnic groups in Canadian society nor the links between ethnicity and inequality. Furthermore, as the example of the role played by the French language in Quebec demonstrates, ethnic differences that are "only" symbolic can be as dynamic as any others.

## Ethnicity in the Canadian Context

While the resurgence of ethnicity has been something of a surprise to most sociologists, Canadian sociologists may be less surprised than others. Sociologists in this country have long acknowledged the significance of ethnicity in Canadian society and have been at the forefront of theory and research on ethnic phenomena.

Ethnic and racial groups are more likely to take an institutional form in Canada than in the United States, Britain, or Germany for two reasons: the special role played by ethnicity in Canadian society, and the official policies of bilingualism and multiculturalism, initiated and promoted by the federal and various provincial governments. These two factors have caused Canadian sociologists to direct much of their attention to two issues: the connection between ethnicity and inequality in Canadian society, and the integration—or lack of integration—of ethnic groups and communities into Canadian society.

John Porter's description of Canadian society as a **vertical mosaic** (1965) stimulated research into the link between ethnicity and inequality. Porter asserts that an individual's ethnicity defined his or her "place" within Canada's stratified social system. Immigrants and their children had little social mobility. Most people in Canada tended to retain their ethnic *entrance status*, that is, their occupational, educational, or social status upon first arrival. Porter's data showed that the groups of British and French origin dominated Canadian society with respect to economics, politics, and status. Other groups fell into place in what was effectively an ethnically divided stratification system—the vertical mosaic—that promoted ethnic community organization. The various minority ethnic groups imitated the earlier example of the French and the British by treating ethnicity less as a matter of individual sentiment than as a form of collective organization that could be designed to meet collective interests.

Hubert Guindon (1967) argues that the cleavage between British and French had a structural impact on the development, nature, and context of ethnic inter-group relations. Following the British Conquest, a pattern of ethnic and religious institutional self-segregation developed between the British and French communities, resulting in two parallel societies. While they did interact somewhat in the areas of politics and work, the two groups maintained a rigorous separation of language, education, religion, residence, and marriage. Although the popular description of Canada's British and French communities as "two solitudes" ignores the important realities of class, status, and political divisions within each of what are often called the **charter groups**, there is nevertheless a sense in which each has lived in a world of its own.

Other minority ethnic groups have formed solitudes of their own. For the Native peoples, isolation on reserves kept them outside the economic and political mainstream of Canadian society. Major immigrant ethnic groups imitated—to a greater or lesser degree—the pattern of institutional self-segregation they found in Canada. Throughout much of Canada's history, the cultural and physical separation of British and French created a climate for newly arriving immigrant groups, a separation that fostered and preserved the differences between them and thereby promoted institutional development within them.

Breton (1964) suggests that the high level of institutional development within ethnic communities explains the lack of integration among ethnic groups in Canada. The idea of institutional development inspired Breton's article on **institutional completeness** (1964), a measure of the degree to which a community offers a range of services to its members. According to Breton, full institutional completeness implies that "members would never have to make use of native institutions for the satisfaction of any of their needs" (1964: 194). By focusing on the level and type of social organization found among ethnic groups, Breton initiated an examination of ethnic

groups in Canada as organized communities (Breton, 1978, 1983, 1984; Breton et al., 1977, 1990).

Does Porter's thesis of the vertical mosaic still explain inequality in Canada? To this hotly debated question we will return later in this chapter. Beyond debate is what Porter has demonstrated: ethnic communities are always elements in some system of stratification. John Rex (1987) notes that they are embedded in a social context in which significant social forces, such as class relations or political interests, cut across the commonalities. Breton (1978) suggests that, in a society such as Canada's, an ethnic community is usually a partial community, one whose members have diverse interests, who participate in other, often competing institutions, and who take on multiple and distinct identities. Most people's participation in their ethnic community is a "sometimes" thing, as the salience of their ethnic identity ebbs and flows with the circumstances in which they find themselves. These circumstances include situations of group conflict, because ethnic communities are among the more important means by which group conflict is expressed. Ethnic groups provide the resources its members use to compete for political, economic, and cultural advantages.

## Ethnicity and Politics

The state in Canada has tended to define ethnic groups as primarily cultural, through such policies as official bilingualism and multiculturalism. But the political character of ethnic group organization cannot be overlooked. Indeed, federal government policy has unintentionally promoted the political character of ethnic group organizations through its funding strategies. Funds tend not to be disbursed to individuals or specialized institutions , but rather to umbrella organizations such as the Canadian Jewish Congress, the National Association of Canadians of Origin in India, and the National Congress of Italian Canadians.

Umbrella organizations become points of contact between the ethnic community and government agencies. The receipt of funds legitimates them as the representative of their ethnic community in the eyes both of the community and of the government. Prominent members of umbrella organizations will be invited to join consultative committees or commissions, to participate in workshops, and to help to legitimate government policy. These individuals may also come to lobby on behalf of their group's interests, and, to the degree that they are seen as "official" representatives of their communities, their views may influence government policy.

There has been a slow but steady reshaping of some ethnic institutions from cultural institutions to representatives of political interest groups. Moreover, different groups sharing common political goals may unite. In Quebec, for example, the key umbrella organizations of the Greek-, Italian-, and Jewish-Canadian communities have worked together in recent years on political issues. They have prepared joint submissions and briefs, formed joint committees, and organized common community political events. Unified action has given these groups far more influence with the government than they could have achieved alone, even if they had separately supported the same policies. Unity provides greater strength—and it clearly identifies the joint structures as political. Politicians have come to recognize the political strength of ethnic organizations and try to curry favour with them in the hope that it will be translated into votes at election time.

Not all groups share equal access to such resources as political advantage, of course. Important differences between groups result from their time of arrival in Canada and the type of reception they experienced.

## Ethnicity and Gender

**Gender** plays a multi-faceted role in society, and the intersection of gender and ethnicity raises numerous questions on a wide variety of issues (see, for example, Stasiulis, 1999). Many of these issues, however, are only just beginning to be acknowledged by social scientists. Until quite recently, gender issues were ignored by researchers studying ethnicity, just as gender was ignored in much of sociology. Indeed, minority women researchers suggest that the concerns of immigrant and minority women have been largely overlooked by what they call "mainstream"—that is, white, middle-class—feminists (Petrovic, 2000). There is now growing recognition of the interconnections of gender, ethnicity, and Canadian society in the areas of immigration policy, the workplace, and the home (Stasiulis, 1999). In looking at the connection between gender and ethnicity it is important to acknowledge the diversity of women and to realize that the problems women face and the solutions they require are not the same for all (Ralston, 2000).

Stasiulis asserts that Canadian immigration policy has tended to make women "dependent on husbands, fathers, and other male relatives, and . . . restricted [in]

opportunities to learn the official languages" (1990: 291). Living in a new and unfamiliar country, often unable to speak the local language, with few friends to provide assistance or offer practical advice, and with little knowledge of the social services available, the lives of immigrant and refugee women are often highly centred on their families and husbands. Immigration policies can leave women trapped in abusive situations from which they do not know how to escape.

Married women often have to work long hours at low pay to supplement the family's income. Nevertheless, many find that their husbands also expect them to take on all the traditional household tasks, which are perceived to be "women's work"—cooking, cleaning, and child care, and other roles, such as serving as "domestic brokers", "organizing and pooling resources . . . to maintain themselves and their families" (Henry, 1994: 60). In addition, there are often domestic tensions caused by the frustrations felt by both men and women as a result of having to work at jobs that are much lower in pay and status than their skills or education would lead them to expect. Frustration can lead to conflict, sometimes even domestic violence. Immigrant women are more vulnerable in such a situation because, as we have seen, they are more dependent on their husbands, more centred on the family, and less likely to be aware of the resources available to them.

Like many other Canadians, immigrants experience the gendered division of labour in the workplace. Historically, immigrant women have tended to work in low-paying, low-status jobs in manufacturing or domestic service. These are precisely the kinds of jobs in which they are most likely to be exploited. Domestics, for example, are usually paid the minimum wage, and many are expected to work extra hours for little or no pay (Bakan and Stasiulis, 1997). In manufacturing, many immigrant women work in factories, some of them illegally, many of them not unionized. These women have no job security, may be paid below minimum wage, and are expected to work over 40 hours a week. Such **exploitation** is possible because immigrant women are unfamiliar with Canadian law and unaware of the existence of agencies designed to protect their rights. Those who are aware of these agencies may still avoid them because they are unable to speak one of the official languages, or simply because they are distrustful of or intimidated by people they see as "officials." It is not surprising that many fear unemployment more than exploitation.

Native women have distinctive concerns, some of which came to the fore during the constitutional debate of the early 1990s. While the male Native leadership advocated the precedence of Aboriginal rights over the Canadian Charter of Rights and Freedoms, the Native Women's Association of Canada argued that Aboriginal rights must not supersede federally guaranteed equal rights for Native women (Krosenbrink-Gelissen, 1993).

Prior to 1985, for instance, as a result of gender discrimination in the Indian Act, Indian women who married non-Indian men lost their Indian status and their right to own property and reside on a reserve. The same was not true for Indian men who married non-Native women. When Indian women took legal action to end this discrimination, they found that the official Native organizations—all dominated by men—opposed their position. Thus, many Native women feel they have not received fair and equitable treatment from Native organizations and have not had their concerns taken seriously. They even fear that Native self-government might cause them to lose their rights under Canada's constitution without granting them equal rights within the Native community. Lilianne Krosenbrink-Gelissen notes that, for this reason, many Native women "oppose the position that [self-government] must be entrenched unconditionally, without a guarantee of gender equality rights" (1993: 361).

For immigrant women, too, community support may be lacking. Research by Amanda McIntyre and Michael Rosenberg (2000) on a number of ethnic women's organizations in Montreal found that these groups frequently were refused money or support by their local ethnic community umbrella organizations. Some people in the community—both men and women—viewed women's organizations as having only one goal, that of "breaking up families." They ignored or disregarded the many programs and services these organizations tried to initiate. Ironically, women active in these organizations sometimes reported that they received little support from mainstream feminists. Feminist groups defined the organizations as "ethnic" rather than "women's" organizations (McIntyre and Rosenberg, 2000).

The links between gender and ethnicity require a new way of thinking about issues related to ethnicity. Indeed, as Stasiulis (1990) suggests, feminists would do well to question their ethnocentric views of women and the positions that women should be taking on a wider variety of issues.

# Patterns of Immigration to Canada

In December 2002, the cover story in *Maclean's* magazine on immigration (Janigan, 2002) asked the question, "How many is too many?" This is the question that has set the context for Canadian immigration policy since Confederation (Palmer, 1991). Although immigration has been a major force in shaping Canadian society, Canada, unlike the United States, is not now and never has been a "nation of immigrants." Immigration has not only played a different and far lesser role in building Canadian society, it has also had a different meaning in the Canadian context.

In the United States, immigrants played a crucial role in the industrialization and modernization of American society, especially in the period between 1880 and 1925. Arriving in huge numbers to fill the enormous demand for labour created by American industry, they were expected not only to merge into American society, but also to contribute to the creation of a new, dynamic society. The United States was a nation of immigrants not only in a numerical sense, but in the central, symbolic, and creative role assigned to immigration. The so-called American Dream was a dream both of achieving personal success and of finding a place in American society—being accepted as a full-fledged US citizen. This dream reflected the **melting-pot** ideology that assumed immigrants would discard all the traditions and distinctions they brought with them, including their ethnic language and national identity, and become nothing other than Americans.

To some extent, the dream and the melting pot were no more than myths. Many immigrants found life in the United States to be one of unending poverty, toil, and exploitation. Some groups, such as blacks and Asians, were entirely excluded from the melting pot. Yet some immigrants found real opportunities, and even those who never "made it" in their own lifetimes could still look forward to having their children take advantage of opportunities they themselves were denied.

Why did immigration never have the same central role in Canadian society? The answer, as so often happens, lies in the attitudes and preferences of the two charter groups, both of which dominated Canada and neither of which sought either to incorporate the other or to absorb new immigrants. The British and the French are known as *charter groups* because they have a special status in Canada, one entrenched in the Canadian constitution, and have effectively determined the dominant cultural characteristics of Canada. Each group has special rights and privileges, especially with regard to the language used in the legislatures, courts, and schools.

At Confederation, almost all Canadians were of either French or British origin. The two groups saw Canada as a political union between them. The goal of immigration was not to alter this political equation, but to provide the human "raw materials" needed to run the factories or farm the land. Immigrants were viewed as fulfilling primarily an economic function; they were acceptable to the majority groups only so long as they were considered neither a cultural nor an economic threat. Simply, an Italian coming to the United States became an American, but an Italian coming to Canada became an Italian Canadian.

## Traditional Immigration

At every stage of Canada's evolution, national immigration policy has preferred certain groups over others. Initially, migrants from Britain or Northern Europe were favoured. This policy was reflected in the ethnic composition of Canada's population as late as 1991, as shown in Figure 8.1. Canadians believed that the British and Northern Europeans would best fit into Canadian society with respect to culture, race, economics—even adaptation to the Canadian winter. Immigration of non-whites was discouraged, and

immigration policy before the late 1960s was racist and exclusionary. The history of migration to Canada for the first century after Confederation was a history of European migration.

Even so, not all Europeans were viewed as equal; nor were they equally welcomed. Early policy discouraged immigrants from Eastern and Southern Europe. Only the failure to attract sufficient immigrants from Britain and Northern Europe forced the government to recruit from elsewhere. Beginning in about 1880, Eastern Europeans were encouraged to come to Canada to farm the West. Ukrainians, Russians, and Poles came in large numbers because of the terrible economic conditions in their homelands at that time. By the turn of the century, Southern Europeans, notably Italians, began arriving to work as manual labourers in the rapidly expanding and industrializing cities of central Canada.

Even between 1900 and 1930, when immigration rates were high, as shown in Figure 8.2, Canada's population did not increase dramatically. Many of the new immigrants simply left Canada; some 50 per cent either moved on to the United States or returned to their homelands. Another factor was the high death rate among immigrants at the turn of the century. Montreal, where many of the early immigrants settled, was an unhealthy city with poor medical facilities. Paul-André Linteau, René Durocher, and Jean-Claude Robert (1983) have pointed out that malnu-

Figure 8.1   **Ethnic Composition of Canada's Population, 1991**

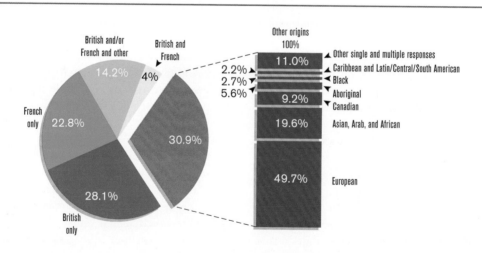

SOURCE: Adapted from Statistics Canada, *Canadian Social Trends*, Catalogue 11-008, Autumn 1993.

trition and disease killed large numbers of immigrants who were impoverished and had no family or friends to help them through hard times.

The most significant factor was the departure of so many of the new immigrants. Why did they leave? Why would people coming from extremely harsh economic or political circumstances not find Canada an attractive place to live? Part of the answer has to do with the enormous pull of the United States, the attraction of the American Dream of equality and opportunity for all. Immigrants to Canada not only found themselves overworked and underpaid, but also realized that the charter groups dominated society and that not all groups were politically or economically equal here.

Another reason for this pattern of emigration was the indifference, or sometimes outright hostility, of Canadians towards the new arrivals. The isolation of Catholic Quebec promoted a distancing from (and outright animosity towards) immigrants, who were seen as weakening the French Catholic character of the province. The British, for their part, were unwilling to absorb immigrants from Eastern and Southern Europe. Their desire was to "keep Canada British," not to have Canada imitate the cultural hodgepodge of the United States.

Attitudes towards immigration became more positive after World War II, a time of economic prosperity when there was a significant demand for the labour that immigrants could provide. By the 1950s, most Canadians no longer looked upon European immigrants as racially different or inferior, but rather as generally desirable. However, immigration from Europe failed to keep up with Canada's demand for labour by the mid-1960s because the economies of Western European countries, initially devastated by World War II, had improved dramatically. At the same time, Eastern European countries, now under the control of communist governments, blocked emigration.

## The New Immigration

Immigration patterns have changed substantially since the late 1960s. Immigrants now are coming in increasing numbers from areas outside of Europe, particularly Asia. In 2001, China, India, Pakistan, the Philippines, and Korea were the top five source countries for immigrants to Canada. Indeed, 16 per cent of all immigrants that year came from China, 11 per cent from India, and 6 per cent from Pakistan; altogether over 42 per cent of that year's immigrants came from the top five countries. The top European source country in 2001 was Romania, from which about 5,600 immigrants arrived, making up only a little more than 2 per cent of all immigrants. Table 8.1 compares the top source countries for Canadian immigrants in the 1990s with those for immigrants who arrived before 1961.

More immigrants than ever before are members of visible minorities—almost 4 million in 2001, near-

Figure 8.2    **Immigration Numbers in Historical Perspective, 1860–2001**

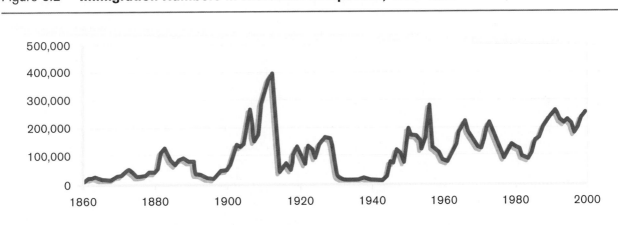

SOURCE: From Citizenship and Immigration Canada's *Immigration Overview, Facts and Figures 2001,* <http://www.cic.gc.ca>. Adapted and reproduced with the permission of the Minister of Public Works and Government Services Canada, 2005.

ly 13.5 per cent of Canada's population. Such people face different problems from those being encountered by European immigrants, problems compounded by several other trends. Almost all immigrants end up in cities; indeed, almost 77 per cent of those who came to Canada in 2001 went to live in Toronto, Vancouver, or Montreal. Toronto by itself received 125,061 immigrants in 2001, almost 50 per cent of the total. This concentration means that visible minorities are, so to speak, more visible than ever in some parts of Canada; at the same time, they remain largely invisible, and therefore unknown, elsewhere.

Moreover, immigration is on the rise after a decline in the mid-1980s—from just over 84,000 in 1985 to over 250,000 in 2001. This increase, combined with the high level of concentration, means that many urban residents are immigrants—44 per cent of the population in Metropolitan Toronto comprising over 2 million people, almost 800,000 of those having arrived since 1990.

To refer to immigration to "Canada," is in one sense a misnomer, since most of Canada does not participate in this immigration. Few immigrants in 2001 chose to live elsewhere in Canada. Only 404 immigrants came to live in all of Newfoundland, only 1,709 came to Saskatchewan, and only about 5,000 settled in Quebec outside of Montreal—about the same number as those who selected Manitoba. In contrast, more than 445,000 immigrants arrived in the Toronto area between 1996 and 2001. This rate of immigration puts enormous strains on the infrastructure of the Toronto region, as well as raising issues of settlement and the adequate provision of services for the new arrivals. Language training alone is a major undertaking, with 45 per cent of the new arrivals in 2001 speaking neither English nor French. If immigrants are to get decent jobs, interact with others, and fully understand their rights, they must be able to speak one of the official languages. Moreover, if immigrants are allowed into Canada in order to benefit the country economically, demographically, and culturally, then most parts of the country are not sharing in that benefit.

Both the numbers and the concentration of immigrants in urban areas tend to perpetuate various problems of integration. One such problem is that, by remaining in the cities, immigrants are contributing to the regionalization of Canada, whose large cities are coming to have very different characteristics from other areas. For example, 88 per cent of Quebec's immigrants live in Montreal, making up 18.4 per cent of the city's population. By contrast, immigrants make up just 2.9 per cent of Quebec City's population, and 1.5 per cent of a city like Trois-Rivières. Since Montreal is also the only major centre in Quebec with a high concentration of anglophones, it may be

Table 8.1    **Top 10 Countries of Birth, Canada, 2001[a]**

| | Immigrated Before 1961 | | | Immigrated 1991–2001[b] | |
|---|---|---|---|---|---|
| | **Number** | **%** | | **Number** | **%** |
| Total immigrants | 894,466 | 100.0 | Total immigrants | 1,830,680 | 100.0 |
| United Kingdom | 217,175 | 24.3 | China, People's Republic of | 197,360 | 10.8 |
| Italy | 147,320 | 16.5 | India | 156,120 | 8.5 |
| Germany | 96,770 | 10.8 | Philippines | 122,010 | 6.7 |
| Netherlands | 79,170 | 8.9 | Hong Kong, Special Administrative Region | 118,385 | 6.5 |
| Poland | 44,340 | 5.0 | Sri Lanka | 62,590 | 3.4 |
| United States | 34,810 | 3.9 | Pakistan | 52,990 | 3.2 |
| Hungary | 27,425 | 3.1 | Taiwan | 53,755 | 2.9 |
| Ukraine | 21,240 | 2.4 | United States | 52,440 | 2.8 |
| Greece | 20,755 | 2.3 | Iran | 47,080 | 2.6 |
| China, People's Republic of | 15,850 | 1.8 | Poland | 43,370 | 2.4 |

[a] Population counts are rounded to the nearest 5.
[b] Includes data up to 15 May 2001.
Source: Adapted from Statistics Canada, *Canada's Ethnocultural Portrait: The Changing Mosaic*, 2001 Census (Analysis series), Catalogue 96F0030, <http://www.statcan.ca/english/IPS/Data/96F0030XIE2001008.htm>.

said that in Quebec, ethnic and linguistic diversity is a characteristic only of Montreal. Indeed, many Montrealers feel that their city is quite different from the rest of Quebec, while many Québécois who do not live in Montreal fear that the city is losing its "French face" (Statistics Canada, 2003a: 58).

---

 8.1

# Global Issues
## Migration in International Context

Migration, whether of immigrants, refugees, or "guest workers," has become a major international phenomenon in the contemporary world. Recently, the United Nations Population Division estimated that 175 million people could be classified as migrants, double the number in 1975. (Migrants are defined by the United Nations as persons who have been residing outside of their country of birth for at least 12 months.) Most of these migrants, 56 million, are in Europe, another 50 million in Asia, and 41 million in North America, including 35 million in the United States and almost 6 million in Canada (United Nations Population Division, 2002: 2).

Because Canada has a high rate of immigration, most Canadians do not realize that immigration is severely restricted by many other nations. Those that do allow immigration usually allow only a limited number of people to arrive in any given year. Germany, for example, enacted a law in 2003 that allows in 50,000 people a year, in contrast to the Canadian immigration target for 2003 of 220,000 to 245,000. Like Germany, many European countries have passed legislation further restricting immigration and the possibility of naturalization (that is, becoming citizens). They have a long history of allowing "foreigners" to enter their countries as labourers, but not of granting them the right to settle permanently or to become citizens. Many countries outside of Europe, too, have large numbers of migrants who neither expect to, nor will be allowed to, become citizens.

In Canada, we do expect immigrants to become full-fledged members of the society. Canada allows immigrants to become citizens after only three years of residence. In contrast, Germany requires "foreigners" to have resided in Germany for 15 years in order to apply for naturalization (Martin, 2002). In Britain, immigrants must take a course on "Britishness" that includes "instruction in modern family life and the need for tolerance of different ethnic groups" (*Migration News*, December 2002).

In most countries, migrants do not have the same rights as citizens, nor are they entitled to the same services or protection of the law. In France, for example, non–European Union citizens are restricted from working in government-owned industries or as pharmacists, as architects, or in 50 other professions. Non-citizens are also subject to the arbitrary whim of legislative and regulative agencies. Recently, the government of Saudi Arabia decided that "foreigners" would no longer be allowed to drive taxis, putting 50,000 people out of work.

Migrants in many nations are often economically exploited and subjected to discrimination; they may even be physically abused. Human Rights Watch, for example, has documented beatings and other forms of "cruel, inhuman, or degrading treatment" of suspected illegal North African migrants (including children) by Spanish authorities. Many countries routinely detain illegal immigrants or refugee claimants. While many Canadians are somewhat concerned about the current high levels of immigration, they do not have the strong negative attitudes towards migrants typically found elsewhere. A poll conducted in November 2002 by the Institute of Conflict Research at Bielefeld University indicated that "52 per cent of men and 58 per cent of women agreed that Germany has too many foreigners, and 24 per cent of men and 31 per cent of women believed foreigners should leave Germany in times of high unemployment" (*Migration News*, January 2003).

This concentration in cities also causes problems for the immigrants themselves, who would be in a better position to compete for jobs if their distribution were more even. Li (2000) found that immigrants formed 32 per cent of the labour market in metropolitan areas of over 1 million people. Furthermore, housing costs and the cost of living in general are higher in the cities; at the time of writing, this is particularly true of Vancouver and Toronto. Finally, concentration may promote **racism** or **prejudice**. Because relatively few Canadians come to know new immigrants, perceptions of them outside of urban centres may be based on stereotypes that are rarely challenged by reality.

Another trend in immigration is that recent immigrants tend to have more education than previous generations of immigrants. In fact, Arnold deSilva (1992) has found that they are better educated than the general population in Canada. This development is a result of immigration policy, which favours those with a high level of education or with job skills that are needed in the labour force. That outcome will also be affected by the existing demand for specific skills, the level of unemployment, and other job-related factors, as well as by the degree to which discrimination is present in the society.

# Patterns of Inter-group Relations in Canada

How are the new immigration trends affecting Canadian society? Not all of the effects are visible yet, but the new immigration is certainly affecting the patterns of relationships among Canada's ethnic groups. In recent years, these patterns have largely been directed by the state, particularly through its promotion of official bilingualism and multiculturalism. Both policies may need to be redefined to reflect the changing ethnic, cultural, and linguistic reality of Canadian society.

### *Bilingualism*

Sociologists often speak of the unintended consequences of social actions and policies. The issues surrounding ethnic group relations in Canada serve as examples of such unintended consequences. In theory, official bilingualism—the government policy of providing services everywhere in Canada in both official languages—seems like a good idea. All Canadians, whether English- or French-speaking, should feel at

home anywhere in Canada. They should feel secure in the knowledge that their government institutions will be able to serve them in their own language, that these institutions are theirs. The net result of bilingualism should be to promote Canadians' sense of identification with the country as a whole, and thereby to promote national unity.

Yet, it has been argued by Guindon (1983) and others that official bilingualism has divided rather than united Canadians. Like any policy designed to please everyone, it seems to have ended up pleasing almost no one. It certainly fails to meet the aspirations of most francophone Québécois, while simultaneously creating tensions and animosities among anglophones, especially those Westerners who are members of non-British minority groups.

Canada's bilingualism policy emerged out of an attempt to deal with the "problem of Quebec." By 1960, the start of the Quiet Revolution, many Québécois felt dissatisfied with the constitutional, political, and fiscal arrangements in Canada, which they perceived as having negative effects on Quebec society and on the status of its francophone citizens. The response of the federal government was to establish the Royal Commission on Bilingualism and Biculturalism in 1963. The Commission's task was to "recommend what steps should be taken to develop the Canadian Confederation on the basis of an equal partnership between two founding races, taking into account the contribution made by other ethnic groups to the cultural enrichment of Canada and the measures that should be taken to safeguard that contribution" (Royal Commission on Bilingualism and Biculturalism, 1970: 3).

Canada's constitutional and linguistic problems have not ended; the Commission failed in its task. Perhaps it did so largely because it defined the key problem in the relationship between the English and French as one of language and thereby failed to address the many other concerns of Quebec—constitutional, political, and economic. This failure made the Commission and its proposals largely irrelevant to most Québécois. Even worse, the solution offered—the federal policy of official bilingualism—served to aggravate rather than solve the real problems, including the linguistic ones. The idea behind bilingualism was that it would allow Québécois to feel at home anywhere in Canada because French services would be available everywhere. A francophone resident of Quebec passing through Moose Jaw, Saskatchewan, for example, would be able to use French in a post office. But Québécois were not complaining about the status of French outside of Quebec—they were complaining about their own status within Quebec.

Bilingualism is not popular in Quebec. Some Québécois assert that, in practice, what bilingualism really means is that francophones are encouraged to learn English. Census data for 2001, almost 40 years after the creation of the Royal Commission, tend to support such a view. The data show that slightly over 17 per cent of Canadians are bilingual, including about 43 per cent of francophones but only 9 per cent of anglophones. Moreover, given that over 65 per cent of Québécois are unilingual francophones, many francophones feel that a policy that promotes bilingualism disadvantages them by effectively locking them out of jobs or obstructing promotion to senior positions. Even many francophones who do speak English also feel disadvantaged; they find it

---

8.2

# Sociology in Action
## Québécois Nationalism

When we look at ethnic distinctions between Canadians, we must inevitably deal with the issue of Quebec and its relation to the rest of Canada. Quebec is not only a province of Canada; in a very real sense, it is also a distinct society within Canada (Fournier, Rosenberg, and White, 1997).

Québécois nationalism is a volatile phenomenon. There are times when it seems quiescent, other times when it flares up and presents a real threat to Canadian unity. Quebec separation is not a new issue—it has been a part of Canada's political history, and has helped shape Canada's political structure, from the time of Confederation on.

It took its modern form in 1960–6, the years of the Quiet Revolution, which were characterized by a profound reorientation of Quebec state action and policy. The provincial government initiated a broad series of reforms in a wide range of areas. Structural changes included the establishment of a Ministry of Education and the implementation of the Quebec Pension Plan. Ideological reforms expressed a new conception of the state as the leading actor in the process of transforming Quebec into a modern, self-assured, and democratic society capable of controlling its own destiny.

The society that emerged from the Quiet Revolution was substantially different from that which preceded it. Quebec's key institutions—in particular the state—had been radically transformed. The Québécois, as they began to call

themselves, felt that in the state and its agencies they finally had the collective tools with which to build their future society. But what type of society would it be? Was a fully developed Quebec society even possible within the confines of the Canadian federation? These questions raised new debates and generated new disagreements within the Québécois community, giving urgent priority to issues of nationalism and language (Monière, 1981).

Language played a significant role in the debates for a number of reasons. The preservation of the French language, despite 200 years of British domination, has been a major accomplishment of the francophone Québécois, a shared source of pride in the past and a collective point of concern for the future. At the same time, the high birth rates that had characterized the francophone community for 200 years went into a steep decline. The influx of non-francophone immigrants reinforced the proportionate decline of the francophone Québécois population since most of these new immigrants chose English as their language of work and the language of education for their children.

The 1976 provincial election put into power the Parti Québécois, a party committed to building Quebec as a French society. A year later, Bill 101 declared French to be "the distinctive language of a people that is in the majority French-speaking [and] is the instrument by which that people has articulated its identity."

insulting to be required to know English in order to get a job within their own overwhelmingly francophone community. As Quebec's Bill 101 expresses it, the consensus among most Québécois is that French—and only French—is to be the "normal and everyday language of work, instruction, commerce and business" in Quebec.

Francophones outside of Quebec, however, do benefit from official bilingualism. Since they are a minority in all provinces but Quebec, official bilingualism serves to protect their linguistic rights and provides them with services and job opportunities. Anglophones within Quebec, 66 per cent of whom are bilingual, also benefit from the federal policy.

Outside of Quebec, many anglophones dislike bilingualism, complaining that they are having French forced upon them on signs and packaging or in government services. In fact, they are not having French forced upon them at all; bilingual signs and services do not replace English, but merely add French. Why is there such resentment about the presence of French?

Breton suggests that the federal government has been engaged in attempting the "reconstruction of the symbolic system and . . . the redistribution of social status among linguistic and ethnocultural groups in Canadian society" (1984: 134). The effect of the policy of bilingualism has been to raise the status of francophones outside of Quebec by giving their language a special status. This, in turn, has had the unintended effect of lowering the relative status of other groups. In western Canada, where groups such as Ukrainians outnumber the French, these groups see official bilingualism as implying that the government considers the French more important than they are. The result is resentment—what Breton calls "status anxieties" and "cultural tensions."

Bilingualism, then, has solved few existing problems but has instead created problems of its own. Indeed, Breton argues that it was the resentment aroused by the bilingualism policy that forced the government to initiate yet another policy: official multiculturalism.

### Multiculturalism

Like bilingualism, official multiculturalism—the government policy of promoting tolerance among cultural groups and helping them preserve the values and traditions important to them—seems a good thing in principle. Who could be opposed to the aims it espouses? Yet, once again, many people question whether an official policy of multiculturalism is truly

beneficial or whether it instead engenders strains in Canadian society and divisions between Canadians.

Multiculturalism became an official government policy in 1971, under Prime Minister Pierre Trudeau, who pointed out in a House of Commons debate that "although there are two official languages, there is no official culture." The federal government then proposed a series of initiatives to promote cultural diversity and tolerance.

How real is cultural tolerance in practice, and how real should it be? Jean Leonard Elliot and Augie Fleras (1992) cite the example of a bullfight organized by a Portuguese group in Ontario. Many Canadians would consider a bullfight to be the cruel mistreatment of an animal; it is, in fact, illegal under Canada's laws. Should it nevertheless be tolerated as part of the Portuguese culture? According to Elliott and Fleras, "We need to ask about the limits of multicultural tolerance. Which cultural differences can be absorbed within a multicultural society without undermining incontestable values and beliefs? The dilemma is self-evident: too many differences can create anarchic conditions which inhibit the effective functioning of a social system. Too many restrictions makes a mockery of multicultural principles" (1992: 293).

Multiculturalism is an inherently limited policy because its focus is ethnic groups as cultural groups and because the activities it promotes are cultural activities. As noted earlier, the policy has given the federal government what some regard to be unwarranted control over which sorts of activities are legitimate for a given group and over who is recognized as an appropriate representative of the group. The result is yet another unintended effect: the politicization of ethnic groups and the corresponding alteration of the equation between government and ethnic communities.

Despite the restrictions in the government's policies on multiculturalism, Canadians tend to be ambivalent about the whole idea. Canadians pride themselves on being a tolerant people who respect others' cultures and traditions and are willing to accept cultural pluralism. Nevertheless, many would like to see a more unified country whose people are committed to being "Canadians" rather than retaining their ethnic languages or loyalties (Kalin and Berry, 1994). Ambivalence about ethnicity shows up in the data gathered by Breton, who found that among members of ethnic groups in Toronto, "a majority of most groups feel that the loss of traditions, customs, or language is a problem . . . [yet] a majority also feel that members of their group should blend and not form communities" (1990: 213).

This ambivalence has its sources in various sociological factors. First, as we have seen, the ambiguous government definitions and policies related to ethnicity seem to have aggravated the ethnic tensions they were designed to ease. Related to this is a shift in the meanings assigned to ethnic groups, from primarily cultural groups to political interest groups. The most dramatic example is offered by the Native peoples, who have organized to become a highly visible political force in Canada. Another factor is the new immigration, along with questions as to the degree to which Canadians are willing to accept visible minorities as members of their society.

"Multiculturalism" may no longer reflect the reality of a society in which more and more people see themselves as "Canadian" rather than as members of minority cultural groups. In the 2001 census, almost 40 per cent of the population—well over 11 million people—indicated their ethnic origin to be "Canadian." Contrast this to 1991, when only about 4 per cent of the people reported their ethnic identity to be Canadian on the census forms, and 1996, when that figure rose to 19 per cent. This change may reflect many factors, but it does indicate that many people in Canada are coming to identify themselves in a new way, one in which their ethnic origin is less significant than their attachment to Canada.

An increase in intermarriages has an impact upon the notion of ethnic culture implicit in multicultural policy. The assumption of multiculturalism is that every Canadian is tied into a specific and distinct heritage culture. Intermarriage not only ties each person, at least to some extent, into the ethnic culture of the spouse, it means that their children have multiple ethnic backgrounds. In 2001, about 11 million people reported having multiple ethnic backgrounds. For such people, policies designed to enhance or maintain ethnic identification may have little significance. Still, groups are not equally likely to intermarry: to date, most intermarriages occur among people of European ancestry.

# Prejudice and Discrimination

The distinction between *prejudice* and *discrimination* is a distinction between attitude and action. Racism is a form of discrimination.

## Prejudice

*Prejudice* refers to the prejudgement of an individual on the basis of characteristics assumed to be common to all members of that individual's group: that is, a stereotype. A prejudice describes someone's attitudes towards a group; it will not necessarily determine how he or she behaves towards that group. To believe that all Native people are alcoholics, that all Newfoundlanders are stupid, or that all Americans are arrogant is prejudice based on stereotypes and myths. The term *prejudice* denotes that such stereotypes and myths cause people to decide in advance what a certain person will be like based on knowing no more than the individual's ethnic group or appearance.

Are Canadians free of ethnic or racial prejudices? The evidence is that we are not. If anything, says Peter Pineo (1977), Canada seems to be a society with strong, distinctive attitudes towards different ethnic and racial groups. John Berry, Rudolf Kalin, and Donald Taylor (1977) found that most Canadians, whatever their ethnic group, tend to have a positive perception of and positive attitudes towards the two charter groups. This finding comes as no surprise considering the dominant political, economic, and symbolic role played by the British and French in Canadian society. These groups have served as role models for most other Canadians, providing an image of what it means to be a Canadian. In sum, Canadians have a positive prejudice in favour of the charter groups.

What about other groups? Here again, we can identify a positive prejudice, at least in how each group views itself. Groups see themselves to be very much like the charter groups, characterizing themselves as "decent," "friendly," "trustworthy," and "clean" (Berry, Kalin, and Taylor, 1977). But more negative attitudes can also be found. Canadians generally see the visible minorities in the least positive light, with Native people, blacks, and East Indians (South Asians) at the very bottom of the scale. Berry, Kalin, and Taylor (1977) found that East Indians, for example, received low scores for being "hardworking," "Canadian," or "clean," the implication being that they are viewed as "lazy," "foreign," and "dirty."

Research done in 1991 showed that most Canadians report themselves to be "comfortable" when in the presence of British-origin Canadians but that the level of comfort decreased significantly for many when in the presence of Muslims, Indo-Pakistanis, or Sikhs (Driedger and Reid, 2000). This type of prejudice is not necessarily a problem in society as long as it is not transformed into the differential treatment of individuals and groups. There is always the danger, though, that prejudice will result in discrimination.

Are Canadians free of ethnic and racial prejudices? The evidence is that we are not. This photograph documents the case in which parents were split over whether to allow 12-year-old Sikh pupil Gurbaj Singh to wear his kirpan, a ceremonial dagger, to a Montreal school. (CP/Ryan Remiorz)

## Discrimination

*Discrimination* refers to the action of treating an individual differently—usually unfairly—because of his or her membership in a particular group or category. Discrimination is based on prejudice, not on the objective features of the individual or groups being discriminated against. Consider an example. As noted earlier, recent immigrants to Canada tend to be well educated and relatively highly skilled. Yet they frequently fail to find work in the occupations for which they have been trained, being forced instead to accept menial, low-status jobs. Patricia Tomic and Ricardo Trumper (1992) give the example of two Chilean economists who, on coming to Canada, found themselves offered jobs as shipping clerks.

Discrimination comes in many forms, some more insidious than others. Blatant discrimination was seen in 1982 in Montreal when a taxi company fired more than 20 Haitian cab drivers. The company announced that the drivers were not being fired because they did not do their job properly, but because the public refused to take cabs driven by Haitians. It claimed to have received many complaints from the public that the Haitians did not know their way around the city

and frequently got lost, that their cabs were "dirty" and "smelled," that they were rude, and that they spoke an "incomprehensible" French. Although the drivers were rehired after extensive media coverage and a public outcry, the incident made evident the degree of prejudice and discrimination in Montreal. Such cases are relatively easy to deal with precisely because they are so obvious. Should public opinion fail to end the discrimination, then human rights legislation and government agencies will do so. Blatant discrimination may pose problems for particular individuals, but as long as instances remain few in number, it does not constitute a problem for society.

Perhaps the most insidious of all forms of discrimination is **institutional** or **structural discrimination**, discrimination that is actually built into the structure of an institution or its method of operation. For example, in a time of economic recession, workers in a company are likely to be laid off on the basis of seniority. Since new immigrants are likely to be at the bottom of the seniority list, they are most vulnerable to losing their jobs. Indeed, the more recently an immigrant arrived, the more likely he or she is to be unemployed (Citizenship and Immigration Canada, 1998). However, immigrants generally have lower unemployment rates than do the Canadian-born—in 1986, the figures were 8.2 per cent for immigrants and 10.8 per cent for native-born Canadians (deSilva, 1992: 11). Unemployment rates among immigrants in the same year were 11.5 per cent for those who arrived between 1978 and 1982 and 16 per cent for those who arrived between 1983 and 1986. It is sometimes claimed that high levels of immigration lead to high levels of unemployment, but the figures do not bear this out. What is clear is that the most recent immigrants are likeliest to be unemployed.

Another example of institutional discrimination is the failure to recognize the credentials of an immigrant professional. The discrimination may not be intentional but may simply reflect the local professional association's difficulty in evaluating whether the foreign credentials are equivalent to Canadian standards. Intentional or not, the effect is to discriminate against immigrants. Yet another example is the common requirement of having a college diploma for a relatively unskilled job, a requirement that penalizes members of poorer minority groups, who are less likely to have completed college. Because these forms of discrimination are hidden or can be justified on the basis of "good reasons," they are often very hard to eliminate.

Most Canadians recognize that there is some degree of prejudice in society, but they think of

Canada as largely free of discrimination. Unfortunately, many researchers, such as Subhas Ramcharan (1982), show that this simply is not so. Given the above-mentioned pattern of institutional self-segregation of ethnic groups, which characterizes most ethnic group relations, institutional discrimination is not only common, but acceptable to most Canadians. Indeed, institutional self-segregation can be characterized as **systemic discrimination** because it is built into the very fabric of Canadian life. Most Canadians prefer to live their lives in communities where they encounter people like themselves. They prefer to deal with doctors, lawyers, bank managers, politicians, and police officers from their own or what they consider to be a similar ethnic group. Systemic discrimination may not be intended; it may simply be the consequence of the preference of ethnic group members to do business with their "own kind." Still, the result is that immigrants, especially members of visible minorities, do not have the same opportunity to obtain jobs or to gain the trust of the established group.

This type of systemic discrimination promotes an *ethnic sub-economy*, which Morton Weinfeld describes as "a network of economic relationships which may link employees, employers, consumers, buyers and sellers, of a specific ethnic group" (1983: 8). The sub-economy provides jobs and opportunities for members of that ethnic community.

However, Norbert Wiley (1967) has pointed out that it can also serve as a mobility trap when ethnic group members find themselves locked into it and out of the larger economy.

### Racism

*Racism* can be defined as a belief that one racial group is superior to others. Racists believe that differences in physical appearance serve as an index to other differences—for instance, personality characteristics, intelligence, honesty, reliability, law-abidingness, and so on. Racism in this sense probably has always existed; it is likely that there have always been people or groups that regarded themselves as superior to everyone else. Racism in the modern sense is different in that it categorizes groups strictly on the basis of physical appearance and offers a "scientific" basis for claims to superiority.

*Scientific racism* is the attempt to categorize human groups into distinct biological classes forming an evolutionary, intellectual, and moral continuum. The theory of scientific racism that emerged in the nineteenth century helped Europeans to justify colonialism and imperialism; it promised a scientific basis for racism that was absolute and impervious to moral, ethical, or religious debate. As developed in Western Europe and the United States, the theory essentially held that the different races resulted from a differential rate of evolu-

8.3

## Human Diversity
### Racism and Institutional Discrimination in Canada: The Case of the Chinese

The treatment of Canada's Chinese immigrants has always served as an index of the country's racial and ethnic climate. Prior to 1948, Canada's treatment of the Chinese was unquestionably racist and the Chinese experienced more systematic, institutional discrimination than any other immigrant group in Canada. Since then, they have experienced a dramatic level of upward social mobility and become one of Canada's most "successful" ethnic groups. Yet racism and misunderstandings persist and Chinese immigrants continue to face a wide variety of problems in trying to integrate into Canadian society.

It was only in 1948 that Chinese Canadians in British Columbia finally received the right to vote in both provincial and federal elections. Indeed, beginning about 1875, legislation in British Columbia had excluded the Chinese from buying Crown land or working as miners, loggers, fishermen, civil servants, pharmacists, or lawyers. The Chinese were not allowed to serve on a jury, to be admitted to provincial homes for the aged, or to obtain a liquor licence.

The federal government, too, sought to discourage Chinese immigration to Canada, imposing a head tax of $50 on Chinese immigrants in 1885, a tax

*continued*

increased to a forbidding $500 by 1903. An even more explicitly restrictive law, the Chinese Immigration Act, was passed in 1923. Until 1947, this Act excluded almost all new Chinese immigrants.

That the Chinese were a cheap and reliable labour force is shown by the preference given them as workers in building the Canadian Pacific Railway. This, however, led to fears that cheap Chinese labour would take away jobs from British Columbia workers and undermine "the position of skilled labour" (Comack, 1985: 75), especially after the completion of the railway. As industrial unions began to form in the 1890s, opposition to cheap Chinese labour became organized and politically popular.

In addition, racist sentiment viewed the Chinese as morally and mentally inferior to whites and as unfit to participate in Canadian society. This racism was tinged with fear of the "yellow peril," the belief that the Chinese were bent on world conquest. Racists such as Edmonton judge Emily Murphy, for example, claimed that opium and other narcotics were being used in an international conspiracy by "foreigners" to bring "about the downfall of the white race" (quoted in Green, 1986: 32). William Lyon Mackenzie King, sent to Vancouver in 1907 to investigate an anti-Oriental riot, urged the federal government to prohibit the recreational use of narcotics in Canada. "To be indifferent to the growth of such an evil in Canada," King said, "would be inconsistent with those principles of morality which ought to govern the conduct of a Christian nation" (quoted in Green, 1986: 27).

Positive attitudes towards the Chinese as "allies" developed during World War II, and racist and discriminatory legislation was largely scrapped by the late 1940s. Since then, Chinese Canadians have become a success story in socio-economic terms. They are better educated than the average Canadian, have a higher income, are more likely to own their own homes, and are more likely to work as professionals. Asians, including Chinese, are coming to Canada in record numbers and are bringing much-needed skills—and money—with them.

Yet racism is far from gone. Headlines in newspapers and magazines, for example, proclaim the danger posed to Canadians by the "new" Asian gangs. Asian immigrants are accused of taking away jobs from "Canadians" and of raising the housing costs in Vancouver. Foreign Chinese students are portrayed as taking away places in universities from Canadians. Some Quebec nationalists accuse the Chinese of being cliquish and of refusing to integrate into Quebec's French culture. Surveys show that many Canadians believe that immigrants, especially visible minorities, are entering Canada too fast and in too high numbers (Ekos Research Associates, 2002).

tion among the peoples of the world. Thus, while some races evolved to a higher level of "humanness," others remained in a lower evolutionary state. Scientific racists argued that it was evolution, not the actions of human beings, that condemned the "inferior" races to low status and to the supervision of the superior.

In Canada, scientific racism was combined with a number of other **ideologies** that reinforced one another. British imperialism, for example, to which many Canadians subscribed, viewed the British as culturally and institutionally superior and therefore best qualified to shoulder the "white man's burden" of civilizing and, of course, ruling "inferior" races. Canadians combined this viewpoint with a sense of moral superiority to the United States, which was seen as a land of unrestrained greed, crime, and vice—characteristics linked to its open immigration policy.

Canadian racists also evolved a unique ideology that equated life in the north with racial superiority. Because of the harsh Canadian winters, they argued, only the northern "races," such as the Anglo-Saxons, Scandinavians, and Germans, could survive in Canada. They went so far as to claim that Canada's climate made its people hard-working, self-reliant, and honest. Again, this perspective was contrasted with a negative image of the United States, whose population was seen as lazy, impulsive, and disorderly, partly as a result of the influence of the warmer American climate (Berger, 1966).

Racism is a form of discrimination. How, then, is it to be differentiated from other forms of discrimination? Few Canadians belong to or support overt racism, such as that promoted by white supremacist groups; racism in Canadian society more often takes the form of institutional or systemic discrimination. While these forms of social organization are not intentionally discriminatory, people with racist views can take advantage of institutional practices and policies to cover their practises of racial discrimination.

Canada among nations today is at the forefront of attempts to prevent racial or other forms of discrimination, whether intentional or not. Employment equity programs and other forms of affirmative action are designed to produce what is termed "equality of result." The federal government and the provincial governments have encouraged the civil service and Crown corporations to hire women, French Canadians, Native people, visible minorities, and the disabled in numbers reflecting their percentages in the population (Abella, 1984; Weinfeld, 1981). In Quebec, for example, an Act Respecting Equal Access to Employment in Public Bodies came into effect in 2001, requiring measures to increase the representation in public bodies of "target groups" such as visible minorities.

## Discrimination in Canadian Society

Have the programs for combatting discrimination worked? Or is Canadian society still characterized by the vertical mosaic? To what extent are new immigrants or visible minorities discriminated against in contemporary Canada? These remain matters of contention among social scientists.

Immigrants almost always enter a new country at a disadvantage. They may not know the language of the new country or be familiar with the customs and routine expectations of the host society. They are likely to be unaware of their legal rights, as well as of the agencies to which they can turn for assistance. They may have difficulty getting their credentials or qualifications recognized. They will lack a network of friends and contacts for support, work, or assistance. They will often have to start at the bottom, whatever their qualifications, in order to prove themselves. Low in seniority or in a subordinate position, they may feel vulnerable at work and may accept lower wages, longer hours, or worse conditions than they are entitled to. None of these obstacles necessarily implies discrimination. Rather, they all are a consequence of the structural disadvantages facing new immigrants. Discrimination is a valid explanation only if these disadvantages are unevenly distributed among new immigrants or if they persist for some groups and not for others.

Evidence concerning the prevalence of discrimination is inconsistent. Clearly, differences do exist. What do they really mean? Will they persist? DeSilva's examination of 1986 census data (1992) led him to conclude that there is no significant discrimination against visible minorities in Canada and that, over time, most immigrants achieve income equality with Canadian-born workers. DeSilva does admit, however, that immigrants from East Asia and the Caribbean do not seem to achieve income equality and that the education and work experience obtained by immigrants before coming to Canada seem to count less then education and work experience within Canada.

However, DeSilva's data assume that members of visible minorities are invariably foreign-born, effectively ignoring the existence of Canadian-born members of visible minority groups. Li (2000) examined the data from the 1996 census, comparing immigrants with native-born Canadians of the same gender, racial origin, and urban location. He found that immigrant men and women "earned either the same or more than their native-born counterparts of the same racial background" (304). Li then took into account such factors as experience and language ability and found that the earnings "advantage" of immigrants disappeared. In fact, he found that immigrant women, whether or not members of visible minorities, had a significant earnings disadvantage, as did immigrant visible-minority men, whereas non-visible-minority immigrant men had a much smaller income disadvantage. (See Table 8.2.)

Li's data indicate a more significant earnings disadvantage than that found by earlier researchers, such as Monica Boyd (1992), who examined 1986 data. Li's analysis used different assumptions, but it may also reflect the increasing earnings disadvantage of more recent immigrants. A recent report on the economic performance of immigrants (CIC, IMDB Profile Series, May 1999) indicates that whereas immigrants with a university degree had employment earnings 20 per cent above the Canadian average in 1981 after only one year in Canada, such immigrants had a 30 per cent earnings disadvantage by 1992. The relative earnings of recent refugees has also deteriorated compared to average Canadians, with refugees in 1992 earning 35 per cent less relative to the Canadian average than in the 1980s (CIC, 1998).

Table 8.2 **Earnings of Immigrants and Native-Born Canadians as Percentage of Earnings of Native-Born Non-visible-minority Men, for Four CMA Levels, 1996**

| | | Gross Earnings | | Net Earnings After Adjusting for Individual Characteristics[a] | | Net Earnings After for Adjusting Individual and Market Characteristics[b] | |
|---|---|---|---|---|---|---|---|
| | | Native-Born Canadian | Immigrant | Native-Born Canadian | Immigrant | Native-Born Canadian | Immigrant |
| *Not CMA* | | | | | | | |
| Non-visible minority | Male | $28,122 | 122% | $29,590 | 86% | $31,657 | 88% |
| | Female | 61% | 70% | 73% | 52% | 75% | 56% |
| Visible minority | Male | 77% | 106% | 98% | 87% | 99% | 89% |
| | Female | 62% | 61% | 83% | 62% | 85% | 66% |
| *Small CMA (<500,000)* | | | | | | | |
| Non-visible minority | Male | $32,821 | 120% | $31,936 | 90% | $32,565 | 89% |
| | Female | 62% | 66% | 71% | 53% | 71% | 52% |
| Visible minority | Male | 71% | 86% | 96% | 76% | 96% | 75% |
| | Female | 51% | 52% | 77% | 57% | 77% | 56% |
| *Medium CMA (500,000–999,999)* | | | | | | | |
| Non-visible minority | Male | $33,182 | 114% | $31,679 | 89% | $31,657 | 88% |
| | Female | 62% | 63% | 72% | 52% | 72% | 50% |
| Visible minority | Male | 56% | 73% | 85% | 65% | 84% | 64% |
| | Female | 46% | 51% | 80% | 54% | 79% | 53% |
| *Large CMA (1,000,000+)* | | | | | | | |
| Non-visible minority | Male | $36,082 | 106% | $33,954 | 85% | $31,913 | 82% |
| | Female | 68% | 68% | 74% | 56% | 72% | 51% |
| Visible minority | Male | 60% | 75% | 88% | 67% | 85% | 62% |
| | Female | 45% | 56% | 79% | 56% | 75% | 51% |

[a] Net earnings are adjusted earnings after differences in individual characteristics and differences in market characteristics have been taken into account. Individual characteristics include industry of work, occupation, full-time or part-time work, years of schooling, years of work experience, experience squared, number of weeks worked, official languages ability, and number of years since immigrated to Canada for immigrants (native-born = 0).
[b] Market characteristics include the level of unemployment in the person's region of residence and the size of immigrants' population as a percentage of the region's total population.
SOURCE: Peter Li, "Earnings Disparities Between Immigrants and Native-Born Canadians," *Canadian Review of Sociology and Anthropology*, 37 (2000): 303. Reprinted by permission of CSAA.

These figures are especially discouraging in view of current policy, which promotes the immigration of skilled workers and professionals. The proportion of immigrants arriving prior to 1986 without a level of education or credentials equivalent to native-born Canadians was much greater than today. Yet, while recent immigrants have a higher level of education and better credentials than those in the past, they are making less money. Credentials are of no benefit if they are not recognized, and *Maclean's* magazine (Janigan, 2002) reports that there are over 344,000 people in Canada whose foreign credentials are not recognized.

Being an immigrant, and especially a member of a visible minority, makes a difference. Put together, these data suggest that the lower income of visible minorities results mainly from structural disadvantages and from their relatively recent time of arrival rather than from overt discrimination. Support for this can be found in the fact that the longer immigrants have resided in Canada, the more likely they are to have an income equal to or greater than the Canadian average.

Research by Frances Henry and Effie Ginzberg (1990) attempted to uncover discrimination against visible minorities in a more direct way. These researchers arranged for equally qualified blacks and whites to apply for jobs in Toronto in 1984. They found that whites were favoured 3:1, with 27 job offers made to whites and only 9 to blacks. This is clear evidence of discrimination. On the other hand, a replication of the study in 1989 had different results, with blacks slightly favoured in job offers: 20 compared with 18 offers to whites (Economic Council of Canada, 1991: 30).

Like more recent immigrants, many European immigrants arriving in the 1950s and 1960s found themselves near the bottom of the occupational and income hierarchy. However, the evidence suggests that they have in large measure been able to move beyond their entrance status. A study by Wsevolod Isajiw, Aysan Sev'er, and Leo Driedger (1993) compared German, Italian, Jewish, and Ukrainian Canadians in Toronto and found that, in all four categories, there had been significant occupational and educational mobility between the first-, second-, and third-generation group members. Hugh Lautard and Neil Guppy approached the issue from another angle, looking at the index of occupational dissimilarity among ethnic groups. In their words, the index of occupational dissimilarity is the "percentage of the ethnic group which would have to have a different occupation in order for there to be no difference between the occupational distribution of the group and the rest of the labour force" (1990: 200). Their figures show that the index of occupational dissimilarity declined for most major ethnic groups between 1961 (when Porter gathered much of his data) and 1986. For Italian Canadians, for example, it declined from 40 to 24, for Jewish Canadians from 59 to 49.

Despite these findings, it would be unrealistic to paint a rosy picture of eventual equality for all. Occupational dissimilarity may have diminished, but it still exists. Remember, too, that not all discrimination is intentional. Institutional and systemic discrimination remain problems in Canada inasmuch as they are built into the very fabric of our society. In difficult economic times, for example, employers might prefer hiring members of visible minorities on the assumption that they could pay them less or provide them with fewer benefits.

Canada as a whole is characterized by income inequality. The "average" income simply masks the discrepancies of poverty and wealth between the members of our society. An ethnic group's success in achieving an "equal" income simply reflects that this group is just as unequal as Canadians are as a whole.

# Ethnicity and the Future of Canada

Can Canadians overcome their regional, ethnic, and linguistic differences in order to keep the country together? Or will the differences that have for so long shaped Canadian society eventually tear it apart? There are no easy answers to these questions. Past policies intended to ease the differences do not seem to have been effective. And while few Canadians expect the resulting problems to be resolved by violence, recent history might give us pause. The 1990 confrontation between Natives and police at Oka, Quebec, near the Kanesatake reserve, escalated very quickly. A police officer was killed, troops were brought in, and a series of ugly incidents erupted outside the area, including the blocking of a bridge by Mohawks near Montreal and the stoning of Mohawks' vehicles by whites. What if Quebec were to choose to separate from the rest of Canada? Most Canadians assume the separation would be peaceful. Inevitably there would be disputes over jurisdictions, money, perhaps even borders. How would these disagreements be resolved in an emotionally charged atmosphere?

Discrimination is another problem related to ethnicity. While Canada remains one of the most tolerant and pluralistic societies in the world, there are disturbing signs that racism, if not more prevalent, has become more acceptable. Canadian society seems to be coping well with institutional and systemic discrimination and racism. However, what is to be done about avowedly racist groups? Should their members be censored or charged with promoting hatred? In answering these questions, we inevitable run into questions of rights. It is hard to make sure that in trying to protect the rights of some, we do not endanger the rights of others. Serving to complicate the situation is the fact that court action against racists serves to give them free publicity and thereby helps them disseminate their ideas.

The Canadian dilemma of trying to keep together a nation composed of people divided by ethnicity, language, and even region will not soon be resolved. Canadians have so far shown a remarkable ability to handle these divisions with very little recourse to violence, oppressive legislation, or the suspension of rights. Perhaps the best solution is to try to understand the different kinds of people who make up this country and make them all feel that they are equally at home in Canada.

## Conclusion

Because of Canada's origin as a political union of two distinct groups—the British and the French—ethnicity and ethnic differences have always played a special role in Canadian society. Contention between the two charter groups has been a part of Canada's history since their first arrival. More recently, the Native peoples have been engaged in political action with a view to achieving self-government. Understanding such issues requires an awareness of ethnicity and its role in Canadian society.

*Ethnicity* refers to the social distinctions whereby groups differentiate themselves from one another on the basis of presumed biological ties. Distinctions are justified on the basis of symbolic markers such as appearance, language, or religion. When the symbolic markers are biological, sociologists use the term *race* to refer to a group.

An *ethnic group* exists to the extent that people are capable of organizing and acting on their ethnic interests or identity. An *ethnic community* is a group

that has evolved a set of common interests, institutions, and identities. Even people for whom ethnicity is irrelevant may be counted as part of an *ethnic category*, a strictly objective measure of how many people share a particular ethnic origin.

Most theories of ethnicity are either pluralistic theories or remedial. Pluralistic theories see ethnic or racial differences among people as natural or inevitable. Remedial theories tend to treat ethnicity as a characteristic of a class or of an industrial society. While they largely discount the role of ethnicity in modern societies, they still try to explain how or why ethnicity may be relevant under certain conditions. The most influential pluralistic theory is that of Barth, who argued that ethnic differences are a consequence of the patterns of social interaction among people that generate boundaries among them. The most popular remedial approach in Canada is to look at the role of the state in defining and promoting ethnic distinctions.

Two issues have dominated Canadian sociologists' research on ethnicity: the connection between ethnicity and inequality in Canada, and the integration of ethnic groups and communities into Canadian society. Porter's description of Canadian society as a vertical mosaic initiated research interest in links between ethnicity and inequality. Porter's work showed that ethnic groups in Canada have been encouraged to retain their distinctive identity and culture and have thereby been locked into accepting limited economic opportunities and retaining their entrance status. Breton's work on institutional completeness gave sociologists an essential tool for measuring an ethnic community's integration into Canadian society and initiated an examination of ethnic groups in Canada as organized communities.

While Canadians pride themselves on being tolerant, prejudice, discrimination, and racism all may be found to some degree in Canadian society. Institutional discrimination, which is built into the very structure and operation of society's institutions, is particularly difficult to eradicate.

Canadian immigration policy has always favoured certain groups over others, initially, migrants from Britain or Northern Europe. Immigration policy before the late 1960s was racist and exclusionary. Since then, immigration patterns have changed substantially, with more immigrants coming to Canada from non-European, especially Asian, countries. As a result, more immigrants than ever are members of visible minorities, who face different problems from those faced by earlier European immigrants.

Inter-group relations in Canada have evolved in a context of bilingualism and multiculturalism. While these official policies were intended to ease tensions between ethnic groups, both have met with only limited success. Currently, transnationalism and the increase in the number of Canadians having multiple ethnic origins are changing the pattern of relations among Canadians. These new patterns are evolving in ways that may soon make both bilingualism and multiculturalism outdated policies.

The most recent research concludes that ethnicity still makes a difference in such factors as income; however, gender often makes a greater difference. The data suggest that the lower income of visible minorities is mainly the result of structural disadvantages and their relatively recent time of arrival, rather than of discrimination.

## ☐ Questions for Critical Thought

1. Suppose you could decide who should or should not be admitted to Canada as an immigrant. On what factors would you base your decisions for admitting immigrants? What factors would you use to keep people out?

2. Would you prefer to be identified as a Canadian or as a member of an ethnic or racial group? Is your own ethnic or racial identity relevant to your everyday life? Are there particular circumstances in which it becomes more relevant?

3. Do you agree that Native peoples should have some form of self-government? Should Aboriginal rights be given precedence over Canada's Constitution and laws? Is Native self-government compatible with women's entrenched equal rights?

4. Are most Canadians racially or ethnically prejudiced? Is it necessary that people be prejudiced for minority groups to suffer discrimination? Can you think of examples of discrimination that may be unintentional but that have negative consequences anyway?

5. Why do ethnic differences appear to be increasing in significance worldwide? Is the world changing in ways that make ethnic identity more relevant to people?

6. Religious and national differences seem to be a source of much conflict in the world today. Do you think ethnic or racial attachments differ in kind from religious or nationalist differences, or are they all part of some broader category of social differentiation? How can we go about overcoming such differences?

7. The extraordinary movement of peoples we see today can be expected to continue and even expand in the future. What kinds of changes might become necessary in how we relate to one another locally, nationally, and globally?

8. Immigrants to Canada are far more likely to obtain Canadian citizenship within the minimum prescribed time than are immigrants to the United States. Why do you think that is? Do immigrants feel a greater need for political and constitutional protections in Canada than in the United States?

## ☐ Recommended Readings

**Vered Amit-Talai and Caroline Knowles**, *Re-situating Identities: the Politics of Race, Ethnicity and Culture* (Peterborough, Ont.: Broadview, 1996).

This reader is one of many new books and collections that are attempting to re-examine and rethink the phenomenon of ethnicity in light of the fundamental social changes that are transforming relations among individuals and groups. This particular collection focuses on transformations of identity both in Canada and elsewhere in the world.

**Raymond Breton**, *The Governance of Ethnic Communities: Political Structures and Processes in Canada* (New York: Greenwood, 1991).

This important book by one of the most influential and respected researchers on ethnicity in Canada examines the way in which the nation's ethnic communities are organized and govern themselves.

**Alan C. Cairns**, *Citizens Plus: Aboriginal Peoples and the Canadian State* (Vancouver: University of British Columbia Press, 2000).

One of Canada's most thoughtful and elegant writers on politics and the state examines the issue of Aboriginal relations with the rest of Canada. In this book, Cairns is less concerned with providing data than with putting forth an argument that all Canadians, including Aboriginal peoples, need to develop a sense of common identity and institutions that can foster common citizenship.

**Madeline Kalbach and Warren E. Kalbach**, *Perspectives on Ethnicity in Canada* (Toronto: Harcourt, 2000).

A first-class collection of readings on Canadian ethnicity covering a wide spectrum of topics.

**Peter S. Li**, *The Chinese in Canada*, 2nd edn (Toronto: Oxford University Press, 1998).

This book remains an essential examination of one of Canada's most significant ethnic groups. This is one of the few books to examine an ethnic group in the context of its interactions with others, especially the impact of racism on the development of the Chinese Canadian community.

## ☐ Recommended Web Sites

**Citizenship and Immigration Canada**
www.cic.gc.ca

The official source of government data on immigration and citizenship issues, and the only site where you can get information on immigration that is more up to date than the census. It is also a source of practical information for people seeking to immigrate to Canada and of government policies and plans.

**Metropolis Canada**
www.canada.metropolis.net/

This is another example of the extraordinary wealth of material available on the internet, as well as of how Canadian sites set an example for the rest of the world. The Metropolis project is an international interdisciplinary program of research on migration, integration, and cultural diversity.

**Transnational Communities Programme**
www.transcomm.ox.ac.uk

Located at Oxford University, the Transcomm Programme has generated a wealth of material written by major scholars and available on the Web site. The material on this site is written at an advanced level.

# part three

> > >

## Social Institutions

In this section we will see that society's major social institutions—families, the educational system, the economy and workplaces, health issues, politics, and religion—persist, change, and interconnect in complicated patterns. The sociological imagination helps us see these linkages and the ways that large changes result from millions of much smaller changes.

# 9

Maureen Baker

> > >

# Families

© W.P. Wittman Limited

## ☐ Learning Objectives

In this chapter, you will:

- learn to differentiate popular myths about family life from actual research results
- gain a clearer understanding of variations in family life
- understand how sociologists have conceptualized and explained family patterns
- gain some insight into several contentious issues in Canadian families
- identify current demographic trends in Canadian families
- understand how predictions are made about family life in the future

# Introduction

This chapter defines *families* and outlines some of the variation in family structure and practices. The different ways that sociologists have discussed and explained family patterns are introduced before we turn our attention to five issues in family life: sharing domestic work; low fertility and assisted conception; child-care concerns; the impact of divorce and repartnering on children; and wife abuse.

# Family Variations

## What Are Families?

Many different definitions of *family* have been used in academic and government research, as well in as the delivery of government programs. Most definitions focus on legal obligations and family structure rather than on how people feel about each other or on what services programs provide. These definitions always include heterosexual couples and single parents sharing a home with their children, but not all definitions encompass same-sex couples. Most definitions include dependent children, while some also take into account childless couples or those whose children have left home. Still others extend the definition of family to grandparents, aunts, uncles, and cousins who share a dwelling.

Sociologists and anthropologists used to talk about "the family" as a monolithic **social institution** with one acceptable structure and common behavioural patterns (Eichler, 1997). Academic researchers used to assume that family members were related by blood, marriage, or adoption and that they shared a dwelling, earnings, and other resources; that couples maintained sexually exclusive relationships, reproduced, and raised children together; and that family members cherished and protected each other. Nevertheless, academics have always differentiated between **nuclear families**, which consist of parents and their children sharing a dwelling, and **extended families**, which consist of several generations or adult siblings with their spouses and children who may share a dwelling and resources. Both kinds of families continue to be a part of Canadian life.

The most prevalent definition used in policy research is Statistics Canada's **census family**, which includes married couples and cohabiting couples who have lived together for longer than one year, with or without never-married children, as well as single parents living with never-married children. This definition says nothing about the larger kin group of aunts, uncles, and grandparents; or about love, emotion, and caring; or about providing household services. Yet a common definition must be agreed on when taking a **census** or initiating policy research.

The Canadian government also uses the concept of **household** in gathering statistics relating to family and personal life. *Household* refers to people sharing a dwelling, whether or not they are related by blood, adoption, or marriage. For example, a boarder might be part of the household but not necessarily part of the family. A gay or lesbian couple might also be considered by the government to be a household, even though they might be living as a married couple. Table 9.1 shows how the Canadian government categorizes families.

In a culturally diverse society such as Canada, it is inaccurate to talk about "the family" as though a single type of family exists or ever did exist. In fact, different cultural groups tend to organize their families

Table 9.1  **Types of Families in Canada, 1981, 1991, and 2001 (Percentages)**

| Type of Family | 1981 | 1991 | 2001 |
|---|---|---|---|
| Legally married couples with children | 55.0 | 48.2 | 41.4 |
| Legally married couples without children | 28.2 | 29.1 | 29.0 |
| Lone-parent families | 11.3 | 12.7 | 15.7 |
| Common-law couples without children | 3.7 | 5.8 | 7.5 |
| Common-law couples with children | 1.9 | 4.2 | 6.3 |
| Same-sex couples as percentage of all couples | N/A[1] | N/A[1] | 0.5 |

[1]Same-sex couples were counted for the first time in the 2001 census, and classified as common-law couples

Source: Vanier Institute of the Family, *Profiling Canada's Families III* (Ottawa: Vanier Institute of the Family, 2004), 40; Vanier Institute of the Family, *Profiling Canada's Families II* (Ottawa: Vanier Institute of the Family, 2000), 31; Statistics Canada, *Dwellings and Households: 1991 Census of Canada* (Cat. no. 93-311) (Ottawa: Statistics Canada, 1992), 130.

differently, depending on cultural traditions, religious beliefs, socio-economic situations, immigrant or indigenous status, and historical experiences, though most Canadians live in nuclear families comprising parents and their children (Vanier Institute of the Family, 2000). When relatives do not share a household but live close by and rely heavily on one another, they are said to be a **modified extended family**.

In the 1950s, American sociologists lamented the isolation of the modern nuclear family, suggesting that extended families used to be more prevalent prior to industrialization (Parsons and Bales, 1955). Since then, historians have found that nuclear families were always the most prevalent living arrangement in Europe and North America (Goldthorpe, 1987; Nett, 1981), but extended families were and still are quite prevalent among certain cultural groups, such as some First Nations peoples, Southern Europeans, and some Asians. They are also more prevalent among those with lower incomes and at certain stages of the family life cycle, for example, in order to provide low-cost accommodation and practical support for young cash-strapped couples, lone mothers after separation, or frail elderly parents after becoming widowed.

Many immigrants come to Canada from countries where people live in extended families, yet the percentage of "multi-family households" (a term used by Statistics Canada that approximates an extended family) declined from 6.7 per cent in 1951 to 1.1 per cent in 1986, when immigration rates were high (Ram, 1990: 44). The explanation for this decline is that most Canadians considered living alone more acceptable and feasible and that immigrants tend to change their family practices to fit in with the host country. In a recent study of immigrants who came to Canada in 1985, 43 per cent lived with established relatives in 1986, but this declined to 26 per cent by 1996 (Thomas, 2001: 18). In contrast, only 11 per cent of Canadian-born people lived with relatives in 1986 compared to 13 per cent in 1996. Living with relatives was more prevalent among female immigrants and among those with lower educational qualifications and lower incomes (Thomas, 2001: 21).

In this chapter, the term *families*, in the plural, will be used consistently to indicate the existence of many different and sociologically acceptable definitions of family structures. Qualified phrases, such as "male-breadwinner families," "lesbian families," and "step-families," will be used for clarification. Although sociological definitions formerly focused on who constitute a family, more researchers and theorists now emphasize what characterizes a family. This approach downplays the sexual preference of the couple and the legality of the relationship, focusing instead on patterns of caring and intimacy (Eichler, 1997).

## Monogamy Versus Polygamy

When George Murdock completed his *World Ethnographic Sample* in 1949, he noted that only about 20 per cent of the 554 societies he studied could be designated as strictly monogamous. In Canada and most industrialized countries, monogamy—being legally married to one spouse at a time—is both social custom and law. Yet many Canadians marry more than once over their lifespan, a situation called **serial monogamy**. In Murdock's study, most societies permitted **polygyny**—being legally married to more than one wife at a time—and were characterized by a *mixture* of polygyny and monogamy.

In some African and Islamic nations, polygyny continues to be practised by wealthier men who can afford to support more than one wife. Wives in polygynous marriages may welcome a new wife to help with household duties and child care, to share work in the fields, or to provide companionship (Leslie and Korman, 1989).

Polygyny is much more prevalent than **polyandry**, the practice of being legally married to more than one husband at a time. The underlying reasons probably are that only one male is needed to impregnate several wives, that questions of paternity and inheritance would arise with more than one husband, and that men have the power to ensure that family practices suit their interests (Baker, 2001a). In recent years, **polygamy**—marriage to more than one spouse at a time—has been prohibited by law in all Western nations because of the assumed difficulties of providing adequate financial and emotional support for more than one partner and because of Judeo-Christian ideas of sexual exclusivity.

## Arranged Versus Free-Choice Marriage

Marriages continue to be arranged in many parts of the world in order to enhance family resources, reputation, and other alliances and because parents feel more qualified to choose their children's partners. The family of either the bride or of the groom may make initial arrangements, but marriage brokers or intermediaries with extensive contacts are occasionally used to help families find suitable mates for their offspring.

9.1

## Global Issues
### A Maori Lone-Mother Family on Social Assistance, New Zealand

"From Friday to Sunday it's pretty much mayhem here. I can have anything up to thirteen kids. Nieces, nephews, the *mokos* [grandchildren], the neighbours. Last weekend I had their baby, a 15-month-old baby from next door. Because they were having a big party and they were out of babysitters and I said, well, just chuck him over the fence and we'll be right and she can sleep here the night so you can . . . pick her up in the morning. So they did that. My niece had to go to a funeral and she's got a 3-week-old baby and she popped her over to me with a little bottle of breast milk as well. So I had those two babies and . . . my son had his friend over for the night because his mother was next door partying and so while everybody does their thing, I have the kids and I had another little girl 'cause her mother was there too and I don't really know them."

———

SOURCE: Maureen Baker, personal interview, 2002.

Marriages are sometimes arranged for Middle Eastern and East Asian immigrants living in Canada. These arrangements may involve returning to the home country to marry a partner selected by family members still living there, or a man and a woman from the same cultural group, living in Canada, may be introduced to each other by family members and may be encouraged to marry. Young people expect to have veto power if they strongly object to their family"s choice, but in the home country considerable pressure exists to abide by the judgement of elders (Nanda, 1991).

Family solidarity, financial security, and potential heirs are considered more important in arranged

Marriages continue to be arranged in many parts of the world in order to enhance family resources, reputation, and alliances. Family solidarity, financial security, and potential heirs are important in arranged marriages. (© Sheriar Hirjikaka, L'image Photography)

marriages than sexual attraction or love between the young people (Baker, 2001a). New marital partners are urged to respect each other, and it is hoped that love will develop after marriage. Arranged marriages frequently are more stable than free-choice unions because both families have a stake in marriage stability. Furthermore, divorce may be legally restricted, especially for women, and may involve mothers' relinquishing custody of their children. In addition, women cannot always support themselves outside marriage in some of these societies.

A **dowry** is sometimes used to attract a higher-status husband, to clinch a marriage agreement between the two families, to contribute to the establishment of the new household, and to furnish a married woman with "insurance" money in case of divorce or premature widowhood. Under this system, families with marriageable daughters must show families with eligible sons that they can provide money or property with their daughter's marriage. If a woman has a large dowry, she can find a "better" husband, which usually means one who is relatively wealthy, healthy, well-educated, and from a respected family. However, the dowry system is a financial burden for poorer families with several daughters and tends to encourage a preference for sons. For these reasons, the dowry system has been outlawed in some countries, such as India, though it continues to operate clandestinely in rural areas (Baker, 2001a; Nanda, 1991).

In other societies that practised arranged marriage (such as eastern Indonesia), the groom's family was expected to pay the bride's parents a **bride price** for permission to marry their daughter. If the bride was beautiful or came from a wealthy or well-respected family, the price would rise. If the groom and his family were short of cash or property, the bride price could sometimes be paid through the groom's labour.

Although dowries and bride prices are associated with arranged marriages, free-choice marriages have retained symbolic remnants of these practices. For example, trousseaus, honeymoons, and the wedding celebration itself are remnants of dowries. The engagement ring and wedding band given to the bride by the groom are remnants of a bride price.

### Patterns of Authority and Descent

Most family systems designate a "head," who makes major decisions and represents the group to the outside world. In both Western and Eastern societies, the oldest male is typically the family head, in a system referred to as **patriarchy**. An authority system in which women are granted more power than men is a *matriarchy*, but matriarchal systems are rare. Some black families in the Caribbean and the United States have been referred to as matriarchal, or at least **matrifocal** (Smith, 1996), as has been the Tchambuli people of New Guinea (Mead, 1935). In both examples, wives and mothers make a considerable contribution to family income and resources as well as to decision-making. Although Canadian families used to be patriarchal, men and women now have equal legal rights and men are no longer automatically viewed as family heads. However, in some cultural communities, men are still regarded as family heads.

When young people marry, they usually consider their primary relationship to be with each other rather than with either set of parents or siblings. In most cases, however, the newly married pair is expected to maintain contact with both sides of the family and to participate in family gatherings, and could inherit from either side of the family. This situation is termed a **bilateral descent pattern**. In other cases, the bride and groom are considered to be members of only one kin group, in a system called **patrilineal descent** if they belong to the groom's family, **matrilineal descent** if they belong to the bride's. Patterns of descent may determine where the couple live, how they address members of each other's family, what surname their children will receive, and from whom they inherit.

In Canadian families, bilateral descent is common for kinship and inheritance, but patrilineal descent has been retained for surnames in some provinces. The surname taken by a wife and by the couple's children has traditionally been the husband's name— a symbol of his former status as head of the new household. This tradition has been changed in Quebec, where brides are required to retain their family name. In Ontario, brides have a choice between keeping their family name and taking their husband's name. Where there is some legal choice, couples may also abide by their cultural traditions.

## Explaining Family Patterns and Practices

All social studies are based on underlying philosophical assumptions about what motivates human society and what is important to emphasize in research. These assumptions, often called *theoretical frameworks*, cannot be proven or disproven but guide our research and help to explain our observations (Klein and White,

1996). In this section, several of the theoretical frameworks used to study families will be examined, including their basic premises, strengths, and weaknesses.

## The Political Economy Approach

The basic thesis of the political economy approach is that people's relation to wealth, production, and power influences the way they view the world and live their lives. Family formation, interpersonal relations, lifestyle, and well-being are affected by such events in the broader society as economic cycles, working conditions, laws, and government programs. This perspective originates in the nineteenth-century work of German political philosophers Karl Marx (1818–3) and Friedrich Engels (1820–95). In *The Origin of the Family, Private Property and the State* ([1882] 1942), Engels discusses how family life in Europe was transformed as economies changed from hunting-and-gathering societies to horticultural, to pre-industrial, and finally to industrial societies.

The political economy approach has been debated and modified over the years. Political economists argue that social life always involves conflict, especially between people who have wealth and power and make social policies and people who do not. Conflicting interests remain the major force behind societal change. In the nineteenth century, men's workplaces were removed from the home, which gradually eroded patriarchal authority and encouraged families to adapt to the employer's needs. Furthermore, many of the goods and services that people formerly had produced at home for their own consumption eventually were manufactured more cheaply in factories. This meant that families eventually became units of shared income and consumption rather than units of production. Once the production of most goods and services took place outside the home, people began to see the family as private and separate from the public world of business and politics. Nevertheless, unpaid domestic labour helps keep wages low and profits high (Bradbury, 2001; Fox, 1980; Luxton, 1980).

The impact of industrialization and workplace activities on family life are the focal point of the political economy approach, based in the belief that economic changes transform ways of viewing the world. Political economists would argue, for example, that the surge of married women into the labour force after the 1960s occurred mainly for economic rather than feminist ideological reasons. The service sector of the economy expanded according to changes in domestic and foreign markets, requiring new workers. While married women had always worked as a reserve labour force, the creation of new job opportunities, as well as inflation and the rising cost of living, encouraged more wives and mothers to accept paid work. These labour market changes led to new **ideologies** about family and parenting. Political economists focus on the impact of the economy on family life, on relations between **the state** and the family, and on the social conflict arising from these political and economic changes. In doing so, they downplay voluntary behaviour and interpersonal relations.

## Structural Functionalism

The basic assumption of **structural functionalism** is that behaviour is governed more by social expectations and unspoken rules than by personal choice. Individuals cannot behave any way they want but must abide by societal or cultural guidelines learned early in life. Deviant behaviour that violates rules is always carefully controlled.

Within this approach, "the family" is viewed as a major social institution that provides individuals with emotional support, love and companionship, sexual expression, and children. Parents help to maintain social order through socializing and disciplining their children. Families co-operate economically and help each other through hard times by sharing resources. They often protect their members from outsiders. Finally, people acquire money and property through inheritance from family members, which suggests that social status is largely established and perpetuated through families.

Talcott Parsons and Robert F. Bales (1955) theorized that with the development of industrialization and the shift to production outside the home, the small and relatively isolated nuclear family began to specialize in the **socialization** of children and in meeting the personal needs of family members (Thorne, 1982). These authors assumed that the family has two basic structures: a hierarchy of generations, and a differentiation of adults into instrumental and expressive **roles**. Parsons and Bales argued that the wife necessarily takes the expressive role, maintaining social relations and caring for others. The husband, on the other hand, assumes the instrumental role, earning the money for the family and dealing with the outside world (Thorne, 1982).

Structural functionalists have been criticized for their conservative position, as they often write about "the family" as though there is one acceptable family form rather than many variations. They believe that behaviour is largely determined by social expectations and family upbringing, and therefore is difficult to alter. Structural functionalists have also implied that a gendered division of labour was maintained throughout history because it was "functional for society," when it may have been functional mainly for heterosexual men (Thorne, 1982). In addition, change is seen as disruptive rather than as normal or progressive, and individual opposition to social pressure has been viewed as "deviance." Consequently, the structural functionalists have not dealt with conflict and change as well as have those taking a political economy approach. Nor have they focused on the dynamic nature of interpersonal relations. For these reasons, many researchers who want to examine inequality, conflict, and change find this theoretical perspective less useful than others to explain the social world.

**Systems theory** accepts many of the basic assumptions of structural functionalism but focuses on the interdependence of family behaviour and the way that families often close ranks against outsiders, even when they are in trouble. The understandings implicit to this approach have been particularly useful in family therapy.

## Social Constructionist Approach

The **social constructionist** approach refutes the idea that people behave according to unwritten rules or social expectations. Instead, it assumes that we construct our own social reality (Berger and Luckmann, 1966). Life does not just happen to us—we make things happen by exerting our will. This approach, also called **symbolic interactionism**, originated with the work of Americans Charles H. Cooley (1864–1929) and George Herbert Mead (1863–1931), who studied how families assist children to develop a sense of self. Within this perspective, the way people define and interpret reality shapes behaviour, and this process of interpretation is aided by non-verbal as well as verbal cues. Social constructionists also theorized that part of socialization is developing the ability to look at the world through the eyes of others and anticipating a particular role before taking it (called **anticipatory socialization**).

Studies using this approach often occur in a small-groups laboratory, using simulations of family interaction and decision-making. Researchers observe the interaction in this kind of setting between parents and children, among children in a playgroup, and between husbands and wives. Sometimes behaviour will be videotaped and the subjects will be asked to comment on their own behaviour, which is then compared to the researchers' observations. Research is often centred on communication processes during everyday experiences, but it is not enough to observe what people *do*. In addition, it is essential to understand how they *feel* and why they feel this way. People's perceptions and their definitions of the situation influence their actions or behaviour. This perspective could be seen as the precursor of postmodernist theory, to be discussed later in this chapter.

## Feminist Theories

**Feminist** theorists have focused on women's experiences, on written and visual representations of women, and on socio-economic differences between men and women. These perspectives developed and proliferated as more researchers concluded that women's experiences and contributions to society had been overlooked, downplayed, or misrepresented in previous social research.

Some feminist researchers have used a **structural approach** to analyze the ways in which inequality is perpetuated through social policies, laws, and labour market practices (Baker, 1995; O'Connor, Orloff, and Shaver, 1999). Others have concentrated on interpersonal relations between men and women, examining non-verbal communication, heterosexual practices, and public discourse (Baines, Evans, and Neysmith, 1998). Still other feminist theorists are attempting to create a more interpretive feminist analysis that takes women's experiences and ways of thinking and knowing into consideration (Butler, 1992; D. Smith, 1999).

Feminists note that housework and child care are unpaid when performed by a wife or mother but paid when done by a non-family member but that, in both cases, the work retains low occupational status and prestige. Although most adult women now work for pay, they continue to accept responsibility for domestic work in their own homes (Bittman and Pixley, 1997; Fox, 2001a; Hochschild, 2001). The unequal division of labour within families, as well as women's "double day" of paid and unpaid work, is considered to interfere with women's attempts to gain employment equity.

*Post-feminists* question the very nature of feminist analysis by arguing that vast differences remain between individual women depending on their unique experiences, social position, and cultural background

(Fraser and Nicholson, 1990). Others criticize the feminist perspective because it glosses over men's experiences or fails to compare men with women; but feminists argue that men's experiences and views are already well represented by traditional social science. Much of social science is now permeated by feminist ideas, especially the work of female scholars. The incorporation of this perspective into mainstream academic theory has been promoted by greater acceptance of the idea that there is no absolute socioloogical truth and that perception and knowledge depend on one's social position (Seidman, 1994).

### Postmodernist Approaches

The postmodernist analysis of families argues that "truth" is relative and depends on one's social position, gender, race, and culture. Furthermore, vast differences exist in family life, and "the traditional nuclear family" is more a myth than a historical reality. In contemporary OECD (Organisation for Economic Co-operation and Development) countries, sexuality is increasingly separated from marriage, and marriage is being reconstructed as a contract that can be ended. Childbearing and child-rearing are no longer necessarily linked with legal marriage, and the division of labour based on gender is continually renegotiated (Elliot, 1996). These demographic and social trends have led to a theoretical reworking of what defines *family* in the twenty-first century.

Another focus is on how families are constructed in everyday language and policy discourse (Muncie and Wetherell, 1995). By deconstructing—or analyzing the origins and intended meanings of beliefs about—"the family," researchers are able to see how images of this institution have been socially constructed and are historically situated. Nancy Fraser (1997) argues that historical conceptions of the nuclear family, upon which many Western countries built their welfare systems, were premised on the ideal of the male-breadwinner/female-caregiver family. Labour market changes (including the casualization and feminization of the workforce) and changing expectations for both men and women have questioned this gender order. Fraser suggests that we need major changes to conceptions both of gender and of the organization of work in order to facilitate a new order based on equity and on recognition of the interdependence of work and family.

The legal assumption of the heterosexuality of couples has also been criticized, and Martha Fineman (1995) proposes a reconceptualization of family away

What defines a family? "Normative heterosexuality" is being questioned by lesbians and gays who seek to legally marry and whose families embrace friends, lovers, co-parents, adopted children, and offspring conceived by alternative insemination. (© Toronto Star 2003)

from the current focus on sexual or horizontal intimacy (between spouses or partners). She argues for abolishing marriage as a legal category and placing greater emphasis on a vertical or intergenerational organization of intimacy (between parents and children). This would redirect attention away from sexual affiliation and encourage policy discussions about support for caring. Elizabeth Silva and Carol Smart (1999) suggest that "normative heterosexuality" is being challenged by lesbians and gays who dispute the old saying, "You can choose your friends, but you can't choose your relatives." These families embrace friends, lovers, co-parents, adopted children, children from previous heterosexual relationships, and offspring conceived through alternative insemination (Weeks, Donovan, and Heaphy, 1998). Critics of the postmodernist approach often argue that too much emphasis is placed on communicating messages and meanings and on minority family situations, rather than on discussing the ways that most people actually live or the influence of socio-economic forces on families (Nicholson and Seidman, 1995).

## Recent Issues in Canadian Families

In the past few decades, many aspects of family life have become viewed as conflictual or even as social problems. In this section, we consider a number of these, with specific reference to Canadian families. First, we examine issues relating to the gendered division of labour.

## *Sharing Domestic Work*

Over the past 20 years, patterns of paid work between husbands and wives have changed dramatically. While 50 per cent of families depended only on the husband's income in 1975, by 1996 only 20 per cent had a single male earner because so many wives have entered the job market (Statistics Canada, 1998a: 22). Families relying on a single wage earner experienced a $4,200 decline in real average income between 1989 and 1996, but the combined income in dual-earner families increased slightly (Statistics Canada, 1998a: 10). Table 9.2 shows that fathers are still more likely than mothers to be working for pay, regardless of the age of their children.

Canadian adolescent women expect to have paid jobs in the future. They tend to perceive household tasks as "women's work," but not as a viable option for themselves, except among working-class girls (Looker and Thiessen, 1999). Furthermore, both adolescent males and adolescent females see jobs normally done by women as less desirable than those typically performed by men.

Research typically concludes that most heterosexual couples divide their household labour in such a way that husbands work full-time and perform occasional unpaid chores around the house, usually in the yard or related to the family car. Most wives are employed for fewer hours per week than their husbands, but they usually take responsibility for routine indoor chores and child care, even when employed full-time. Wives are also expected to be "kin keepers" (Rosenthal, 1985), which includes maintaining contact with relatives, organizing family gatherings, and buying gifts. In addition, wives and mothers usually retain responsibility for "emotional work," such as

soothing frayed nerves, assisting children to build their confidence, and listening to family members' troubles (Baker, 2001a).

Despite this prevalent division of labour, wives who are employed full-time tend to perform less housework than those who work part-time or who are not in the labour force (Marshall, 1993). Wives employed full-time may lower their housework standards, encourage other family members to share the work, or hire someone to clean their houses or care for their children. Yet women continue to retain all or most of responsibility for indoor housework and child-rearing tasks, including the hiring and supervision of cleaners and care providers (Bittman and Pixley, 1997; Luxton, 2001). Many employed mothers report feeling exhausted and drained by their attempts to earn money and take most of the responsibility for child care and homemaking (Beck-Gernsheim, 2002; Fox, 1980; Hochschild and Machung, 1989).

Younger, well-educated couples with few or no children are more likely to share domestic work more equitably. Some wives in dual-earner families are employed full-time but still retain sole responsibility for housework, especially older women and those who did not complete high school (Marshall, 1994). Wives' bargaining power may increase slightly when they earn an income comparable to their husbands', as these wives are better able to persuade their husbands to do more housework and they tend to be less willing to relocate with their husbands' jobs (Marshall, 1993).

According to the 1998 Canadian Time Use Survey, married men aged 25 to 44 with children and employed full-time spent 23.1 hours a week on unpaid work (including volunteer work), compared to 34.3 hours for the same category of women; at the same time, women spent about 10 hours less per week than men on paid work (Vanier Institute of the Family, 2000: 79). An unsatisfactory division of housework with their partner was given as a valid reason for

Table 9.2 **Labour Force Participation Rates for Mothers and Fathers with Children Under 15 Years of Age, 2001 (Percentages)**

| Family Type | Mother | Father |
| --- | --- | --- |
| Single lone parent with youngest child under 6 | 60 | 76 |
| Married parent with child under 6 | 71 | 83 |
| Single lone parent with youngest child 6–14 | 76 | 94 |
| Married parent with youngest child 6–14 | 81 | 94 |

Source: Vanier Institute of the Family, *Profiling Canada's Families III* (Ottawa: Vanier Institute of the Family, 2004), 74. Reprinted by permission of The Vanier Institute of the Family.

divorce by 17 per cent of respondents in a 1995 Canadian study, but men were more likely to hold this attitude than women (Frederick and Hamel, 1998).

Why do wives accept the responsibility for housework even when they work for pay and prefer more sharing? Lorraine Davies and Patricia Jane Carrier (1999) examined the division of labour in dual-earner Canadian and US households using 1982 data, which allows them to say little about the current division of labour. Nevertheless, they concluded that the hours of work and the income earned by marital partners are less important than marital power relations in determining the allocation of household tasks. These power relations are influenced by gender expectations, opportunities, and experiences in the larger society, and gender intersects with race, ethnicity, and social class to influence these relations.

Only 1 per cent of Canadian families have adopted a role reversal, with the husband performing domestic work and child care at home while the wife works full-time (Marshall, 1998). In these families, most of the men are unemployed and have not necessarily chosen this lifestyle. Other North American research suggests that unemployed husbands feel that they would lose power in their marriages if their wife earned most of the household income, and that this view is shared by the wider community (Potuchek, 1997).

## Low Fertility and Assisted Conception

The emergence of common-law marriage, same-sex partnerships, divorce, and remarriage has complicated marriage and family relationships in the twenty-first century, but reproductive and genetic technologies may be in the process of fundamentally reshaping families (Eichler, 1997). This reshaping includes separating biological and social parenthood, changing generational lines, and creating the possibility of sex selection. A wide range of procedures have now become routine, such as egg retrieval, in-vitro fertilization, and reimplantation into a woman's womb. Frozen sperm and embryos make conception possible after their donors' death, postmenopausal women can bear children, and potential parents can contract surrogates to bear children for them (Baker, 2001a).

Eichler (1996) argues that reproductive technologies tend to commercialize human reproduction: we can now buy eggs, sperm, embryos, and reproductive services—all of which are produced and sold for profit. These technologies tend to raise the potential for eugenic thinking and enable us to evaluate embryos on their genetic makeup. Prenatal diagnoses allow us to choose whether or not a fetus is worthy of being born (Eichler, 1996). However, we have very little research on the impact of these technologies on family life, such as how parents involved in artificial insemination reveal their children's background to them and how children deal with this knowledge.

Most men and women intend to reproduce, as Figure 9.1 indicates. Fertility is important for social acceptance and gender identity, and conception problems contribute to feelings of guilt, anger, frustration, depression, and to marital disputes (Doyal, 1995). Low fertility may be caused by many factors, including exposure to sexually transmitted diseases, long-term use of certain contraceptives, workplace hazards, environmental pollutants, hormonal imbalances, and lifestyle factors such as tobacco smoking, excessive exercise, a large consumption of caffeine or other drugs, and prolonged stress (Bryant, 1990). The probability of conception also declines with women's age. Some couples spend years trying to become pregnant, while others place their names on adoption waiting lists. The number of infants available for adoption, however, has dramatically decreased in the past two decades with more effective birth control and with social benefits that enable single mothers to raise their own children. Consequently, more couples with fertility problems are turning to medically assisted conception.

*Infertility* is usually defined as the inability to conceive a viable pregnancy after one year of unprotected sexual intercourse, although many fertile people take longer than that to conceive. This short-term definition encourages some fertile couples to seek medical attention prematurely. Access to reproductive technologies is often limited to those considered most acceptable as parents: young heterosexual couples in a stable relationship with no previous children. Private clinics charging fees, however, may be less selective, and many women around 40 years of age approach fertility clinics for assistance. Most treatments last for several months and involve the use of drugs that can produce side effects such as depression, mood swings, weight gain, and multiple births. Some treatments continue for years.

Fertility treatments are also expensive, although those who end up with a healthy baby may find these costs acceptable. And although many individuals pay privately for medically assisted conception, any complications will probably be treated within the public health system. The chances of complications following IVF are higher than with natural conception; about 25

Figure 9.1   **Number of Children that Women and Men Intend to Have, by Age Group, 1995[a]**

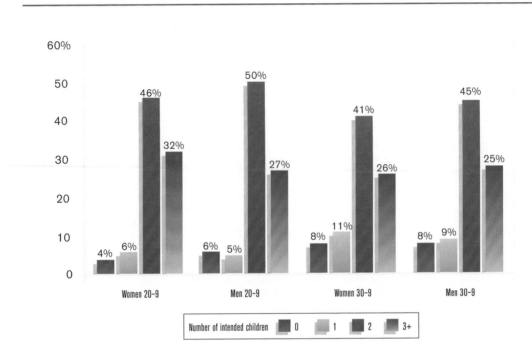

[a] As measured by the question, "What is the total number of children you intend to have, including those you have now and are currently expecting?" The proportion responding "don't know" ranged from 12 per cent among women aged 20–9 and men aged 30–9 to 14 per cent among women aged 30–9.
SOURCE: Adapted from Dave Dupuis, "What Influences People's Plans to Have Children?" *Canadian Social Trends,* Catalogue 11-008 (Spring 1998).

per cent of IVF pregnancies end in miscarriage (Baird, 1997). Furthermore, the success rate is not always as high as couples anticipate. British research indicates that in vitro fertilization ends in success for fewer than one-third of those who embark on it (Doyal, 1995: 149) and for only about 15 per cent per treatment cycle. The probability of producing a live birth from IVF declines substantially with age, and among women aged 40 to 44 the chance is only 5.5 per cent. With donor eggs, however, the probability of having a live birth increases to 17.7 per cent per IVF cycle for women aged 40 to 44 (Human Fertilisation and Embryology Authority, 1997). A higher number of multiple births also results from medically assisted conception. Medical births and their complications tend to use greater public health resources and also place financial and time constraints on new parents.

Those unable to reproduce even with the assistance of medical technology have sometimes turned to surrogacy arrangements. Surrogate mothers are usually low-income women who view pregnancy and childbirth as a relatively easy way to earn money, while the childless couple is often financially well off (McDaniel, 1988). P. Baird (1997) suggests that commercial surrogacy arrangements are unethical because they are premised on the idea that a child is a product that can be bought on the market and because they allow women to be exploited. In the United States, the substantial cost of surrogacy arrangements means that the commissioning couple is likely to be of a much higher economic and educational status then the woman gestating, and the brokers work on behalf of the paying couple (Baker, 2001a).

Eichler (1997) argues that reproductive and genetic technologies represent a quantum leap in complexity by blurring the role designations of mother, father, and child. For the child in a surrogacy relationship, who is the mother—the woman who gave birth or the woman who was part of the commissioning couple? What does it now mean to be a father? Does a man become a father if he impregnates a woman but has no social contact with the child? Does he become a father when he contracts another woman to use his sperm to make a baby, which he then adopts with his legal wife? Although sociologists have always been interested in the impact of absent fathers on family life, they are now talking about the "new absent fathers": sperm donors (Jamieson, 1998: 50). Social researchers are also interested in the increasing number of lesbian couples who are using self-insemination to create families without men (Albury, 1999; Nelson, 1999).

Sociologists and feminists have been ambivalent about medically assisted conception. On the one hand, it offers hope and opportunities for parenthood for those who might otherwise be excluded. However, some of the technologies are experimental and intrusive. These technologies also medicalize the natural act of childbearing, reinforce the pressure for all women to reproduce, and provide costly services unavailable to the poor. Feminist scholars have also been concerned that patriarchal societies will use sex selection to reinforce the cultural preference for sons rather than daughters and that working-class women will be exploited, both financially and emotionally, through surrogacy arrangements. These scholars seem to be most supportive of new reproductive technologies when they discuss self-insemination within lesbian relationships (Nelson, 1999), perhaps because of the assumption that unequal power relationships and coercion are minimized (Baker, 2001a).

---

 **9.2**

## Open for Discussion
### Medically Assisted Conception

"We tried IVF [in-vitro fertilization] and we got pregnant the first time. So it was very successful and obviously we are very pleased. I would say the IVF process was very cruel, even though we succeeded. I take my hat off to people who have it two or three times because it was extremely tough. It is very impersonal. You can't fault the treatment or the staff, but all the injections, different phases—it's like a roller coaster. You think you're ahead. Then you have a setback, bad news.

"One of the most stressful times for me was when I was in the room and they were harvesting the eggs from [my wife's] ovaries the first time—one egg. It felt terrible because we were hoping to get twelve. We got five off the second, so that was great but you still feel pretty disappointed. Then they fertilize and you only get two embryos and we were pretty depressed. Then a day later, we were up to four, so we were elated. Their goal was to try for five or six to choose. We had four, but one was a bit dodgy so we had three good embryos—you get that news a day later and you're down a little bit. Then during the IVF we had always envisaged that they would insert two embryos, which is extremely common—most peo-

ple have two put in. We only had one because [my wife's] uterus is a bit dodgy and they didn't want twins with a uterus shaped like that. They didn't want a prem [premature] baby, so all of a sudden you think that your chances are halved, which wasn't quite true. Then we had three great embryos and they chose the best one and it took, which is very pleasing. The other two are cryogenically frozen just like Austin Powers, waiting for their day in the sun."

*(Interviewer: "Amazing isn't it, when you think of the technology?")*

"Yes it is, and we wouldn't have got pregnant otherwise. . . . One of the senior doctors said that this was just the start and there were plenty more ups and downs. We are in the process now where there is lots of worry. [My wife] is worried about what she should and shouldn't eat. She worries that the baby will be born with some fault because she didn't take enough care. I'm very much in the reassuring mode—I'm sure it will be fine. I'm sure that once it is born then more worries start. It is an intriguing game, becoming a parent, I'd say."

---

SOURCE: Maureen Baker, personal interview, 2002.

### The Cost and Regulation of Child Care

The dramatic increase in the proportion of employed mothers within the past 40 years has led to a higher demand for non-family child care and to public concerns about the need to regulate the quality of care. Yet the demand still outstrips the supply, the assurance of quality continues to be a problem, and child-care costs are unaffordable for many parents.

Since the 1960s, Canadian governments have provided subsidized spaces for low-income and one-parent families, generally in not-for-profit centres or licensed homes. However, there are insufficient spaces for eligible families. Two-parent families with higher incomes must pay the full cost, but the Canadian government provides income-tax deductions for employed parents requiring child care to maintain their employment. These tax deductions, however, cannot be used by a substantial minority of parents because they are unable to obtain receipts from caregivers working informally within the underground economy (Clevedon and Krashinsky, 2001).

Many not-for-profit child-care centres have long waiting lists. Furthermore, they do not usually accept children under the age of two unless they are toilet-trained. Even if space is available, parents want to ensure that the centre employs an adequate number of staff to keep the infants clean, fed, and stimulated. In addition, some parents are concerned about the spread of infectious diseases in centre care. Finding a qualified babysitter to come to the child's home or who will welcome an extra child in her home is also difficult. Although licensed family homes are available in most jurisdictions, sitters usually operate outside these regulations (Doherty, Friendly, and Oloman, 1998).

Sitter care is unregulated by any level of government, yet it remains the most prevalent type of child care for employed parents. Grandparents (usually grandmothers) are sometimes able and willing to provide child care while the parents are at work, and care by grandmothers can save money, provide culturally sensitive care, and create a more solid bond between generations. Yet it could also lead to disagreements about child-rearing techniques between the parents and the grandparent, who is likely to have retained more traditional cultural values. Child-care concerns have encouraged some mothers to remain at home to care for their own children, although most can no longer afford this option.

In two-parent families, employed parents may be able to share child rearing if they work on different shifts. In the past, the majority of physical care and emotional support was given to the child from the mother, but today's fathers are taking a more active role in child care and nurturing. (© Harry Cutting Photography www.harrycutting.com)

Most centre-based care operates during regular office hours, but some parents need child care in the evening and weekends. In two-parent families, employed parents may be able to share child-rearing if they work on different shifts, but it is difficult to maintain their own relationship or to engage in family activities. Parents whose children have special needs experience special problems. Before institutions and hospitals were built in the 1960s, mothers were the main caregivers of these children. This source of unpaid labour is once again being examined as a way to reduce health and chronic care costs with policies of deinstitutionalization since the 1980s. Yet many mothers are now in the labour force, and without some remuneration and community assistance, they will be unable to supervise their disabled children (or frail relatives) because of their own work responsibilities.

Many parents and activists are concerned about the quality of care both in licensed centres and by babysitters in private homes. In some jurisdictions (such as Alberta), neither the employees of child-care centres nor babysitters are required to have special training. These jobs pay the minimum wage or less, and centres have difficulty attracting and retaining trained workers. A number of advocacy groups have formed around child-care concerns. These groups have asked governments to tighten regulations; to improve training, fringe benefits, and pay for child-care workers; and to allocate more public money to child care for employed parents. However, the extent of government involvement in the funding and regulation of child care remains contentious in many jurisdictions.

Some conservative politicians assert that child care is a family matter that should be of no concern to governments or employers. Yet conservative women's lobby groups, such as REAL Women of Canada, have argued for more income-tax relief for single-earner families and for higher social benefits to allow women to make a choice about working for pay or caring for their children at home (Baker and Tippin, 1999). For governments to provide mothers with a real choice, however, the social benefits would need to approximate women's potential earnings. This suggests that taxes would have to rise considerably.

### *Divorce and Repartnering: The Impact on Children*

When divorce rates increased in the 1970s and 1980s, researchers began to devote their attention to the social consequences, especially for children. Many studies concluded that children from one-parent fam-

ilies experience more negative outcomes than do children from two-parent families, including lower educational attainment, behavioural problems, delinquency, leaving home earlier, premarital pregnancy for girls, and higher divorce rates when they marry, among many others. The main research question typically focused on whether negative outcomes result from the parental conflict during marriage, the trauma of separation, the absence of a father, or some other factor. As Figure 9.2 shows, mothers typically retain custody of the children.

Despite negative media attention given to single-parent families, most children from these families do not experience problems, although they have a higher risk of problems than do children from two-parent families. Furthermore, when studies control for changes in family income after marital separation, the incidence of problems declines, although it does not disappear (Elliott and Richards, 1991; Kiernan, 1997). The Canadian National Longitudinal Survey on Children and Youth (NLSCY) found that about 19 per cent of children from low-income families headed by a lone mother experience a conduct disorder, compared to 9 per cent of children from two-parent families. For those from higher-income families, this percentage drops to 13 per cent for lone-mother families and 8 per cent for two-parent families (Lipman, Offord, and Dooley, 1996: 8). Socio-economic conditions, however, are not always held constant.

Many lone-parent families experience economic disadvantage *before* divorce as well as after, as people from lower socio-economic groups tend to have higher rates of bereavement, separation, and divorce (Rodgers and Pryor, 1998). When children are raised in low-income families, they are likely to suffer disadvantages that continue into adulthood. Furthermore, more children live in poverty in English-speaking countries than in Nordic nations, as Table 9.3 indicates. Using British National Child Development Study data, Kathleen Kiernan (1997) found that children from separated families were more likely than those from intact families to experience low earnings, low family income, unemployment, and social housing as adults.

Distinguishing between the impact on children of low socio-economic status and of parental separation is difficult for researchers. Lower status after separation seems to be a mediating factor for some outcomes but not for others. It accounts for a decline in educational attainment but not for rates of delinquency, psychosomatic illnesses, cigarette smoking, or heavy drinking in adulthood (Hope, Power, and Rodgers, 1998). Even

Figure 9.2  **Dependent Children by Party to Whom Custody Was Granted, 1995 and 2002**

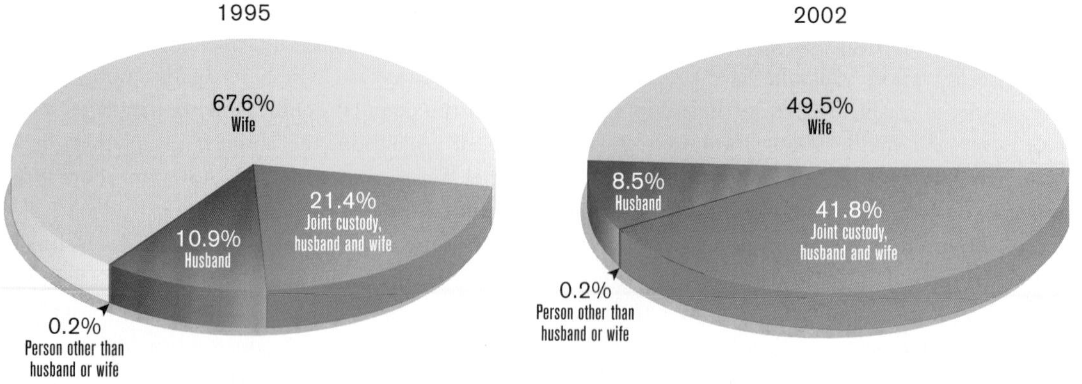

1995

67.6% Wife
21.4% Joint custody, husband and wife
10.9% Husband
0.2% Person other than husband or wife

2002

49.5% Wife
8.5% Husband
41.8% Joint custody, husband and wife
0.2% Person other than husband or wife

Source: Adapted from Vanier Institute of the Family, *Profiling Canada's Families III* (Ottawa: Vanier Institute of the Family, 2004), 38. Reprinted by permission of The Vanier Institute of the Family.

in intact families, being raised in lower socio-economic households is associated with negative behavioural outcomes. These include delayed school readiness, lower educational attainment, a greater number of serious childhood illnesses, childhood accident rates, premature death, high rates of depression, high rates of smoking and alcohol abuse as young adults, and more trouble with school authorities and the law, to name only a few (National Longitudinal Survey of Children and Youth [NLSCY], 1996). For this reason, social researchers and theorists must consider socio-economic status as an important variable in all discussions of the outcomes of children after divorce.

Many studies indicate that children who live with their mothers after divorce are likely to experience diminished contact with their fathers and to suffer

distress from this loss (Cockett and Tripp, 1994; Funder, 1996; Furstenberg, Morgan, and Allison, 1987). As children grow older, the time they spend with the non-resident parent decreases, and some lose contact completely. The amount of access that non-resident fathers have to their children is not the deciding factor in children's adjustment after their parents separate, however, as access is mediated by inter-parental conflict. Frequent contact with their father may negatively impact on children's well-being if there is a high amount of conflict between father and child or between parents over the children (Amato and Rezac, 1994). If conflict is absent or contained, children both want and benefit from frequent contact with both parents (Mitchell, 1985). In general, a close relationship with both parents is associated

Table 9.3  **Child Poverty Rates[1] in Selected OECD Countries, Late-1980s to Early-2000s**

| Country | Late-1980s to Early-1990s | Late-1990s to Early-2000s |
|---|---|---|
| Finland | 2.3 | 2.8 |
| Norway | 5.2 | 3.4 |
| Sweden | 3.0 | 4.2 |
| Belgium | 3.8 | 7.7 |
| Netherlands | 8.1 | 9.8 |
| Canada | 15.3 | 14.9 |
| United Kingdom | 18.5 | 15.4 |
| United States | 24.3 | 21.9 |

[1]Child poverty rate is defined as the percentage of children living in families whose income is less than 50 percent of the median adjusted disposable income for all persons

Source: The United Nations Children's Fund (UNICEF), The State of the World's Children 2005 (New York: UNICEF, 2004), 28.

with a positive adjustment in children after divorce (Rodgers and Pryor, 1998). Furthermore, whether or not the father continues to pay child support may influence both the children's adjustment and the socio-economic status of the lone-parent family.

Adult children of divorced parents are more likely than those from intact marriages to end their own marriages with divorce (Beaujot, 2000). This may result from poor role models in childhood, from the simple observation that there is "life after marriage," or from the fact that divorce becomes more personally acceptable as a solution to an unhappy marriage if it has already happened in one's own family.

No simple or direct relationship between parental separation and children's adjustment is apparent, although many studies do find differences between children from intact and separated families. Parental separation clearly adds stress to children's lives through changes in relationships, living situations, and parental resources. Although most studies find that psychological and behavioural stress are prevalent for children from separated parents, few studies conclude that psychological disturbance is severe or prolonged (Emery, 1994). Instead, most research finds that the first two years after separation require adjustments by both parents and children.

Never-married mothers who become pregnant before their education is completed are particularly vulnerable to low income as well as to disciplinary problems with their children (Dooley, 1995). These mothers often repartner within a few years of the child's birth, but the socio-economic disadvantages of bearing a child at a young age may linger. Their children are most likely to spend their childhood in one or more stepfamilies, which are often conflictual (Marcil-Gratton, 1998). These factors may partially account for higher rates of behavioural problems in the children of never-married mothers.

Research suggests that stepfamilies are difficult to establish and that considerable negotiation is required to maintain them. Children living in stepfamilies are at the same risk of behavioural problems and distress as children growing up in lone-parent families. Neither increased household income nor having two adults in the home ensures good outcomes for these children (Pryor and Rodgers, 2001). One explanation is that parental conflict and separation have a lasting effect on children. Another is that step-parents do not relate to their stepchildren with the same warmth and concern as they do to their biological children because they do not share their genes and have not spent their formative years together.

Although researchers usually study separation and divorce as negative life events, parents often experience relief and contentment after the initial adjustment of leaving an unhappy marriage. This is reflected in their general outlook and in their interactions with their children. Consequently, most researchers agree that children living in stable lone-parent families are better off than children living in conflict-ridden two-parent families (Booth and Edwards, 1990). Furthermore, children of employed lone mothers tend to accept more egalitarian gender roles, as they see their mothers supporting the family and managing tasks that were previously defined as "men's jobs" (Baker, 2001a). This suggests that separation and divorce could have positive as well as negative outcomes for both parents and children.

## Wife Abuse

Beginning in the 1980s, when domestic violence appeared to be on the increase, sociologists became more interested in studying this phenomenon. Feminist sociologists argue that the very term *family violence* implies that this behaviour is randomly distributed within families, whereas men actually are the perpetrators in the vast majority of cases that come to the attention of police and social workers (Dobash et al., 1992).

The Canadian Urban Victimization Study found that in cases of "spousal violence," physical abuse is not an isolated event. Some abused women are assaulted on numerous occasions by their male partners and have sought help many times from friends, neighbours, social workers, and the police. Furthermore, separated women are more likely to be assaulted than divorced or married women (Johnson, 1990). Women are more vulnerable if they see their partner as the head of the household and if they are financially dependent on him. The larger society also condones such behaviour: violence is used as a form of entertainment in films and sports events. This tends to normalize violence as a means of resolving conflict.

Longitudinal US survey research by Murray Strauss and Richard Gelles (1990) concluded that marital violence actually decreased in the United States throughout the 1980s even though the reporting of this behaviour increased. They contend that reporting was influenced by the women's movement, by police campaigns to prosecute perpetrators, and by the availability of more options for women wishing to leave violent marriages. Yet they also make the controversial claim that women are as likely as men to abuse their partners, although they acknowledge that this behaviour is less likely to be reported to the authorities, is less consequential in terms of physical harm, and is often is a form of self-defence. Walter DeKeseredy (2001) criticizes the conflict tactics scale used by Strauss and Gelles, which counts incidences of violence but fails to examine their social context. He agreed that women's "violence" against men is often in self-defence.

Wife abuse may represent men's rising concern that they are losing authority in their families, especially those men who are experiencing unemployment or other personal problems. This kind of violence is also aggravated by alcohol and substance abuse but represents much more than an interpersonal problem. The fact that most victims of reported violence are women and that separated women are often the targets indicates important social patterns in this behaviour relating to gender and power.

In the past, the police failed to respond in a serious way to calls about violent wife abuse because they thought women did not want charges laid or would later withdraw them (Johnson, 1990). Policies have now been implemented in most jurisdictions for police to charge men who batter. Yet many wives remain with abusive partners because of shortages of low-income and temporary housing, an inability to support themselves and their children, and a lack of knowledge about where to turn for assistance. Abuse is also permitted to continue because some women feel that they deserve it, especially those abused as children and those who suffer from low self-esteem.

In addition, many women fear reprisal from spouses or former spouses who have threatened to kill them if they go to the police or tell anyone about an incident. The enormous publicity recently given to women killed by their partners indicates that, in many cases, fear of reprisal is entirely justified.

Women's groups, social service agencies, police, and researchers have developed new ways of dealing with violence against women in intimate relationships. Many of the programs are crisis-oriented and focused on women, helping them develop a protection plan that could involve laying charges against a spouse or ex-spouse, finding transitional housing, engaging a lawyer, and, if necessary, acquiring social assistance to cover living costs. Through either individual counselling or group therapy, battered wives are also helped to restructure their thinking about violence and to view it as unacceptable, regardless of their own behaviour.

The male abuser is now more often charged with an offence. He is also given opportunities for counselling, including accepting responsibility for his acts of violence rather than blaming his partner, learning to control his emotions, developing better communication skills, and learning non-violent behaviour from male role models. Action against family violence has also included sensitization workshops for professionals, such as teachers and judges, to increase their knowledge of program options and of the implication of this form of violence for women, their families, men who batter, and the wider society (DeKeseredy,

### 9.3    Sociology in Action
#### The Emotional Scars of Family Violence

"I was raped by my uncle when I was 12 and my husband has beat me for years. For my whole life, when I have gone to the doctor, to my priest, or to a friend to have my wounds patched up, or for a shoulder to cry one, they dwell on my bruises . . . that's for sure. . . . I don't look like anything like I did 15 years ago, but it's not my body that I really wish could get fixed. The abuse in my life has taken away my trust in people and in life. It's taken away the laughter in my life. I still laugh, but not without bitterness behind my laughter. It's taken away my faith in God, my faith in goodness winning out in the end, and maybe worse of all, it's taken away my trust in myself. I don't trust myself to be able to take care of the kids, to take care of myself, to do anything to make a difference in my own life or anyone else's. That's the hurt I would like to fix. I can live with my physical scars. It's these emotional scars that drive me near suicide sometimes."

SOURCE: Walter S. DeKeseredy and Linda MacLeod, *Woman Abuse: A Sociological Study* © 1997. Reprinted with permission of Nelson, a division of Thomson Learning: www.thomsonrights.com. Fax 800-730-2215.

2001). In addition, support services have been provided for families in high-risk circumstances.

Money is a major impediment to establishing new programs and transitional housing, even though governments at all levels have voiced their concern about violence against women and children. Transition houses are usually funded by private donations, staffed by volunteers, and operated with uncertain resources. Follow-up therapy and counselling may also be necessary for the entire family, but these services cost money to establish and maintain. Despite the serious nature of marital violence, new program funding for the rising number of reported victims and their abusers is difficult to find.

A correlation has been noted between "courtship" violence and marital violence. K. O'Leary and colleagues (1989) found that the probability of spouse abuse in the United States was over three times greater if violence had also occurred during courtship. They also found that adults who abuse their spouses or children have often come from families where their parents engaged in similar behaviour.

Three broad explanations of marital violence arise from these studies. The intergenerational theory suggests that solving conflicts through physical or verbal violence is learned from early family experiences. The solution within this perspective focuses on improving conflict resolution and parenting skills in order to reduce marital violence. A second theory sees marital violence as a misguided way of resolving conflicts that is used by husbands who feel that their authority within the family is being threatened. The solution to the problem within this systems framework is to offer therapy sessions to men or couples to improve their communication skills, learn to control emotions, and become more assertive about their feelings and needs without resorting to violence.

In contrast, feminist theories argue that "marital violence" is actually "male violence" perpetrated by some men against their female partners. This behaviour is symptomatic of women's lack of interpersonal power in families, the way in which the patriarchal state has permitted husbands to control their wives, and the social acceptability of violence towards those considered most vulnerable (Baker, 2001a). Changing public attitudes towards physical and sexual abuse means that more people now report such activity and that social services are needed to assist them. Consequently, this kind of behaviour, which always existed, now appears more prevalent.

These theories are not entirely incompatible: not everyone becomes abusive who has witnessed abuse

or who feels threatened by lack of power in their workplace or at home. Furthermore, everyone lives in a society that condones certain kinds of violence and a lower status for women. None of the theories alone can explain the perpetuation of violence in intimate relationships. Yet it is clear that violence against women and children cuts across national, cultural, and class boundaries and is not confined to marriage or cohabitation. In fact, women who are separated appear to be more vulnerable than married women (Johnson, 1990).

## Overview of Canadian Family Policies

Late in the nineteenth century and early in the twentieth century, Canadian governments (both federal and provincial) developed ways to count their citizens and to register marriages, births, adoptions, divorces, and deaths. They also established child welfare legislation, offered married women more political rights and control over their property, equalized the guardianship rights of mothers and fathers over their children, and established basic social services. As Table 9.4 indicates, income security programs for families were developed mainly from the 1940s to the 1970s, and governments tightened abuse and neglect laws as well as the enforcement of child support during the 1980s and 1990s (Baker, 2001a; Ursel, 1992).

There will always be a need for governments to regulate certain aspects of family life, especially to protect vulnerable family members and to assist those in serious financial difficulty. Families also require health and social services to ensure healthy and safe pregnancy, childbirth, and childhood, and these services need government regulation and financial support. Regulation of life events by the state is designed to prevent incestuous and bigamous marriages, adoptions by "inappropriate" parents, and hasty divorces and to ensure that spouses and parents understand and fulfill their basic support obligations. Governments also gather basic statistics about populations in order to plan future social services and facilities. They need to be able to predict the size and structure of the future labour force and the numbers of future voters, taxpayers, and consumers. Some of these statistics also prove useful for the business sector in their marketing and growth plans.

Throughout Canadian history, the extent of government involvement in the "private" realm of the family has been debated, although these debates have usually focused on the provision of income support.

Table 9.4  **The Establishment of Social Benefits in Canada**

| | |
|---|---|
| Family Allowance | • A universal allowance created in 1945 and paid to mothers for each child<br>• Replaced by the targeted Child Tax Benefit in 1993 |
| Old Age Pension | • Established in 1926 as a pension for those with low incomes<br>• Converted to a universal pension in 1951 |
| Mothers/Widows Pensions | • Developed around 1920, but date varies by province |
| Unemployment Insurance | • Established as a federal social insurance program in 1941<br>• Maternity benefits added in 1971<br>• Now called Employment Insurance |
| Hospital/Medical Insurance | • Hospital insurance established nationally in 1958<br>• Medical insurance established in 1966 (commonly called "medicare") |
| Canada Pension Plan | • Established in 1966, and financed by contributions from employees, employers, and government<br>• Also pays survivors benefits and disability benefits to contributors |
| Spouses Allowance | • Established in 1975 as an income-tested pension for spouses aged 60–4 of old age pensioners, mainly women |
| Child Tax Benefit | • The former Family Allowance and tax deductions and credits for children were rolled into this targeted tax benefit for lower- and middle-income families in 1993<br>• Replaced by the Canada Child Tax Benefit in 1998 |
| Parliamentary resolution to end "child poverty" | • All-party agreement in 1989 |
| Canada Child Tax Benefit | • The Child Tax Benefit and the Working Income Supplement were rolled together to form this benefit in 1998 |

Recently, federal and provincial governments have trimmed the costs of social services and focused more on "personal and family responsibility" rather than on social support or the payment of social benefits. At the same time, they have tightened laws on spousal and child abuse, but these laws have been difficult to enforce because this behaviour often occurs within the privacy of people's homes and without witnesses. The careful monitoring of at-risk families suggests that the state regulates family life as a form of **social control** as well as merely for information-gathering or future planning.

## Conclusion

Family life has changed substantially over the past few decades, but intimate relationships remain central to most people's lives. At the same time, cultural variations are becoming more prevalent with new immigration sources. More people are creating their own intimate arrangements, but governments continue to clarify the rights and responsibilities of family members in these new arrangements. Cohabitation and

divorce are now more prevalent that a generation ago, while legal marriage and fertility are declining. Nevertheless, popular support for intimate relationships remains strong.

Social scientists have used different theoretical frameworks to study the similarities and variations in family life, each emphasizing different aspects and issues. The five theoretical frameworks presented in this chapter suggest that theorists differ in their focus within family studies. Five of the many conflictual issues in family life discussed include: (1) the sharing of domestic work; despite dramatic increases in women's paid work, wives still do the lion's share of housework and child care; (2) the apparent rise in infertility and feminist and sociological concerns about medically assisted conception; (3) the cost and quality of care of the children of employed parents, making it difficult, especially for mothers, to combine paid work and child rearing; (4) the contradictory evidence of the impact of separation, divorce, and repartnering on children, suggesting that remarriage is not always the best solution for children; and (5) wife abuse and why it continues.

## □ Questions for Critical Thought

1. In your opinion, does the way "family" is defined make a difference? Why or why not?
2. Would you expect societies that practise arranged marriages to have more stable and happier marriages than societies that allow free-choice marriage? Why or why not?
3. How would you explain the perpetuation of family violence, with reference to (a) feminist perspectives, (b) structural functionalism, and (c) political economy theory?
4. Why are more young people living together without legal marriage? Does this behaviour indicate a rejection of "family"?
5. Is parental divorce detrimental to children?
6. Should fertility clinic services be covered by government health care? Why or why not?
7. Should governments contribute more to child-care services for employed parents?
8. Is there any reason to believe that Canadian birth rates will rise again in the near future?

## □ Recommended Readings

Walter DeKeseredy, "Patterns of Family Violence," in *Families: Changing Trends in Canada*, 4th edn, edited by Maureen Baker (Toronto: McGraw-Hill Ryerson, 2001), 238–66.
   This chapter discusses recent research and theorizing about various forms of family violence, including wife abuse, child abuse, sibling violence, and elder abuse.

Margrit Eichler, *Family Shifts: Families, Policies, and Gender Equality* (Toronto: Oxford University Press, 1997).
   Eichler examines major new shifts affecting families today, including gender equality as a legal and moral principle and the potential impact of biotechnology.

Lynn Jamieson, *Intimacy: Personal Relationships in Modern Societies* (Cambridge, Mass.: Polity, 1998).
   The author discusses whether a new type of intimacy is being sought in Western societies or if relationships still are shaped fundamentally by power and economic considerations.

Susan A. McDaniel and Lorne Tepperman, *Close Relations: An Introduction to the Sociology of Families* (Scarborough, Ont.: Prentice-Hall Allyn and Bacon, 2000).
   This Canadian text provides an overview of research on and theories of family life.

Vanier Institute of the Family, *Profiling Canada's Families II* (Ottawa: Vanier Institute of the Family, 2000).
   This book contains numerous tables and charts about family trends, as well as discussion about the research's relevance.

## □ Recommended Web Sites

**Centre for Families, Work and Well-Being**
**www.worklifecanada.ca**
   The Web site of the Centre for Families, Work and Well-Being at the University of Guelph contains information about research projects.

**Childcare Resource and Research Unit**
**www.childcarecanada.org**
   The Web site of the Childcare Resource and Research Unit at the University of Toronto includes Canadian and cross-national research and other material on child-care issues.

**Statistics Canada**
**www.statcan.ca**
   Statistics Canada provides a wide range of family-related census documents and statistics.

**Vanier Institute of the Family**
**www.vifamily.ca**
   The Vanier Institute of the Family provides educational material, news items, and research on Canadian families.

# 10

Juanne Clarke

> > >

# Health Issues

© Digital Vision

## ☐ Learning Objectives

In this chapter, you will:

- see how health, illness, and disease are distinct in the sociology of health, illness, and medicine

- learn that health, illness, disease, and death are integrally related to the social world through a number of intermeshing levels

- examine medicare as a system that embodies five principles: portability, universality, comprehensive coverage, public administration, and accessibility

- see how privatization is increasing in the Canadian medical system

- learn that medicalization is a powerful cultural force

# Introduction

Health is inextricably linked to the social order. Its very definition, its multitudinous causes, and its consequences all are social. What is considered healthy in one culture may not necessarily be considered to be healthy in another. What was thought of as good health at one time is not the same as what is considered to be good health at another. Rates of sickness and death vary across time and place. Social classes differ in their definitions of good health. What a woman considers health may be different from a man's definition of health. Moreover, **class** and **gender** seem to operate in ways that lead to different levels of health and sickness and different rates of death.

It is unlikely that you have heard of or suffered from lake-fever or intermittents. I also doubt that you have used quinine, pepper, or whisky as a treatment when you were ill, although many of you may have your own family healing traditions, such as chicken soup, mustard plaster, or brandy for a cold. Yet the diseases and the treatments of the nineteenth century were as fervently believed in as we believe in treating cancer with chemotherapy, radiation, and surgery today.

The experiences of new immigrants from various parts of the world to all of the provinces in Canada provide interesting insights into some of the culturally distinct threads of the Canadian "mosaic" of health's meanings. The interpretation of "health" varies not only historically and culturally, but also between men and women, people of differing educational and social class backgrounds and religious traditions, and so on. Think a little about how your male and female friends, your brothers and sisters, and your parents differ with respect to how they think about and act with regard to what they consider sickness. Think, too, about how illness and medicine are portrayed on television programs such as *ER*.

The sociology of health issues is not only about health, **illness**, and **disease**, but also about medical or health systems of diagnosis, prognostication, and treatment. Conventional medicine—sometimes called **allopathic medicine** because it treats by means of opposites, such as cutting out or killing germs, bacteria, or other disease processes through chemotherapy, surgery, or radiation—is taken for granted in much of the Western world. In fact, much of the history of the sociology of health and medicine assumes the primacy of the work of the allopathic system and its practitioners. However, naturopathic (treatment through "natural" remedies and procedures, such as herbs or massage), chiropractic (treatment through spinal adjustment), and homeopathic medicine (treatment with similars), all examples of CAM, or *complementary and alternative medicines*, are of increasing importance in the Western world. The second part of this chapter will investigate some of the most important trends and social policy issues in the area of medical sociology, including **medicalization**, the future of the health-care system, and **privatization**.

# Theoretical Perspectives

Four theoretical **paradigms** considered to be the most significant ways of approaching and understanding health and medicine sociologically are: structural functionalism, conflict theory, symbolic interactionism, and feminism.

## *Structural Functionalism*

From the **structural functionalist** perspective, health is the normal and normative position or behaviour in the social system. In a stable society, all institutional forces work together to create and maintain good health for the population. Your university or college assumes your good health as it organizes its courses and exams—you probably have to get a letter from a doctor for exemption from writing a test or an exam. The smooth functioning of societies depends on the good health of its members. Societies are organized to support a population up to an average **life expectancy** and at a given level of health and ability. This normative standard of health and normative age at death are reinforced by political, economic, cultural, and educational policy.

It has been suggested, for example, that the reason that governments continue to allow cigarette smoking is because to do so reaps economic benefits, through the high levels of taxation, for the **state**. Not only does the availability of cigarettes with their high taxation rate contribute to the income of the state, but the relatively fast death from lung cancer as compared to other cancers, for instance, saves the government in health-care costs. Although this may be too cynical an analysis, it makes clear interesting and thought-provoking social structural ways of thinking about the potential relationships between the health and life expectancy of a population and the institutional and political forces of the population.

Assertions about the interrelationships among institutions all fit within the structural functionalist theoretical perspective. A classic statement of this perspective is found in the work of Talcott Parsons (1951), in particular in his concept of the **sick role**. The sick role is to be thought of as a special position in society. It exists to prevent **sickness** from disrupting the "ongoingness" of social life. The sick role also provides a way of institutionalizing what might otherwise become a form of deviant behaviour. It does this by articulating certain rights for those who claim sickness in a society so long as they fulfill certain duties.

In Parsons's thinking, there are two rights and two duties for those who wanted to claim sickness and engage in the sick role. The *rights* include the right to be exempted from normal social **roles** and the right to be free of blame or responsibility for the sickness. The *duties* are to want to get well and to seek and co-operate with technically competent help. However, that these theoretically derived ideas do not always have empirical support is evident in a number of ways. For example, it is well known that the right to be exempt from the performance of social roles depends in part on the nature of the sickness. A hangover, for instance, may not be considered a good enough reason to claim the sick role as an excuse for an exam exemption. There is also a great deal of evidence that people with AIDS were seen as culpable, especially in the early days of the disease in North America—in fact, it was called the "gay plague" by some (Altman, 1986). And not everyone is expected to want to get well. Indeed, those with a chronic disease such as multiple sclerosis are expected to accept their condition and to learn to live with it. Parsons assumed the dominance of allopathic medicine in his statement that a sick person was to get technically competent help. Today, however, many people believe that the best help may not always come from allopathic medicine even though it is the state-supported type of medical care. Indeed, a substantial minority—approximately 40 per cent—of North Americans now rely on complementary and alternative medicines, or CAMs (Statistics Canada, 2001a: 17; Eisenberg et al., 1998).

## Conflict Theory

From the perspective of **conflict theory**, health and ill health result from inequitable and oppressive economic conditions. The primary focus of analysis is the distribution of health and illness across the **social structure**. Questions driving this perspective include, Are the poor more likely to get sick? Is the **mortality rate** (the frequency of death per a specified number of people over a specified period of time) among the poor higher than among the rich? Are women more likely than men to get sick? Do men die at younger ages? Does racism affect the **morbidity** (sickness) **rate** (the frequency of sickness per a specified number of people over a specified period of time)? Health is seen as a good that is inequitably located in society.

A classic statement of this position is found in the work of Friedrich Engels, who co-authored works with Karl Marx. In his book *The Condition of the Working Class in England* ([1845] 1994), Engels demonstrates the negative health consequences of early **capitalism**. He describes how the development of capitalism advanced mechanism in agriculture and forced farm workers off the land and into the cities to survive. Capitalists in the cities sought profit regardless of the costs to the well-being of the workers. Owners maintained low costs for labour through poor wages and long hours of back-breaking work in filthy and noisy working conditions. Even children worked in these unhealthy circumstances.

As a consequence, poor labourers and their families lived exceedingly rough lives in shelters that offered little or no privacy, cleanliness, or quiet. They had very little money for food, and the quality of the foodstuffs available in the cities was poor. The slum-like living conditions were perfect breeding grounds for all sorts of diseases, and because of the high density of living quarters, the lack of facilities for toileting and washing, and the frequent lack of clean drinking water, the morbidity and mortality rates in the slums were very high. Infectious diseases such as tuberculosis (TB), typhoid, scrofula, and influenza spread quickly and with dire results through these close-quartered and malnourished populations.

Epidemics were almost common in nineteenth-century industrial cities, where overcrowding, overflowing cesspits, piles of garbage all around, and unsafe water were the norm. Only when there were new discoveries in bacteriology did it become clear that many of the worst diseases were spread by bacteria and viruses in the water, air, and food; then governments started to enact public health measures. These new prevention policies included sewage disposal, garbage removal, clean filtered drinking water, and hygienic handling of food. The death rates began to abate (Crompton, 2000). Table 10.1 shows how, even in the 1920s in Canada, infectious diseases such as influenza, bronchitis, and pneumonia, TB, various stomach and digestive ailments such as gastritis, and communicable diseases were important causes of death.

Conflict theory also has been given a feminist emphasis, as in the work of Hilary Graham. In *Women, Health and the Family* (1984), Graham documents how inequality affects the various types of home health-care work done by women in order to protect the good health of their families. In particular, she articulates four different components of women's home health-care work: (1) maintaining a clean, comfortable home with an adequate, safe, and balanced diet as well as supportive social and emotional intra-familial relations; (2) nursing family members when they feel ill or are debilitated; (3) teaching family members about health and hygiene, including such things as sleeping, bathing, cleaning, and toileting; and (4) liaising with outsiders regarding the health-care needs of family members, such as taking children or a partner to the doctor, clinic, hospital, or dentist.

As Graham notes, the ability of women to fulfill these four roles varies significantly depending on the educational, socio-economic, health, spiritual, emotional, and financial resources that women have or to which they are able to gain access. Moreover these resources are inequitably distributed over the socio-economic hierarchy.

## Symbolic Interactionism

Interpretation and meaning are the hallmarks of sociology within the **symbolic interactionist** perspective. What is the meaning, for example, of anorexia and bulimia? Are they medical conditions? Are they the result of a moral choice? Or could they be thought to be "socio-somatic" conditions, that is, caused by society (Currie, 1988)? Various authors have attributed them to women's "hunger strike" against their contradictory positions, against culturally prescribed images, and against lack of opportunities in contemporary society. They have been conceptualized as a means "through which women, both unconsciously and consciously, protest the social conditions of womanhood" (Currie, 1988: 208). There is often a stigma attached to the person with HIV/AIDS, cancer, depression, inflammatory bowel disease, diabetes, or asthma. Some people think these ailments connote morality or immorality in the sufferers. Good health is even associated with being a good person.

Table 10.1  **Leading Causes of Death, Canada, Twentieth Century**

|  | Cause of Death[a] | Rate per 100,000 |
|---|---|---|
| 1921–5 | All causes | 1,030.0 |
|  | Cardiovascular and renal disease | 221.9 |
|  | Influenza, bronchitis, and pneumonia | 141.1 |
|  | Diseases of early infancy | 111.0 |
|  | Tuberculosis | 85.1 |
|  | Cancer | 75.9 |
|  | Gastritis, duodenitis, enteritis, and colitis | 72.2 |
|  | Accidents | 51.5 |
|  | Communicable diseases | 47.1 |
| 1996–7[b] | All causes | 654.4 |
|  | Cardiovascular diseases (heart disease and stroke) | 240.2 |
|  | Cancer | 184.8 |
|  | Chronic obstructive pulmonary diseases | 28.4 |
|  | Unintentional injuries | 27.7 |
|  | Pneumonia and influenza | 22.1 |
|  | Diabetes mellitus | 16.7 |
|  | Hereditary and degenerative diseases of the central nervous system | 14.7 |
|  | Diseases of the arteries, arterioles, and capillaries | 14.3 |

[a] Disease categories are not identical over time.
[b] Rates are age-standardized.
SOURCE: Adapted from the Statistics Canada publication, *Canadian Social Trends*, Catalogue 11-008, Winter 2000, p.13.

One contemporary study that uses the symbolic interaction perspective is Michael Hardey's investigation of illness stories posted on the Internet (2002). In his investigation, Hardey argues that illness home page accounts demonstrate the processes whereby, in a global economy, ill people have transformed themselves from mere passive recipients of diagnosis and medical treatments at the behest of the powerful doctors into consumers and producers of health information and care. Home pages offer explanations for illness, advice, solutions, and products and services to those who read them. They provide space for people to portray themselves as experts with regard to particular diseases. These pages can be read for the meanings that people associate with illness and other topics related to a symbolic interactionist perspective.

### Feminism

**Feminist** health sociology recognizes the centrality of gender to social life as well as to inequity in the worlds of and in relations between men and women. Feminist health sociology investigates whether, how, and why men and women have different health and illness profiles, as well as different causes and average ages of death. Feminist health sociology also includes consideration of such things as **ethnicity**, sexual preference, and ability/disability as fundamental characteristics of social actors and social life. These axes of inequality are therefore central issues to be included in designing research, uncovering social injustice, and planning and making social change.

Women's health has been a central issue and in many ways a major impetus for the recent women's movement. The health-related book *Our Bodies, Our Selves*, when first published in 1971 by the Boston Women's Health Collective, became a major rallying document for women. Translated into many languages, and more recently revised and updated, the book offers a radical critique of medical practice and medicalization as well as women's views of their own health, sickness, and bodies.

Another work within the feminist paradigm is Anne Kasper and Susan Ferguson's *Breast Cancer: Society Shapes an Epidemic* (2000), which suggests that among the reasons for the growing incidence (number of new cases in a year) and prevalence (number of cases within a given population) of the disease is that it is primarily a women's disease and is therefore not given the serious and systematic research attention that it would have received had it been primarily a male disease. Contributions to this book by scholars and practitioners from a wide variety of fields, including sociology, zoology, social and health policy, anthropology, law, and biology, examine the social and political contexts of breast cancer as a social problem, arguing that gender, politics, social class, race, and ethnicity have affected the type of research that is done, the types of treatments that have become dominant, the rates of growth in the morbidity and mortality of breast cancer, and even the ways in which the disease is experienced by women. Indeed, they suggest that one of the reasons for the continuance of the epidemic is not only that it is primarily a women's disease, but also that it is located in their breasts.

Kasper and Ferguson's collection provides a thought-provoking look at one of the major causes of worry, sickness, and death among women in Canada and the United States. Despite the fact that both heart disease and lung cancer are more frequent causes of death for Canadian women, women in Canada fear breast cancer more and even think of their breasts as essentially flawed and vulnerable to disease (Robertson, 2001). This is undoubtedly related to the enormous mass media attention the disease has received in the last 15 years or so. During this time, first in the United States and then in Canada, powerful lobby groups of women activists founded highly successful breast cancer advocacy coalitions, lobbied governments and corporations, and received substantial increases in the funding levels for research into the disease and its treatment. There is, of course, a painful irony in the fact that the increased attention and financial investment have been coupled with a proliferation of stories in the mass media that have served to increase anxiety and fear of risk of disease among Canadian women.

# The Sociology of Health, Illness, Disease, and Sickness

At the broadest level, sociologists compare within and between societies around the world and over time with respect to the rates of, causes of, and treatments for health and sickness and to rates and causes of death. Here, factors such as wars, famine, drought, epidemics, natural disasters, air and water quality, quantity and quality of foodstuffs, transportation safety, level and type of economic development, technology, available birth control, immunization, antibiotics, medicalization, culture, and political economy all are considered relevant.

At the next level, sociologists examine morbidity and mortality within societies and cultures and compare people of different social class backgrounds, educational levels, genders, religiosity, rural/urban locations, occupations, ethnicities, family statuses, and so on. A further level of investigation concerns the way socio-psychological factors, such as level of stress and sense of coherence, are implicated in illness, disease, and sickness.

The next level is an examination of the relationships between various "lifestyle" behaviours, such as smoking, seat-belt use, alcohol consumption, diet, risk-taking behaviours, sexual activity and protection, and drug use. Finally, the existential considerations, including the meaning and the experience of morbidity and mortality to individuals, are studied. Figure 10.1 shows these links, beginning from the person.

This separation of investigation into levels is artificial and done only for reasons of analytical clarity. In fact, each of the levels influences all the other levels.

### Comparative Analyses

### The Changing Health of Canadians

People generally live longer and healthier lives today than they did in the past. The increase in health and the decrease in mortality rates over the past 150 years has been substantial. In the nineteenth century, infectious and communicable diseases such as cholera, typhoid, diphtheria, and scarlet fever were responsible for enormous levels of suffering and death for early Canadians. Wound infections and septicemia were frequent results of dangerous and unhygienic working, living, and medical conditions. Puerperal fever killed many women during and after childbirth. The health experiences of early Canadians have been well described in some general non-fiction (see, for example, Bliss, 1991, 1992) and in personal memoirs, such as Susannah Moodie's *Roughing It in the Bush* ([1852] 1995), on settler life in the 1800s. Even fiction can help us understand how people have experienced health. Margaret Atwood's *The Edible Woman* ([1968] 1994), for example, foreshadows the contemporary issue of eating-disorder attitudes and behaviours.

In 1831, the average life expectancy for Canadian men and women was 39.0 years—38.3 for women, and 39.8 for men (Clarke, 2000: 50). Today, life expectancies are about double this for Canadian men and women. Today's women can expect to live to 81, men to 75 (Crompton, 2000: 12). What has happened to cause this dramatic shift? You might think first of medical interventions and vaccinations. However, the

most important causes of the increase in life expectancy are related to public health measures that were able to forestall the spread of disease. These included improved nutrition, better hygiene through sanitation and water purification practices, and advances in birth control. Interventions such as these brought the average life expectancy to 59 in the 1920s and, largely because of dramatic declines in infant mortality, to 78 in 1990–2 (Crompton, 2000: 12).

In the 1920s, the most common causes of death became heart and kidney disease, followed by influenza, bronchitis, and pneumonia, and the diseases of early infancy. Widespread use of newly discovered vaccines and antibiotics (vaccines against diphtheria,

### Figure 10.1    **Components of Health**

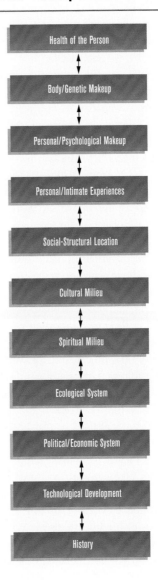

Health of the Person

Body/Genetic Makeup

Personal/Psychological Makeup

Personal/Intimate Experiences

Social-Structural Location

Cultural Milieu

Spiritual Milieu

Ecological System

Political/Economic System

Technological Development

History

tetanus, typhoid, and cholera were developed in the late nineteenth and early twentieth centuries, and antibiotics were introduced in the 1940s) made a significant difference in the twentieth century (Crompton, 2000). While heart disease remains the most common cause of death, it has declined dramatically over time, probably as a result of lifestyle changes such as declines in smoking and dietary fat, improvements in exercise, and better medical treatments. Lower infant death rates today have resulted primarily from better nutrition and improved hygiene in pregnancy, secondarily from medical and technological advances. For example, prematurity, a frequent cause of infant death in the past, is now both more often prevented through educational programs and prenatal care and well managed in hospital.

The incidence of such diseases as measles, scarlet fever, and whooping cough was cut almost to zero until some people abandoned the vaccines in the 1990s. For a short time, the incidence of these diseases increased, but by the late 1990s they had declined again when public health authorities became alerted to the issue and became more diligent about universal vaccinations in Canada.

One other important feature of the declines in mortality or gains in life expectancy is the gap between men and women and how this gap has changed over time (see Table 10.2). From 1920 to 1922, women lived an average of two years longer than men; from 1990 to 1992, they lived an average of six years longer than men. Part of the explanation for women's greater benefit from the changes of the twentieth century relates to the decline in maternal mortality over this period. Another part of the explanation is the greater tendency for men to engage in risk-taking behaviours such as cigarette smoking and drunk driving.

Today, among the most important causes of death are, for men, cardiovascular disease, followed by diseases of the heart and then cancer, and, for women, cardiovascular disease, followed by cancer and then diseases of the heart. The rates per 100,000 for men are 316.9, 238.7, and 234.7, and for women, 193.8, 150.3, and 134.8, respectively (Statistics Canada, 2001a).

These rates do not take age into account. *Potential years of life lost*, or **PYLL**, is a statistical representation of death that does take age into account: the younger the average age of death for a given disease, the greater the number of years of life lost. PYLL allows us to see the years of life lost by disease type, taking 70 years as the cut-off age point. Here the rank order of the top four causes of death changes: all cancers were responsible for 302,585 deaths, accidents for 228,106,

diseases of the heart for 145,394, and suicide for 108,488 (Statistics Canada, 1996a: 116).

These two sorts of information have different implications for such things as government health promotion planning. For example, the PYLL figures tell us that younger people are more likely to die of accidents and suicide and that the numbers of deaths in these categories are large. One can then consider what sorts of things might be done to prevent particular categories of accidents and suicides as compared to the chief causes of death—those sometimes called "diseases of civilization"—cancer and cardiovascular and heart diseases.

### Intra-societal Analyses

#### Social Inequality and Health

The degree of inequality has been increasing in Canada, especially recently, in the last decade of the twentieth century and into the twenty-first century. As an illustration, consider the following statistics. In 1996, the top 20 per cent of the Canadian population earned 43.2 per cent of the total income, while the bottom 20 per cent earned 2.3 per cent (Ross and Roberts, 1999: 26). Over the decade of the 1990s this disparity grew substantially (Yalnizyan, 1998).

Poverty exacerbates health problems from birth onward. In 1996, the poverty rate in Canada was 18 per cent, the child poverty rate 21 per cent (Raphael, 2001: 226). Poor women are more likely to bear low-birth-weight babies. Low birth weight is associated with myriad negative health, disability, learning, and behavioural effects. Children born in the poorest neighbourhoods in Canada (the lowest 20 per cent) live shorter lives, by 2 to 5.5 years. They also tend to spend more of these shorter lives with some degree of disability. Individuals living within the poorest neighbourhoods are also more likely than the well-off to die of almost every disease (Wilkins, Adams, and Brancker, 1989). *The Health of Canada's Children* (Canadian Institute of Child Health, 1994) noted that children at the lower end of the social hierarchy have a greater variety of both health and development deficits than those higher up on the socio-economic status ladder. Note that these results, like the Whitehall study results, are situated in the context of a nationally funded medical care system.

Although substantial links between income inequality and both ill health and death have been demonstrated, Canadian health policy continues to involve substantial investments in the health-care system rather than community-level interventions such as

Table 10.2  **Life Expectancy at Birth (Years), over Time, by Province, and by Gender**

|  | Both Sexes | Males | Females | Difference |
|---|---|---|---|---|
| **Canada** | | | | |
| 1920–2 | 59 | 59 | 61 | 2 |
| 1930–2 | 61 | 60 | 62 | 2 |
| 1940–2 | 65 | 63 | 66 | 3 |
| 1950–2 | 69 | 66 | 71 | 5 |
| 1960–2 | 71 | 68 | 74 | 6 |
| 1970–2 | 73 | 69 | 76 | 7 |
| 1980–2 | 75 | 72 | 79 | 7 |
| 1990–2 | 78 | 75 | 81 | 6 |
| 2000–2 | 80 | 77 | 82 | 5 |
| **1990–2** | | | | |
| Newfoundland and Labrador | 77 | 74 | 80 | 6 |
| Prince Edward Island | 77 | 73 | 81 | 8 |
| Nova Scotia | 77 | 74 | 80 | 6 |
| New Brunswick | 78 | 74 | 81 | 7 |
| Quebec | 77 | 74 | 81 | 7 |
| Ontario | 78 | 75 | 81 | 6 |
| Manitoba | 78 | 75 | 81 | 6 |
| Saskatchewan | 78 | 75 | 82 | 7 |
| Alberta | 78 | 75 | 81 | 6 |
| British Columbia | 78 | 75 | 81 | 6 |
| **2000–2** | | | | |
| Newfoundland and Labrador | 78 | 76 | 82 | 4 |
| Prince Edward Island | 79 | 76 | 81 | 5 |
| Nova Scotia | 79 | 76 | 82 | 6 |
| New Brunswick | 79 | 77 | 82 | 5 |
| Quebec | 79 | 77 | 82 | 5 |
| Ontario | 80 | 78 | 82 | 4 |
| Manitoba | 79 | 76 | 81 | 5 |
| Saskatchewan | 79 | 76 | 82 | 6 |
| Alberta | 80 | 77 | 82 | 5 |
| British Columbia | 81 | 78 | 83 | 5 |
| Yukon[1] | 77 | 74 | 80 | 6 |
| Northwest Territories[1] | 76 | 73 | 80 | 7 |
| Nunavut[1] | 69 | 67 | 70 | 3 |

[1]Data should be interpreted with caution due to small underlying counts of births and deaths.

Source: Adapted from Statistics Canada, "Life Expectancy at Birth," available online at <http://www.statcan.ca/english/Pgdb/health26.htm>, accessed 30 December 2004; Statistics Canada, *The Daily* (27 September 2004), available online at <http://www.statcan.ca/Daily/English/040927/d040927a.htm>, accessed 30 December 2004.

a guaranteed annual wage, job creation, a national day-care program, or proactive prenatal care for low-income mothers. This preferential funding persists despite the fact that repeated studies have documented that interventions at these levels would have more widespread effects on the health of the population than do medical initiatives directed towards individuals.

## Social Capital

It is clear from all types of research done both today and in the past, and in our and in other societies, that social **status** and health are related. Much of this analysis compares individuals who differ in health and social status. However, when the level of analysis moves from the individual to the society as a whole, the link between status and health remains. Societies with greater degrees of inequality have poorer over-all health outcomes regardless of their overall wealth. With respect to rates of health and illness, the overall wealth of a society appears to be less important than the degree of inequity among societal members.

This interesting paradox needs explanation.

**10.1**

# Human Diversity
## Health and Aboriginal Canadians

One of the most troubling health issues faced by Canadians today is the relatively poor health and shorter lives of Aboriginal Canadians. For example, in the Northwest Territories, where more than half of the population is Aboriginal, the life expectancy is five years less for women (at 75) and four years less for men (at 70) than that of other Canadians (Helwig, 2000: 681). This is largely due to the higher mortality rates among Aboriginal people.

Among the factors that have been used to understand this difference are the higher rates of alcohol use and cigarette smoking, and higher rates of certain infectious diseases, including tuberculosis and some sexually transmitted diseases. While the higher level of physical activity among the Inuit confers some cardiovascular benefits, it also contributes to their accident rate, which is twice the national average.

Following are some highlights of the *NWT*

*Health Status Report* (1999), covering territory that is now the Northwest Territories and Nunavut:

- More NWT residents reported (self-perceived) very good or better health status (91 per cent) than other Canadians (85 per cent).
- The incidence of binge drinking in the Northwest Territories is three times the frequency in the rest of the population, and 26 per cent of NWT residents are heavy drinkers, compared with 9 per cent in the rest of Canada.
- Forty-five per cent of the population smoke tobacco, compared to 30 per cent in the rest of Canada.
- The tuberculosis rate is nine times, the chlamydia rate seven times, that of the rest of Canada.
- The chief cause of injury-related deaths in the Northwest Territories are, in order, vehicular accidents, suicide, and drowning.

Explanations for the individual-level correlation have suggested that people with higher incomes, higher occupational prestige scores, and higher educational levels are more able to prevent ill health through eat-

ing and drinking wisely, avoiding serious threats to health such as cigarette smoking and excessive alcohol consumption, and engaging in prescribed early detection such as mammograms and PSA (a test for

**10.2**

# Sociology in Action
## Canada's Guide to Health?

**Canada's Guide to Health?**
1. Don't smoke.
2. Exercise regularly.
3. Drink alcohol only in moderation.
4. Minimize the amount of fat in your diet.
5. Reduce stress.
6. Don't use marijuana or other street drugs.
7. Get eight hours of sleep a night.
8. Follow Canada's Food Guide.
9. Have a yearly check-up.
10. Reduce the amount of sugar in your diet.

**A Sociologist's Version**
1. Don't be poor.
2. Don't be born to a teenage mother.
3. Don't be born into a poor family.
4. Don't be a member of a racialized group.
5. Don't live on the streets or in temporary or poor housing.
6. Don't drop out of school.
7. Don't live in a polluted environment.
8. Don't lose your job.
9. Don't work at manual labour.
10. Don't be a woman.

prostate cancer). When those in these higher levels become sick, they are able to get immediately to the doctor and to take advantage of the most sophisticated and effective new treatments.

But why would the degree of inequality in a society be more important than the average living standard and income of persons in a society in predicting health and illness outcomes? A recently developed theoretical explanation is that the degree of social cohesion, social capital, or trust is the link between inequity and health (Mustard, 1999). A society characterized by inequity is one in which "there is a pronounced status order" (Veenstra, 2001: 74). As people compare themselves to one another, it is possible—indeed, likely—that those lower in the status hierarchy "will feel this shortcoming quite strongly, given the width of the gap, and consequently will suffer poorer health" (75). This may result from "damaging emotions such as anxiety and arousal, feelings of inferiority and low self-esteem, shame and embarrassment, and recognition of the need to compete to acquire resources that cannot be gained by any other means" (75).

A number of researchers have suggested that societies with high degrees of inequality are also low in *social cohesion* (or *social capital*), and it is social cohesion that mediates between social status and illness. Social cohesion is thought to be evident in societies to the extent that people are involved in public life and volunteer to work together for the good of the whole. A society with little social cohesion might, for instance, be dominated by market values and characterized by transactions in the interest of profit. Current social policies in Canada that favour market dominance over state intervention exacerbate the degree of inequity in society.

Many researchers are now looking at the processes whereby societies in which there is a high degree of citizen involvement, communication, and community feeling (social cohesion or social capital) maintain relatively high levels of good health.

### The Existential Level

People around the globe and even within the variety of cultures and classes within Canada experience illness in different ways. Popular conceptions of illness compete and overlap, too. One compilation of popular notions of illness includes illness as choice, illness as despair, illness as secondary gain, illness as a message of the body, illness as communication, illness as metaphor, illness as statistical infrequency, and illness as sexual politics (Clarke, 2000).

"Illness as choice" refers to the notion that we choose when to become sick, what type of illness we will have, and so on. In other words, illness episodes are a reflection of the deep tie between the mind and the body. That illness is a sort of despair is a related notion—the idea being that illness results from emotional misery or reflects unresolved grief and unhappiness.

The notion of secondary gain emphasizes the benefits sometimes derived from illness—for instance, an ill student might not be able to write an exam for which he or she also happens to be unprepared. Closely related to this notion is the philosophy of illness that suggests that physical symptoms are a means through which the body is trying to communicate a message to the world. And related to this, in turn, is the idea that the symptoms are meant to reflect a particular message, a particular set of unmet needs. For example, a cold, with its running nose and eyes, may be said to represent a frustrated desire to cry.

Susan Sontag (1978) describes some of the metaphors attached to diseases such as tuberculosis,

Many women with eating disorders see themselves as much bigger than they are. What social forces do you think contribute to this? (GettyImages/ Tony Latham)

AIDS, and cancer. One disease metaphor portrays a disease as an enemy and the subsequent necessity for a war against the disease. Illness as statistical infrequency, in contrast, is simply a numerical definition that names as "illness" a bodily functioning or symptom that is infrequent in the population.

Finally, the idea that illness reflects gender politics is related to the **patriarchy** of the medical profession and its consequent tendency to see women's bodies as basically flawed and women's behaviours as more likely to be pathological (for example, meriting psychiatric diagnosis) than those of men. These medical views reflect gender and gender roles in society (see Clarke, 2000). All of these different popular conceptions of illness have been taken up at one time or another by Canadian researchers.

## Sociology of Medicine

The sociology of medicine examines the location, definition, diagnosis, and treatments of disease. It includes an examination of the health-care institutions such as hospitals, clinics, co-operatives, and home care, along with medically related industries and the training, work, and statuses of medical and nursing professions and other health-care providers today and in historical context.

Because the history of the twentieth century has been characterized by the increasing dominance of allopathic medicine and its spreading relevance to more of life (Zola, 1972), the term *medicalization* (the tendency for more and more of life to be defined as relevant to medicine) has provided an important conceptual framework for critical analysis. We will turn now to a discussion of the medical care system in Canada today.

### The Canadian Medical Care System

Our present medical care system was first implemented in 1972 after a Royal Commission on Health Care (Hall, 1964–5), under Justice Emmett Hall, recommended that the federal government work with the provincial governments to establish a program of universal health care. While hospitalization and some medical testing had been covered before that, the new program was designed to cover physicians' fees and other services not already covered under the Hospital Insurance and Diagnostic Services Act (1958).

Four basic principles guided the program. The first was universality. This meant that the plan was to be available to all residents of Canada on equal terms, regardless of prior health record, age, income, non-membership in a group (such as a union or workplace), or other considerations. The second was portability. This meant that individual benefits would travel with the individual across the country, from province to province. The third was comprehensive coverage: the plan was to cover all necessary medical services, including dentistry, that required hospitalization. The fourth was administration. This referred to the fact that the plan was to run on a non-profit basis.

The Canada Health Act of 1984 added a fifth principle, accessibility. The costs of the plan were to be shared by the federal and provincial governments in such a way that the richer provinces paid relatively more than the poorer provinces; thus, the plan would also serve to redistribute wealth across Canada. Doctors, with few exceptions (found mostly in community health clinics), were not salaried by the government. Instead, they were and continue to be private practitioners paid by the government, usually on a fee-for-service basis.

### Privatization

Despite the presence of the universally available and federally supported national medical care system, there is considerable evidence of privatization within the system. Moreover, the degree of privatization varies across the provinces. Approximately 75 per cent of the Canadian system is presently public, 25 per cent private (Fuller, 1998). These figures, however, exclude physicians, who are in a somewhat anomalous position because though most receive money from the state, they do so usually as private entrepreneurs compensated on the basis of the number of patients they see and the type of diagnosis and treatment they offer.

The private aspects of the Canadian system are dominated by multinational corporations involved in providing a variety of health-related goods and services, including additional medical insurance, information technology services, food and laundry for hospitals, long-term and other institutional care, drugs, medical devices, and home care (Fuller, 1998). The most important impetus for growth in the medical system is in the private sector, particularly in drugs and new (and very expensive) technologies such as MRI, CAT scan, and mammography machines and other increasingly popular diagnostic technologies, such as the PSA test for prostate cancer (Fuller, 1998).

Table 10.3 portrays the increase in personal expenditures on medical care from 1975 to 2004.

These older women seem to be energetic and engaged in life. They are providing one another with social support. (*Health Canada web site and Media Photo Gallery*, Health Canada, http://www.hc-sc.gc.ca. Reproduced with the permission of the Minister of Public Works and Government Services Canada, 2005.)

Notice especially the dramatic increases in private expenditures for other health-care professionals (for example, providers of complementary and alternative health care) and for drugs.

There is considerable debate today about whether or not Canada can continue to afford a publicly funded and universally available medical care system. The mass media are full of stories of overcrowded emergency rooms and impossibly long waiting lists

(Canadian Health Services Research Foundation, 2002). These sorts of concerns often seem to lead to the argument that the problem is the publicly funded system. Consistent with the move to the political right both in Canada and throughout the Western world is an emphasis on the value of the free market, arguing that a private health-care system would be both more efficient and more cost-effective. However, evidence from a wide variety of sources

Table 10.3 **Total and Private Sector Canadian Health Expenditure by Use of Funds, 1975, 1990, and 2004**

| | Total Health Expenditure | | | Private Sector Health Expenditure[1] | | |
|---|---|---|---|---|---|---|
| | 1975 | 1990 | 2004[2] | 1975 | 1990 | 2004[2] |
| Hospitals | 44.7 | 39.1 | 29.9 | 11.0 | 14.4 | 7.9 |
| Other institutions | 9.2 | 9.4 | 9.6 | 11.3 | 10.2 | 8.5 |
| Physicians | 15.1 | 15.2 | 12.9 | 0.9 | 0.6 | 0.7 |
| Other professional | 9.0 | 10.6 | 11.2 | 33.0 | 35.3 | 34.2 |
| Drugs | 8.8 | 11.4 | 16.7 | 31.7 | 29.9 | 33.8 |
| Capital | 4.4 | 3.5 | 4.5 | 5.5 | 2.5 | 3.5 |
| Public health & administration | 4.5 | 4.2 | 6.7 | – | – | – |
| Other health spending | 4.3 | 6.7 | 8.6 | 6.6 | 7.3 | 11.5 |
| Total | 100.0 | 100.0 | 100.0 | 23.8[3] | 25.5[3] | 30.1[3] |

[1]Includes out-of-pocket expenditures made by individuals, claims paid by health insurance firms, private spending on health-related capital construction, and privately funded health research
[2]Forecast
[3]Represents percentage of total health expenditure

Source: Canadian Institute for Health Information, *National Health Expenditure Trends 1975–2004* (Ottawa: Canadian Institute for Health Information, 2004), 108–9, 114–15.

does not support this point of view (Canadian Health Services Research Foundation, 2002). For example, Calgary, Alberta, recently moved to some degree of privatization: cataract surgery services are now bought from private companies. This has resulted not only in more costly cataract surgery but also in longer waiting times than in the nearby cities of Lethbridge and Edmonton.

US studies on the effect of governments' buying of medical services from private companies also demonstrate problems with privatization. For instance, dialysis and kidney transplants are funded through the federally run Medicare program, which buys services from both for-profit and not-for-profit dialysis centres. Johns Hopkins University researchers compared over 3,000 patient records and found that the for-profit centres had higher death rates, were less likely to refer patients for transplants, and were less likely to treat children with the dialysis method most likely to be of benefit to them (Canadian Health Services Research Foundation, 2002).

Most US-based research suggests that for-profit (private) care costs more, pays lower salaries to staff, and incurs higher administrative costs but does not provide higher-quality care or greater access. Between 1990 and 1994, for-profit hospitals billed approximately $8,115 (US) for every discharged patient, whereas not-for-profit hospitals charged $7,490 per person even though quality of care, according to some indices, was better in not-for-profit institutions. For instance, not-for-profits tend to provide higher rates of immunization, mammography, and other preventive services (Canadian Health Services Research Foundation, 2002). People lose, on average, two years of life when they are treated in for-profit hospitals (Devereaux et al., 2002: 1402).

It has also been claimed that private systems offer more choice. The inference is that public systems are restrictive because of bureaucratic government interference. In fact, however, the interference by insurance companies in medical decision-making in private, for-profit systems appears to be more problematic than state interference. The other aspect of the argument for choice is that a combined system would allow individuals the possibility of choosing between private and public services for different services. This argument, by and large, flies in the face of the repeatedly confirmed value orientations of Canadians, who continue to identify medicare as one of Canada's most important social programs.

## Medicalization

*Medicalization* is the tendency of more and more of life to be defined as relevant to medicine. Irving Zola (1972) is one of the social theorists who has been critical of this process. He defined *medicalization* as including the following four components:

1. an expansion of what in life and in a person is relevant to medicine
2. the maintenance of absolute control over certain technical procedures by the allopathic medical profession
3. the maintenance of almost absolute access to certain areas by the medical profession
4. the spread of medicine's relevance to an increasingly large portion of living

The first area of medicalization is the expansion of medicine from a narrow focus on the biomechanics of the human body to a broader concern by medicine with the "whole" person. The second area refers to the fact that there are things that only doctors are allowed to do to the human body, such as surgery. The third refers to the fact that doctors, through medicine, have been able to transform into medical problems areas of life such as pregnancy and aging that were formerly viewed as normal, neither as pathological nor as medically relevant processes. The fourth pertains to the way in which medicine increasingly has jurisdiction in areas formerly considered to be of relevance to the criminal justice or religious systems, such as criminality and alcohol addiction.

Medicalization has been shown to be evident in the tendency for more and more of life to be defined by the medical profession. Ivan Illich (1976) attributes the growth of medicalization to bureaucratization. Véase Navarro (1975) claims that medicalization, or medical dominance, is more related to class and class conflict, in particular the upper-class background and position of physicians. He also relates medicalization to the work of physicians who operate as entrepreneurs in the definition of health and illness categories and their relevant treatments.

## Disease Mongering

Furthering this argument about the role of capitalism in the growth of medical dominance is the instrumental role that the pharmaceutical corporations play in "disease mongering." Through a series of suggestive

10.3

# Sociology in Action
## Population Aging

You have probably heard the concern voiced that as the population ages in the next several decades in Canada as a result of the aging of the baby-boom generation, the strain will be felt in our health care system. In fact, people over 65 are more likely to be ill than adults at other ages. Moreover, they are also more likely to use the health care system when they are ill.

Recent research from the Canadian Health Services Research Foundation demonstrates that the increasing use of the health care system by seniors is not the result of their increasing numbers in the population, but rather of their relatively higher utilization rates. There is evidence that it is not the sick seniors who are responsible for the increase in costs, but rather *healthy* seniors. For example, the rate of doctor visits by the well in Manitoba increased by 57.5 per cent for visits to specialists and by 32.0 per cent for visits to general practitioners between the 1970s and 1983. Rates for unhealthy seniors increased by only 10 per cent or less (Canadian Health Services Research Foundation, 2001: 1–2). It appears, then, that the elderly routinely receive more care than they formerly did. The cost of health care increases because of the simple aging of the population is estimated to be only 1 per cent of total health care costs. The significant impact of population aging, then, appears to be the result of overtreatment of the elderly, including such interventions as flu shots, hip replacement, and cataract surgery (Canadian Health Services Research Foundation, 2001).

Examine the accompanying figure. What is the obvious explanation for what is portrayed? What do you think are the more complex and interesting explanations?

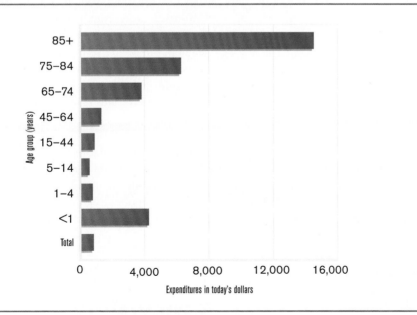

**Estimate of Total Provincial Government Per Capita Health Care Expenditures by Age Group, Canada, 1998–9**

SOURCE: *In Search of Sustainability: Prospects for Canada's Health Care System* (Ottawa: Canadian Medical Association, 2001), p. 26. Reprinted by permission of the publisher © 2001 Canadian Medical Association.

anecdotes, Ray Moynihan, Iona Heath, and David Henry (2002) argue for critically examining the ways in which the pharmaceutical industry plays a significant role in defining as diseases conditions for which they have developed an effective drug. The researchers illustrate this practice through descriptive case histories of a process whereby a drug is manufactured and then a disease is newly highlighted as problematic. Three cases are highlighted: a baldness tonic for men, a drug for "social phobia," and osteoporosis in aging women.

Ostensibly involved in public education about new diseases and treatments, and often working alongside doctors and consumer groups, the pharmaceutical industry has promoted as problematic conditions that may well be better seen as part of life. For example, the medicalization of baldness by Merck occurred after the development of their anti-baldness drug, Propecia, in Australia. Around the time of the patenting of the drug, a major Australian newspaper reported on a new study that indicated that about one-third of men experienced hair loss (Hickman, 1998). Further, the article emphasized, hair loss sometimes led to panic and other emotional difficulties and had a negative impact on job prospects and well-being. At the same time, the paper featured news of the establishment of an International Hair Study Institute. What the newspaper failed to report was that both the study and the institute were funded by Merck and that the "expert" quotations were from the public relations firm hired by Merck.

These two steps are just illustrations of some strategies used by pharmaceutical industries who have been advised in Britain's *Pharmaceutical Marketing* magazine to "establish a need and create a desire" (Cook, 2001, cited in Moynihan et al., 2002). The report cited is based on several anecdotes. More and systematic research on the extent of these practices is needed, but even these few examples raise questions about what may be invisible and unregulated attempts to "change public perceptions about health and illness to widen markets for new drugs" (Moynihan et al., 2002: 891).

### The Socio-economic Background of Medical Students in Canada

There are substantial differences between the backgrounds of medical students and those of the rest of the Canadian population. Doctors are not drawn, in a representative way, from all across the socio-economic and socio-demographic variation of the whole population of citizens.

Specifically, medical students are more likely to have had fathers who were doctors. This continues to be true today. In 1965, 11.8 per cent of medical students had fathers who were doctors. Today, 15.6 per cent do (Dhalla et al., 2002: 1032). Rural students, in contrast, were under-represented in the mid-1960s and continue to be under-represented today. Whereas 30.4 per cent of Canadian high school students lived in rural areas in 1965–6, only 8.4 per cent of the medical students did. Rural students are slightly better represented today (Dhalla et al., 2002: 1032). In 1965–6, the fathers of 7.5 per cent of the population had attended university, while 38.0 per cent of the fathers of medical students did so. Today, 39.0 per cent of the fathers of medical students had graduate or doctoral degrees, compared with only 6.6 per cent of the whole population of the same age (Dhalla et al., 2002: 1032). With respect to gender, however, significant changes have occurred. In 1965–6, 11.4 per cent of the medical students were female. Now about half are (Dhalla et al., 2002: 1032). Medical students continue, however, to be less likely than the general population to be Aboriginal or black (Dhalla et al., 2002).

These findings are important in practical terms as well. For example, medical students who are from rural areas are more likely to practise in (under-serviced) rural areas. And poorer people have poorer health outcomes, yet students from the poorest neighbourhoods are seven times less likely to attend medical school than those from the richest neighbourhoods (Dhalla et al., 2002).

The trend towards privatization in Canadian universities can only exacerbate these discrepancies in adequate representation of medical students. Rising tuition fees in Ontario since 1997 have already affected the equitable representation of doctors. Although family incomes, as self-reported by students in medical schools, have increased, these students are graduating with more debt, are more likely to consider potential income when choosing a place to practise, and are more likely to report financial stress while in school (Kwong et al., 2002).

## Conclusion

In many ways, health issues are fundamentally social issues. The rates, definitions, and meanings of illness, sickness, disease, and death have varied and continue to vary around the world and over time. Within

Canadian society, these differences, particularly in rates, reflect culture and social structure and mirror inequality and marginalization. They are affected by large external physical forces such as characteristics of the physical environment and by smaller lifestyle, existential, and psycho-social factors.

Medical care is dominated by allopathic medicine today. However, a sizable minority of Canadians are now choosing complementary and alternative care.

Still, evidence continues to indicate the dominance of medical definitions of reality (*medicalization*) in many parts of life. There is, as well, increasing evidence of the manipulation of medicalization by the pharmaceutical industry and its entrepreneurial disease-defining work. While there is substantially more privatization in the Canadian medical care system today, it has tended not to reduce costs or to provide better medical service but the reverse.

## □ Questions for Critical Thought

1. What are the implications of developing health policy on the basis of the mortality rate from the chief causes of death in Canada as compared to PYLL?
2. Discuss the evidence for an increasingly medicalized society.
3. What are the costs and benefits of medicalization?
4. Assess the opportunities for social cohesion in your college or university. Are there things available to you to do in class or extracurricularly that give you chances to get to know and trust people from different programs and years at your university?
5. What challenges to your health are evident in your school? In your answer include challenges related to the physical plant, the organization of learning and testing, and the social life available to students.
6. Discuss the water or air quality of the town where you are going to school. Discuss the strategies that you have used to get information about the air or water quality. Assess the quality of the information to which you have gained access.
7. Examine three magazines that you commonly read for their health-related messages. Include both articles and advertisements in your analysis. Consider the portrayal of issues such as gender, ethnicity, and social class in your discussion.
8. Compare the sense of coherence and social cohesion. To what extent are these concepts related to one another?

## □ Recommended Readings

David Coburn, Carl D'Arcy, and George Torrance, eds, *Health and Canadian Society: Sociological Perspectives*, 3rd edn (Toronto: University of Toronto Press, 1998).
    This excellent reader on the topic of medical or health sociology in Canada provides an overview of the socio-historical development of the medical system, health-care costs, and the health status of Canadians.
Nicholas J. Fox, *Postmodernism, Sociology and Health* (Toronto: University of Toronto Press, 1994).
    This book takes up poststructuralism and modernism in social theory and examines how they might change our conventional understandings of health, illness, the human subject, the body, and so on.
Anne Kasper and Susan J. Ferguson, eds, *Breast Cancer: Society Shapes an Epidemic* (New York: St Martin's Press, 2000).
    This reader is written with a multi-disciplinary perspective, including sociology, women's health activism, environmentalism, medicine, health policy, and health management.
Michael Rachlis and Carol Kushner, *Strong Medicine: How to Save Canada's Health Care System* (Toronto: HarperCollins, 1994).
    This is a critique of the current medical care system written by a physician and a journalist. The authors advocate fundamental structural reform in the interests of quality and efficiency while maintaining universal medical care.

☐ **Recommended Web Sites**

**Health Canada**

**www.hc-sc.gc.ca**

Health Canada, a government department, provides health-related information on topics such as healthy living, health care, diseases and conditions, health protection, and media stories. You can also find here the latest statistics regarding health, illness, death, PYLL, medical care system characteristics, and current issues.

**National Network on Environments and Women's Health**

**www.yorku.ca/nnewh/english/nnewhind.html**

This is one of the five federally funded Centres of Excellence for Women's Health. It focuses on the impact of three key environments on women's health workplaces, including paid and unpaid work, unemployment and labour force restructuring and adjustments, health systems (both conventional and unconventional forms of health care), formal and informal practices, women's understandings of health and health risks, and policy.

**The National Women's Health Information Center**

**www.4woman.gov**

This is the Web site of the Office on Women's Health and the Department of Health and Human Services of the US federal government—an excellent site for the latest findings regarding health research, particularly as it pertains to women (there is also an internal link to men's health issues included on the home page).

**Statistics Canada**

**www.statcan.ca**

Statistics Canada publishes myriad studies on Canadian society, including statistics relevant to morbidity, mortality, disease incidence, birth rates, and so on. The journal *Canadian Social Trends*, census data, and *The Daily* all can be accessed here.

# 11

Terry Wotherspoon

# Education

© W.P. Wittman Limited

## Learning Objectives

In this chapter, you will:

- understand how and why formal education has become a central social institution in Canada and other nations
- learn the main dimensions associated with the growth of formal education systems
- gain a critical understanding of various forms of lifelong learning beyond formal education
- understand the major theoretical perspectives and theories that sociologists employ to explain educational institutions, practices, and outcomes
- understand the relationships between education and social inequality
- explore how education and educational outcomes are shaped by relationships between educational institutions and participants and the social contexts within which those institutions operate
- critically understand contemporary debates and controversies over major educational issues

## Introduction

The chief economist for the World Bank recently highlighted the importance of education as "critical to participation and productivity in economic life." "A healthy, literate labor force," he said, "will both increase the amount of growth realized from establishing a sound investment climate and strongly reinforce the poverty reduction benefit from that growth" (Stern, 2002: 21). Probably few people would take issue with these comments. What do they mean, though, to people in different situations?

Sociologists are interested in several issues associated with educational processes and outcomes and in the environments within which education operates. Questions that sociology addresses include:

- Why is formal education so important in contemporary societies, and how did it get to be that way?
- What are the main dimensions of education and education systems in Canada and other nations?
- How do sociologists explain the growth of education systems and the outcomes associated with education for different groups?
- What are the main educational experiences and outcomes for different social groups?
- What are the main challenges facing education systems in Canada and other nations?

## The Changing Face of Education

Education is generally understood as the formal learning that takes place in institutions such as schools, colleges, universities, and other sites that provide specific courses, learning activities, or credentials in an organized way. *Informal learning* also occurs as people undertake specific activities to learn about distinct phenomena or processes. Both formal and informal education are part of the broader process that sociologists call **socialization**, which refers to all direct and indirect learning related to humans' ability to understand and negotiate the rules and expectations of the social world.

A comparison of today's educational settings and classrooms with those of a century ago yields both striking similarities and profound differences. Massive, architecturally designed complexes have replaced self-contained one- or two-room wooden buildings; sophisticated equipment often takes the place of chalk and slate boards; and most students are exposed to a diverse range of teachers, subject choices, and work projects unthinkable in 1900. Today's students and teachers are likely to exhibit a far greater array of personal, stylistic, and cultural variation than was apparent a century ago and have access to many more learning and community resources.

Despite these changes, the casual visitor to classrooms in either time period would not be likely to mistake schools for other settings. Groupings of children and youth, under the instruction and regular scrutiny of adult teachers, are guided through both regimented activities—at least for part of the time in rows or other arrangements of desks—and periods allocated for recreation or personal expression. Education is a unique **social institution** at the same time as it reveals characteristics that are integral to the society in which it operates.

### Dimensions of Educational Growth

Educational expansion accelerated rapidly after the Second World War. In 1951, over half (51.9 per cent) of all Canadians aged 15 and over had less than a Grade 9 education, while just under 2 per cent had a university degree and only about 1 in 20 aged 18 to 24 was enrolled in university (Clark, 2000: 4–6; Guppy and Davies, 1998: 19). At the beginning of the twenty-first century, by contrast, Canadians have unprecedented levels of education, distinguishing Canada with one of the most highly educated populations in the world.

Table 11.1 provides an overview of the increasing educational attainment of Canadians in the last half of the twentieth century. The proportion of the population who had less than a Grade 9 education diminished rapidly, especially in the 1960s and 1970s. And while very few had taken or completed post-secondary studies at the start of the period, over half of the population had at least some post-secondary education by 2001. The average number of years of formal education held by Canadians rose from just under 12.5 at the beginning of the 1990s to nearly 13 by 1998, ranking Canada second only to Germany, where the average was just over 13.5 (Organization for Economic Co-operation and Development [OECD], 2001: 19). Growing emphasis on the importance of formal education and credentials has been matched by three interrelated factors: the overall expansion of educational opportunities and requirements, increasing levels of educational attainment among people born in Canada, and recent emphasis on the selection of highly educated immigrants.

The fact that many people did not have substantial amounts of formal education in the late nineteenth and early twentieth centuries was not as sig-

Many aspects of schooling have changed dramatically over time, although the core structure of classroom life has also retained some constant elements. In the early twentieth century, only three out of five children attended school, often for limited periods of time. Both teachers and students, like those depicted here in a Model School in Vancouver in about 1907, were supervised closely to emphasize routine habits, discipline, conformity, and common values. Most people today have more educational options that are considered essential parts of lifelong learning. (City of Vancouver Archives, SGN 1586, Photographer C. Bradbury)

nificant as it may seem in retrospect, because only a few occupations required educational credentials. Most people relied on schools to provide some basic skills and knowledge, discipline, and social training, and as a service to provide something for children to do when their parents were too busy to attend to them. Formal learning was often subordinate to other concerns. School superintendents and other educational authorities devoted their efforts to enforcing school attendance and improving the quality of instruction in schools. Annual reports and other documents maintained by provincial education departments are filled with references to concerns such as the need to maintain proper order and discipline in

Table 11.1 **Educational Attainment in Canada, by Percentage of Population Aged 15 and over, Selected Years, 1951–2001[a]**

|  | Less than Grade 9 | Grades 9 to 13 | Some Postsecondary | University Degree | Median Years of Schooling |
|---|---|---|---|---|---|
| 1951 | 51.9 | 46.1 | – | 1.9 | – |
| 1961 | 44.1 | 53.0 | – | 2.9 | – |
| 1971 | 32.3 | 45.9 | 17.1 | 4.8 | 10.6 |
| 1981 | 20.1 | 44.3 | 27.6 | 8.0 | 11.8 |
| 1986 | 17.3 | 43.0 | 30.2 | 9.6 | 12.2 |
| 1991 | 13.9 | 43.0 | 31.7 | 11.4 | 12.5 |
| 1996 | 12.1 | 40.7 | 34.0 | 13.3 | 12.7 |
| 2001 | 9.8 | 39.0 | 35.7 | 15.4 | – |

[a] Figures may not add up to 100 because of rounding.
SOURCE: Compiled from Statistics Canada, census data and *Education in Canada*, annual series.

the classroom; attention to habits and duties; routine procedures and daily records of pupil attendance, school visitors, and recitations drawn from various subjects; and the desire for teachers who were not so much good instructors as proper role models with good manners and high moral standing. (See Lawr and Gidney, 1973, for examples.)

Early advocates of public **schooling** promoted schooling as an efficient enterprise that would serve the public or general interest. Other institutions or sites, such as families, churches, and businesses, were narrower and more selective in scope.

The education system adopted a degree of flexibility that made it possible to integrate new tasks and curricula. School authorities had to make concessions when funds to build and run schools or hire the preferred quality of teachers were scarce. Some people resented having to pay or to be taxed for schooling. Schools could also be victims of their own success, as demands for education or population growth in communities outpaced the ability to provide school facilities, textbooks, teaching materials, and qualified teachers. In many parts of Canada, especially in smaller communities and rural areas, school operations remained highly uncertain or irregular until well into the twentieth century because of sporadic pupil attendance, an inability to attract and retain teachers, lack of funds, or disputes between school board and community members. A single teacher provided the schooling for all grades that were offered in rural one-room schools, whereas cities and larger districts tended to have better-equipped schools with a full range of programs and a complement of trained, more specialized teachers.

Gradually, centralized schools and districts replaced smaller units across Canada. School district consolidation began in 1900, though amalgamation into larger schools and school districts did not fully take hold until the period between the mid-1940s and the late 1960s. Amalgamation has continued since then, accelerating in the 1990s when the number of school boards in some provinces, including Alberta and Quebec, was cut by over half. In New Brunswick, all school boards were abolished between 1996 and 2001. Consolidation was hastened by financial and administrative difficulties in many districts and by the development of transportation networks and support linkages that made it easier to concentrate schools in selected centres. By 1970–1, there were just over 16,000 public schools in Canada (a figure that has declined moderately into the early twenty-first century), nearly 10,000 below the number that had operated a decade earlier (Statistics Canada, 1973: 104).

Pressure to build and maintain larger schools intensified as more people began to stay in school longer, extending into and beyond the high school years. The **baby boom** that occurred after the Second World War resulted in cohorts of children of unprecedented numbers entering and moving through the school system. The figures in Table 11.2 demonstrate that, while total enrolment in Canadian public elementary and secondary schools in 1950 was just over double what it had been in 1900, enrolment doubled again over the next decade and a half. The average number of pupils per school increased in Canada from 66 in 1925–6 to 156 in 1960–1 and nearly doubled over the next decade to reach 350 in 1970–1, a level that has remained relatively stable since then (Manzer, 1994: 131).

The data in Table 11.2 demonstrate how formal education has expanded throughout the life course. Children have begun their schooling at progressively younger ages over the past five decades. Kindergarten is now compulsory in most Canadian jurisdictions, and many children also attend various preschool and early childhood education programs.

Meanwhile, people have been extending their formal education well past high school into post-secondary studies. The larger cohorts of students moving through schools and completing high school, combined with increasing emphasis on higher education in particular fields and more general reliance on educational credentials as a means for firms to select employees, contributed to massive growth in post-secondary studies. The data in Table 11.2 demonstrate that, in 1950–1, only about 69,000 people were enrolled in full-time university studies, but university enrolment exploded to over 200,000 by the mid-1960s and approached 600,000 by 2000.

A similar pattern followed in other post-secondary institutions, which until the 1960s had encompassed mostly specific occupational and vocational certification programs in areas such as nursing and teacher education as well as pre-university studies in Quebec and other provinces. However, the introduction and expansion of the community college system in the 1960s and 1970s provided numerous options for post-secondary study both for students seeking certification in specialized trades or vocations and for students taking courses that could be employed for university credit. Sociologists have been concerned with issues related to the bureaucratic organization of education and educational inequality as school size and complexity increased.

Table 11.2 **Full-Time Enrolment in Canada, by Level of Study, Selected Years, 1870–2000 (in Thousands)**

| | Pre-elementary | Elementary and Secondary | Non-university Postsecondary | University Undergraduate | University Graduate |
|------|------|------|------|------|------|
| 1870 | – | 768 | – | 2 | – |
| 1880 | – | 852 | – | 3 | – |
| 1890 | – | 943 | – | 5 | <1 |
| 1900 | – | 1,055 | – | 7 | <1 |
| 1910 | – | 1,318 | – | 13 | <1 |
| 1920 | – | 1,834 | – | 23 | <1 |
| 1930 | – | 2,099 | – | 32 | 1 |
| 1940 | – | 2,075 | – | 35 | 2 |
| 1950 | – | 2,391 | – | 64 | 5 |
| 1955 | 103 | 3,118 | 33 | 69 | 3 |
| 1960 | 146 | 3,997 | 49 | 107 | 7 |
| 1965 | 268 | 4,918 | 69 | 187 | 17 |
| 1970 | 402 | 5,661 | 166 | 276 | 33 |
| 1975 | 399 | 5,376 | 221 | 331 | 40 |
| 1980 | 398 | 4,709 | 261 | 338 | 45 |
| 1985 | 422 | 4,506 | 322 | 412 | 55 |
| 1990 | 473 | 4,669 | 325 | 468 | 64 |
| 1995 | 536 | 4,895 | 391 | 498 | 75 |
| 2000 | 522 | 4,867 | 407[a] | 591[a] | – |

[a] 1999.

SOURCE: Compiled from various editions of Dominion Bureau of Statistics/Statistics Canada, census data and "Education at a Glance," *Education Quarterly Review*.

## *Education in the Learning Society*

The organization and nature of schooling across Canada remain varied. Initiatives to implement greater conformity and consistency across jurisdictions run parallel with increased numbers of alternative schools and educational services. Educational diversity is a product, in part, of the fact that elementary and secondary education is a formal jurisdiction of the provinces under constitutional legislation, while other forms of education, including adult and post-secondary education and vocational training, are controlled, operated, or funded by a variety of governments (federal, provincial, and First Nations) and by private sources. Increased emphasis on education and training has been accompanied by considerable expansion of educational opportunities and programs offered at all levels. Many people are turning to additional sources, such as distance education and Web-based course offerings that originate both within and outside Canada.

Schooling is compulsory for Canadians aged 5 to 16 in most provinces, however, most people engage in education well beyond these limits. The widespread use of terms such as *information society*, *learning society*, and **lifelong learning** signifies the central place that education holds within the context of what is commonly designated as the **new economy** or *knowledge-based economy*. The new economy has gained prominence through increasing reliance on rapidly changing information technologies and scientific advancements that have affected not only business and the workplace, but virtually every major sphere of social life. Learning is central to all dimensions of the new economy, including the need to train qualified personnel; to conduct research for continuing innovation; to develop, test, and market new products and services within firms; to process the vast amounts of new information being created; and to ensure that people have the capacities to employ new technologies at work and at home (Wolfe and Gertler, 2001). In this climate, what counts is not so much the knowledge that we acquire as the capacity to learn and apply that knowledge to emerging situations. People are expected not simply to learn more, but to develop adaptive ways of learning.

These expectations have contributed to extensive levels of and variations in educational qualifications and experiences. With respect to formal learning, nearly 6.4 million Canadians (about one-fifth of the entire population) identified in Table 11.2 are engaged in full-time schooling, and well over 300,000 more are involved in part-time studies. Between one-quarter and one-third of the population that has completed initial education indicate, as well, that they are involved in some adult education, whether in the form of in-person, correspondence, or private courses, workshops, apprenticeships, or arts, crafts, or recreation programs (Statistics Canada and HRDC, 2001: 13).

The phenomenon of informal learning has also attracted growing attention. *Informal learning* involves distinct efforts arranged and undertaken by individuals or groups to acquire new knowledge that can be applied to work, personal, or community circumstances. Such activities include initiatives to learn a new language on one's own or with other people, to learn computer skills or software programs, or to gain competencies that can be used for volunteer work or family situations. Surveys in Canada and the United States estimate that over three-quarters of the adult population undertake well over 300 hours of informal learning projects per person every year. Even among adults with a university degree, nearly half (48

per cent) report that they are engaged in adult education, and nearly all people, regardless of education, are heavily involved in informal learning activities (Livingstone, 1999: 36–7; Statistics Canada and HRDC, 2001: 18).

Canada ranks high on international comparisons of education, although Canadians are not unique in their growing pursuit of education and training. Among the nine Organization for Economic Co-operation and Development (OECD) nations represented in Figure 11.1, Canada has the highest proportion of the population with formal educational credentials beyond high school and ranks second, behind the United States, with respect to the percentage of the population with a university degree.

Emphasis on formal training and lifelong learning is a phenomenon associated with **globalization** and competitiveness across national settings. Throughout the twentieth century, the degree to which a population was educated came to be recognized as a significant indicator of modernization and development status. The more education one has, the higher the chances are to have a good job, better income, good health status, and many other factors positively associated with a high standard of living. Conversely, rates of poverty, unemployment, crime, serious illness and

Figure 11.1 **Level of Education and Functional Literacy in Selected OECD Countries, 1996[a]**

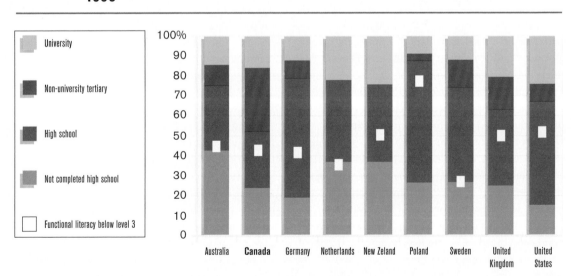

[a] Percentage distribution of the population 25 to 64 years of age, by the highest completed level of education (1996) and level of functional literacy proficiency (1994–5).
SOURCE: Adapted from Statistics Canada, *Learning a Living: A Report on Adult Education and Training in Canada*, Catalogue 81-856, May 2001.

injury, and other less desirable indicators rise when formal education is limited.

Many nations are accelerating the pace of educational advancement as they undertake economic and human resource development strategies aimed at the production of new knowledge and a more highly trained workforce. The importance of education for the new economy is highlighted in the titles of numerous recent research reports and discussion papers produced by governments; Canadian examples include *High School May Not Be Enough* (Human Resources Development Canada and Statistics Canada, 1998), *Learning a Living in Canada* (Skill Development Leave Task Force, 1983), and *Knowledge Matters: Skills and Learning for Canadians* (Human Resources Development Canada, 2002). Consequently, governments, businesses, and agencies concerned with economic development stress the need to expand education well beyond compulsory levels in order to foster both economic growth and non-economic benefits such as improved health, the ability to use skills for non-monetary purposes, and the intrinsic desire to learn (OECD, 2001). The prevailing sentiment is that, with a few variations, "overall, individuals will need more and more knowledge and skills, and our society will need a class of highly educated and trained people to prosper" (LeBlanc, 1994: 15).

Regardless of the widespread acceptance of and participation in education as an essential feature of contemporary life, not everyone encounters and benefits from education in the same way. Educational experiences, outcomes, and achievements differ considerably among individuals and groups and are interpreted in different ways.

# Alternative Accounts of Educational Growth and Development

Several major theoretical perspectives that have been applied to an understanding of the education system are outlined here: the structural-functionalist approach, symbolic interactionist and interpretive theories, conflict theory, feminist theories, and more recent integrative orientations to the analysis of education.

## Structural Functionalism

**Structural functionalism** examines education, like any other aspect of society, in terms of its contributions to social order and stability. Education gains importance in modern societies as an institution that provides participants with the core understandings, capabilities, and selection criteria necessary to enable them to fit into prescribed social and economic roles. As society becomes more complex and specialized, schools and other educational institutions take on many of the functions previously managed by families, communities, and religious organizations to ensure that children and youth—and eventually adult learners, also—are equipped for work and adult life.

The structural-functionalist perspective presents an image of the properly functioning society as one in which the **transition** from early childhood and family life into schooling and eventually the labour force is relatively seamless, relying on the co-ordination and integration of all key components. Disruptions and changes are posed as problems of adjustment, either within the social system or by individuals who do not "fit." Social pathologies, like the need for periodic automobile maintenance or health checkups, must be repaired through proper diagnosis and treatment in order to maintain the system in a state of healthy balance.

Émile Durkheim, who wrote extensively about education in his efforts to establish sociology as a distinct scientific discipline in the early twentieth century, described education as "the means by which society perpetually re-creates the conditions of its very existence" ([1922] 1956: 123). Within each person education cultivates knowledge as well as moral obligation and commitment to other members within a social framework governed by definite rules, regulations, and expectations.

Talcott Parsons (1959) later extended this analysis to a North American context, highlighting the two central functions that schooling fulfills within contemporary societies. First, schooling allocates individuals into selected occupational pathways and social positions in order to match social requirements with the available pool of skill, talents, and interests. Second, it socializes people by providing them with the general aptitudes and knowledge they need to operate successfully in their society and by preparing them more specifically for the adult roles that they will occupy. Schooling is organized in such a way that people move in the primary grades from home environments where highly personal, emotional ties prevail, through the senior grades, which are marked by progressively greater degrees of competition, merit, and instrumentality intended to prepare the individual for integration into work and other institutional settings crucial to adult life.

Robert Dreeben (1968) shows further the importance of school practices, in and out of the classroom, in cultivating characteristics essential for contemporary work and public life. Four essential **norms** are independence (acting by oneself), achievement (actions to meet accepted standards of excellence), universalism (treatment of others in an impartial way based on general categories), and specificity (emphasizing as important selected characteristics of the individual as opposed to the person as a whole).

Structural functionalism offers a possible explanation of educational expansion both by connecting schooling with the growth of complexity in the occupational structure and by highlighting its increasing importance to citizenship in industrialized societies. A related form of analysis, sometimes referred to as *technical functionalism*, links educational growth with the increasing technical sophistication of jobs and knowledge production (Bell, 1973). Functionalist analysis typically assumes a broad social consensus about what should be taught in schools and how educational institutions should be organized. Moreover, it tends not to question either the legitimacy of educational credentials to determine entry into specified labour market positions or the fairness of the way the education system operates.

Functionalist analysis also tends to portray deviation from these ideals as abnormalities or temporary problems that warrant minor reforms rather than challenges to the education system as a whole. It offers a description of what schools should be like, within liberal democratic ideologies, more than an explanation of how extensive schooling came about. Functionalism presents education as a meritocratic ideal, a means to enable people to gain opportunities for social or economic success regardless of their social backgrounds. Societies require a careful fit among capability, talent, effort, training, and jobs as social tasks become more complex and specialized. These claims have led to subsequent research into the definition and measurement of educational inequality, calling into question the degree to which educational realities match the needs of industrial democratic societies.

*Human capital theory*, an approach with some affinity to structural functionalism, emphasizes education's role as a critical tool for developing human capacities to create and apply new knowledge. The human being is regarded as an input, along with material and economic resources, that contributes to economic productivity and development. **Human capital** can be enhanced when adequate investment is made in the form of proper training, education, and social

support; this approach has been used to justify massive investment by governments that contributed to the significant enrolment growth in post-secondary education observed in Table 11.2. More recently, human capital theory has been revisited as attention turns to the importance of advanced training and educational credentials in the "knowledge" society.

Despite evidence that levels of employment, income, and other benefits improve with educational attainment, structural functionalism and related theories, such as human capital theory, are unable to account for the presence of persistent inequalities in educational opportunities, outcomes, and benefits. The theoretical emphasis on consensus limits consideration of actual differences in educational values, content, and practices; of how some things are incorporated into schooling while others are not; and of how these differences affect people from different social backgrounds. Alternative theoretical approaches to education attempt to address some of these issues.

## Symbolic Interactionism and Microsociology

*Interpretive analysis* examines such questions central to the sociological study of education as how schooling contributes to the development of personality and **identity**, how some forms of knowledge and not others enter into the curriculum, and how students and teachers shape the learning process both in and outside of the classroom. Interpretive analysis evaluates the meanings and possibilities that social actors bring to social settings. Willard Waller depicts schools as "the meeting-point of a large number of intertangled social relationships. These social relationships are the paths pursued by social interaction, the channels in which social influences run. The crisscrossing and interactions of these groups make the school what it is" ([1932] 1965: 12). Peter Woods (1979) explores schooling as a series of **negotiations** among teachers, students, and parents, expressed in such phenomena as how pupils select the subjects they take, the role of humour and laughter in the classroom and staff room, and teacher reports on student progress. Howard Becker (1952) shows how teachers' backgrounds influence their construction of images of the ideal pupil, which in turn affect how they treat and assess students.

These examples illustrate symbolic interactionists' depictions of societies and institutions as fluid rather than fixed entities. Institutional patterns are the result of recurrent daily activity and of people's capacities to shape, interpret, reproduce, and modify social arrangements through their social relations. *Ethno-methodology*, a variant of interpretive sociology, examines in detail the methods or approaches that people draw upon to construct a sense of reality and continuity in everyday life. Understood this way, the likelihood that classrooms in one place resemble those in another is less a product of a given model of schooling than an outcome of actions based on images about what is expected of us and how we are supposed to act.

Symbolic interactionism and ethnomethodology offer interesting insights, but they tend to fail to account for broader concerns and limiting factors by focusing too much on the details of ongoing social activity. Classroom dynamics or how one interprets the curriculum cannot be understood fully without reference to educational policy, power structures, social change, and persistent social inequalities that strongly influence educational processes and outcomes.

Some researchers have combined interpretive sociology, with its insights into practical social activity, with other approaches that pay greater attention to the social contexts within which social action takes place. Several British sociologists, under the banner of the "new sociology of education," extended this analysis by attempting to break down barriers between **micro-** and **macrosociology**, and by shifting attention away from educational problems defined by educational administrators and policymakers. Their concern is with how educational knowledge and practices are socially constructed and become part of the "taken for granted" assumptions that guide the actions and understandings of teachers and other educational participants. This work has focused "on the curriculum, on the 'educational knowledge' imparted by the school, and on the school's conception of 'what it is to be educated'" (Blackledge and Hunt, 1985: 290). Furthering this analysis, Basil Bernstein (1977) highlights the various ways that **power** and control enter into the authority structure of schools and classrooms as well as through the expectations and assumptions around which the curriculum and educational policies are framed. Bernstein's contributions to a systematic understanding of micro and macro levels of analysis have influenced writers working within diverse theoretical traditions (Sadovnik, 1995).

## *Conflict Theory*

Samuel Bowles and Herbert Gintis (1976), like structural functionalists, emphasize schools' role as mechanisms to select and prepare people for different posi-

tions in labour markets and institutional life. Their Marxist orientation, however, perceives schools' inability to fulfill the democratic ideology, namely, that all people have fair chances to succeed. The labour market is conditioned more by **capitalist** interests than by general consensus about social values and needs. Bowles and Gintis posit education, historically, as "a device for allocating individuals to economic positions, where inequality among the positions themselves is inherent in the hierarchical division of labor, differences in the degree of monopoly power of various sectors of the economy, and the power of different occupational groups to limit the supply or increase the monetary returns to their services" (1976: 49).

Conflict theorists emphasize that education-related inequalities are not simple imbalances that can be eradicated with minor modifications or reforms. Deeply rooted relations of domination and subordination create persistent barriers to opportunity and advancement. This critical sociological orientation denies the functionalist and human capital theory accounts of educational expansion as being a result of rising technical requirements of jobs. Different **social groups** are understood to employ education and educational ideologies as tools to pursue and safeguard their own interests. Employers rely on formal educational credentials, quite apart from the actual skills demanded by the job, to screen applicants and assess a person's general attributes. Professions control access to education and to certification as a way to preserve the status and benefits attached to their occupations. New knowledge and technological advancements in such areas as medicine, nursing, teaching, engineering, and information-processing may appear to produce a demand for increasingly more advanced, specialized training. But more often, credential inflation occurs as occupations preserve special privileges by simultaneously claiming the need for superior qualifications and restricting entry into these kinds of jobs (Collins, 1979).

Technological developments are not necessarily accompanied by increasing skill requirements for many jobs. Machines and information technology often substitute routine technical operations for human input or lead to new jobs in which people are required to do little but read gauges, respond to signals, or input information. Under these conditions, schools may be said to function more as warehouses to delay people's entrance into the labour force and dissipate dissatisfaction with the economy's failure to provide sufficient numbers of satisfying jobs than as places where effective learning and occupational training take place. Harry Braverman suggests that "there is no longer any place for the young in this society other than school. Serving to fill a vacuum, schools have themselves become that vacuum, increasingly emptied of content and reduced to little more than their own form" (1974: 440). Capitalism, in this view, has contributed less to skills upgrading through technological advancement than to an ongoing process that erodes working skills, degrades workers, and marginalizes youth.

Other conflict theorists highlight the biases and inequalities that are produced directly or indirectly through the curriculum and classroom practices. Students and parents have different understandings, resources, and time that affect the extent to which they can participate in and benefit from educational opportunities. Government cutbacks and changes to school funding formulas exacerbate many of these inequalities. In Ontario, for instance, many schools

---

**11.1**

# Sociology in Action
## Dimensions of Educational Participation

In Canada and most other nations, educational participation rates and attainment levels are increasing, regardless of social background. Sociologists have debated the extent to which these trends do or do not reflect education's ability to fulfill its promise to provide social and economic opportunity, especially in relation to demands associated with labour markets that require more skilled and highly qualified workers.

Exploration of these issues offers a useful opportunity to apply a *sociological imagination*, described by C. Wright Mills (1959) as the ability to link one's personal biography or background and circumstances with historical sensitivity to wider social structures and processes.

Begin by examining your own educational and career pathways. What level of formal education have you attained so far? What level would you like to attain? What other kinds of education (such as informal learning through self-directed or group study, special interest courses, adult education, or on-the-job training) have you engaged in? Have there been any gaps or interruptions in your studies? What experiences (positive or negative) have affected your interest and ability to gain the level of education you desire or have completed? What jobs (if any) have you been engaged in? What is the relationship between your educational background, including any specific skills, knowledge, or credentials you have, and the job itself? (Examine both the starting qualifications for the job and the actual tasks

involved in the job.) What future employment do you desire, and how is this related to your educational plans and qualifications?

Second, consider your own educational experiences in relation to your social background and context. How typical or different are your own educational and work experiences in comparison with your family and members of other social groups you have associated with (such as your grandparents, parents, childhood peers, and community members) or those you consider yourself part of now? Relate your educational experiences and aspirations to other important characteristics or aspects of your social background (including your gender, race, ethnicity, family income, regional and national origin, place of residence such as urban or rural, age, and other factors your consider important).

Third, engage in broader comparisons between your own education and working experiences and those of others. Examine data from various studies cited in this chapter, and from extensive records maintained on the Statistics Canada Web site. What is the relationship between your experiences, those of other persons from your family and home community, and wider trends evident from these data?

Finally, explain the major patterns and conclusions derived through your inquiries. What do these findings reveal about the nature of education and its social and economic importance?

report difficulty raising funds even for basic school materials and supplies: "Funding levels are so low, parents are having to make up for programs that aren't paid for—so then it depends on where you live and who you are. . . . There is a growing concern about equity. There is a growing gap between the 'have' and 'have-not' schools" (L. Brown, 2002: A1, A26).

In post-secondary education, decreased government funding has led to rising tuition fees, which has been accompanied by higher costs for textbooks and technology support, living expenses, and other factors. It is now increasingly difficult for students without sufficient resources or unable or unwilling to take on mounting student loans to attend colleges and universities. Conflict analysis also points to concern about the growing reliance by educational institutions on corporate donations and sponsorships to make up for shortfalls in government funding.

Conflict theories of education, in short, stress that expectations for schooling to fulfill its promise to offer equal opportunity and social benefits to all are unrealistic or unattainable within current forms of social organization. Barriers that exist at several levels—access to schooling, what is taught and how it is taught, ability to influence educational policy and decision-making, and differential capacity to convert education into labour market and social advantage—deny many individuals or groups the chances to benefit from meaningful forms and levels of education. Conflict theories offer varying assessments of what must be done to ensure that education can be more democratic and equitable. Some analysts stress that educational institutions and organizations themselves must be transformed, while others suggest that any kinds of school reform will be limited without more fundamental social and economic changes to ensure that people will be able to use, and be recognized for using, their education and training more effectively.

### Feminist Theories

**Feminist** analyses of schooling share similar observations with other conflict theories, though with an explicit emphasis on the existence of and strategies to address social inequalities based on **gender**. Feminist theory stresses that social equity and justice are not possible as long as males and females have unequal power and status though **patriarchy** or gendered systems of domination. In the eighteenth century, Mary Wollstonecraft ([1792] 1986) saw access to education as a fundamental right for women; by being denied

such a right historically, women were degraded as "frivolous," or a "backward sex." Later waves of feminism have continued to look to education as a central institution through which to promote women's rights, opportunities, and interests.

There are multiple "feminisms" in the analysis of education, rather than a single feminist orientation; each poses different questions for educational research and proposes different explanations and strategies for change (Gaskell, 1993; Weiner, 1994). In general, though, feminist analysis shows that influential mainstream studies of schooling have often concentrated on the lives of boys and men, with insufficient recognition that girls and women have different experiences and little chance to voice their concerns. Much research in the 1970s and 1980s focused on how such things as classroom activities, language use, images and examples in textbooks and curriculum material (including the absence of women and girls in many instances), treatment of students by teachers, and patterns of subject choice reflected gender-based stereotypes and perpetuated traditional divisions among males and females (Kenway and Modra, 1992).

Feminist analysis seeks to do more than simply demonstrate how these social processes contribute to inequalities, in order to change the conditions that bring these practices about. This focus has shifted as some aspects of the agenda on women's rights and issues have advanced successfully while specific barriers continue to restrict progress on other fronts. For instance, school boards have policies, enforced through human rights legislation, to restrict sexist curricula and to prohibit gender-based **discrimination** in educational programs and institutions. Rates of educational participation and attainment by females have come to exceed those for males. Yet there remains a need for greater progress in getting girls to take courses or programs in computer programming, engineering, and some natural sciences and to remove gender-based barriers in other areas of schooling.

Feminist analysis of education also explores the gender structure of the teaching force. The feminization of teaching, as female teachers came to outnumber male teachers by the end of the nineteenth century, carried significant implications for the occupation and its members. Teachers often lack the professional recognition that might otherwise accompany the demands and training their work involves. Teachers—and women teachers in particular—have been heavily regulated by governments and by school boards. During the early part of the twentieth century, guidelines often specified such things as what teachers could wear, with whom they could associate, and how they should act in public (Wotherspoon, 1995). Until the 1950s, legislation in many provinces required women to resign their teaching positions upon marriage. Although today's teachers have much greater personal and professional autonomy than those of the past, teachers' lives and work remain subject to various forms of scrutiny, guidelines, and informal practices that carry gender-based assumptions or significance. Female teachers predominate in the primary grades, while men tend to be overrepresented in the upper grades and in post-secondary teaching positions, especially in the most senior teaching and educational administrative positions.

Feminist analysis also addresses interrelationships among gender and other social factors and personal characteristics. Gender-based identities, experiences, and opportunities are affected by race, region, social class, and competing expectations and demands that people face at home, in the workplace, and in other social spheres (Acker, 1999). Students and teachers from different backgrounds encounter diverse experiences, concerns, and options, even within similar educational settings, which in turn affect subsequent educational and personal options.

### Emerging Analysis and Research in the Sociology of Education

Educational researchers make distinct choices about which theoretical positions are most useful or relevant to their analysis. *Critical pedagogy* draws from different theoretical positions, including conflict theory and feminist theory, both to explore how domination and power enter into schooling and personal life and to seek to change those aspects that undermine our freedom and humanity (Giroux, 1997; McLaren, 1998). Anti-racism education shares similar orientations, stressing further ways in which domination builds upon notions of racial difference to create fundamental inequalities among groups that are defined on the basis of biological differences or cultural variations (Dei, 1996).

Pierre Bourdieu (1997a; Bourdieu and Passeron, 1979) has explored how **social structures** become interrelated with the meanings and actions relevant to social actors. Bourdieu, as a critical theorist, emphasizes that education contributes to the transmission of power and privilege from one generation to another as it employs assumptions and procedures

that advantage some groups and disadvantage others. Educational access, processes, and outcomes are shaped through struggles by different groups to retain or gain advantages relative to one another. However, the mere fact that people hold advantageous degrees of economic, social, and cultural resources does not guarantee that these will be automatically converted into educational advantage. Competition for educational access and credentials increases as different groups look to education to provide a gateway into important occupational and decision-making positions.

Canadian research, influenced by Bourdieu's analysis and other integrative approaches such as life course theory, demonstrates the complex interactions among personal and social structural characteristics that affect the pathways taken by children and youth through education and from schooling into work and other life transitions (Andres Bellamy, 1993; Anisef et al., 2000). In order to understand schooling fully, one must take into account several interrelated dimensions, including:

- how educational systems are organized and what happens inside schools
- how school experiences are made sense of and acted on by various educational participants
- the relationships between internal educational processes and external factors, including governments and agencies that set and administer educational policy, employers that demand particular kinds of education and training and that recognize particular types of credentials, political frameworks composed of competing values and ideologies about what education should be all about and how resources should be allocated for education in relation to other priorities, and broader structures of social and economic opportunity and inequality
- the relations among transformations that are occurring on a global scale with more specific economic, political, and cultural structures that alternatively provide opportunities for and systematically exclude democratic participation by specific social groups (Apple, 1997; Torres, 1998).

## Educational Participants

Educational institutions reveal considerable complexity in their organization and composition. Comprehensive schools may have 2,000 to 3,000 students and dozens of teachers and support staff, while colleges and universities can exceed the size of small cities. Consequently, sociologists are interested in questions related to the changing nature of who attends and works in these institutions (with respect to gender, racial, ethnic, religious, socio-economic, and other factors), what positions they occupy, and what barriers and opportunities they encounter.

Sociologists are interested in much more than simply how the curriculum and formally structured activities affect students' learning and chances for success. Educational organization, rules, expectations, and practices also contain a **hidden curriculum**, the unwritten purposes or goals of school life. School life has a daily rhythm, through repeated variations between structured learning situations and informal interactions, channelling students into selected directions and contributing to taken-for-granted understandings about order, discipline, power relations, and other aspects of social life (Lynch, 1989). These educational processes are likely to reflect selected interests or issues while they ignore others. Benjamin Levin and J. Anthony Riffel observe that "low socio-economic status is more strongly associated with poor educational outcomes than any other variable. Yet educators are quite ambivalent about the meaning of poverty for their work and the conduct of schooling" (1997: 117). Schooling occasionally has limited connection with—and produces negative consequences for—the students and communities it is intended to serve (Dei et al., 2000; Royal Commission on Aboriginal Peoples, 1996).

Two mechanisms—referred to as *silencing* and the *banking model*—illustrate how common educational practices can have indirect and unequal consequences for students, their identities, and their educational experiences and outcomes. *Silencing* refers to practices that prevent educational participants from raising concerns that are important to them (such as when teachers do not give students the opportunity to talk about current events or matters of student interest), as well as to indirect processes that make students question their own cultural background or that discourage parents from talking to teachers because of their discomfort with the authority represented by the school. The *banking model* of **pedagogy** (Freire, 1970) refers to educational practice in which material is pre-packaged and transmitted in a one-way direction, from the educator to the student. This practice limits the forms of knowledge that are presented as valid, leaving students from alternative backgrounds with a sense that their experiences, questions, and capacities are invalid or irrelevant.

Many educators have modified their approaches as they have gained sensitivity to the impact of their actions on students and have responded to new skill priorities in areas such as critical thinking. However, educators are under considerable pressure to balance public demands for improvement in the quality of education with attention to the multi-faceted problems and interests they must deal with in their work. As resources and energies are directed to special needs students or to programs to accommodate students from diverse cultural backgrounds, there tends to be less time and funding for core areas that must also be covered.

The high profile given to concerns such as bullying and violence in the classroom and schoolyard is in part symptomatic of tensions encountered by both staff and students. Teachers are becoming increasingly frustrated with many aspects of their jobs as they find they are given little time and recognition for all that they are called on to do (Council of Ministers of Education Canada, 1996). While teachers are considered to be professionals, with the expectation that they are responsible for planning and carrying out educational functions, their professional status is constrained by extensive regulations and scrutiny.

## Educational Policy, Politics, and Ideologies

Educational policy is established and administered in a variety of ways across jurisdictional settings. Many nations, like Sweden and Japan, have highly centralized systems of education. Canada and the United States, by contrast, do not have uniform or centralized education systems because education is constitutionally defined as an area of provincial and state authority. Canada exhibits what Paul Axelrod describes as an "educational patchwork, particularly in comparison with the more uniform approaches of other countries" (1997: 126). In nearly all nations, however, competing demands for more co-ordinated educational planning, national standards, and consistency across jurisdictions coexist with competing reforms seeking greater responsiveness and accountability to local concerns (Manzer, 1994).

Provincial and territorial governments in Canada have the authority to create legislation and guidelines that outline virtually all aspects of the education system, including how it is organized, the school-year length, curriculum and graduation requirements, teacher qualifications and certification, and educational funding. The specific details related to setting and carrying out educational policies and operating schools normally are delegated to elected local school boards or similar regional bodies.

In recent years almost all provinces and territories have begun to propose and initiate significant changes to the ways in which education is organized and administered, particularly at the school board or district level. Since the early 1990s, for instance, many provinces (Newfoundland and Labrador, Quebec, Alberta, and, for a five-year period, New Brunswick) have cut the number of school boards by more than half, while new bodies, including parents' advisory councils, have been established to replace or supplement school boards' roles in these and other jurisdictions (Council of Ministers of Education Canada, 2001).

Public education at elementary, secondary, and post-secondary levels have experienced significant financial changes since the early 1990s. Total educational expenditures in Canada dropped by more than $760 million between 1995 and 1996, with an overall decrease from 8 to 7 per cent of the nation's gross domestic product (GDP, or total expenditures) between 1992 and 1996 (Statistics Canada, 2002a: 49). Since the mid-1990s, renewed levels of educational spending have become more selective or targeted in nature. Selected educational priority areas, such as materials, innovation, and training related to new technologies, have expanded, whereas other areas have languished. Figure 11.2 shows that provincial and territorial governments are the predominant source of education funding in Canada but that there is growing reliance on private and individual sources.

These fiscal trends have placed burdens of higher costs on students and others who have come to be defined as "educational consumers." Educational inequalities increase when students from less privileged backgrounds cannot afford to enrol and remain in advanced educational programs. Post-secondary tuition fees doubled during the 1990s and have continued to grow dramatically. Increases in the numbers of students incurring student debt and in the extent of student debt loads have accompanied rising costs of education and living expenses (Bouchard and Zhao, 2000).

Similarly, elementary and secondary schools more often are forced to choose among having to pay higher costs, fundraising to cover educational expenses, and cutting school programs and services. An advocacy group in Ontario has expressed concern about what it views as the "growing gap between the 'have' and 'have-not' schools" following changes to the school funding formula in that province. Among their findings from responses from 841 schools are the following:

- Fifty-two per cent of schools said that they raise funds for classroom supplies, up from 31 per cent in 1997.
- Twenty-four per cent of schools raise funds for textbooks, up from 21 per cent in 1997.
- Sixty-two per cent of schools say they raise funds for library books, compared to 56 per cent in 1997. (L. Brown, 2002: A26)

Educational funding decisions are accompanied by growing concern over the extent to which educa-

Figure 11.2  **Total Educational Spending in Canada, by Direct Source of Funds**

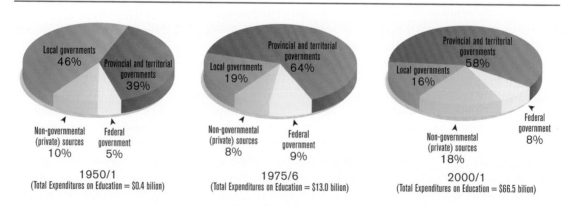

SOURCES: Based on data from Statistics Canada, *Historical Compendium of Education Statistics: From Confederation to 1975* (Ottawa: Statistics Canada, 1978); Statistics Canada, *Advance Statistics of Education* (Ottawa: Statistics Canada, annual); and Statistics Canada, *Education Quarterly Review* (2002), 8: 3.

tion systems are able to prepare learners for contemporary economic and social conditions. There are competing viewpoints (often expressed through concerns about educational quality and excellence) about what role governments should play within this changing environment.

Neo-conservative critics have advocated for governments and the services they deliver, including education, to operate more like businesses guided by market principles. High-quality education is defined in terms of the excellence of educational "products," measured by such things as standardized test scores, parental choice, and public accountability. Parents and learners are commonly viewed, in this way, as "consumers" who should have the opportunity to approach education with the tools to make personal choices about the kinds of schooling they desire (like decision-making about other purchases, with the added importance that it is their children and not some material object that is of concern).

These criticisms have had some impact on education systems, particularly as governments look for ways to restrict expenditures and reorganize public services. Some observers view the recent directions in educational reform as a dangerous shift in public priorities to serve the needs of vocal interest groups who are more concerned with preserving the narrow interests of their own families or groups rather than a commitment to community participation and high-quality education (Osborne, 1999). Matters of educational quality, accountability, and choice are often framed by a focus on a limited number of factors that can be measured in quantifiable terms, such as standardized test results. These kinds of indicators, and the manner in which they are interpreted, can be misleading when they do not account for the full range of activities and competencies encompassed by schooling. Ironically, many reforms that claim to increase educational "choice," public accountability, and decentralization of educational decision-making have the effect, in fact, of concentrating control over such matters as finance, curriculum, and provincial testing at the provincial or territorial level or in central bodies outside of formal education systems (Gidney, 1999; Kachur and Harrison, 1999).

## Education, Work, and Family

Changes in the nature and composition of learners' families and the varied demands from workplaces for particular kinds of qualified labour-force participants

have made it even more crucial to understand how education systems interact with other institutions.

Children and their parents undergo substantial stress as they experience family breakdown, economic crises induced by job layoffs or persistent poverty, or difficulties in securing adequate child-care arrangements. Family, work, and community responsibilities create multiple demands on both children's and parents' time, making it difficult for them to provide strong support for schools' learning and extracurricular activities that rely on extensive student–parent interaction. Tensions often spill over from one site of social life to another, expressed in public concern over phenomena such as bullying, violence, gang warfare, and "risk" among children and youth. Unfortunately, these issues frequently are viewed or reported in a highly sensationalist way that distorts the true nature of childhood and youth activity and that ignores the strong motivations and positive contributions to leadership and mutual support prevalent among much of the student population.

Students, teachers, and educational environments face additional stresses through the growing general emphasis on education as an entry point to subsequent occupational and economic success. Taking their cue from the market model of education, many parents view their children's education as an investment, making significant demands on their children (in order to guarantee high performance) and on teachers and educational administrators (in order to deliver a high-quality product that will yield the best results in the marketplace). Parents and community members from diverse backgrounds have divergent expectations about the way education should be organized and delivered. Some immigrants, for instance, may feel the Canadian education system is too unstructured and undemanding in comparison with the systems they were familiar with prior to arriving in Canada, while others take the opposite view (Campey, 2002). Aboriginal people look to schools to reconcile their needs to prepare youth for a meaningful place in global society with those to make strong connections with indigenous people, their cultural heritage, and their contemporary circumstances (Royal Commission on Aboriginal People, 1996).

## Education and New Technologies

Education, like other institutions, has been significantly affected by the introduction of computers and other new technologies. Information technology, in a few cases, has indeed revolutionized education. Some institutions have replaced traditional instructional settings with fully wired teaching/learning centres in which participants can not only communicate with each other, but also draw upon material and interact with individuals on a global basis (Gergen, 2001). Schools in remote regions have gained access to varied learning resources and connections through the Internet and through initiatives such as SchoolNet, which aims to provide Web-based learning resources to all Canadian schools. Adults can subscribe to an unprecedented range of continuing and post-secondary study options. Schools and universities are just beginning to explore fully the opportunities that new technologies are making available to them (even though the World Wide Web was originally developed, in part, as a tool that could be used to produce and share new knowledge among university-based researchers).

New technologies and their use in and impact on education give rise to several important questions. Levin and Riffel, reviewing alternative perspectives on the role that new technologies play in school settings, conclude that "it may be that technology is not living up to its promise because it has been seen as an answer to rather than a reason to ask questions about the purposes of schools and the nature of teaching and learning" (1997: 114). Two issues are especially critical in this respect.

First, a significant "digital divide" separates those who have access to computers and electronic connections—and the skills and know-how to use and take advantage of new technologies—and those who do not. This divide is most commonly posed in global terms, distinguishing richer, more technologically developed nations, such as those in North America, Europe, parts of Southeast Asia, and Australia and New Zealand, from developing nations in Asia, Africa, and Latin and South America. Canada, in this regard, is in a highly favourable situation in comparison to all, or nearly all, other nations, with one of the highest proportions of its population who use and own computers and employ Internet connections at home and at work. However, even within regions and nations, regular access to computers and the ability to employ them regularly at higher levels depend on such factors as a steady job, income and education levels, gender, social class, and racial characteristics (see Figure 11.3).

Issues related to the adoption of computer technologies in education reflect more enduring concerns about the relationship between what happens in the classroom and structures and processes outside of schooling. Educational practices are strongly influenced by social, technological, and economic developments and innovations, though they also have their own peculiarities and rhythms. Demands for education to prepare people for the changing workplace sit side by side with parallel demands for producing better citizens as well as individuals with the multiple competencies needed to function in a global society.

## Educational Opportunities and Inequalities

Questions about the relationship of education with social inequality and opportunity structures have long been central to the sociological study of education. This is due, in large part, to public expectations about education's contributions to social and economic advancement in post-industrial or knowledge-based societies. Despite compelling evidence that much of this promise has been fulfilled, significant inequalities persist in educational experiences and outcomes.

Differences between groups are apparent within the significant increases in levels and rates of educational participation and attainment across the population as a whole. One of the most striking trends within the general pattern of educational growth has been the strong advancement of educational opportunities for women, particularly in post-secondary education. With respect to the increase in overall education levels during the period between 1951 and 1991, Neil Guppy and Scott Davies point to two key trends related to gender: "First, at the low end of the educational distribution, men remained less likely than women to complete at least Grade 9 and this difference did not narrow over the 40-year interval. Second, at higher education levels, women have surpassed the lead that men clearly held in 1951" (1998: 87). Among persons most likely to have completed their education recently, the proportion of the population in the 20- to 29-year-old age cohort with a post-secondary degree or diploma increased from 37 per cent for both men and women in 1981 to 51 per cent for women and only 42 per cent for men in 1996 (Statistics Canada, 1998b: 1). By 1999, nearly three out of five (57.6 per cent) of all persons who received university degrees were women, although the reverse was true at the highest end, where 61 per cent of Ph.D.s were awarded to men (based on Statistics Canada, 2002a: 43; see also Table 11.3).

The shift in the gender balance of educational attainment has drawn attention to other aspects of

Figure 11.3 **Internet Home Access Among Households by Income Level**

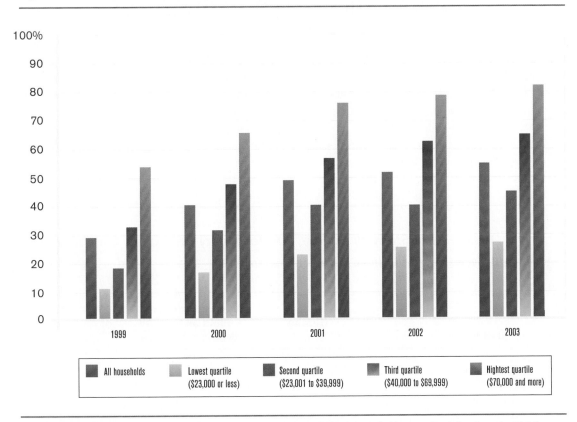

SOURCE: Adapted from Statistics Canada, *Internet Use in Canada* (56F0003XIE). (Ottawa: Statistics Canada, 2004). Available at <http://www.statcan.ca/english/freepub/56F003XIE/index.htm>, accessed 29 December 2004.

education. Findings from numerous surveys that girls have begun to outperform boys on a number of indicators have generated controversy over suggestions that gender inequality has reversed to the point that the education system is now "failing" boys. For example, the comprehensive Programme for International Student Assessment (PISA), conducted in 2000 to compare student performance in core areas, posed a concern for policy-makers that girls in Canada and the 31 other participating nations consistently demonstrated stronger test outcomes in reading (Bussière et al., 2001). However, the PISA findings also demonstrate the complex nature of gender inequalities in education. Few pronounced gender differences appear in performance in areas of mathematics and science. Moreover, the survey highlights how similarities and differences based on gender cannot be understood without reference to a broad array of other family, school, and individual characteristics, notably family socio-economic background (Bussière et al., 2001).

Many gender-related differences are obscured through simple comparisons between boys' and girls' test results (Epstein et al., 1997). Women outnumber men in post-secondary enrolment and graduation, but there are strong gender differences in fields of study and types of training programs (see Table 11.3). Programs in areas such as business, management, and commerce, some arts and social sciences, protection and correction services, and languages are relatively popular among both men and women. Women are much more heavily concentrated in a few fields such as education, nursing, and social work or social services. Men tend to be more widely dispersed over more fields but outnumber women considerably in areas such as engineering and electrical technologies, computer science, and primary industries.

Differences in fields of study reflect a combination of personal choices and circumstances, institutional characteristics (such as cues or levels of comfort and discomfort that direct students into some areas and away from others or the compatibility between particular programs and responsibilities to care for dependent children), and broader socio-economic factors (Statistics Canada, 1998b; Wotherspoon, 2000). Employment options and life pathways are generally associated with the kinds of education and credentials that people attain. Nonetheless, rising levels of education do not always translate fully into gains in labour market positions, incomes, and other equitable outcomes for women (Kenway et al., 1998).

As is the case with gender comparisons, educational differences between racial and ethnic groups appear to have disappeared or diminished significantly in recent decades (Guppy and Davies, 1998).

Immigration policies have simultaneously emphasized the recruitment of immigrants with high educational credentials and made Canada less dependent on immigrants from Western Europe and the United States. These policies have contributed to a growing proportion of highly educated or professionally qualified visible-minority immigrants who place a high value on their children's educational advancement. Racial diversity has been accompanied by increasing sensitivity to the impact of racial discrimination and other mechanisms that historically have excluded or discouraged racial minority students from advancing through the Canadian education system.

Table 11.3 **Top Fields of Study by Gender, Postsecondary Graduates, Canada**

**Community College Diplomas Granted in Career Programs, 1997–8[a]**

*Women*

| Rank | Field of Study | Number of Graduates | Women Graduates in Field as % of All Women Graduates | Women as % of All Graduates in Field |
|---|---|---|---|---|
| 1 | Management and administration | 9,198 | 17.4 | 62.3 |
| 2 | Social services | 5,271 | 10.0 | 86.7 |
| 3 | Nursing | 4,952 | 9.4 | 88.0 |
| 4 | Secretarial science | 4,471 | 8.5 | 93.0 |
| 5 | Arts | 4,365 | 8.3 | 58.4 |
| 6 | Health-related technologies | 4,156 | 7.9 | 77.5 |
| 7 | Educational and counselling services | 3,665 | 6.9 | 93.3 |
| 8 | Protection and correction services | 2,233 | 4.2 | 48.8 |
| 9 | Arts and sciences | 1,966 | 3.7 | 58.7 |
| 10 | Computer science and mathematics | 1,748 | 3.3 | 32.0 |
| **Total Women Graduates** | | **52,909** | **79.4** | **57.9** |

*Men*

| Rank | Field of Study | Number of Graduates | Men Graduates in Field as % of All Men Graduates | Men as % of All Graduates in Field |
|---|---|---|---|---|
| 1 | Management and administration | 5,566 | 14.5 | 37.7 |
| 2 | Computer science and mathematics | 3,718 | 9.7 | 68.0 |
| 3 | Electrical/electronic technologies | 3,542 | 9.2 | 92.8 |
| 4 | Arts | 3,109 | 8.1 | 41.6 |
| 5 | Protection and correction services | 2,341 | 6.1 | 51.2 |
| 6 | Arts and sciences | 1,384 | 3.6 | 41.3 |
| 7 | Merchandising and sales | 1,364 | 3.5 | 47.3 |
| 8 | Health-related technologies | 1,210 | 3.1 | 22.5 |
| 9 | Environmental and conservation technologies | 1,079 | 2.9 | 61.0 |
| 10 | Primary industries | 894 | 2.3 | 81.1 |
| **Total Men Graduates** | | **38,450** | **63.0** | **42.1** |

*(continued)*

Table 11.3  **(cont.)**

**University Bachelor's and First Professional Degrees, 1998**

*Women*

| Rank | Field of Study | Number of Graduates | Women Graduates in Field as % of All Women Graduates | Women as % of All Graduates in Field |
|---|---|---|---|---|
| 1 | Education | 11,435 | 15.5 | 74.2 |
| 2 | Business, management, and commerce | 7,045 | 9.6 | 48.5 |
| 3 | Psychology | 6,756 | 9.2 | 78.0 |
| 4 | Languages | 5,595 | 7.6 | 75.5 |
| 5 | Sociology | 4,290 | 5.8 | 76.0 |
| 6 | Biology | 3,834 | 5.2 | 60.4 |
| 7 | Nursing | 3,084 | 4.2 | 93.0 |
| 8 | Physical education | 2,244 | 3.0 | 56.7 |
| 9 | Social work | 2,096 | 2.8 | 84.9 |
| 10 | Law | 1,830 | 2.5 | 52.4 |
| | **Total Women Graduates** | **73,593** | **65.5** | **58.9** |

*Men*

| Rank | Field of Study | Number of Graduates | Men Graduates in Field as % of All Men Graduates | Men as % of All Graduates in Field |
|---|---|---|---|---|
| 1 | Business, management, and commerce | 7,466 | 14.6 | 51.5 |
| 2 | Engineering | 6,598 | 12.9 | 80.1 |
| 3 | Education | 3,983 | 7.8 | 25.8 |
| 4 | Computer science | 2,530 | 4.9 | 79.4 |
| 5 | Biology | 2,515 | 4.9 | 39.6 |
| 6 | Economics | 1,930 | 3.8 | 60.2 |
| 7 | Psychology | 1,900 | 3.7 | 22.0 |
| 8 | Languages | 1,818 | 3.5 | 24.5 |
| 9 | Physical education | 1,712 | 3.3 | 43.3 |
| 10 | History | 1,686 | 3.3 | 51.2 |
| | **Total Men Graduates** | **51,268** | **62.7** | **41.1** |

[a] Figures have been rounded.
SOURCE: Data derived from Statistics Canada, *Education in Canada, 2000* (Ottawa: Statistics Canada, 2001), 126–46.

Nonetheless, as in the case of gender inequalities, much of the analysis of racial and ethnic inequality in education points to a complex series of factors and interactions that do not lead to any straightforward conclusions. The short answer to the question of whether some groups are advantaged or disadvantaged in relation to racial and ethnic criteria is, "It depends." Guppy and Davies (1998), in common with many other commentators who have reviewed census data and education indicators over time, observe that Canadians in most categories (based on gender, race, region, age, class, and other factors) have benefited from the expansion of education systems. However, specific groups, including Aboriginal people, those from working-class backgrounds, francophones within Quebec, Portuguese Canadians, and the disabled, continue to face strong disadvantages relative to most other groups. Social class has a strong impact on post-secondary attendance and educational attainment. These general trends are compounded by considerable variation in educational success and attainment within groups.

Research on education for Aboriginal people is instructive in this regard. Many significant initiatives have been undertaken as researchers, policy-makers, and educators have come to acknowledge the combined impact of significant barriers to educational advancement faced by Aboriginal people. Education has long been regarded by Aboriginal people, as for any other group, as an important vehicle for gaining meaningful employment and social participation.

Many First Nations, for instance, expressed their desire in the treaty-making process in the nineteenth century to have access to formal education in order to keep pace with contemporary social and economic demands.

However, subsequent developments, including the legacy of frequently destructive residential schooling, lack of acceptance or discriminatory treatment in provincial schools, and other social, cultural, and eco-

11.2

# Human Diversity
## Education for Canada's Aboriginal People

The educational experiences of Aboriginal people in Canada are instructive for an understanding of how education can both advance and restrict social and economic opportunities. Historical practices and inequities have contributed to a legacy of widespread failure, marginalization, and mistrust, but considerable optimism also accompanies many new initiatives.

Many Aboriginal people in the late nineteenth century looked to schooling as a way to ensure integration into contemporary societies. Tragically, while some education-related treaty promises were fulfilled, the residential school system and continuing problems with other forms of educational delivery had devastating consequences that many Aboriginal communities and their members are still struggling to cope with. The report of the Royal Commission on Aboriginal Peoples (1996) endorsed the long-standing principle of First Nations control over education along with other measures to ensure that all educational institutions would provide more receptive schooling for Aboriginal people.

Mixed results have been accomplished so far, as one of the co-chairs of the Royal Commission has observed:

Considering the primary importance of children in aboriginal cultures, it is not surprising that education was one of the first sectors where aboriginal nations and communities are now administered locally, and where possible they incorporate aboriginal languages and cultural content in the curriculum. . . .

More young people are staying in school to complete a high-school diploma, though a gap still exists between graduation rates of aboriginal and non-aboriginal people. . . . Aboriginal youth are especially vulnerable. They are less likely than mature adults to have attained academic and vocational credentials and they are hardest hit by unemployment. (Erasmus, 2002: F6–7)

The accomplishment of educational improvement is a difficult one in the context of considerable diversity among Aboriginal populations and their educational options, aspirations, and circumstances. Some successful schools or programs, for instance, have developed strong foundations in Aboriginal cultures and indigenous knowledge systems, while others have been more concerned to provide services oriented to students' immediate needs and future plans. Marlene Brant Castellano, Lynne Davis, and Louise Lahache, reviewing recent trends, conclude that

the promise of education is that it will enable Aboriginal people to sustain well-being while meeting their responsibilities in the circle of life. Those responsibilities are seen to reach further today than in any previous generation. Fulfilling the promise will require preparing successive generations to participate fully in their own communities and to assume their place as Aboriginal citizens and peoples in global society. (2000: 255) nomic factors, have left Aboriginal people's overall education levels (especially for Registered Indians who live on reserve) well below national levels (Schissel and Wotherspoon, 2003). Data from the 1996 census reveal that "despite general improvements in educational attainment, Aboriginal people in [the 20- to 29-year-old] age group remained only one-half as likely to have a post-secondary degree or diploma, one-fifth as likely to have graduated from university and over twice as likely not to have completed high school" (Statistics Canada, 1998b: 7).

Sociologists and other researchers have identified numerous factors, such as cultural differences, lack of individual motivation and family or community support, and social and educational discrimination, to explain these educational inequalities. In fact, a complex chain of interrelated cause-and-effect mechanisms is usually involved. Increasing attention has been paid to the importance of early childhood development and to the family and social environments in which children are raised for the development of literacy and language skills, thinking processes, and other capacities that are central to educational success. These conditions, in turn, depend on the

socio-economic circumstances of parents, the availability of support networks in the home and community, labour market opportunities for parents and students coming out of the education system, the extent to which people in particular communities or regions have access to high-quality educational programs and services, and numerous other factors. There are strong associations between social class or socio-economic background and educational attainment. Parents' education levels and household income are strong predictors, both independently and in combination with one another, of the likelihood that a person will continue into post-secondary education (Knighton and Mirza, 2002).

Educational institutions are implicated in these broader processes in several ways. Schooling makes a difference in such ways as how well institutions are equipped to deal with students from diverse cultural and social backgrounds; the kinds of relationships that prevail between and among teachers, parents, and students; curricular objectives and materials; standards for assessing and evaluating students; and the general social climate within educational institutions. Social class and cultural differences are evident, for instance,

Historical developments, including the often damaging legacy of residential schooling, lack of acceptance or discriminatory treatment in provincial schools, and other social, cultural, and economic factors, have left Aboriginal people's overall education levels well below national levels. In February 2003, the *Globe and Mail* reported that Ottawa would make $35 million available over the next two years for issues such as stopping the high turnover among teachers in some First Nations schools. (Patti Gower/*Globe and Mail*)

in the grouping and streaming of students into specific educational programs that contribute, in turn, to diverse educational pathways.

## Conclusion

We have examined several dimensions of education and their relevance for sociological inquiry. The phenomenal growth of formal systems of education since the nineteenth century and the accompanying increases in general levels of education throughout the population are linked to a strong degree of public faith in the ability of education to contribute simultaneously to individual development and to address social needs for knowledge, innovation, and credentials. Educational growth, processes, and outcomes are being studied from four major theoretical perspectives: (1) structural functionalism, which analyzes education in terms of its contributions to dominant social and economic requirements; (2) symbolic interactionism and microsociology, which highlight the roles and interactions of various participants within educational processes; (3) conflict theories, which emphasize education's contributions to social inequality and power relations; and (4) feminist theories, which stress gender-based educational differences. The significance of formal schooling to the experiences and social and economic opportunities of different social groups is changing, particularly with respect to gender, race and ethnicity, and social class. All groups have benefited from educational expansion, though in varying degrees. Adequate sociological analysis of education requires an ability to integrate an understanding of what happens in and as a result of formal education with the social context in which education is situated.

## ☐ Questions for Critical Thought

1. Why is education in most nations organized formally through schools and related institutional structures rather than through some other arrangement, such as families or community-based agencies? To what extent should education be a private as opposed to a public responsibility?
2. Explain how and why employers and other agencies have come to rely on formal educational credentials or qualifications as legitimate mechanisms to determine applicants' eligibility for positions in their organizations.
3. Compare and contrast schooling (formal education) with other major social institutions, including businesses, families, prisons, and religious organizations. Describe and explain the major similarities and differences.
4. What is the impact of emerging emphases on lifelong learning and the new economy on education systems? Explain and critically discuss the changes (or lack of change) you have identified.
5. What factors account for the rising levels of education in Canada and other, similar nations? Discuss and explain the extent to which increasing levels of education are required to perform essential tasks associated with new technologies and information systems in a global economic framework.
6. Discuss the extent to which education is, and should be, organized in the interests of the communities in which educational institutions are located as opposed to interests shaped by national and global concerns. Illustrate this with reference to your own educational experiences.
7. To what extent has education in Canada fulfilled its promise to provide greater opportunities for social and economic advancement to all social groups? Explain your response with reference to at least three different theoretical frameworks.
8. Discuss the relative impact that particular social groups or forces (including students, teachers, administrators, parents, policy-makers, and selected interest groups) have had on educational decision-making and processes. To what extent are the arrangements you describe satisfactory, and to what extent should they be changed? Justify and explain your answer.

## ☐ Recommended Readings

**Madeleine Arnot, Miriam David, and Gaby Weiner,** *Closing the Gender Gap: Postwar Education and Social Change* **(Cambridge, UK: Polity, 1999).**

> This book highlights the closing and apparent reversal of the gender gap in education, detailing the processes by which girls' and boys' educational experiences and outcomes have changed in recent decades.

**Sandro Contenta,** *Rituals of Failure: What Schools Really Teach* **(Toronto: Between the Lines, 1993).**

> Contenta discusses how schools' hidden curricula both restrict future prospects for many students and limit the extent to which true education is accomplished through schooling.

**Neil Guppy and Scott Davies,** *Education in Canada: Recent Trends and Future Challenges* **(Ottawa: Statistics Canada, 1998).**

> This book analyzes census data for a comprehensive overview of major trends and indicators in education and related areas, and presents a concise discussion of the relevant literature employed to interpret and explain the findings.

**A.H. Halsey, Hugh Lauder, Phillip Brown, and Amy Stuart Wells, eds,** *Education: Culture, Economy, and Society* **(New York: Oxford University Press, 1997).**

> This is one of the most comprehensive collections of analyses of education from various perspectives in sociology and other disciplines, containing influential chapters from different national settings.

**Terry Wotherspoon,** *The Sociology of Education in Canada: Critical Perspectives* **(Toronto: Oxford University Press, 1998).**

> Various dimensions of Canadian education are explored from a critical orientation that emphasizes inequalities based on class, race, gender, region, and other factors.

## ☐ Recommended Web Sites

**Educational Resources Information Center (ERIC)**
**www.eric.ed.gov**

> The ERIC database is a comprehensive collection of information (mostly abstracts of journal articles and reports) on various aspects of and fields related to education, including sociology of education. It is a valuable reference tool and starting point for research into both contemporary and historical educational issues.

**Sociology of Education Section, American Sociology Association:**
**www.asanet.org/soe**

> This site is directed primarily to professionals and researchers engaged in the field. However, it contains a summary description of the sociology of education and emerging issues and many useful links to other databases and relevant sites.

# 12

Pamela Sugiman

> > >

# Work and
the Economy

© PhotoDisc, Inc.

## ☐ Learning Objectives

In this chapter, you will:

- come to understand the different types of paid and unpaid work that people carry out in this society

- examine the different ways in which work has been socially organized by employers

- be introduced to some of the main concepts used in the sociological analysis of work

- learn some of the recent trends in employment

- discover how workers experience work and sometimes resist management control

- recognize the impact of the new flexibility strategies on workers who are located differently in a society stratified by race, gender, and class

## Introduction

Most of us will spend the better part of our lives working, because work is central to our economic well-being. Work is also a social product and, as such, it is subject to **negotiation** and change by human actors. And it matters to us individually: people seek meaning in the work that they perform—there is a close relationship between work, life, and **identity**.

In recent years, some social commentators have predicted the demise of work. In this view, people will invest more time in leisure activities and will be shaped primarily by their relationship to the consumer economy. But try to imagine a life without work. What would it be like if you never held a job? Unless you were incredibly wealthy, unable to work as a result of disability or poor health, or willing (or forced) to live on social assistance or handouts on the street, it is unlikely that you could live without work. Most of us will spend the bulk of our days working; the majority will work for someone else, on another's terms. A recognition of the strong link between work and life calls for a critical examination of the world of work.

Most Canadians view the work they do as a given. Work is something that we either have or do not have (Gorz, 1999), that we must prepare ourselves for, that we must escape at the end of a day or the end of a career. Discussions of work, therefore, tend to revolve around a specific, narrowly circumscribed set of concerns, namely, job growth, unemployment, and job-related training (Lowe, 2000). But just as we need to face up to the fact that work is what we will do for the good part of our lives, it is also important to understand that there is nothing inevitable about the way in which work is presently organized. Work is a social product. The way work is structured, the nature of jobs, the rewards of work—these are all the products of **social relationships** between different groups of people. As such, over time and across cultures, work has taken varied forms.

Although most of us work in order to survive and to live comfortably, we also work for more than mere economic survival or comfort of living. Sociologist Graham Lowe (2000) highlights the importance of moving discussions of the quantity of work (unemployment statistics, job counts, and work hours) to its quality. After all, the quality of work matters to workers, young and old. According to Workplace 2000, this country's first national work-ethic study, when

Canadian workers were asked what they would do if they won a million dollars, only 17 per cent said that they would quit their jobs and never work again; 41 per cent of respondents claimed that they would remain in their current job, 17 per cent would embark on a different career, and 24 per cent would start their own business (Lowe, 2000: 52). Canadians still have a strong attachment to work.

To understand work fully, we need to consider the wider economy in which it is situated. We may define the *economy* as a social institution in which people carry out the production, distribution, and consumption of goods and services. Discussions of the economy are sometimes presented in an inaccessible language that easily mystifies those untrained in the discipline. Talk of gross domestic product, gross national product, inflation, and recession can be confusing. Yet it is critical that we understand how economic systems function because they have a direct bearing on how we live. The economy and our location in it shapes, for instance, the quality of health care, housing, diet and nutrition, consumer spending, and lifestyle. The economic system is, furthermore, linked to a nation's political system, to people's conceptions of democracy and citizenship, and to general measures of success and failure.

## World Economic Systems

Economic systems are not abstract entities. They are structured and contested, shaped and reshaped, by the people who inhabit them. They further reflect relations of **power** and inequality. In Canada, we presently live in a society based on a system of **capitalism**. As such, there are blatant as well as subtle manifestations of inequality. We observe extremes of wealth and poverty every day. A businessman rushing to pick up a $1,500 suit from Holt Renfrew walks quickly past a homeless person squatting on the corner. A Filipina nanny on a temporary work permit spends her days taking someone's children to Montessori school, piano lessons, and dance class. On her way home, she buys their groceries. At night, she returns, tired, to her small room beside the furnace in the basement of the family's well-appointed home. We live in a society in which economic inequalities are complexly wound up with inequalities based on **gender**, **race**, and **ethnicity**.

## Pre-industrial, Pre-capitalist Societies: Hunting and Gathering

Early human societies rested on a system of production and exchange called *hunting and gathering*. Hunting-and-gathering (also called *foraging*) societies were characterized by a simple *subsistence economy*—relatively small groups of people lived off the land (gathering nuts, berries, and other forms of wild vegetation), hunting game, and, in some cases, fishing. Such societies were characterized by considerable physical mobility as groups would move from one geographic location to another in accordance with the food and water supply. Production among hunter-gatherers was largely for *consumption*, or immediate use. In other words, food gathered would be divided among people and eaten with little excess, or *surplus*. Without the accumulation of surplus, a system of exchange was minimal, and there was no private accumulation of wealth. Hunting-and-gathering societies are thus considered to be among the most egalitarian in human history.

Furthermore, the division of labour among hunter-gatherers was simple, based on sex and age. Women tended to perform gathering activities, often with children in tow, while men hunted. Some anthropologists have argued that this sex-based division of labour did not translate, however, into inequalities between the sexes. While men and women performed different functions, the divisions were not as rigid as they are currently. As well, the work that women performed was not devalued. Indeed, insofar as hunting-and-gathering societies looked largely to vegetation (and not scarce meat) for their dietary needs, women made a greater productive contribution to the maintenance of the group than did men.

## Agricultural Societies

The development of *agriculture* (the breeding of animals, the cultivation of plants, and human settlement) brought about many changes in the social and economic organization of societies. These changes were connected to an increase in productive power, a more dependable and stable food supply, and the accumulation of surplus and establishment of market exchange.

Prior to the nineteenth century, Canada was largely an agricultural society based on a *family economy*: most economic activities were located in or nearby family households. The **household** thus served both as a place of work and as a residence. This type of economy, furthermore, featured a more elaborate division of labour (than in the past) based on age and sex (Nelson and Robinson, 2002). Family survival during this period, though, depended on the interdependent and collective labours of household members. Work was organized according to the market, but also according to nature, seasonal cycles, and personal need.

## Capitalism

Unlike earlier economic systems, capitalism is based on private ownership of the **means of production**, an exchange relationship between owners and workers, an economy driven by the pursuit of profit, and competitive market relations.

In order to understand capitalism, let us turn to the ideas of the social theorist Karl Marx. Marx ([1867] 1967) wrote about the profound changes he observed in nineteenth-century England. He witnessed in England a gradual but dramatic transition from a feudal agricultural society to an industrialized, capitalist economy. Under capitalism, the capitalist class (or **bourgeoisie**) owns the means of production, while the majority of people, the working class (or **proletariat**), does not. *Means of production* is a concept that refers to wealth-generating property, such as land, factories, machines, and the capital needed to produce and distribute goods and services for exchange in a market. While many of us own a car, a computer, or perhaps a house, these items do not constitute the means of production insofar as they are for our personal use only (a place to live, a tool for writing your research papers) and not for the production of wealth.

In a capitalist society, furthermore, capitalists and workers are engaged in a relationship of unequal exchange. As workers do not own the means of production, they have no choice but to sell their labour to a capitalist employer in exchange for a wage. Working people are forced into this relationship because in this type of economy, it is almost impossible to survive without money. One can try to feed a family with the produce of a home vegetable garden, wear homemade clothes, and live without electricity, but at some point it is necessary to purchase market goods and services. For example, you will need to buy fabric, sewing needles, seeds, and a plot of land.

The capitalist class organizes production (work) with the specific goal of maximizing profits for personal wealth. For this reason, it structures work in the most efficient way imaginable, pays workers the lowest possible wages, and extracts the greatest amount of labour from the worker within a working day. And, lastly, capitalism is based on a freely competitive market system and therefore a *laissez-faire* ("hands-off") government. Under capitalism, the market forces of supply and demand are supposed to determine the production and distribution of goods and services, with no government interference.

## Capitalism and Industrialization

People sometimes use the terms *capitalism* and *industrial society* interchangeably. However, conceptually, they are distinct. While *capitalism* is a broad economic system, *industrialization* refers to a more specific process that has consequences for the nature and organization of work as well as for the division of labour.

In Canada, as in England, industrialization resulted in a transformation of capitalist production. The rise of industrial capitalism in the late nineteenth and early twentieth centuries constituted one of the most fundamental changes in our society. Industrialization involved the introduction of new forms of energy (steam, electricity) and of transportation (railroads), **urbanization**, and implementation of new machine technology, all of which contributed to the rise of the factory system of production and the manufacture and mass production of goods. These changes greatly facilitated and heightened capitalist production. As well, and in profound ways, they have shaped how people have worked and organized their lives.

The proliferation of factories led to the movement of work from homes and small artisanal workshops to larger, more impersonal sites, to the concentration of larger groups of workers under one roof, and to the introduction of *time discipline* (by the clock), in addition to the more specialized division of labour.

This displacement of work, furthermore, removed men from the home and family. While single women were employed in some textile factories, married women were prohibited from most factory jobs. Many women thus continued to work in the home or were employed as domestics in private households, took in boarders, or did other people's laundry in exchange for a small cash sum (Bradbury, 1993). These changes in the economy had far-reaching consequences for the construction of femininity, masculinity, marriage, and family life.

During the period of industrial capitalism economic inequalities became increasingly visible and conflict between classes grew. While successful cap-

italists made huge amounts of money, working-class men toiled in factories or mines for a pittance, women combined long hours of domestic drudgery with sporadic income-generating activities, and children were sent off to work in factories or domestic work. Many people lived in poverty and misery.

## Family Capitalism

In the mid- to late nineteenth century, industrial capitalism was in its early stages. Throughout this period, a small number of individuals and families owned and controlled most of the country's wealth—its major companies and financial institutions. Because wealth accrued from business enterprises was `passed on within families, from generation to generation (for example, the Fords and Rockefellers in the United States and the Eatons and Seagrams in Canada), this era is aptly termed that of *family capitalism*.

## Corporate Capitalism

The subsequent phase of economic development, occurring in the late nineteenth to mid-twentieth centuries, is called *corporate* (or *monopoly*) *capitalism*. This phase witnessed the movement of ownership from individuals and families to modern corporations (and their shareholders). A *corporation* is defined as a legal entity distinct from the people who own and control it. As an entity legally equivalent to a "person," the corporation itself may enter into contracts and own property. This separation of enterprise from individuals has served to protect owners and chief executives from personal liability and from any debts incurred by the corporation. It also is protected from many sorts of reprisals because it possesses rights and freedoms similar to those of individuals.

Insofar as the Canadian economy has traditionally been resource intensive, many of the corporations that have dominated our industrial development have been American-owned. Consequently, Canadians have witnessed the establishment of numerous branch plants of companies whose head offices are located in the United States (for example, IBM Canada and GM Canada). This position of subordination has raised important concerns about our political sovereignty, our culture, and our distinctiveness as a people and a nation.

Under corporate capitalism, furthermore, there has been a growing concentration of economic power (that is, power in the hands of a few large corporations). One way in which capitalists have increased their economic power is through mergers. By merging, large corporations have been able to create situations of monopoly and oligopoly. A corporation has a *monopoly* when it has exclusive control over the market. Obviously, this situation is undesirable for consumers, as it restricts their market "choices." The Canadian government has implemented certain controls to curb the monopolization of an industry.

An *oligopoly* is the control of an industry by several companies. The insurance, newspaper, and entertainment industries are characterized by oligopolistic control. Increased revenue by way of mergers and acquisitions is obviously desirable to corporate owners but may occur at the expense of industrial development and employment. In 1996, profits of the top 500 firms internationally increased by 25.1 per cent, while assets grew by 3.5 per cent and the number of employees grew by a mere 1.1 per cent (International Labour Organization, n.d.). (See also Table 12.1.)

### Welfare Capitalism

In the real world, of course, examples of pure capitalism and pure socialism cannot be found. In Canada, as well as in parts of Western Europe, the economy is market-based while government intervenes in the form of regulations and controls. Economists call this type of system *welfare capitalism*. Under this system, state-sponsored programs such as universal health care and public education address the needs of particular groups of people in the country. Many government controls, such as tax credits for corporations, act in the interest of business.

In our society, the means of production are owned both by private citizens and by governments. In spite of moves towards their **privatization**, we still have a number of *Crown corporations* (businesses owned by the federal or provincial governments)—such as Canada Post, the Canadian Broadcasting Corporation (CBC), and the Canada Mortgage and Housing Corporation (CMHC).

### Socialism

Marx (Marx and Engels, [1848] 1986) believed that in a capitalist society, workers would eventually revolt against their **exploitation**, develop a consciousness of themselves as a class, and overthrow the system of capitalist production, replacing it with a socialist economy. He did not make clear how this revolution was to proceed (except that it would be led by a communist party). In the first stages after victory, workers would establish a "dictatorship of the proletariat" and the economy would be socialized. This would involve the elimination of private property and public ownership of the means of production (in other words, it would give workers control). Once this had been accomplished, **the state** would gradually wither away and socialism would give way to *communism*. Under communism, work would be organized on the basis of a radically different division of labour. In particular, the production and distribution of goods and ser-

### Table 12.1 **The 10 Largest Employers in Canada, 2001**

| Rank | Company (Year End) | Location of Head Office | Number of Employees | Revenue per Employee ($) | Profit per Employee ($) |
|------|--------------------|-------------------------|---------------------|--------------------------|-------------------------|
| 1 | Loblaw Companies (De01) | Toronto | 114,000 | 118,912 | 4,939 |
| 2 | Onex Corp. (De01) | Toronto | 87,300 | 275,968 | 9,141 |
| 3 | Bombardier Inc. (Ja02) | Montreal | 80,000 | 272,555 | 4,886 |
| 4 | BCE Inc. (De01) | Montreal | 75,000 | 343,947 | 6,973 |
| 5 | Hudson's Bay Co. (Ja02) | Toronto | 71,000 | 105,037 | 1,025 |
| 6 | Magna International (De01)[a] | Aurora, Ont. | 67,000 | 165,985 | 8,657 |
| 7 | Royal Bank of Canada (Oc01) | Toronto | 57,568 | 443,337 | 41,881 |
| 8 | Sears Canada (De01) | Toronto | 56,000 | 120,114 | 1,680 |
| 9 | Quebecor Inc. (De01) | Montreal | 54,000 | 216,254 | −4,476 |
| 10 | Nortel Networks Corp. (De01)[b] | Brampton, Ont. | 52,600 | 324,030 | −521,787 |

[a] Figures reported in $US and annualized in previous 3 through 5 years.
[b] Figures reported in $US.
SOURCE: Excerpted and adapted from "50 Largest Employers," *Globe and Mail Report on Business Magazine* (2002); available at <http://top1000.robmagazine.com/2002/employers/employers.htm>, accessed 29 May 2003. Reprinted with permission from The Globe and Mail.

vices would be in accordance with ability and need within the population, rather than shaped by market forces and the pursuit of profit for individual gain.

Like capitalism, socialism and communism have never existed in a pure form. Many revolutions, successful and not, have been attempted in its name (for example, the Bolshevik revolution in Russia in 1917, China's in 1949, and Cuba's in 1959), but these societies have never reached the vision laid out by Marx. During the 1980s, the Soviet Union experienced a series of economic and political crises that ultimately led to the disintegration of its economic base and political structures. This economic crisis was based on the inability of this form of "command economy" to adapt rapidly to the changing global economy. The last two decades have witnessed the breaking up of the former Soviet empire and attempts by Russia and the various "new" countries, such as Hungary, Czechoslovakia, Poland, Ukraine, Latvia, Estonia, and Lithuania, to make the transition from command economies to capitalist ones, or some variation between the two (Storey, 2002).

According to Robert Storey, "for the present, capitalism seems triumphant. If so, however, given the historical and contemporary inequalities, not to mention capitalism's intimate association with war and environmental degradation, it is a triumph that has many human and natural costs" (2002).

## The Global Economy

Today, economic activity knows no national borders. Most large companies operate in a global context, setting up businesses in Canada, the United States, and various parts of Asia, Africa, and India. These firms may be called *transnational* (or *multinational*) companies. The head offices of transnational corporations are located in one country (often the United States), while production facilities are based in others. We see the products of the global economy everywhere we turn. Look at the clothes you wear, the car you drive, the food you eat. Where are they from? In the course of their assembly, products of the new global economy typically move through many nations.

Clearly, the goal of transnational corporations is profit. Capitalists are rapidly moving beyond national boundaries in an effort to secure the cheapest available labour, low-cost infrastructure (power, water supply, roads, telephone lines), and production unencumbered by health and safety regulations, minimum-wage and hours-of-work laws, maternity provisions, and the like. Unprotected by legislation and typically without union representation, labour in **developing countries** is both cheaper and easier to control than workforces in Canada.

Critics have pointed to the negative cultural, social, and economic consequences of **globalization**. Some argue, for example, that globalization has resulted in a homogenization of **culture**. Media giants AOL Time Warner and Disney, for instance, distribute many of the same cultural products (television shows, films, videos, books) to audiences across the globe. Among many other holdings, AOL Time Warner owns more than 1,000 movie screens outside of the United States and the second largest book publishing business in the world. Admittedly, corporate capitalists of the early twentieth century wielded great power, but the power of transnational firms in the current era is immense. According to Anthony Giddens, "half of the hundred largest economic units in the world today are nations; the other half are transnational corporations" (2000: 315).

Furthermore, global capitalism has had an uneven impact on groups of people both within Canada and around the world. Media exposés of children sewing Nike soccer balls in Pakistani sweatshops for the equivalent of six cents an hour have brought worldwide attention to sweatshop abuses in the garment and sportswear industries. More hidden, says the Maquiladora Solidarity Network, are the teenage girls, often single mothers, who sew clothes in the maquiladora factories of Central America and Mexico for major North American retailers such as Wal-Mart, The Gap, and Northern Reflections (Maquiladora Solidarity Network, 2000). Some of these are 12- and 13-year-olds working illegally, while others, 15- and 16-year-olds, are legal employees. Both groups of young people, however, work 12- to 18-hour days, often without overtime, under unsafe conditions and in the face of physical, verbal, and sometimes sexual abuse.

It is no coincidence that many sweatshop employees are women, and of colour—people who have no choice but to endure these conditions in order to survive. Garment manufacturers in Central America's free trade zones, Mexico's maquiladora factories, and Asia's export processing zones say that they prefer to hire young girls and women because "they have nimble fingers. Workers suspect that children and young people are hired because they are less likely to complain about illegal and unjust conditions. And more importantly, they are less likely to organize unions" (Maquiladora Solidarity Network, 2000). We are seeing the intensification of divisions of labour, globally, along the lines of class, sex, and race.

These developments, furthermore, have direct consequences for the organization of work, and for the collective power of working people in Canada. Many Canadians now work under the constant threat of company relocation to lower-cost areas. And this has resulted in a weakening of the political power of workers and their unions. In light of this threat, many people in Canada have agreed to concessions (that is, giving up past gains) such as pay cuts, loss of vacation pay, and unpaid overtime. In a study of clerical workers employed at a major telecommunications firm, Bonnie Fox and Pamela Sugiman (1999) found that top management relied on television monitors in the employee cafeteria to broadcast warnings that jobs would be lost if the workers did not make special efforts (including concessions) in the interest of the firm's survival. One employee explained, "the axe is falling. People are afraid....They'll do what they need to do to keep their jobs" (Fox and Sugiman, 1999: 79). In the long term, the lingering threat of job loss affects the standard of living in the country as a whole.

# The Capitalist Economy: Where People Work

Most of us contribute to the economy in one way or another. And just as the economy undergoes change throughout history, so too does our relationship to work. With the expansion of some economic sectors and the contraction of others, our opportunities for employment at certain kinds of jobs also change. Social scientists identify four major economic sectors in which people in this country find employment: primary and resource industries, manufacturing, the service sector, and social reproduction.

## Primary Resource Industry

Years ago, most Canadians worked in *primary* (or *resource*) *industry*. It is likely that your grandparents or great-grandparents performed primary-sector work. Though not always for pay, **First Nations** people have had an important history in the resource industry (Knight, 1996). Work in the primary sector involves the extraction of natural resources from our environment. Primary-industry jobs may be found, for instance, in agricultural production (farming, skilled and unskilled agricultural labour), ranching, mining, forestry, hunting, and fishing.

Throughout the eighteenth and nineteenth centuries, the primary sector represented the largest growth area in Canada. However, in the twentieth century, it began a dramatic decline. Many forces have contributed to its contraction, notably the demise of small family farms and small independent fishing businesses, along with a corresponding rise in corporate farming (or "agribusiness") and large fishing enterprises. These developments have resulted in dwindling opportunities for many people. Moreover, because of the geographic concentration of primary-sector jobs, this decline has devastated some towns (for example, Elliot Lake, Ontario) and entire regions (for example, Atlantic Canada) and entire resources (the cod stocks off the eastern seaboard).

## Manufacturing

Into the twentieth century, growing numbers of Canadians began to work in the *manufacturing* (or *secondary*) *sector*. Manufacturing work involves the processing of raw materials into usable goods and services. If you make your living by assembling vans, knitting socks, packing tuna, or piecing together the parts of Barbie dolls, you are employed in manufacturing. Though the popular image of a manufacturing employee is a blue-collar male, the industry's workforce now reveals much more diversity along the lines of sex, race, and ethnicity.

On the whole, the manufacturing sector in Canada has experienced a slower decline than primary industry. The decline in manufacturing began in the early 1950s. In 1951, manufacturing represented 26.5 per cent of employment in Canada, but by 1995, the employment share of manufacturing had been cut nearly in half, to 15.2 per cent (Jackson and Robinson, 2000: 11). Manufacturing continues nonetheless to be an important employer of Canadians. Job losses in manufacturing are largely attributable to technological change and the relocation of work to various low-wage sectors in Mexico, parts of Asia, and the southern United States.

## The Service Sector

In *The End of Work* (1995), Jeremy Rifkin wrote about the relationship between job loss and technological change. Rifkin predicted that technological innovation would result in the loss of a great many jobs (except for an elite group of knowledge workers such as computer technicians and scientists) and would thus constitute an end to work. For various reasons, Rifkin's predictions have not come true. First, many employers prefer to hire dirt-cheap human labour rather than purchase expensive machines. Second, unions have exerted some power

12.1

Nike's presence in China is estimated at 50 contracted factories, manufacturing sneakers and clothing and employing approximately 110,000 workers. Forty percent of Nike's footwear is produced in China. The Sewon factory is a South Korean investment that has produced exclusively for Nike since 1989. Average wages for a worker in a shoe factory in South Korea are US $2.49/hour, or more than twelve times the cost at Sewon. Is it any wonder that Nike produces such a considerable amount of shoes and garments in China?

The New York–based National Labour Committee (NLC) researchers uncovered that working time is excessively long and three factories show evidence of gender and age discrimination. These factories prefer to hire young, single women, specifically stating in job recruitment advertisement that proof of marital status is necessary for the application. One company fires employees at the age of 25 when they become "used up" (exhausted).

Nike's Code of Conduct guarantees that ". . . partners share the best practices and continuous improvement in . . . management practices that recognize the dignity of the individual" and that "there shall be no discrimination based on race, creed, gender, marital or maternity status, religious or political beliefs, age, or sexual orientation." Obviously, on these points, Nike has failed in China.

———

SOURCE: Canadian Labour Congress, "Nike in China," *Sweatshop Alert* (November 2000), 9; available at <www.clc-ctc.ca>, accessed 16 July 2003.

### Nike in China: Five Factories

| Factory | Location | No. of Workers | Wages ($US) | Working Hours | Time Off | Remarks |
|---|---|---|---|---|---|---|
| Sewon | Jiaozhou City, Shandong Prov., Liuhizai Ind. Area | 1,500, mostly women aged 18–25 | Base wage: 20¢/hr | 11- to12-hr shifts, 6 days/wk | 1 day/wk | Sewon would not hire 27 yrs of age |
| Hung Wah & Hung Yip Keng Tau | Huijou City, Guangdong Prov. | 2,000–2,500, mostly women aged 16–32 | Average: 22¢/hr | Peak season: 15-hr shifts, 7 days/wk | 1 day/mo. | Workers never heard of Nike's Code of Conduct; 12/room |
| Keng Tau | Keng Tau Industrial Zone | 1,000–1,200 | 11–36¢/hr | Peak season: 14 hrs/day, 7 days/wk | 1 day/mo. | No overtime premium; 16/room |
| Tong Ji | Chongzhan Prov. | 500 migrant workers | Average: 27¢/hr | 57.5 hrs/wk | 1 day/wk | Nov. 1999: 72.5 hrs/wk |
| Wei Li | Guangdong Prov. | 6,100, mostly women aged 16–25 | Average: 56¢/hr | Normal: 8 hrs/day, 5 days/wk; Peak: 12-hr shift | Normal: 2 days/wk; Peak: 1 day/ 2 wks | Employs only single women; require certificate of marital status |

SOURCE: China Labour Bulletin and National Labour Committee.

in resisting the wholesale implementation of techno-logical change. And third, a massive number of new jobs have been created in the rapidly expanding ser-vice (or tertiary) sector. Study after study demon-strates that employees who lost jobs in manufacturing have been absorbed by the service industry. Indeed, many of you reading this no doubt currently are employed in part-time or temporary service jobs. If so, you are not unlike many Canadians.

In recent years, the service sector has expanded dramatically. From 1951 to 1995, the employment share of this sector more than doubled, from 18 per cent to 37.1 per cent. The rise of the service industry has been linked to the development of a post-indus-trial, information-based economy and to the rise of a strong consumer culture. All of this has resulted in a growing need for people to work in information-processing and management, marketing, advertising, and servicing. In the course of a day, you will encounter dozens of service-sector employees. Airline reservation agents, taxi drivers, teachers and profes-sors, daycare staff, bank employees, computer techni-cians, crossing guards, librarians, garbage collectors, and Starbucks barristas—these all are service workers.

The service sector embraces a wide range of jobs so dissimilar that some people speak of a *polarization of work*. In other words, there are some "good," highly skilled, well-paid jobs at one end of the spectrum and many "bad," poorly paid, dead-end jobs at the other. Jobs in retail trade and food services are at the low end of the hierarchy, while those in finance and busi-ness, health, education, and public administration tend to be at the high end.

The experience of service work is also qualita-tively different from that of manufacturing. Much service employment involves not only the physical performance of a job, but also an emotional compon-ent. In the face of an intensely competitive market, how does a company vie for customers? Service. And service rests on a big smile and artificially personal-ized interactions. In *The Managed Heart* (1983), Arlie Hochschild explored the emotional work of flight attendants. According to Hochschild, emotional labour, typically performed by women, is potentially damaging to workers because it involves regulating one's emotional state, sometimes suppressing feelings and often inventing them.

Also problematic is the frequently tense relation-ship between workers and their bosses. Low-end ser-vice work is characterized by low-trust relationships. With the expectation that their workforces will have only weak loyalties to the company and its goals, man-agers attempt to control employees largely through close direction and surveillance (Tannock, 2001). It is now common practice for employers to use electronic equipment to monitor telephone conversations between employees and clients and to install video security cameras to keep an eye on retail clerks. Another form of surveillance, more common in the United States than Canada, is drug testing (through urinalysis) of prospective employees. Such testing is standard, for example, at Wal-Mart stores (Ehrenreich, 2001). But at the same time that such work is subject to routinization and close surveillance, it necessitates high levels of self-motivation and investment on the part of the workers. In consequence, the most com-mon complaint among workers in low-end service jobs is a high level of stress (Tannock, 2001).

## Social Reproduction

All of the work we have discussed so far is conducted in what social scientists call the *sphere of production*. Production typically occurs in the public world of factory, office, school, and store. Moreover, it involves monetary exchange. The study of work in this coun-try has largely been biased towards production. When we think of work and workers, who comes to mind? Steelworkers, garment workers, plumbers, secretaries, farmers, and lawyers. What is common to all of these occupations? They are all done in exchange for money—a wage, salary, or income.

However, in Canada as well as in other parts of the world, many people spend hours and hours each day doing work that is not officially recorded as part of the economy. This type of labour may be called **social reproduction**. Social reproduction involves a range of activities for which there is no direct eco-nomic exchange. Often, though not always, this work is performed within family households. Typically, it is done by women. We do not view as economic activ-ity the hours women (and less often men) spend buy-ing groceries, planning and cooking meals, washing dishes, folding laundry, chauffeuring children, buying clothes, vacuuming, managing the household budget, caring for aging relatives, supervising homework, and cleaning the toilet bowl. The instrumental value of such activities has long been hidden. Rather than viewed as work, these activities are deemed a labour of love (Luxton, 1980).

But what would happen if women and other fam-ily members no longer performed this labour? How would it get done? Equally important, who would pay for it? If capitalist employers or the state had to ensure that workforces got fed, clothed, nurtured, and counselled, what would be the cost? These kinds of questions perplex economists and social statisticians. Says economist Marilyn Waring, breast-feeding, for example, is "a major reproductive activity carried out only by women, and this thoroughly confuses statisticians' and economists' production models. The reproduction of human life also seems conceptually beyond their rules of imputation. But bodies most certainly have market prices" (1996: 86). In the United States, the cost of reproducing another life ranges from $1,800 for artificial insemination to $36,000 for a surrogate mother to carry the child. This, notes Waring, is the equivalent of $5.35 (US) per hour over a 280-day pregnancy (1996: 86). According to a Canadian estimate, if unpaid work were replaced for pay, it would be worth $275 billion to the Canadian economy (GPI Atlantic, n.d.).

The system of capitalism benefits tremendously from the performance of unpaid labour. Yet the unpaid services of housewives and other family members are not only excluded from traditional economic measures, for many years sociologists did not even consider them to be "work." This is perplexing insofar as such work is essential to basic human survival and to the quality of our lives.

### The Informal Economy

Hidden from official growth figures—as well as from public conscience—is a wide range of economic activities that are not officially reported to the government. These activities make up the **informal** (or *underground*) **economy**. Some are legal; others are not. They include, for example, babysitting, cleaning homes, sewing clothes, peddling watches, playing music on the streets, gambling, and dealing drugs. As you make your way through the downtown areas of most major cities in Canada and the United States and almost anywhere in the developing world, you will see people of all ages trying to eke out a living in the informal sector. The so-called squeegee kids who can be found at congested intersections of Canadian cities are also part of this world of work.

Of course, we do not know the precise size of the underground economy. We have only estimates of its share of officially recognized economies. Here, we see much variation across the globe. In Africa, the informal economy has been estimated to involve 60 to 70 per cent of the labour force and to produce close to one-quarter of the continent's output. According to the International Labour Organization (ILO), the infor-

mal sector absorbs three-quarters of new entrants into the African labour force. In Mexico, beginning in the 1990s, the informal economy was estimated to contribute between 25 and 40 per cent of the country's gross domestic product (GDP), providing work for roughly one-quarter of the economically active population (Kilgour, 1998: 2–3).

There have long been informal economies in most nations. However, this sector has grown in importance, largely because of economic hardship related to restructuring, globalization, and their effects of dislocation and forced migration. Increasingly, people are turning to "hidden work" in order to survive in the midst of contracting opportunities in the formal economy. It has become a safety net of sorts for the poorest groups in society. Without doubt, workers in this sector have had to be enterprising. Some are highly motivated and possess valuable skills; others lack formally recognized credentials. Unfortunately, most people who rely on the informal economy for a living face precarious, unstable "careers" in unregulated environments.

## Managerial Strategies of Control

### Scientific Management

In order to assess the new world of work, it is important first to understand the old one. So let us briefly go back in time. Since the days when Marx observed the rise of the factory system, capitalist goals of efficiency and profit-making have shaped the organization of work. Writing in the nineteenth century, Marx declared that work should be a central source of meaning and satisfaction in a person's life. In his words, "the exercise of **labour power**, labour, is the worker's own life-activity, the manifestation of his own life" (cited in Rinehart, 2001: 13). But he noted that for most labouring people, work had lost meaning and creativity. Under capitalism, the worker "works in order live. . . . Life begins for him where this activity ceases" (cited in Rinehart, 2001: 3).

By the early twentieth century, with the spread of mass production, much work (most notably in manufacturing) was being further divided into ever more unconnected and meaningless parts. The twentieth century witnessed the large-scale implementation of **scientific management**, one of the most influential and long-lasting managerial strategies. Scientific management, a method of organizing work and controlling workers, was introduced by American engineer

Frederick Winslow Taylor. After its founder, scientific management is also referred to as Taylorism.

Taylor applied the principles of "science" to the performance of human labour. On the basis of his close observations of workers performing their jobs, he broke work processes down into simple tasks, each of which could be timed and organized into formal rules and standardized procedures. Taylor believed that once the work was subdivided, workers did not need to understand the entire process of production. Scientific management, in this sense, resulted in the separation of mental and manual labour, the conception of work from its execution. In short, it contributed to the deskilling of the worker.

Also in the twentieth century, Henry Ford, founder of the Ford Motor Car Company, applied the principles of scientific management (in tandem with the bureaucratic organization of work) to mass production of the automobile. Even if you have never stepped foot in an auto manufacturing plant or other mass production facility, you are probably familiar with the assembly line. Richard Edwards (1979) called the moving assembly line an example of "tech-nical control." *Technical control* refers to the control of a workforce not directly by supervision (for example, by a foreperson), but rather indirectly by a machine.

While early researchers highlighted the application of Taylorism to manufacturing, this principle now applies to many different types of work. In one form or other, scientific management has been implemented in offices (Lowe, 1987), schools, hospitals, and restaurants. Esther Reiter (1991) describes how the fast-food industry has carefully broken down the process of serving a burger from laying down the buns to evenly spreading the ketchup to distributing precisely half an ounce of onions. The total preparation time for a Burger King Whopper is 23 seconds—no more, no less.

Critics have argued that work broken down into simple parts, though efficient and rational, results in degradation and dehumanization (Braverman, 1974). Marx introduced the concept of "alienation" to describe the consequences for working people. **Alienation** is a structural condition of powerlessness that is rooted in a worker's relationship to the means of production. Insofar as workers have little or no

The assembly line has been called an example of technical control. This refers to the control of the workforce not directly by supervision (for example, a foreperson), but rather indirectly by a machine. (© Getty Images)

control over their labour, work is no longer a source of fulfilment. According to Marx, under these conditions, workers become estranged from the products of their labour, from the work process itself, from each other, and from themselves (Rinehart, 2001).

Faced with the problem of alienated workforces, some employers have attempted to motivate workers with financial incentives. In the 1930s, Henry Ford introduced the "Five Dollar Day." In that era, five dollars constituted a relatively high rate of pay that supposedly would cover the living costs of not only the male autoworker but also of his (dependent) wife and children. Decades later, J.H. Goldthorpe and colleagues' study of workers' orientations to work (1969) further supported the view that some people have an instrumental relationship to work. In this view, people can be compensated for meaningless work. Work can be a means to an end rather than an end in itself.

There are two essential problems with the assumption that money makes up for the meaninglessness of work. First, only a minority of employers do in fact compensate their employees for performing degrading and dehumanizing work. In the popular media, we hear stories about $30 hourly wage rates for auto and steelworkers. But we must keep in mind that Ford, GM, and Stelco workers represent the privileged of the working class. Most employers are not willing to pay high wages—though they can be forced to do so, under the pressure of strong unions such as the Canadian Auto Workers and the United Steelworkers of America. Consequently, the majority of people do not receive high monetary compensation. Most Canadians perform boring jobs and are not paid handsomely for doing so.

Second, this view overlooks the importance of workers' needs for *intrinsic satisfaction*—the need of human beings to find meaning in the work that they perform. As stated, whether they are Supreme Court judges, car assemblers, letter carriers, caretakers, or retail clerks, people need to find meaning in the work that they perform day in and day out. We have a basic human need for respect and dignity at work (Hodson, 2001). This holds whether you are a man or woman, Canadian-born or a recent immigrant or a migrant labourer, in middle age or youth, in a part-time job or a career.

### The Early Human Relations School

In the 1930s, social psychologists and managerial consultants began to recognize this basic human need.

In a series of experiments at the Western Electric Company's Hawthorne plant in Chicago, an industrial psychologist named Elton Mayo discovered that attention to workers resulted in a significant improvement in their productivity. The Hawthorne studies played an important role in spawning a new school of management thought known as the **human relations** approach. The basic idea on which the human relations approach rests is that if managers want productive, motivated workers, they should recognize workers' social needs.

In contemporary workplaces, many early human relations principles are embedded in an array of organizational initiatives such as "human resource management," "total quality management," and "quality of work life" programs. Employee-of-the-week schemes, employee suggestion boxes, quality circles, and job enrichment all reflect such managerial methods. All of these schemes highlight employee motivation by promoting a discourse of co-operation (rather than conflict) between managers and workers, with the belief that happy workers are better workers.

A fundamental problem with the human relations approach to managing, however, is that such programs do not constitute real workplace democracy. Under such schemes, employers often create the illusion that workers are important and respected, their ideas valued and rewarded, but there is no real redistribution of power and control. Over time, employees begin to recognize the limits of their involvement. Moreover, some research has demonstrated that workers' suggestions for organizing work may backfire against them, resulting in layoffs for some and in the further rationalization of the work process for those who remain (Robertson et al., 1993).

## The Social Organization of Work Today

### Revolutionary New Technology

Today, popular writers and scholars alike are talking about the emergence of a new world of work rooted in a "knowledge society"—a world that offers opportunity, an increase in leisure time, an experience of work far more positive than in the past. Are these assertions accurate? Do people now have better jobs than their parents and grandparents? Have we rid the economy of many of the low-paying, dead-end, and routine jobs that characterized the past? In short, has work been transformed?

According to Daniel Bell (1973), the answer to these questions is "Yes." In *Post-industrial Society*, Bell argues that we are now living in a post-industrial era, a new information economy, one based on the use of sophisticated microelectronic technology. With the decline of Taylorized manufacturing jobs and the rise of knowledge work, argues Bell, people are becoming highly skilled and jobs are becoming intrinsically rewarding.

Admittedly, most people agree that the new technology may eliminate routine, repetitive tasks, thereby freeing people to perform more challenging work. Think, for example, about preparing a research paper without a computer, printer, and access to the Internet. Moreover, the technology has had a positive impact on job creation. In fact, in Canada, information technology has created more jobs than it has eliminated. In a comparison of firms that relied extensively on sophisticated information technology with other, low-tech firms, the Conference Board of Canada found that the former produced more jobs than the latter (Lowe, 2000).

Notwithstanding these findings, some sociologists argue that, at the same time, the technology has created new forms of inequality and exacerbated old ones. While it has resulted in new, more challenging jobs for some people, many others have lost their jobs (or skills) as a result of technological change in the workplace. In the **service economy**, for instance, employers have relied extensively on computers and the new microelectronics to streamline work processes. In banking, many of the decisions (such as approving a bank loan) that used to be made at the discretion of people are now governed by computer. And the introduction of automated bank machines has made redundant the work of tens of thousands of tellers. In some industries, computers have taken over the supervisory function of employee surveillance. With state-of-the-art computer equipment, and without the direct intervention of a supervisor, firms can now effectively enforce productivity quotas and monitor workers, especially those who perform highly routine tasks (Fox and Sugiman, 1999).

Another problem is that the technology is rapidly changing. Competence with the technology thus necessitates continually learning new skills and making ongoing investments in training. Often workers themselves assume the costs of such training. In the past, says Graham Lowe, employment was based on an implicit understanding of loyalty in exchange for job security; today, this idea has been replaced with a system based on "individual initiative and merit." Workers who go above and beyond, who contribute what managers sometimes call "value added," who hone their skills—these are the workers who will be recognized and rewarded (2000: 61).

Moreover, opportunities for extra job-related training are unequal. Not surprisingly, they are closely linked to an employee's income and level of education. Lowe notes that only 3 in 10 Canadian workers annually receive training related to their present or future employment (2000: 65). University graduates are twice as likely as high school graduates to be involved in such training. One in 5 workers who earns less than $15,000 participates in training, compared to half of those earning in excess of $75,000.

### Flexible Work

Some writers are extolling the benefits of related innovations in management methods. In business circles today, one hears buzzwords such as "workplace restructuring," "downsizing," and "lean production." All of these concepts are part of a new managerial approach called *flexibility*. Flexibility (most often in tandem with "technological innovation") has, as they say, "held out the hand of promise." It has been promoted as an improvement over the old human relations approach and an alternative to the Taylorist and Fordist methods that have long stripped workers of control and dignity (Sennett, 1998). Critics, on the other hand, say differently. Smart, young managers trained in the postmodern language of flexibility may introduce seemingly new forms of managing and organizing work and adapt them to an increasingly competitive and precarious global context, but on close inspection, they claim, such strategies are firmly grounded in time-worn approaches.

Most contemporary flexibility strategies are based on one or a combination of two approaches: *numerical flexibility* and *flexible specialization* (also called *functional flexibility*). **Numerical flexibility** involves shrinking or eliminating the core workforce (in continuous jobs, and full-time positions) and replacing them with workers in *non-standard* (or *contingent*) *employment*. **Non-standard work** is a term used to describe various employment arrangements such as part-time work, temporary (seasonal and other part-year) work, contracting out or outsourcing (work that was previously done in-house), and self-employment. Non-standard work is, in short, based on an employment relationship that is far more tenuous than those of the past (Jackson and Robinson, 2000).

When you hear about non-standard work, what comes to mind? If you are like most Canadians, you think of jobs in the fast-food or retail industries—so-called "McJobs." But in the current economy, non-standard work arrangements now characterize most spheres of employment. We need look no further than the university or college, for example, to see the employment of people in non-standard jobs. In these institutions of higher learning, you may discover that many of your courses are taught by part-time or sessional instructors, some of whom hold Ph.D.s, others of whom are graduate students. These are individuals who are paid by the university to teach on a course-by-course or session-by-session basis. Sessional or part-time instructors typically do not work on a full-time basis, and they seldom receive assurances of stable employment.

According to many scholars of work, non-standard labour represents the fastest growing type of employment in this country (see, for example, Jackson, 2005; Vosko, 2000). While 6 per cent of all employed persons worked part-time (fewer than 30 hours per week) in 1975, that proportion had risen to over 18 per cent by 1997 (Nelson and Robinson, 2002: 239). Today, non-standard work represents about one-third of all jobs. Though this form of employment may be found in all industries, it is most typical of sales and service.

Many writers have cogently argued that the growth of non-standard work is closely linked to the corporate goals of flexibility and global restructuring (Harvey, 1989). Not unlike the "reserve army of labour" described by Karl Marx, non-standard employees provide owners and managers with a ready supply of labour to "hire and fire" as the market demands. Employers invest minimally in these workers and offer them only a limited commitment. In order to remain competitive in the global market, it is argued, corporations must reduce labour costs through downsizing (that is, laying off permanent, full-time workers and replacing them with part-time, temporary, and contract labour; Duffy, Glenday, and Pupo, 1997).

Yet, unyielding market forces notwithstanding, there is also evidence that "precarious jobs have become the norm much faster in some countries than in others" (Jackson and Robinson, 2000: 50). For example, in the United States, non-standard work grew quickly in the 1980s, but in comparison to Canada, in the 1990s, its growth has been limited by low unemployment. Moreover, in much of Europe, unions and employment laws have (until recently) limited the growth of contract work and substandard part-time work. In the Netherlands, a country known for having one of the most flexible labour markets in continental Europe, part-timers receive equal wages

and benefits with full-time employees, and contract workers must be given a permanent job within a specified time period (Jackson and Robinson, 2000).

Another offshoot of the increasingly precarious relationship between employers and workers is the growth in self-employment. In the 1990s, one driving force behind self-employment was the move of large firms and governments to contract out work that had formerly been performed in-house by a core workforce (Jackson and Robinson, 2000). In fact, throughout the 1990s, growth in self-employment was a leading labour market trend. In 1998, self-employed individuals accounted for 18 per cent of all employment in Canada, and between 1989 and 1997, self-employment constituted about 80 per cent of all job growth (Lowe, 2000).

Contrary to romantic images of the self-employed as benefiting from flexible work schedules, autonomy, and economic success, research indicates that they are not always better off than their waged or salaried counterparts. Most self-employed people work alone, often in small enterprises. Only a minority run companies that employ others (Lowe, 2000). Furthermore, they tend to work excessively long hours and, on average, accrue about the same earnings as regular employees. In addition, gender-based pay differentials are more pronounced among the self-employed, and work is highly polarized. In other words, recent growth in self-employment has been especially strong at the top of the job hierarchy (for example, among engineers and accountants) and at the bottom (for instance, among domestic cleaners and salespeople).

Part-time and temporary workers tend to be women and young people, though not exclusively. Because of these demographics, people assume that the casual employment relationship is not problematic; indeed, some believe it to be desirable. Admittedly, there are individuals who choose non-standard work in the hope that it will offer heightened flexibility to facilitate the competing demands of job and family or job and school. Yet many other people accept these employment terms on an involuntary basis, largely because they have no alternatives. Moreover, studies suggest that many non-standard work arrangements do not in fact provide employees with greater flexibility (Vosko, 2000) or that they offer flexibility only to favoured employees (Sennett, 1998).

Furthermore, non-standard workers as a group receive relatively low wages and few benefits. Consequently, many people who rely on this type of work must resort to holding multiple jobs in an effort to make ends meet. People carve out a living by stringing together a host of low-paying, part-time, and temporary jobs. Often this involves moonlighting or doing shift work, situations that no doubt put added strain on families.

Interestingly, along with the expansion of the non-standard workforce, there has been an increase in overtime work for full-time employees. And while there has been a significant rise in overtime hours for both sexes, men are especially likely to work beyond the standard 40-hour week. As well, the lengthening of the workday has been more pronounced among managers than among employees. And on the whole, more of this overtime is unpaid. Paid overtime tends to be concentrated in unionized workplaces and in blue-collar manufacturing and construction jobs (Jackson and Robinson, 2000). Unpaid overtime, in comparison, is more marked in the female-dominated public sector, such as in teaching and social work (suggesting that women are more likely to put in overtime without pay), as well as among managers and professionals.

Among the many reasons for the recent increase in overtime work is that, first, and as a result of downsizing and restructuring, to get the job done the remaining employees simply must put in longer hours. According to Andrew Jackson and David Robinson, "the survivors have to pick up the work of those who have left as a result of layoffs or early retirement" (2000: 86). Fear of future job loss is also a potent factor behind putting in extra hours. In a "survival-of-the-fittest" corporate culture, long hours are viewed as evidence of effort and commitment. Undoubtedly, many workers also internalize the ethic of doing more with less, particularly those who are serving the public and helping to make up for cuts through unpaid work. In short, in the face of general labour market uncertainty, many core employees feel pressured to work overtime, whether or not they so desire. As a result, we now have, "side by side, underemployment and overemployment, with high levels of insecurity and stress on all sides" (Duffy, Glenday, and Pupo, 1997: 57).

In light of these trends, for most Canadians, the concept of a career is a remnant of the past. The gold watch for 50 years of continuous service to the same company is not attainable in the new workplace scenario. Says Richard Sennett, "flexibility today brings back this arcane sense of the job, as people do lumps of labor, pieces of work, over the course of a lifetime" (1998: 9). Living in this era of economic uncertainty, with the attendant worry about layoffs and job loss, is, not surprisingly, a major source of stress for people in Canada (Jackson and Robinson, 2000).

Another component of the new flexibility is **flexible specialization** (or *functional flexibility*, often called

*flex spec*). Flexible specialization involves multi-skilling, job rotation, the organization of workers into teams, and the concentration of power—without the centralization of power. Flexible specialization has been called the antithesis of the system of production embodied in Fordism (Sennett, 1998). Under the new system, the old auto assembly line has been replaced by "islands of specialized production." These new work units allow businesses to respond quickly to fluctuations in market demand, especially in industries such as fashion and textiles where there is a short product life.

Typically, flex spec is also accompanied by a goal of co-operation and flexible arrangements between labour and management rather than adversarial relations based on strict contractual agreements. Where Taylorist management strategies have rationalized production by eliminating the need for workers to make decisions, a flex-spec organization attempts to eliminate "waste" by employing workers' knowledge of their jobs in the rationalization process. Working in teams, employees are given responsibility for scheduling, planning the work, rotating workers among jobs, and meeting quotas (Fox and Sugiman, 1999). By increasing workers' responsibility, team organization diminishes the need for supervision—although it provides employees with no added authority.

Finally, information technology has been an integral component of flexibility strategies. Flexible specialization is suited to high technology: "Thanks to the computer, industrial machines are easy to reprogram and configure. The speed of modern communications has also favoured flexible specialization, by making global market data instantly available to a company" (Sennett, 1998: 52). Unlike the earlier mechanization, the new telecommunications technology enables employers to easily relocate work from one site to another, thereby scattering workforces to various parts of the country, continent, or world. As a result of teleworking, you can make a hotel reservation or check your credit level from Hamilton, Ontario, and be speaking to a reservation agent or debt collector in Tennessee. Likewise, with the availability of portable computers, fax machines, cell phones, and e-mail connections, some people may simply do their work from home rather than in an office or factory. Work can now follow people home.

### Flexibility for Whom?

We may now point to a polarization of jobs. At one end of the spectrum are the good jobs, at the other the bad. There is no bulging middle. There has, in other words, been a widening of inequalities. Good jobs offer decent pay and intrinsic rewards (fulfillment, autonomy, the opportunity to exercise know-

12.2

# Sociology in Action
## Don't Work Too Hard

Hard work never killed anyone! This is an old and familiar phrase. Teenagers are likely to hear it from their parents when they are asked to shovel the snow. Steelworkers, miners, and loggers hear it bellowed at them by their supervisors when they do not want to clean out the steel-making furnace, work overtime to dig out extra coal, or climb a steep hill to get to the next stand of trees.

But hard work does injure and kill. In 1998, just over 3 Canadian workers died every working day from an occupational injury, and 1 in 18 workers was injured at work. This represented one occupational injury every 9 seconds. In 2002, the Ontario Workplace Safety and Insurance Board registered over 350,000 claims for workplace-based injuries.

Canadian workers are injured and killed on the job in at least three ways. First, some jobs, such as mining, logging, and fishing, are very dangerous, and accident and fatality rates are unacceptably high. Second, accident rates are related to how fast and how long a person works at a job. The more hours a person works in a day, the greater the likelihood of an accident. Why? Fatigue. If you get tired shovelling snow, you can stop. If you are paid according to the number of widgets you produce, you are likely to push yourself beyond safe limits. And if you are manipulating a fast-paced machine with sharp cutting tools, even a brief lapse in attention can result in serious injury. Third, years of working hard can lead to various work-related diseases that are both debilitating and fatal.

The change from an industrial to a "post-industrial" or "information" society has altered the patterns of accidents somewhat. Over 30 years ago, the dominant form of injury compensated by provincial compensation boards involved crushed or severed limbs. Now it is various forms of strains and sprains, especially of the lower back and upper limbs. These injuries now represent approximately half of all workplace injuries, and their severity is increasing.

But this is just the tip of the iceberg. These numbers apply overwhelmingly to injuries caused by workplace accidents. But what about occupational disease? Numerous studies link long-term exposure to toxic substances and chemicals such as asbestos, lead, benzene, and arsenic to cancer and other deadly or debilitating diseases.

The problems associated with compensating occupational diseases are many and complex. How does a worker prove that exposure to a toxic chemical caused their cancer—especially if they changed jobs over the years and they smoked cigarettes? While some researchers believe that upward of 25 per cent of all cancers can be linked to the workplace, only about 2 per cent of all compensation claims are for occupational diseases. Every year, thousands of Canadians get ill and die from a work-related illness. The problem is that they don't know it.

Workers and unions in Canada have protested this alarming health and safety situation. In the late 1970s, these protests resulted in the passage of occupational health and safety laws that gave workers the right to know about the substances they were working with, the right to participate with management in identifying unsafe and unhealthy working conditions, and the right to refuse to do work they believed to be unsafe. While these rights apply to the majority of workers, unionized workers are most knowledgeable about their health and safety rights and are most likely to exercise them on a regular basis.

In 1994, Sean Kells, a 19-year-old from Mississauga, Ontario, was killed when flammable liquid he was pouring into a vat was ignited by electricity. It was his third day on the job. The plant in which he was working was not unionized. He had received no safety training or safety information from his employer. He was not aware of his health and safety rights, including his right to refuse unsafe work. He might still be alive if his employer had obeyed the law.

Know your rights. And don't work too hard.

SOURCE: Robert Storey, Labour Studies Program and Department of Sociology, McMaster University (2003). Printed with permission of the author.

ledge and acquire skill). But while the new information society has created some good jobs, these are not held by all, or even most, people in this country.

And whether they work in the primary, manufacturing, or service economy, as manual labourers or as professionals, people are facing increasing uncertainty in the labour market. Downsizing, the resulting increase in non-standard employment, and the **globalization of work** all have contributed to this uncertainty. Says Sennett, "What's peculiar about uncertainty today is that it exists without any looming historical disaster; instead it is woven into the everyday practices of a vigorous capitalism. Instability is meant to be normal" (1998: 31).

# The Changing Face of Labour: Diversity among Workers

Just as places of work have changed dramatically over time, so, too, has the workforce itself. Workplaces today, whether offices, factories, hospitals, or classrooms, are becoming increasingly diverse. Only a minority of families relies on a single paycheque. First Nations people make up a growing proportion of the paid labour force in certain geographic areas. People of colour, some of whom are immigrants to this country, many Canadian-born, currently have a stronger-than-ever presence, particularly in big cities such as Vancouver, Toronto, and Montreal. As well, the workforce has become more highly educated and younger. As a result of these changes, students of work must turn their attention to some pressing new problems.

### Gendered Work

The participation of women in the paid labour force has increased steadily over the past four decades. In Canada today, women constitute approximately 45 per cent of the labour force (Statistics Canada, 2001b: 8). Most striking has been a rise in the employment rates of married women and mothers of children under the age of six. Recent census data indicate that the two-breadwinner (also called *dual-earner*) family is now the norm. Gone are the days of *The Adventures of Ozzie and Harriet*.

Decades—indeed, over a century—of struggle and activism by feminists have resulted in important gains. Paid work is one arena in which these gains have been most prominent. In Canada, we now have employment equity legislation (albeit limited) in the federal government and laws enforcing equal pay for work of equal value. It is important to remember, though, that

many of these breakthroughs are relatively recent. Into the 1950s, companies and governments still restricted the employment of married women, overtly defined work as "female" and "male," and upheld gender-based seniority systems (Sugiman, 1994).

Today, many young women and men entering the labour force are unaware of the blatant sexual inequalities of the past. Whether or not they self-identify as feminists, women today are building their careers on a feminist foundation. If not for the challenges posed by women's rights activists, university lecture halls would be filled exclusively by men, women would not be permitted entry into the professions or management, and paid employment would simply not be an option after marriage.

But just as women's historical breakthroughs are instructive, so, too, are the persisting inequalities. In spite of a dramatic increase in female labour-force participation, women and men are by no means equal in the labour market. The **social institution** of work is still very much a gendered one. It is important that women have made inroads in non-traditional fields of manual labour, the professions, and management and administration, but the majority of women remain concentrated in female-dominated occupations such as retail salesperson, secretary, cashier, registered nurse, elementary school teacher, babysitter, and receptionist, while men are more commonly truck drivers, janitors, farmers, motor vehicle mechanics, and construction trade helpers, for example. Particularly troubling is the finding that Canadian women who have completed university or community college are three times more likely than their male counterparts (24 per cent and 8 per cent, respectively) to move into a clerical or service job (Nelson and Robinson, 2002: 226). To the extent that occupational segregation by sex has lessened somewhat over time, it is more because of the entry of men into female-dominated occupations than the reverse.

As well, women (as well as youth of both sexes) are more likely than men to be employed on a part-time and temporary basis. For years now, women have made up approximately 70 per cent of the part-time workforce in Canada. And while the majority of the self-employed are men, the 1990s witnessed a rapid growth in women's self-employment. In comparing the sexes, we also see that self-employed men are more likely than self-employed women to hire others—male employers outnumbered females three to one—and that businesses operated by men are more likely to be in the goods sector whereas female-run businesses are likely to be in the less lucrative service sector (Nelson and Robinson, 2002: 242).

These trends—labour market segregation by sex and the over-representation of women in precarious employment—have contributed to gender-based differences in earnings. From 1967 to 1997, the pay gap between women and men employed full-time and full-year narrowed from 58 per cent to 72 per cent (Jackson and Robinson, 2000: 19), yet the narrowing of this wage gap was largely the result of an increase in time worked for women and of falling or stagnant wages for men, with only a modest increase in women's earnings. In addition to this, gender-based earnings differentials may, to a large degree, be attributed to women's concentration in part-time and temporary work. When we compare women employed on a full-time basis with their male counterparts, the gap narrows—though, as noted above, it does not disappear.

All women are not, of course, in the same position. Immigrant women, women of colour, and First Nations women bear the brunt of income and occupational polarization by sex. In consequence, their average annual earnings are disproportionately low. In her research on various categories of women, Monica Boyd (1999) concludes that earnings differentials increase between Canadian-born women and foreign-born women, especially when the latter group are of colour and when they are not fluent in English or French. In addition, foreign-born women who are currently residents of Canada are more likely than Canadian-born women to be employed in particular segments of the service sector—namely, those that are typically labour-intensive, poorly paid, and dominated by small firms (Vosko, 2000). While men of colour are concentrated in either professional occupations or service jobs, women of colour are more likely than Canadian women as a whole to perform manual labour. First Nations women likewise are concentrated in service or clerical work (First Nations men are more likely to perform manual labour than other kinds of work).

Faced with multiple forms of **discrimination**, working-class women of colour and some female immigrants have come to occupy job ghettos. Indeed, many of the jobs that are typically performed by working-class people of colour have a "hidden" quality: the work they do is not noticed; the workers are rendered invisible. All too often, we regard private domestic workers and nannies, hotel and office cleaners, taxi drivers, health-care aides, and dishwashers—all of whom perform indispensable labour—as simply part of the backdrop (Arat-Koc, 1990; Das Gupta, 1996). Not only are they physically out of sight (in basements, in kitchens, working at night when everyone else has gone), they are out of mind.

Social scientists have produced reams of statistics documenting sex-based inequalities in employment, but we can speak of the gendering of work in many other ways, some not easily quantifiable. Joan Acker (1990) writes about the process by which jobs and organizations become gendered, regardless of the sex of job holders. The bureaucratic rules and procedures, hierarchies, and informal organizational culture may rest on a set of gender-biased assumptions, for example. In her book *Secretaries Talk* (1988), Rosemary Pringle highlights how gendered family relationships are reproduced in workplace relations between bosses (fathers) and secretaries (wives, mistresses, daughters). Pringle describes how male bosses determine the boundaries between home and work, public and private, whereas "secretaries do not have this luxury. Male bosses go into their secretaries' offices unannounced, assume the right to pronounce on their clothes and appearance, have them doing housework and personal chores, expect overtime at short notice and assume the right to ring them at home" (1988: 51).

Many formal and informal mechanisms prevent women from entering male-dominated occupations. Cynthia Cockburn (1983) explores how a culture of manhood became a part of the printing trade. For years, the link between masculine identities, masculine culture, and the printing trade was so strong that the occupation was completely impenetrable to

Many of the jobs in job ghettos are performed by working-class people of colour. This work has a hidden quality: the work is not noticed. All too often, we regard these workers—nannies, maids, taxi drivers, dishwashers—simply as part of the backdrop. (© Fotosearch)

women. Sugiman (1994) describes how women attempted to carve out for themselves "pockets of femininity" in the male-dominated auto plants of southern Ontario during the Second World War. By the war's end, however, women's presence was no longer welcome. Most were hastily dismissed from the industry.

Today, many young women plan to both have a professional career and raise a family, but they are not quite sure how they will combine the two. Feminist researchers have demonstrated how the very concept of "career" is gendered. It is one that has been built on a masculine model. Career success depends on the assumption of a wife at home—a helper who will pick up the children from school, arrange dinner parties, and generally free the "breadwinner" to work late at nights or on weekends and for out-of-town business travel.

Feminist analysis has called attention, furthermore, to the complex link between paid and unpaid labour, employment, and family. With two breadwinners, both of whom are spending increasing hours in their paid jobs, families are under enormous pressure (see Figure 12.1). While the demands of paid work have risen over time, so, too, have pressures on family life. Government restructuring and cutbacks in resources have affected public daycare, after-school programs, special-needs programs, and care of the elderly and the disabled. Who picks up the slack? The family. One consequence has been an intensification of (unpaid) family work and growing tensions within families as people try to cope.

In a study of working-class families in Flin Flon, Manitoba, Meg Luxton (1980) introduced the concept of a *double day* of labour—the combination of paid and unpaid labour that must be performed in the course of a day. Usually, notes Luxton, this double burden is carried by women. Every day, millions of people put in a "second shift" of unpaid labour after they get home from their paying jobs. According to Hochschild (Hochschild and Machung, 1989), this second shift amounts to one extra month of 24-hour days of work per year. Hochschild (1997) also speaks to the experiences of millions of North American families in her study of the "time bind". The time bind has resulted in overworked, stressed people and in the downsizing and outsourcing of family responsibilities. Children are cranky, parents are rushed, and the concept of "leisure" is laughable. Hochschild suggests that rather than leave families with the "leftovers" of paid work, people should start challenging employers to consider more seriously the conflicting needs of family and employment.

## Race and Racialized Work

The trends we have so far discussed (precarious work, heightened job insecurities, and underemployment) have clearly had a disproportionate impact on groups who have long faced discrimination in the labour market and in society as a whole: women, people of colour, and Native people. But though we now have an abundance of research on the gendering of work, sociologists in Canada have paid far less attention to the relationship between race, citizenship, and employment.

Barriers faced by people of colour, by Native people, and by immigrants are demonstrated most often in unemployment and earnings disparities. Native people comprise only a tiny percentage of the working-age population (2.3 per cent), yet this group is growing rapidly and already constitutes a sizable share of the labour force in some cities (Jackson and Robinson, 2000: 70). **Unemployment rates** for Native people are disturbingly high, more than double that for the Canadian population as a whole (24 per cent for Native men and 22 per cent for Native women; Nelson and Robinson, 2002: 228). In addition, only one in three Native people was employed in a full-time, continuous job in 1996, and this proportion was even lower for those who live on reserves (Jackson

Figure 12.1 **Measures of Time Scarcity**

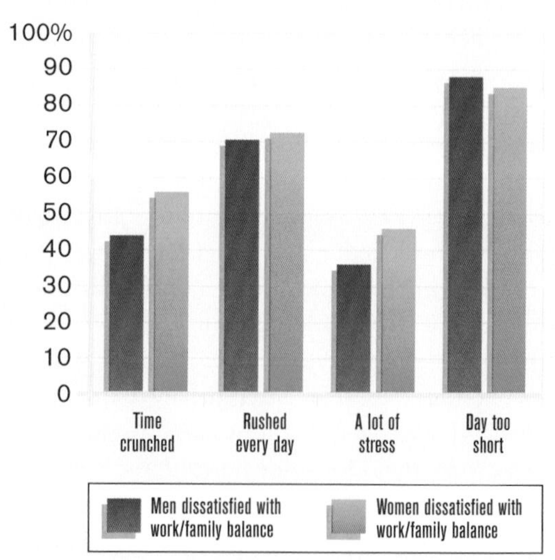

SOURCE: Adapted from Statistics Canada, *General Social Survey*, 1998

and Robinson, 2000: 71). Close to half of the off-reserve Native population lives in poverty.

The category "people of colour" is quite diverse, containing significant differences according to class, education, and citizenship status. In Canada, about 1 in 10 workers is defined as being of colour (the official census term is *visible minority*), and over 80 per cent of this group are relatively recent immigrants (Jackson and Robinson, 2000: 69). Today, immigrants of colour (compared to earlier generations of immigrants) are finding it extremely difficult to close the employment gap with native-born Canadians (see Figure 12.2). In 1996, the average employment income for immigrants who arrived between 1986 and 1990 was 18 per cent lower than the earnings of non-immigrants. For those who immigrated after 1990, earnings were 36 per cent lower. And these gaps persist even when we control for age and education. On average, recent immigrants are younger than the labour force as a whole, but they also have more schooling. One problem is that foreign credentials are not always respected in Canada, thus contributing to a high concentration of immigrants of colour in low-wage jobs (Jackson and Robinson, 2000: 69–70).

Likewise, in 1995, the unemployment rate for workers of colour was 14.2 per cent compared to 10.1 per cent for all workers. Black Canadians in particular experienced a relatively high unemployment rate of 19.3 per cent, almost double the Canadian average (Jackson and Robinson, 2000: 70). It is not surprising, then, that roughly 45 per cent of black households in Canada live in poverty. Furthermore, there is evidence of race-based inequities in earnings: people of colour earn about 15 per cent less than the total Canadian workforce (Jackson and Robinson, 2000: 70). Among this group, the pay gap is much greater for men than women (though we must consider that women generally have much lower earnings than men). These lower earnings are in part a result of this group's concentration in low-paying, relatively low-skilled jobs, their under-representation in skilled jobs, and their higher rates of unemployment.

Though telling, these statistics reveal only one dimension of the research on disadvantaged groups. It is equally important to recognize that because of racial and cultural differences, people experience the work world in distinct ways. In their study *Who Gets the Work*, Frances Henry and Effie Ginzberg (1985) found striking incidences of discrimination directed at job seekers. For example, when whites and blacks with similar qualifications applied for entry-level positions than had been advertised in a newspaper,

whites received job offers three times more often than did black applicants. Similarly, of the job seekers who made inquiries by telephone, those who had accents (especially South Asian and Caribbean) often were quickly screened out by employers.

Much of the role played by the Canadian state in promoting or facilitating racialized work (Schecter, 1998) has been documented. Agnes Calliste (1993) notes that between 1950 and 1962, Canadian immigration authorities admitted limited numbers of Caribbean nurses, but under different rules from those applied to white immigrant nurses. Black nurses were expected to have nursing qualifications superior to those demanded of whites. Several scholars (Arat-Koc, 1990; Bakan and Stasiulis, 1994) have also discussed the role of the Canadian state in addressing the need for cheap child-care workers by importing women from the developing world (the Caribbean and the Philippines, in particular) to perform domestic labour without granting them full citizenship rights.

Often, jobs and occupations become racialized (that is, to adopt a racial label) as a result of formal and informal barriers that prevent their holders from exiting (Calliste, 1993; Das Gupta, 1996). In a study of black workers in automotive foundries, Sugiman

Figure 12.2 **Distribution of Annual Earnings by Racial Category, 1999 (Percentage in Earnings Group)**

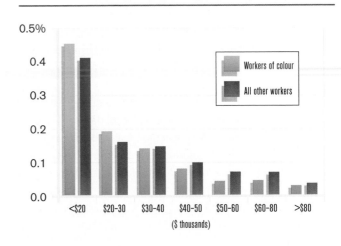

SOURCE: From 'Workers of Colour' by Andrew Jackson, in *Falling Behind: The State of Working Canada, 2000*, Andrew Jackson, David Robinson, Bob Baldwin, and Cindy Wiggins (Ottawa: Canadian Centre for Policy Alternatives/Canadian Labour Congress, 2000). Reprinted by permission of the Canadian Centre for Policy Alternatives. www.policyalternatives.ca.

12.3

# Human Diversity
## Migrant Farm Workers in Canada

Summer brings the promise of warm, sunny days and the prospect of fresh Ontario-grown produce. Tempting supermarket produce displays belie the fact that thousands of invisible hands, more than 100,000 workers in Ontario's agricultural sector, including many migrant workers, have been hard at work planting and harvesting these crops. . . .

Agriculture is a staple in Ontario's economy, but its mainstay is no longer the family farm. Farming is big business. Leading Canada, Ontario shipped more than seven billion dollars of agrifood to the world in the first 11 months of 2001, a 13 per cent increase over the same period in 2000. In the last decade, Ontario's agrifood exports have tripled. . . .

While the structure of the agricultural industry may have changed, the nature of the work has not. Planting and harvesting is labour intensive, some would say back-breaking. Exposure to toxic substances, like pesticides, and the potential to contract disease from biological hazards are daily health threats. For some the work can be deadly. . . .

Last May, 20 migrant agricultural workers from Leamington spoke out about their working and living conditions. They didn't call the Ministry of Labour office but instead contacted the nearest Mexican consulate. Within days they were sent back to Mexico. . . .

For more than 30 years, migrant workers like these have been regularly employed on Ontario farms to meet short-term labour demands during peak seasons. Farm owners have traditionally failed to find sufficient Canadian labour to perform the work many characterize as poorly paid, unskilled, but most likely rejected for its gruelling nature.

The Seasonal Agricultural Workers Program (SAWP), created in 1966, was a response to farm owners' appeal for government assistance to address these ongoing labour shortages. The program, administered by Human Resources Develop-

ment Canada (HRDC), provides migrant workers for a period of six weeks to eight months from Mexico and Commonwealth Caribbean countries. An agreement between the participating countries also includes guidelines and an employment contract entered into by the worker, employer, the Canadian government and the worker's home country.

The program currently operates in Alberta, Manitoba, Ontario, Quebec and Nova Scotia. Of the 16,705 migrant workers employed in Canada under the program in 2000, 90 per cent worked on Ontario farms, 60 per cent are from Mexico.

Farm work in Ontario pays little more than minimum wage at $7.25/hour. Other legal rights, however, are less than minimum. While some may be entitled to health benefits, Ontario agricultural workers are not entitled to overtime pay and are exempt from hours of work legislation. Like other workers they pay Employment Insurance premiums. In 2000, $11 million was deducted from migrant farm workers and their employers yet they do not qualify to collect the benefit.

Toiling almost invisibly on farms, migrant workers are part of the community but have few social, economic or legal support systems. . . . Last December [2001] the Supreme Court of Canada in Dunmore v. Ontario (Attorney General) ruled agricultural workers' exclusion form the *Labour Relations and Employment Statute Law Amendment Act* violates workers' right to freedom of association guaranteed by the *Charter of Rights and Freedoms*.

———

SOURCE: Workers Health and Safety Centre, Ontario, Canada. Excerpts from 'Cultivating Health and Safety: Labour and community partners extend a hand to agricultural workers' from <www.whsc.on.ca/Publications/atthesource/summer2002/cultivatinghs.pdf>, accessed 28 May 2003. First published in *At the Source*, Summer 2002; a publication of the Workers' Health and Safety Centre. Reprinted by permission.

(2001) found that after years of intense discrimination, workers themselves may circumscribe their "choices". Over the course of many decades, most black men remained where they had started—in the foundry. In

the words of one foundry worker, "Their idea was, 'well, the white man don't want you up there no how, so why . . . put yourself in a position where you know you're not wanted'" (Sugiman, 2001: 102).

### Youth

In Canada today, youth (persons between the ages of 15 and 24) constitute a much smaller share of the population than in past years (Lowe, 2000: 110). Yet the youth labour market is expanding at a significant rate. Young people still receive relatively little attention in studies of work. But young people today are facing harsh economic conditions, with the youth unemployment rate roughly 50 per cent higher than that of the population as a whole. Throughout the 1990s in Canada, the overall high unemployment rate, government deficit-cutting, public- and private-sector downsizing, and various other wage-reduction strategies resulted in a contracting job market. In consequence, large numbers of youth withdrew from the labour market, returning to school or staying in school for longer periods (Lowe, 2000: 109).

The research presents us with a woeful picture. Study after study suggests that young people are in important ways no different from the majority of Canadian workers. They want high-quality work—work that is interesting and challenging and that provides a sense of accomplishment (Lowe, 2000). And youth have been increasing their human capital to acquire such jobs. Notably, young people are acquiring more education. (While a university degree does not guarantee a job, young people are still better off if they have the formal credentials.) But while Canadian youth are better schooled on the whole, they are also working less, and in jobs for which they feel they are overqualified. Young people are those workers most likely to be employed in such low-paying service-sector jobs as fast-food restaurants, clothing stores, and grocery stores. For most students, contingent work is all that is available.

Some writers argue that the youth labour market makes a perfect accompaniment to the new goals of managerial flexibility. Employers invest in the belief that young people will have a limited commitment to the goals of the firm and that they expect to stay in jobs temporarily, as a stop-gap measure discontinuous with their adult careers and identities (Tannock, 2001). Stuart Tannock explains that youth partially accept the popular **ideology** that positions them "as a separate class of workers who deserve less than adult workers do. Good jobs are predominantly the privilege of adulthood. Young workers must be content at first to spend their time in a tier of lower-quality service and retail employment. Dreams of meaningful work must be deferred" (2001: 109). Many young people compare themselves not to other workers across the spectrum, but exclusively to other youth workers (Sennett, 1998).

Consequently, youth are more pliable and passive. Also, because their jobs are viewed as transient, youth are less likely to become unionized. All of these features render them an extremely exploitable source of labour.

But as Tannock (2001) points out, youth are not stop-gap workers simply because they are young: they are stop-gap workers also because of the poor conditions under which they have to labour—conditions that have been created by employers in the service sector. But despite the popular view that young people are not especially concerned about their conditions of work, much evidence now points to the contrary: "Teenagers and young adults working in these industries, who expect to have long lives ahead of them, worry that their jobs, which are supposed to be meaningless, stop-gap places of employment, will have lasting and detrimental effects on their bodies and future life activities" (Tannock, 2001: 54).

# Workers' Coping and Resistance: The Struggle for Dignity and Rights

### Finding Meaning in Work

Regardless of the many differences among Canadian workers today, one point remains clear: most Canadians want personally fulfilling work (Lowe, 2000). People have a powerful desire to maintain dignity at work (Hodson, 2001). Some of us are fortunate to hold jobs that offer challenge, jobs in which we can exercise autonomy and from which we can reap fruitful economic rewards. But even the "good jobs" are not always meaningful. And many jobs are rarely rewarding. How do people cope with their work?

Sociologists have found that no matter how meaningless the job, people seek meaning in their work. Sometimes this is done through the culture of the workplace. People who have boring, routine jobs, for example, may make a game out of their work, varying repetitions, altering pace and intensity, imagining the lives of customers. As well, the social component of work (peer relations) is frequently a source of pleasure. In some workplaces, employees regularly exchange gossip, flirt, engage in sexualized play, share personal problems, debate politics, ridicule management. Relationships with co-workers often make the job itself more bearable, if not meaningful. In cases where the organization of work permits such exchanges, the lines between employment and leisure can become blurred.

### 12.4

## Open for Discussion
#### "We Don't Need No Education"

At an individual level, the command to "get educated" is like a mantra, repeated ad nauseam to hapless teenagers, the unemployed, displaced workers and any other unfortunates who appear to need free advice from their more comfortable acquaintances. At a policy level, meanwhile, the clarion call to educate, educate, educate provides a handy catchall solution for just about any economic or social problem imaginable: poverty, low productivity, globalization, inequality.

[But] the claim that Canada is being held back by a shortage of skills and knowledge is absurd. On the contrary, there is a vast and wasteful underutilization of the abundant skills and knowledge that our citizens already possess. . . . Close to two-thirds of young adults in Canada now complete a college or university degree program by the time they turn 30. According to the World Bank, our post secondary enrollment rates are the highest in the world.

Yet millions of Canadians are employed in positions that do not come close to fully utilizing their existing skills and knowledge. One-quarter of the 8 million Canadian workers with post secondary education report that they are over qualified for their jobs; one-quarter of all university and college graduates in Canada are employed in clerical, sales and menial service positions; and close to 30 per cent of all Canadians living in poverty have at least some post secondary education. So much for education being a one-way ticket to prosperity.

. . . Self-righteous hectoring about education and the knowledge economy is especially disingenuous when we remember that the well-educated, comfortable classes actually require vast output of unskilled, low-paid labour in order to continue living in the style to which they have become accustomed. Imagine, for example, what would happen if the entire low skill workforce

suddenly went back to school and then burst back into the economy with Internet startups and consulting practices. Who would then do the dishes, clean the professional offices and mind the children? The age-old lament of the wealthy, "it's hard to find good help these days," would resonate with a dramatic urgency. Ultimately, both the employers of unskilled workers and the consumers of their services benefit from their lousy salaries, and their lack of formal education is simply a convenient excuse for their poverty.

If the great unskilled proletariat actually followed the nominal advice of those above them and bettered themselves through further education, then the system would need to quickly recreate another unskilled proletariat—through immigration and/or through the recruitment of new internal pools of "disempowered" labour. If we are genuinely concerned about ditch diggers, we'll save the lecture about how they should invest in their human capital. Our economy needs more ditch diggers—and dishwashers and janitors and labourers and secretaries and cashiers and manufacturers and waiters and drivers.

Further education may be extremely valuable for these Canadians, but they don't need it to do their jobs well and it won't guarantee them a better standard of living. Higher minimum wages, more effective unions, and other efforts to directly regulate and improve the wages and conditions of their work will do a lot more for them than investing in human capital.

We need the labour of these workers. And there's no inherent economic reason (other than the greed of their employers and their customers) that they shouldn't receive a decent income.

———

SOURCE: From Jim Stanford, "We Don't Need No Education," *This Magazine* (July/August 2001), 15–16.

Job satisfaction studies suggest that work is not all that bad. Most people report they are generally satisfied with their jobs (Lowe, 2000). On close examination, though, discontent broods near the surface. At

the same time that they report satisfaction, a majority of workers say that their jobs are somewhat or highly stressful; that they are not sufficiently involved, recognized, and rewarded; and that their talents are underutilized (Lowe, 2000). High rates of absenteeism, oppositional attitudes, slacking off, pilfering, and even destruction of company property also occur. Some workers simply quit their jobs. But in the face of a competitive job market, family responsibilities, consumer debt, and, for some, few marketable skills, this is not a viable option. Furthermore, even though many people claim to like their jobs, they add that they do not want their own children to end up doing the same kind of work (Sennett, 1988).

Faced with unfair, unsafe, and sometimes unchallenging work, there will be discontent. Workers will find ways to make changes, to resist. Individual acts of coping and resistance may give workers the feeling of agency and control, but insofar as they are individual acts, they rarely result in a fundamental or widespread change in conditions of work. In order to effect large-scale change, people must resort to collective measures.

## Professions and Negotiating Professional Control

Securing professional control is an option for middle-class people who possess formally recognized credentials and can claim expertise in an area. When we think of a *professional*, who comes to mind? Physicians, psychiatrists, dentists, lawyers, engineers, accountants. Some sociologists (proponents of trait theory) have attempted to define *professionals* with reference to a checklist of characteristics (Freidson, 1970). This checklist includes, for example, possession of a body of esoteric or abstract knowledge, reliance on a specialized technical language or vocabulary, and membership in associations that control entry and membership in the occupation through licensing, accreditation, and regulation.

Critics, however, argue that trait theory does not fully explain how and why some occupations become defined as professional while others do not. Rather than list a series of traits that define a profession, Terence Johnson (1972) highlights the resources available to different occupational groups that have enabled physicians, psychologists, and lawyers to define themselves as distinct from other groups such as managers, clerical workers, and massage therapists. In focusing on the process of professionalization, critical theorists have noted that at the heart of the struggle to professionalize are relations of power and control. Feminist scholars have recently offered a more nuanced analysis of how **patriarchy** (a system of male dominance), too, structures the process of securing professional authority and control (Witz, 1992).

## Labour Unions and Labour's Agenda

The struggle to professionalize is not one in which many Canadians will be engaged. Greater numbers of people in Canada, and globally, turn to another form of collective action to secure their rights and dignity in the workplace: they look to unionization. Just as campaigns to secure professional control have had a middle-class base, the struggle to unionize in this country has traditionally been one of white men in blue-collar jobs. In the latter part of the twentieth century and into the present time, however, increasing numbers of women, people of colour, white-collar workers, and middle-class employees have joined the ranks of the labour movement.

When most of us think of unions, strikes come to mind. Some of us may view trade unionists as just a bunch of greedy, overpaid workers demanding higher wages and, in the process, disrupting our health care, transportation, communication, or garbage collection. We may owe this perception to dominant media representation of unions, their members, and their leaders.

But the labour movement in this country goes far beyond this narrow and unfair characterization. The basic premise of the organized labour movement is to take collective action through the process of bargaining a contract. This *collective agreement* is the outcome of days, weeks, or even months of negotiations between two parties: worker representatives and company representatives. The contract is a legally binding document signed by both the employer and the union. Only if the two parties cannot reach an agreement is there potential for strike action. The actual incidence of strikes in Canada is, in fact, low. In 2001, the estimated work time lost through strikes and lockouts was 0.07 per cent, one-sixth the level of 20 years earlier (Statistics Canada, 2002f: 3). The strike is usually a measure of last resort. The vast majority of contracts that come up for renewal are settled without resorting to strike action. Indeed, some would argue that the leadership of unions acts to contain militancy on the part of its rank-and-file membership.

Workers in the nineteenth century first struggled to secure union representation to protect themselves against excessively long workdays, extremely hazardous work environments, low pay, and blatant favouritism on the job. Critical to the survival of the labour movement in Canada was the passage of the Rand formula at the end of the Second World War. The Rand formula, named for Supreme Court Justice Ivor Rand, ensured the automatic deduction of union dues by the employer in a unionized workplace.

Today, labour–management conflict arises over a host of issues. Not only are wages an item of dispute, but companies and union representatives also negotiate benefits packages, job security, the implementation of technological change, outsourcing, concessions, and anti-harassment policies. The struggles of union members won for Canadian workers in offices, stores, and factories the right to refuse unsafe work, the right to participate in company-sponsored pension plans, and, in some cases, access to on-site daycare centres.

The gains of unionized workers, moreover, spill over into the wider society. Both unionized and non-unionized workers now have employment standards, (un)employment insurance, a standard workday of eight hours, a five-day workweek, overtime premiums, vacation pay, health benefits, and sick-leave provisions. Unions have been pivotal in lobbying governments to introduce worker-friendly provincial and federal legislation.

### Union Membership

In the first half of 2002, union membership in Canada was 3.9 million (of 12.8 million paid employees), which represented a slight increase from 3.8 million in 2001. Women accounted for nearly all of this increase. In 2002, the rate of union membership among women was 30.2 per cent, for the first time matching that of men (at 30.3 per cent; Statistics Canada, 2002f: 1). In part, growth in female membership reflects the high rate of unionization in the (female-dominated) public service (for example, in Crown corporations, public schools, and hospitals). It is also, in part, a result of recent union organizing in private services (Jackson and Robinson, 2000). In comparison, the unionization rate for men has dropped since the 1960s. This is largely attributable to a shrinking proportion of jobs in traditionally male-dominated and heavily unionized sectors such as primary/resource, manufacturing, and construction (Jackson and Robinson, 2000).

Union membership also varies with terms of employment. Almost one in three full-time employees belongs to a union, compared to one in four part-time workers. Similarly, close to one in three permanent employees is a union member compared to about one in four non-permanent employees (Statistics Canada, 2002f: 2). We can, furthermore, see variations by age. Employees aged 45 to 54 (41.6 per cent) are more likely to be unionized than those aged 15 to 24 (13.3 per cent). Education is also a factor. A higher-than-average unionization rate can be found among men with post-secondary credentials (34.7 per cent) and those with less than a Grade 9 education (34 per cent). For women, the highest rate is for those with a university degree (40 per cent), reflecting unionization in health care and teaching (Statistics Canada, 2002f: 3).

Global comparisons reveal that the rate of union membership in Canada is higher than those in the United States and Japan and lower than those in most Western European nations. The dramatic decline in union membership in the United States has been a particular source of concern. The US unionization rate fell from 30 per cent at the end of the 1960s to less than 15 per cent in the current period (Jackson and Robinson, 2000: 25). This drop can be explained by a variety of forces, not the least of which are the electoral success of anti-union governments and the growth of anti-union employers such as Wal-Mart and Radio Shack. The assault on trade unions has been blatant in the United States.

### The Union Advantage

There is absolutely no doubt that unionization benefits workers. Collective bargaining has secured for employees advantages in wages, benefits, job security, and extended health plans. This has been called the *union advantage.* The union wage premium in particular is greatest for (traditionally disadvantaged) workers who would otherwise be low-paid. Unionization tends to compress wage and benefit differentials and thereby promote an equalization of wages and working conditions among unionized workforces (Jackson and Robinson, 2000). In 2001, for example, average hourly earnings of unionized workers in Canada were $20.29, while for non-unionized workers, they were $17.22. For part-time unionized and non-unionized workers, the figures were $17.31 and $10.60, respectively. Unionized part-time workers also tended to work more hours per week than their non-unionized counterparts. Consequently, their average weekly earnings were nearly double ($343.94 compared to $181.65; Statistics Canada, 2002f: 3).

The advantages of unionization to women are perhaps the most obvious. In 2001, unionized women working full-time received on average 90 per cent of the hourly earnings of their male counterparts, and female part-time workers earned 9 per cent more than men who were in part-time work (Statistics Canada, 2002f: 3). It is also notable that women in unionized jobs are more than twice as likely to be included in pension plans as women in non-unionized jobs (Jackson and Robinson, 2000).

12.5

# Sociology in Action
## McDonald's and Unions

A Quebec trade union has signed a labour contract with a McDonald's fast-food franchisee, the first in North America and only the second in the world.

"We had so many problems, so much repression," said Jean Lortie, a division president with the Quebec Confederation of National Trade Unions in Montreal. "But we didn't give up."

It took more than a year of often bitter negotiations to get a contract with the fast-food outlet in the tiny resort town of Rawdon, in the Laurentians north of Montreal. The process, Mr Lortie said, was so unpleasant and lengthy that by the time the union won only two of the 25 original signatories were still on staff.

The CNTU nearly became the first union in the world to get a labour contract with McDonald's, but a French union signed up a McDonald's restaurant only six weeks ago, said Len Ruel, area director of the Canadian Auto Workers in British Columbia.

The French union had to strike for six months to get a contract. By contrast, the Quebec contract was negotiated through the normal arbitration channels without a work stoppage. "All parties negotiated in good faith," said Maureen Kitts, a spokeswoman for McDonald's Restaurants of Canada Ltd in Toronto. She said McDonald's pays fair and equitable wages. Employees often start at the minimum legal wage with merit increases that are based on performance.

Rawdon is the first Canadian McDonald's outlet to sign a labour contract. Several other Canadian outlets have been certified by provincial labour authorities, but were unable to reach a first contract.

Ms Kitts said an outlet in Squamish, BC, was the first to be certified in North America. But Mr Ruel said the company decertified that union before he was able to negotiate a first contract.

Unions have organized other outlets in recent years, notably in Orangeville, Ont., in Montreal and in St-Hubert, Que.

But Mr Lortie said those outlets were closed or decertified shortly after. Another outlet, in the United States, was bulldozed by the franchisee shortly after it was certified, Mr Ruel said. "The company does everything it can to stop the union," he said.

With the first contract, the McDonald's workers in Rawdon will get a base pay of $7 an hour and a raise of 10 cents every six months on the job. "It's not a very good deal, but it's a start," Mr Lortie said. "This is the first time that everybody will get the same wage. There will be no favouritism."

More important, he said the workers will get seniority rights and layoff protection, a key factor in a resort town where the work is highly seasonal. The company has also agreed to stiffer safety regulations, a contentious issue in a restaurant that fries potatoes in boiling oil.

The labour contract in Rawdon will not apply to other McDonald's outlets because it is owned by an independent franchisee.

The two union leaders said McDonald's fought hard to stop the union coming in. They say the company and the franchisee harassed the union leaders by moving them to midnight shifts, giving them dirty jobs or by neglecting to call them into work.

"They had so many problems, they quit," Mr Lortie said. "They were only getting $7 a hour, so it wasn't worth it for them.

"We had to rebuild the union from scratch after they pushed out the union officers," he added. "It was a tough job to implement the new agreement."

SOURCE: Oliver Bertin, "Quebec Union's Labour Contract with McDonald's Is Landmark," *The Globe and Mail*, 18 Apr. 2002. Reprinted with permission from The Globe and Mail.

According to the 1995 *World Employment Report* of the International Labour Organization (ILO), the idea is erroneous that unions or good labour standards are the "fundamental cause of unemployment, and it is important to recognize the positive impacts for society in terms of greater equality and less poverty"; collective bargaining efforts should be regarded as an "important source of social well-being" (Jackson and Robinson, 2000: 96).

# Conclusion

## *Work in the Future, Our Future as Workers*

Workers and unions, of course, have limited powers. While newspaper headlines promote the "big" collective bargaining gains of the most strongly organized unions, most unionized workers across the country are struggling to attain basic rights that others managed to secure years, if not decades, ago. Every day, in small workplaces, employees (unionized and non-unionized) negotiate their rights. More often now than in the past, these are women, people of colour, the disabled—not members of the dominant groups in this country.

Their struggles have been difficult, and continue to be so, particularly in the context of the current assault on unions. In Ontario, the Harris-led Conservative government, for example, curbed the power of the Ontario Labour Relations Board by introducing legislation to remove the Board's right to give union certification to workers who have faced (illegal) intimidation by anti-union employers. The power of workers and their movements is being even more severely circumscribed by the aggressiveness of global capitalists, many of whom are openly supported by networks of governments in both developing and developed nations. Whether you work part-time at The Gap, labour a 60-hour week in a steel factory, freelance as a consultant, or find sporadic office employment through a temporary help agency, you are faced with a challenge.

Regardless of theoretical perspective or political agenda, scholars today are debating the nature of the challenge of the transformation of work. Young people entering the labour market for the first time and middle-aged people confronting reconfigured jobs and refashioned workplaces are both part of this transformation. Workers, young and old, must work in order to survive, to nurture families, to participate in life. Given this reality, it is crucial to know the debate, engage in it, and perhaps transform the world of work according to your own vision.

## ☐ Questions for Critical Thought

1. Think about where you are located in the economy. If you are not currently employed, where do you plan to find work? How does this depart from your parents' and grandparents' work histories? What factors have shaped (or constrained) your work-related aspirations?

2. Some employers believe that if you pay a worker more money (and offer better benefits), then you can compensate her or him for the boredom of work, loss of control, and lack of autonomy on the job. What do you think about this belief?

3. Think about the work that you perform in the course of an average day. What proportion of this is paid and what unpaid? Do you believe that we should define unpaid domestic activities as "work" that is of economic worth? If you were asked to calculate the economic worth of unpaid domestic labour, what factors would you take into account?

4. Most people in Canada today take the new computer technology for granted, but as a sociologist, you must take a closer, critical look. Consider some of the ways in which computer technology has reshaped employment opportunities and the nature of work.

5. A prevailing view is that the youth today are merely "stop-gap" workers and that young people themselves are not concerned about the nature of the jobs they perform. Why should sociologists bother writing about youth at work?

6. Do you believe that who you are (that is, female or male; Aboriginal, or of Asian or European or African descent; young or middle-aged; working-class; educated) is an important indicator of the type of work that you will perform? If so, in what ways? If not, explain.

7. Even though women's labour-force participation rate is now almost the same as men's, there are many persisting gender-based inequalities in employment. Identify some of these inequities. What are some of the formal and informal barriers to equality between women and men in the labour market today? How would you confront them?

8. Labour unions have long faced challenges in capitalist societies. Some people would argue that today union leaders and members face new challenges, perhaps more formidable than those of the past. Identify and discuss some of the new challenges that confront the labour movement in this country.

## ☐ Recommended Readings

**Barbara Ehrenreich, *Nickel and Dimed: On (Not) Getting By in America* (New York: Henry Holt, 2001).**
An extremely readable sociological (and personal) comment on "getting by" as a low-wage worker in the new economy. Ehrenreich, a sociologist, travelled throughout the United States, working as a hotel maid, a waitress, a cleaner, and a Wal-Mart clerk. She describes the hardship and indignity of her work.

**Randy Hodson, *Dignity at Work* (Cambridge: Cambridge University Press, 2001).**
Based on an examination of 109 organizational ethnographies, Hodson sensitively highlights the ways in which workers search for dignity and self-worth on the job.

**Graham S. Lowe, *The Quality of Work: A People-Centred Agenda* (Toronto: Oxford University Press, 2000).**
A refreshing and informative empirical analysis, by one of Canada's experts on the sociology of work, of the quality of work performed by Canadians today.

**Richard Sennett, *The Corrosion of Character: The Personal Consequences of Work in the New Capitalism* (New York: Norton, 1998).**
A meaningful, eloquent critique, by one of America's finest sociologists, of the consequences of the new flexible workplace on individual lives and moral identity.

**Stuart Tannock, *Youth at Work: The Unionized Fast-Food and Grocery Workplace* (Philadelphia: Temple University Press, 2001).**
An excellent, engaging study of youth at work. Tannock gives voice to young people themselves, their experiences and concerns, while at the same time offering a rigorous critique of the low-end service economy today.

## ☐ Recommended Web Sites

**Canadian Centre for Occupational Health and Safety (CCOHS)**
**www.ccohs.ca**
The CCOHS, based in Hamilton, Ontario, promotes a safe and healthy working environment by providing information and advice about occupational health and safety issues.

**CorpWatch**
**www.corpwatch.org**
CorpWatch is a San Francisco-based organization that monitors and critiques corporate-led globalization through education and activism. It seeks to foster democratic control over corporations by building grass-roots globalization—a diverse movement for human rights, labour rights, and environmental justice.

**International Labour Organization (ILO)**
**www.ilo.org**
The ILO was founded in 1919 and is now an agency of the United Nations. Its mandate is to promote and realize standards, fundamental principles, and rights at work.

***Labour/Le Travail***
**www.mun.ca/cclh/llt/**
*Labour/Le Travail* is the leading academic journal for labour studies in Canada. Founded in 1976, the journal publishes historical and contemporary articles on all aspects of work in Canada.

# 13

Augie Fleras

> > >

# Mass Media
# Communication

© PhotoDisc, Inc.

## ☐ Learning Objectives

In this chapter you will:

- learn to account for media in understanding patterns of social behaviour

- see the social dimensions of mass media communication through the relationship of media in society

- see how the relationship between media and society is created, maintained, challenged, and transformed by government policy

- see mass media communication as social construction in advancing hidden agendas and in defence of dominant ideology

- find out how intellectual and technological changes have created an identity crisis for the mass media

- discover the importance of fostering media literacy to navigating through the perils and promises of twenty-first-century Canada

# Introduction

## *Media in Society/Society in Media*

If someone were to ask you about crime in Canada, how would you respond to questions like "How much crime?" "What kind is most common?" "Who is most likely to commit crime?" "Who are the most common victims?" "What is the criminal justice system (from cops to courts to corrections) doing about fighting crime?" and "How successfully?" Each of these questions would elicit responses depending on the person and context, but it is highly unlikely that any response would reflect first-hand experience; after all, few of us have experienced crime directly as either victim or villain. Moreover, even those among us who have had this misfortune cannot confirm whether our experiences are typical or the exception.

Chances are your understanding of crime, criminals, and criminal justice is derived from exposure to **mass media**. Television programming relies on crime fighting as prime-time fodder; movies without a criminal dimension are few indeed; and news in general (but local news in particular) is consumed with highly charged stories of "cops" and "robbers" (Fleras, 2004). Nevertheless, concern is growing over media coverage of crime, which many see as misleading (Perlmutter, 2000), others as contradictory (Surette, 1998). However valid these assessments of media–crime relations, there is more to mass media than crime coverage. What we know, do, or believe is no less influenced by the content and structure of mass media communication:

- What is the primary source of sex education for young people, especially in terms of relating to the opposite gender at physical, emotional, and social levels? Is this knowledge based on parental advice or high school instruction? Probably not.
- Why do many continue to obsess over body weight and image even though we should know better than to judge others—and ourselves—by appearances?
- How do each of us become "gendered"—that is, develop concepts of what it means to be male and female in a world where conventional gender scripts are increasingly contested and evolving?
- Where do most of us obtain insights into the politics of diversity that embrace Canada's racial(ized) relations, ethnic diversity, and Aboriginal peoples? People tend to accept media versions as true because they have no reason not to. But can these sources of information be trusted?

- Why are some individuals prone to violence and anti-social behaviour? Is it because of something "in here" (inherited) or because of something "out there" (acquired)? How is the link between the "in here" and the "out there" mediated?
- Why are certain individuals admired as role models to emulate while others are demonized as problem people?

Each of the above questions points to mass media communication as an explanatory factor. Upon reflection, one realizes the degree to which our knowledge of the world "out there" is media-driven—often without much personal awareness or individual resistance. In the absence of personal experience for understanding social reality, mass media provide a preliminary and often primary point of contact about what is going on, why, and how. Their pervasiveness and persuasiveness are such that media messages appear inextricably linked with concepts of self-understanding, our relationships with each other, our place in society, our perception of Canada, and our understanding of social reality in lives generally.

Few would cavalierly dismiss the importance of mass media communication as windows of information. Rather than a frivolous diversion for amusement or distraction, the mass media (the plural of *medium*) are influential in framing what we see, think, and experience and how we relate to others. Media coverage draws our attention to some aspects of reality as normal and necessary—in large part by telling us what issues to think about, how to think about these issues, and whose voices will prevail in the discussions. Other aspects are deemed to be inferior or irrelevant because of how issues are verbally framed. In short, far from reflecting an already given social reality, the media contribute to its very construction as a convention—especially during times of diversity, change, and uncertainty. When the mass media provide an accurate reading of the world we inhabit, they appear to be doing their job. But when conflict-driven and celebrity-hungry coverage results in distortion or omission—either deliberately or inadvertently—the media should be criticized for doing a disservice to society and its members.

The conclusion seems inescapable: the mass media exert a powerful influence on society. Conversely, a changing society plays an equally powerful role in shaping the content of mass media communication. And it is this mutually reinforcing relationship—the theme of media in society and society in the media—

that informs this chapter. We will emphasize the social dimensions of mass media communication by addressing the dynamic nature of media–society relations. One side of this two-way process is the study of media in society. Media create an impact on society by establishing public discourses that define what is necessary, normal, and acceptable; alternative viewpoints are deemed to be unacceptable or a threat. Media outcomes also exert an effect on individuals, ranging from good to bad to in-between, depending, of course, on personal and social factors. The other side of the analytical divide is the focus on society in the media. Changes in society may trigger changes in media content, particularly when historically marginalized groups enlist media in challenging the prevailing distribution of power and privilege. This double articulation—media in society, society in the media—secures a conceptual framework for unpacking a relationship both complex and contested as well as evolving and incomplete.

## Defining Mass Media Communication

To say we live in a media(ted) world is surely an understatement. The magnitude of media is nothing less than astonishing. Just about everyone in Canada and the United States owns a television and a radio, has access to movies and magazines, reads some portion of a newspaper (either print or on-line), and routinely downloads or texts messages. Even those in the developing world are hopping aboard the media express, although it is estimated that nearly half of the world's population has yet to make their first phone call, let alone to have dial-up Internet service. The Internet offers access to about 2.5 billion publicly accessible documents (the "surface Web") while the "deep Web" (which contains information that requires membership fees) may be 500 times larger. The world produces about 31 million hours of original TV programming each year—enough to rivet even the most dedicated couch potato with 35 centuries of non-stop viewing. There are 66 million book titles in existence worldwide, in contrast to the modest 1,338 books held at the Sorbonne Library in Paris in the thirteenth century, regarded as the largest library in Europe at that time. To cap it off, the year 2002 produced 5 exabytes ($10^{18}$ bytes, or about 1 million MB) of information worldwide, or 500,000 times of all the holdings in the US Library of Congress (Lyman and Varian, 2003; Potter, 2005). Such a voluminous amount of information is ungraspable. Who, then, can

be surprised when people's minds drift into auto pilot for refuge from this info-glut?

For something so common and routine, the concept of mass media communication has proven difficult to define. Simply, the concept of mass media communication can be defined in three ways: (1) what it looks like, (2) what it is supposed to do, or (3) what it *really* does. Compounding the challenge of definition are the conventions that refer to a broad range of structures and activities encompassed by mass media communication. While *media* may refer to any device for transmitting information to a large audience, including newspapers, magazines, radio, television, film, and the Internet, media sociologists generally speak of *media* as *industries* or *businesses* that own or control interests in radio and television programming, production, and broadcasting; movies, theatres, and film distribution rights; music companies; newspaper, magazine, and book publishing; and Internet services and content providers (Kendall et al., 2004). The inception of new (computer-mediated) technologies has further reinforced references to media as content and as an institution of delivery (Maule, 2003).

Mass media and **mass communication** are analytically distinct yet mutually related concepts. *Mass media* generally refers to structures or institutions, while communication, in turn, connotes process and messages. The mass media have customarily been defined in terms of a distinct product distributed in a distinctive way, namely, books, magazines, newspapers, radio, music, film, video, television (Hoskins et al., 2004). Traditional media content is conveyed by print, electronically, or by photography (on film); in a digital world, this content can be distributed via the Internet or through vertically integrated systems of text, audio, and video content ("**convergence**"). Mass media, then, include technologically based communication structure (or institution) involving the centralized production and technology-mediated distribution of information and entertainment (Lorimer and Gasher, 2002). By contrast, *mass communication* consists of a process by which messages are encoded, transmitted, and decoded as well as transformed by this three-stage process. Mediating technologies are incorporated into the production and distribution of centrally produced and mechanically distributed messages. In short, *mass media communication* can be defined as the institutionalized process for producing and distributing centrally produced messages by way of mediating technologies.

The next issue in definition is, What are media supposed to do? Does watching (or listening to) public broadcasting elicit a different experience compared to commercial radio or television (Starowicz, 2003)? Is there yet another response that characterizes people's involvement with community media sources (including ethnic and alternative media)? The fact that most people acknowledge a difference is consistent with typologies of media based on what is being communicated, why, how, and with what purpose. Three media models can be discerned because of their underlying logic: commercial, public, and community.

- *Commercial (private) media* are those that many see as populist because of their commitment to give audiences what they want. Commercial media are privately owned, concerned primarily with making money or profit (usually through advertising or subscriptions) by providing consumers with safe and formulaic content, and generally reject any social responsibility for actions and outputs that do not entail the bottom line.
- *Public (or public interest) media* are viewed as elitist because of their mandate to provide audiences

### 13.1

# Human Diversity
## Ethnic Media: Putting
## Multiculturalism to Work in Canada

A distinction between mainstream media and ethnic media is widely acknowledged. Mainstream media include those private or public outlets that cater to the general public. By contrast, ethnic media are thought to target a specific ethnic minority. Ethnic media represent a flourishing industry in Canada. Canada's first ethnic papers were written in German and published in Halifax at the end of the eighteenth century; *Das Museum Canada* appeared in 1835 in the Waterloo region; and the black papers had come on the scene by the 1850s (including the *Provincial Freeman* and *The Voice of the Fugitive*). Today, about 350 ethnic papers cater to their audiences on a daily, weekly, monthly, or twice-yearly basis. As well, there are ethnic radio stations and programming and multicultural TV programming, such as Omni 1 and 2, which tap into Canada's ethnic diversity. Finally, Aboriginal peoples media, begun on CBC radio in the 1920s, now includes the Aboriginal Peoples Television Network (APTN), created in 1999, on our cable system.

Ethnic media originated for a variety of reasons, both reactive and proactive (Riggins, 1992). On the reactive side, ethnic and racialized minorities reacted to their exclusion from the mainstream presses except as problems or troublemakers. Their role in Canada's political,

social, and economic life was also glossed over or distorted—in effect making it doubly important for an outlet to reflect and reinforce their interests and concerns as both "new Canadians" and Canadian-born minorities. On the proactive side, ethnic media provide stories of interest and relevance to ethnic minorities by relying on a language, perspective, and tone that resonate more deeply with audiences.

In short, ethnic media play both inward- and outward-looking roles within ethnic communities (Silverstone and Georgiou, 2005). Identity and community are fostered through stories that secure social cohesion, foster cultural maintenance, and convey information about the homeland. The emergence of digital technology in an era of global migration has enabled transnational (or diasporic) communities to maintain contact with far-flung members (Karim, 1998). Ethnic media also provide an integrative function by providing ethnic minorities with information about fitting in and settling down in Canada. As well, they may assume an advocacy role by pointing out injustices that confront the ethnic community. This dual function creates an ambiguity. On one hand, ethnic media are monocultural because they cater to single-minority audiences. On the other, the existence of ethnic media collectively contributes to Canada's multicultural landscape.

with a product they are perceived to need. Public media are government- or taxpayer-owned, focused largely on providing a product that enlightens citizens across a broad range of programming with a special emphasis on "highbrow" material, and geared to maximizing public good or national interests.

- In contrast with the vastness and remoteness of private or public media, *community media* are generally perceived as inclusive and localized. Community media are geared towards providing a service for those minority audiences whose interests and concerns are largely ignored by mainstream media. Community media tend to be locally owned and to reflect localized interests, and content is directed at empowering those who have been marginalized. Included under community media are *alternative* and *ethnic* media.

The expression "mass media communication" sounds innocent enough. But mass media do more than communicate; more accurately, they communicate by manipulating patterns of persuasion to achieve a desired effect. Used largely by governments and private interests, media serve as instruments of persuasion for conveying notions of right from wrong, acceptable from unacceptable, and normalcy from deviance. Mass media are not simply conveyors of someone else's information. They are loaded instead with values, priorities, and hidden agendas that draw attention to some aspects of reality as normal and necessary while discrediting others as irrelevant or inferior. Consider the commercial media: they are not in the business of informing or entertaining per se. Nor do they see themselves as agents of enlightenment or progressive social change. On the contrary, commercial media exist primarily for one reason: to make money for themselves and their shareholders by persuading people to watch their content, purchase advertised products, and buy into a consumerist lifestyle.

The centrality of advertising to commercial media draws attention to several paradoxes that initially may appear counter-intuitive to the reader. First, consider the relationship between advertising and programming. Contrary to popular belief, advertising is not a disruption to programming, given its centrality in financing commercial mass media. Put baldly, television programming can be interpreted as an interruption to the main function of mass media—to make profits through advertising. Second, audiences are not the main customers for commercial media; rather,

advertisers are the main customers, while audiences are primarily a commodity for sale to advertisers. Third, while we normally think of ourselves as "watching TV," it is just as accurate to say that television is watching *us*—monitoring our viewing habits and conveying this information to marketing and advertising agencies. These inversions serve as a reminder of the complexities that inform the relationship of media to society.

## Rethinking Media Communication: From "Mass" to "Interactive"

The concept of mass media means something different today than in the past. Media discourses were once littered with references to "mass audiences," "mass messages," and "mass society." For many, the notion of mass media was synonymous with a piece of furniture in the corner of a family room, expensive and immobile, with everyone huddled around the "tube" to watch their favourite evening programs on over-the-air network stations (with "bunny ears" to improve black-and-white reception). Radios—from big boxy sets to portables—were equally popular as sources of mass information and mass entertainment, as was a rotary dial telephone, an evening paper, letters delivered by a postal service, and a movie on weekends at a single-screen or drive-in theatre. Choices were limited: media information and mass entertainment were prepackaged and beamed from a central source, drip-fed to audiences largely at media convenience—not yours—at a predetermined time and place, with the same standardized package for everyone.

How times have changed! Instead of describing a system of mass production of standardized goods for mass delivery to a homogeneous mass, references to "mass media" now invoke everything and everywhere, everybody and anytime. Thanks to the marvels of computer-mediated communication, we live in a wired/wireless world where everyone is connected but no one is in charge. Unlike the days of one-to-many mass communication, people in a networked society can now communicate on a many-to-many or many-to-one basis for the first time in history, at a chosen time or on demand, across borders and on a global scale, and without undue central interference. Televisions are increasingly part of a sophisticated home entertainment centre that taps into cable, digital, and satellite technology for selection beyond belief. Blogs (personal Internet diaries as opinion pieces) are now promoted as the new journalism by drawing attention to overlooked stories, encouraging discussion and debate where none existed before, and providing a kind of feeder system for an increasingly beleaguered traditional media. Evening papers have given way to morning versions, with most having an Internet edition to ensure cutting-edge coverage over the competition. Mobile wireless phones with a capacity to do almost anything are *de rigueur* for anyone who wants to impress or connect. To compensate for loss of advertising revenue because of downloading or commercial-stripping devices such as PVR (personal video recorders) and TiVo, advertising is more intrusive than ever, including advertisements in even so-called commercial-free zones, such as product placement in movies. Movies remain a prime source of entertainment even if many prefer to download them because of cost or convenience. Finally, the Internet has proven to be every bit as revolutionary as the printing press. The Internet has transformed everything from how we interact and create "virtual" communities, to changes in how goods (books and music) and services (travel) are created and marketed, purchased, and consumed. Its promise to draw the world closer together—a kind of global village of interconnected intelligences—may yet prove a reality (De Kerckhove, 1997).

Until recently, the concept of "mass" was pivotal to conventional studies of mass media communication. Mass media institutions produced mass messages for mass audiences in hopes of creating mass responses. References to "mass" included the notions of a large and widely dispersed audience, large scale in delivery and consumption, unidirectionality and impersonality in distribution, standardized content, and mass production for a one-size-fits-all market. Communication involved a largely linear process from one to many, that is, a transmission of information or entertainment from a central source to a vast audience, with limited degree of feedback. Predictably, then, mass media communication was defined as a technologically driven process of one-way communication by which standardized and mass-produced content was impersonally conveyed to a large and amorphous audience.

But technology, especially computer technology, appears to have taken the "mass" out of mass media communication. This "de*mass*ification" process has profoundly influenced the creation, distribution, and consumption of media messages, with corresponding shifts in how people process media information:

- The explosion of cellular and on-line communication has catapulted the consumer ("audiences") into the limelight as the centre of attention in a media world (Grewal, 2005).
- Instead of producing a standardized pitch for everybody, media messages are increasingly customized around the needs and anxieties of market niches.
- Instead of conveying messages from one to many, as might be expected with centralized sources, the Internet can be described as a pattern of person-to-person (or "interpersonal") communication on a mass scale. Four possibilities prevail: one to many (spam), one to one, many to many, and many to one.
- Instead of restricting media to a one-way system of communication, structures are in place to allow

 **13.2**

# Sociology in Action
## It's a Media World

The urge to communicate across time and space is one of the more fundamental impulses of the modern era. Many of us spend our waking hours surrounded—and swamped—by a flood of media images, messages, and narratives. The average North American spends more than half of his or her waking hours in some media-related activity—more than any other daily endeavour, from sleeping to socializing (Biagi and McKie, 2001). Try using a diary to keep track of all the mass media communication you encounter on a daily basis, from the time you wake up to the time you go to sleep. Include all your media exposure, both deliberate (for example, watching television) and accidental (driving by a billboard), as well as the amount of new (computer-mediated) media compared to conventional media. What does your media exposure look like?

interaction by way of feedback and exchange. Communication is no longer monological (directed one way) but rather dialogical, involving a two-way process of dialogue. In this sense, "media communication" can be visualized as a verb involving a process of interaction and construction rather than as a noun for mass consumption.

- Historically, mass media communication was perceived as a powerful force with the capacity to persuade or constrain, thus requiring some kind of regulation to ensure control over the (public) airwaves. Audiences were generally seen as absorptive sponges that uncritically absorbed media messages without much resistance or reflection. Today audiences are seen as active and interactive—that is, as rational consumers who negotiate the meaning of media messages according to needs, personality, and circumstances.

- Media effects are increasingly couched in non-deterministic frames of reference. Effects are no longer defined as direct, uniform, and causal; emphasis instead is on the indirect, varied, and negotiated. Growing disillusionment over discovering the causal basis of media effects has shifted scholarly attention towards (a) understanding meaning (how people process media information) and (b) constructing media as constructed texts. In other words, attention has shifted from how media make and remake people to how people make the media do work for them.

The trends are unmistakable: a mechanistic approach to media-society relations is no longer tenable. Endorsed instead is a new pattern of media communication involving a technologically driven process of interactive communication in which active audiences engage with customized content to create a variety of outputs. To be sure, both interactive and mass media communication remain powerful forces of persuasion with the potential to convince, challenge, confirm, delude, or change. But their power lies not in telling people what to think, but in telling us what to think *about*, by framing (or organizing) issues in a way that promotes a preferred reading. Audiences are no longer regarded as cultural dopes who are easily duped or robotically manipulated. Instead, audiences are seen as rational beings with a capacity to negotiate meanings depending on the situational context. With technology having taken the "mass" out of mass media communication, mass media are now in a position to customize messages around increasingly fragmented (niche rather than mass) audiences.

Three implications are immediately discernible. First, reference to media as "verb" or "doing" or "creating" is increasingly displacing conventional notions of media as "noun" or "thing for consumption." Second, the expression "interactive media communication" is gradually displacing the concept of "mass" as the preferred frame of reference. To get some idea of the distinction, Table 13.1 compares mass with interactive media along ideal–typical grounds. Third, appearances are deceiving: despite growing customization and interactivity, the "mass" in mass media continues to matter. Mass media are becoming more concentrated than ever through mergers and convergence because of a belief that bigger is better. This contradictory tension exerts a powerful impact and effect on society and its members.

# Media in Society

Every society is under pressure to survive and prosper. The keys to prosperity and survival appear five-fold: first, to foster some degree of national identity as basis for securing both internal and external sovereignty; second, to nurture a sense of national unity by instilling a sense of community through shared values; third, to ensure economic prosperity for all its members; fourth, to promote co-operation and consensus through the right kind of socialization; and fifth, to impose some degree of control to ensure conformity and order (Fleras, 2005).

## *Canada-Building and the Media*

Canada is no exception to these imperatives for building society. But a series of challenges complicates the attainment of a cohesive and distinctive society in Canada. These challenges include:

- *Geography*. The sprawling land mass called Canada poses problems related to unity and identity. Just one quick look at a topographic map of North America clearly reveals an anomaly: the east–west axis on which Canada was constructed goes against the grain of a natural north–south division. The Pacific regions of Canada and the United States have more in common (geographically speaking) with each other than with the rest of the country. Similarly, commonalities exist between the Prairie provinces and the American Midwest, between the Great Lakes region (including Quebec) and the American north-central belt, and between the Atlantic provinces and the Northeast states.

Table 13.1 **Media Models/Communication Discourses**

|  | From Mass Media Communication | to Interactive Media Communication |
|---|---|---|
|  | media as noun (thing) | media as verb (process) |
| Relationship | monological (one-way) | dialogical (two-way) |
| Flow of messages | top down (authoritarian) | bottom up (democratic/anarchic) |
| Content | standardized | customized |
| Target | mass audience (broadcasting) | market niche (narrowcasting) |
| Perception of audience | mass/passive | active/interactive |
| Media effects | deterministic<br>a) domination (social control)<br>b) socialization (thought control) | non-deterministic<br>a) contested<br>b) resistance |
| Focus of media studies | explaining why by<br>  measuring behaviour | understanding how by<br>  interpreting meaning |

- *Demography.* Canada's population of 31 million is not evenly distributed across the country but concentrated primarily within a 150-kilometre radius of the American border. Large parts of Canada are sparsely populated and remote from major urban centres.

- *Diversity.* Canada is an extremely diverse society because of current immigration patterns. Canada's diversity includes Aboriginal peoples (who are diverse among themselves), the descendants of the original colonists (French and English), and nearly 200 different ethnic groups representing immigrants or descendants of immigrants. However, much of the new diversity is not spread across Canada but concentrated in four major regions: Montreal, southern Ontario, the Edmonton–Calgary corridor, and the lower BC mainland and Vancouver.

- *History.* Canada has long been subject to colonial pressures that have compromised its development. French colonization was replaced by English colonization, which in turn was superseded by American economic colonization that continues into the present.

- *Location.* Canada derives benefits from its location next to the world's most formidable economic and military power. Yet such proximity has played havoc with defining national identity and securing Canadian sovereignty from the colossus to the south (Fleras, 2005).

Let's face it: Canada's status as a society is hardly conventional. Canada lacks many of the integrative functions that inform European societies or the United States. There is no common language, culture, or history to bind Canadians. Revolutionary origins or founding myths to foster a sense of peoplehood are no less absent. Instead, Canada must be interpreted as a socially constructed community in constant need of shoring up and repair work. In the absence of orthodox society-binding elements, Canada has historically embraced the mass media to provide an electronic glue—a railroad of the mind—for holding Canadians together. For media to discharge their obligations in advancing national and public interests, the airwaves were defined as public spaces—a virtual public square where Canadians could meet on common ground and communicate with each other (Taras, 2001).

The Broadcasting Acts of 1932, 1968, and 1991 secured a blueprint for advancing national interests through radio and later television programming. CBC radio first aired in 1936 in hopes of blunting the free-market incursions of American radio. The introduction of CBC television in 1952 provided Canadians with an alternative to American programming. The establishment of the CRTC (Canadian Radio and Television Commission, now the Canadian Radio-television and Telecommunications Commission) in 1968 continued the regulatory efforts of earlier agencies through the granting of licences for radio and television stations, ensuring each complied with the provisions of the Broadcasting Act and the terms of the licence. The imposition of quotas for minimum Canadian content on radio and television soon followed.

The value of public broadcasting and regulatory systems remains contested (Taras, 2001). For some, both a global market economy and the border-busting imperatives of modern technology have rendered obsolete the concept of social engineering through a public broadcaster. For others, the threat of eroding

Canada's integrity and identity by globalization and technology confirms the need for a public broadcaster. For still others, it is not a case of either/or, but of both/and—that is, how to provide Canadians with a public service that is consistent with emergent realities. In any case, there is no denying the impact of the public broadcaster in re-contouring the shape of Canadian society.

## Media Impacts

What is the impact of mass media communication on society? Do the mass media contribute to the creation of a stable and cohesive society? Are the media more likely to generate competition, conflict, and divisiveness, or is it more accurate to say that media are inseparable from those meaningful social interactions at the core of human society? Responses to these questions are varied, of course, but vary with how society is theorized: that is, as consensus, as conflict, or as construction. Each of these sociological theories of society—**functionalism**, **conflict theory** (including Marxist and feminist), and **symbolic interactionism**—endorses fundamental premises (foundational knowledge) about society (or social reality) with respect to the nature of society, why it exists as it does, how it is constructed, who gets what, and why. These sociological theories of social reality (or society) can then be compared by examining how the media contribute to the organization and dynamics of society.

### Sociological Theories of Social Reality

*Functionalist* theories embrace the idea of social reality (or society) as an integrated whole of parts that collectively contribute to the survival of society. Children need to be socialized, goods and services must be produced and distributed, a sense of meaning and continuity must be instilled, and some degree of social control is indispensable. Functionalism begins with the premise that every society is built around the dynamics of constancy, community, and consensus. It concludes with the notion that institutions must be interpreted on grounds of their contribution to societal order and stability. Functionalist theorizing also argues that a stable and co-operative society cannot survive without securing a normative value consensus through the internalization of appropriate values and beliefs.

The mass media contribute to attaining this moral consensus. First, the media create an enlightened and informed population as a prerequisite for a stable and prosperous social order. Second, the transmission, circulation, and reinforcement of core values and key norms help in defining what is right or wrong, desirable or acceptable. The media help in setting the agenda, conferring and legitimizing status, defining which issues are important, and constructing identity through role-modelling. Third, a sense of connectedness is generated through collective engagement and common shared experiences. Fourth, exposure to media enhances the possibilities of a cosmopolitan outlook, with its potential to eliminate inward-looking provincialisms.

In contrast to the functionalist emphasis on system equilibrium, normative consensus, and institutional integration, a *conflict* perspective portrays society as a contested site of unequal yet competing groups perpetually engaged in a struggle for scarce resources related to **power**, wealth, and prestige. The mass media are seen as critical in creating and maintaining inequality through content and coverage that reinforce the prevailing distribution of power and resources. Media content is filled with values and agendas promoting the rich and powerful while diminishing the needs and aspirations of those who are poor and powerless. Confrontation and conflict over who gets what are inevitable under these conditions: those in positions of power, property, and privilege will do everything—both consciously and inadvertently—to secure their status, while those who occupy marginal positions will struggle to achieve greater parity.

**Marxist** conflict perspectives endorse a class-based analysis. For Marxists, social inequality and class conflict over the production of wealth are keys to a theory of society. Social relations can be reduced to two competitive forces. The media industry itself is owned and controlled by big business; not surprisingly, media content tends to reflect, reinforce, and advance their interests at the expense of others (Winter, 2001). In other words, the bottom line is profit, with the result that coverage is organized to maximize advertising revenue and audience ratings. **Feminist** conflict perspectives tend to see gender conflict as a source of inequality in society. The interplay of sexism and androcentrism with **patriarchy** denies women full and equal participation in society. Media contribute to this gendered inequality; after all, media are not a neutral communication but reflect the interests of those whose agendas have historically informed media content and messages.

Both functionalist and conflict perspectives rely on society as a basic point of departure. Society is portrayed as external to individuals: that is, it is logically prior to and determinative of human behaviour through a process of internalization known as **socialization**, including by mass media. For functionalists, human behaviour is generated by knowledge of those rules, roles, and relationships that cumulatively contribute to societal stability and order. For conflict theorists, social behaviour is derived from those forces that dominate or exploit as opposing groups engage in continuous competition over scarce resources. Mass media are seen as contributing to both outcomes—in opposition at times, but simultaneously at other times.

By contrast, *symbolic interactionist* theories of society disagree with this assessment of social reality. They disdain conventional theories of society as having needs or class interests. There is even greater dislike of determinist theories that reduce humans to robots who mechanically respond to external stimuli or impersonal forces. Interactionists see society as a human accomplishment—a dynamic process created and recreated by social actors who define situations and go about their business of constructing realities through social action. The social world we inhabit is defined as formative, emergent, and **negotiated** because of this interplay between structure (out there) and meaning (in here).

Symbolic interactionism differs from functionalist and conflict perspectives in defining media–society relations. Attention is drawn to the role of media as a social construction that is both constructed and constructing—"constructed," because media constitute a constructed reality in their own right rather than anything natural or normal, with their own set of agendas and biases, created by individuals in meaningful interaction who make choices and take chances (albeit within a broader context not necessarily of their making), and "constructing," because of media involvement in the social construction of reality, that is, how people incorporate the media in helping to define realities and to act on these definitions in creating human social life. Table 13.2 summarizes the relationship between society and media from the perspective of these sociological theories of society.

## Generating Public Discourses

The impact of the mass media on society can be discerned in a second way. Media outputs do not have a direct impact on society. Rather, media impacts are generated by articulating public discourses about what is normal and necessary. Attention is drawn to some aspects of reality as acceptable or superior, while other aspects are glossed over as inferior, irrelevant, or threatening. This agenda-setting activity is interpreted differently by each of the sociological theories of social reality. For functionalists, media messages contribute to the smooth functioning of society; for conflict theorists, domination and control is the result; and for symbolic interactionists, this agenda is itself under constant construction. These discourses or debates then become the basis by which individuals become informed—or misinformed—about the society they live in. Box 13.3 provides an excellent example of how media discourses can distort people's understanding of social reality while simultaneously creating a social climate that clashes with public interests.

## *Media Effects*

Fascination with mass media communication is animated by the topic of **media effects**. What influence do media have on people's attitudes and behaviour? Are media effects powerful, direct, and long-lasting, or are they indirect, diffused, short-term, and highly variable depending on context, person, criteria, and consequences? Why are some people seemingly so susceptible to media messages? And how do we prevent a repeat of the media-inspired teenage shootings at Columbine or at Red Lake First Nations? Sociological interest in media effects coincides with sociology's commitment to understand or explain human behaviour by situating it within the broader context. Students are no less intrigued by media effects but often take a narrow view of the link with people's behaviour. High-profile tragedies are often cited as evidence of media effects. However, because

## Table 13.2 **Sociological Theories of Society and the Place of the Media**

|  | **Functionalism** | **Conflict** | **Interactionism** |
|---|---|---|---|
| Nature of society | integrated whole | site of inequality | dynamic process |
| Normal state of society | stability and order | competition, change contradiction, conflict | social construction of reality |
| What holds society together | consensus | power/force | defining situations |
| Role of media in society | contribute to order/stability | contribute to inequality | part of the definitional process |

# Sociology in Action

"If it bleeds, it leads; if it scares, it airs": A Case Study of the Media Coverage of Crime

Much of what we know about crime, criminals, and the criminal justice system is gleaned from the mass media. Most of us (thankfully) rarely have first-hand experience with this dimension, with the result that the media provide our first and often our only point of contact with the criminal world. Crime news is packaged as objective and newsworthy, but it conceals the production values behind the decision-making, with the result that audiences come to believe that news media coverage of crime is accurate and representative rather than a constructed convention. And, yet, are the media telling us the whole truth, nothing but the truth, about the world out there?

What do the media, including newscasting, TV programming, and movies, tell us about crime, criminality, and control? First, rates of crime are increasing—at least judging by the volume of crime stories in news, TV programs, and movies. Second, much of this crime is violent, involving grisly homicides and "shoot 'em up" encounters between "cops" and "crooks." References to white-collar crime, including workplace, environmental, and corporate crime, are generally downplayed. Third, it's a dangerous world out there because of violent crimes perpetrated by strangers ("the stranger is danger"). Fourth, criminals are not like us, but a breed apart, with a tendency to be ruthlessly calculating and cold-blooded or irrationally impulsive. Finally, the criminal justice system usually catches the culprit by way of careful investigative work by detectives who splice together evidence from, say, forensic scientists.

So much for "reel" reality. What about *real* reality? First, crime rates (including youth crime rates) have declined both in Canada and the United States since the early 1990s. Second, most crime is categorized as property crime, while homicides, abductions, and attempted homicides—the stuff of news, TV, and films—are relatively rare. Third, strangers, not family and

friends, inflict most of the violent crime. Fourth, criminals are not from Mars but a lot like us earthlings. They want the same things as we do (success, popularity, money) but resort to unconventional (criminal) means to attain those goals. And most of us engage in petty criminal acts on a daily basis, from jaywalking to pinching office supplies. Fifth, most crime is solved not by police work alone but as a result of community input. Criminologist David Bayley (1994) has estimated that police solve as few as 4 per cent of crimes without the assistance of community members.

In short, media depictions of crime, criminality, and criminal justice appear to be at odds with the real world. Some would argue that what appears in the news or in entertainment is the exact opposite of what really happens (Surette, 1998). Others take a softer position (Perlmutter, 2000): media coverage emphasizes what occurs least often and under-reports what happens most frequently. In either case, a structural (systemic) bias appears, ignoring those aspects of social reality inconsistent with the news values of a prevailing news paradigm (Fleras, 2004). But all agree on why this distortion occurs: in this celebrity-crazed era, crime sells because of drama, emotion, excitement, and visuals, and audiences never seem to tire of crime shows—especially among the most desired demographics.

As a reader you may want to conclude with a shrug and a "so what." Watching televised crime is simply a form of entertainment or fantasy that most people recognize as such and dismiss accordingly. But media depictions of crime may generate public discourses about social reality that influence public opinion and public policy. Individuals may be attracted to policing for the wrong reason, thanks to the media-inspired excitement of collaring crooks, and may subsequently engage in forms of law enforcement that are inappropriate or discriminatory. Politicians may pass laws on fighting crime based on what they see on TV or in the news—even if these laws fail to address the problem or to offer appropriate solutions. The news media tend to ignore the contextual basis of crime, thus reinforcing the blaming of individual offenders. Conservative ideologies capitalize on public fears when advancing a diet of vigilantism, stricter laws, longer prison terms, and tougher policing. Moreover, news may reinforce racial

stereotypes because of its fixation with violent or street crime (Benson, 2005).

Finally, audiences are known to overestimate the amount of street crime, presumably because of constant exposure to media crime (Gerbner and Gross, 1976). This overestimation can make people internalize a disproportional fear of being victimized by crime (Altheide, 2002). The concept of society suffers accordingly when people lose the trust that greases the interactional basis of a healthy social reality.

such incidents are seen as isolated and infrequent, many people dismiss media effects as something that happens only to other people (Potter, 2005).

Perceptions of media effects are highly varied, even contradictory. For some, excessive exposure to media breeds passivity (couch potatoes); for others, aggressiveness is the result. For some, such exposure contributes to crime by glamorizing criminal role models; for others, it contributes to collective consensus by fostering shared values regarding right and wrong. For some, media trivializes reality; for others, public debate and social action are fostered. For some, the media are little more than "dumbing down" to the lowest common denominator; for others, the effect is cognitively empowering. As Rob Salem, TV critic for the *Toronto Star*, points out, a 24 January 2005, episode of the hit series *24* involved the lives of 21 distinct characters and 9 primary narrative threads within 44 minutes of viewing time (Salem, 2005). Opinions remain polarized: to one side, public support for the magic-bullet theory of media effects persists—that is, media are powerful and persuasive because audiences uncritically absorb media messages and blindly act on them. To the other side are skeptics and media scholars. According to this line of thinking, audiences are not like empty wheelbarrows that can be filled with media content and pushed around with impunity (Fleras, 2003). To the contrary, they are generally perceived as active and interactive agents who take the initiative in negotiating and interpreting media messages. Not surprisingly, mass media are increasingly seen as sites of contestation, that is, a kind of social battleground for an ongoing struggle between media's preferred meaning and the oppositional meanings that audiences bring to the forum.

Media effects are not restricted just to individuals. Institutions, also, are affected by the media in ways both direct and indirect, in the long term and in the short run. Political institutions have changed dramatically because of the media. Instead of old-fashioned speech-making and backroom deals, politics is increasingly driven by opinion polls, slick and expensive negative ads, and media-savvy spin doctors for improving the appearance of candidates (McChesney, 1999). Other institutions, such as the family, are undergoing change because of social pressures that the media amplify. For example, many argue that media create a higher demand for consumer products, which means longer working hours for individuals, with a corresponding influence on patterns of parenting, parent–child relations, and even the notion of media as a shared experience. Finally, media effects cannot be seen in isolation but must be seen within the broader context of other influences (Potter, 2005). We live in a complex society where a variety of forces are constantly at work, often at cross-purposes to each other; media are but one set of important players in the accelerating pace of life. And because media-driven institutions remain influential, as W. James Potter (2005) reminds us, we can conclude that media exert an indirect effect on individuals through these institutions.

### Media Violence and Violent Behaviour

Exploring the link between television violence and violent behaviour exposes the paradoxes of causality. The question is straightforward enough: Is there a causal relationship between violence in the media and violent behaviour? Many would say yes. Over 3,000 studies since the late 1940s have explored this relationship, with the vast majority indicating some kind of relationship, ranging from the causal to the correlational (see Freedman, 2002). Many academics and professional bodies have come to the same conclusion (Grossman and DeGaetano, 1999; Macbeth, 2001). Others are not so sure, and argue that media provide a convenient scapegoat, thus enabling us to overlook contributing factors such as poverty. Not surprisingly, the general public is confused by competing claims: to one side are researchers and child advocates who assume the worst; to the other side are Hollywood industry representatives who tend to underplay the effects of media violence (Bushman and Anderson, 2001).

Put bluntly, there are many difficulties in uncovering a causal relationship between media violence and violent behaviour, and that makes it doubly important to problematize this relationship by exposing the complexities inherent in establishing a causal link (Potter, 2005). Questions abound: Do media exert a similar influence on everyone who watches them, or do negative effects depend on types of portrayals of violence, types of viewers, and types of environment? Does the type of media make a difference? Do boys and girls respond differently? Are cartoons more likely than police shows to elicit violent reactions? To what extent are video games a culprit? Do violent films such as *Sin City* or *Kill Bill* glamorize the cult of killing by making killing look cool? Should films like *Natural Born Killers* be interpreted as a satire on media fascination with serial killers? Do serious but violent films such as *Saving Private Ryan* have the same effect on audiences? The debate over the nature of the relationship is more than academic: if media violence is the problem at interpersonal and societal levels, any effective solution must be consistent with how the problem is defined.

Violence may be a universal phenomenon insofar as no human group is without it, yet this universality has not made it easier to explain or control. As is often the case, much of the debate hinges on what exactly constitutes violence, both in real life and in the media. Of particular note is the need to **operationalize** (convert abstract concepts into measurable properties) such terms as *media violence*, *violent behaviour*, and *causality*. What do we mean by violence? Is war violence? Is self-defence violence? Are documentaries about violence, violence? Is professional sport a site of violence? Is violence the same as conflict, aggression, deviance, or anti-social behaviour? Is it only about physical harm, or should its definition include emotional and psychological abuse? Does it have to be deliberate, or can violence be inadvertent and accidental? Is vio-

lence still violence when approved by the state, legally sanctioned, or endorsed by social norms?

Violence on television appears to have taken the brunt of criticism for misleading Canada's youth. To some extent, the criticism appears deserved. Graphic portrayals that convey pain may be one thing; random depictions of violence as a joke may be quite another (that is, the differences between *Home Alone* and *Pulp Fiction* and *The Matrix*). Television routinely takes what is harrowing about violence and transforms it into something exciting, ennobling, or empowering. Thus, what would by all accounts be a sordid and grisly event is sanitized into something relatively painless or harmless—even redemptive—and no amount of moralizing about evil or pain disrupts its "cool" effect. Violent encounters are portrayed as humorous, exciting, and glamorous in advancing the entertainment demands of prime-time audiences and video-gamers. Those routinely engaged in these actions rarely are punished. If anything, a glamorized form of masculine violence is likely to enhance perpetrator status and stature; after all, negotiation and compromise for solving problems tend to be time-consuming and inconclusive. By contrast, violent solutions are clear-cut and unambiguous.

But is there a causal relationship? If so, what precisely is the nature of this relationship between media violence and violent behaviour? Does televised violence provide the cues, establish models, reinforce existing patterns, and stimulate learning of new behaviour? Substantial evidence suggests that media violence influences people's attitudes and beliefs (Brannigan and Hardwick, 2001). New attitudes may be formed in some cases; more often, existing attitudes may be reinforced. Sustained exposure may create a more callous and indifferent attitude to the suffering of others, together with an unwillingness to do something about it. Sustained exposure may also exaggerate viewers' fear of becoming victims in a world perceived to be more violent and dangerous than it really is (Gerbner and Gross, 1976).

What about causation? Does television viewing cause violent behaviour? If so, what precisely is the nature of this imitative effect? Does exposure to violence lead to imitation, or is television a poor medium of socialization since nobody takes it seriously? Consider how the media–behaviour relationship may prove correlational rather than causal because of the difficulties in isolating causes from effects in a society where competition and aggression are the norm rather than the exception. In a society saturated with competition and conflict, causal relations may be impossible to detect. And what about the possibility that the causal arrows work in reverse? That is, more violence-prone individuals may be drawn to violent fare on television, thereby reinforcing pre-existing dispositions? Even more intriguing is the possible absence of any direct relationship between media and behaviour. For example, exposure to TV violence may even reduce social violence if portrayed from a victim's point of view, according to Dr Jurge Grimm of Germany's Mannheim University (editorial, *Christchurch Press*, 25 July 1996).

Evidence to date points to a balanced cautiousness: To isolate one medium as a primary culprit while ignoring other sources is simplistic. But to ignore the effects of media on human behaviour is both irresponsible and dangerous. We need to move away from a dogma of media determinism without discarding the possibility that media effects are real but tend to be negotiated, indirect, and situational—with the result that certain groups are more likely to transform violent media messages into violent actions. And while some deny any direct causal links, most studies and parents continue to believe prolonged exposure is unhealthy, proving yet again that when it comes to media, perception *is* reality.

# Society in Media

Until recently, most media studies tended to frame mass communication as a relatively self-contained system. A fixation with the construction, distribution, and consumption of media messages prevailed over their placement within a broader context. Increasingly, however, attention is directed at the relationship of society to mass media, including new ways of framing issues related to **class**, **race**, and **gender**. Pressure is mounting to portray a reality that is respectful of diversity and gender rather than coverage from a purely "pale-male" perspective. To date, however, patterns of minority inclusiveness have proven both shallow and tokenistic and rarely challenge traditional images of minorities as inferior, irrelevant, remote in time and place, problem people, and not-quite-Canadian. The gendered nature of mass media communication persists as well. Women and men continue to stand in a different relationship to media institutions and messages because of male privilege as the unquestioned norm in processing what we see or hear. Finally, media institutions continue to be owned and controlled by big business and corporate interests. Depictions of working classes and the poor tend to be slanted accordingly.

Of course, not everyone agrees with this assessment. According to one line of thinking, mainstream media do not exist to inform or entertain. Nor do they exist to promote progressive social change or advance social engineering. Media exist to make money by making the right kind of noise regardless of the consequences for society at large. Others disagree, and argue that all mass media, but especially broadcast media such as TV and radio that employ the public airwaves to convey their messages, have a responsibility because of the power they wield to inform, persuade, and enlighten. Such oppositional views have resulted in ongoing debates over the role of society in media.

## *Media and Minorities*

Canada is widely known—and renowned—as a multicultural society. Such an observation can be operationalized at several levels. First, Canada is multicultural in terms of demographic fact. Nearly 19 per cent of Canada's population is foreign-born (second-highest in the world after Australia, at 22 per cent), with about 14 per cent identifying as visible minorities and another 3 to 4 per cent as Aboriginal. This multicultural diversity is expected to expand in the foreseeable future to incorporate 51 per cent of the population in Toronto and Vancouver by 2017, thanks to immigration patterns from so-called non-conventional sources. Second, Canada is multicultural because of a dominant ideology that endorses tolerance and diversity as a core value—at least in theory (Fleras, 2002). Third, Canada is multicultural at an official level. Multiculturalism originated as an all-party policy agreement in 1971, then was entrenched in the Constitution Act as an interpretive principle (that is, nothing in the Charter of Rights and Freedoms is to be interpreted in a manner inconsistent with the enhancement and preservation of Canada's multicultural character) and then accorded statutory standing with passage of the Multiculturalism Act in 1988. Fourth, Canada is multicultural because of a commitment to put the principles of multiculturalism into practice. Mainstream institutions are expected to be inclusive of diversity by improving institutional rules of reward, procedures for hiring and promotion, removal of discriminatory barriers, and delivery of services or products.

Canada's mass media are no exception to this commitment to inclusiveness. Even if racialized minorities fall outside the "preferred" demographic as measured by disposable income (Starowicz, 2003), mainstream media are under pressure to move over and make space—pressure from government regulation, minority assertiveness, and commercial imperatives to capitalize on diversity or risk losing revenue and credibility. Until recently, however, the mass media did not fare well in responding to diversity. Media portrayal of migrants and minorities left much to be desired (Mahtani, 2002). Mainstream news media were reproached for their unbalanced and biased coverage of those migrants and minorities who continue to be insulted or typecast by defamatory images and demeaning assessments (Fleras and Kunz, 2001). A fixation with the sordid and sensational produces coverage that exaggerates the exception while disregarding the normal and routine. Minorities and migrants remain vulnerable to questionable coverage in which they are: miniaturized as irrelevant or inferior, demonized as a social menace to society, scapegoated as the source of all problems, "othered" for being too different or not different enough, refracted through the prism of Eurocentric fears and fantasies, and subjected to double standards that lampoon minorities regardless of what they do or don't do. Consider the typecasting: African Canadians were routinely slotted into the categories of athletes and entertainers or street thugs with attitudes (Gray, 1995); individuals from Asia were math whizzes or martial arts masters (Hanamoto, 1995); Aboriginal peoples were warriors or welfare bums (Valaskakis, 2005); and Jews were victims or perpetrators, heroes or anti-heroes (Omer, 2005). Media misrepresentation can be further categorized as normalizing invisibility but problematizing visibility, namely, the framing of minorities and migrants as invisible, stereotyped, problem people, adornments (props or tokens), and whitewashed (Alia, 1999; Henry and Tator, 2002; Lambertus, 2004; Wilson, Gutierrez, and Chao, 2003).

Media have reacted to this criticism: media processes such as advertising have embraced inclusiveness to capitalize on the marketing muscle of ethnic minorities (Fleras and Kunz, 2001). Blatant stereotypes are no longer tolerated within advertising, except to spoof the stereotyping of minorities in the past. Both film and television have explored and expanded the range of characters involving women and men of colour across a broader range of contexts. Canada's news media have taken steps to improve the representation of migrants and minorities. Initiatives range from more diversity training for journalists to less race-tagging (assigning a racial label to victim or perpetrator) without good reason, to reduction in the kind of language that minorities find offensive. And yet each step forward is undermined by one step back (Murray, 2002). With several exceptions, a business-as-usual mindset prevails in an industry that appears impervious to change (Infantry, 2005, see also Task Force, 2003). Both Aboriginal peoples and visible minorities remain

under-represented in areas that count (success), but over-represented in areas that don't count (failure) and misrepresented across all areas. Nowhere is this more evident than in newscasting, where coverage of minorities reinforces a perception of news as a medium of the negative (Fleras, 2004; also Henry and Tator, 2002; Hier and Greenberg, 2002).

Have mainstream media responded to the challenges of diversity in a manner consistent with the promises of multiculturalism (May, 2004)? Modest improvements notwithstanding, the principles of multiculturalism have yet to infiltrate Canada's mainstream media. Much of the lukewarm response can be traced to a combination of factors, including fear or ignorance, institutional structures and organizational culture, and news values implicit within the prevailing news paradigm with its emphasis on conflict, problems, and deviancy. Cultural diversity continues to be framed within the demands of meeting market expectations, program success, and public perceptions as prime reference points (May, 2004). Insofar as they are refracted through the prism of whiteness, minority women and men continue be victimized by a Eurocentrism that privileges whiteness as the norm or standard of acceptability by which others are judged because of who they aren't rather than who they are (Benson, 2005). Differences are difficult to convey as a result of this Eurocentric commitment to liberal universalism. A liberal commitment to universality (a belief that our deep-down similarities are more important than skin-deep differences) induces a superficial pluralism that does not resonate well with those Canadians who want differences to be taken seriously in defining who gets what, and why (Maaka and Fleras, 2005). For example, Canadian news media appear to be better equipped to handle multicultural issues than those involving the more radical politics (and demands) of Aboriginality. In brief, the relationship between media and minorities in a multicultural Canada is likely to remain as awkward and contested as ever—despite demographic changes to the contrary—without a fundamental change in how (news) media information is processed.

### Gendered Media

Many regard the women's movement of the 1970s as one of the more profound transformations of the twentieth century. The transformations went beyond simply improving the lot of women or that of rescripting the status and role of women in society. The women's movement also challenged the foundational

## 13.4

# Human Diversity
## Minorities in the News Media

How do mass news media portray minority women and men? In a balanced and objective manner, as might be expected of a mainstream institution within a multicultural Canada? Think again.

For one year (26 April 2004 to 25 April 2005), I collected data on the news media portrayal of minorities from Canada's two national papers. All newspaper headlines and headers about migrants, Aboriginal peoples, and minorities were collected from the *National Post* and the *Globe and Mail*. Inclusion of an article headline was restricted to (a) an event in Canada involving ethnic, race, or Aboriginal relations, migration and settlement, immigration and multiculturalism, racism and discrimination, or conflict and crime involving minorities, (b) its placement in the news or business section (rather than entertainment or sports), and (c) an explicit reference to a minority or diversity dimension in a headline or accompanying photo. The survey, sample, and results were intended to be informational rather than scientific, given the high level of subjectivity in such an exercise.

The results proved interesting, if not altogether unexpected. The *National Post* published 375 stories related to minorities or diversity over the year, with only 12 that could be conclusively defined as positive. The rest of the references involving minorities clearly indicated or implied their status as "troublesome constituents"—that is, people who are problems, have problems, or create problems. The *Globe and Mail* published 372 stories involving minorities or diversity, with approximately 46 positive entries. This does not mean that there is a deliberate bias in advancing such a distorted coverage. Rather, it may reflect a combination of subliminal Eurocentric assumptions regarding normalcy and acceptance, in addition to systemic biases involving prevailing news values that privilege conflict and problems as newsworthy (Fleras, 2004). But regardless of who or what is at fault, the impact of such slanted coverage in shaping public discourses clashes with Canada's multiculturalism ideals.

principles of a largely patriarchal constitutional order, in the process redefining the notions of justice and equality. All mainstream institutions came under pressure to rethink their business-as-usual approach in order to foster an organizational climate commensurate with women's concerns, realities, and aspirations.

The media have no reason to be excepted from closer scrutiny (Nelson, 2006). Like many institutions, the media possess an ambivalent relationship with the genders. The media continue to be gendered in the same way that society at large remains gendered, despite superficial changes that have barely modified the rules of engagement in what structurally remains a "white guys'" game. Media texts are deeply and persistently encoded in a sexualized way with respect to structures, priorities, operating procedures, and messages. Men and women also tend to use the media differently and for different purposes, with the result that gender becomes a key variable in the production, transmission, and interpretation of media messages. The genders benefit disproportionately

between each other from an institution that many people perceive as patriarchal in structure, androcentric in process, and sexist in outcomes. Predictably, then, images of women in general and of minority women in particular tend to reflect a male gaze revolving around a host of male-dominated images, fantasies, fears, and projections (Jiwani, 1992).

Historically, media conveyed messages about women as inferior or irrelevant (Nelson, 2006). Women tended to be marginalized or trivialized as situationally demanded by mainstream media, including news, advertising, programming, and film. Usually they were relegated to the maternal/domestic domain, stereotyped by way of mis- and under-representations, objectified to the point of dehumanization, victimized by body images that linked success with "ampleness," and typecast as the second sex whose worth lay in appearances and value in relationships to the men in their lives (from father to husband to sons). A relatively small number of roles were open to women, including that of mother, wife, girl next door, spinster in the making, whore or saint, and castrating bitch. By reinforcing female sexuality as the key to social power, mainstream media constantly barraged women with images (indeed, fantasies) of perfection that were difficult to achieve without eroding a healthy self-image (Kilbourne, 2000).

Does this assessment hold true in the new millennium? Media representations of gender and gender relations are proving a paradox: gender depictions today are much more diverse than in the past, continually changing, subject to multiple interpretation and ambiguous readings, and highly contested. The representation of women in the media has improved considerably from the one-dimensional days of *Father Knows Best*. Women are no longer routinely banished to the outer fringes of media reality. Their emergence as eager consumers with substantial disposable spending power has increasingly seen to that (Graydon, 2001).

But improvements are not the same as transformation; nor is there any suggestion that the transformation is unfolding to everyone's satisfaction. Women continue to be evaluated as objects of male fantasy or as superficial subjects in need of constant consumer-driven pampering. Powerful women are routinely found—from those who want to kick butt (from *Xena* to *Buffy the Vampire Slayer*) to those who have no qualms about admiring male butts (from *Sex and the City* to *Desperate Housewives*). And yet heroines generally conform to fairly rigid standards of beauty: thin, pretty, and preferably blonde (Nelson, 2006).

In short, the situation appears to be in flux and disarray, although when it comes to who gets what, it's still a man's world (Fleras, 2003). Mainstream mass media remain patriarchal in structure and function—designed by, for, and about male interests and priorities, with the result that there is an androcentric tendency to reflect, reinforce, and advance male experiences, realities, and agendas as normal and necessary. For media women (both women in media and media in women) the interplay of mixed messages is proving both empowering and progressive yet dispiriting and regressive, in effect confirming Susan Douglas's prescient conclusion that media may be a woman's best friend as well as her very worst enemy (Douglas, 1994).

## Social Class and Media

Canada's mainstream media do not exist in a political or economic vacuum. Mass media are situated within a capitalistic framework that has intensified the rational and quick accumulation of profit. The media themselves have become (in)corporatized into larger conglomerates for control of the information/entertainment package from start to finish. Not unexpectedly, mainstream media have evolved into intensely competitive business ventures whose bottom-line mentality prevails over national interests. The development of media industries into turbo-charged money-making machines not only dictates media decisions and institutional design; a profit-driven mindset also generates a conflict of interest between private gain and public good.

The combination of media mergers, cross-media ownership, and concentration of ownership poses a potentially serious problem for a democratic society (Gans, 2003). About 10 corporations dominate the global media market at present, compared to nearly 50 firms just 20 years ago (Kendal et al., 2004). Media ownership has become increasingly concentrated into a few large companies with monopolistic control over media content, production, and distribution, thus putting unprecedented political and economic power in the hands of a few (Croteau and Hoynes, 2003). In Canada, five companies control most newspapers and television stations, while, in the United States, five giant corporations control the major TV news divisions: NBC, ABC, CBS, Fox, and CNN. Five book companies control nearly 80 per cent of the market (Ryan and Wentworth, 1999). The film industry is so highly concentrated that seven companies claim nearly 90 per cent of the market; large companies are buying up smaller film firms while granting them some freedom to explore and innovate without losing control of the overall process. The recording industry is controlled by six global corporations with ownership of just over 80 per cent of the market. As with film, these large corporations are buying up smaller companies while conceding some degree of artistic licence.

Why worry about media conglomerates becoming cash cows? Haven't media always been businesses with at least one eye cocked towards the bottom line? Besides, is big always bad? Media processes such as newscasting may even benefit from improved economies of scale and access to scarce resources. Yet criticism of corporate concentration abounds (Winter, 2001). The scope and content of news may suffer when business decisions define what is newsworthy. As Herman and Chomsky (1988) remind us, powerful interests can fix the parameters of debate and discourage public opinion; government and the corporate elite will monopolize access to what even-

# Open for Discussion
## The Tyranny of the Thin

Many women are thought to have a poor self-image of their bodies. Rampant cases of eating disorders and yo-yo dieting binges coupled with obsessive exercise regimes are but part of how this problem manifests itself. Few will be startled by this obsession with physical appearance (including beauty, youthfulness, and thinness). The media are complicit in advancing the notion of thinness as the contemporary cultural ideal of feminine beauty (Kilbourne, 2001; McCabe et al., 2005). Thin is in, as everyone knows, and living fat on a skinny planet is nothing less than a recipe for social disaster.

Images of thin are everywhere: women's magazines routinely put twig-like models on covers to attract sales; television programs with skinny actors such as Calista Flockhart (*Ally McBeal*) are proven winners; and the emaciated casts of *Survivor* continue to waste away to prisoner-of-war proportions. The careers of box-office twiglets such as Gwyneth Paltrow and Cameron Diaz soar in contrast to the flagging careers of normally sized starlets such as Kate Winslet (Nelson, 2006). And for many girls, their sensitivity to weight and body image begins with exposure to emaciated ("waif-like") fashion models whose surgically altered bodies are idolized as proportions to strive for. With such pressure to be nubile, young, and thin, who can be surprised when many women confess that the prospect of shedding a few pounds would bring them greater happiness than career success or domestic bliss?

Admittedly, most of us know that we should not judge people by their appearance. Nevertheless, our actions continue to be governed by perceptions of our bodies as a basis for judging others and ourselves (Graydon, 2001). Yes, many are critical of the cultural contradictions that prevail. But what can be done since women (and men to some extent) are forced to live inside these contradictions (Kilbourne, 2000)? The field day enjoyed by the tabloid press in lampooning the ballooning Kirstie Alley is testimony to the cruelties of being plump in an age of the twig (although in this case, the actress may have had the last laugh by starring in a successful sitcom titled *Fat Actress*). And yes, most people endorse the virtues of more wholesome body size, yet rejecting thinness runs the risk of being perceived as lacking self-discipline and control. Women and men may extol the virtues of inner beauty, including confidence, health, and attitude, but when push comes to shove, the body prevails. Just ask Renée Zellweger, whose wholesomeness in *Bridget Jones's Diary* was quickly transformed into boniness in time for the 2001 Academy Awards.

No one should be surprised by how a mediated society conspires against women (Wolf, 1991). Powerful cultural messages exert pressure for conformity to a particular shape and size, neither realistic nor attainable for most individuals (except for about a dozen airbrushed supermodels, as the Body Shoppe ads like to remind us). These impossible standards are then used as a weapon to foster personal disenchantment when the fat hits the fan. Both advertising and the beautification industry (from aerobic centres and dieting fads to cosmetics and plastic surgery) rely on revenue from breeding guilt and fanning discontent by exploiting gaps in individual self-esteem. Media profits depend on unrealistic images of women whose exacting standards can be attained through considerable expense and relentless discipline. Not unexpectedly, sales that cater to the outer body, namely, cosmetics, exercise gizmos, and weight-loss supplements, continue to escalate. In a capitalist society anchored around packaging and appearances, any move towards acceptance of inner beauty that does not enhance the sales of some product is bad for business. In a society that no longer reveres spiritual or intellectual achievement, all that is left is the body, both as a metaphor for success and as a standard for assessment.

tually is defined as news; large advertisers can dictate the terms of newscasting; and media owners can influence what will or will not appear. Or consider the view of Ben Bagdikian (1997), who warns us that the fewer the number of owners, the narrower the range of media outputs.

The proliferation of conglomerates has ominous overtones for a freedom-loving society (Winter, 2001; Kent, 2003). The danger of media concentration to democratic ideals is fourfold. First, it rests in the blending of editorial and commercial content to create an undemocratic hybrid. Second, there are dangers in advancing the interests of those who own or control the media to the exclusion of those who don't. Third, ratings-driven media are less interested in advancing a public service and more focused on generating revenue. And fourth, a concentration of media power may restrict the range of content by squeezing out diversity or the common Canadian. The abuse of power by a mass media monopoly can-

not be underestimated. Not only are Canadians betrayed into conflating profits with public good, consumerism with citizenship, information with propaganda, and new symbolic wants with fundamental needs (Nesbitt-Larking, 2001; Taras, 2001), they also have been misled about life at the margins in Canada and abroad.

# Conclusion

## Media-Proofing for a Twenty-First-Century Canada

This chapter has focused on the social dimensions of media–society relations, with special emphasis on mass media influences on society and, conversely, societal influences on mass media communication. Four dynamics appear to have reconfigured the social dimensions of Canada's mainstream media in recent years (see Attalah and Shade, 2002). First, technologi-

---

 **13.6**

## Global Issues
### Media and Social Class

The commercial imperative may exert a powerful if largely unarticulated influence in shaping media contents (Hackett et al., 2000; Winter, 2001). Although the relationship between class and media is unmistakable given how class permeates media content and underlies media industries, there is a dearth of studies on how class and inequality are portrayed in television or newscasting (Benson, 2005; Croteau and Hoynes, 2003).

Nevertheless, certain global patterns are discernible. For example, the ownership and control of profit-oriented commercial mass media by the rich and powerful may indirectly influence how social class is portrayed. In suggesting that some people are more valuable than others, media content is slanted towards depictions of the middle classes and professionals, whereas (with several exceptions) the working classes, labour unions, and the unemployed or poor are ignored or demeaned as less than human (Butsch, 1992). Class enters into news content

as well (Croteau and Hoynes, 2003). News tends to highlight issues of concern to middle-class readers, while the organizational culture of journalism favours coverage of those with privileged access to the news industry. Advertising is no less class-driven. Advertisers are keenly interested in the socio-economic status of those affluent media consumers, and adjust their content accordingly.

Class also seems to play a role in how audiences interpret media messages. Middle-class viewers read media content differently than do working-class viewers, thereby reinforcing a key sociological theorem: that where we are socially located in society in terms of social class (as well as race, gender, and so on) will profoundly influence how we see, think, and experience the world around us (see Martin, 1997). This observation also reminds us that mass media and media communication are hardly neutral but are systemically classed as well as gendered and racialized.

cal changes, from the Internet to digitalization, have transformed how media content is produced and transmitted, as well as audience consumption of these outputs. Second, both technology and globalization have intensified the relatively free flow of information across increasingly porous borders, thus exerting additional pressure for regulatory control to protect national interests. Third, historically disadvantaged groups are demanding greater inclusiveness within those media institutions that once excluded or exploited them. Inclusiveness goes beyond adding a splash of colour to programming or content, but entails a fundamental shift in how things are done. Fourth, commercial pressures are increasing, reflected in the creation of larger media corporations through convergence, mergers, and vertical monopolies. Each of these themes—commercialization, inclusiveness, globalization, and technology—has irrevocably altered the mediascape by transforming the relationship of media to Canadian society.

Such transformative change has sharpened the need for improved media literacy skills. Our media age puts an onus on media-"proofing" as an essential survival skill for seeing through those powerful forces that define and distract, conceal and evade, or shape and control. With increased media concentration and monopolistic control of information, we need to know who owns what, what kind of information they are circulating, why, and what kind of impact they have in shaping public opinion and influencing people's behaviour (McChesney, 1999). People need to recognize how the mass media—as discourses in defence of dominant ideology—contain values and myths that cloak aspects of social reality. An unequal status quo, which has the intent or effect of empowering some at the expense of others, is thus reinforced. In short, as money-making machineries of meaning, the mass media must be exposed for what they are: powerful socially constructed vehicles of persuasion that not only set agendas by concealing complex systems of thought control and corporate advancement, but also frame issues in ways that advance patterns of power and privilege (Fleras, 2003).

To be sure, many people think they are reasonably media literate; after all, those of us weaned on iPods, BlackBerries, and PDAs (personal digital assistants, now with TV coverage capabilities) can compile a huge music library thanks to MP3s, download Hollywood blockbusters, text message with friends, blast away at Play Station (virtual) villains, vote for *American Idol* finalists with the press of a button, and see through the phoniness of advertising pitches (Hassan, 2004). And yet those same media-savvy individuals with an endless propensity towards technological wizardry are precisely those who continue to be misinformed about the nature and purpose of mass media. True, there is widespread knowledge about the gee-whiz aspects of mass media technology, but there is less wisdom about how media messages are produced and consumed, who controls the media, the economics of the industry, and the sometimes subtle ways media manipulate our emotions, personalities, and core values (Lasn, 1999; Potter, 2005). Put bluntly, the media are not stupid: as audiences become

## 13.7 Open for Discussion
### Double Standards in the Media

Are women in media exposed to double standards? Consider the following: a cover story in the 18 April 2005 issue of *Maclean's* magazine focused on Belinda Stronach, the rich and attractive Conservative MP (now a Liberal cabinet minister) who many had dubbed as having sufficient star power to assume party leadership one day. In the first paragraph we are reminded that she stepped into the party's convention centre wearing a "vivid green Hugo Boss leather jacket," "striped satin skinny pants," "a chunky pearl necklace," and "taupe stilettos." On the third page of the article was a three-quarter-page photo spread of her splashy fashion sense. Finally, towards the end of the article, we are informed that on day two of the convention she wore "a tailored pinstripe suit," "a crisp white shirt," and "crocodile stilettos." None of the males in the story were described by their sartorial splendour.

more informed and cynical, the media are finding new ways of co-opting this citizen strength and transforming it into a consumer weakness. The consequences of this cat-and-mouse game are hardly immaterial: those who allow any medium to program their grasp of social reality by programming their viewing habits run the risk of being manipulated for corporate goals.

Do the media give people what they want, or have audiences become conditioned to accept less than they deserve? The acquisition of "media smarts" provides a starting point for unmasking those underlying structures, internal logics, and hidden agendas that tend to inflame rather than inform, to excite rather than enlighten, and to simplify rather than reveal complexity (Traverse, 2003). Consider the paradoxes at the heart of media dynamics. As mass media become more complex, for example, the messages they communicate become increasingly simple (Zingrone, 2001). Television news from CNN or Newsworld can convey faster-paced information, yet their coverage of complex issues shrinks to little more than a sound blip. News media tend to simplify complex human events such as the Iraq conflict for easy consumption, yet they may also render complex through obsessive coverage trivial events for low-cost entertainment purposes (Michael Jackson, anyone?). The alternative is unthinkable—or, as caustically claimed by Frank Zingrone (2001), the truth might put you out of business. Not surprisingly, programming is increasingly sanitized and formulaic for fear of alienating audiences or frightening off advertisers.

Media-proofing for a twenty-first-century Canada must begin by taking media seriously. Life and social reality as we have come to know them would be starkly different without the persuasiveness of mass media communication, and yet, like the air we breathe, this pervasive force is rarely taken into consideration in shaping thought and activity (Croteau and Hoynes, 2003). Our lives are so saturated with media messages that because of their repetitiveness and ubiquity many people are oblivious to their obviousness. Media are much more than a transmission technology for conveying information about reality: media *are* reality. Media inform and infuse our perception of reality, with the result that the world "out there" is not lived per se except within the framework of media images, symbols, and representations (Fiske, 1994). Media create the images around which reality is constructed and—through repeated exposure—confer legitimacy on the constructed images as necessary and normal. The challenge in media-proofing is relatively straightforward: to reclaim power from the media by learning to read between the lines, so to speak, thus repositioning the media around people-as-priorities rather than upon corporate goals.

Admittedly, a sense of perspective is critical: mass media are the source of neither good nor of evil in the world, nor are they the all-encompassing solution to the world's problems. Their influence in shaping human behaviour and solving societal problems rests somewhere between these extremes. In that mass media articulate and transmit powerful images and narratives regarding what is acceptable, normal, and necessary, mass media communications are influential in shaping our attitudes (Why do I think like I do?), identities (Why am I like I am?), and behaviour (Why do I behave the way I do, and why do others behave as they do?). Inasmuch as this relationship has proven complex and conflicted, not readily deconstructed but easily discerned, and subject to endless discussion and debate, a critically informed inspection of media–society relations is both timely and relevant. The alternative is a paralysis that not only cripples public discourses, but also robs ordinary Canadians of the information required for taking appropriate political and social action.

## ☐ Questions for Critical Thought

1. Media are known to exert a powerful influence on institutions. Professional sports is no exception as an institution that has changed dramatically because of media influence from scheduling and marketing, to the padding of financial pockets for athletes, owners, television networks, and advertisers. How have the media influenced the evolution of professional sports such as hockey or football?

2. Discuss the impact and implications of taking the "mass" out of mass media communication. Explore the possibilities with respect to media content, media delivery, and audience reception. Also indicate how these changes in "de-massifying" the media may alter how media scholars study mass media communication.

3. The concept of **hegemony** is premised on the goal of winning people's hearts and mind without any awareness that their attitudes are changing. Are you personally influenced by what you see or hear in the media? How might media shape your thoughts and actions?

4. The media are more than passive or neutral conveyors of somebody else's information. In what ways are the media themselves both gendered and racialized, as well as classed?

5. The news media have been criticized for manufacturing consent. Conversely, advertising comes in for criticism for manufacturing *dis*content. What is the difference between the two? You might consult the discussions of crime and media and the tyranny of the thin (Box 13.5) to assist in your response.

6. How has media-proofing become a more essential coping skill? What should the goals of media-proofing be, and how might it be accomplished?

7. How do private, public, and community media differ in terms of structure, functions, and process? Do changes in the level of public funding for media matter? Why or why not?

8. How does the relatively interactive nature of Internet communications affect the media–society relationship? Can Internet communications change other media interactions as well? Or are Internet communications less different than they appear to be?

## ☐ Recommended Readings

**David Croteau and William Hoynes, *Media/Society: Industries, Images, and Audiences*, 3rd edn (Thousand Oaks, Calif.: Sage, 2003).**

Croteau and Hoynes address an array of media issues in the United States, but much of the material is also relevant for a Canadian context.

**Susan Douglas, *Where the Girls Are: Growing Up Female with the Mass Media* (New York: Random House, 1994).**

This is one of those rare books that manages to be entertaining yet informative at the same time; priceless in demonstrating how media can be a woman's best friend or worst enemy depending on the context and criteria.

**David Taras, *Power and Betrayal in the Canadian Media* (Peterborough, Ont.: Broadview, 2001).**

Taras's critique of the CBC is an eye-opener, but his plea to strengthen Canada's national public broadcaster situates the criticism and concern within a constructive perspective.

## ☐ Recommended Web Sites

**Canadian Broadcasting Corporation**
**www.cbc.ca**

The CBC is Canada's national public broadcaster; its Web site includes a significant range of archival material.

**Canadian Association of Broadcasters**
**www.cab-acr.ca**

The Canadian Association of Broadcasters is the national voice of Canada's private broadcasting industry.

**DiversityWatch**
**www.diversitywatch.ryerson.ca**

Run by Ryerson University's School of Journalism, DiversityWatch is an excellent site for information on media and diversity.

# 14

Randle Hart,
Peter R. Sinclair,
and John Veuglers

> > >

# Politics and
# Social Movements

© Dick Hemingway

## ☐ Learning Objectives

In this chapter, you will:

- discover the value of comparing different societies

- review and evaluate competing perspectives on democratic societies

- consider the global dimensions and implications of many political issues

- grasp why women, the poor, and minority ethnic groups have been poorly represented in political life

- review the theoretical approaches to the study of social movements

- read about key debates within the study of social movements

- see how empirical research is used to test and criticize social movement theories

- learn how social movements are embedded in national and international (global) politics

# Introduction

This chapter is largely about the use of power for political ends. As we will see, power is exercised in the political arena by political parties, elected legislators, and civil servants, among others. In politics, **the state** is the chief actor, using its great power and resources to control and change people's behaviour. Of interest to students of political sociology is the relation between the state and the economy—between political actors, on the one hand, and the largest corporations, dominant social classes, and major economic groupings such as consumers and workers' unions, on the other. No less important is the relation between the state and civil society, between political actors and those institutions that make up the everyday lives of ordinary people—families, schools, churches, communities, and so on. In this context, social movements represent the political arm of civil society. This chapter pays particular attention to social movements, how they form, and how they influence both civil society and the state.

# Core Concepts

## *Politics and Power*

**Politics** is the process by which individuals and groups act to promote their interests, often in conflict with others. Politics is intimately connected to **power**. In all spheres of action, power reflects the extent to which available resources both constrain and enable people's actions (Giddens, 1979). Resources provide the means for action, but they also provide a limit on what action is possible. Following Max Weber ([1908] 1978), one of sociology's outstanding social theorists of the early twentieth century, *power* is often defined as the ability of a person or group to achieve their objectives, even when opposed. Power typically becomes concentrated in society because some people consistently have greater discretionary power in controlling what others do (Barnes, 1988). However, in some situations power is more or less equal, as in most friendships.

Thus, power is about the capacity to act in a desired way, and politics is the process of mobilizing these capacities. Politics is most visible when it involves struggle between opposing forces, but it is also evident in what people do to avoid conflict and maintain their domination. Examples include controlling agendas and the timing of decisions, even how other people define

their interests (Lukes, 1974). John Gaventa (1980) demonstrated the way power could be maintained for generations through his investigation of why Appalachian miners remained politically inactive, despite much poverty, from the late nineteenth century until 1975. Apart from brief periods when recessions weakened the position of landowners and mine operators, this local elite wielded effective power. In particular, the poor miners and their families accepted existing conditions because their opponents controlled not only vital resources—jobs, houses, land, stores, access to medical facilities, even the local electoral process—but also the opinion-forming institutions of the area: schools, churches, and the media.

Power is hidden in relationships and can be observed only when those subject to it actively resist. However, opposition will be rare if people believe they have no chance of successfully resisting the demands being placed on them; and it will not appear when power holders enjoy **authority**, which may be defined as power considered legitimate by those subject to it.

## *Types of Authority*

Clearly, to hold authority over others is a critical resource in the conduct of politics. Where authority is widely accepted, politics will be likely to follow peaceful, established patterns, but when it does not exist, intense conflicts are probable sooner or later. To understand how authority becomes established, the work of Max Weber, almost a century ago, remains important. Weber ([1908] 1978) identified three types of authority according to the grounds on which it was accepted by those subject to it. These types seldom appear in pure form because actual relationships usually involve combinations.

**Traditional authority** is evident when the reason people obey is because that is the way things have always been done. The power holder enjoys "the sanctity of immemorial traditions" (Weber, [1908] 1978, vol. 1: 215) and may expect obedience as long as these established rules are followed. Examples include chiefs and elders who ruled tribal societies by customary practice and acceptance of their rights. Authority of this type is more secure when it is grounded in the belief that it derives from a revered spiritual source, so that to oppose one's leader would also be to oppose one's god.

**Charismatic authority** rests on belief in the exceptional qualities of an individual person, someone of exemplary or heroic character who reveals how life will unfold, perhaps involving new social values and patterns of conduct. The person with charisma is thought to be able beyond the capacity of ordinary people to resolve problems and may build a devoted following, sometimes rooted in religious faith, as with the Judeo-Christian prophets, or in secular **ideologies**, as with Mao Zedong and Adolf Hitler. Charismatic leaders are innovative, even revolutionary, but their authority is fragile, being dependent on their personal qualities and the appearance of results.

**Rational-legal authority** is based on formally established rules, procedures, and standards of expertise in which an individual's acknowledged right to command is limited to his or her formal position. Personal characteristics both of the office holder and of those subject to command are irrelevant to the conduct of business. It is expected that each person will be treated as any other, which gives rise to formal procedures both for appointment to positions and for the treatment of citizens. This form of authority is characteristic of **bureaucratic** structures, both public and private, where those in higher-ranked positions may command those in lower positions within the limits of their jurisdiction. Thus, the manager who attempts to obtain sexual services from a secretary engages in behaviour considered illegitimate in that context. Specialized knowledge or expertise is another modern basis of authority.

Modern states develop bureaucratic structures based on claims to rational-legal authority, though this authority is backed by the capacity to use force should there be opposition. Of course, bureaucratic officials, in practice, are at times corrupt (which

## 14.1

# Sociology in Action
## The Impact of Research on Political Practice: The Aalborg Project

Social research can have an effect on what is studied by helping to change the way people conduct their affairs. Bent Flyvbjerg's investigation of Aalborg's transportation system (1998) uncovered how effectively the local business elite was able to bypass formal democratic processes and achieve its objectives over a period of 15 years. However, Flyvbjerg (2001) was also committed to research that would be critical and reflexive. This required placing the results of his research back into the political arena in the hope that improvements might take place—here, in the functioning of democracy. Flyvbjerg therefore presented his results in the mass media and in public meetings. For example, he demonstrated that, contrary to expectations, traffic accidents in the centre of Aalborg increased over the life of the plan without officials apparently noticing, and that "the increase in accidents was caused by city officials allowing the rationality of the Chamber of Industry and Commerce to slowly, surely, and one-sidedly, influence and undermine the rationality of the Aalborg project" (Flyvbjerg, 2001: 157).

Initially, those whose positions were threatened by his evidence challenged Flyvbjerg by claiming his information was inaccurate, but a determined defence of that evidence was eventually accepted by the alderman responsible for city planning. After that, dialogue developed. *Dialogue* is understood as a respectful exchange of ideas, a requirement of the democratic process, in contrast with mere rhetoric and polemic, which impede informed judgment.

As the public debate proceeded, the alderman and his officials realized that reports about the research were influencing the public and that the Aalborg plan had to change. They could no longer defend what was demonstrably not working, especially as the project was by this time receiving much international attention. A new plan emerged based on an open democratic process. The city government invited a variety of interest groups to join the planning and implementation processes. The European Union, inspired by Flyvbjerg's research and determination that it should be noticed outside the academy, recognized this new practice by commending Aalborg for its innovative, democratic planning process.

means that some people are treated with special favour in return for unofficial personal payments) or obstructionist. These departures from the rules weaken the legitimacy of the bureaucracy and may increase the likelihood of radical opposition to the regime in control of the state.

Although power and politics are dimensions of all **social relationships**, "politics" in common use refers, in the first instance, to processes of government and regulation within and between modern states. This more specific understanding of politics is our focus here.

**Political institutions** are established rules and procedures for the conduct of political affairs, including the government of society. They constitute a network of power relationships. Specialized political institutions were evident in some form in most earlier societies but became more complex in the industrial countries of the modern world. There is no uniform course of development, but several important trends can be identified: increasing scale of government, growing political intervention in social affairs, the rise of the nation-state, and various forms of bureaucratic administration (Bottomore, 1979). These political institutions constitute networks of power that we can analyze in light of their internal structures and their links to the rest of society. Special interest groups, **social movements**, and political parties connect various segments of the public to the state, which is the core political frame of contemporary complex societies.

In modern societies, state institutions are both objectives of political struggle and resources in these struggles. In Weber's famous definition, the state is "a human community that (successfully) claims the monopoly of the legitimate use of physical force within a given territory" ([1922] 1946: 78). However, tyrants, dictators, and zealots can rule effectively for long periods. Unless we insist that states exist only when rule is legitimate, another definition is called for. Thus the state may be considered to be that set of procedures and organizations concerned with creating, administering, and enforcing rules or decisions for conduct within a given territory. Here, legitimacy is not assumed.

Modern nation-states certainly vary in scale, but typically they are complex, with legislatures, governments, public bureaucracies, police, a judiciary, and a military force. Given the complexity and scale of these states, it is misleading to assume that "the state" is coherently unified; in practice, the parts are loosely integrated and often work at cross-purposes. Canada's

federal Department of Finance, for example, may wish to reduce taxes at the same time as the Department of Health and Welfare is pushing for a better-funded health-care system. The federal structure also creates layers of government with overlapping jurisdictions and potential conflicts.

# The Emergence of Modern States

Why do societies developed the different types of institutions that characterize their political lives? Why, for instance, has liberal democracy remained so firmly entrenched in Sweden and the United States while it was so weak in Germany and Italy earlier in the twentieth century that fascism overthrew it? Why did China and Russia choose socialism while India opted for the capitalist, democratic route? Why have so many attempts at nation-building ended in military dictatorship and other forms of authoritarian government? Although no one has answered all these questions adequately, several have risen to the challenge with impressive theories.

## Moore's Alternate Paths

Among the seminal works of political sociology is Barrington Moore's investigation of the conditions that led to the major forms of the modern state: democracy, fascism, and communism. Moore's *Social Origins of Dictatorship and Democracy* (1969) is a comparative assessment of these alternate paths. The key examples of the capitalist path to democracy are Britain, France, the United States, and, more recently and less securely, India. The path to fascism is exemplified by Germany and Japan in the second quarter of the twentieth century. Moore takes the former Soviet Union and the People's Republic of China as the essential illustrations of the path to communist development. He explains the various paths in terms of the relationships among the agrarian classes. Particularly relevant to life in Canada is Moore's identification of the conditions for the emergence of democracy, which he saw as involving the elimination of arbitrary government and of mass participation in the making of rules.

According to Moore, the first condition is that neither the monarchy nor the landed aristocracy should be able to dominate each other consistently. A central power must bring some semblance of order to the nobility, yet where the Crown holds absolute power for too long, democracy cannot flourish.

Moore cited the histories of China, Russia, and Germany in support of this point. Second, in the absence of urban dwellers to counteract the landed aristocracy when it challenges royal power, democratic impulses falter. In Moore's own words, "No bourgeois, no democracy" (1969: 418). In Germany, for example, the weakness of the towns led to a lack of pressure to expand the scope of aristocratic demands in a democratic direction. Next, the development of commercial agriculture by the landed aristocracy is central to democratic resistance to the monarchy. In England, for example, the nobles became commercial farmers, displacing the peasantry. This social change provided the basis of common interests between the nobility and the urban bourgeoisie. The fourth condition is that there should be no massive reservoir of peasants that might be mobilized as capitalism develops, either to fascist ends or in a communist movement. The United States never had a "peasant problem," while in England the peasantry was drastically reduced in numbers. The final condition is that a revolutionary break with the past should occur. In this context, Moore points to the English Civil War, the French Revolution, and the American Civil War as vital components of democratic development. Without such a break, democratic tendencies will not become strongly entrenched.

Moore was reluctant to generalize from these conditions to evaluate the fate of contemporary societies because he was sensitive to the fact that the early development of some societies necessarily changes the circumstances encountered by others. Nevertheless, his analysis remains a significant achievement.

### Skocpol's Theory of Social Revolutions

Theda Skocpol stresses the importance of **social revolutions**, which she defines as "rapid, basic transformations of a society's state and class structures" (1979: 4). Skocpol treats states as key parts of the **social structure** that contribute to bringing about social change. She also stresses a society's international environment far more than Moore, arguing that modern social revolutions occur only in countries situated in disadvantaged positions in the international arena. This international context is increasingly important.

Like Moore, Skocpol places great weight on the actions of the peasantry. She demonstrates that France, Russia, and China were characterized by conditions favourable to political crisis and peasant revolt. For instance, Russia before 1917 was a bureaucratic, absolutist state dominated by the czar, who claimed to rule by divine right. Its nobility was politically weak, its agriculture backward. Conflicts with other societies placed Russia under pressure by revealing its military and economic weakness. Despite the land reforms of the nineteenth and twentieth centuries that eliminated feudalism, rents and redemption payments continued to impoverish the peasants. However, through their close-knit village communities, they could be mobilized against the existing order. Peasant revolts against private landed property contributed to the defeat of the state in 1917 and helped bring the Bolsheviks to power. Internal pressure alone could not bring down the czarist state, which stumbled into its final crisis as a result of military defeats during the First World War. Wisely, Skocpol does not conclude her analysis with the rise to power of a new regime but recognizes that the process of revolutionary state-building can last for decades. In all three of her cases, state-building was encouraged by popular mobilization against counter-revolutionaries and foreign powers. The outcomes were states larger, more centralized, more bureaucratic, and more concerned to mobilize the masses than the ones they replaced.

Despite the majestic sweep of Skocpol's analysis and the range of evidence mustered in support, she leaves room for argument and extension: the differences in the origins and the outcomes of the three main cases are considerable, and general theories of nation-building are difficult to square with the historically specific factors that condition each of her examples. Emphasizing the general structural conditions of change can lead to the neglect of the role of creative human activity.

# Modern State Institutions

States vary in the degree to which power is centralized, civil rights are equally distributed, opposition is permitted, and military forces are subject to civilian control—essential dimensions for the analysis of state political institutions. The forms of the state are usefully summarized as *authoritarian*, *totalitarian*, and *liberal-democratic*. Since the nineteenth century, the idea of nationhood to many cultures means that a society within the territorial boundaries of a state is often referred to as a *nation-state*, even though state and national boundaries rarely coincide perfectly. We shall see that attempts in the last 50 years to establish truly national states have often generated severe conflict.

## Authoritarian States

In authoritarian states, public opposition is forbidden and the population as a whole is under great pressure to accept and comply with the expectations of political leaders. At a minimum, authoritarian leaders insist on compliance in all public life and depend on control by military force to maintain their positions if challenged.

Absolutist monarchies, which combine tradition and force to control the population, were common in pre-industrial societies in which the labour of ordinary people supported an elite. Although this type of state became rare in the late twentieth century, one example was the regime of the Shah of Iran prior to that country's Islamic revolution of 1979. Some contemporary states, such as Saudi Arabia, come close to this model.

Military dictatorships have frequently taken power in Asian, African, and Latin American countries following their independence from colonial rule. Usually these seizures are claimed to be temporary measures until corruption or ethnic conflicts can be solved. Military regimes lack popular legitimacy and may be short-lived. At times, experimental democratic regimes and military dictatorships replace each other in a cyclical pattern.

## Totalitarian States

Totalitarianism is more extreme than authoritarianism because it involves intervening in and controlling all aspects of both public and private life. It demands cultural homogeneity in every important respect. Nazi Germany is considered an exemplar of totalitarianism in which the Nazi Party (the National Socialist German Workers' Party) mobilized cultural institutions (mass media, schools, religion) to promote its ideals and eliminated any opposition through imprisonment and genocide of the Jewish people and others. Such states usually function in alliance with established classes and corporations, although the rhetoric of their leaders may be populist; for example, they may appeal to the anger of ordinary people, who may be suffering economic pain or political humiliation, by selecting visible minorities as targets for extremist action.

Socialist states, of which the former Soviet Union is the prime example, are totalitarian but ideologically quite different from those already discussed in that they are committed to a revolutionary transformation of capitalism (hence the rationalization for controlling all political, cultural, and economic institutions without permitting open dissent) in order to break the old order and bring a new socialist society to life. In the Soviet Union, most productive property was collectively owned, but control was centralized in the bureaucracy of the Communist Party rather than dispersed among collectives or workers.

In practice, totalitarian homogeneity never existed in the Soviet Union. Although the Soviet state was highly centralized, it was not a monolithic entity that excluded all debate and dispute. Even in the years before Mikhail Gorbachev's leadership (1985–91), interest groups and factions struggled for control within the Communist Party. There was, for example, long-standing competition between advocates of a more decentralized economic system and those who believed that modern information-processing technologies could permit centralized planning to a high degree, even in a complex industrial economy. Until the 1980s, the latter position dominated, but the rise of Gorbachev and his commitment to a more decentralized structure—to the reform of state socialism from within—changed the balance, with serious consequences for the whole system.

## Liberal-Democratic States

Literally, *democracy* means rule by the people, but who is to be granted status as "the people" and how ruling takes place can vary enormously. *Direct democracy*, in which all citizens discuss and vote on all issues of importance to them, can function effectively only in small settings such as utopian communities or the classical Greek city-states. That said, liberal-democratic states are characterized by institutions that allow representation of the views of ordinary citizens through political parties that compete for the power to govern. These states may be *constitutional monarchies*, like Norway and Canada, in which the head of state is a hereditary position, or *republics*, like France and the United States, in which the head of state is elected.

At the heart of democracies are their election practices. These electoral institutions are quite varied. Some create legislatures by electing members from small areas (*constituencies*) within the state. In a sense, such societies (such as the United Kingdom and Canada) conduct a set of mini-elections all at the same time. Other democracies count votes for the whole society and candidates are elected from a party list in proportion to the party's share of the total votes cast. These *proportional representation* systems are found in many countries, including Israel and Italy.

The rapid spread of democracy has been one of the world's great dramas over the last 50 years. Democratization proceeded rapidly in the twentieth century. In 1900, no society qualified as fully democratic because the first democracies of Europe, North America, Australia, and New Zealand restricted voting rights to men. After 1945, many societies emerged from colonial rule, sometimes to continuous democratic politics (like India), sometimes to unstable democracies with periods of military rule (like Nigeria). In addition, many Latin American states formally established in the nineteenth century did not transform effectively to democratic institutions until the latter part of the twentieth century. Although China continues to try to maintain authoritarian central control in political life while opening the economy to market rules, it has proven exceptionally difficult to restrict individual freedom to the marketplace in socialist societies.

Despite 70 years of control and persuasion in the Soviet Union, as soon as popular sentiments were unleashed communist institutions were swept away. After 1989, when the Soviet Union and its East European allies collapsed, the spread of democracy accelerated dramatically for several years with the appearance of fledgling democratic political institutions. Although few commentators foresaw the end of the USSR until it was practically upon us, hindsight suggests plausible factors leading to its collapse. Perhaps the most significant of these are the internal contradictions between state socialism and a lack of legitimacy. The need to raise productivity and living standards, which increasingly required more individual initiative and "company" autonomy in some kind of market system, conflicted with the need to maintain central control of the social structure (Sinclair, 1982). A system created on the basis of bureaucratic control and centralized planning could not easily be reconciled with the decentralization required by effective local initiatives. Openness and criticism could not be contained once genuinely released. The second factor, lack of legitimacy, had to do with popular frustration resulting from inadequate material living conditions in comparison with the advanced capitalist societies, resentment against authoritarian rule, and the suppression of ethnic and religious cultural identities. In the case of the nations of Eastern Europe, hostility towards the USSR as a colonizing power was an additional factor.

# Perspectives on the Democratic State

Sociologists have attempted to explain the politics of the modern state by analyzing the connection between political institutions and the **social groups** of which society is composed. Sociological theories of the state revolve around the question of whose interests are represented in institutions and actual policies. (See Table 14.1 for summary statements.) Do all these approaches provide part of the answer, or does the evidence fit some better than others?

## Old Foes: The Ruling Elite and Pluralism

Until the 1970s, the chief contending perspectives stressed either elite domination or pluralism. The "ruling elite" approach pointed to a small clique that effectively dominated political decisions on all matters of central interest to its members. C. Wright Mills argued for the existence of a power elite at the national level in the United States—"those political, economic and military circles which as an intricate set of overlapping cliques share decisions having at least national consequences" (1956: 18). This power elite was not a fixed group whose members, in conspiratorial fashion, made all decisions; rather, it was composed of people who knew each other, shared an upper-class background, and consulted each other on issues of fundamental importance to society. Other researchers identified elites that effectively controlled decision-making at the local level (Hunter, 1953). Thus, the vision of elite domination encompassed all levels of the state.

Mills believed that the corporate elite was the most powerful segment of the power elite. Closer to Marx's concept of the ruling class is William Domhoff (1990), who believes that the corporate wealthy (about 1 per cent of the US population) are able to limit government to actions that serve the interests of the capitalist class. Similarly, Wallace Clement (1975) describes at length a ruling class in Canada intimately interconnected at the highest levels of corporate power and between private boardrooms and the national government.

The image of the state implicit in "ruling elite" theory is one that puts little emphasis on administra-

Table 14.1    **Key Features of Perspectives on Liberal-Democratic States**

|  | Social Bias of the State | Basis of Political Power | Possibility of Major Change |
|---|---|---|---|
| Power/Ruling elite | Captive of the elite: leading members of state, military, and especially economic elite | Common socialization process and control of key political resources | Highly unlikely because the mass public lacks effective organization |
| Pluralism/Elite competition | Neutral arena for debate: wide range of interest groups and public as a whole benefit | Success in persuading electorates in open competition plus interest group mobilization | Normal rotation of parties and effective interest groups; no structural change |
| Neo-Marxism | Serves the capitalist class and, to a lesser extent, the service class | Control of wealth and, indirectly, of the political elite | Unlikely but occasionally possible through revolutionary class action |
| Autonomous state | State elite and more powerful interest groups | Control of means of force, taxation, and votes | Possible if balance of resources shifts among key social groups |
| Feminism | Reflect male values and organizations; state helps maintain patriarchy | Male control of institutional patterns; limited participation by women | Unlikely without radical transformation of gender attitudes |

tion. Instead, it focuses on policy, which is linked to the interests of those who hold key institutional positions. In all cases, this theory agrees that the interests of ordinary people are ignored whenever they might clash with those of the elite. Without explicitly writing about the state, these theorists create a vision of the state as necessarily anti-democratic. The state becomes nothing more than a means of domination, even when policy is couched in formally democratic procedures.

Mills and his followers wrote partly in criticism of pluralism, whose advocates presented a benign view of American democracy as a forum in which any person or group had a fair chance of being represented. In turn, they were attacked by those identifying a pluralist structure in US politics. Robert Dahl (1961), for example, cautioned that Mills had merely pointed out a group with high potential for control but had failed to demonstrate that this group actually dominated decision-making. Dahl insisted, furthermore, that only issues on which a clear difference of position could be observed in public debate ought to be considered. He also adopted the restrictive view that power is not exercised in situations where people are persuaded by others to adopt their attitudes. Dahl's own research, particularly in the city of New Haven,

Connecticut, led him to conclude that democracy was alive and well in the America of the 1950s.

The pluralist approach recognizes that modern states all have intermediate organizations between government and the people—namely, parties and interest or lobby groups, which represent those with particular issues to promote in the state. Interest groups try to influence parties but rarely offer their own candidates for election because their objectives are limited to particular issues. Pluralists claim that no one interest is able to dominate the state and that democracy is protected by the competition between interests. Political leaders will be swayed by mass opinions because of their desire to win elections.

If pluralism is correct, the more disadvantaged groups in society (workers, women, minorities, and the poor) will not consistently lose to other groups. The pluralist position is justified to the extent that these groups sometimes achieve their objectives. Rights to organize and strike, the extension of the franchise to women, equal-pay legislation, medicare, language legislation, land claims agreements with Aboriginal peoples, unemployment insurance, and welfare state payments are among the most important state actions that point to an element of pluralism in the Canadian system. This system might be viewed as one of elite competition for popular support. However, these policies could also be interpreted as elite concessions, implemented because they were socially and politically expedient. Clearly, an extreme ruling elite perspective is unwarranted, but so is the uncritical image of a political system functioning without bias.

A fundamental problem for the pluralist perspective is that men and elites dominate political parties, the key groups in the political system. Moreover, representation in Parliament shows a strong class bias that has persisted throughout Canada's history. White-collar workers in routine jobs (clerical and sales) and blue-collar workers—the majority of the population in the twentieth century—have always been severely under-represented, whereas business and middle-class professionals have dominated all parliaments. The increasing proportion of people from business and administration reflects the growing significance of corporate managers. Recently, the number of lawyers in office has declined sharply while that of other professional groups, mainly educators and social scientists, has increased.

The extent to which Canada's tiny capitalist class occupies the pinnacles of state power has also been the subject of considerable research by such sociologists as John Porter (1965), Clement (1975), Denis Olsen (1980), and John Fox and Michael Ornstein (1986), although much of this work is now outdated. During the nineteenth century, the wealthy regularly were directly represented in the state apparatus; in the late twentieth century, this became less common, but connections were still close.

For the years 1946–77, Fox and Ornstein (1986) investigated the convergence between those in leading state positions and those sitting on the boards of Canada's largest corporations. At the federal level, they examined the cabinet, deputy ministers, major Crown corporations, the Senate, senior courts, and the Governor-General; at the provincial level, cabinets, deputy ministers, major Crown corporations, and lieutenant-governors. In addition, they looked at the 20 largest universities and the 15 largest hospitals. They found that, "overall, more than 3300 ties connect the 148 state organizations and 302 private organizations" (1986: 489–90). Manufacturing and finance firms were especially well connected to the federal cabinet, the Senate, and the state bureaucracy. Provincial governments were much less likely than the federal government to be linked to corporations. Moreover, the degree of convergence increased substantially over the three decades. The weight of this evidence is behind a "ruling elite" position.

## Political Economy Perspectives

Since the late 1960s, political economy perspectives have dominated discussions about the state, which is seen as the core of the political system. For the most part, modern thinkers abandoned the old Marxist view, associated with Vladimir Ilyich Lenin, that the state was merely the instrument of capital designed to solve periodic problems of accumulation. Although they have disputed the degree to which the state should be seen as the captive of capital, neo-Marxists usually consider the state to be structured or even programmed so that it acts in the long-term interests of capitalists as a class. Consequently, these authors de-emphasize the evidence that workers appear not to be against capitalism, and see reformist labour or social democratic parties as fulfilling a need for capitalism to make concessions in order to maintain legitimacy and continuity. Similar to ruling elite theory, the liberal-democratic processes are thought to function at a secondary level in the power structure.

Nicos Poulantzas (1978) developed the *neo-Marxist* perspective most fully, arguing that the state must be relatively autonomous from class conflict in the production process if it is to serve the needs of the dominant class. Here, *autonomy* does not mean independence from class control, but rather that the state is not directly representing dominant class interests. The main role of the state is to attain cohesion by "individualizing" the workers—that is, by contributing to their sense of **identity** as individuals and as part of a nation rather than as members of a class. Legal and ideological structures resting on claims of equality among citizens conceal from workers the fact that they are engaged in class relations. To achieve this outcome, the state may act to protect certain economic interests of the dominated classes, but it never challenges the political power of the dominant class. The state may have to resist certain short-term demands of capitalists (for example, reduced taxes and reduced public spending) to meet the long-term needs of capitalism as a whole (for example, maintaining an appropriately educated labour force). From this perspective, the expansion of public welfare against capitalist opposition is interpreted as a move to shore up the future of capitalism by smoothing over some of the discontent engendered by unemployment, poor health care, and unequal access to education.

Skocpol (1979) and Fred Block (1980), among others, put forward another theory, that of the *partially autonomous state*. These theorists claim a genuinely independent source of power for state officials based on the resources of the state that these officials control. This position challenges Marxist theory by claiming, first, that the continuation of capitalism is not necessary; second, that other forms of state or institutional action might meet the "needs" of capitalism; and, third, that much state action is opposed by those for whom it is thought to be essential.

Block's answer to the central question of why state managers should act in the interests of capitalism is that they need capitalists to continue investing, or the state will lose income and political legitimacy. Nevertheless, state intervention often takes a form opposed by capital, because the state is forced to respond to working-class political pressure and because state managers have an interest in expanding their sphere of influence. Depending on the relative flow of power among these groups, state policies can be expected to oscillate. In this model, the state becomes a third effective force, although it is tied to the perpetuation of capitalist interests.

In a more radical version of this thesis, Skocpol argues persuasively that the state should be recognized as a "structure with a logic and interests of its own not necessarily equivalent to, or fused with the interests of the dominant class in society or the full set of member groups in the polity" (1979: 27). Here we are directed to the interests of state actors themselves, as well as to the process of policy formation, to explain the policy that is actually produced. Skocpol does acknowledge that the state often protects dominant class interests, but not in all circumstances—in particular, not when such protection would threaten political stability. Hence, according to Skocpol, "the state's own fundamental interest in maintaining sheer physical order and political peace may lead it—especially in periods of crisis—to enforce concessions to subordinate class demands" (1979: 30). Skocpol charges neo-Marxists with a failure to accord sufficient independence to state and party and with an unjustified insistence that the state must work towards the reproduction of capitalism. Without accepting the idea that politics is a free-for-all competition among equals, this position goes some way towards the pluralist interpretation by recognizing that the capitalist class is not consistently dominant.

As indicated earlier, Canadian data show substantial links between capital and the state—certainly substantial enough to permit direct input of capitalist interests into the state arena. Fox and Ornstein conclude, however, that "the data demonstrate nothing like a fusion of state and capital" (1986: 502). Thus, a simplistic view of the state as the instrument of capital will not hold true.

The state elite is not a mere tool of capital. One reason for the independence of the state elite is that capitalists seldom present a united front on specific policies; another is that the state controls such key resources for independent action as legal authority, lawful force, and information. The elite accommodates deprived groups to some degree in order to guarantee the legitimacy and stability of the political structure in which their own careers are located. That said, it is also true that the ideological compatibility between the state elite and Canadian capitalists, together with the complementarity of their interest in maintaining the social structure from which they benefit, works to inhibit radical institutional change.

### Feminist Perspectives

Most theories of the state focus on class issues to the exclusion of **gender** and **ethnicity**. By contrast, feminist theory makes gender a central component in the analysis of politics and the state, as it does for social life generally. Specifically, the **feminist** perspective has brought attention to the state as a contributor to the subordination of women and as an institution permeated by gender inequality. However, there is no single feminist position. Judith Allen (1990), for example, has even asserted that feminists have no need for a theory of the state because the concept of the state is too vague and unitary to be applicable to women's political strategies, which must focus on specific local conditions or "sites."

Nonetheless, other feminists have considered state theory important. In an influential paper, Mary McIntosh (1978) argues that the state supports a system in which men control women in the household, where they work without pay to maintain capitalism's labour force, and from which they can be drawn as needed to supply cheap labour. Referring mainly to the United Kingdom, McIntosh reviews how the state indirectly subordinates women by staying out of certain areas such as family life, which are left to the control of men, and through legislation, such as husbands' tax allowance, which privileges the employed, married men. In a very real sense, McIntosh contends, women are hidden in the family or household to serve the needs of men and capitalism.

Jill Quadagno claims with justification that the explanation of the development of the welfare state has emphasized class analysis, while ignoring the welfare state's "organization around gender" (1990: 14).

Feminist theorists often claim that welfare programs maintain male dominance insofar as their rules of eligibility favour male breadwinners. Women are more often subject to means tests for social assistance programs, whereas men are more likely to qualify for universal entitlement programs. However, Quadagno notes that some social programs could advance women's interests by reducing their dependence on men. But the development of "gender-equal policies" requires women to mobilize as effective political actors. The latter point is effectively supported by Quadagno's analysis of the defeat of the US Family Assistance Plan in 1972. Had it been implemented, this program would have improved the economic position of both women and blacks in the southern states.

Quadagno's view is consistent with the work of Varda Burstyn (1983), a Canadian feminist, who also identifies the state as acting to maintain domination both by capitalism and by men. Burstyn explains the gender-biased actions of the state largely by the massive extent to which men occupy higher-level state positions. The most extreme bias in the state's structure is the inadequate representation of women. Canadian women did not achieve federal voting rights until 1918—in Quebec, not until 1940. The 65 women elected between 1921 and 1984 amount to 0.8 per cent of all elected members of the House of Commons (Brodie, 1985: 2–4). Since then, the situation has improved, with women constituting 21.1 per cent of MPs in 2002 (Library of Parliament, 2002), the same percentage as their share of cabinet positions. Still, Sylvia Bashevkin's generalization that the more powerful the position, the fewer the women (1985) remains apt for both party and state. Only one woman has been prime minister—Kim Campbell, who served for several months in 1993 until her Progressive Conservative government was defeated.

Does representation matter? While there is no reason to expect that women hold views different from men on many issues, the interests of women would be more effectively represented if they were present in decision-making positions. Manon Tremblay's analysis of women in Parliament in the mid-1990s (Tremblay, 1998) gives some support to this position. Although women's issues (women's rights and traditional areas of women's involvement, such as elder care) were marginal in House activities, when discussion did take place women were more involved than men. Women MPs accorded greater importance than did men to women's issues; they were more likely to report interest in these matters and to feel that they should be given priority. Yet differences were moder-

ate. Regardless of whether or not women would be better protected by their greater political participation, their absence from positions of power is unacceptable, since it seems to rest purely on the ascriptive criterion of gender.

The position of Canadian women in politics is intermediate when compared with other societies. In the Scandinavian countries and the Netherlands, women fare much better, holding over 35 per cent of electoral seats in 2003, while the United States, with 14 per cent, did not rank in the top 50.

Women are dismantling the bastions of male political dominance, but the process is slow and depends on reorienting attitudes towards gender roles. Although some men are sensitive to women's issues, male-controlled legislatures in Canada and elsewhere have been slow to act on many matters of importance to women. As of 2005, there was still no national daycare policy. Publicly funded daycare facilities do not meet demand. Furthermore, child-care workers are unable to earn the professional salaries that would justify the necessary training and commitment. In the labour market generally, part-time workers are disproportionately women and receive inferior job protection. Legislation that would end pay discrimination in the private sector based on gender has been slow to arrive and is difficult to enforce. These are only a few examples of the gender-related problems that remain to be solved in Canada and most other societies.

# Democracy and Politics in Canada

## Party Politics and the Electoral System

A **political party** is an organization dedicated to winning political power by controlling government. In liberal democracies, this means winning a general election. Canada is a federation with a complex structure in which the powers of legislation are divided between federal and provincial governments. The organization of parties mirrors this institutional arrangement, and securing as much electoral support as possible within this structure is the key to their success.

At the federal level, only the Liberal and the former Progressive Conservative parties have ever governed, and the Liberal Party has been dominant. Until the 1990s, these two parties competed with each other for control of the state by following a brokerage strategy in which the parties would attempt to appeal to diverse social groups in order to establish a winning combination. Usually, this meant avoiding controversial ideological issues and adopting broadly similar positions on major issues. An exception was the 1988 election campaign in which the Conservatives championed free trade and claimed victory after a bitter struggle, although the two parties opposing free trade with the US—the Liberals and the New Democratic Party—gained many more votes than the victorious Tories.

Canada's electoral system has several advantages. Citizens may be able to approach their local member of Parliament (MP), although it would be impossible for everyone actually to do so. More important, this system usually produces a majority, and thus a stable government. But it clearly makes some people's votes more influential than others, depending on where they live, and often produces a Parliament that does not reflect the wishes of the population as a whole, as the 1988 election outcome suggests.

## Political Participation

Participation in the political process varies from informal discussion, listening to media reports, and voting to more demanding activities such as attending meetings, assisting with campaigns, contacting politicians in order to influence them, even running for office. For most Canadians, political participation is limited to discussion and voting for candidates to the various levels of government. However, it appears that the public is becoming increasingly cynical about politicians; turnout at elections is falling, with federal elections now attracting about 70 per cent of eligible voters.

Sociologists are interested in the social characteristics that may influence participation. However, a great deal of research has demonstrated that no necessary link exists between a person's social background and the party he or she supports. Harold Clarke's team (1991) examined the variables of class, gender, ethnicity, religion, region, community size, and age, and found that they all have some effect on Canadians' voting preferences, but much less than political variables such as prior voting record, concern about immediate issues, and the image of the party leader. Nonetheless, in 2000 the Liberal Party could not have won without the strong support outside Quebec of Catholics (54 per cent) and Canadians of non-European ethnicity (70 per cent; Gidengil et al., 2001: 28). Region was more critical than it had been in earlier elections, with the right-wing Alliance Party powerful west of Ontario (where Liberals were much weaker) but unable to break through in eastern

Canada, where Progressive Conservatives and especially Liberals were stronger. Women supported the NDP much more than did men, whereas men were more drawn to the Alliance. Age and language were critical to voting in Quebec, where those under 55 and francophones were more likely to support the separatist, social democratic Bloc Québécois.

Class is not a defining force in contemporary Canadian politics, but economic issues and beliefs do influence the choices of many voters. Thus, outside Quebec, those who believed in giving increased priority to market forces were more attracted to the Alliance and Progressive Conservative parties in 2000 (since merged as the Conservative Party), while those with the opposite view favoured Liberals and the social democratic NDP; social conservatives preferred the Alliance to the Progressive Conservative Party (Gidengil et al., 2001).

A crude theory in which voting behaviour inevitably follows from social experience is obviously untenable. A more useful sociological account, influenced by **symbolic interactionist** theory, starts from the assumption that voting is an interpretive action to which people carry assumptions from their prior experience, filtered through their social positions and possibly their previous commitments to a party. Usually they have incomplete information and incomplete understanding of how the political system operates. Typically, the strongest parties play down social issues and try to emphasize the quality of their leaders (or record in office) to cope with whatever problems exist. To achieve overall victory, care will be taken not to appear too closely linked to the interests of any particular group. In the end, voters make choices that respond only partially to social and cultural factors. Of course, for decades in Quebec, the priority of cultural concerns and the issue of independence have made political life more ideological and socially influenced. Nonetheless, voting does not really determine state policy—it provides legitimization for those who control it.

## Neo-conservatism and Privatization

After decades of expansion of the welfare state and standards of living, many countries faced problems of inflation, lower economic growth, and budget deficits in the 1970s and 1980s. Continued demands for better public education and health care were incompatible with pressure to reduce taxes. Many states seemed to be suffering from or on the brink of what some called a "crisis of legitimation" (Habermas, 1975; Offe, 1984). With welfare state policies under severe stress, political space opened up for more conservative policies. These policies stressed eliminating public deficits by reducing expenditure, stimulating the economy by cutting taxes, and withdrawing the state from the economy by privatizing existing public enterprises and contracting to the private sector for services previously provided by public employees. Sometimes **privatization** sales have been legitimized as contributions to debt reduction. The promotion of "free" market forces and a smaller state is at the core of this new conservatism, which has found favour with many voters, especially those who would benefit from tax reductions and who have the capacity to purchase services for themselves.

In Canada, this trend has been evident not only in the rise of the Canadian Alliance, but also in practices of various provincial governments, especially Conservatives in Ontario (under Mike Harris) and Alberta (Ralph Klein) and Liberals in British Columbia (Gordon Campbell). However, all levels of government have participated to some degree. For example, the federal government sold Air Canada to the private sector, and most of Petro-Canada, the highly successful national oil company, can now be purchased on the stock market. Airport security was subcontracted prior to the terrorist attacks of 11 September 2001. The privatization of basic public goods, such as power and water supply, is proving to be controversial: many people are concerned that prices will rise in the long term once supply is in corporate hands. Thus, the decision to sell Ontario Hydro in a mammoth public share offering proved difficult to implement in 2002 as citizen groups mobilized in opposition.

Certainly among the most critical issues is the reform and increased privatization of health care, which was on the political agenda for some years and the subject of several investigations, most recently the Romanow Commission on the Future of Health Care in Canada, which reported in 2002. As of 2003, the federal government insisted that it would use its power to maintain standards across Canada, including universal access. Nevertheless, there have been signs of creeping privatization, especially in Alberta, and considerable dispute continues between the federal government and the more conservative provincial administrations. Canadians worry about what is happening to their health-care system when they see so many publicized delays in accessing specialist services and when hospital emergency rooms are frequently

overflowing. The 2003 SARS outbreak in Toronto brought such concerns to the forefront again as the hospital system appeared close to collapse. Several hospitals had to be diverted from their normal activities, and medical staff were required to function under dangerous and stressful conditions. Some are convinced that privatization or a two-tier system is necessary, while others prefer a reform of the existing system and the injection of the necessary funds to make it work properly.

# Social Movements

Political change more dramatic than an election may be brought about by social movements. A *social movement* consists of like-minded organizations that co-ordinate the voluntary actions of non-elite members of society and offer a program for changing the way society distributes social goods. People form a social movement when they voluntarily work together to influence the distribution of social goods. A *social good* is anything that a particular society values. Familiar examples include money, honour, peace, security, citizenship, leisure time, political power, and divine grace. There are probably no universal social goods, because no two societies have exactly the same set of values. Furthermore, social goods vary historically. They emerge and disappear as values change or traditions lose relevance (Walzer, 1983).

Social goods are scarce—in part, that is why they are valuable—and some individuals or groups get more of them than others do. How people make sense of such inequalities depends on *ideologies*, sets of ideas that justify how social goods are distributed. *Dominant ideologies* defend existing inequalities by making them seem right. *Counter-ideologies* challenge the justice of the existing social system, promote alternative values and goals, and present a plan for change. Promoting counter-ideologies is a goal of social movements.

Social movements try to achieve change through the voluntary co-operation of the relatively powerless. These people may contribute financial or other material resources, recruit new members, or spread a counter-ideology. They may also participate in strikes, sit-ins, boycotts, demonstrations, protest marches, violent action, or civil disobedience. The efforts of social movements can be focused on changing attitudes, everyday practices, public opinion, or the policies and procedures of business and government.

Social movements are easier to understand when compared and contrasted with other phenomena studied by sociologists (Diani, 1992). A *social trend*, for example, is simply a changing pattern of social behaviour, whereas a social movement is a co-operative effort to achieve social change from below. The rising labour market participation of women is a social trend; a group of volunteers who fight for gender equality is a social movement. Certainly, social movements influence some social trends. For instance, feminist movements may encourage the trend for women to enter the paid workforce. However, many social trends—such as changing fashions or unemployment patterns—may be scarcely affected by social movements.

A *pressure group* is an organization that aims to influence large institutions, particularly the state. A social movement is one kind of pressure group. However, other pressure groups—known as *interest groups*—represent the specific concerns of farmers, employers, medical doctors, ethnic groups, and so on. Interest groups restrict their membership and rely heavily on a professional staff rather than volunteers. Moreover, recognition by the government often gives them semi-official or even official status. Like social movements, interest groups use public opinion to put pressure on political or economic elites. But membership in social movements is more open, and their ideologies typically appeal to people from different walks of life.

Since social movements depend on voluntary participation, they are *voluntary associations*. However, not all voluntary associations seek deeper changes in the distribution of social goods. Some provide social or health services; others organize leisure activities or unite the followers of a spiritual doctrine. Voluntary associations that only help people to accept or enjoy the existing social system are not social movements.

While social movements try to change the distribution of social goods, political parties try to win and keep political power. In principle, a social movement becomes a political party when it fields candidates in elections. The Green parties in Germany, France, and Italy, for example, have grown out of environmental movements in these countries. In practice, the difference between social movements and political parties is sometimes hazy. Parties that have grown out of social movements often retain features from their past. They may be more sectarian or may rely heavily on grassroots supporters. These features foster a strong party identity, but they may also discourage outsiders from joining.

Finally, not all groups with non-elite, voluntary members who aim to reallocate social goods are necessarily social movements. A *counter-movement* may have

Demonstrations belong to a repertoire of contention that also includes strikes, violent action, and civil disobedience. These may have influence on public opinion, government policies, or business practices. In this photograph, citizens are protesting in front of the Ontario legislature against cuts to the public education system. (© Dick Hemingway)

all of the characteristics of a social movement, but with one important difference: a counter-movement arises *in response to* a social movement. Three conditions must be met for counter-movements to appear:

1. A social movement must be seen as successful (or as gaining success).
2. A social movement's goals must be seen as a threat to another group.
3. Allies must be available to support mobilization of the counter-movement.

While some counter-movements (such as the National Rifle Association in the US) wish to defend the status quo against a perceived threat by social movements, others (such as the anti-abortion movement) emerge when a state or government agency has ambiguous policies or is internally divided on a particular social issue (Meyer and Staggenborg, 1996).

# Theoretical Approaches to Social Movements

Different beliefs about society separate the four main approaches to social movements. The **breakdown approach** assumes that stability is the basis of social order and that **culture** is the major determinant of action. The **resource mobilization approach** assumes that social order is based on competition and conflict and that interests are the fundamental cause of action. The **identity-based approach** and the **political process approach** draw selectively from the other two. Both assume that social order rests on an unsteady resolution of conflict and that culture is the major determinant of action. Table 14.2 summarizes the assumptions that underlie these four perspectives.

## *The Breakdown Approach*

The breakdown approach builds on a view of society developed by the French sociologist Émile Durkheim (1858–1917) and later by the American founder of **structural functionalism**, Talcott Parsons (1902–79). Both thought that shared **norms** and **values** hold society together. The breakdown approach holds that rapid, thorough, or uneven change in society weakens the social bonds that promote social order. Social disintegration, in turn, encourages the formation of groups advocating radical change.

The assumptions of the breakdown approach underlie **relative deprivation theory**, which claims that radical social movements result from feelings of fear and frustration. According to James C. Davies (1962), revolutions and rebellions are preceded by two phases. The first phase is characterized by economic and social progress. More and more social goods become available—food becomes more plentiful, for example, or the rights of citizens expand—and

expectations rise. But if a sharp reversal follows—if food suddenly becomes scarce and costly, or if authorities ban opposition parties and the free press after a period of liberalization—rising expectations are no longer met. In the second phase, the gap between what people expect and what they actually get grows ever wider. Rebellion results when anxiety and frustration become widespread and intense.

Critics of relative deprivation theory point out that the most frustrated members of society are not the only people who fight for radical change. Revolutions, especially successful ones, also are led and supported by people from the middle and upper classes. Moreover, relative deprivation theory does not provide a convincing link between people's feelings and revolution. Surely the people of Haiti, for instance, have endured many decades of anxiety and frustration under brutal dictatorships. Yet their dissatisfaction has not led to revolution. A great deal must happen before individual grievances will translate into major changes such as the toppling of a political regime.

Like relative deprivation theory, Neil Smelser's **systemic theory** highlights the role of social breakdown in the growth of social movements. But instead of focusing on individuals, as relative deprivation theory does, Smelser looks at society as a whole. He sees society as a set of linked elements that work to maintain stability. Social movements reflect the breakdown of stability, but they do not form unless six conditions are met (Smelser, 1963):

1. *Structural conduciveness.* Social conditions must give people a chance to unite for change. If people remain isolated, they cannot pool their efforts.
2. *Structural strain.* The dominant ideology must be viewed with dissatisfaction or uncertainty.
3. *Growth and spread of a generalized belief.* Potential participants in social movements must share a counter-ideology that binds them together.
4. *A precipitating factor.* This is the straw that breaks the camel's back—some event so serious that people finally decide to fight for change.

## Table 14.2 **Approaches to the Study of Social Movements**

| | | Primary Cause of Social Action | |
| --- | --- | --- | --- |
| | | **Culture** | **Interests** |
| **Underlying Societal Dynamic** | Consensus | • breakdown approach | • *undeveloped approach* |
| | Conflict | • identity-based approach<br>• political process approach | • resource mobilization approach |

5. *Mobilization*. People's readiness for action must have an outlet; they must be able to join a social movement.

6. *The response of authorities*. Because the state is so powerful, its response affects a social movement's chances of survival and success.

Smelser's systemic theory improves on relative deprivation theory. It corrects the overemphasis on individuals by specifying group and societal factors involved in the rise of social movements. Moreover, systemic theory recognizes that shared grievances alone will not bind protestors together. For a movement to last, protestors must share a counter-ideology, a set of ideas that gives them guidelines to work together for change. Finally, the theory brings mobilization into the picture. Personal dissatisfaction alone will not form a social movement, no matter how widespread the grievance.

Unfortunately, Smelser's theory rests partly on circular reasoning. On the one hand, he defines social mobilization for action as a response to strain in generalized belief. But he also lists mobilization for action, strain, and generalized belief among the six factors that cause social movements. In this respect, his theory is a restatement of what needs to be explained, not an explanation (Aya, 1990).

Contrary to the assumptions of the breakdown approach, social conflict may be a normal feature of social life. If this is so, then the breakdown of value consensus and stability may not explain the formation of social movements. Breakdown theory has also been accused of treating social movements as ailments. Yet many sociologists welcome the movements against war, racism, sexism, pollution, bureaucracy, and present educational systems as positive signs of healthy protest against injustice and alienation.

Finally, critics argue that it is misleading to treat social movements as outbursts of uncontainable emotion. Experience suggests that participation in social movements may involve the same kind of calm and rational decision-making found in other areas of life. This interpretation underlies the resource mobilization approach.

## The Resource Mobilization Approach

The resource mobilization approach challenges the image of social movements as unusual, impermanent, or disorderly. Instead, it assumes that social movements are quite similar to other organizations. They are managed by leaders whose decisions are no less calculating than anyone else's. Some sociologists go so far as to treat social movement organizers as entrepreneurs who have a "product" to sell.

Unlike business entrepreneurs, however, social movement entrepreneurs must deal with *free-riding*—non-co-operation in the attainment of a good that will be available to all members of the community. For movement leaders, the solution is to make their "product" appealing in the competitive market for potential members' time, energy, and resources. From this perspective, social movement propaganda is a form of marketing that advertises the benefits of joining (Jenkins, 1983).

Proponents of the resource mobilization approach argue that the breakdown approach is wrong in assuming that satisfaction with the social order is the normal state of affairs. Instead, dissatisfaction is built into society. There will always be people with grievances because social goods are unequally distributed. But grievances alone do not make a social movement. What social movements do is lift grievances out of the shadows, giving them ideological form and propelling them into public life.

The resource mobilization approach puts power at the centre of analysis. Power is not something one has: one can only be in a position that confers power, for power means having the ability to carry out one's wishes. As the German sociologist Max Weber (1864–1920) put it, *power* refers to a person's or group's chance of fulfilling their goals even when others would have it otherwise ([1908] 1978: 926).

The source of power is control over resources. Control creates *leverage*, the ability to get others to do what one wants. What represents a resource in any given situation varies, but three kinds of power stand out. One is *economic power*, which is based on control over the means of material production: land, energy, capital, technology, labour, factories, raw materials, and so forth. Another is *political power*, based on control over the means of legitimated violence: the police and the armed forces. A third is *ideological power*, which is based on control over the means of producing and disseminating **symbols**: schools, churches, newspapers, publishing houses, television and radio, film and advertising companies, and the like. The resource base for each of the three kinds of power differs. Nonetheless, control over any resource allows elites to shape the lives of the powerless.

Social movements must compete against other social institutions for the scarce resources necessary to start and operate an organization. The resource mobilization approach therefore searches for the social conditions that affect social movements' control over resources, and focuses on the strategies that translate power into success.

There are two perspectives on resource mobilization: the utilitarian and political conflict perspectives (Ramirez, 1981). While both assume that actors (whether individuals or groups) are rational and seek to maximize self-interest, each addresses somewhat different problems.

The **utilitarian perspective** focuses on how individuals promote their own interests. The free-rider problem is a central concern, with the proponents of this perspective asking how and why selective incentives attract volunteers and cut down on free-riding. It also studies the relationships between social movements and how rewards motivate social movement entrepreneurs.

Critics of the utilitarian perspective have stressed the limited applicability of the free-rider problem. The assumption that social movements attract support only by providing selective incentives may misconstrue people's reasons for joining. Instead, people may join a movement simply because it seems headed for success. Or they may join because they identify with other members of the social movement and believe the group will benefit if its members work together (Barry, [1970] 1978). Finally, norms of fairness may override concerns about efficiency. Pressures to conform may lead people to join social movements, irrespective of selective incentives (Elster, 1989). Such considerations are ruled out by an exclusive focus on the free-rider problem. The utilitarian perspective forgets that people are ruled by more than self-interest. Further, it forgets that social movements are groups, so they cannot be explained by individualistic decisions alone.

The **political conflict perspective** focuses on how parts of society (typically classes) promote collective interests. Although not a Marxist approach, it tends to stress issues central to the Marxist tradition: working-class mobilization, class conflict, and revolution. Hence, analysis from this perspective usually tries to explain the origins of class **solidarity**. Studies in the political conflict tradition also search for factors that determine the success and failure of class-based movements, including class alliances, pre-existing social ties that foster communication and group action, and ties with other groups and political authorities.

In recent decades, sociologists working from the political conflict perspective have reduced an earlier emphasis on class strength and class alliances. Simultaneously, they have lent more attention to the state. Because it is so powerful, the state can tip the balance in favour of one class over another. Thus, domestic and international events affecting the state may decide the fate of a revolution. A thorough analysis of social movements will pay attention to the state's power, and a subtle analysis of social movements will respect the complexity of state–society relations.

The resource mobilization approach represents a clear advance over the breakdown approach. It underscores the normality of social movements by drawing attention to their similarities with other organizations. Nevertheless, this approach has some shortcomings, too. First, it runs the danger of missing some important differences between social movements and other organizations. They have different resources, career cycles, and relationships with government authorities as well as with other social movements. They also exhibit distinctive modes of acting, organizing, and communicating (Tarrow, 1988). The image of human action conveyed by the resource mobilization approach has also been criticized as too voluntaristic. It exaggerates the extent to which social movements reflect careful planning and successful strategy. People often act with only vague or conflicting goals in mind. The goals of social movements often emerge and change as situations evolve. The voluntarism of the resource mobilization approach contains another drawback: this approach neglects political and international contexts, and it neglects the manner in which culture shapes—and is shaped by—participation in social movements.

### The Identity-Based Approach

The identity-based approach squarely confronts neglect of culture inherent in the resource mobilization approach. Major intellectual influences on this approach include neo-Marxists who have treated ideas and consciousness as stakes in class and political struggle, such as the Italian Antonio Gramsci (1891–1937), and theorists associated with Germany's Frankfurt School (Held, 1980). According to the identity-based approach, dominant interpretations of reality uphold class, gender, racial, and other inequalities. Progressive social movements must therefore challenge the dominant culture.

The identity-based approach criticizes the resource mobilization approach for forgetting that neither the goals of social movements nor the way they calculate the best means of achieving them is self-evident. Norms and values are created in and by social movements. Hence, the formation of social movements' goals needs to be explained (Nedelmann,

1991). Moreover, the resource mobilization approach takes for granted the sense of community that creates identity and a willingness to work together. How people define themselves depends very much on whom they identify with—on what community, with its unique norms and values, they feel they belong to. Effective social movements redefine identities by changing or reinforcing people's sense of community.

The *new social movement* (NSM) perspective focuses largely on identity. It proposes that social movements can be laboratories for more progressive forms of social interaction (Melucci, 1989). The breakdown and resource mobilization approaches define the success of social movements in terms of change in economic or political institutions. The NSM approach defines success differently. To be sure, it does not deny the desirability of change in dominant institutions. However, the more important struggle takes place in civil society, those areas of social interaction that stand largely outside of the state and the market. In fact, theorists claim that new social movements have come about since the 1960s because state and economic practices have increasingly encroached on people's everyday lives. Slogans such as "the personal is political" are meant to express how everyday life is pervaded by government and corporate activities, as well as by dominant cultural ideas that create inequality.

According to this approach, civil society offers greater chances for freedom, equality, and *participatory democracy*, a system of decision-making in which all members of a group exercise control over group decisions. Indeed, new social movements are, in part, characterized by institutional arrangements wherein their members try to organize according to the ideals of equal participation. This is what social movements are good at, and striving for other kinds of success risks perverting these ideals (Cohen, 1985).

Generally, new social movements are said to be distinctive from previous forms of collective action. The appearance of these new social movements may be explained by a value shift (Inglehart, 1990b). With relative economic and political stability in Western societies, the cultural value of social goods has changed. In the past, social movements were concerned primarily with the redistribution of social goods that provided sustenance and security, such as money, job security, and welfare rights. The new social movements, in contrast, are said to be concerned primarily with cultural recognition. In other words, these movements attempt to have their subcultural practices understood and in some cases legitimated by the dominant culture.

The work of French sociologist Alain Touraine (1981) exemplifies the identity-based approach. Touraine originally studied the French workers' movement, but during the 1960s, he became interested in the feminist, student, peace, and ecological movements. Unlike movements promoting the interests of a specific group, these new social movements had goals based on more universal values. They also displayed an innovative interest in participatory democracy. Touraine has urged sociologists analyzing social movements to follow an *intervention approach*—that is, to abandon professional detachment and contribute to social change by actively sharing insights and ideas with the people they are studying.

Like resource mobilization approaches, the identity-based approach tends to be voluntaristic in its emphasis on people's potential for actively challenging and changing society. It focuses on altering the shared understandings that maintain patterns of domination. Consequently, it, too, often ignores the structures of economic and political opportunity that shape the destinies of social movements.

Also, while identity-based theories lean towards abstraction in their language and scope, identity-based studies tend to be descriptive and narrowly focused. These characteristics point to a gap between theory and research.

## The Political Process Approach

While the breakdown, resource mobilization, and identity-based approaches have been useful for understanding social movements, in recent years scholars have attempted to create a synthesis. The political process approach is generally attributed to Peter Eisinger's study of movements during the 1960s (1973). Eisinger argued that collective action depends on the structure of local political opportunities at the institutional and governmental levels. Charles Tilly (1978), an early proponent of the political process approach, built on this idea by showing how nation-states can manipulate the political terrain to stymie the activities of social movements. Tilly argues that the rise of nation-states gave rise to the national social movements of the early modern era in Europe. New political ideas that helped to create nation-states also generated grievances that led people to act collectively. These national social movements had characteristics that set them apart from previous forms of collective action (see also Tarrow, 1998).

The political process approach assumes that the *polity* (the organized political society) can be characterized by its opportunities and constraints. *Opportunities* involve almost anything that provides reasons and resources for people to mobilize—so long as the political climate is not so oppressive that people cannot mobilize without fear or great difficulty. Political opportunities may include economic crises, laws ensuring the right to assemble, a history of previous collective action, even accidents that show the need for social change. *Constraints* include anything within the polity that may act as a barrier to the mobilization and survival of a social movement. Political constraints include a repressive police state, inexperience with collective action, even a lack of communication among a social movement's participants. Opportunities and constraints go hand in hand: no polity is completely open or completely closed.

Slogans such as "the personal is political" are meant to draw attention to the ways in which everyday life is pervaded by dominant values that promote inequality. Environmental, feminist, gay and lesbian, peace, and anti-poverty organizations in British Columbia and other provinces have formed coalitions based on shared understandings of social injustice. (© Dick Hemingway)

The breakdown approach assumes that some form of social or political crisis is needed for people to act collectively. By contrast, the political process approach assumes that collective action is an ongoing social phenomenon. In other words, the breakdown approach assumes that social movements arise from *outside* the polity but enter the political terrain when there are reasons to do so. Conversely, the political process approach assumes that social movements have a historical position *within* the polity and that the frequency of social movement activity changes according to opportunities and constraints (Tarrow, 1998).

Fluctuations in the opportunities and constraints influencing the frequency of collective action create a *cycle of contention* (Tarrow, 1998). A rise in the cycle means that social movements have created or met new opportunities and have made room for the rise of other movements. Protest events among Native groups in Canada rose dramatically between 1989 and 1991, peaking in 1990. This increase can be attributed to the 78-day armed uprising at Oka, Quebec, over municipal plans to expand a golf course over a Mohawk burial ground. In support of the Kanesatake Reserve at Oka, nearby Mohawk bands at Kahnawake and Akwesasne, as well as bands across Canada, increased their protest activities.

Like the resource mobilization approach, the political process model focuses on institutions. Specifically, this approach looks at *mobilizing structures*, which include levels of informal and formal organization (McCarthy, 1996). An example of **informal organization** is a friendship network. When the cycle of contention is at its lowest point—when there are relatively few (or no) active social movement organizations—the network of friendships among demobilized movement participants keeps the spirit of collective action alive. These latent, or buried, networks explain why social movements arise when political opportunities appear and when constraints are eased (Melucci, 1989). Although informal communication alone cannot give rise to a social movement, it can become an important resource for mobilization.

The analysis of **formal organization** looks at the inner dynamics of social movements. These generally include leadership structures, flows of communication, the entry and exit of members, and the means of identifying, obtaining, and utilizing resources. By studying mobilizing structures, sociologists can understand the institutional processes whereby movements rise, persist, and decline.

The study of social movement organizations also includes inter-organization dynamics, such as *movement coalitions*. A coalition results when two or more social movement organizations share resources, such as information, in the course of pursuing a common good. Coalitions can be temporary or enduring, and they can bridge different types of movements. Environmental, feminist, gay and lesbian, labour, peace, and anti-poverty organizations in British Columbia, for example, have formed coalitions based on shared understandings of social injustice (Carroll and Ratner, 1996).

According to the identity-based approach, social movements develop subcultural understandings of the world. These understandings form the basis for identifying and acting on social grievances. These also provide movement participants with the resources needed to create activist identities.

The political process approach uses frame analysis to analyze how movements create novel understandings of the world. Drawing on Erving Goffman's concept of framing processes (see Goffman, 1986), *collective action frames* are "action-oriented sets of beliefs and meanings that inspire and legitimate the activities and campaigns of a social movement organization" (Benford and Snow, 2000: 614). Collective action frames are the communal understandings of a social movement, and these understandings are used to identify and promote grievances. The process whereby individuals adopt the ideology and methods of a particular movement organization is called *frame alignment* (Snow et al., 1986).

Finally, social movements may use collective action frames as strategic resources. To mobilize general support for their cause, movements promote their own ideologies in the wider culture. If a social movement's framing of injustice and its solution are accepted in society, then it has created its own political opportunities. If a movement is unsuccessful, however, it risks adding to its own difficulties.

As William Gamson and David Meyer observe, the political process model has been "used to explain so much, it may ultimately explain nothing at all" (1996: 275). While somewhat overstating their case, these critics are concerned that if variable after variable is included in the model, the explanation is no longer parsimonious. The model loses simplicity and thus its explanatory appeal.

Doug McAdam (1996) provides two solutions to this problem. First, he suggests restricting this concept to include only four variables:

- the openness of the state;
- the stability of alliances among elite members of society;
- support within the elite for a particular movement;
- the level of state repression.

Second, McAdam argues that opportunities and constraints are different for each type of social movement. For example, the elements of the political structure that give rise to revolutionary movements likely will be different from those that give rise to identity-based movements. Revolutionary movements usually identify most of their political opportunities within the state system, whereas identity-based movements are likely to find most of their opportunities within the cultural practices of civil society (McAdam, 1996).

# The Analysis of Social Movements

Why do some movements succeed, while others fail? To find an answer to this question, we will examine two social movements: the Canadian women's movement and agrarian social movements.

## *Unity and Diversity in the Canadian Women's Movement*

Social movements need both diversity and unity. In the history of the Canadian women's movement, diversity of membership and of experience has helped the movement adapt to a range of situations. Diversity has also encouraged recognition of the many faces of gender inequality. By maintaining a stock of alternative views and ideas, ideological diversity readies the movement for social change. Unity, in turn, gives the movement strength. A one-woman strike, boycott, or sit-in scarcely represents a threat to dominant institutions. But women who are individually powerless gain leverage by acting together. Unified, they can disrupt patriarchal institutions and pressure authorities into finding new solutions.

Though diversity and unity are beneficial, they pull social movements in opposite directions. Diversity tends to impede unity and may lead to factionalism. Unity tends to suppress diversity and may stifle flexibility and innovation. As in any complex social arrangement, there can be no either/or choice for social movements: survival and efficacy dictate a balance between diversity and unity. The story of the first and second waves of the Canadian women's movement illustrates this dilemma.

The first wave of feminism in Canada began in the late nineteenth century and ended in 1918. During this period, women formed organizations for the protection and education of young single women, such as the Anglican Girls Friendly Society and the Young Women's Christian Association (YWCA). Women's groups also protested against child labour and poor working conditions and pressed for health and welfare reforms.

Feminists of the first wave differed in their religious, class, and ethnic backgrounds. While many were Protestant, others were not. Anglo-Saxon women from the middle and upper classes predominated, especially among the leadership, and language divided anglophone and francophone feminists. Moreover, women's organizations had diverse goals. But the battle for women's voting rights unified the movement. By 1916, women had won the right to vote in provincial elections in Alberta, Saskatchewan, and Manitoba. Canadian women received the federal franchise in 1918.

As with many other social movements, success led to decline. The fight for voting rights had given the women's movement a common goal. When this goal was attained, the movement lost unity and momentum. Certainly, women did not stop pushing for change after winning the right to vote. Some worked within the labour movement; others continued to fight for social reform or female political representation. Yet after 1918, the Canadian women's movement became fragmented, and four decades would pass before it regained strength (Wilson, 1991).

The second wave of the movement rose out of the peace, student, and civil rights movements of the 1960s. In some cases, organizations advanced the women's cause by branching out. For example, a Toronto organization called the Voice of Women (VOW) was founded in 1960 as a peace group. But the VOW gradually adopted other women's issues, and by 1964 it was promoting the legalization of birth control.

The social movements of the 1960s also spurred women in other ways. Women in the student movement came to realize that many male activists were sexist. This drove home the extent of gender inequality and the need to organize apart from men. Through the New Left movement, women discovered that socialism helped make sense of gender inequality. More generally, the cultural upheaval of the 1960s encouraged women to question their position in private and public life.

As a distinct women's movement emerged in the late 1960s and early 1970s, so did internal diversity. Some members were revolutionary Marxists, while others were socialists, liberals, or radical feminists. At times, those who favoured grassroots activism criticized those who worked through high-profile official committees such as the Canadian Advisory Council on the Status of Women. The specific concerns of lesbian, non-white, immigrant, or Native women were often ignored or marginalized by mainstream women's groups. Finally, issues of language and separatism split women's organizations in Quebec from those in the rest of Canada.

Still, the movement found bases for unity. In 1970, a cross-Canada caravan for the repeal of the abortion law attracted much publicity. The caravan collected thousands of petition signatures, showing women what could be achieved through collective action. Since then, other coalitions have formed around the issues of daycare, violence against women, labour, and poverty. Women's groups have also worked together on International Women's Day celebrations.

During both its first and second waves, then, the Canadian women's movement has organized around many issues. The diversity of its concerns and perspectives not only reflects the many faces of gender inequality, but also promotes a diffusion of the movement's ideas and its survival in the face of changing social conditions. However, serious internal arguments may exhaust activists. Although factions permit the coexistence of different constituencies, they draw attention and energy away from common interests that can unite diverse organizations. When the time for action comes, a movement may lose effectiveness if its factions do not set aside their differences. At the same time, the success of the women's movement, like that of all social movements, also depends on balancing the trade-offs between diversity and unity (Briskin, 1992).

### The Roots of Agrarian Protest in Canada

A study by Canadian sociologist Robert J. Brym (1980) shows why regional differences between farming economies have affected agrarian social movements in Alberta, Saskatchewan, and New Brunswick. The ideology and popularity of these movements and their links with other social groups all depend on the type of farming found in each region.

During the 1930s, agrarian protest grew rapidly in the Prairie provinces, but not in New Brunswick.

Much of this difference can be explained by the degree to which farmers' livelihoods were affected by the market. In the West, farmers concentrated on producing beef or wheat, both for the rest of Canada and for export. Hence, western ranchers and wheat farmers faced similar economic pressures. Eastern Canada set the tariffs on manufactured goods, the rates for railroad freight and bank credit, even the prices of beef and wheat. United by common economic interests, western farmers responded by creating marketing, consumer, and other voluntary associations that stressed co-operation.

In New Brunswick, by contrast, farmers practised mixed agriculture. Their primary productive goal was meeting their economic needs without selling what they produced or buying what they needed—strictly speaking, they were peasants rather than farmers. Since changes in market prices hardly affected them, they had little reason to defend themselves by forming co-operatives. Historical and geographical factors also mattered. While the dominance of shipping and timber interests had hampered the commercialization of agriculture in New Brunswick, the province's poor soil and rugged terrain confined farming to river valleys and the coastline. Finally, New Brunswick farmers were not only more isolated than those in the West, they also had much smaller debts. Farmers in New Brunswick were therefore much less likely to form associations. In 1939, for instance, membership in farmers' co-operatives per 1,000 rural residents over 14 years of age was 32 in New Brunswick, compared with 326 in Alberta and 789 in Saskatchewan (Brym, 1980: 346).

Thus, the greater radicalism of western farmers stemmed from high solidarity and a loss of control over their **means of production**. But the two western provinces diverged in their approach to agrarian protest. Alberta's Social Credit Party was right-wing, while Saskatchewan's CCF (Co-operative Commonwealth Federation, the predecessor of today's New Democratic Party) was left-wing. What accounts for this divergence?

In Alberta, a leftist agrarian party known as the United Farmers of Alberta excluded small-town merchants and others seen as exploiters of farmers. During the difficult Depression years of the 1930s, however, co-operation between farmers and merchants increased when they saw that their economic fortunes were connected—if farmers did badly, so would local businesses, and vice versa. With the support of right-wing merchants, teachers, professionals, and preachers, the new Social Credit Party spread

from Calgary to the small towns of southwestern Alberta. Eventually, Social Credit reached farmers and won their support too, but the party never lost the right-wing ideology of its urban roots.

In Saskatchewan, on the other hand, the CCF maintained strong ties between farmers and the left-wing urban working class. Of the CCF leadership, 53 per cent were farmers and 17 per cent workers, while of the Social Credit Party 24 per cent were farmers and none were workers (Brym 1980: 350). Thus, the differing class backgrounds of the farmers' allies help to explain differences in the ideologies of agrarian movements in Saskatchewan and Alberta.

Brym's study suggests that economic factors affect the formation of social movements, as well as which ideological direction they take. Agricultural producers such as prairie farmers are more likely to protest if there is a downturn in the capitalist economy because their livelihood, unlike that of producers in New Brunswick, depends on the market. Furthermore, the organization of a protest movement is hampered when potential supporters lack pre-existing social ties or work in isolation from other potential supporters. Finally, the alliances of a social movement affect both its ideology and its chances of success.

## Is the Future of Social Movements Global?

The world is going through an accelerated bout of **globalization**. While this is hardly new, some sociologists claim the level of global interdependence and the scale of global interaction are becoming more complex, too. Capital and commodities, information and ideas, people and their cultures are criss-crossing the globe, and these interactions are changing the world's societies.

Many social movements recognize that globalization is changing the political terrain. New opportunities and constraints are appearing that force social movements to adapt their strategies, resources, and ideologies. Recall Charles Tilly's research (1978) on the development of the nation-state in Europe: the rise of new forms of social protest was a product of the rise of nations. Will globalization also give rise to new, global forms of protest?

Some environmental, human rights, and health and anti-poverty organizations, such as Greenpeace International, the Sea Shepherd Society, the World Conservation Union, Amnesty International, Oxfam, and Médecins sans frontières, as well as a variety of anti-globalization movements, aim to operate in a global polity. These organizations take the globe as their site of struggle while simultaneously operating in specific locations. In other words, organizations such as these claim to "think globally but act locally." Their strategy is clear: concerted efforts in locations throughout the world will alter the negative social and environmental effects of globalization.

The link between globalization and social movements has not gone unnoticed by sociologists. German sociologist Ulrich Beck (1996) claims that globalization creates opportunities for new forms of collective action that operate outside the politics of the nation-state, in the politics of what Beck calls a "world risk society." Beck suggests that ordinary people in all societies have been socialized to understand that the modern world is full of human-created hazards. Widely publicized dangers, such as the radioactive cloud that drifted from a nuclear reactor in Chernobyl (in Ukraine, at that time part of the Soviet Union) to the rest of Europe in 1986, have forced people to acknowledge that many political issues transcend borders. For Beck, the emerging recognition of global risks marks a new reality for social movements.

Greenpeace International is a good example of a global, or *transnational*, social movement that appears to have adapted to this world risk society. Greenpeace originated in the late 1960s, and its earliest members were environmental activists from Canada and the United States. From the start, this environmental movement was concerned with global issues and it organized protests throughout the world.

Greenpeace has developed its own political opportunities by creating unique forms of global diplomacy (Beck, 1996). It often operates outside the boundaries of the nation-state, such as on the high seas, where individual nations have no legal jurisdiction (Magnusson, 1990). Conscious of the influence of the international media, Greenpeace rallies support by organizing global boycotts that challenge governments and corporations to change their environmental policies and practices. Through these media events, Greenpeace attempts to stir up moral indignation while recognizing that different cultures have various understandings and experiences of global environmental dangers (Eyerman and Jamison, 1989).

Not all sociologists agree that globalization has created a fundamentally new political reality. Leslie Sklair (1994) argues that global politics are very much like national politics, simply on a larger scale. For Sklair, organizations such as Greenpeace International

mirror the organizational structures of transnational corporations. He suggests that the global environmental movement consists of transnational environmental organizations whose professional members make up a global environmental elite. This elite plays an ideological game with the transnational corporate and governmental elite: each side attempts to have its version of the environmental reality accepted as the truth. For Sklair, this is politics as usual.

Sociologists also question whether the rise of *supranational organizations*, such as the European Union (EU), will bring about new forms of collective action that link activists across national boundaries. Although the EU does constitute a new political terrain, Doug Imig and Sidney Tarrow (2001) have found that collective action in Europe remains strongly rooted within the nation-state. While Europeans have many grievances against the EU, most of the protest against it is domestic rather than transnational. This may simply indicate that activists have yet to develop new transnational strategies and linkages. Nevertheless, domestic politics remain a viable political arena for voicing concerns about the EU (Imig and Tarrow, 2001).

Today the world is more intricately connected than in the past. New social issues have arisen as a result, and there are now social movements that attack globalization. Each has to identify guilty institutions and actors, however, and states and corporations remain the best choice because they are largely responsible for the policies and practices that promote globalization.

Generally, two characteristics are needed for a social movement to be truly global. First, a social movement must frame its grievances as global grievances. Many environmental organizations do this. By framing environmental risks as global risks, the environmental movement hopes to demonstrate that environmental degradation affects everyone. Second, to be global a social movement needs to have a worldwide membership and organizational structure. On a global scale, membership and frame alignment probably are supported by communication technologies such as e-mail and the Internet. Alternatively, a global movement can arise through a long-term coalition or network of movement organizations. For example, indigenous peoples across North and South America, Australia, and New Zealand have united against the ongoing effects of colonialism and to ensure that the rights of indigenous populations everywhere are recognized.

## Conclusion

Politics in Canada and around the globe is changing quickly as people grapple with major technological, environmental, and social forces impinging on their lives. While long-term effects of such developments as genetic engineering are debated, the critical political questions are: Who is in control? and What will be permitted?

In the early twenty-first century, some forces imply that decentralization and fragmentation are the likely course of societies in the years to come. After all, cultural groups struggle for political autonomy (like Quebec) and others advocate a smaller role for the state in many ways, from privatization to more partnerships with non-state actors. Probably these forces are weaker than the integrating, regionalizing, and even globalizing tendencies associated with high-speed communication, cultural diffusion of tastes and values, an international division of labour, corporate concentration, world-level environmental problems, North–South inequality, and new or more powerful transnational organizations.

Does this globalization mean the eclipse of the state (Strange, 1996)? Most likely not within the next 20 years. So far, despite the tendencies mentioned, there is little sign that any global decisions, whether taken in political institutions, such as the United Nations, or by other assemblies, such as inclusive meetings on AIDS or climate change, can be effective if the most powerful states are unwilling to support them.

We live in difficult and dangerous times in which no country is truly isolated from external economic, cultural, and political forces. To that extent, life is internationalized, if not fully globalized. Violent conflicts spill over national borders. Maintaining the civil rights of all people is one of the greatest political challenges that societies face in the early twenty-first century.

Much of this work will be done by social movements. Sociologists seek to explain how and why social movements form, continue, and dissolve. Comparative studies of movements can help to determine whether or not any common features point to a general explanation or whether existing explanations hold for different situations. And historical studies reveal how social movements change over time.

Early forms of collective action were poorly organized and relatively sporadic. Often their grievances were tied to local affairs, and thus their targets

February 2003 saw worldwide peace rallies in opposition to the war expected to be waged by the United States against Iraq. In a global outpouring of anti-war sentiment, millions of protestors gathered in all of the capitals of America's traditional allies: London, Rome, Paris, and Ottawa. In this photograph, anti-war activists brave −30 degree Celsius temperatures to protest against any Canadian involvement in a possible war with Iraq. (CP/Jonathan Hayward)

were usually local elites. With the rise of nation-states, however, new kinds of social movements appeared. These movements were highly organized and often identified social issues that stemmed from structural conditions such as economic inequality and narrow political representation. They also routinized protest activities: different social movements learned to apply similar methods of protest, such as the mass demonstration. The rise of new social movements in the second half of the twentieth century marks another change. These movements are more concerned with gaining cultural recognition than with the redistribution of social goods. So even though NSMs tend to use traditional forms of protest, they are more concerned with the politics of everyday life than with the traditional politics of governance.

While issues and methods of protest have changed over time, the success of collective action is always linked to the social and political climate. In other words, social and political changes can create opportunities for social movements, or they can create constraints. According to a theory developed by Herbert Kitschelt (1993), present conditions in Canada have created opportunities that may lead to an increase in social movement activity. To understand why, short- and long-term social movement dynamics must be distinguished. Support for social movements usually rises when political parties and interest groups fail to channel citizens' demands. Social movements can then mobilize support, attract resources, and forge alliances among protest groups. However, according to Kitschelt, this surge in social movement activity peaks as resources dwindle, as political parties begin to take up citizens' concerns, and as people's interest

in collective mobilization wanes. Social movement activity then falls, only to rise again the next time organizers capitalize on frustration with parties and interest groups. In other words, the short-term pattern of movement activity is cyclical.

The long-term trend, by contrast, is towards an increase in the number of social movements. In the wealthy capitalist democracies, social movement activity has grown steadily since the 1960s. Established parties and politicians have proven increasingly incapable of providing satisfactory solutions to such issues as nuclear power, toxic waste disposal, resource management, abortion rights, pornography, and equal rights. Today, many Canadians share a distrust of established politicians, political parties, and interest groups. The extent of citizen discontent should not be exaggerated, however. Recent federal elections have shown that an established party like the Liberals can still attract much support. Nevertheless, many burning public issues—citizen participation, the environment, and gender, ethnic, and Native rights—often elude both parties and interest groups. The current climate in Canada favours an expansion of social movement activity. Of course, whether organizers will actually exploit this situation remains to be seen. The outcome will depend on social movement leaders and on the political establishment's ability to co-opt them.

## ☐ Questions for Critical Thought

1. Electoral institutions ensure that political leaders are responsive to the interests of the population as a whole. Do you agree or disagree with this statement?
2. What changes have occurred since 1980 in women's participation in the legislatures and cabinets of liberal democracies? Discuss some of the differences you observe. How would you explain these findings?
3. Select an issue that has been important during the last year in the province or municipality where you live. Using media sources, try to determine who was able to exercise power. What theory of the state best explains what you observed?
4. Collect information on the size of public-sector employment relative to private-sector employment in Canada's provinces. Try to explain any variations among the provinces.
5. Find an ideological statement from a social movement, such as a flyer or leaflet, a brochure or members' newsletter, a Web site, or an interview with a movement representative. What are the movement's ideals, goals, and plan of action? What social goods does the statement value, disparage, or neglect? How does the statement use emotional appeals to make its message more persuasive? Is the movement offering selective incentives to attract new members? What kinds of people are most and least likely to be persuaded by this statement?

6. All sociological theories make **ontological** assumptions. In other words, theorizing about the social world requires particular assumptions about how it operates (for example, social conflict versus social consensus). How can empirical research on social movements be used to refute or confirm the ontological assumptions of social movement theories?
7. Social movements disseminate ideas and hope to influence the general public. What is the role of the media in this process? How might new media technologies change social movement strategies, processes, and internal organization?

## ☐ Recommended Readings

Brian Barry, *Sociologists, Economists and Democracy* (Chicago: University of Chicago Press, [1970] 1978).

This lucid review and critique of "rational choice" and cultural approaches remains pertinent to theoretical debates on social movements among sociologists and is a good source for readers interested in exploring structural functionalism, the role of values, and the free-rider problem.

William K. Carroll, ed., *Organizing Dissent: Contemporary Social Movements in Theory and Practice*, 2nd edn (Toronto: Garamond, 1997).

The ideological stance, choice of subject matter, analytical styles, and emphasis on identity-based approaches found in this edited volume exemplify the dominant trends in studies of Canadian social movements.

Murray Knuttila and Wendee Kubik, *State Theories: Classical, Global and Feminist Perspectives*, 3rd edn (Halifax, NS: Fernwood, 2000).

*State Theories* is a thorough review of recent theorizing about the state.

Manon Tremblay and Caroline Andrew, eds, *Women and Political Representation in Canada* (Ottawa: University of Ottawa Press, 1998).

This collection is a useful overview of issues that are particularly significant for women.

## ☐ Recommended Web Sites

American Sociological Association, Section on Collective Behavior and Social Movements
www.asanet.org/sectioncbsm

This is a good starting place for more information on the sociological study of social movements. Read *Critical Mass*, the section's newsletter, to be informed of new publications, conferences, and the latest research.

Canadian Election Study (CES)
http://math.yorku.ca/ISR/ces.htm

The results of investigations into the 1997 and 2000 federal elections may be obtained at this site, from which various academic presentations may be downloaded.

Centre for Social Justice
www.socialjustice.org

This organization was established in 1997 and is based in Toronto. Its goals are to foster national and international social change through research and advocacy.

Global Solidarity Dialogue
www.antenna.nl/~waterman/dialogue.html

This is a good starting place for information on global social movements. The site provides research, news, and discussion on social movements throughout the world, as well as information on globalization.

# part four

> > >

# Canadian Society and the Global Context

This part discusses Canada's place in a global context and its implications for Canadians. Today, we humans are trying to find ways of achieving peace in a world pulled apart by ideologies, racial and cultural conflicts, and competition for scarce natural resources. We are all connected in global networks of organizations, institutions, markets, and alliances. The fate of humanity depends on how willingly and well we can co-operate despite a poor history of past peaceful co-operation; sociology may well have a role to play in showing how groups and nations can work together.

# 15

William Michelson,
Frank Trovato, and
G. Keith Warriner

> > >

# Population, Urbanization, and the Environment

© W.P. Whittman Limited

## ☐ Learning Objectives

In this chapter, you will:

* see how the "population explosion" is a recent phenomenon

* compare the demographic transition histories of industrialized and developing countries

* explore the implications of Malthusian theory of population growth and available resources

* consider the Marxist perspective on overpopulation

* see how the existence and prevalence of cities reflects societal and world conditions

* examine the extent to which cities affect behaviours

* examine global population growth and its relationship to poverty and development

* critically assess terms such as sustainable development, scarcity, and carrying capacity

## Introduction

This chapter ambitiously covers three central topics in modern sociology—urban sociology, environmental sociology, and demography (or the study of population). What these three fields share is an interest in the physical or material backdrop of social life. Unlike many of the concepts discussed in this book—for example, culture or deviance—the topics of this chapter are not fully open to social definition. They are the contexts within which people and societies must operate. In that sense, the natural environment is a context; so is human life—its boundedness by birth and death and migration—which is the subject matter of demography. Urban sociology is about how built environments reflect human ingenuity and planning; however, space—like time—is a context of human life and forms the backdrop of urban life.

Moreover, these three topics are related in obvious and not-so-obvious ways. Obviously, the environment is significantly affected by population growth, migration, and the large-scale gathering of people in cities. Equally obviously, **urbanization** affects migration patterns and even birth and death rates. More subtly, the environment shapes settlement and migration patterns, ordinary rates of birth and death, and even large-scale demographic crises such as wars, epidemics, and natural disasters.

## World Population

World population today and tomorrow must be understood in the broader context of human history. Ansley Coale (1974) divides population history into two broad periods: the first, from the beginning of humanity to around 1750, a very long era of slow population growth; the second, relatively brief in historical terms, one of explosive gains in human numbers. According to Coale (1974: 17), the estimated average annual growth rate between 8000 BCE and 1 CE was only 0.036 per cent per year. In modern times, the trajectory of population growth has followed an exponential pattern (1, 2, 4, 8, 16, . . .). Since the early nineteenth century, each successive billion of world population has arrived in considerably less time than the previous one. World population reached the 1 billion mark in 1804, and topped 2 billion 123 years later, in 1927. Thirty-four years later, the world witnessed its third billion. The 4 billion mark was reached in 1974, only 14 years later (Birg, 1995: 85). In 2003, the population of the world was 6.3 billion (Population Reference Bureau, 2003).

World population growth rates peaked at just over 2.0 per cent during the 1960s and early 1970s. In recent decades the growth rate has been declining to its present level of 1.3 per cent (Population Reference Bureau, 2003). This trend is expected to continue into the foreseeable future, so that by the year 2050 the growth rate of the world might be as low as 0.5 per cent per year—a rate of growth not seen since the 1920s (Bongaarts and Bulatao, 2000: 20; Eberstad, 1997; Lutz, 1994). This remarkable reduction will result from anticipated declines in fertility and mortality over the next half-century. This "central" scenario projection suggests a population in 2050 of just under 9 billion.

During this century, population growth will occur unevenly across the major regions of the world. Most of the projected growth will take place in the **developing countries**, especially in the poorest nations, where rates of natural increase are currently in the range of between 1.6 and 2.5 per cent annually. Though fertility has been declining in many developing countries, natural increase remains high because of the faster pace of the mortality declines. Africa's

Most industrialized nations have been experiencing a baby dearth in recent years. In Italy, the pope has urged the population to have more children in order to solve the "birth rate problem." In Spain, women are being asked to reproduce for the sake of the nation. (Vince Streano/CORBIS)

share of the world's population will increase rapidly, regardless of its devastating experience with the HIV/AIDS epidemic (Eberstadt, 1997). The growth rate for the **developed countries** is only 0.1 per cent per year; in nations such as Germany, Italy, and Japan, annual rates of natural increase have been close to zero or even slightly negative (Population Reference Bureau, 2002).

Some of the anticipated population growth for the world over the next 50 years is unavoidable. Even if current fertility rates worldwide were to decline suddenly to the replacement level of 2.1 children per woman, substantial population growth would occur, at least until about the third decade of this century (Eberstadt, 1997). This growth is due to the powerful effects of **population momentum** (Bongaarts and Bulatao, 2000; Lutz, 1994). That is, because of past high fertility and mortality declines, the proportion of the world's population in the reproductive ages (roughly ages 15–49) has been growing and is expected to continue to grow over the next several decades. Even with their much reduced fertility rates, today's large parental cohorts will be bringing more babies into the world than ever before. Indeed, even the "low variant" projection by the United Nations (2003), which assumes large declines in fertility, shows a population of about 7.4 billion in 2050. But under this low variant, the population of the world would peak around 2030, then start a course of indefinite decline. That is, the 7.409 billion number in 2050 under the "low variant" scenario would be part of a downward trend in world population (Eberstadt, 1977). Of course, we must recognize that predicting population growth is an inexact science; the projections depend largely on changes in fertility, which can be a rather unpredictable variable. Even small changes in fertility can have dramatic effects on the results.

Over the course of this century, all populations in the world will become older, the result of decades of fertility declines worldwide. Countries with more rapid and sustained fertility reductions will experience greater degrees of demographic aging. For example, Italy, with one of the lowest fertility rates in the world, will see its potential support ratio—the number of persons of working age (15–64) per older person—drop by the year 2050 to less than 2, from its current ratio of about 4. In 2050, 16 per cent of the world population is expected to be over the age of 65. (In 2000, the percentage was close to 7.)

# Theories of Population Change

Two influential themes can be identified in the literature regarding the interrelationship of population and resources. The first proposes that curbing population growth is essential for maintaining a healthy balance between human numbers, resources, and the sustainability of the environment; the second characterizes population as a minor or inconsequential factor in such matters. Thomas Malthus and Karl Marx (with Friedrich Engels) are the principal thinkers representing these opposing views. Before examining their ideas, let us review another influential theory of population dynamics: the demographic transition theory.

## Demographic Transition Theory

The **demographic transition** theory was first developed on the basis of the experience of Western European countries with respect to their historical pattern of change in birth and death rates in the context of socio-economic modernization. In general terms, the theory can also describe the situation of the developing countries, though the structural conditions underlying changes in vital rates are recognized as being substantially different from the European case (Kirk, 1996; Teitelbaum, 1975). The demographic transition of Western societies entailed three successive stages: (1) a pre-transitional period of high birth and death rates with very low population growth; (2) a transitional phase of high fertility, declining death rates, and explosive growth; (3) a final stage of low mortality and fertility and low natural increase. (The second stage may be divided into early and late Stage 2.) By the early 1940s, most European societies had completed their demographic transitions (see Figure 15.1).

Crude birth and death rates in the ancient world probably fluctuated between 35 and 45 per 1,000 population (Coale, 1974: 18). With gradual improvements in agriculture and better standards of living, the death rate declined, though fertility remained high. During the second stage, the excess of births over deaths was responsible for the modern rise of population—the so-called population explosion (McKeown, 1976). With gradual modernization and socio-economic development, during the mid and late nineteenth century, birth rates in Europe began to fall,

Figure 15.1    **The Classical Demographic Transition Model and Corresponding Conceptual Types of Society**

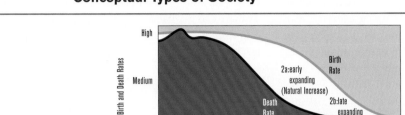

| Stage | Fertility | Mortality | Population Growth | Economy |
|---|---|---|---|---|
| 1. Pre-industrial | High, fluctuating | High, fluctuating (low life expectancy) | Static to very low | Primitive or agrarian |
| 2. Early industrial | High | Falling | High, explosive | Mixed |
| 3. Modern urban industrial | Controlled: low to moderate to sub-replacement levels | Low (high life expectancy) | Low to moderate to negative | Urban industrial to post-industrial |

SOURCE: Adapted from Glenn Trewartha, *A Geography of Population: World Patterns* (New York: Wiley, 1969), 45, 47.

first in France and then in other countries. In the early 1930s, Western nations had attained their lowest birth rates up to that point in their histories; the death rate was also quite low by historical standards, and a new demographic equilibrium had been reached. In pre-transition times, the low growth rates were the result of humans' lack of control over nature and acceptance of fate; the end of the demographic transition came from incremental successes over nature—agricultural development, industrialization, urbanization, economic growth, and modern science and medicine.

Coale (1969, 1973) extensively investigated the causes of the European fertility transition. Theorists had proposed that in pre-transitional societies, conscious family limitation was absent, economic development and urbanization preceded the onset of fertility declines, and a drop in mortality always occurred prior to any long-term drop in the birth rate (Davis, 1945; Notestein, 1945; Thompson, 1929, 1944). But the empirical evidence uncovered by Coale failed to support some of these propositions.

For instance, one important discovery was that economic development is not always a precondition for a society to experience the onset of sustained declines in fertility (though economic development would help speed up the transition). Coale concluded that sustained fertility declines in a society would take place when three preconditions were met: (1) fertility decisions by couples must be within the calculus of conscious choice, that is, cultural and religious norms do not forbid couples to practise family planning, nor do they promote large families; (2) reduced fertility must be viewed by couples as economically advantageous; and (3) effective methods of fertility control must be known and available to couples (Coale, 1969, 1973; Coale and Watkins, 1986).

Having long completed their mortality and fertility transitions, the industrialized countries have gained widespread economic success; their populations enjoy a great deal of social and economic security and well-being. Couples in these societies see little need to have large families. In many developing countries, however, entrenched cultural norms and traditions favour high fertility; parents tend to view children as a source of security in an insecure environment (Cain, 1983; Caldwell, 1976). Nevertheless, over recent decades much progress has been made in raising the prevalence levels of contraceptive practices. Organized family planning programs have played a major role in this trend (Caldwell, Phillips, and Barkat-e-Khuda, 2002). New evidence suggests a growing number of developing nations are now approaching the end of their demographic transitions, and others in the poorer regions of the world (for example, sub-Saharan Africa) have recently begun their fertility transitions (Bulatao, 1998; Bulatao and Casterline, 2001).

Figure 15.2 displays in schematic form the demographic transitions of the West and of the contemporary developing countries, the latter subdivided into "transitional" and "delayed transition" societies. Examples of transitional populations are India, Turkey, China, Indonesia, Taiwan, Thailand, Mexico, and countries in Latin America and the Caribbean. Delayed transition societies are found in sub-Saharan Africa, southern Africa, and southwest Asia (for example, Afghanistan, Pakistan, and Bangladesh). In both these cases, mortality reductions have been fairly rapid. In the European historical context, health improvements occurred more gradually in response

to incremental socio-economic advancements and economic modernization. In the developing countries, declining death rates have been achieved through family planning, public health programs, and other medical interventions offered by the industrialized countries (Preston, 1986b).

### Malthusian Theory

Thomas Malthus (1766–1834) was an ordained Anglican minister and professor of political economy in England. His most famous work, *An Essay on the Principle of Population*, was published in 1798. This treatise has had a lasting influence on subsequent theorizing about population matters. At the time, a number of scholars had already contributed serious thoughts on the question of population and resources. For instance, the Enlightenment theorists Jean-Jacques Rousseau, Marie Jean Antoine Nicolas de Caritat, Marquis de Condorcet, and William Godwin viewed population growth as a positive development (Overbeek, 1974). A growing population would help stimulate economic growth, and with further advances in civilization a natural tendency for subsistence would increase faster than population. Malthus reacted strongly to such optimistic views; he was less optimistic about mankind's capacity to maintain a sustainable balance between available resources and

Figure 15.2 **Schematic Representation of Demographic Transition: Western, Delayed, and Transitional Models**

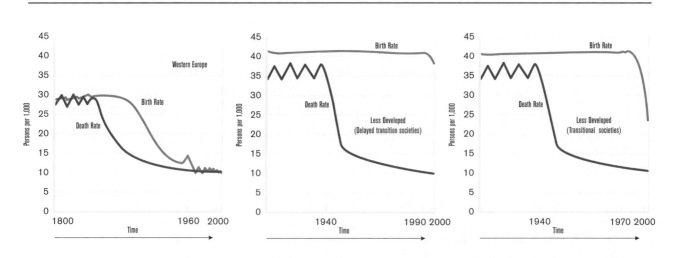

SOURCE: Adapted from Glenn Trewartha, *A Geography of Population: World Patterns* (New York: Wiley, 1969), 45, 46.

population growth. He set out to warn humanity about the dangers of unchecked population growth.

Alan Macfarlane identifies three fundamental themes in Malthus's *Principle of Population*. The first is that human beings are very strongly motivated by a desire for sexual intercourse. If uncontrolled, this will naturally lead to the second fact: high fertility among humans. If this high fertility is combined with a moderately low rate of mortality, early and frequent mating will lead to rapid population growth. Finally, this rate of growth is likely to outstrip food production. Economic resources, in particular food production, cannot keep pace with this population growth within a basically agrarian economy largely dependent on human labour (Macfarlane, 1997: 12–13).

Malthus assumed that humans tend to increase in numbers beyond the means of subsistence available to them. Mankind, he argued, lives at the brink of subsistence. Population, left unchecked, tends to double once every generation; it thus follows a geometric, or exponential, progression (1, 2, 4, 8, 16, 32, . . .). The food supply, on the other hand, tends to grow arithmetically (1, 2, 4, 6, 8, 10, . . .). Under this scenario, in the long term, population would eventually outstrip food and other essential resources.

As a solution to this problem, Malthus proposed that population could be kept in equilibrium through the activation of two different mechanisms. The first is what he called *positive checks* (also referred to as *vice and misery*). These are conditions that raise the death rate and thus serve to reduce population—famine, pestilence, war, and disease. The second, and more desirable alternative, would be widespread exercise of *preventive checks* (also referred to as *moral restraint*) to curb population growth—the imposition of the human will to curtail reproduction through celibacy, postponed marriage, and sexual abstinence. By postponing marriage until people were in an adequate position to maintain a family, individuals and society would both gain economically: by working longer before marriage, people would save more of their incomes, thus helping to reduce poverty and raise the overall level of well-being. Malthus considered abortion and contraception to be immoral.

Malthusian theory has provoked strong reactions. One criticism is that Malthus failed to appreciate fully the resilience of humanity when faced with difficult problems. Throughout history, humanity has shown a remarkable ability to solve many of its predicaments. Writers point out that progress in science, technology, and socio-economic well-being has evolved in

tandem with explosive population growth and that the agricultural and industrial revolutions arose in response to problems and demands arising from a rapidly growing population (Boserup, 1965, 1981; Fogel and Costa, 1997; Simon, 1995, 1996).

Malthus suggested that population and food supply must be in balance. But exactly what constitutes an "optimum" population size is difficult, if not impossible, to specify. Perceptions of the "optimal," in this sense, are highly dependent on available resources to a society, as well as on consumption patterns and the degree of economic activity and production. Consumption and production are closely tied to a society's cultural standards for material comfort and demand for consumer products. As described by Paul Ehrlich and J.P. Holdren (1971), the potential impact of population on the environment is multiplicative. That is, the effect of the population depends partly on its size and growth, but also on a society's level of affluence and technological complexity. In a slow-growing population with strong material expectations, the potential for environmental and resource depletion may be greater than in a fast-growing population with lower levels of material aspirations and technological sophistication. The more developed the society, the higher the expected standard for "basic" necessities. As material aspirations rise, so do levels of consumption and expenditures by the public. Increased consumer demand for material goods spurs economic activity; greater levels of economic activity heighten the risk of environmental damage because of increased pollution and resource depletion (Ehrlich and Ehrlich, 1970, 1990).

Industrial societies may be facing an inversion of the Malthusian scenario (Woolmington, 1985). In these societies, overpopulation is no longer the threat Malthus advocated. Rather, the seeds of systemic instability in these societies may lie more in their reliance on endless economic growth and consumption. Rather than population pressing on resources, as was proposed by Malthus, the economy now presses the population to consume—economic growth and stability depend on this. However, in the long term, the spiral of consumption and production may not be sustainable in slow-growing or declining populations (Woolmington, 1985).

Finally, Malthus's insistence on the unacceptability of birth control is inconsistent with his advocacy of curbing rapid population growth. The reality is that people throughout the centuries have always resorted to some means of birth control at one time or another.

### The Marxist Perspective on Population

Marxist scholars have refuted the Malthusian principles. They contend that population is a secondary issue to the pernicious problems of widespread economic inequality and poverty. Large families arise from poverty. With Friedrich Engels, Marx advocated the elimination of hunger, poverty, and human suffering through the radical restructuring of society to ensure the equitable distribution of wealth and resources (Marx and Engels, [1845–6] 1970). As for poor developing nations, their population predicament can be traced to their relative economic deprivation. In response to Malthus's principle that population grows geometrically, the Marxist view proposed that scientific and technological solutions tend to progress geometrically. Scientific and technological progress could be used to relieve human suffering.

The Marxist perspective is grounded in the idea that socio-economic inequality is a root cause of human problems and suffering. However, in matters of population control, Marxist skepticism of the role of population in human problems is now largely ignored (Petersen, 1989). China—a communist state—has outwardly rejected the Marxist doctrine of population. Chinese officials have recognized that slowing population growth through concerted family planning policies is, in the long term, essential to societal well-being (Bulatao, 1998; Caldwell, Phillips, and Barkat-e-Khuda, 2002; Haberland and Measham, 2002). With few exceptions, developing countries now embrace population policies that are consistent with neo-Malthusian principles. Family planning and reproductive health programs are recognized by governments as critical means in their quest to curb population growth.

### Contemporary Perspectives on Population

Neo-Malthusian scholars—the contemporary followers of Malthus—believe that the world's population has been growing too fast and that the planet is

Is the poverty shown in this photograph a result of overpopulation or of unequal access to resources and opportunities? This is a shantytown just outside of the commercial district in Buenos Aires, Argentina. (Mariana Bazo/Reuters)

already close to reaching critical ecological limits. Unlike Malthus, however, neo-Malthusians view contraception and family planning as a key element in population control (Ehrlich and Ehrlich, 1990). The neo-Malthusian view implies that the world would be a better and safer place if it contained fewer people. An expanding population in conjunction with excessive consumerism and economic production will, in the long term, lead to the depletion of essential resources and to ecological breakdown.

Neo-Marxist scholars place less emphasis on the centrality of population as a source of human predicaments. Focusing on population as the root cause of human suffering obscures the reality that the world is divided into wealthy and relatively poor regions and that this divide is widening rather than narrowing. Neo-Marxists alert us to the extreme consumerism of wealthy regions and their overwhelming economic and political influence over less advantaged nations. In addition, the **globalization** of capital—seen by many other observers as the key to emulating the "success story" of the West—often exacerbates, rather than diminishes, socio-economic disparities within and across societies. Investigations by neo-Marxist scholars tend to focus on regional inequalities in resources and wealth and on the political and economic dependence of developing countries on the developed nations. Some nations enjoy inordinate power and influence over others (Gregory and Piché, 1983; Wimberley, 1990). In this connection, Andre Gunder Frank (1991) has coined the phrase "the underdevelopment of development" to refer to the overwhelming influence and control the world's major economic powers hold over the developing countries. Development, it is argued, primarily serves the interests of the most powerful nations. Aid received by the poor nations comes at the cost of being in a persistent state of dependence on the providers.

Other writers concerned with the complex interactions of population, environment, and resources take a revisionist stance on such questions. Revisionists are neither neo-Marxists nor neo-Malthusians (Ahlburg, 1998; Cincotta and Engelman, 1997; Clarke, 1996; Evans, 1998; Furedi, 1997; National Research Council, 1986). Julian Simon (1995, 1996), for instance, has written that population growth historically has been, on balance, beneficial to humankind—people are the "ultimate resource," Simon contends.

The US National Research Council's report on population, environment, and resources (1986) exemplifies a revisionist perspective. This report proclaimed that, in some cases, population may have no discernible relationship to some of the problems often attributed to it. The report also concludes that the relationship of population to depletion of exhaustible resources is statistically weak and often exaggerated. Indeed, income growth and excessive consumption are more important factors in this sense: a world with rapid population growth but slow increases in income might experience slower resource depletion than one with a stationary population but rapid increase in income. It was also found that reduced rates of population growth would increase the rate of return to labour and help bring down income inequality in a country.

The National Research Council (NRC) also suggested that while rapid population growth is directly related to the growth of large cities in the **Third World**, its role in urban problems is most likely secondary. Ineffective or misguided government policies may play a more important role in the development of urban problems. Moreover, the NRC has noted that although it is often assumed in the literature that reducing population growth leads to a reduction in poverty and income inequality, in fact this relationship holds to a certain point only. For instance, if the population of Bangladesh were halved, its status as a poor nation would not change appreciably; it would move from being the second poorest nation in the world to thirteenth poorest (National Research Council, 1986). Many factors beyond rapid population growth are responsible for poverty (Keyfitz, 1993).

## The First Cities

The emergence of cities in about 3500 BCE truly represented something new under the sun and marked a change in human history. Cities could not have developed without the growth of new economic opportunities for industry and trade, or without a food surplus that allowed occupational differentiation. Perhaps the most elementary conception of a city is that it must contain at least some non-agricultural workers. The effect of cities on the rest of society was therefore immediate and direct: the rural sector had to grow a surplus of food to feed the urbanites. Creating stable and predictable agricultural surpluses required simultaneous developments throughout the whole society in technology and **social structure** in geographic areas, such as Mesopotamia and the Indus Valley, that could support intensive agriculture (Adams, 1966). Innovations of importance for urbanization included irrigation; bronze metallurgy for ploughing and cutting instruments; the domestication of animals; stone mortars;

the selective cultivation of rich, non-perishable foods such as grains and dates; wheeled carts and sailing vessels for transport; and building bricks for permanent settlements.

Like technology, social organization evolved, and the division of labour beyond age and sex became a legacy to later cities and societies. One aspect of the enhanced division of labour was *vertical stratification*—differentiation in the degrees of responsibility and power. For instance, the responsibility of some individuals was to see that, by providing technological support and controlling delivery, the farmers produced surpluses for the non-agricultural workers. Another aspect of the division of labour was *horizontal stratification*—different job specializations even at the same level of power and prestige. Full-time soldiers, artists, and producers of consumer goods appeared in the urban settlements, while farmers could become ever more specialized. From the beginning, then, cities had heterogeneous populations with complex, usually coercive relationships with the rest of society. Although the farmers did obtain products and the often dubious benefits of laws and protection, they relinquished some of their food under terms beyond their control.

This relationship between urban and rural people may appear current. However, there have been enormous changes over time in the balance between the two groups, reflecting developments in the central elements of technology and social organization. For example, technology was at first barely adequate for producing the necessary food surplus.

## Paths to Urban Development

The development of industry based on non-living energy sources such as coal and steam is commonly given credit for a substantial shift in the population balance from rural to urban. Powered industry reflected societal developments in technology and accentuated the division of labour. The same advances in science and engineering that made possible large-scale factories with machinery also led to innovations in agricultural technology that enabled fewer farm workers to grow food more intensively and on larger holdings.

In technologically advanced societies, a surplus of agricultural labour therefore became available for newly emerging, specialized city jobs. These workers were pushed from the countryside and pulled to cities. They became specialists in housing, food, transportation, financial services, warehousing distribution, and much more; several specialists were needed

to provide the services and supplies for every factory worker. This led to a growth in urban population by what is called the *multiplier effect*—population growth several times the number accounted for by factory workers alone.

Technically, observers think of urbanization as the proportion of a nation's population living in settlements of a certain minimum size. Statistics Canada, for example, defines an urban area as having a population of at least 1,000 with a population density of at least 400 per square kilometre. Just two centuries ago, only about 3 per cent of the world's population lived in settlements of 500 or more inhabitants. A city about the size of the current Vancouver metropolitan area would have been the largest in the world. Today's technologically advanced nations have urbanization levels exceeding 75 per cent.

If you look at the development of urbanization in historical perspective, as in the timeline represented by Figure 15.3, you see that it took many thousands of years of human life for the prerequisites for cities to occur and then to lead to the establishment of urban settlements in various parts of the world. The ingredients of modern cities have only become known in the last few minutes in the day of mankind. Indeed, the predominantly urban society is largely a phenomenon only of the past 60 years of the 50,000 or so of known human history. During this recent time, however, the tempo of technological innovation and societal adaptation has grown phenomenally. Considering that powered industry only came about in the eighteenth century, electricity in the nineteenth, and the automobile, telephone, radio, television, airplane, computer, nuclear power, and much more even later, it is increasingly difficult to predict or imagine what cities and society will be like even in the next decade.

Canada and the United States belong to a club of industrial nations with reasonably similar, high rates of urbanization. According to the United Nations Centre for Human Settlements (2001), the more developed nations of the world had a mean urbanization level of 76.0 per cent in the year 2000, compared to 39.9 for less developed regions. Canada is just about on this level, with 77.1 per cent urbanization, as is the United States, with 77.2 per cent. Although this represents a relatively steady level of urbanization for the more developed nations in the past 20 years, it is an increase of about one-third in the urbanization levels of less developed nation during this recent time (Gold, 2002: 3).

The highly industrialized continents of the Americas, Europe, and Oceania all have mean urban-

Figure 15.3 **Timeline of Significant Events in the Development of Urbanization**[a]

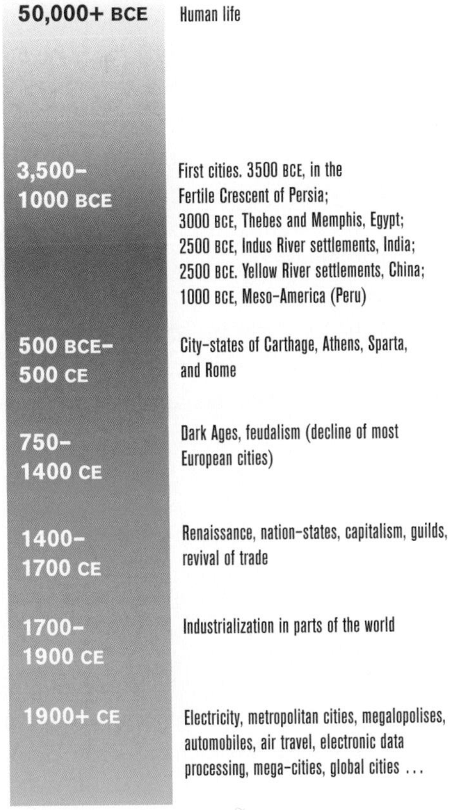

|  |  |
|---|---|
| **50,000+ BCE** | Human life |
| **3,500–1000 BCE** | First cities. 3500 BCE, in the Fertile Crescent of Persia; 3000 BCE, Thebes and Memphis, Egypt; 2500 BCE, Indus River settlements, India; 2500 BCE, Yellow River settlements, China; 1000 BCE, Meso-America (Peru) |
| **500 BCE–500 CE** | City-states of Carthage, Athens, Sparta, and Rome |
| **750–1400 CE** | Dark Ages, feudalism (decline of most European cities) |
| **1400–1700 CE** | Renaissance, nation-states, capitalism, guilds, revival of trade |
| **1700–1900 CE** | Industrialization in parts of the world |
| **1900+ CE** | Electricity, metropolitan cities, megalopolises, automobiles, air travel, electronic data processing, mega-cities, global cities … |

[a]Not to scale.

ization levels of over 70 per cent, compared to much lower levels for Africa and Asia. The former levels, however, have been relatively steady for two decades, while the latter levels have increased by about one-third during this time, suggesting the possibility of future international convergence in the spread of urbanization.

Nonetheless, a concentration on such large land masses obscures differences in levels of industrialization within them. Hence, a focus on national urbanization levels shows that Western Europe has some of the highest levels in the world (for example, Belgium at 97.3 per cent, the United Kingdom at 89.5 per cent), while some nations in Eastern Europe have less urbanization (for example, Romania at 56.2 per cent,

Croatia at 57.7 per cent). Australia and New Zealand are at the 85 per cent level, while the smaller islands in Oceania bring down the regional mean level. Japan has a markedly higher urbanization rate than many other Asian nations that have not as yet achieved the same level of industrialization (United Nations Centre for Human Settlements, 2001).

Nations with low urbanization rates may nonetheless have very large cities. Indeed, many of the largest cities in the world are found in less developed nations. The economic and technological contexts in which cities become established are important to understanding their size and distribution within their nations.

The urban population in Western industrial societies is distributed quite evenly across a number of reasonably sized settlements, as capital and technology are diffused. In less developed nations, it is concentrated in the single very large metropolis in the country or in a region. Most of the extremely large cities in the Third World, such as Bombay, Calcutta, and Shanghai, were centres from which foreign imperial powers exported the nation's or region's raw materials for industrial production in the home countries. This was called *imperialism*. Mattei Dogon and John Kasarda (1988) suggest that these urban settlements grew to such size as obvious destinations for the rural poor, despite the virtual absence of an industrial economic base in both the cities and the countries at large. Urban populations in such situations are typically underemployed, poor, and predominantly male.

When more people reside in a city than would be expected from its economic base, *overurbanization* is said to occur. Then, when the technology and infrastructure catch up to overurbanized cities that are already large, they become huge. Cities of 10 million or more persons are called mega-cities, and the majority of them are in less developed nations. Often their expansion is accompanied by environmental degradations of many kinds: air, water, hazardous wastes, road accidents, and noise (Hardoy, Mitlin, and Satterthwaite, 2001).

## Globalization and Global Cities

Although industrialization is held largely responsible for high rates of urbanization, the recent trend of globalization has led to added growth and wealth in a few cities with extensive development of corporate organization, finance, telecommunications, and air

**15.1**

# Sociology in Action
## The Gap Between the Real World and Formal Measures

Documenting various aspects of urbanization demonstrates many of the measurement challenges facing sociologists more generally. For example, the basic measure of urbanization—the percentage of persons in a nation living in urban areas—depends on a standard definition of what constitutes an *urban area*. In some nations, it means a municipality of 5,000 persons. In others, the threshold is only 1,000 persons, while in yet others, it is as high as 10,000 persons. Beijing, for example, is known to have at least 3 million undocumented residents on top of the nearly 11 million officially reported as legal residents.

The degree to which census organizations are able to accurately count urban and rural populations is variable. The size of large cities also reflects how wide an area of settlement is considered to be part of a given city. Urban regions—larger than a named municipality—are often considered a logical unit on which to present city size figures. But how such regions are defined and then measured varies greatly from place to place and from time to time. Mexico City, for example, might be considered the world's largest city were different approaches to measurement taken. Therefore, descriptive and analytic numbers should be understood in terms of the best efforts of researchers and knowledge of the criteria they employ, rather than as absolutely objective and fully comparable facts.

transportation. These favoured cities, known as **global cities**, manifest high levels of technology. As David Thorns puts it, "Global cities are now the key sites for the control, coordination, processing and distribution of knowledge that makes them the engines of growth within the present stage of capitalist development" (2002: 54). They are vital centres for the flow of information, direction, and money, and they do not have to be on the doorstep of the heavy industries they indirectly control and co-ordinate. Global cities reflect the presence of interacting financial enterprises through highly concentrated and prominent office buildings (Castells, 1989; Sassen, 1991).

Saskia Sassen (1991) argues that such cities as New York, London, and Tokyo have achieved more prominence than their manufacturing base might suggest, while large cities based more fully on manufacturing (such as Detroit in the United States and Manchester in England) do not gain global status because they do not need the same degree of white-collar employment right at hand. Toronto is considered a minor global city, and Vancouver is active in this respect on the Pacific Rim. One might well consider whether globalization can be viewed as a modern form of imperialism, in which profits and consumer products

flow from around the world to the home country rather than raw materials for home-country industries and their wage workers.

In Canada, as in the United States, economic factors pull people to cities rather than push them away from rural areas, and women typically outnumber men in the urban context. As of 2001, the majority of people in every Canadian province and territory except Prince Edward Island and Nunavut were city-dwellers. Thus, high levels of urbanization are not confined to Ontario and Quebec, with their predominant cities. The overall urbanization rate documented by the 2001 census in Canada is 79.7 per cent. The relatively large recent growth of Toronto and Vancouver is related to major global functions, while cities such as Winnipeg, Montreal, and Hamilton, though still major centres within the Canadian context, lack the same level of international roles with which to boost their employment and population.

## Urbanism

One of the reasons sociologists are interested in cities is the popular belief that life in cities differs from life in other forms of settlements. Research findings over many years have shown that the issue is subtler than simple urban–rural differences. The path to understanding urbanism is a good example of the convergence of different theories and the research done to document them.

## Classical Approaches

Early approaches to urbanism seemed to make the assumption that urban contexts cause certain forms of behaviour in a very direct way. This viewpoint is known as *determinism*, since it presupposes that a given set of conditions determines behavioural outcomes.

Does life in an urban context differ systematically from that in a rural context? Many classical analysts have thought so. Gideon Sjoberg (1960), for example, found that job specialization and the complexity of production and marketing that accompanied industrialization required standardization in weights, measures, currencies, pricing, and financial interaction. For the system to work, rational, exact actions became necessary. Other theorists, such as Max Weber, Sir Henry Maine, Ferdinand Tönnies, and Émile Durkheim, used different words but made similar observations that urban life is more likely to involve rational, universalistic, impersonal, and logistically oriented behaviours than had been the case in earlier rural settings. Noting that German urbanites had to pay constant attention to contextual signals—lights, signs, footsteps, whistles, and the like—Georg Simmel (1950a) summarized these observations by saying that the head, rather than the heart, dictates most urban behaviours.

The best-known ideas on urbanism may be attributed to Louis Wirth's 1938 article "Urbanism as a Way of Life." Wirth believed that cities have three defining characteristics—large numbers of inhabitants, high densities, and heterogeneous populations—each accounting for important aspects of an urban way of life. Large numbers lead to the impossibility of knowing all persons, and hence to the relative absence of intimacy in most interpersonal relationships. Human relations become segmented into many largely anonymous, superficial, transitory contacts. At the same time, high density fosters human diversification and specialization. Social distance is established to maintain personal space in response to the inescapable presence of close physical contact with diverse persons. Nonetheless, accentuated friction inevitably arises, and formal means of **social control**—notably, uniformed police—assume prominence in cities. Despite, or per-

haps because of, such close proximity, complex patterns of segregation take shape. Finally, heterogeneity makes it difficult for individuals to be constricted by rigid social structures, as in rural areas. Urban individuals more often find themselves in varied social settings and groups. Both upward and downward mobility, with the resultant greater feelings of instability and insecurity, are more likely in cities.

Although classical approaches to urbanism never achieved total consensus, their legacy was sobering. Any societal gains derived from greater division of labour, rationality, and personal freedom seemed to be counterbalanced by unending suspicion, distrust, and isolation.

## Modern Social-Psychological Approaches

Modern social psychologists have been particularly taken with the earlier theoretical themes dealing with urban life as situated in the impersonal presence of great numbers of strangers, some of whom represent annoyance at the least, and, more seriously, risk. Lyn Lofland wrote a valuable analysis of how people relate to each other in cities, with the germane title, *A World of Strangers* (1973). In it, she stresses that people minimize interpersonal interaction as a way to maximize public order (that is, safety). In recent work (Lofland, 1998), she delves into how urbanites have a love-hate relationship with public spaces. She suggests that even though people potentially access unparalleled experiences in the congregating spaces of large cities, the public realm has been largely neglected, given the ambivalence urbanites have about contact with strangers.

Stanley Milgram made a noteworthy development of Simmel's notion of impersonal signals bombarding urbanites. Using modern systems analysis, Milgram characterizes urban life as sensory overload: "City life, as we experience it, constitutes a continuous set of encounters with overload, and of resultant adaptations" (1970: 1462). He describes a variety of ways in which urbanites cope with overload. All of them are literally textbook examples of the *Gesellschaft* side of Tönnies's classical theoretical dichotomy between *Gemeinschaft* and *Gesellschaft*—figuratively, "heart" versus "head"—as describing **social interaction** in societies.

One common strategy for coping with overload is to tune out what is found to be overburdening: anything from drunks and poverty to negative consequences of public- or private-sector policies or practices that benefit only some. Increasing numbers of people live literally on the streets of Canada. Many citizens have taken active ameliorative roles in food drives, food banks, and night patrols for the homeless, but the context of everyday life for many involves passively working around difficult situations.

In another coping strategy, urbanites are said to avoid aiding strangers who need help in an effort to avoid trouble themselves. Much research followed the public shock that resulted when, in 1964, Kitty Genovese was murdered after appealing for help outside the windows of at least 38 onlooking neighbours in a New York City apartment house. The research suggested that the more people are there, the less likely any individual is to intervene. People are more likely to intervene if they feel that they are needed in the absence of others.

Urbanites also minimize involvement by taking action to remove themselves from easy contact with strangers. They buy telephone answering devices or subscribe to voice mail services, institute scripted menus to provide information, fail to list their telephone numbers (this is certainly the case for ubiquitous cellphones), filter visitors through secretaries and assistants, travel by private automobile, and live in segregated (and, increasingly, guarded) buildings and **neighbourhoods**. Ironically, at the same time, the same people are in greater contact than ever with those they know, through the medium of electronic mail.

People use a range of coping procedures in public places. They pretend not to see each other (for example, on beaches) and tolerate other lifestyles except where these represent clear and present dangers. They follow unspoken but definite rules about how much distance to keep from others for particular purposes, where they sit (for example, on buses or in libraries), and the way they walk (Hall, 1966; Sommer, 1969).

Urbanites, however, are not totally isolated beings. In some public settings people expect to interact with other persons in ways that they don't during most public encounters. Churches, bars, and sporting events, for example, all provide the opportunity for positive interactions among persons with similar interests and objectives.

People wanting to communicate to others their personal **identity** once relied on clothing in general, and uniforms in particular, to provide a basis for secure interaction without previous personal acquaintance. In smaller settings, the family name was noteworthy, and it still is in some circles. However, in urban circles in which consumer goods like clothing are rampant and family connections may be obscure, personal credentials (transcripts, credit cards, and so on) and home addresses help complete the introduction, for good and for ill. According to Janet Abu-Lughod, "the larger neighborhood or even the city can take on an important symbolic and social meaning, serving as a source of identity ('I come from Grosse Pointe')" (1991: 338).

Urban life in a world of strangers: a subway station. (William Michelson)

### The Subcultural Theory of Urban Life

Is it really some aspect of the city that calls for coping behaviours such as those described by Milgram? Albert Reiss Jr (1959) found that the anonymous, segmented, and impersonal relations noted by Wirth reflected occupation more than residence. For instance, men living in rural areas with non-farm jobs had daily contact patterns resembling those of their urban counterparts.

In contrast to the deterministic approach of the classical thinkers, other sociologists adopt a *compositional* perspective, according to which behaviour reflects the composition of the population. Herbert Gans (1967), for example, explains suburban behaviour not in terms of the physical nature of the area, but in terms of the social class background and life-cycle characteristics of the population in the suburb he studied. The nature and extent of their contact with neighbours, their participation in organizations, and their interest in schools all reflected middle-class backgrounds and the presence of families with young children. In short, exponents of the compositional approach believe that urban life reflects the most salient features (for example, class, ethnic background or race, religion, age, and sex) of the particular population groups living in particular cities or their constituent parts.

In *The Urban Experience* (1976), Claude Fischer attempts to reconcile deterministic and compositional theories and to go beyond them. Fischer argues that Wirth was right in stressing the significance of large numbers of persons in cities. But Fischer does not see the numbers as providing various direct effects; rather, he considers their primary importance as providing the nucleus for various specialized **subcultures** within cities. It is the particular compositions of the various subcultures that influence so-called urban lifestyles.

Fischer calls his approach the *subcultural theory* of urban life. Which subcultures become significant in a given city depends on many macroscopic characteristics of cities: their economic base, sources of migration, climate, and more. Within highly urbanized societies, cities of different sizes and in different locations may be functionally specialized. This does not mean that they are monolithic in terms of their activities or resident populations, but there are distinct tendencies regarding who chooses to live and work there and, hence, which subcultures take root. It is unusual for even a city specializing in industry to have more than 25 per cent of its jobs in manufacturing because of the need for complementary and supportive activi-

ties, yet the difference between 25 per cent and 10 per cent spells a big difference in the critical mass of a blue-collar subculture. Hamilton, Ontario, with its huge steel mills, differs substantially in its ways of life from nearby London, an insurance and financial centre—not to mention from Victoria, British Columbia, with its combination of government jobs, retirees, mild weather, and afternoon tea. However, the largest national cities tend to be diverse economically, with their population size supporting varied subcultures and lifestyles. It takes a Toronto, not a Truro, to supply the critical masses for creating the world's most ethnically diverse city, where the varied ethnic communities enjoy rich cultural lives and where these cultural groups exist side by side with youth, yuppie, gay, sports, criminal, and endless other subcultures.

Does Fischer's subcultural theory invalidate the generalizations made by urban social psychologists about such problems as overload, anonymity, and coping adaptations? In subsequent work, Fischer (1982) shows that the personal contact patterns of urbanites are more firmly concentrated in specialized groupings (which in cities means subcultures) than those of people living in smaller communities and rural areas. Similarly, big-city dwellers are likely to trust their closest neighbours but not urbanites in general.

## Ecology of Cities

Since urban behaviour patterns reflect subcultural cleavages, we might expect the physical structure of cities to reflect and reinforce these patterns. Examining the city in ecological terms strongly supports such an expectation. We know that most cities are made up of distinct parts. The ecological perspective addresses the nature of these parts and what kinds of patterns they form.

### Cities, Suburbs, and Metropolitan Areas

While urbanization levels in Canada show that Canadians live predominantly in cities, they do not reveal in what types of settlements or where within them we live. Do most Canadians live in large or small cities, in central cities or suburbs?

A common pattern in technologically advanced societies has been the buildup of population beyond the borders of older cities and into newer municipalities immediately adjacent. These are commonly called *suburbs*, although the word is often applied to areas that simply look newer and less crowded than

**15.2**

# Open for Discussion
## Diversity, Stereotyping, and Hiring

Both selective interaction and avoidance behaviours accompany urbanism. Identification with those like oneself and distrust of those very different can lead to stereotyping and social problems. The situation is particularly problematical when those with power and authority are not sufficiently sensitive to the nuances of subcultures that are different from their own. The widespread issue as to whether police officers profile members of minority groups would not be as keen if subcultures were not perceived as significantly separate. Recognition of these problems underlies current attempts to incorporate minorities more fully into police and fire departments and into the teaching profession, as well as to expand human rights programs.

the centres of the traditional cities. Montreal and Vancouver, for example, have many suburbs, while much of Calgary and Edmonton appears suburban.

Large cities and their suburbs may represent different municipalities, but in terms of everyday behaviour and economic activity, they form an entity known as a **metropolitan area**. Many people live in one part of a metropolitan area and work in another; there is, for instance, an active interchange between Vancouver and New Westminster.

Statistics Canada defines a **census metropolitan area (CMA)** as an area comprising one or more large cities (totalling at least 100,000 inhabitants at the previous census) in the centre (the urban core) together with surrounding areas that are economically and socially integrated on a day-to-day basis with the urban core (1992: 29). On the basis of these criteria, some CMAs include a central city and many municipalities extending a considerable distance from the urban core, while others consist of a single municipality. The makeup of a CMA reflects the size of the urban area, its history, and the amount of land suitable for expansion under the control of the central city. Toronto extends as a functional entity almost as far as Hamilton (that is, through Oakville), while Saskatoon not only includes nearly all the residents in its vicinity but also controls undeveloped land for future development. There are 27 CMAs in Canada. Although these metropolitan areas take up only a tiny fraction of the land in Canada, they were home to more than 19 million of Canada's 2001 population of 30 million—just short of two-thirds of the national population (Statistics Canada, 2001 census data). Canada's urban population is not dispersed into many small cities and towns across the landscape—it is highly concentrated in metropolitan areas.

Many people have an image of the city as an older municipality with a high density and buildings that are large and striking or old and grey. The suburbs are, somehow, something else. This view, however, needs revision. Most residents of Canadian and American metropolitan areas are suburbanites, even if we discount the great numbers of people in the newer cities—largely in the western regions of both countries—who live in typically suburban conditions. The suburban segments of most CMAs grew between 1991 and 2001, continuing previous trends in the distribution of population within metropolitan areas. This distribution is essential to an understanding of the pattern of local areas and lifestyles in metropolitan areas. Whereas people previously focused on the central city and spoke in stereotyped terms about the suburbs and suburbanites, now it is essential to recognize that a major and still-growing share of the urban population lives outside of traditional central cities.

## Metropolitan Population and Land-Use Patterns

How are people and their subcultures patterned within metropolitan areas? Several theories have been proposed to answer this question.

From studies of Chicago, Ernest Burgess (1925) identified the *concentric ring* land-use and stratification pattern of cities. At the heart of this pattern is the *central business district (CBD)*, consisting of the principal private- and public-sector offices, department stores, and hotels. The CBD is serviced by public transit to make it the most accessible place in the city. Burgess assumed that the CBD would be the only major centre in the city and that it would continue to grow indefinitely. Because of this growth, the land around the CBD would be held speculatively for future profit. Before upgrading, the *zones in transition* would be used, without maintenance or improvement, for rooming houses, transient hotels, and other impermanent uses. They would contain the poorest, newest migrants, the criminal element, and prostitutes—all subcultures requiring short-term affordable housing and, in many cases, anonymity. The more regularized sectors of the population would be distributed in rings around both the CBD and the zones in transition, in proportion to their ability to pay for greater amounts of land increasingly far from these two areas, as well as for the cost and time involved in longer commutes. Thus, working-class communities would be surrounded by the middle class, which in turn would be surrounded by the upper class. In short, according to Burgess, major land uses would claim the city centre through market-mechanism competition, while residential areas would be distributed at varying distances from the CBD according to income.

Another member of the Chicago School of urban sociology, Robert E. Park (1925), labelled as "**community**" the forms of behaviour thought to arise because "birds of a feather flock together." Within a given ring, local communities that were homogeneous by ethnic or religious background would form within boundaries formed by major streets, railways, parks, and the like. Park called these communities *natural areas* because no one rationally planned their location—they were simply a function of land value (thought to lie beyond the control of individuals) and incidental boundaries. According to this view, the critical mass of people in subcultures could exercise a strong influence on individual behaviour through their physical proximity in the natural area.

The concentric ring pattern is far from universal, however; it has been demonstrated to exist in few places outside Chicago. Indeed, in many settings outside the United States, the rich occupy the city centres while the poor are left outside of the benefits of urban infrastructure.

Ironically, Homer Hoyt (1939), another researcher in Chicago, discovered a rather different pattern. Hoyt's *sectors* resemble pieces of a pie, extending from the centre outward without interruption. Hoyt noted that certain amenities, such as waterfront parks, and eyesores, such as freight railways, extended outward. People of means would try to live within view of the amenities; those of few means would follow the tracks; still others would locate themselves in-between. One side of town would become better

than another, if only because it was upwind from centrally located industries.

A third approach is Chauncy Harris and Edward Ullman's *multiple nuclei theory* (1945), which states that each land use or subculture is located according to unique criteria having to do with the proximity of other land uses. Heavy industry, for example, wants to be near railroads and highways but doesn't need to be as accessible to consumers as do retailing land uses. Head offices draw fine restaurants, banks, and law offices to their vicinity, while universities attract fast-food chains and bookstores. The result is a city with many diverse centres whose locations are not in a fixed geometric pattern.

A statistical process called *factorial ecology* lets sociologists analyze census statistics for local areas of a given city to determine the patterns shown by such dimensions. Robert Murdie (1969) drew a number of conclusions in his pioneering analysis of Metro Toronto: that family size increased with distance from the centre, that social class segregation was in sectors from the centre outward, and that ethnic groups lived in unique clusters of multiple nuclei. He demonstrated that a single city could show several different patterns, depending on the criterion. No one pattern of land use characterizes all cities.

# The Environment and Ecological Scarcity

As the world's population has grown to an unparalleled size and more and more people have gathered in cities, human concern has turned increasingly to the impact on the natural environment.

Issues of ecological scarcity have long been of considerable interest to environmental sociologists. *Scarcity* involves problems associated with the overuse of natural resources, leading to their exhaustion, or with their waste or destruction by contamination or misuse. The immense reliance of societies on natural resources and the extent to which this reliance influences social arrangements as well as prospects for social change often go unrecognized. Sociological interest in resource scarcity therefore addresses questions of world population growth, global carrying capacity limits, and the relationship between development and scarcity.

## *Population Growth*

The startling statistics on population growth presented earlier in this chapter explain why Earth's population has been likened to a time bomb threatening to destroy the planet. Population pressure is regarded as one of the most serious environmental threats, contributing to resource exhaustion, destroying species and habitat, causing pollution, and taxing the capacity of agricultural systems. It is a major factor in such diverse ecological disasters as famines in Africa, global warming, acid rain, the garbage crisis, and the spread of disease. While we have not yet arrived at the theoretical limits for food production on the planet, they will be reached by the year 2100, with a projected population of 11.2 billion (World Commission on Environment and Development, 1987: 98–9).

The most serious environmental problems affect mainly the more than 5 billion people in the developing countries of Latin America, Africa, and Asia—80 per cent of the global population. Here, among the 172 nations classified by the United Nations as "less developed countries" (LDCs), 99 per cent of global population natural increase—the difference between numbers of births and numbers of deaths—occurs. By the end of the first quarter of the twenty-second century, the world's more developed countries (MDCs) will begin experiencing negative natural increase, and all of the global population increase will come from the less developed world (US Bureau of the Census, 1999: 10). It is not surprising, then, that environmental scientists and population experts generally agree that the way to avoid reaching the limits of the global carrying capacity is to reduce the birth rates of developing nations.

### Sustainable Development

The concept of **sustainable development** grew out of the perspective that economic development and environmental conservation are compatible goals. First appearing during the 1972 United Nations Conference on the Human Environment in Stockholm, the principle gained widespread support over the next three decades and was the focus of various international conferences and reviews, including the 1987 Brundtland Commission and the 1992 and 2002 Earth Summits. Sustainable development calls for the conciliation of several apparently competing ends: environmental integrity; the protection of ecosystems and biodiversity, and the meeting of human needs; and positive economic growth and equitable distribution of the benefits of the environment and resources among social classes and across nations. While the idea of the existence of ecological limits is clearly ingrained in sustainable development,

and while there is an insistence on strict resource husbandry, the principle is unabashedly pro-development.

After initial enthusiasm, certain environmentalists have come to regard sustainable development with skepticism. Some see it as no more than a legitimization of development under the guise of assisting the poor. An extension of this view is that sustainable development is an excuse for further incursions by Western nations into the Third World for the sole purpose of profit. In the words of Wolfgang Sachs, "Capital, bureaucracy and science . . . the venerable trinity of Western Modernization declare themselves indispensable to the new crisis and promise to prevent the worst through better engineering, integrated planning and sophisticated models" (1991: 257). Finally, more than a few environmentalists claim that the principles of ecology, as well as the scientific community, are being co-opted to support the further destruction of nature on the grounds of scientific rationality.

## The Environment and Social Theory

Environmental sociology has its theoretical bases in several sociological traditions. Among these is the field of **human ecology**, a sociological perspective with important ties to the work of Émile Durkheim. More recently, human ecology has been revised for the insights it provides for environmental sociology. Another theoretical topic debated by environmental sociologists concerns whether their field should be seen as constituting a paradigm shift for sociology in general. The division between the order and conflict schools so prevalent elsewhere in sociology is also a characteristic feature of environmental sociology. More generally, there has been broad debate over the relevance of sociology's classical theoretical traditions to the study of environmental issues. Contemporary theoretical approaches include the concept of the **risk society**, developed by Ulrich Beck. Finally, **social constructionism**, a perspective found elsewhere in sociology, has become a prominent approach within environmental sociology.

### Human Ecology

The science of ecology is central to the study of environmental issues; *human ecology* is the application of the same approach to sociological analyses. Human ecology emerged under the direction of Robert Park and Ernest Burgess at the University of Chicago during the

1920s (Park and Burgess, 1921; Park and McKenzie, 1925; Theodorson, 1961, 1982). Much as the science of ecology studies plant and animal communities, human ecology sought to explain human spatial and temporal organization by concentrating on the dynamic processes of competition and succession that influence human social organization. Park and Burgess and their students studied how Chicago's rapidly changing society physically accommodated increases in population and changes in the industrial and cultural organization of the city. Their approach, and that of their successors, was to focus on symbiosis, the dynamic interdependencies that bind people together in communities and lead to particular living arrangements.

In developing the concept of human ecology, Park was greatly influenced by Durkheim's *The Division of Labor in Society* ([1893] 1964). Durkheim addressed the development of social complexity from human population growth and density. As populations grow, the threat to available resources is crucial from a sociological viewpoint because it leads to competition and conflict. Problems of resource scarcity can therefore affect societal organization.

Durkheim's work was appealing to early human ecologists because of their interest in *sustenance activities*—the routine functions necessary to ensure the survival of a population from generation to generation (Hawley, 1950). Humans have a greater capacity for adapting to resource scarcity than any other organism, an ability labelled *competitive co-operation*. Adaptive responses include reductions in per capita consumption, increases in production through technology or more intensive resource exploitation, changes to distribution networks, and decreases in competition because of emigration from the community or an increased division of labour (Micklin, 1973; Schnore, 1958). Through such adaptive mechanisms, involving reciprocal cause-and-effect processes between the population and its vital resources, a state of equilibrium is reached. Park and Burgess (1921) postulated that competition and co-operation are the key forms of human exchange by which organized populations seek to maintain equilibrium within a dynamic environment.

Beginning in the mid-1950s, Park and Burgess's theory underwent significant revision to correct what are commonly regarded as major shortcomings: an over-emphasis on the spatial arrangements of populations at the expense of understanding societal–environmental relations, and the neglect of **culture** and values (Dunlap and Catton, 1979a, 1979b; Hawley, 1981). Moreover,

while highly influenced by the conceptual approaches and terminology of ecology, early human ecologists concentrated on human social organization and patterns and did not include other species or aspects of the natural world in their analyses. They therefore veered away from a concern about environmental issues. During the 1950s, the *ecological complex* (Duncan and Schnore, 1959; Hawley, 1950), which viewed societies as being constituted of four interrelated dimensions—population, organization, environment, and technology (POET)—substantially revised the conceptual basis of human ecology. But even after this reformulation, human ecologists continued to use the concept of environment in socio-cultural, symbolic terms (Dunlap and Catton, 1983; Michelson, 1976).

# The Environment and Social Movements

The environmental movement has proven to be among the most successful and enduring social movements of all time. Few other recent movements can match it in terms of sustained activity, size of following, and ability to affect the lives of so many people. It has even changed our language, with such terms as NIMBY ("not in my back yard") and *environmentally friendly product* entering the vernacular. The first Earth Day, staged 22 April 1970, was impressive, drawing some 20 million people (Dunlap and Gale, 1972), and Earth Day has since grown to become an international annual event—Earth Week, celebrated in 180 countries. Today few people admit to not supporting environmentalism; in fact, most people claim to be environmentalists (Dunlap, 1992). The environmental lobby, institutionalized as a significant player in government decision-making, is further evidence of the movement's impressive success.

The environmental movement has changed significantly over the years, often appearing to share little with its student-activist beginnings. The movement seems less angry today, but at the same time far more meticulous and deliberate in its approaches, often more at home in the corridors of power than on the protest line. The discussion that follows offers a look at the several strands of the contemporary environmental movement.

## *Progressive Conservation*

Contemporary environmentalism traces its roots to the **progressive conservation** movement of the late nineteenth century in the United States (Fox, 1985; O'Riordan, 1971). Led by such reformers as Gifford Pinchot and John Muir, the founder of the Sierra Club, progressive conservation was a reaction against the unchecked destruction of nature during this period of freewheeling capitalism. The wanton environmental damage caused by private ownership of resources led to widespread public support for placing limits on the private use of land. Progressive conservation was instrumental in the creation of the national parks system in the United States, the increase of government control over public lands, and the founding of such conservation groups as the Sierra Club and the Audubon Society.

Reflecting a period in which science and technology were revered, progressive conservation sought to formulate and implement "scientific management" of the environment. Two alternative science-based approaches to environmental management emerged. The preservationists, led by John Muir, advocated setting aside and protecting wilderness so that its natural, aesthetic, recreational, and scientific values could remain undisturbed for the benefit of future generations. Consumptive wildlife users, on the other hand, promoted conservation for utilitarian ends. Led by Pinchot and supported by President Theodore Roosevelt, this group wanted lands to be set aside mainly for recreational needs, but also for logging, mining, and grazing. American conservation policies in the early twentieth century tried to accommodate both sides of the debate through the creation of a liberal policy of greater government control over both private enterprise and public lands.

### Mainstream Environmentalism

One legacy of the progressive conservation movement was the legitimization of government involvement in the economy and the environment. The responsibility for maintaining some balance between environmental preservation and economic growth is mainly the province of government planners and politicians. Hence, progressive conservation set the scene for the current relationship between business and government. The main beneficiaries of this policy are the large corporations, which, while gaining controlled access to resources, have paid little in resource rents. Some observers regard the sustainable development movement as a new expression of the principle of consumptive wildlife use. Meanwhile, the voices of the early preservationists, calling for envi-

ronmental protection on moral, scientific, and aesthetic grounds, have largely gone unheard.

According to Robert Cameron Mitchell, Angela Mertig, and Riley Dunlap (1992), the other legacy of progressive conservation can be seen in the relationship between contemporary mainstream environmentalists and the government. Early preservationists quickly learned that they had to co-operate with the consumptive wildlife users and the Roosevelt administration or they would have little hope of making progress towards environmental protection. By now, environmentalists have become highly skilled at working as partners with government and developers in reaching compromise on environmental decisions. The inevitable result is trade-offs on preferred environmental solutions. Rik Scarce (1990: 15) reports that most environmental organizations admit to having no specific approach or plan for the environment other than saving what they can. Such muddling through has resulted in some checks on development, but also in serious environmental losses. Rarely have the mainstream environmental groups been in a position to claim complete victory in their efforts to stop a development or save an ecosystem.

Contemporary mainstream environmentalism is increasingly in the form of inside lobbying, politicking, and consultation, and relies mainly on its well-organized bureaucracies for success (Mertig, Dunlap, and Morrison, 2002). The leaders tend to be highly educated environmental professionals, often having backgrounds in public administration or environmental law and holding permanent, salaried positions. Fundraising and research are essential to successful competition with large corporations over the fate of resources. The individual member is far more likely to write a cheque or the occasional letter to an elected representative than to take part in a sit-in or blockade.

Many mainstream environmentalists argue that only through these increasingly well-organized, well-funded, professional organizations have environmental review and assessment become a permanent part of economic planning. Critics such as William Devall (1992) have suggested, however, that these same organizations are too accommodating to development interests, their leaders too close to their opposite numbers in business and government and too secure in their professional status. Still others are critical of mainstream environmentalism in general, arguing that it has long suffered from elitism. Various writers have pointed out the middle- or upper-class origins and high educational levels of environmental leaders and members of mainstream environmental organizations (Humphrey and Buttel, 1982; Morrison and Dunlap, 1986). However, it is also important to note that supporters of the environmental movement—if not those actually involved in it—tend to be drawn widely from across the social class spectrum (Mertig and Dunlap, 2001). A related criticism levelled at mainstream environmentalism is that the programs or policies advocated may lead to reductions in resource-based jobs or even in wholesale plant closures because of the high costs of environmental regulation or the protection of a given wilderness area (Schnaiberg, 1975). Such economic events are likely to have the most adverse effects on the working class and the poor.

### The New Ecologies

Mainstream environmentalism is one wing of the larger environmental movement. The new ecologies are a range of approaches within environmentalism with a number of features. First, they are all critical of mainstream environmentalism for its failure to address ecological problems by taking into account the systems of dominance in social relations that help to create those problems. Inequality among nations and regions enhances competition for scarce resources and thereby increases environmental harm. The new ecologies argue that the key to solving environmental problems is the promotion of social equity and self-determination, which will allow peoples and nations to meet their needs while maintaining ecological integrity (Gardner and Roseland, 1989).

Another distinguishing feature of the new ecologies, according to Nicholas Freudenberg and Carol Steinsapir (1992), is their devolved character. Hierarchical relations of authority between the membership and leaders or between the branches of each organization are rejected as being inconsistent with the prevailing thesis of human equality with nature rather than domination over it. This essentially ecocentric (and preservationist) stance is yet another characteristic of these groups, which tend to be sharply critical of any anthropocentric tendency to "manage" the environment—an approach mainstream environmentalists seem all too willing to accept.

Finally, the new ecologies tend to outline specific principles for environmental reform consistent with their broad vision of the human–nature relationship, rather than simply muddling through. They are also far less willing than the mainstream to accommodate

solutions in the interest of political and economic expediencies. Indeed, some radical arms of the new ecologies movement advocate the use of illegal, even violent, actions to win environmental disputes. While these radicals are in the minority, mainstream environmentalists admit to having been helped by them in reaching compromises more favourable to the environment—their "mainstream" proposals appear reasonable in comparison to the unbending demands and extremism of the radicals (Scarce, 1990).

Thus far, we have enumerated the similarities among the new ecologies. Now we look at three of these movements in order to highlight their differences.

### Eco-feminism

Eco-feminism represents the partnership of ecology and feminism. It is founded mainly on shared opposition to hierarchy and domination. Feminists argue that the subordination of women by men has been achieved through the ability of men to employ conceptual frameworks that place women at a disadvantage. According to Val Plumwood (1992), these include hierarchical frameworks that justify inequality; dualism, which justifies exclusion and separation; and rationality, which justifies logic and control. By advancing these three conceptual preferences, men have succeeded in legitimizing their domination over both women and nature.

The logic of domination holds that by virtue of the distinctiveness of men from nature and of men from women, together with the greater rationality of men, the domination of men over both women and nature is reasonable. In other words, eco-feminists argue that exactly the same male-controlled value system is used to justify both patriarchal human relations and the exploitation of nature.

Feminism and environmentalism connect, then, at the point of recognizing the similarities in the ways men treat women and nature. If one form of domination—of men over women—is wrong, then all forms of domination are wrong, including that of humans over nature. To be a feminist therefore compels one to be an environmentalist. Moreover, eco-feminists argue, inasmuch as environmentalists recognize and reject the domination of men over nature, they must also reject the domination of men over women. Therefore, all environmentalists must be feminists (Warren, 1990).

### Social Ecology

Social ecology has become a major pillar of philosophical thought in contemporary environmentalism.

Founder Murray Bookchin (1989) has articulated this philosophy over two decades. Social ecology advances a holistic world view of the human–nature partnership based on community. Bookchin identifies the dualism and domination informing current human–nature relations as products of human ideology and culture through which society has become defined as distinct from and superior to nature. While he acknowledges that culture and technology do distinguish society from nature, Bookchin rejects their separation. Rather, society springs from nature, reworking it into the human experience. Society always has a naturalistic dimension, and social ecology is tries to describe how both the connectedness and the divergences between society and nature occur. Appropriate technology, reconstruction of damaged ecosystems, and human creativity will combine with equity and social justice to produce an ecological society in which human culture and nature are mutually supportive and evolve together. Social ecology envisions a society in harmony with nature, combining human-scale sustainable settlement, ecological balance, community self-reliance, and participatory democracy.

### Deep Ecology

Deep ecology is among the most intriguing of the new ecologies, as well as the most controversial. The name was coined in 1973 by Norwegian philosopher Arne Naess. Defining contemporary environmentalism as "shallow" ecology, Naess (1973) argued that its advocacy of social reforms to curb problems of pollution and resource depletion identifies it as concerned mainly with protecting the health and affluence of the developed countries. By contrast, deep ecology is concerned with the root causes of environmental crisis and inspired by the understanding derived through personal experiences as humans in nature. The most distinctive aspect of deep ecology is its biocentric emphasis. Deep ecologists believe that all life forms have an equal right to exist and flourish. Humans in society, having become to a greater or lesser extent divorced from nature, must become aware of their role as one among many life forms, as opposed to seeing themselves as the kindly (or not so kindly) caretakers of nature. Therefore, while deep ecology shares with the other new ecologies the rejection of anthropocentrism, it goes beyond the humanistic, ecocentric ecology of human–nature coexistence. Deep ecologists desire humans to have the least possible effect on the planet and respect ecological integrity above all else (Tokar, 1988).

Deep ecology also emphasizes self-realization, the extension of the environmentally conscious individual's self beyond his or her personal needs to include the environment as a whole. The idea that human insight and experience are enhanced by contact with nature follows logically from biocentrism.

Deep ecologists believe that an important practical consequence of self-realization is the obligation to strive actively to prevent environmental destruction. The emphasis on direct action has particularly inspired the best-known of the deep ecology groups, Earth First!, which advocates the use of whatever means are necessary to save wilderness areas. Earth First! has garnered much attention—and criticism—for the use of ecological sabotage ("ecotage")—illegal force intended to block actions perceived as harming the environment (Taylor, 1991). "Monkey wrenching"—disruption by such covert and unlawful means as removing survey stakes, destroying machinery, or spiking trees—is controversial even within Earth First! These tactics stand in sharp contrast with the more widely accepted civil disobedience strategies of other radical environmentalists. Civil disobedience involves public protest for a cause, and while the marches or blockades may result in the protestors' being charged with civil crimes, there is a strong commitment to non-violence.

### Grassroots Environmentalism

While the roots of environmentalism date back to the preservationist movement of the nineteenth century, the publication of Rachel Carson's *Silent Spring* (1962), which detailed the impact of pesticides on ecosystems and human health, led to a concern for health assuming significance along with conservation and preservation as environmental goals. We weren't just protecting animals and ecosystems for aesthetic or economic reasons; these needed to be protected for our own essential well-being. The current era of environmentalism has increasingly focused on the dangers associated with industrial pollution and placement of pollution sources in residential communities. New grassroots forms of environmentalism have emerged in recent years with this as the mandate.

### The Toxic Waste Movement

The toxic waste movement is a branch of environmentalism unlike either the mainstream environmental movement or the new ecologies. On the one hand, the well-funded and organized mainstream environmental organizations, such as the Sierra Club, rely on professional leadership and a skilled staff, along with well-placed connections within the power structure, savvy insight into the political process, and a large public base of followers willing to provide financial support or to lend their voices to back a cause. On the other hand, the new ecologies have fewer material resources but are inspired and maintained by the ideology and shared values of the members.

The toxic waste movement reflects few of the tendencies of either of these more general arms of the environmental movement. The movement is, in a sense, all the disputes and protests by myriad groups opposed to perceived environmental threats present in their own communities and neighbourhoods. Diffuse in its focus, the toxic waste movement is associated with all manner of protest against everything from proposed developments, such as a new landfill, factory, or highway, to those connected with pollution caused by an existing industry. What unites the toxic waste movement is a common focus on perceived health threats to the community. The movement is intrinsically grassroots in its composition and approach, constituted typically of groups of formerly uninvolved citizens now struggling in their cause to stop a development or clean up pollution while facing the efficient and well-funded opposition of industry and/or government.

The toxic waste movement may be the fastest growing branch of environmentalism (Szasz, 1994). It is also in many ways far less distinguishable than the other types of environmentalism. For one thing, there is little in the way of national organizing bodies, or even communication among the various local groups. This extreme decentralization means that local protestors have very few resources, outside of their own means, on which to draw in developing their plans of opposition. Mainstream environmental organizations typically employ professional social movement organizers to guide their agendas, but local toxic waste protestors rarely have the backgrounds or resources required to mount a well-managed and effective campaign. Valuable skills may be learned as the protest develops, but as these campaigns are often also short-lived, such knowledge may not be passed on.

Characteristic of the toxic waste movement is the high proportion of its members who are women and homemakers, minorities, and those from lower socio-economic backgrounds (Brown and Masterson-Allen, 1994). Toxic waste activists also tend to be older, politically conservative, and trusting of existing institutions, laws, and regulations. The movement's high composition of women and homemakers is in keeping with its principal focus on preserving human health, especially that of children, in the face of an immediate threat from a nearby development or pollution source. These groups' membership is on average less educated than that found within mainstream environmentalism and the new ecologies, and their protests are more emotional than those of these other groups, which prefer to emphasize rational opposition based on scientific and legal evidence.

Unlike the new ecologies, ideology is not a prominent factor relating to either the formation or the reasoning of toxic waste groups. Toxic waste activists are motivated by the presence of a nearby environmental threat and are conditioned by their experiences in responding to it. Initially apolitical and naive in the art of protest, the lessons learned at the hands of the authorities and corporations may compel a loss of innocence leading to personal transformations (Aronson, 1993). Along with bringing lifestyle and value changes, such personal reconsideration may also prompt new skepticism about the political process, along with mistrust of the authorities, business, and scientific experts.

Grassroots toxic waste protest is often dismissed as NIMBYism by those who disagree with its ends, and it is true that self-interest often is an underlying motivation. Nevertheless, if the threat is real, why should self-interest depreciate the legitimacy of the group's goal? In addition, a general increase of concern over health risk from pollution and development helps to move the toxic waste movement towards a more formally defined foundation of support and new allegiances. This is seen, for example, in connection with the general movement to supplant NIMBY with NIABY—"not in anyone's back yard"—indicative of the reduced emphasis on self-interest, as well as with LULU ("locally unwanted land uses"), reflective of the greater sensitivity to the broader public interest currently sought in the development of many municipal land-use plans (Freudenburg and Pastor, 1992).

## Environmental Justice

Recently, another new grassroots movement, known as the **environmental justice** (EJ) movement, has emerged, with an agenda going beyond the traditional concerns of conservation and preservation common to most environmentalism. The EJ movement has ties to the toxic waste movement, but is also altering the focus of environmentalism generally to include broader concerns with regard to the societal inequities that result from industrial facility siting and industrial development.

While the environmental movement has long been concerned with the risks to human health from industrial pollution, only recently has awareness developed over the distributional risks associated with these effects. Various US studies have documented the inequitable distribution of environmental hazards (Bryant and Mohai, 1992; Bullard, 1990; Hofrichter, 1993), showing, for the most part, that low-income and racial-minority populations are disproportionately being affected by poor environmental quality resulting from exposure to industrial pollution, workplace pollution, and contaminated water and lands. A similar finding for low income and the likelihood of exposure to contamination risk was found in a comparison of pollution sites across Toronto, Hamilton, and Niagara Falls, Ontario (Nabalamba, 2001), and lower socio-economic status has often been found to be a prevalent condition within Canada's worst-polluted neighbourhoods.

Various explanations have been offered for the inequitable distribution of environmental burdens. One position reflects economic or market dynamics, suggesting that "sound" business decisions and the need to reduce costs may be grounds for locating potentially polluting industrial facilities (Kriesel, Centner, and Keeler, 1996; Oakes, 1996). It points to economic efficiency within the marketplace as the central criterion that guides what results as the unfair distribution of environmental risks to the poor. Industry's desire to minimize costs specifically associated with land or property values is seen as a major contributing factor to the disproportionate exposure to environmental pollutants. The suggestion is that this unequal risk occurs because cost-efficient industrial areas with low property values are also likely to be near areas with low residential property values and therefore a concentration of low-income populations.

Another rationale given for why the poor face greater pollution risk is the "path of least resistance" argument (Higgins, 1994; Hofrichter, 1993). This suggests that low-income and minority communities end up with a disproportionate share of disposal and polluting industrial facilities and poor environmental quality in general because they have less political clout than the more affluent communities.

Finally, a more contentious explanation cites "environmental racism" among private-industry and government decision-makers as being behind the disparities found in the uneven distribution of polluting industrial facilities (Bryant and Mohai, 1992; Bullard, 1990). This position draws largely on interpretations of evidence from the United States that show race to be a major factor in who is likely to be exposed to pollution risk. Hence, when race stands out as being significantly associated with the location of new disposal and polluting industrial facilities, racism is targeted as influencing the decision-making process.

## Conclusion

The history of the human population can be subdivided into two broad stages: a very long period of slow growth, from the beginning of humankind to about 1750, followed by a relatively recent phase of explosive growth. As a legacy of the population explosion that took place in the modern era and that continues in many developing countries, the world faces challenges heretofore unforeseen in the history of humanity.

Three demographic trends seem inevitable over the course of this new century: the population of the world will become older; the developing countries will grow much more than the developed countries; and there will be intense pressure on highly industrialized countries to accommodate an even larger share of immigrants from developing countries than they do currently. The implications of this eventuality will be far-reaching: with increased immigration, the highly industrialized receiving nations will become even more racially and ethnically heterogeneous. Given its relatively long history of immigration and its multicultural orientation, Canada seems well positioned to deal with this reality. For the countries that are relatively new immigrant-receiving societies in Western Europe (many of which until recently were sending nations), the adjustment process to this emerging reality poses difficult challenges. Their conceptions of nationhood may need to be modified in view of the changing racial and ethnic composition of their societies.

Cities are not immutable structures with predictably deterministic effects on human beings. They are a part of societies and of social changes, and are a reflection of people's conscious actions. Cities may be large and complex, but—for good or for ill—they are subject to human agency and organization. In many respects, cities mirror on an impressive scale the interacting agendas of individuals, groups, cultures, and nations. As in other areas of sociological inquiry, analysis and research help clarify what goes on around us and provide a basis for shaping contexts and structures in useful ways. It remains for everyone to benefit from such knowledge by taking conscious steps for the common good.

Either societies will change to achieve environmental integrity, or they will be changed by environmental contamination and resource depletion. Social change on behalf of the environment is therefore one of the most pressing global issues.

If sociology can be said to make one substantial contribution to the understanding of ecological crisis, it is the recognition that environmental problems are social products. This understanding goes beyond descriptions of how individuals or firms contribute to environmental degradation, and the solutions suggested involve more than promoting more environmentally responsible behaviours or technologies.

While such approaches may help deal with an immediate situation, they ultimately do more harm than good by deflecting attention from the real roots of environmental problems and the discovery of long-term solutions. In short, social systems must change in order that global disaster may be averted. What this chapter has illustrated, as dramatically as any in the book, is the remarkable, inescapable relationship between finite human individuals, their enduring, collectively created environment, and their often taken-for-granted natural environment. Sociologists must never forget that human systems and the environments in which they are nested all disappear in the end, but they have different life trajectories and all influence one another. All living things are also dying things whose survival and decline are inextricably connected on Planet Earth. Humans, despite their grand achievements—of which cities rank among the grandest—cannot escape this fact.

## □ Questions for Critical Thought

1. Describe how populations change. What are the demographic components of change?
2. What is atypical about the current stage of the demographic history of the world? Describe the relationship of demographic transition to the history and projected future of the human population. Are there any certainties about the future population of the world?
3. Assess the theories of Malthus and Marx on the matter of population and its relationship to contemporary issues concerning resources and the environment. Discuss how contemporary perspectives on population matters relate to the Malthusian and Marxist theories of population.
4. What role does technology play in contemporary urbanization and in the growth or decline of specific Canadian cities?
5. Do you think that everyday interpersonal behaviour varies more in an urban–rural comparison or between critical masses of subcultures within cities?
6. What are the largest subcultures in your area? Do they have different ways of life that make an impact on the area?
7. Environmental sociologists argue that ecological problems are social problems; that is, they exist because of the nature of social arrangements and social organization. Discuss this idea by selecting one or more environmental problems and suggesting how they might have been avoided or reduced if alternative social arrangements had existed.
8. The concept of sustainable development is key to much economic planning, but its critics often argue that it is being used mainly as a rationale for allowing more economic growth at the expense of the environment. Can economic growth and environmental quality coexist? Is sustainable development the answer for saving the planet?

## ☐ Recommended Readings

**Roderic Beaujot and Kevin McQuillan,** *Growth and Dualism: The Demographic Development of Canadian Society* **(Toronto: Gage, 1982).**
This book is an important introduction to Canada's population. The authors' historical overview of the development of Canada's population is particularly insightful.

**Lyn H. Lofland,** *The Public Realm: Exploring the City's Quintessential Social Territory* **(New York: Aldine de Gruyter, 1998).**
Lyn Lofland is one of the leading students of urbanism. In this recent book, she examines in a thorough and engaging way how people adapt to urban spaces.

**W.W. Rostow,** *The Great Population Spike and After: Reflections on the 21st Century* **(New York: Oxford University Press, 1998).**
The author takes a careful look at the populations of the industrial and developing countries, how they have been changing, and how they will change over the course of the new millennium.

**Mathis Wackernagel and William Rees,** *Our Ecological Footprint: Reducing Human Impact on the Earth* **(Gabriola Island, BC: New Catalyst, 1996).**
This book introduces the metaphor of the ecological footprint, a term used to refer to the productive land needed in order to sustain different lifestyles.

## ☐ Recommended Web Sites

**The Community Web**
**www.commurb.org**
The Web site of the American Sociological Association's Section on Community and Urban Sociology has a section of featured writings and photographs about contemporary topics and issues.

**Earth Day Network Ecological Footprint Quiz**
**www.earthday.net/footprint/index.asp**
A number of Web sites allow on-line calculation of your ecological footprint, the amount of productive land needed to sustain an individual's lifestyle. This one from the Earth Day organization calculates your ecological footprint based on information you provide on your consumption, housing, and travel patterns.

**United Nations Population Division**
**www.unpopulation.org**
The *United Nations Demographic Yearbook* contains a wealth of demographic information by country. Another key product from the United Nations is the *Human Development Report*.

# 16

Michael R. Smith

# Global Society

© W.P. Whitman Limited

## Learning Objectives

In this chapter, you will:

- identify the major international organizations that are the focus for much of the debate on globalization

- learn the four main forms of globalization: international political agreements, trade and capital flows, the mobility of populations, and cultural diffusion

- distinguish between globalization effects in rich and poor countries

- see how constraint on policy choice is present whether countries enter into treaties or not

- see that overall there is little evidence of net and aggregate harmful effects of globalization, and there is some evidence of positive effects

- examine how "global cities" play a critical role in the globalization process

- explore the two main forms of the cultural diffusion argument

- set current concerns with globalization within a broader historical context

## Introduction

On 12 August 1999, a group of about 200 people vandalized a McDonald's restaurant under construction in Millau, in southern France. They were led by José Bové, a sheep farmer from the region. Bové is a different sort of farmer. He spent most of his childhood in Berkeley, California, while his French parents were teaching at the University of California, before returning to France at the age of 15. Prior to the McDonald's incident, he had led several agriculture-related protests—to recover agricultural land used by the French military, to ban the feeding of growth hormones to calves, to destroy a stock of transgenic (genetically modified) corn. He was in Seattle in 1999 to protest at a World Trade Organization (WTO) meeting, and returned to North America to protest at another one in Quebec City in 2001. In 2002, while awaiting the outcome of his appeal against a prison sentence for the McDonald's incident, he led a group in Brazil that, among other things, pulled up crops of genetically modified corn and soybeans. Bové has become a symbol of anti-globalization protest. His targets reflect a number of the areas of concern about the process.

There is the WTO itself. Created through negotiations among governments, it enforces international trade rules on member countries. Anti-globalization protestors criticize the lack of citizen involvement in such negotiations, claiming that corporations have privileged access to governments so that treaties reflect corporate interests rather than the interests of the broader population.

Countries use tariffs (taxes on imported goods), quotas (restrictions on the quantity of incoming goods), and subsidies (cash transfers or tax relief) to protect domestic producers. The WTO's assumption is that international trade is a good thing, that tariffs, quotas, and subsidies obstruct international trade. The WTO is a forum for negotiating their reduction or elimination.

The WTO also has a quasi-judicial responsibility. Governments that think other countries protect their industries in ways that are incompatible with treaty obligations can appeal to the WTO, which then rules on the matter and prescribes sanctions to impose on the offending country, usually including the right of other countries to impose retaliatory tariffs. For example, when the United States government, in response to steel industry lobbying, imposed a 30 per cent tariff on steel imports, the European Union appealed to the WTO. All this limits national policy autonomy. Thus, a country like France that uses sub-sidies to maintain a strong national film industry is likely to run afoul of the WTO. Bové and others regard this as an inappropriate limit on national policy autonomy.

Then there is the issue of health and safety. In the 1990s, some people in Britain developed a human variant of bovine spongiform encephalitis (BSE, or "mad cow disease"), apparently from the consumption of meat from British cattle. Other countries responded by closing their markets to British beef imports on health grounds. WTO regulations permitted this. Other health or safety issues are less clear. In North America, for example, hormones are often added to livestock feed to accelerate growth. This is less common in Europe. Several European governments claim that hormone-fed beef is a health hazard to those who consume it. North American producers contest that claim, arguing that European cattle producers are asserting this health effect as a pretext, that the real European objective is to protect domestic producers against more efficient North American competition. Bové and others contest the right of the WTO to adjudicate this sort of issue.

Finally, there is a broader resistance to the diffusion of a foreign **culture**, particularly US culture. Bové can wax lyrical on the virtues of small-scale local production and high-quality food. On his own farm, he produces one particular culinary gem: Roquefort cheese. The contrast with the industrial agriculture and standardized distribution that underpins the success of McDonald's Corporation is obvious. Bové and his supporters vandalized a McDonald's because they regarded it as a symbol of the intrusion of American culture.

Clearly, Bové is not enthused by globalization, at least in its current form. The same animus with respect to globalization that has expressed itself in his political career stimulates much of the academic, and quasi-academic, debate on the subject. It is an area of diatribes. On one side of the debate, globalization (in its current form) is iniquity incarnate (see, for example, Klein, 1999). On the other side, critics of globalization are treated as fools or knaves, or both (for example, Burtless, 1998). Let us try to bring some detachment to the issue.

## What Is Globalization?

There is much debate on what **globalization** means (see Guillén, 2001), but the underlying idea is fairly clear: international processes intrude on the preferences and behaviour of national and local populations. The word *intrusion* is chosen deliberately: it has a pejorative connotation. In much of the relevant writing, so does *globalization*. That writing often associates globalization with the loss of things that ought to be valued. Beyond this, things get more complicat-

ed, as globalization takes many forms. We will consider globalization as political arrangement, as economic process, as mobility and transnational **social networks**, and as cultural diffusion.

## 16.1

# Open for Discussion
## The International Monetary Fund (IMF)

Before the Second World War, there had been a period of competitive currency devaluations that reduced international trade. The Bretton Woods negotiators established the IMF to address this problem.

Countries can maintain or create jobs by exporting goods to other countries. How much they export will depend, in part, on the prices of the goods they produce. There are two ways of cutting the prices of export goods. First, producers can reduce the costs of production in the country's own currency. Thus, Canadian manufacturers might use energy or labour more efficiently. Alternatively, the country's currency can be devalued. The Canadian dollar depreciated by about 35 per cent between 1974 and 2002. This led American consumers to buy more Canadian goods than they would otherwise have done. The devaluation has reduced the price of Canadian products in US dollars. Think about this in terms of the current relative cost of snowboarding to an American paying in US dollars for a visit to a Canadian ski mountain as opposed to a Canadian paying for a visit to a US ski mountain.

During the Great Depression of the 1930s, many people lost their jobs in Europe and North America. Several countries tried to create employment by devaluing their currencies. But any advantage gained if one country devalues its currency is lost if its commercial rivals devalue their currencies. Something like this happened during the 1930s—there was a wave of competitive devaluations (Kindleberger, 1986). The Bretton Woods negotiators concluded that export industries had been damaged and jobs destroyed by competitive devaluations. The reason for this is that exporting and importing are much riskier where prices are subject to substantial change through relative currency price changes.

The IMF was set up to deal with this problem. Suppose, for example, that an early frost damages the coffee crop of a Third World country that is substantially dependent on coffee exports. This is likely to cause a temporary fall in government revenues since there will be less income to tax. This fall in revenue would be likely to lead to a government deficit. And government deficits tend to put pressure on currency values. (Part of the decline of the Canadian dollar from the 1970s to now is probably explained by the large deficits of Canadian governments from the mid-1970s until the early 1990s.) So where there is temporary pressure on a country's currency, the IMF may make a loan to that country—at less than commercial interest rates—to allow its government to cover the temporary revenue shortfall.

This is fairly non-controversial. The problem occurs where the government of a country like, say, Argentina, accumulates a large debt over a substantial period of time. The IMF may still make a loan to help the Argentinian government deal with its problems, but in such cases the IMF is mandated to encourage governments to adopt "sound economic policies." This usually means reductions in government expenditures, balancing budgets, and privatization. The rationale for privatization is that loss-making government-run enterprises contribute to government debt. The IMF also assumes that private ownership implies improved efficiency. It makes these sorts of policies conditions for the receipt of a loan.

But cutting government expenditures usually means reducing education and welfare spending, and privatization sometimes leads to layoffs. There are sometimes real costs for significant parts of the populations of countries receiving IMF loans. It is these that generate the hostility of anti-globalization protesters toward the IMF.

## Globalization as Political Arrangement

After the Second World War, the United States and Britain—and, to a lesser extent, other countries—negotiated the framework for subsequent international economic arrangements. They produced the Bretton Woods agreement, named after the resort in New Hampshire where the main negotiations took place. Bretton Woods created the International Monetary Fund and the World Bank. Each has become a *bête noire* to anti-globalization protestors.

The IMF and the World Bank encourage "**sound economic policies**" in the **Third World**, usually including cuts to government expenditures and the reinforcement of the private sector. The WTO (successor to the General Agreement on Tariffs and Trade, GATT) limits the discretion of governments with respect to tariffs, quotas, and subsidies. Critics oppose these organizations because of their definition of "sound economic policies" and also because of the role of rich, powerful countries in their design. The Bretton Woods agreement was only one of several proposed arrangements for managing post-war international trade, but the relative economic power of the United States after the Second World War meant that its preferences largely prevailed (Skidelsky, 2000). The IMF, World Bank, and WTO commitments to market solutions reflect the policy preferences of a set of Western nations—in particular, the United States.

Moreover, beyond international organizations, outcomes are also shaped by naked power. Take the softwood lumber dispute between Canada and the United States. For a number of reasons, but particularly because of the depreciation of the Canadian dollar, the US lumber industry has lost market share to Canadian producers. In response, it has pressured US politicians to look hard at Canadian practices, claiming that, in violation of trade rules, Canadian governments have found ways to subsidize the industry. Using threats, the US government has forced Canada to adopt policies that raise the price of lumber exports into the United States, including, at various times, both export taxes and quotas (Grafton, Lynch, and Nelson, 1998).

## Globalization as Economic Process

Consider, first, rich countries. Trade exposes owners and employees to competition. Third World competitors mostly pay markedly lower wages. They may either drive rich-country producers out of business or force them to cut the wages of their employees in order to compete (Wood, 1994).

Then there are **multinational corporations**. Nortel, Bombardier, and Inco are Canadian examples. Other things being equal, managers of these companies are likely to locate factories and offices where costs are lower and the political environment more congenial. Low taxes, less restrictive labour laws, and government reticence to intervene in the economy are likely to attract them. So, in competition for investment, countries may cut taxes, reduce services, weaken labour laws (health and safety regulations, statutory protections against dismissal, trade-union protections), and refrain from other policies offensive to foreign investors.

International agreements limit the policy choices of the countries that sign them. Some of the passions that this arouses are clearly expressed in these photographs. A protestor shouts at the police; Quebec City, Summit of the Americas protests, April 2001. The police response follows. (Dru Oja Jay/Dominionpaper.ca)

16.2

After World War II, the large European countries were in appalling financial shape. But global growth depended on their return to financial health. Countries such as the United States and Canada were in better economic shape but needed European countries rich enough to absorb their exports. The International Bank for Reconstruction and Development (IBRD) was the policy response to this problem. It was created to provide loans to governments to fund investments in devastated European countries—say, the reconstruction of a rail network.

The World Bank evolved out of the IBRD, which is now one part of the World Bank Group. But its mission has changed. By the mid-1950s, European countries had substantially recovered, so the IBRD shifted to providing loans to "credit-worthy poor countries." It was reoriented to the Third World.

Other elements of the World Bank Group, with the dates of their establishment, are the International Financial Corporation (1956), which helps to finance the private sector in the Third World; the International Development Association (1960), which funds programs to alleviate long-term poverty (in recent years, it has, for example, funded female education and anti-AIDS programs); the International Centre for Settlement of Investment Disputes (1966), which mediates disputes between private investors and countries (for example, a dispute involving the claim by a private company that the government of Albania expropriated its property); and the Multilateral Investment Guarantee Agency (1988), which encourages private-sector investments in Third World countries by providing insurance against political risk (such as civil war).

Like those of the IMF, these purposes seem entirely worthy. But the IBRD directs its loans to "credit-worthy countries." This puts pressure on borrowers to balance their budgets. At the same time, the International Finance Corporation, the Multilateral Investment Guarantee Agency, and the International Centre for Settlement of Investment Disputes are all designed to reinforce the private sector. Those who would prefer a larger role for the public sector in development might object to this.

---

There are also enormous flows of **finance capital** between countries. So-called **hot money** usually accumulates in countries where interest rates are higher and the local currency more stable (Sassen, 2002). This also limits policy options. Government policies designed to stimulate the economy normally involve lower interest rates, but lower interest rates may lead to a flight of "hot money" out of the country as investors seek the highest rate (for a given level of political and economic stability).

A government confronting a high **unemployment rate** may wish to reduce interest rates, hoping that doing so will create jobs. Lower interest rates imply lower mortgage payments, which stimulate the housing market. Lower rates also reduce entrepreneurs' cost of borrowing, which encourages job-creating investment. But interest-rate reductions may precipitate a decline in the value of a country's currency.

For various reasons, a government may be reluctant to see the value of its currency fall. Insofar as this is the case, it may avoid policies that lead to a reduction in interest rates (Andrews, 1994). Thus, the unemployment rate in Canada in the early 1990s was well over 10 per cent, but the government of the time did not substantially stimulate the economy. It chose instead policies that had the effect of supporting the value of the Canadian dollar, and the unemployment rate rose fairly dramatically (see Fortin, 1996). The anti-globalization interpretation of this is that Canadian government policy was limited by the development of an international market for capital, with ever-larger flows of "hot money" between countries.

Parallel damage may be inflicted on the Third World. Despite lower labour costs, Third World producers are sometimes undercut by exports from rich countries. Here is a particularly pathetic example:

rich-country charities receive donations of second-hand clothes, but "with more donations than they can use, the charities unload their surplus on wholesalers who buy it in the West for a few pennies a pound, then ship it [to Zambia] and sell bales of it to . . . street retailers at a markup of 300 to 400 per cent" (Jeter, 2002: A1). The local population buys the goods for reasons of both price and taste. Items with sports logos are particularly popular in some African markets. There used to be relatively lively textile and apparel industries in Zambia. These have now been seriously damaged by competition from second-hand European and North American goods.

Most damage to domestic industries in Third World countries, however, comes from **capital-intensive** industries. Capital-intensive production in rich countries—particularly agriculture—can often lead to lower sale prices, despite the relatively high cost of labour in the rich countries. The effects are compounded where agriculture is heavily subsidized, as is the case for many US and European agricultural products. Some development analysts believe that it is only possible for Third World countries to develop their own industries if those industries are protected or encouraged—with tariffs, quotas, or subsidies. But doing so would go against the policy preferences of the WTO, the World Bank, and the IMF, all of which press for liberalized trade and have sanctions available if a country chooses protectionism.

This brings us to the Third World and capital markets. Lenders often regard Third World countries as too risky for investment, so those countries are compelled to turn to international organizations—the World Bank or, during financial crises, the IMF—as sources of loans or as guarantors of private-sector loans. But these loans come with strings attached, of the sort discussed earlier—requirements that markets be opened and that the country adopt a "sound economic policy."

### Globalization as Mobility and Transnational Social Networks

Products imported from the Third World might force down rich-country wages, but migration from the Third World to rich countries may have the same effect. In either case, wages of unskilled (usually meaning poorly educated) employees in rich countries are most likely to be affected. There has been a large unskilled migration into the United States, both legal and illegal. One result of this is competition between poorly educated Latin American migrants and, disproportionately, poorly educated African Americans. Some think that this competition has forced down wages of unskilled workers in the United States—of African Americans in particular (Stevans, 1998).

The Canadian situation is a little different. A points system determines eligibility for some immigrant classes. Would-be migrants are given points for education and in-demand skills (as well as other things). Those with enough points are admitted. This system for selecting immigrants is thought to have reduced the magnitude of unskilled immigration to Canada (but see Reitz, 1998). Europe has also experienced post-war migrations. The fundamental point, though, is that international migration—mainly from poor to rich countries—is a common experience across rich countries.

These migrations create transnational social networks. Most migrants settle in cities. The main destinations of migrants to Canada are Toronto, Montreal, and Vancouver, where they create their own communities, sometimes retaining close ties with other members of their family or ethnic group in other cities in the world. The same thing happens on a larger scale in New York, Los Angeles, and London. This creates what Alejandro Portes (1997) calls *transnational communities*, with identities and economic interests shaped by their inter-city relations.

At the other end of the social scale, claims Saskia Sassen (2002), international cities develop a distinctive elite. This elite manages international commercial flows—the movements of goods, services, and capital that have become these cities' main economic vocation—and, to some degree, becomes detached from national loyalties. Bankers in London engaged in the financing of international trade, for example, become less concerned with British domestic policy issues. Rather, their transnational economic and social ties become increasingly important (Sassen, 2002; see also Arthurs, 1999, on Canada).

### Globalization as Cultural Diffusion

Hollywood is the most conspicuous worldwide projector of a particular culture, through the process called **cultural diffusion**. The US movie and television industry has aggressively marketed itself throughout the Americas and Europe (Segrave, 1998). It probably shapes the world views of receiving populations. What Hollywood projects is heterogeneous (it is a long way from Woody Allen to Clint

Eastwood to Arnold Schwarzenegger), but it is unlikely to reflect the range of preferences and opinions in the rest of the world. It must substantially embody cultural judgements, knowledge, or ignorance of those producing movies and television. Hollywood's ignorance extends even to its most immediate northern neighbour; Pierre Berton (1975) describes one film that took place during a blizzard in Saskatchewan—in July!

American cultural influence is not confined to Hollywood. US universities train graduate students from the rest of the world and produce a disproportionate share of the world's academic output. US multinational companies transmit employment practices to other countries (Merten, 1997). That is, American multinational corporations have similar ways of hiring (recruitment and evaluation methods), of promoting, and of dealing with grievances (among other things). When they set up branches in Belgium, or Brazil, or Barbados, they bring those practices with them. They change the culture of employment in those countries. To varying degrees, so do multinationals based in other countries.

## The Effect of Globalizing Mechanisms

Two linked themes run through this discussion so far. One is that globalization is a homogenizing process. Political, economic, and cultural pressures create societies that look increasingly similar. Such homogenization may be regarded as undesirable in general—a process through which the diversity and richness of cultures is replaced with the grey monotone of a standard international practice. A displacement of consumption from, say, Roquefort cheese or similarly distinctive products to McDonald's might be a symbol of this process. The other theme specifies what seem to be identifiably bad outcomes of the globalization process. The destruction of Zambia's indigenous clothing industry might be an example of this. The limits placed on government choices of economic and social policy by international organizations and by international trade and capital flows are often also regarded in this way.

Consider the four broad globalizing mechanisms identified above in light of these concerns.

American cultural influence extends across the globe. This striking photograph was taken in an open-air market in Kabul, Afghanistan. Even in countries where America is not favoured, an impressive array of US-made running shoes are ready for sale. (Steve McCurry/Magnum Photos)

## Treaties and International Organizations

### Constraint in Principle

International organizations and common markets are created through treaties. Treaties are international contracts, so, like the contracts associated with a mortgage, a marriage, or a mutual fund purchase, they impose constraints on signatories. Further, sovereign nations can sign or not sign such agreements. Several European countries, for example, chose not to become members of the European Economic Community (now the European Union, or EU) when it was first created and some still remain outside it. Had the 1987 federal election in Canada gone differently—and it could easily have done so—the Canada–US Free Trade Agreement (FTA) would not have been signed. The initiative to create the North American Free Trade Agreement (NAFTA) came from the United States and Mexico. The Canadian government inserted itself into the process when it seemed it would be left out (Robert, 2000)—it was concerned that a NAFTA without Canada might mean that Mexico would replace Canada as the principal trading partner of the United States.

Of course, a picture of sovereign governments free to choose between courses of action would be a gross misrepresentation. Self-defence motivated the Canadian government to negotiate the FTA. Rising protectionist sentiment in the United States in the 1980s led to threats of unilateral imposition of tariffs and quotas. The FTA was conceived to shelter Canadian exporters from this protectionist wave. The threat of protectionism, then, constrained the Canadian government to pursue a trade agreement.

Similarly, Third World countries that borrow from the World Bank, or rich or poor countries that borrow from the IMF, do so because other options seem less appealing. There is no such thing as unconstrained choice. Still, there is some choice. The core of the debate on globalization is about whether or not the amount of constraint has increased.

### Constraint in Practice

Do the sorts of treaties associated with globalization imply increased levels of constraint? To answer this question we need first to determine as compared to when constraint might have increased.

Consider these two examples. From 1876 to 1884, King Leopold of Belgium created his own personal second kingdom, in what became the Congo, ushering in a period of spectacular brutality (Anstey, 1966; Hochschild, 1998). Indigenous males were conscripted into the production of rubber, or their lives were disrupted as they fled the Belgian troops sent to conscript them. Among other atrocious acts, mutilation was used as a form of labour discipline. In areas of British conquest in southern Africa, European farmers displaced the indigenous population. That population was then subjected to taxes. The idea was that the need to pay taxes in cash would force the native population to seek employment on settler farms (Crush, 1987). Coercive activities of various sorts were common across the various European empires in Africa and elsewhere. *This* was constraint.

Treaties and international organizations, moreover, are often methods for escaping or limiting other sorts of constraint. Take, for example, the case of the Bretton Woods agreement of 1944. Part of it committed signatories to maintain approximately fixed rates of exchange between their currencies. This ruled out (or made more difficult) one particular policy choice: competitive devaluation. Bretton Woods was a means for escaping the macroeconomic policy constraints imposed by competitive devaluations, with which governments had to deal during the interwar period.

Treaties, then, embody chosen constraints. How binding are those constraints? Post-war trade agreements were supposed to create a level playing field across countries, so that only the most efficient producers would thrive, irrespective of country of location.

But consider the following case. In 1999, a Taiwanese computer chip company proposed siting a plant in a suburb of Montreal. As encouragement, the Quebec government agreed to invest $400,000 in the company and offered the company a tax holiday worth about a billion dollars and training grants of several million dollars. The municipality targeted promised half the cost of necessary infrastructure investments, with water supplied at a discount. Further subsidies were sought from the federal government, but that support, in the amounts sought, was not forthcoming and the project was dropped. All these promises—and this is the important point—were made despite the fact that they were probably inconsistent with international trade agreements to which Canada is a signatory. This example is not unique (Smith, 2001b).

Canada is not alone in evading trade treaty obligations. It may offend less than other rich countries. The United States aggressively subsidizes its agriculture and in March 2002 imposed a 30 per cent tariff on steel imports that, a year later, was ruled illegal by the WTO. The European Union is no better. Treaties do constrain signatories, but it is important to understand that the degree of compliance is highly variable. Further evidence of this is the substantial body of legal writings dealing precisely with the problem of increasing the likelihood of treaty compliance. We live in a world where treaty violation is frequent (Chayes and Chayes, 1995).

Governments regularly confront choices. On the one hand, there is the possibility of inconsistent mutual regulation through a treaty. On the other hand, there is the possibility of inconsistent mutual regulation in the absence of a treaty. The latter, no-treaty situation will often involve a tit-for-tat approach to disputes—one country limits trade to protect its vulnerable industries, another country punishes the first country by closing off its domestic market to the first country's major export industries, and so on. Or countries might consecutively devalue their currencies, as during the interwar period. Or they might do both.

Constraint is present in both situations. What matters is the relative benefits of different kinds of constraint. Since treaties spell out rules for international relations, they will usually be preferable. Rules mean that treaty implications for signatories are relatively predictable, except where treaty enforcement is very inconsistent indeed. Critics of the IMF, the World Bank, and the WTO say interesting things about the harmful consequences of these institutions' actions. However, in the final analysis, our judgement of them and other international organizations requires the specification of feasible alternative arrangements and their consequences.

### Trade and Investment: Rich Countries

Critics of globalization tend to focus on two negative consequences for rich countries of increased trade and more mobile investment. One suggests that increased trade—particularly with the Third World—worsens the pay and employment situation of the less skilled and of workers in general. Another argues that, to create an investment-friendly environment and attract increasingly footloose capital, rich countries adopt less generous social policies. This is the "**race to the bottom**" argument.

### Employment and Wages

Most trade is between rich countries. Roughly speaking, the world's rich countries are members of

the Organization for Economic Co-operation and Development (OECD). Figure 16.1 shows that from 1970 to 1998, over two-thirds of imports into OECD countries originated in other OECD countries. There was no downward trend in the share of OECD-originating imports. Finally, imports from members of the Organization of the Petroleum Exporting Countries (OPEC) account for a significant share of total non-OECD imports. But the bulk of imports from these countries is petroleum. Few OECD countries compete in the oil market.

But perhaps the variation in pay levels between rich countries is sufficient to undermine Canadian and US wages. For example, the gap between wages in Canada and the United States, on the one hand, and Greece and Portugal, on the other, is fairly wide. In fact, however, the evidence seems to suggest that trade is not forcing down wages in richer countries.

Price competition is supposed to put pressure on the wages of richer countries, and low-wage countries should be able to sell into high-wage countries at a lower price. But were this process underway, one might expect those industries in rich countries exposed to more trade to be less able to raise their prices than industries exposed to less trade or altogether sheltered from trade. They might even be forced to lower their prices. Research on both the United States and Europe, however, has found no link between the amount of trade in the goods of a particular industry and price trends in that industry (Slaughter and Swagel, 1997). In fact, rich-country prices have proven to be robust in the face of international competition. This suggests that trade exerts little pressure on rich-country wages.

Another issue is the effect of trade on unemployment. For Canada, a good test of this is provided by events following the FTA and NAFTA (Smith, 2001b), which came into force on 1 January 1988 and 1 January 1994, respectively. Each reduced barriers to competition with the United States. The second also reduced barriers with Mexico, a low-income country. Unemployment in Canada did rise after the FTA, but the FTA's implementation coincided with a recession—unemployment rose elsewhere at the same time. NAFTA, in contrast, was implemented in the early part of an upswing in the economy. Unemployment was falling before it was signed and continued to fall after it was signed. Evidence indicates, however, that the largest post-FTA declines in employment were concentrated in industries subject to the largest tariff cuts. All this suggests that some workers lost their jobs because of the trade agreements but that the agreements' aggregate net effect on unemployment was negligible.

But if particular workers were damaged by these agreements, perhaps this is evidence of trade's gener-

ally harmful effect on unskilled employees in particular. Rising earnings inequality is usually cited in support of this interpretation (e.g., Bernard and Jensen, 2000). It is sometimes thought to reflect the down-

**16.3**

# Open for Discussion
## Protectionism vs Free Trade

Tariffs, quotas, and subsidies are all forms of protectionism. *Tariffs* are taxes imposed on goods when they enter a country. They raise prices to importers and therefore to consumers. *Quotas* limit the quantity supplied of the goods to which they are applied. A reduced supply usually also implies a higher price. Why would anyone favour policies that increase the prices of goods? *Government subsidies* involve the transfer of income from those who pay taxes to the private owners of the firms receiving the subsidies. Why might taxpayers wish to enrich other private owners—often foreign—most of whom are very rich? Here are some arguments for one or another of these protectionist measures:

1. The removal of tariffs or quotas exposes a previously protected industry to low-cost foreign competition. Many consumers will benefit from lower prices, but the benefit per consumer is likely to be small. In contrast, industry employees will likely suffer large costs. Either their pay will be cut to match the competition, or they will lose their jobs. This implies a transfer of income from producers to consumers.
2. Protectionist measures might be adopted to punish another country that already has quotas, high tariffs, or industrial subsidies. This can encourage another country to change its policies. Recent increases in subsidies to agricultural producers in the United States might be seen as retaliation against even higher subsidies in the European Union.
3. Already-established firms have an advantage: they have invested in plant and equipment over a long period of time, developed local expertise in production processes, and created networks of suppliers and customers. For a new entrant to an industry to match all this would be very costly indeed. Consequently, a

country might protect domestic producers for the first decades of their operation so that they can build up to a competitive scale of operation. This is called the *infant industry argument*. It suggests that transitional protection is appropriate.

4. It is in the interests of countries to have high-technology industries because profits and wages in them are higher than in other industries. This is because of monopoly power. Scale economies in the aircraft industry, for example, are so large that, worldwide, only a small number of producers is feasible. Patents legalize pharmaceutical monopolies for specified numbers of years. Even without patent rights, the knowledge frontier of high-technology industries is continually being pushed outward so that technology and products are progressively improved. This makes it hard to enter an industry or, if a new firm does so, to catch up. Most countries recognize this. Japan protected its computer industry for many years. European governments have subsidized Airbus Industries. In such an environment, protectionism may be necessary to assure a high-technology industry presence (see Johnson, Tyson, and Zysman, 1990).

There are, of course, pro–free trade responses to each of these arguments:

1. It is better to liberalize trade and provide temporary help (unemployment insurance, retraining) to those who lose their jobs through foreign competition.
2. Retaliation against the protectionism of others leads to a mutually harmful tit-for-tat spiral.
3. In practice, protected "infant industries" rarely "grow up."
4. High-technology industries are not as distinctive as the protagonists of protectionism claim.

ward pressure on the earnings of the unskilled (the uneducated) exerted by Third World competition. But only a small number of countries—in particular the United States and the United Kingdom—have experienced large and sustained increases in earnings inequality (Atkinson, 2000; Card and DiNardo, 2002; Wolfson and Murphy, 1998). Earnings inequality rose in Canada from about 1975 to about 1985 and has been stable or falling since (Card and DiNardo, 2002; Wolfson and Murphy, 1998). In still other countries—Italy and Germany—there was no increase at all (Atkinson, 2000). Yet all of these countries have been exposed to globalization. Further, earnings inequality stopped rising in the United States in about 1993 while world trade continued to increase.

### The Race to the Bottom

Social programs rest on tax collections. But corporations are lured by cuts in corporate taxes and in the income taxes to which high-earning managers are liable. So, it is argued, competitive tax cuts cause cuts to social programs.

This argument is plausible. But the available evidence tends not to support it. Nancy Olewiler (1999) has found that there were large differences between OECD countries in the tax rates imposed on corporations and individuals, that there were large differences between tax rates in Canada and the United States, that there was no evidence of a convergence in tax rates over time across OECD countries, and that taxes had tended to rise rather than fall in the periods studied.

Consistent with this, huge social policy divergences persist. The income protection provided to those who lose their jobs, get sick, or incur hard-to-manage family obligations (for example, those of single mothers) remain much more generous in Sweden and Germany, say, than in the United States. A substantial literature documents the persistence of social policy variation despite globalization (see, for example, Kitschelt, 1999). Figure 16.2 shows just how wide the variation in social spending remains, with social spending as a percentage of GDP (gross domestic product) in Sweden about twice that of Japan. Note, furthermore, the variation in methods of social spending: all of Norway's involves direct spending by the government, whereas about one-quarter of spending in the United States involves private social benefits, either legally stipulated (such as occupational health and safety premiums) or voluntarily provided (such as employer-funded pensions).

## Figure 16.1 OECD Imports

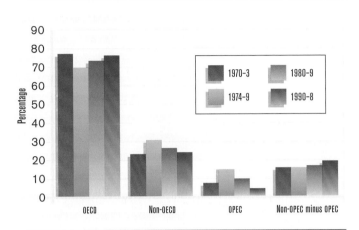

SOURCE: Based on Organisation for Economic Co-operation and Development (OECD), *OECD Historical Statistics, 1970–1999* (Paris: OECD, 2001), 118.

### What Prevents Convergence?

Given the criticisms of globalization, one might wonder why international trade and investment with the Third World do not lead to rising unemployment and falling wages among unskilled workers in rich countries.

One reason is that the magnitudes of the economic changes associated with globalization are often exaggerated. Paul Hirst and Grahame Thompson (1996) have observed that only at the beginning of the 1990s did trade as a percentage of GDP equal and begin to exceed the figure for 1913. And William Watson (1999) notes that in some countries, including Canada, investment as a percentage of GDP was much larger in the late nineteenth and early twentieth centuries than it is currently. Some caution, then, is warranted with respect to the novelty of the globalization process.

Another reason is that in capitalist economies many jobs are both destroyed and created (Davis, Haltiwanger, and Schuh, 1996). Changing technology and tastes, as well as globalization, lead to declines in employment in some firms and industries. These declines in employment sometimes involve layoffs, but they are also often managed through attrition. The same changes in technology, taste, and opportunities on the international market, however, lead to expansions in employment in other sectors. As a result, while particular groups of employees may be harmed by globalization (as was the case for the FTA in Canada), the aggregate effect may be modest.

Figure 16.2  **Net Public and Private Social Expenditures as a Percentage of GDP**

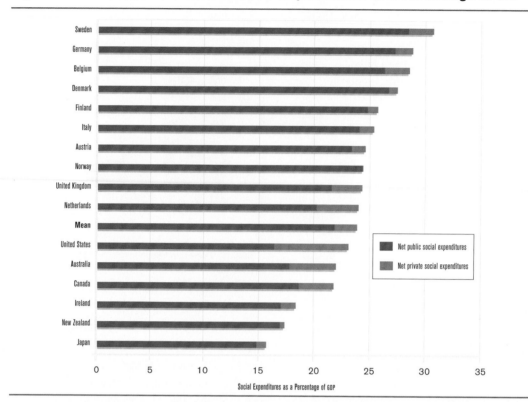

<sup>a</sup> Social benefits include old-age cash benefits, disability cash benefits, occupational injury and disease benefits, sickness benefits, services for the elderly and the disabled, survivors' benefits, family cash benefits, family services, active labour market policies, unemployment compensation, housing benefits, public health expenditures, and other contingencies, such as cash benefits to those on low incomes.

SOURCE: Willem Adema, *Net Public Social Expenditures* (Paris: OECD, 2001), 27–8. Reprinted by permission of the OECD.

Still another reason is that many governments of countries with greater exposure to the international market have chosen to invest more heavily in social programs than have those with less exposure. Other things being equal, trade as a percentage of GDP is higher in small countries such as the Netherlands, Belgium, Sweden, and Canada than it is in large countries such as Germany, the United Kingdom, or, in particular, the United States (perhaps because of economies of scale). At the same time, social programs are, on average, more generous in the first set of countries than in the second (though Germany diverges from the second group pattern).

What explains this association? Dani Rodrik (1997) notes that countries with a large share of their economy engaged in trade are likely to be particularly hard hit during downturns in the economic activity of their principal trading partners. To compensate for this vulnerability, governments of small countries like the Netherlands have developed generous welfare states. In their case, globalization has led to more generous social policy rather than to a race to the bottom.

A final problem with the "race to the bottom" argument is that the "bottom" may not be the outcome preferred by managers of multinational corporations. Suppose that you are a manager of a multinational company. What factors might affect your decision with respect to where to locate your head office? You would certainly prefer a reasonably safe city—it is harder to recruit and keep high-quality employees who confront a significant likelihood of being mugged, assaulted, or burgled. So investments in a police force are required, as well, probably, as investments in social programs that provide a living standard adequate to reduce the likelihood that the poor will feel inclined to mug, assault, or burgle. Since few people enjoy being solicited by beggars or passing people sleeping in doorways, you may want to see some programs established to help the homeless.

In addition, you almost certainly do not want to be exposed to infectious diseases. Investments in public health reduce the likelihood of contracting, say, tuberculosis. You would want traffic jams kept under control. In a large **metropolitan area**, that would require (very costly) investments in mass transit. You might also like to see a rich cultural life in your city. Universities tend to elevate the cultural lives of their host cities. Even in the United States, universities are substantially funded through taxes. If you want an opera, ballet, symphony orchestra, a set of museums, and a theatre district, you would also have to expect to be taxed to make possible subsidies to these cultural institutions. Along these lines, there are more high-paid head office jobs in New York City than in, say, Birmingham, Alabama. Taxes are markedly lower in Birmingham than in New York, but so are public services. Many would think that the quality of life is also inferior in Birmingham. The preservation of better jobs certainly requires some public spending, possibly a lot of it.

## *Trade and Investment: Poor Countries*

What about the Third World? Is the case of the Zambian apparel industry exemplary? The answer to this question is yes—and no.

The Indian textile industry in the early nineteenth century provides a classic example of destructive trade. It was destroyed by competition from Britain, causing considerable suffering among local weavers (Rothermund, 1993). Contemporary writers within the "fair trade" tradition are convinced that there are many more such examples (for example, Suranovic, 1997). Clearly, the export from the United States and Europe of (often subsidized) agricultural products makes the development of a viable commercial agriculture in several Third World countries more difficult. That is the "yes" part of the answer.

But the issue is complicated. In an exhaustive review of evidence, Peter Lindert and Jeffrey Williamson (2001) show that, over two centuries, between-country inequality has risen. By the mid-1990s, the gap between rich and poor countries was greater than it had been at the beginning of the nineteenth century. Clearly, this rise coincides with a huge increase in economic integration at the international level. Is this evidence of the harmful effects on poor countries of globalization?

Not really. The long-term rise in inequality between countries originates in the improvement in

Crowded bridges crossing the Canada–US border reflect the enormous volume of trade between the two countries, a volume that increased after the FTA and NAFTA. But Canada depends more heavily on its trade with the United States than the United States depends on Canada. This is an important source of policy constraint. (Jason Kryk Photo)

average incomes in those countries that integrated into the world economy. Inequality rose as the European countries that created the modern world economy became rich after 1600. It increased further as countries like Japan, Taiwan, Singapore, Korea, Mexico, and Brazil opened up to the world economy and competed successfully. Japan's success in the 1980s in the export of automobiles and consumer electronics is a good example of this. Japan, Taiwan, and countries like them became richer than did the Third World countries that failed to integrate themselves into the global economy. At the same time, other poor-country economies remained closed. Where that was the case, their populations failed to get any richer. This pattern is reflected in Figure 16.3.

Trends in inequality within Third World countries that have opened themselves to the international market provide further evidence consistent with this interpretation. Inequality has risen within the so-called East Asian tigers as well as in China, Mexico, and Brazil. This is, in part, because regions that are more integrated into the world economy have become richer while the regions that have not been integrated remain as poor as they ever were. For example, in the southern coastal part of China, where export industries are located, incomes are rising. In the interior and the north, which remain largely unintegrated into the world economy, incomes have failed to rise. The Chiapas region in Mexico provides another interesting case. This region has experienced significant political unrest and persistent poverty. Not surprisingly, Chiapas is relatively excluded from the international economy, as compared to other parts of the country (Lynn, 2002).

For both the Third World and rich countries, then, the character of the economic effects of globalization seems broadly similar. Some workers (and their families) have been harmed by processes associated with globalization—for example, weavers in the nineteenth-century Indian textile industry, agricultural producers in Third World countries excluded from commercial markets by cheap food imports from rich countries, and many employees in the apparel industries of rich countries since the Second World War.

But it is difficult to discern harmful net and aggregate economic effects of globalization. On the contrary, international trade has been the main route to the relative prosperity of the richer countries in the world economy. Nor does the evidence yet suggest that trade and investment flows lead to a race to the bottom in social policy, in part because relatively generous social programs and other forms of government spending may often be a requisite for trade and investment, at least where higher-paid jobs are involved.

# Social Networks and the Movement of Populations

## *Global Cities and Global Networks*

Globalization disperses economic activity across countries. This creates a problem of co-ordination (Sassen, 1991, 1996, 2002). The international flow of goods and contracts and the financing of that flow require "a system for the provision of such inputs as planning, top-level management, and specialized business services" (Sassen, 1991: 29). These inputs are most efficiently co-ordinated within a small number of very large cities. New York, London, and Tokyo are at the top of the global hierarchy of cities providing

Figure 16.3 **Trade Policy and the Third World**

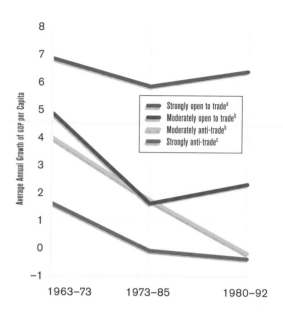

a [Strongly open] Hong Kong, South Korea, and Singapore.
b [Strongly anti-trade] 1963–73: Argentina, Bangladesh, Burundi, Chile, Dominican Republic, Ethiopia, Ghana, India, Pakistan, Peru, Sri Lanka, Sudan, Tanzania, Turkey, Uruguay, and Zambia. In the two later periods, Chile, Pakistan, Sri Lanka, and Turkey became more open, while Bolivia, Madagascar, and Nigeria joined the strongly anti-trade group.
c The composition of the intermediate groups can be found in the original World Bank source used by Lindert and Williamson.
Source: Adapted from Peter H. Lindert and Jeffrey G. Williamson, *Does Globalization Make the World More Unequal?* (Cambridge, MA: National Bureau of Economic Research, 2001).

this co-ordination. Toronto falls in the upper part of the hierarchy, with Montreal some way behind.

The development of **global cities** has created two sorts of network, each globally oriented. One is made up of the economic decision-makers in global cities—bankers, specialists in commercial insurance, international lawyers, brokers of various kinds, and so on. Because in their day-to-day work they deal with international issues, and because this implies they are part of international social networks, their political orientations also tend to be international. Their loyalties shift towards their international network and away from the nation-state in which they are located.

The second network is quite different. It is made up of those at the bottom of the hierarchy within global cities. In these cities, immigrants from Third World countries create an ethnic underclass. Several mechanisms are involved in this. Traditional ways of life have been disrupted by the spread to the Third World of commercial agriculture and resource extraction (mining and logging) to supply rich countries with coffee, sugar, lumber, bauxite, and so on. Direct foreign investment has created manufacturing jobs in Third World cities, further disrupting traditional ways of life. Manufacturing plants often disproportionately recruit young women. The geographic mobility entailed loosens the traditional ties of those women, making overseas migration more likely. Direct foreign investment in the Third World, then, creates a population pool detached from the social roots that would be likely to keep them in their countries of origin. These are the potential migrants.

Then there is the character of the demand for labour in the global city. Those who co-ordinate global economic flows have high incomes. They consume lots of personal services; "the increase in the numbers of expensive restaurants, luxury housing, luxury hotels, gourmet shops, boutiques, French hand laundries, and special cleaners that ornament the urban landscape illustrates this trend" (Sassen, 1991: 9). Many of these activities are both labour-intensive and poorly paid. They provide jobs that immigrants are willing, and that native labour is unwilling, to fill.

The immigrants filling these low-paid service-sector jobs are usually distinguished by skin colour, language, or both. They tend to be the objects of **discrimination**. Imperfectly integrated into the host society because of discrimination, immigrants retain their loyalties to family and former neighbours in their countries of origin. They, too, are part of larger transnational networks. Once immigrant communities get established in a global city, they facilitate the migration of others by providing information, cash, sponsorship (for example, through the family reunification component of Canadian immigration policy), contacts, or employment. The result of all this is immigrant communities substantially estranged from their host society but that remain part of, and contribute to, the nurturing of a dense pattern of social relations with their countries of origin.

In Sassen's account, these ties with the country of origin often provide economic opportunity to migrants. They can use the ties to develop more or less lucrative business relationships. They can involve themselves in the import and export of goods from their home countries. Relatives brought in to work in family businesses provide both cheap and reliable labour. Like the elites, the immigrants in global cities develop an extra-national orientation, but, obviously, for different reasons.

## Global Cities and Global Networks: Hypotheses and Evidence

According to Sassen, then, globalization challenges the nation-state. It does so by creating core groups at both the top and the bottom of the hierarchy, groups whose political orientation is shaped by international networks rather than country of residence.

There is a further effect that connects with the discussion earlier. In rich countries, the development of an elite that prospers through the co-ordination of global interchanges and of an underclass largely made up of immigrants increases inequality. The gap between the business elite and the ethnic underclass means that global cities are highly unequal. Since the global business elite earn very high salaries and the ethnic underclass very low ones, inequality tends to increase in the broader society.

As we have seen, the evidence on trends in earnings inequality is mixed (M. Smith, 1999). There have been increases in some societies, but not in all of them. The clearest increase took place in the United States, but even there the level of inequality stopped increasing after 1993 (Card and DiNardo, 2002).

Jeffrey Reitz (1998) has compared the effects of immigration on inequality within cities in three countries—the United States, Canada, and Australia. He shows that outcomes depend heavily on the particular institutional environment within which immigration takes place. Immigrants, in fact, do relatively (but not absolutely) worse in the United States. That is, their income difference with the native population is larger in the United States than it is in Canada and Australia. This is because stronger unions and higher minimum wages prop up immigrant earnings in these latter two countries.

Where the possible effects of immigration on the employment and earnings of the domestic working class are concerned, on balance, the evidence suggests a very small negative effect on the least skilled (e.g., Borjas, Freeman, and Katz, 1997).

This raises a further interesting question. How is it that such a large flow of mainly unskilled immigrants can have such a small effect on the wages and employment probabilities of native unskilled workers? Gregory DeFreitas (1998) proposes the following explanations. The arrival of immigrants increases not only the supply of labour, but also the demand for all sorts of goods being produced by non-immigrants. The proportion of the self-employed among immigrants is also high. Many create their own jobs. In addition, and related to the sort of argument made by Sassen, immigrants often occupy jobs that native labour avoids. Many of these jobs would remain unfilled for longer, or not be created at all, were immigrants unavailable to occupy them. Overall, the evidence tends to suggest smaller employment and wage effects of immigration than some of the writing inspired by Sassen would suggest.

Note also that, as compared to earlier periods of history in immigrant-receiving countries like Canada and the United States, immigrants are a fairly small percentage of the total population. In Canada in the decade before World War I, for example, immigrants made up almost 30 per cent of the population; the equivalent current figure is about 17 per cent (Badets and Chui, 1994: 9; Marr, 1992: 19). Canada experienced a larger immigrant "shock" at the beginning of the twentieth century than at the end of it.

As for the question of the location of loyalty within global cities, the political orientations of powerful city elites may shift from the national to the global. They may, for example, become preoccupied with the elimination of obstacles to international trade and investment flows. The sequence of liberalizing policies associated with the GATT and its successor, the WTO, as well as the creation of regional trade associations and agreements such as the EU and NAFTA, would be broadly consistent with this. But protectionist forces remain strong in all countries, including the United States. Because the small size of their domestic markets requires that they engage heavily in trade, much of the pressure to restrict discretionary protectionism originates in countries such as Canada and Australia, where the leading global cities are not located.

With respect to the political orientation of immigrants at the lower end of the income distribution, Portes (Portes, 1999; Portes, Guarnizo, and Landolt, 1999) has made the following observations. First, immigrant groups vary in the extent to which their members remain oriented to their country of origin. Second, they are more likely to do so where the group was formed by a political convulsion, leading to the simultaneous migration of large numbers of people (for example, Cubans in the United States);

where the group arrives with a culture that provides it with the skills and motivations to develop businesses with contacts to the homeland; where the group confronts fairly clear discrimination in the destination country; and where the government of the country of origin expends funds and effort to develop and maintain ties with expatriate communities.

Third, concerns with the "cultural integrity and solidarity of the receiving society" are probably exaggerated (Portes, 1999: 469). Foreign-born people make up only 17 per cent of the population in Canada and under 10 per cent in the United States. Even if their relationship to the host society is problematic, as an aggregate, immigrants are fragmented into their different ethnicities so that it is hard for them to avoid converging with the majority (host) culture to some degree. Finally, where the cultivation of transnational commercial activities enriches members of a particular immigrant group, it decreases the likelihood of the development of a hostile, adversarial culture within subsequent generations.

# Cultural Homogenization

## Causes of Cultural Convergence

While some writers have worried about the fragmentation of cultures within countries as a result of immigration, others have worried that a process of standardization has been underway *across* countries. Two different mechanisms might produce this outcome. Many societies are exposed to general processes that might lead to the development of shared **beliefs** and behaviours. Or the United States may be a particular, overwhelming source of standardizing cultural practices. What processes might be producing standardization across countries?

First, **capitalism** itself has standardizing effects. It implies common economic and social structures—property ownership, a labour force with varying skills, banks and stockbrokers that mobilize and transfer capital, and so on (Holton, 1998; see also Bromley, 1999).

Second, countries have imposed cultural practices on other countries. When they decolonized, France and Britain bequeathed boundaries, education systems, civil services, and government institutions to a range of countries in Africa and the Middle East. Modern Japanese institutions bear the heavy stamp of practices imposed by the United States after the Second World War.

**16.4**

When forced to encounter them, people have to make sense of each other's cultures. Across regions and countries, those cultures often seem strikingly different. Making sense of culture will always require simplification. Whatever English Canadian culture might be, it is almost certainly somewhat different in Newfoundland and in Alberta. Within Newfoundland, custom and practice are likely to vary from an upper-middle-class district of St John's to, say, Corner Brook, or Fogo. Each level of aggregation requires a greater degree of simplification.

Simplification is always likely to create misleading impressions. These misleading impressions may or may not be pernicious. But they are particularly likely to be pernicious where there is a large power asymmetry between two cultures. This is the starting point for Edward Said's much-celebrated *Orientalism* (1978). There is a long history of European attempts to apprehend the Middle East–the "Orient" upon which Said focuses. That attempt has involved a combination of academic enquiry into, and casual observation of, the languages, customs, and politics of the region. The interpretations generated in this way, in turn, have shaped Western government policies.

Nineteenth-century philological researchers concluded that European languages originated in Semitic languages of the Middle East. But whereas European languages had continued to evolve, the Semitic languages remained in a state of "arrested development" (Said, 1978:

145). Said's point is that this presumption of European superiority pervades subsequent Orientalist writing. For example, he makes much of distinctly crass and vulgar comments on Arab women by the otherwise distinguished French novelist Gustave Flaubert, which rested on casual observations made during his travels in the Orient.

Said's general thrust, it should be clear, is to demonstrate that the Orientalist intellectual tradition established for Western statesmen the inferiority of the Arab world relative to the West. It provided a legitimation for forceful interventions by European powers in the Middle East. Thus, there was a "theme of Europe teaching the Orient the meaning of liberty" (Said, 1978: 172). Interventions in the Middle East using force could be justified as part and parcel of the "White man's burden," to use Rudyard Kipling's nineteenth-century expression.

While the bulk of Said's book deals with the construction of the idea of the Orient in France and Britain, in the last part of it he argues that the same condescending tradition informs post–World War II US policy in the region. The general point here is that the attempt to diffuse cultures has sometimes involved brute force–armies dispatched, monarchies toppled, and systems of education and government inspired by Western European or American ideas imposed on local populations, whether they wanted them or not.

Third, increasing living standards—wherever they occur—shift popular preoccupations. The populations in Western countries have sufficiently high income that most people do not have to worry about the prospects of malnutrition, starvation, or homelessness. The quality of life therefore becomes more salient. People worry about personal development, cultural enrichment, and consumption more generally. Moreover, the development and spread of **education** and **mass media** increase average political skills

within the population. A better-informed populace is better able to hold political leaders accountable. Consequently, these shifts in preoccupations get translated into policies consistent with the changed preferences. This has happened (with lags) across rich industrial countries (Inglehart, 1977, 1990a).

Fourth, a large volume of more specialized communication between nations—publications, conferences, diplomatic transactions—concerns a range of broader political issues. Since no single power centre, no world government, controls those communications, multiple models get introduced into political debate. For John Meyer (for example, Meyer, 2000), this has allowed many non-governmental organizations (NGOs) to insert themselves into political debate and develop alternative policy models that sometimes change government policy. Examples of this are the emergence to policy salience at the international level of human rights and environmental concerns, producing more or less binding international agreements (the Kyoto Accord), coercive political measures (NATO's bombing of the former Yugoslavia), and shared policy priorities (a commitment to create the education system required by a "knowledge society"). These are a source of social, economic, and political convergence.

Fifth, the policies of many governments in the 1980s shifted to the right, Patricia Marchak (1991) argues, in response to the concerted urging of a set of think-tanks located in several countries, but with links among them. The Cato Institute in the United States, the Kiel Institute in West Germany, the Mont Pélérin Society in Geneva, the Institute for Economic Affairs in Britain, and the Fraser Institute in Canada celebrat-

ed and advocated free-market solutions to problems, or what they saw as problems. They continue to do so. This common, well-financed network, Marchak claims, generated policy convergence across countries. There was **privatization** (in Canada, for example, the CN railroad network was privatized). There was deregulation, in particular of financial markets. And by the 1990s, many countries had scaled down the magnitude of government expenditures, or were trying to.

Alternatively, increasing similarities across countries may reflect US hegemony. There is a rising volume of communication between countries using the Internet (Holton, 1998). A disproportionate share of it is in English. This increases the value of the language and the exposure to ideas and preferences originating in English-language media. But while the English language is the primary medium of communication in several societies (including Canada), the sheer volume of communication originating in the United States arguably swamps all other sources. Table 16.1, which summarizes shares of cultural imports into Canada by country or region of origin, documents the relative dominance of the United States.

### Table 16.1 **Shares of Cultural Imports[a] into Canada, 1996–2000**

| | Share (%)[b] | | | | | % Change 1996 to 2000 |
|---|---|---|---|---|---|---|
| | **1996** | **1997** | **1998** | **1999** | **2000** | |
| *North America* | | | | | | |
| United States | 85.5 | 85.5 | 84.2 | 83.4 | 82.2 | −3.9 |
| Other | 0.2 | 0.3 | 0.4 | 0.4 | 0.6 | 200.0 |
| Total North America | 85.7 | 85.8 | 84.6 | 83.8 | 82.8 | −3.4 |
| *Western Europe* | | | | | | |
| United Kingdom | 3.0 | 3.3 | 3.5 | 3.3 | 3.6 | 20.0 |
| France | 3.3 | 3.3 | 3.6 | 3.6 | 3.6 | 9.1 |
| Germany | 0.8 | 0.6 | 0.8 | 0.8 | 0.8 | 0.0 |
| Other | 2.5 | 1.9 | 2.0 | 2.2 | 1.9 | −24.0 |
| Total Western Europe | 9.6 | 9.1 | 9.9 | 9.9 | 9.9 | 3.0 |
| *Asia* | 4.1 | 4.5 | 4.8 | 5.5 | 6.4 | 56.1 |
| *Other Regions[c]* | 0.6 | 0.7 | 0.7 | 0.8 | 0.9 | 50.0 |
| **Total** | **100.0** | **100.0** | **100.0** | **100.0** | **100.0** | |

[a] "Cultural industries" are defined as books and printing services, newspapers and periodicals, other written materials, music and other recordings, printed music, visual arts, architectural plans, other pictorial material, advertising material, and exposed film.

[b] Columns may not add up to 100 because of rounding.

[c] "Other regions" include European countries not listed above, Middle East, Africa, Central and South America, and the Antilles.

SOURCE: Adapted from Cindy Carter and Michel Durand, "Market Opportunities: International Trade of Culture Goods and Services," Statistics Canada, Catalogue 87-004, *Forum on Culture*, 12 (2000): 7.

Businesses and consecutive US administrations have deliberately attempted to break down regulatory obstacles to US cultural products. Jack Valenti, for one, president of the Motion Picture Association, a US lobby group, is an indefatigable crusader for the removal of barriers to the entry of US-produced films (McCarthy, 2002). From Henry Ford to McDonald's, the success of the mass marketing of US companies has transformed the tastes and behaviour of consumers and the menu of business models from which investors can draw (Fantasia, 1995; Ritzer, 2000). Some part of whatever cultural convergence may be taking place is likely to reflect the sheer pervasiveness of the United States and its institutions.

Still, there is no consensus that cultural convergence is taking place, let alone on the origins of that convergence, whether in processes common across countries or in US cultural hegemony.

### Trying to Make a Judgement

The following things can reasonably be said. Ronald Inglehart (1990a) has assembled a significant body of longitudinal data from surveys conducted in rich countries. These data suggest some shift to a wider preoccupation with quality-of-life issues, evidence of cultural convergence in rich countries. However, nationalist sentiments in a number of countries and regions have grown—in Quebec, in the Basque region in Spain, in Scotland within the United Kingdom, and, tragically, in a virulent form in the Balkans. Nationalism can be viewed as a forcible assertion of distinctness (Anderson, 1983). It suggests exactly the opposite of cultural convergence. So, for that matter, does the flow of migrants into global cities, where those migrants retain strong connections not only within their migrant communities but also with their countries of origin. Moreover, since many of those migrants are flowing into the United States and shaping US culture, it seems implausible to argue that cultural diffusion is a one-way street.

The case for cultural convergence or for US cultural hegemony is not overwhelming. However, in a thoughtful article on this, Christoph Brumann says that it strikes him "how much the general debate relies on ad hoc impressions instead of more systematic empirical observation" (1998: 498), but that "pending further empirical support, I still think that a slow *decrease* in the total number of distinct cultural elements or traits . . . paralleling a rampant *increase* of the possible as well as the actual *combinations* of these elements is the best working hypothesis about

current world cultural developments" (499).

What Brumann means by this is that modern communications diffuse cultural traits (a process called **cultural diffusion**) between countries (hence the "*combinations*") but that the number of traits tends to decline as the diffused traits replace or modify others in the recipient countries. Popular music in many countries, for example, absorbs musical characteristics from other countries, creating new combinations that appear across those countries. But some of the original national musical forms disappear as these combinations replace them. This is well illustrated by the conservation work of several late nineteenth- and early twentieth-century European composers. Leos Janácek and Zoltán Kodály in Czechoslovakia, Béla Bartók in Hungary, and Gustav Holst and Ralph Vaughan Williams in England all travelled to the countryside of their respective countries to discover and record examples of folk musical forms. They feared the loss of their national musical traditions because of the cultural dominance of Germany, Italy, and France (Schonberg, 1997). Even in France, which has resisted US cultural influences with some vigour, American cinema, cuisine, language, and management practices now exist alongside what might be regarded as "authentic" French forms (Gordon and Meunier, 2001). In some cases, the US forms likely replace, as well as exist alongside, French forms. Or it is possible that existing forms are displaced by new, Franco-American ones. This conclusion about cultural diffusion seems plausible. But the evidence will not support a claim that goes beyond plausibility.

## Conclusion

Different groups of humans have been bumping into each other throughout human history. Thirty thousand years ago, Neanderthals were driven to extinction through contact and competition with the earliest form of modern humans, the Cro-Magnons (Balter, 2001). Two thousand years ago, the Roman Empire was influencing lives from Western Europe to the Middle East (Gibbon, [1776–88] 1994). Five hundred years ago, a set of European explorers (Magellan, Columbus, Champlain, and others) pushed farther the limits of Western influence (Fernández Armesto, 1995). One hundred years ago, the European empires were attempting to regulate—and were certainly disrupting—lives in areas of conquest spanning the globe (Samson, 2001). The time in-between those events was filled with contact and disruption, often involving amounts of taken-for-granted brutality that challenge modern sensibilities. All this is to say that the facts of contact, constraint, and disruption do not in themselves make distinct what we call contemporary globalization.

What is clearly distinctive about modern relations between individuals and organizations in different countries is the speed and capacity of communication. "Hot money" flows are usually seen as the clearest expression of this (but see Smith, 2001a). More important, though, is the fact that modern communications have enhanced the degree to which control can be effectively exercised over large distances and have made it possible to run a multinational corporation, in which a single organization can co-ordinate production and marketing in different countries. This seems not to imply homogeneity of social and economic policies across countries, but there are strong reasons to believe that the multinational corporation

is an effective vehicle for diffusing both business practices and tastes. One need not endorse Bové's actions to recognize that the McDonald's Corporation has changed consumer preferences in a wide range of countries and that in doing so it is forcing indigenous competitors in those countries to change their way of doing business.

Still, it remains clear that the idea of a global society is a chimera, an illusion. It certainly does not yet exist, and there is no prospect of it in the medium term. The range of social and economic forms remains huge, the WTO and the IMF notwithstanding. What we do confront, as in the past, is a set of international influences and options that constitute both constraints and possibilities. An intelligent reaction to the processes associated with globalization involves discussion of which responses to those constraints are most sensible and which options should be embraced.

## ☐ Questions for Critical Thought

1. Four components of globalization have been identified: political arrangements, economic processes, the mobility of populations, and cultural diffusion. Do they all have to move in the same directions? For example, is it possible to have common practices created by treaties and liberalized trade while populations are prevented from moving and cultures are protected against processes of diffusion from elsewhere?

2. Would Third World countries be better off without the IMF and the World Bank?

3. Is it sensible to expect investors to always prefer lower taxes? If not, for what purposes are they likely to favour taxes, and for what purposes are they likely to oppose them?

4. Sassen argues that the development of global cities changes the political context in the countries in which the cities are located. Assuming her analysis is correct, do you judge the implications of this to be good, bad, or neutral? For whom?

5. Over the post-war period, treaties and the international organizations those treaties have created (such as the WTO) have been designed to limit the capacity of governments to use law (through tariffs and quotas) and taxpayers' money (through subsidies) to protect their domestic industries from international competition. Suppose those treaties and international organizations did not exist. Who would gain and who would lose?

6. The Third World is filled with desperately poor people who work at very low wages. In a context of free trade, how is it possible for rich-country employees to keep their jobs?

7. How do the processes associated with globalization affect labour markets and social policy in rich countries?

8. Does Hollywood matter? If so, how?

## □ Recommended Readings

**Thomas J. Courchene, ed.,** *Room to Manoeuvre? Globalization and Policy Convergence* **(Montreal and Kingston: McGill-Queen's University Press, 1999).**

> This is an excellent collection of essays dealing with the implications for Canada of trade agreements and technology, including suggestions by William Watson that the claims about globalization are overstated.

**Mauro Guillén, "Is Globalization Civilizing, Destructive or Feeble? A Critique of Five Key Debates in the Social Science Literature,"** *Annual Review of Sociology* **27 (2001): 235–60.**

> This is a quite even-handed treatment of the issue by a sociologist who allows that the process may be thought of as going back "to the dawn of history."

**Robert J. Holton,** *Globalization and the Nation-State* **(New York: St Martin's, 1998).**

> This excellent, balanced treatment of globalization contains a useful analysis of the process of cultural diffusion.

**Saskia Sassen,** *The Global City* **(Princeton, NJ: Princeton University Press, 1991).**

> Sassen is the main source on the social and political consequences of international migration. She attributes large political and economic effects to it.

## □ Recommended Web Sites

**Fair Trade Watch**

**www.fairtradewatch.org**

> This Web site maintained by the United Steel Workers of America provides useful, though unsympathetic, information on the WTO and other international organizations and agreements. It can also be used as a glossary for trade jargon.

**World Bank**

**www.worldbank.org**

> The World Bank is as unpopular with anti-globalization protestors as the IMF, and its Web site provides some evidence of its concern with its image.

**World Trade Organization (WTO)**

**www.wto.org**

> The WTO provides both a forum for the negotiation of liberalized trade and investment and a quasi-judicial apparatus issuing judgements on complaints about infractions of trade laws. This Web site is an extremely useful source on what the WTO actually does.

# References

Abella, Rosalie. 1984. *Equality in Employment: A Royal Commission Report*. Ottawa: Commission on Equality in Employment.

Abu-Lughod, Janet L. 1991. *Changing Cities: Urban Sociology*. New York: HarperCollins.

Acker, Joan. 1980. "Women and Stratification: A Review of Recent Literature." *Contemporary Sociology*, 9: 25–34.

———. 1988. "Class, Gender, and the Relations of Distribution." *Signs*, 13: 473–97.

———. 1990. "Hierarchies, Jobs, and Bodies: A Theory of Gendered Organizations." *Gender and Society*, 4: 139–58.

———. 2000. "Rewriting Class, Race, and Gender: Problems in Feminist Rethinking." In *Revisioning Gender*, edited by Myra MarFerree, Judith Lorber, and Beth Hess, 44–69. New York: AltaMira.

Acker, Sandra. 1999. *The Realities of Teachers' Work: Never a Dull Moment*. London: Cassell.

Adams, Tracey L. 1998. "Combining Gender, Class, and Race: Structuring Relations in the Ontario Dental Profession." *Gender and Society*, 12: 578–97.

———. 2000. *A Dentist and a Gentleman: Gender and the Rise of Dentistry in Ontario*. Toronto: University of Toronto Press.

Adams, Robert M. 1966. *The Evolution of Urban Society*. Chicago: Aldine.

Adler, Patricia A., and Peter Adler. 1995. "Dynamics of Inclusion and Exclusion in Preadolescent Cliques." *Social Psychology Quarterly*, 58, no. 3: 145–62.

Agnew, Robert. 1985. "A Revised Strain Theory of Delinquency." *Social Forces*, 64, no. 1: 151–67.

Agnew, Robert, and Lisa Broidy. 1997. "Gender and Crime: A General Strain Theory Perspective." *Journal of Research in Crime and Delinquency*, 34: 275–306.

Ahlburg, Dennis A. 1998. "Julian Simon and the Population Growth Debate." *Population and Development Review*, 24: 317–27.

Albas, Dan, and Cheryl Albas. 1993. "Disclaimer Mannerisms of Students: How to Avoid Being Labelled as Cheaters." *Canadian Review of Sociology and Anthropology*, 30: 451–67.

Albury, Rebecca M. 1999. *The Politics of Reproduction*. Sydney, Australia: Allen and Unwin.

Ali, Jennifer, and Edward Grabb. 1998. "Ethnic Origin, Class Origin and Educational Attainment in Canada: Further Evidence on the Mosaic Thesis." *Journal of Canadian Studies*, 33: 3–21.

Alia, Valerie. 1999. *Un/Covering the North: News, Media, and Aboriginal People*. Vancouver: University of British Columbia Press.

Allcorn, Seth. 1997. "Parallel Virtual Organizations: Managing and Working in the Virtual Workplace." *Administration and Society*, 29: 412–39.

Allen, Judith. 1990. "Do We Need a Theory of the State?" In *Playing the State: Australian Feminist Interventions*, edited by Sophie Watson, 21–37. London: Verso.

Altheide, David. 1997. "The New Media, the Problem Frame and the Production of Fear." *Sociological Quarterly*, 38: 645–66.

———. 2002. *Creating Fear: News and the Construction of Crisis*. New York: Aldine de Gruyter.

Altman, Dennis. 1986. *AIDS in the Mind of America*. New York: Doubleday-Anchor.

Alvarez, Rodolfo. 2000. "The Social Problem as an Enterprise: Values as a Defining Factor." *Social Problems*, 48: 3–10.

Alwin, Duane F. 1984. "Trends in Parental Socialization, Detroit, 1958–1983." *American Journal of Sociology*, 90: 359–82.

———. 1990. "Historical Changes in Parental Orientations to Children." In *Sociological Studies of Child Development*, vol. 3, edited by Patricia Adler and Peter Adler, 65–86. Greenwich, Conn.: JAI Press.

Amato, P.R., and S.J. Rezac. 1994. "Contact with Nonresident Parents, Interparental Conflict, and Children's Behavior." *Journal of Family Issues*, 15: 191–207.

Anderson, Benedict. 1983. *Imagined Communities: Reflections on the Origin and Spread of Nationalism*. London: Verso.

Anderson, R.A., et al. 1999. "7a-Merhyl-19-Notestosterone (MENT) Maintains Sexual Behavior and More in Hypogonad Men." *Journal of Clinical Endocrinology and Metabolism*, 78: 711–16.

Andres Bellamy, Lesley. 1993. "Life Trajectories, Action, and Negotiating the Transition from High School." In *Transitions: Schooling and Employment in Canada*, edited by Paul Anisef and Paul Axelrod, 136–57. Toronto: Thompson Educational.

Andrews, David M. 1994. "Capital Mobility and State Autonomy: Toward a Structural Theory of International Monetary Relations." *International Studies Quarterly*, 38: 193–218.

Anisef, Paul, Paul Axelrod, Etta Baichman-Anisef, Carl James, and Anton Turritin. 2000. *Opportunity and Uncertainty: Life Course Experiences of the Class of '73*. Toronto: University of Toronto Press.

Anstey, Roger. 1966. *King Leopold's Legacy: The Congo Under Belgian Rule, 1908–1960*. London: Oxford University Press.

Apple, Michael W. 1997. "What Postmodernists Forget: Cultural Capital and Official Knowledge." In *Education: Culture, Economy, and Society*, edited by A.H. Halsey, Hugh Lauder, Phillip Brown, and Amy Stuart Wells, 595–604. New York: Oxford University Press.

Appleton, Lynn M. 1995. "Rethinking Medicalization: Alcoholism and Anomalies." In *Images of Issues: Typifying Contemporary Social Problems*, 2nd edn, edited by Joel Best, 59–80. New York: Aldine de Gruyter.

Arat-Koc, Sedef. 1990. "Importing Housewives: Non-citizen Domestic Workers and the Crisis of the Domestic Sphere in Canada." In *Through the Kitchen Window: The Politics of Home and Family*, 2nd edn, edited by Meg Luxton, Harriet Rosenberg, and Sedef Arat-Koc, 81–103. Toronto: Garamond.

Archibald, W. Peter. 1976. "Face-to-Face: The Alienating Effects of Class, Status and Power Divisions." *American Sociological Review*, 41: 819–37.

———. 1978. *Social Psychology as Political Economy.* Toronto: McGraw-Hill Ryerson.

Armstrong, Pat. 1991. "Understanding the Numbers: Women in the Film and Television Industry." In *Toronto Women in Film and Television, Changing Focus: The Future for Women in the Canadian Film and Television Industry*, 3–38. Toronto: Toronto Women in Film and Television.

Armstrong, Pat, Carol Amaratunga, Jocelyne Bernier, Karen Grant, Ann Pederson, and Kay Willson, eds. 2001. *Exposing Privatization: Women and Health Reform in Canada.* Aurora, Ont.: Garamond.

Armstrong, Pat, and Hugh Armstrong. 1983a. "Beyond Sexless Class and Classless Sex." *Studies in Political Economy*, 10, Winter: 7–43.

———. 1983b. *A Working Majority: What Women Must Do for Pay.* Ottawa: Canadian Advisory Council on the Status of Women.

———. 1993. *The Double Ghetto: Canadian Women and Their Segregated Work.* Toronto: McClelland & Stewart.

———. 2000. "Equal Pay for Work of Equal Value". Report prepared for the Public Service Alliance of Canada, in *Canadian Postal Workers vs Canada Post*, Ottawa: Canadian Human Rights Commission.

Aronson, Hal. 1993. "Becoming an Environmental Activist: The Process of Transformation from Everyday Life into Making History in the Hazardous Waste Movement." *Journal of Political and Military Sociology*, 1: 63–80.

Arthurs, Harry. 1999. "Constitutionalizing Neo-conservatism and Regional Economic Integration." In *Room to Manoeuvre? Globalization and Policy Convergence*, edited by Thomas J. Courchene, 17–74. Montreal: McGill-Queen's University Press.

Atkinson, Anthony B. 2000. *Increased Income Inequality in OECD Countries and the Redistributive Impact of the Government Budget.* Helsinki: World Institute for Development Economics Research, United Nations University.

Attalah, Paul, and Leslie Regan Shade, eds. 2002. *Mediascapes: New Patterns in Canadian Communication.* Toronto: Nelson.

Atwood, Margaret. [1968] 1994. *The Edible Woman.* Toronto: McClelland & Stewart.

Axelrod, Paul. 1997. *The Promise of Schooling: Education in Canada, 1800–1914.* Toronto: University of Toronto Press.

Aya, Rod. 1990. *Rethinking Revolutions and Collective Violence: Studies on Concept, Theory, and Method.* Amsterdam: Het Spinhuis.

Babbie, Earl R. 1988. *The Sociological Spirit: Critical Essays in a Critical Science.* Belmont, Calif.: Wadsworth.

Badets, Jane, and Tina W.L. Chui. 1994. *Canada's Changing Immigrant Population.* Ottawa: Statistics Canada.

Baer, Doug. 1999. "Educational Credentials and the Changing Occupational Structure." In *Social Inequality in Canada: Patterns, Problems, and Policies*, edited by James E. Curtis, Edward G. Grabb, and Neil L. Guppy, 92–106. Scarborough, Ont.: Prentice-Hall Allyn and Bacon.

Bafoil, François. 1998. "Weber critique de Marx: Elements d'une interpretation de la crise des systèmes bureaucratiques communistes." *L'Année sociologique*, 48: 385–415.

Bagdikian, Ben. 1997. *The Media Monopoly*, 5th edn. Boston: Beacon.

Baines, Carol T., Patricia M. Evans, and Sheila Neysmith, eds. 1998. *Women's Caring: Feminist Perspectives on Social Welfare*, 2nd edn. Toronto: Oxford University Press.

Baird, P. 1997. "Individual Interests, Societal Interests, and Reproductive Technologies." *Perspectives in Biology and Medicine*, 40: 440–52.

Bakan, Abigail, and Daiva K. Stasiulis. 1994. "Foreign Domestic Worker Policy in Canada and the Social Boundaries of Modern Citizenship." *Science and Society*, 58, no. 1: 7–33.

———. 1997. *Not One of the Family: Foreign Domestic Workers in Canada.* Toronto: University of Toronto Press.

Baker, Maureen. 1995. *Canadian Family Policies: Cross-national Comparisons.* Toronto: University of Toronto Press.

———. 2001a. *Families, Labour and Love: Family Diversity in a Changing World.* Vancouver: University of British Columbia Press.

———. 2001b. "Paid and Unpaid Work: How Do Families Divide Their Labour?" In *Families: Changing Trends in Canada*, 4th edn, edited by Maureen Baker, 96–115. Toronto: McGraw-Hill Ryerson.

Baker, Maureen, and David Tippin. 1999. *Poverty, Social Assistance and the Employability of Mothers: Restructuring Welfare States.* Toronto: University of Toronto Press.

Bales, Robert F. 1950. *Interaction Process Analysis: A Method for the Study of Small Groups.* Chicago: University of Chicago Press.

Balter, Michael. 2001. "What—or Who—Did in the Neanderthals?" *Science*, 293: 1980–1.

Bancroft, John. 2002. "Biological Factors in Human Sexuality." *Journal of Sex Research*, 39: 15–21

Bandura, Albert. 1973. *Aggression: A Social Learning Analysis.* Englewood Cliffs, NJ: Prentice-Hall.

Barnes, Barry. 1988. *The Nature of Power.* Cambridge, UK: Polity.

Barry, Brian. [1970] 1978. *Sociologists, Economists and Democracy.* Chicago: University of Chicago Press.

Barth, Fredrik, ed. 1969. *Ethnic Groups and Boundaries: The Social Organization of Culture Difference.* Boston: Little, Brown.

Bartsch, Robert, Theresa Burnett, Tommye Diller, and Elizabeth Rankin-Williams. 2000. "Gender Representation in Television Commercials: Updating an Update." *Sex Roles*, 43: 735–43.

Bashevkin, Sylvia. 1985. *Toeing the Lines: Women and Party Politics in English Canada.* Toronto: University of Toronto Press.

Bassett, Isabella. 1985. *The Bassett Report.* Toronto: Collins.

Baumrind, Diana. 1971. "Current Patterns of Parental Authority." *Developmental Psychology Monographs*, 4: 1–107.

Bayley, David. 1994. "International Differences in Community Policing." In *The Challenge of Community Policing*, edited by D.P. Rosenbaum, 278–84. Thousand Oaks, Calif.: Sage.

Beaujot, Roderic. 2000. *Earning and Caring in Canadian Families.* Peterborough, Ont.: Broadview.

Beck, Ulrich. 1996. "World Risk Society as Cosmopolitan Society? Ecological Questions in a Framework of Manufactured Uncertainties." *Theory, Culture, and Society*, 13, no. 4: 1–32.

Becker, Howard. 1952. "Social Class Variations in the Teacher–Student Relationship." *Journal of Educational Sociology*, 25: 451–65.

———. 1963. *Outsiders: Studies in the Sociology of Deviance*. New York: Free Press.

———. 1982. *Art Worlds*. Berkeley: University of California Press.

Beck-Gernsheim, Elisabeth. 2002. *Reinventing the Family: In Search of New Lifestyles*. Cambridge: Polity.

Beiser, Morton, Feng Hou, Ilian Hyman, and Michel Tousignant. 1999. "Immigrant Mental Health." Human Resources Development Canada, *Applied Research Bulletin*, Fall: 20–2.

Belknap, Joanne. 1996. *The Invisible Woman: Gender, Crime and Justice*. Belmont, Calif.: Wadsworth.

Bell, Daniel. 1973. *The Coming of Post-industrial Society*. New York: Basic Books.

———. 1975. "Ethnicity and Social Change." In *Ethnicity: Theory and Experience*, edited by Nathan Glazer and Daniel P. Moynihan with Corinne Saposs Schelling, 141–74. Cambridge, Mass.: Harvard University Press.

Belsky, Jay. 1985. "Exploring Individual Differences in Marital Change Across the Transition to Parenthood: The Role of Violated Expectations." *Journal of Marriage and the Family*, 47: 1037–44.

Benford, Robert D., and David A. Snow. 2000. "Framing Processes and Social Movements: An Overview and Assessment." *Annual Review of Sociology*, 26: 611–39.

Benson, Rodney. 2005. "American Journalism and the Politics of Diversity." *Media, Culture & Society*, 27: 5–20.

Berger, Carl. 1966. "The True North Strong and Free." In *Nationalism in Canada*, edited by Peter Russell, 3–26. Toronto: McGraw-Hill Ryerson.

Berger, Peter, and Brigitte Berger. 1975. *Sociology: A Biographical Approach*. 2nd edn. New York: Basic Books.

Berger, Peter, and Thomas Luckmann. 1966. *The Social Construction of Reality: Treatise in the Sociology of Knowledge*. Garden City, NY: Anchor.

Bernard, Andrew B., and J. Bradford Jensen. 2000. "Understanding Increasing and Decreasing Wage Inequality." In *The Impact of International Trade on Wages*, edited by Robert C. Feenstra, 227–61. Chicago: University of Chicago Press.

Bernstein, Basil. 1977. "Class and Pedagogies: Visible and Invisible." In *Power and Ideology in Education*, edited by Jerome Karabel and A.H. Halsey, 511–34. New York: Oxford University Press.

Berry, John W., Rudolf Kalin, and Donald M. Taylor. 1977. *Multiculturalism and Ethnic Attitudes in Canada*. Ottawa: Minister of Supply and Services.

Berton, Pierre. 1975. *Hollywood's Canada: The Americanization of Our National Image*. Toronto: McClelland & Stewart.

Best, Joel. 1999. *Random Violence: How We Talk About New Crime and New Victims*. Berkeley: University of California Press.

———. 2001. *Damned Lies and Statistics: Untangling Numbers from Media, Politicians and Activists*. Berkeley: University of California Press.

Biagi, Shirley, and Craig McKie. 2001. *Media Impact: An Introduction to Mass Media*. Toronto: Nelson.

Bibby, Reginald. 2001. *Canada's Teens: Today, Yesterday and Tomorrow*. Toronto: Stoddart.

Bielby, William, and James Baron. 1984. "Men and Women at Work: Sex Segregation and Statistical Discrimination." *American Journal of Sociology*, 91: 759–99.

Bies, Robert J., and Thomas M. Tripp. 1996. "Beyond Distrust: 'Getting Even' and the Need for Revenge." In *Trust in Organizations: Frontiers of Theory and Research*, edited by Roderick M. Kramer and Tom R. Tyler, 246–60. Thousand Oaks, Calif.: Sage.

Birg, Herwig. 1995. *World Population Projections for the 21st Century: Theoretical Interpretations and Quantitative Simulations*. Frankfurt: Campus Verlag; New York: St Martin's.

Birke, Lynda. 1999. *Biology, Bodies and Feminism*. Edinburgh: Edinburgh University Press.

Bittman, Michael, and Jocelyn Pixley. 1997. *The Double Life of the Family: Myth, Hope and Experience*. Sydney, Australia: Allen & Unwin.

Blackledge, David, and Barry Hunt. 1985. *Sociological Interpretations of Education*. London: Routledge.

Blackwell, Judith C. 1992. "Mental Illness." In *Deviance: Conformity and Control in Canadian Society*, edited by Vincent F. Sacco, 172–202. Scarborough, Ont.: Prentice-Hall.

Blau, Peter M. 1963. *The Dynamics of Bureaucracy*. Chicago: University of Chicago Press.

Bliss, Michael. 1991. *Plague: A Story of Smallpox in Montreal*. Toronto: HarperCollins.

———. 1992. *Banting: A Biography*. 2nd edn. Toronto: University of Toronto Press.

Block, Fred. 1980. "Beyond Relative Autonomy: State Managers as Historical Subjects." In *The Socialist Register, 1980*, edited by Ralph Miliband and John Saville, 227–40. London: Merlin.

Bloemraad, Irene. 2002. "The North American Naturalization Gap: An Institutional Approach to Citizenship Acquisition in the United States and Canada." *International Migration Review*, 36: 193–228.

Blumer, Herbert. 1937. "Social Psychology." In *Man and Society: A Substantive Introduction to the Social Sciences*, edited by E.P. Schmidt, 148–98. New York: Prentice-Hall.

———. 1969. *Symbolic Interactionism: Perspective and Method*. Englewood Cliffs, NJ: Prentice-Hall.

Blustain, Sarah. 2000. "The New Gender Wars." *Psychology Today*, Nov./Dec.: 43–8.

Bohm, Robert M. 1997. *A Primer on Crime and Delinquency*. Belmont, CA: Wadsworth.

Bonacich, Edna. 1972. "A Theory of Ethnic Antagonism: The Split Labor Market." *American Sociological Review*, 37: 547–59.

Bongaarts, John, and Rodolfo Bulatao, eds. 2000. *Beyond Six Billion: Forecasting the World's Population*. Washington, DC: National Academy Press.

Bookchin, Murray. 1989. *Remaking Society*. Montreal: Black Rose.

Booth, Alan, and John N. Edwards. 1990. "Transmission of Marital and Family Quality over the Generations: The Effect of Parental Divorce and Unhappiness." *Journal of Divorce*, 13: 41–58.

Boritch, Helen. 1997. *Fallen Women: Women, Crime and Criminal Justice in Canada*. Toronto: Nelson.

Borjas, George J., Richard B. Freeman, and Lawrence F. Katz. 1997. "How Much Do Immigration and Trade Affect Labor Market Outcomes?" *Brookings Papers on Economic Activity*, 1: 1–67.

Boserup, Ester. 1965. *The Conditions of Agricultural Growth: The Economics of Agrarian Change Under Population Pressure*. Chicago: Aldine.

———. 1981. *Population and Technological Change: A Study of Long-Term Trends*. Chicago: University of Chicago Press.

Boston Women's Health Collective. 1971. *Our Bodies, Our Selves*. Toronto: New Hogtown Press.

Bottomore, Tom. 1979. *Political Sociology*. London: Hutchinson University Press.

Bouchard, Brigitte, and John Zhao. 2000. "University Education: Recent Trends in Participation, Accessibility and Returns." *Education Quarterly Review*, 6, no. 4: 24–32.

Bourdieu, Pierre. 1997. "The Forms of Capital." Translated by Richard Nice. In *Education: Culture, Economy, and Society*, edited by A.H. Halsey, Hugh Lauder, Phillip Brown, and Amy Stuart Wells, 46–58. Oxford: Oxford University Press.

Bourdieu, Pierre, and Jean-Claude Passeron. 1979. *The Inheritors: French Students and Their Relations to Culture*. Translated by Richard Nice. Chicago: University of Chicago Press.

Bourne, Paul, Liza McCoy, and Myra Novogrodsky, eds. 1997. "Gender and Schooling." *Orbit*, 28, no. 1: special issue.

Bowlby, Jeffrey, and Kathryn McMullen. 2002. *At a Crossroads: First Results for the 18- to 20-Year-Old Cohort of the Youth in Transition Survey*. Ottawa: Human Resources Development Canada.

Bowles, Samuel, and Herbert Gintis. 1976. *Schooling in Capitalist America: Education Reform and the Contradictions of Economic Life*. New York: Basic Books.

Boyd, Monica. 1992. "Gender, Visible Minority, and Immigrant Earnings Inequality: Reassessing an Employment Equity Premise." In *Deconstructing a Nation: Immigration, Multiculturalism, and Racism in '90s Canada*, edited by Vic Satzewich, 279–321. Halifax, NS: Fernwood.

———. 1999. "Integrating Gender, Language and Visible Minority Groups." In *Immigrant Canada: Demographic, Economic and Social Challenges*, edited by Shiva S. Halli and Leo Driedger, 282–306. Toronto: University of Toronto Press.

Boyd, Susan B., ed. 1997. *Challenging the Public/Private Divide: Feminism, Law and Public Policy*. Toronto: University of Toronto Press.

Bozeman, Barry, and Hal G. Rainey. 1998. "Organizational Rules and the 'Bureaucratic Personality'." *American Journal of Political Science*, 42: 163–89.

Bradbury, Bettina. 1993. *Working Families: Age, Gender, and Daily Survival in Industrializing Montreal*. Toronto: McClelland & Stewart.

———. 2001. "Social, Economic, and Cultural Origins of Contemporary Families." In *Families: Changing Trends in Canada*, 4th edn, edited by Maureen Baker, 69–95. Toronto: McGraw-Hill Ryerson.

Braithewaite, John. 1979. *Inequality, Crime and Public Policy*. London: Routledge and Kegan Paul.

Brannigan, Augustine, and Kelly Hardwick. 2001. "Pornography in the Mass Media and the Panic over Sex Crimes in Canada." In *Communications in Canadian Society*, 5th edn, edited by C. McKie and B., 295–307. Toronto: Thompson.

Braverman, Harry. 1974. *Labor and Monopoly Capital: The Degradation of Work in the Twentieth Century*. New York: Monthly Review Press.

Breton, Raymond. 1964. "Institutional Completeness of Ethnic Communities and the Personal Relations of Immigrants." *American Journal of Sociology*, 70: 193–205.

———. 1978. "Stratification and Conflict Between Ethnolinguistic Communities with Different Social Structures." *Canadian Review of Sociology and Anthropology*, 15: 148–57.

———. 1983. "West Indian, Chinese and European Ethnic Groups in Toronto: Perceptions of Problems and Resources." In *Two Nations, Many Cultures: Ethnic Groups in Canada*, edited by Jean Leonard Elliott, 425–43. Scarborough, Ont.: Prentice-Hall.

———. 1984. "The Production and Allocation of Symbolic Resources: An Analysis of the Linguistic and Ethnocultural Fields in Canada." *Canadian Review of Sociology and Anthropology*, 21: 123–44.

———. 1989. "The Vesting of Ethnic Interests in State Institutions." In *Multiculturalism and Intergroup Relations*, edited by James S. Frideres, 35–55. New York: Greenwood.

———. 1990. "The Ethnic Group as a Political Resource in Relation to Problems of Incorporation: Perceptions and Attitudes." In Raymond Breton, Wsevolod W. Isajiw, Warren E. Kalbach, and Jeffrey G. Reitz, *Ethnic Identity and Equality: Varieties of Experience in a Canadian City*, 196–255. Toronto: University of Toronto Press.

Breton, Raymond, Jean Burnet, Norbert Hartmann, Wsevolod Isajiw, and Jos Lennards. 1977. "The Impact of Ethnic Groups on Canadian Society: Research Issues." In *Identities: The Impact of Ethnicity on Canadian Society*, edited by Wsevolod Isajiw, 191–213. Toronto: Peter Martin.

Breton, Raymond, Wsevolod Isajiw, Warren Kalbach, and Jeffrey G. Reitz. 1990. *Ethnic Identity and Equality: Varieties of Experience in a Canadian City*. Toronto: University of Toronto Press.

Briskin, Linda. 1992. "Socialist Feminism: From the Standpoint of Practice." In *Feminism in Action: Studies in*

*Political Economy*, edited by M. Patricia Connelly and Pat Armstrong, 267–93. Toronto: Canadian Scholars' Press.

Brock, Deborah R. 1998. *Making Work, Making Trouble: Prostitution as a Social Problem*. Toronto: University of Toronto Press.

Brodie, Janine. 1985. *Women and Politics in Canada*. Toronto: McGraw-Hill Ryerson.

———, ed. 1996. *Women and Canadian Public Policy*. Toronto: Harcourt Brace.

Bromley, David G., and Anson D. Shupe, Jr. 1981. *Strange Gods: The Great American Cult Scare*. Boston: Beacon.

Bromley, Simon. 1999. "Marxism and Globalization." In *Marxism and Social Science*, edited by Andrew Gamble, David Marsh, and Tony Tant, 280–301. Urbana: University of Illinois Press.

Brower, Ralph S., and Mitchel Y. Abolafia. 1997. "Bureaucratic Politics: The View from Below." *Journal of Public Administration Research and Theory*, 7: 305–31.

Brown, Louise. 2002. "Two-Tier Grade Schooling Feared." *Toronto Star*, 31 May, A1, A26.

Brown, Phil, and Susan Masterson-Allen. 1994. "The Toxic Waste Movement: A New Type of Activism." *Society and Natural Resources*, 7: 269–87.

Brumann, Christoph. 1998. "The Anthropological Study of Globalization: Towards an Agenda for the Second Phase." *Anthropos*, 93: 495–506.

Bryant, Bunyon, and Paul Mohai, eds. 1992. *Race and the Incidence of Environmental Hazard: A Time for Discourse*. Boulder, Colo.: Westview.

Bryant, Heather. 1990. *The Infertility Dilemma: Reproductive Technologies and Prevention*. Ottawa: Canadian Advisory Council on the Status of Women.

Brym, Robert J. 1980. "Regional Social Structure and Agrarian Radicalism in Canada: Alberta, Saskatchewan and New Brunswick." In *People, Power and Process: A Reader*, edited by Alexander Himelfarb and C. James Richardson, 344–53. Toronto: McGraw-Hill Ryerson.

Bulatao, Rodolfo. 1998. *The Value of Family Planning Programs in Developing Countries*. Santa Monica, Calif.: Rand.

Bulatao, Rodolfo, and John Casterline, eds. 2001. "Global Fertility Transition." *Population and Development Review*, 27 (suppl.).

Bullard, Robert. 1990. *Dumping in Dixie: Race, Class and Environmental Quality*. Boulder, Colo.: Westview.

Burgess, Ernest. 1925. "The Growth of the City: An Introduction to a Research Project." In *The City*, edited by Robert E. Park, Ernest Burgess, and R. McKenzie, 47–62. Chicago: University of Chicago Press.

Burstyn, Varda. 1983. "Masculine Domination and the State." In *The Socialist Register, 1983*, edited by Ralph Miliband and John Saville, 45–89. London: Merlin.

———. 1999. *The Rites of Men: Manhood, Politics and the Culture of Sport*. Toronto: University of Toronto Press.

Burt, Ronald S., and Marc Knez. 1996. "Trust and Third-Party Gossip." In *Trust in Organizations: Frontiers of Theory and Research*, edited by Roderick M. Kramer and Tom R. Tyler, 68–89. Thousand Oaks, Calif.: Sage.

Burtless, Gary. 1998. *Globaphobia: Confronting Fears About Open Trade*. Washington, DC: Brookings Institution.

Bush, Diane Mitsch, and Roberta G. Simmons. 1981. "Socialization Processes over the Life Course." In *Social Psychology: Sociological Perspectives*, edited by Morris Rosenberg and Ralph Turner, 133–64. New York: Basic Books.

Bushman, Brad, and Craig A. Anderson. 2001. "Media Violence and the American Public." *American Psychologist*, 56: 477–89.

Bussière, Patrick, Fernando Cartwright, Robert Crocker, Xin Ma, Jillian Oderkirk, and Yanhong Zhang. 2001. *Measuring Up: The Performance of Canada's Youth in Reading, Mathematics and Science*. Ottawa: Statistics Canada.

Butler, Judith. 1992. "Contingent Foundations: Feminism and the Question of 'Postmodernism'." In *Feminists Theorize the Political*, edited by Judith Butler and Joan W. Scott, 3–21. New York: Routledge.

Butlin, George, and Jillian Oderkirk. 1996. *Educational Attainment: A Key to Autonomy and Authority in the Workplace*. Ottawa: Statistics Canada.

Butsch, Richard. 1992. "Class and Gender in Four Decades of Television Situation Comedy: Plus ca change. . . ." *Critical Studies in Mass Communication*, 9 :387–99.

Butters, Jennifer, and Patricia Erickson. 2002. "Addictions as Deviant Behaviour: Normalizing the Pleasures of Intoxication." In *New Perspectives on Deviance: The Construction of Deviance in Everyday Life*, edited by Lori G. Beaman, 67–84. Toronto: Prentice-Hall Allyn and Bacon.

Cain, Mead. 1983. "Fertility as an Adjustment to Risk." *Population and Development Review*, 9: 688–702.

Cairney, John. 1999. "Socio-economic Status and Self-Rated Health Among Older Canadians." *Canadian Journal on Aging*, 19: 456–77.

Caldwell, John C. 1976. "Toward a Restatement of Demographic Transition Theory." *Population and Development Review*, 2: 321–66.

Caldwell, John, James F. Phillips, and Barkat-e-Khuda, eds. 2002. "Family Planning Programs in the Twenty-First Century." *Studies in Family Planning*, 33, no. 1: special issue.

Calliste, Agnes. 1993. "Sleeping Car Porters in Canada: An Ethnically Submerged Split Labour Market." In *Work in Canada: Readings in the Sociology of Work and Industry*, edited by Graham S. Lowe and Harvey Krahn, 139–53. Scarborough, Ont.: Nelson.

Calvert, Barbara, and Warren R. Stanton. 1992. "Perceptions of Parenthood: Similarities and Differences Between 15-Year-Old Girls and Boys." *Adolescence*, 27: 315–28.

Campey, John. 2002. "Immigrant Children in Our Classrooms: Beyond ESL." *Education Canada*, 42, no. 3 (Summer): 44–7.

Canadian Health Services Research Foundation. 2001. "Myth: The Aging Population Will Overwhelm the Healthcare System." Ottawa: Canadian Health Services Research Foundation.

———. 2002. "Myth: For-Profit Ownership of Facilities Would Lead to Better Health Care." Ottawa: Canadian Health Services Research Foundation.

Canadian Institute of Child Health. 1994. *The Health of Canada's Children: A CICH Profile*. Ottawa: Canadian Institute on Child Health.

Card, David E., and John DiNardo. 2002. *Skill Biased Technological Change and Rising Wage Inequality: Some Problems and Puzzles*. Cambridge, Mass.: National Bureau of Economic Research.

Carley, Kathleen. 1989. "The Value of Cognitive Foundations for Dynamic Social Theory." *Journal of Mathematical Sociology*, 14, nos 2–3: 171–208.

———. 1991. "A Theory of Group Stability." *American Sociological Review*, 56: 331–54.

Carre, Dominique, and Sylvie Craipeau. 1996. "Entre delo-calisation et mobilité: analyse des strategies entrepre-neuriales de teletravail." *Technologies de l'information et société*, 8: 333–54.

Carroll, William K. 1987. "Which Women Are More Proletarianized Than Men?" *Canadian Review of Sociology and Anthropology*, 24: 465–95.

Carroll, William K., and Robert S. Ratner. 1996. "Master Framing and Cross-movement Networking in Contemporary Social Movements." *Sociological Quarterly*, 37: 601–25.

Carson, Rachel. 1962. *Silent Spring*. Boston: Houghton Mifflin.

Cassidy, Barbara, Robina Lord, and Nancy Mandell. 2001. "Silenced and Forgotten Women: Race, Poverty and Disability." In *Feminist Issues: Race, Class and Sexuality*, 3rd edn, edited by Nancy Mandell, 75–107. Toronto: Prentice-Hall.

Castellano, Marlene Brant, Lynne Davis, and Louise Lahache. 2000. "Conclusion: Fulfilling the Promise." In *Aboriginal Education: Fulfilling the Promise*, edited by Marlene Brant Castellano, Lynne Davis, and Louise Lahache, 251–5. Vancouver: University of British Columbia Press.

Castells, Manuel. 1989. *The Informational City: Information Technology, Economic Restructuring, and the Urban-Regional Process*. Cambridge, Mass.: MIT Press.

Centre for Research and Information on Canada. 2001. "Quebec Sovereignty: An Outdated Idea." [Press release]. Ottawa: Centre for Research and Information on Canada.

Chappell, Neena L., and Nina L. Colwill. 1981. "Medical Schools as Agents of Professional Socialization." *Canadian Review of Sociology and Anthropology*, 18, no. 1: 67–79.

Chasteen, Amy L. 2001. "Constructing Rape: Feminism, Change, and Women's Everyday Understandings of Sexual Assault." *Sociological Spectrum*, 21: 101–39.

Chayes, Abram, and Antonia Chayes. 1995. *The New Sovereignty: Compliance with International Regulatory Agreements*. Cambridge, Mass.: Harvard University Press.

Chesney-Lind, Medea. 1997. *The Female Offender: Girls, Women and Crime*. Thousand Oaks, Calif.: Sage.

Chippendale, Nigel. 2002. *Access to Post-secondary Education in Canada: Facts and Gaps: Conference Report*. Ottawa: Canadian Policy Research Networks for the Canadian Millennium Scholarship Foundation. Available at <www.cprn.ca/en/doc.cfm?doc=59>, accessed 19 June 2003.

Chodorow, Nancy. 1978. *The Reproduction of Mothering*. Berkeley: University of California Press.

Cincotta, Richard P., and Roberta Engelman. 1997. *Economics and Rapid Change: The Influence of Population Growth*. Washington: Population Action International.

Citizenship and Immigration Canada. 1998. *The Economic Performance of Immigrants: Immigration Category Perspective*. Available at <www.cic.gc.ca/english/srr/research/res3aiii.html>, accessed 26 July 2003.

———. 1999. *The Economic Performance of Immigrants: Education Perspective*. Available at <www.cic.gc.ca/english/srr/research/res3aii.html>, accessed 26 July 2003.

Clark, S.D. 1995. *State and Status: The Rise of the State and Aristocratic Power in Western Europe*. Montreal: McGill-Queen's University Press.

Clark, Susan, and Andrew S. Harvey. 1976. "The Sexual Division of Labour: The Use of Time." *Atlantis*, 2, no. 1: 46–65.

Clark, Terry, and Seymour Martin Lipset. 1991. "Are Social Classes Dying?" *International Sociology*, 6: 397–410.

Clark, Warren. 2000. "Education." *Canadian Social Trends*, Winter: 3–7.

Clarke, Harold D., Jane Jensen, Lawrence Leduc, and Jon H. Pammett. 1991. *Absent Mandate: The Politics of Discontent in Canada*. 2nd edn. Toronto: Gage.

Clarke, John I. 1996. "The Impact of Population Change on Environment: An Overview." In *Resources and Population: Natural, Institutional, and Demographic Dimensions of Development*, edited by Bernardo Colombo, Paul Demeny, and MaF. Perutz, 244–68. Oxford, UK: Clarendon.

Clarke, Juanne N. 2000. *Health, Illness, and Medicine in Canada*. Toronto: Oxford University Press.

Clement, Wallace. 1975. *The Canadian Corporate Elite*. Toronto: McClelland and Stewart.

Clement, Wallace, and John Myles. 1994. *Relations of Ruling: Class and Gender in Postindustrial Societies*. Montreal: McGill-Queen's University Press.

Clevedon, Gordon, and Michael Krashinsky. 2001. *Our Children's Future: Child Care Policy in Canada*. Toronto: University of Toronto Press.

Cloward, Richard A., and Lloyd E. Ohlin. 1960. *Delinquency and Opportunity: A Theory of Delinquent Gangs*. New York: Free Press.

Coale, Ansley J. 1969. "The Decline of Fertility in Europe from the French Revolution to World War II." In *Fertility and Family Planning: A World View*, edited by S.J. Berhman, Leslie Corsa, and Ronald Freedman, 3–24. Ann Arbor: University of Michigan Press.

———. 1973. "The Demographic Transition Reconsidered." In International Union for the Study of Population, *Proceedings of the International Population Conference*, vol. 1, 53–72. Liège, Belgium.

————. 1974. "The History of the Human Population." *Scientific American*, special issue: 15–25.

Coale, Ansley J., and Susan Cotts Watkins, eds. 1986. *The Decline of Fertility in Europe: The Revised Proceedings of a Conference on the Princeton European Fertility Project.* Princeton, NJ: Princeton University Press.

Coats, Patricia B., and Steven Overman. 1992. "Childhood Play Experiences of Women in Traditional and Nontraditional Professions." *Sex Roles*, 26, nos 7/8: 261–71.

Cockburn, Cynthia. 1983. *Brothers: Male Dominance and Technological Change.* London: Pluto.

————. 1991. *In the Way of Women: Men's Resistances to Sex Equality in Organization.* Ithaca, NY: ILR Press.

Cockett, Monica, and John Tripp. 1994. *The Exeter Family Study: Family Breakdown and Its Impact on Children.* Exeter, UK: University of Exeter Press.

Cohen, Albert K. 1966. *Deviance and Control.* Englewood Cliffs, NJ: Prentice-Hall.

Cohen, J.L., and J.H. Davis. 1973. "Effects of Audience Status, Evaluation, and Time of Action on Performance with Hidden-Word Problems." *Journal of Personality and Social Psychology*, 27: 74–85.

Cohen, Jean L. 1985. "Strategy or Identity: New Theoretical Paradigms and Contemporary Social Movements." *Social Research*, 53: 663–716.

Coleman, James W. 1987. "Toward an Integrated Theory of White Collar Crime." *American Journal of Sociology*, 93: 406–39.

Collier, Gary, Henry L. Minton, and Graham Reynolds. 1991. *Currents of Thought in American Social Psychology.* New York: Oxford University Press.

Collins, Randall. 1979. *The Credential Society: An Historical Sociology of Education and Stratification.* New York: Academic Press.

Comack, A. Elizabeth. 1985. "The Origins of Canadian Drug Legislation: Labelling Versus Class Analysis." In *The New Criminologies in Canada: State, Crime, and Control*, edited by Tom Fleming, 65–86. Toronto: Oxford University Press.

Comninel, George C. 1987. *Rethinking the French Revolution: Marxism and the Revisionist Challenge.* New York: Verso.

Conley, James. 1999. "Working-Class Formation in Twentieth-Century Canada." In *Social Inequality in Canada: Patterns, Problems, and Policies*, edited by James E. Curtis, Edward G. Grabb, and Neil L. Guppy, 20–34. Scarborough, Ont.: Prentice-Hall Allyn and Bacon.

Connell, R.W. 1995. *Masculinities.* Berkeley: University of California Press.

Connelly, Patricia M. 1978. *Last Hired, First Fired.* Toronto: Women's Press.

Conrad, Peter, and Joseph Schneider. 1980. *Deviance and Medicalization: From Badness to Sickness.* St Louis, Mo.: Mosby.

Constant, David, Lee Sproull, and Sara Kiesler. 1996. "The Kindness of Strangers: The Usefulness of Electronic Weak Ties for Technical Advice." *Organization Science*, 7, no. 2: 119–35.

Cook, J. 2001. "Practical Guide to Medical Education." *Pharmaceutical Marketing*, 6: 14–22.

Cooley, Charles Horton. 1902. *Human Nature and Social Order.* New York: Scribner.

————. [1909] 1962. *Social Organization: A Study of the Larger Mind.* Glencoe, Ill.: Free Press.

Cooperstock, Ruth, and Henry Lennard. 1987. "Role Strain and Tranquilizer Use." In *Health and Canadian Society: Sociological Perspectives*, 2nd edn, edited by David Coburn, Carl D'Arcy, George M. Torrance, and Peter New, 314–32. Markham, Ont.: Fitzhenry & Whiteside.

Council of Ministers of Education, Canada. 1996. *Enhancing the Role of Teachers in a Changing World. Report in response to the International Survey in Preparation for the Forty-Fifth Session of the International Conference on Education.* Toronto: Council of Ministers of Education, Canada.

————. 2001. *The Development of Education in Canada: Report of Canada.* Toronto: Council of Ministers of Education, Canada.

Coverman, Shelly. 1983. "Gender, Domestic Labour Time and Wage Inequality." *American Sociological Review*, 48: 623–37.

Crockett, Lisa, Mike Losoff, and Anne C. Petersen. 1984. "Perceptions of the Peer Group and Friendship in Early Adolescence." *Journal of Early Adolescence*, 4, no. 2: 155–81.

Crompton, Susan. 2000. "Health." *Canadian Social Trends*, 59: 12–17.

Croteau, David, and William Hoynes. 2003. *Media/Society: Industries, Images, and Audiences.* 3rd edn. Thousand Oaks, Calif.: Sage.

Crozier, Michel. 1964. *The Bureaucratic Phenomenon.* Chicago: University of Chicago Press.

Crush, Jonathan. 1987. *The Struggle for Swazi Labour, 1890–1920.* Kingston, Ont.: McGill-Queen's University Press.

Cuneo, Carl. 1985. "Have Women Become More Proletarianized Than Men?" *Canadian Review of Sociology and Anthropology*, 22: 465–95.

Cunningham, Mick. 2001. "The Influence of Parental Attitudes and Behaviors on Children's Attitudes Toward Gender and Household Labor in Early Adulthood." *Journal of Marriage and the Family*, 63, no. 1: 111–23.

Curra, John. 2000. *The Relativity of Deviance.* Thousand Oaks, Calif.: Sage.

Currie, Dawn. 1988. "Starvation Amidst Abundance: Female Adolescents and Anorexia." In *Sociology of Health Care in Canada*, edited by B. Singh Bolaria and Harley D. Dickinson, 198–215. Toronto: Harcourt, Brace, Jovanovich.

Dahl, Robert. 1961. *Who Governs? Democracy and Power in an American City.* New Haven, Conn.: Yale University Press.

Das, Mallika. 2000. "Men and Women in Indian Magazine Advertisements: A Preliminary Report." *Sex Roles*, 43: 699–717.

Das Gupta, Tania. 1996. *Racism and Paid Work.* Toronto: Garamond.

Davies, James C. 1962. "Toward a Theory of Revolution." *American Sociological Review*, 27: 5–19.

Davies, Lorraine, and Patricia Jane Carrier. 1999. "The Importance of Power Relations for the Division of Household Labour." *Canadian Journal of Sociology*, 24: 35–51.

Davies, Scott. 1999. "Stubborn Disparities: Explaining Class Inequalities in Schooling." In Social Inequality in *Canada: Patterns, Problems, and Policies*, edited by James E. Curtis, Edward G. Grabb, and Neil L. Guppy, 138–50. Scarborough, Ont.: Prentice-Hall Allyn and Bacon.

Davis, Charles R. 1996. "The Administrative Rational Model and Public Organization Theory." *Administration and Society*, 28: 39–60.

Davis, Kingsley. 1945. "The World Demographic Transition." *Annals of American Academy of Political and Social Sciences*, 237: 1–11.

Davis, Kingsley, and Wilbert E. Moore. 1945. "Some Principles of Stratification." *American Sociological Review*, 10: 242–9.

Davis, Steven J., John C. Haltiwanger, and Scott Schuh. 1996. *Job Creation and Destruction*. Cambridge, Mass.: MIT Press.

Dawe, Alan. 1970. "Two Sociologies." *British Journal of Sociology*, 21: 207–18.

Day, Shelagh, and Gwen Brodsky. 1998. *Women and the Equality Deficit: The Impact of Restructuring Canada's Social Programs*. Ottawa: Status of Women Canada.

De Vos, George, and Lola Romanucci-Ross. 1982. *Ethnic Identity: Cultural Continuities and Change*. Chicago: University of Chicago Press.

DeFreitas, Gregory. 1998. "Immigration, Inequality, and Policy Alternatives." In *Globalization and Progressive Economic Policy*, edited by Dean Baker, Gerald Epstein, and Robert Pollin, 337–56. Cambridge: Cambridge University Press.

Dei, George J. Sefa. 1996. *Anti-racism Education: Theory and Practice*. Halifax, NS: Fernwood.

Dei, George J. Sefa, Irma Marcia James, Leeno Luke Karumanchery, Sonia James-Wilson, and Jasmin Zine. 2000. *Removing the Margins: The Challenges and Possibilities of Inclusive Schooling*. Toronto: Canadian Scholars' Press.

De Kerckhove, Derrick. 1997. *Connected Intelligence: The Arrival of the Web Society*. Toronto: Sommerfield.

DeKeseredy, Walter. 2001. "Patterns of Family Violence." In *Families: Changing Trends in Canada*, 4th edn, edited by Maureen Baker. Toronto: McGraw-Hill Ryerson.

Dery, David. 1998. "'Papereality' and Learning in Bureaucratic Organizations." *Administration and Society*, 29: 677–89.

DeSilva, Arnold. 1992. *Earnings of Immigrants: A Comparative Analysis*. Ottawa: Economic Council of Canada.

Deutschmann, Linda. 1998. *Deviance and Social Control*. Toronto: Nelson.

Devall, William B. 1992. "Deep Ecology and Radical Environmentalism." In *American Environmentalism*, edited by Riley Dunlap and Angela G. Mertig, 51–62. Philadelphia: Taylor and Francis.

Devereaux, P.J., Peter T.L. Choi, Christina Lacchetti, Bruce Weaver, Holger J. Schünemann, Ted Haines, John N. Lavis, Brydon J.B. Grant, David R.S. Haslam, Mohit

Bhandari, Terrence Sullivan, Deborah J. Cook, Stephen D. Walter, Maureen Meade, Humaira Khan, Neera Bhatnagar, and Gordon H. Guyatt. 2002. "A Systematic Review and Meta-analysis of Studies Comparing Mortality Rates of Private For-Profit and Private Not-for-Profit Hospitals." *Canadian Medical Association Journal*, 166: 1399–1406.

Dhalla, Irfan A., Jeff C. Kwong, David L. Streiner, Ralph E. Baddour, Andrea Waddell, and Ian Johnson. 2002. "Characteristics of First-Year Students in Canadian Medical Schools." *Canadian Medical Association Journal*, 166: 1029–35.

Di Martino, Vittorio. 1996. "Télétravail: à la recherche des règles d'or." *Technologies de l'information et société*, 8: 355–71.

Diani, Mario. 1992. "The Concept of Social Movement." *Sociological Review*, 40: 1–25.

Dobash, R. Emerson, Russell P. Dobash, Margo Wilson, and Martin Daly. 1992. "The Myth of Sexual Symmetry in Marital Violence." *Social Problems*, 39: 71–91.

Dogon, Mattei, and John Kasarda, eds. 1988. *The Metropolis Era*. Beverly Hills, Calif.: Sage.

Doherty, Gillian, Martha Friendly, and Mab Oloman. 1998. *Women's Support, Women's Work: Child Care in an Era of Deficit Reduction, Devolution, Downsizing and Deregulation*. Ottawa: Status of Women Canada.

Domhoff, G. William. 1990. *The Power Elite and the State: How Policy Is Made in America*. Hawthorne, NY: Aldine de Gruyter.

Dooley, Martin. 1995. "Lone-Mother Families and Social Assistance Policy in Canada." In *Family Matters: New Policies for Divorce, Lone Mothers, and Child Poverty*, edited by Martin Dooley, Ross Finnie, Shelley A. Phipps, and Nancy Naylor, 35–104. Toronto: C.D. Howe Institute.

Douglas, Susan. 1994. *Where the Girls Are: Growing Up Female with the Mass Media*. New York: Random House.

Doyal, Lesley. 1995. *What Makes Women Sick: Gender and the Political Economy of Health*. New Brunswick, NJ: Rutgers University Press.

Dreeben, Robert. 1968. *On What Is Learned in School*. Reading, Mass.: Addison-Wesley.

Driedger, Leo, and Angus Reid. 2000. "Public Opinion on Visible Minorities." In *Race and Racism: Canada's Challenge*, edited by Leo Driedger and Shiva S. Halli, 152–71. Ottawa: Carleton University Press.

Duffy, Ann, and Rina Cohen. 2001. "Violence Against Women: The Struggle Persists." In *Feminist Issues: Race, Class and Sexuality*, edited by Nancy Mandell, 134–65. Toronto: Prentice-Hall.

Duffy, Ann, Dan Glenday, and Norene Pupo. 1997. *Good Jobs, Bad Jobs, No Jobs: The Transformation of Work in the 21st Century*. Toronto: Harcourt Brace.

Duffy, Ann, Nancy Mandell, and Norene Pupo. 1989. *Few Choices: Women, Work and Family*. Toronto: Garamond.

Duncan, Otis Dudley, and Leo F. Schnore. 1959. "Cultural, Behavioral and Ecological Perspectives in the Study of Social Organization." *American Journal of Sociology*, 65: 132–45.

Dunlap, Riley. 1992. "Trends in Public Opinion Toward Environmental Issues: 1965–1990." In *American Environmentalism*, edited by Riley Dunlap and Angela G. Mertig, 89–116. Philadelphia: Taylor and Francis.

Dunlap, Riley, and William Catton, Jr. 1979a. "Environmental Sociology." *Annual Review of Sociology*, 5: 243–73.

———. 1979b. "Environmental Sociology: A Framework for Analysis." In *Progress in Resource Management and Environmental Planning*, edited by Timothy O'Riordan and R.C. d'Arge, 1: 57–85. Chichester, UK: Wiley.

———. 1983. "What Environmental Sociologists Have in Common (Whether Concerned with 'Built' or 'Natural' Environments)." *Sociological Inquiry*, 53, nos 2/3: 113–15.

Dunlap, Riley, and Richard P. Gale. 1972. "Politics and Ecology: A Political Profile of Student Eco-activists." *Youth and Society*, 3: 379–97.

Dunn, Judy. 1986. "Growing Up in a Family World: Issues in the Study of Social Development in Young Children." In *Children of Social Worlds: Development in a Social Context*, edited by Martin Richards and Paul Light, 98–115. Cambridge, UK: Polity Press.

Durkheim, Émile. [1893] 1964. *The Division of Labor in Society*. Translated by George Simpson. New York: Free Press.

———. [1895] 1964. *The Rules of Sociological Method*. Translated by S. Solovay and John Mueller. New York: Free Press.

———. [1897] 1951. *Suicide: A Study in Sociology*. Translated by John A. Spaulding and George Simpson. New York: Free Press.

———. [1912] 1965. *The Elementary Forms of Religious Life*. Translated by Joseph Ward Swain. New York: Free Press.

———. [1912] 1995. *The Elementary Forms of Religious Life*. Translated by Karen E. Fields. New York: Free Press.

———. [1922] 1956. *Education and Society*. Translated by Sherwood W. Fox. Glencoe, Ill.: Free Press.

Dworkin, Ronald W. 2001. "The Medicalization of Unhappiness." The Public Interest, Summer: 85–99.

Ebaugh, Helen. 1988. *Becoming an Ex: The Process of Role Exit*. Chicago: University of Chicago Press.

Eberstadt, Nicholas. 1997. "World Population Implosion?" *The Public Interest*, 129: 3–20.

Economic Council of Canada. 1991. *New Faces in the Crowd: Economic and Social Impact of Immigration*. Ottawa: Economic Council of Canada.

Edwards, Richard. 1979. *Contested Terrain: The Transformation of the Workplace in the Twentieth Century*. New York: Basic Books.

Ehrenreich, Barbara. 2001. *Nickel and Dimed: On (Not) Getting By in America*. New York: Henry Holt.

Ehrlich, Paul R., and Anne H. Ehrlich. 1970. *Population, Resources, Environment: Issues in Human Ecology*. San Francisco: Freeman.

———. 1990. *The Population Explosion*. London: Hutchinson.

Ehrlich, Paul R., and J.P. Holdren. 1971. "The Impact of Population Growth." *Science*, 171: 1212–7.

Eichler, Margit. 1996. "The Impact of New Reproductive and Genetic Technologies on Families." In *Families: Changing Trends in Canada*, 3rd edn, edited by Maureen Baker, 104–18. Toronto: McGraw-Hill Ryerson.

———. 1997. *Family Shifts: Families, Policies, and Gender Equality*. Toronto: Oxford University Press, 1997.

Eisenberg, David M., Roger B. Davis, Susan L. Ettner, Scott Appel, Sonja Wilkey, Maria Van Rompay, and Ronald C. Kessler. 1998. "Trends in Alternative Medicine Use in the United States, 1990–1997: Results of a Follow-up National Survey." *Journal of the American Medical Association*, 280: 1569–75.

Eisinger, Peter K. 1973. "The Conditions of Protest Behaviour in American Cities." *American Political Science Review*, 67: 11–28.

Ekos Research Associates. 1999. "Federal Liberals Riding High, Sovereignty Movement Dormant." [Press Release]. Ottawa: Ekos Research Associates.

———. 2002. *CBC/Ekos Poll: Public Attitudes Towards Immigration*. Ottawa: Ekos Research Associates.

Elliot, Faith Robertson. 1996. *Gender, Family, and Society*. London: Macmillan.

Elliott, Jean Leonard, and Augie Fleras. 1992. *Unequal Relations: An Introduction to Race and Ethnic Dynamics in Canada*. Scarborough, Ont.: Prentice-Hall.

Elliott, J., and M. Richards. 1991. "Parental Divorce and the Life Chances of Children." *Family Law*, 481–4.

Elster, Jon. 1989. *The Cement of Society: A Study of Social Order*. Cambridge: Cambridge University Press.

Emery, Robert. 1994. "Psychological Research on Children, Parents, and Divorce." In *Renegotiating Family Relationships: Divorce, Child Custody, and Mediation*, edited by Robert Emery, 194–217. New York: Guildford.

Engels, Friedrich. [1845] 1994. *The Condition of the Working Class in England*. Translated by W.O. Henderson and W.H. Chaloner. Stanford, Calif.: Stanford University Press.

———. [1882] 1942. *The Origin of the Family, Private Property and the State*. New York: International Publishers.

England, Paula. 1982. "The Failure of Human Capital Theory to Explain Occupational SeSegregation." *Journal of Human Resources*, 17: 358–70.

England, Paula, George Farkas, Barbara Kilbourne, and Thomas Dou. 1988. "Explaining Occupational SeSegregation and Wages: Findings from a Model with Fixed Effects." *American Sociological Review*, 53: 544–58.

Ennett, Susan T., and Karl E. Bauman. 1996. "Adolescent Social Networks: School, Demographic, and Longitudinal Considerations." *Journal of Adolescent Research*, 11: 194–215.

Entwisle, Doris, and Leslie Hayduk. 1988. "Lasting Effects of Elementary School." *Sociology of Education*, 61: 147–59.

Epstein, Debbie, Jannette Elwood, Valerie Hey, and Janet Maw. 1997. *Failing Boys? Issues in Gender and Achievement*. Buckingham, UK: Open University Press.

Erasmus, Georges. 2002. "Why Can't We Talk." Excerpted from the 2002 Lafontaine-Baldwin Lecture. *Globe and Mail*, 9 March, F6–7.

Erikson, Erik. 1982. *The Life Cycle Completed: A Review.* New York: Norton.

Erikson, Kai T. 1966. *Wayward Puritans: A Study in the Sociology of Deviance.* New York: Wiley.

Ermann, M. David, and Richard J. Lundman. 1996. "Corporate and Governmental Deviance: Origins, Patterns, and Reactions." In *Corporate and Governmental Deviance: Problems of Organizational Behavior in Contemporary Society*, edited by M. David Ermann and Richard J. Lundman, 3–44. New York: Oxford University Press.

Estes, Carroll L. 1999. "The New Political Economy of Aging: Introduction and Critique." In *Critical Gerontology: Perspectives from Political and Moral Economy*, edited by Meredith Minkler and Carroll L. Estes, 17–35. Amityville, NY: Baywood.

Evans, L.T. 1998. *Feeding the Ten Billion: Plants and Population Growth.* Cambridge: Cambridge University Press.

Eyerman, Ron, and Andrew Jamison. 1989. "Environmental Knowledge as an Organizational Weapon: The Case of Greenpeace." *Social Science Information*, 28, no. 1: 99–119.

Falkenberg, Loren. 1988. "The Perceptions of Women Working in Male-Dominated Professions." *Canadian Journal of Atlantic Studies*, June: 77–83.

Faludi, Susan. 1991. *Backlash: The Undeclared War Against American Women.* New York: Doubleday-Anchor.

———. 1999. *Stiffed: The Betrayal of the American Man.* New York: HarperCollins.

Fantasia, Rick. 1995. "Fast Food in France." *Theory and Society*, 24: 201–33.

Fausto-Sterling, Anne. 1985. *Myths of Gender.* New York: Basic Books.

———. 2000. *Sexing the Body: Gender Politics and the Construction of Sexuality.* New York: Basic Books.

Feld, Scott L. 1982. "Social Structural Determinants of Similarity Among Associates." *American Sociological Review*, 47: 797–801.

Fernández Armesto, Felipe, ed. 1995. *The European Opportunity.* Aldershot, UK: Variorum.

Filion, Normand. 1998. "The Management of Self-Discipline: Social Norms and Cultural Surveillance." Paper presented at the annual meeting of the International Sociological Association.

Fineman, Martha A. 1995. *The Neutered Mother, the Sexual Family, and Other Twentieth Century Tragedies.* New York: Routledge.

Fischer, Claude S. 1976. *The Urban Experience.* New York: Harcourt Brace Jovanovich.

———. 1982. *To Dwell Among Friends: Personal Networks in Town and City.* Chicago: University of Chicago Press.

Fiske, John. 1994. *Media Matters: Everyday Culture and Political Change.* Minneapolis: University of Minnesota Press.

Fleras, Augie. 2002. *Engaging Diversity: Multiculturalism in Canada.* Toronto: Nelson.

———. 2003. *Mass Media Communication in Canada.* Toronto: Nelson.

———. 2004. "Misrepresenting Diversity: Rethinking the News Values of a Prevailing News Paradigm." Paper presented to a Media and Diversity conference, Siegen University, Germany, 25 June.

———. 2005. *Social Problems in Canada: Conditions, Challenges, and Constructions.* Toronto: Pearson/Prentice Hall.

Fleras, Augie, and Jean Lock Kunz. 2001. *Representing Diversity: Media and Minorities in a Multicultural Canada.* Toronto: Thompson.

Flyvbjerg, Bent. 1998. *Rationality and Power: Democracy in Practice.* Chicago: University of Chicago Press.

———. 2001. *Making Social Science Matter.* Cambridge: Cambridge University Press.

Fogel, Robert W., and Dora L. Costa. 1997. "A Theory of Technophysio Evolution, with Some Implications for Forecasting Population, Health Care Costs, and Pension Costs." *Demography*, 34: 49–66.

Fortin, Pierre. 1996. "The Great Canadian Slump." *Canadian Journal of Economics*, 29: 761–87.

Fournier, Marcel, Michael Rosenberg, and Deena White, eds. 1997. *Quebec Society: Critical Issues.* Scarborough, Ont.: Prentice-Hall Canada.

Fox, Bonnie, ed. 1980. *Hidden in the Household: Women's Domestic Labour Under Capitalism.* Toronto: Women's Press.

———. 1988. "Conceptualizing 'Patriarchy'." *Canadian Review of Sociology and Anthropology*, 25: 163–83.

———. 1989. "The Feminist Challenge: A Reconsideration of Social Inequality and Economic Development." In Robert J. Brym with Bonnie J. Fox, *From Culture to Power: The Sociology of English Canada*, 120–67. Toronto: Oxford University Press.

———, ed. 2001a. *Family Patterns, Gender Relations.* 2nd edn. Toronto: Oxford University Press.

———. 2001b. "Reproducing Difference: Changes in the Lives of Partners Becoming Parents." In *Family Patterns, Gender Relations*, 2nd edn, edited by Bonnie Fox, 217–302. Toronto: Oxford University Press.

Fox, Bonnie, and John Fox. 1986. "Women in the Labour Market, 1931–1981: Exclusion and Competition." *Canadian Review of Sociology and Anthropology*, 23: 1–21.

———. 1987. "Occupational Gender Segregation of the Canadian Labour Force, 1931–1981." *Canadian Review of Sociology and Anthropology*, 24: 374–97.

Fox, Bonnie, and Pamela Sugiman. 1999. "Flexible Work, Flexible Workers: The Restructuring of Clerical Work in a Large Telecommunications Company." *Studies in Political Economy*, 60: 59–84.

Fox, James Alan, and Jack Levin. 2001. *The Will to Kill: Making Sense of Senseless Murder.* Boston: Allyn and Bacon.

Fox, John, and Michael Ornstein. 1986. "The Canadian State and Corporate Elites in the Post-war Period." *Canadian Review of Sociology and Anthropology*, 23: 481–506.

Fox, Stephen. 1985. *The American Conservation Movement: John Muir and His Legacy.* Madison: University of Wisconsin Press.

Frank, Andre Gunder. 1991. "The Underdevelopment of Development." *Scandinavian Journal of Development Alternatives*, 10, no. 3: 5–72.

Fraser, Nancy. 1997. "After the Family Wage: A Postindustrial Thought Experiment." In Nancy Fraser,

*Justice Interruptus: Critical Reflections on the 'Postsocialist' Condition*, 41–66. New York: Routledge.

Fraser, Nancy, and Linda Nicholson. 1990. "Social Criticism Without Philosophy: An Encounter Between Feminism and Postmodernism." In *Feminism/Postmodernism*, edited by Linda Nicholson, 19–38. London: Routledge.

Frederick, Judith. 1995. *As Time Goes By . . . : Time Use of Canadians*. Ottawa: Statistics Canada.

Frederick, Judith, and Janet E. Fast. 1999. "Eldercare in Canada: Who Does How Much?" *Canadian Social Trends*, Autumn: 27–30.

Frederick, Judith, and Jason Hamel. 1998. "Canadian Attitudes to Divorce." *Canadian Social Trends*, no. 48: 6–11.

Freedman, Jonathan. 2002. *Media Violence and its Effects on Aggression*. Toronto: University of Toronto Press.

Freidson, Eliot. 1970. *The Profession of Medicine: A Study in the Sociology of Applied Knowledge*. New York: Harper and Row.

Freire, Paulo. 1970. *Pedagogy of the Oppressed*. Translated by Myra Bergman Ramos. New York: Herder and Herder.

Freud, Sigmund. [1923] 1974. *The Ego and the Id*. Translated by James Strachey. London: Hogarth.

———. [1938] 1973. *An Outline of Psychoanalysis*. Translated by James Strachey. London: Hogarth.

Freudenberg, Nicholas, and Carol Steinsapir. 1992. "Not in Our Backyards: The Grassroots Environmental Movement." In *American Environmentalism*, edited by Riley Dunlap and Angela G. Mertig, 27–38. Philadelphia: Taylor and Francis.

Freudenburg, William, and Susan Pastor. 1992. "NIMBYs and LULUs: Stalking the Syndromes." *Journal of Social Issues*, 48, no. 4: 39–61.

Frideres, James S. 1988. *Native Peoples in Canada: Contemporary Conflicts*. Scarborough, Ont.: Prentice-Hall.

Funder, Kathleen. 1996. *Remaking Families: Adaptation of Parents and Children to Divorce*. Melbourne, Australia: Australian Institute of Family Studies.

Furedi, Frank. 1997. *Population and Development: A Critical Introduction*. New York: St Martin's.

Furstenberg, Frank F., S. Philip Morgan, and Paul D. Allison. 1987. "Paternal Participation and Children's Well-Being After Marital Dissolution." *American Sociological Review*, 52: 695–701.

Galarneau, Diane, and Jim Sturrock. 1997. "Family Income After Separation." *Perspectives on Labour and Income*, 9, no. 2: 19–28.

Gamson, William A., and David S. Meyer. 1996. "Framing Political Opportunity." In *Comparative Perspectives on Social Movements: Political Opportunities, Mobilizing Structures, and Cultural Framing*, edited by Doug McAdam, John McCarthy, and Mayer Zald, 275–90. New York: Cambridge University Press.

Gannagé, Charlene. 1986. *Double Day, Double Bind: Women Garment Workers*. Toronto: Women's Press.

Gans, Herbert J. 1967. *The Levittowners: Ways of Life and Politics in a New Suburban Community*. New York: Pantheon.

———. 1979. "Symbolic Ethnicity: The Future of Ethnic Groups and Culture in America." *Ethnic and Racial Studies*, 2: 1–20.

———. 2003. *Democracy and the News*. New York: Oxford University Press.

Gardner, Julia, and Mark Roseland. 1989. "Thinking Globally: The Role of Social Equity in Sustainable Development." *Alternatives*, 16, no. 3: 26–35.

Garfinkel, Harold. 1956. "Conditions of Successful Status Degradation Ceremonies." *American Journal of Sociology*, 61: 420–4.

———. 1997. "A Conception of and Experiments with 'Trust' as a Condition of Concerted Stable Actions." In *The Production of Social Reality: Essays and Readings in Social Interaction*, edited by J. O'Brien and P. Kollock, 396–407. Thousand Oaks, Calif.: Pine Forge Press.

Garson, Barbara. 1972. *All the Livelong Day: The Meaning and Demeaning of Routine Work*. New York: Doubleday.

Gaskell, Jane. 1992. *Gender Matters from School to Work*. Milton Keynes, UK: Open University Press.

———. 1993. "Feminism and Its Impact on Educational Scholarship in Canada." In *Contemporary Educational Issues: The Canadian Mosaic*, 2nd edn, edited by Leonard L. Stewin and Stewart J.H. McCann, 145–60. Toronto: Copp Clark Pitman.

———. 2001. "The Reproduction of Family Life: Perspectives of Male and Female Adolescents." In *Family Patterns, Gender Relations*, 2nd edn, edited by Bonnie Fox, 217–32. Toronto: Oxford University Press.

Gaskell, Jane, and John Willinsky, eds. 1995. *Gender In/forms Curriculum: From Enrichment to Transformation*. Toronto: OISE Press.

Gaventa, John. 1980. *Power and Powerlessness: Quiescence and Rebellion in an Appalachian Valley*. Urbana: University of Illinois Press.

Geary, David. 1998. *Male, Female: The Evolution of Human Sexual Differences*. Washington, DC: American Psychological Association.

Geary, David C., and Mark V. Flinn. 2001. "Evolution of Human Parental Behavior and the Human Family." *Parenting, Science and Practice*, 1: 5–61.

Geertz, Clifford. 1973. *The Interpretation of Cultures: Selected Essays*. New York: Basic Books.

Gerbner, George, and Larry Gross. 1976. "The Scary World of a TV's Heavy Viewer." *Psychology Today*, April, 41–5.

Gergen, Kenneth. 2001. "From Mind to Relationship: The Emerging Challenge." *Education Canada*, 41, no. 1: 8–11.

Ghalam, Nancy. 2000. "Attitudes Toward Women, Work and Family." *Canadian Social Trends*, 3.

Gibbon, Edward. [1776–88] 1994. *The History of the Decline and Fall of the Roman Empire*. London: Allen Lane.

Giddens, Anthony. 1971. *Capitalism and Modern Social Theory: An Analysis of the Writings of Marx, Durkheim, and Max Weber*. Cambridge: Cambridge University Press.

———. 1979. *Selected Problems of Social Theory*. London: Macmillan.

———. 2000. *Introduction to Sociology*. 3rd edn. New York: Norton.

Gidengil, Elizabeth, André Blais, Richard Nadeau, and Neil Nevitte. 2001. "Making Sense of the Vote: The 2000

Canadian Election." Paper presented at the annual meeting of the Association for Canadian Studies in the United States.

Gidney, R.D. 1999. *From Hope to Harris: The Reshaping of Ontario's Schools*. Toronto: University of Toronto Press.

Gilbert, Neil. 1997. "Advocacy Research and Social Policy." *Crime and Justice*, 22: 101–48.

Giroux, Henri. 1997. *Pedagogy and the Politics of Hope: Theory, Culture, and Schooling: A Critical Reader*. Boulder, Colo.: Westview.

Glassner, Barry. 1999. *The Culture of Fear: Why Americans Are Afraid of the Wrong Things*. New York: Basic Books.

Glazer, Nathan, and Daniel P. Moynihan, eds. 1975. *Ethnicity: Theory and Experience*. Cambridge, Mass.: Harvard University Press.

Glenn, Evelyn Nakano. 2000. "The Social Construction and Institutionalization of Gender and Race: An Integrative Framework." In *Revisioning Gender, edited by Myra Marx Feree, Judith Lorber, and Beth B. Hess*, 3–43. New York: AltaMira.

Goffman, Erving. 1959. *The Presentation of Self in Everyday Life*. Garden City, NY: Doubleday–Anchor.

———. 1961a. *Asylums: Essays on the Social Situation of Mental Patients and Other Inmates*. New York: Doubleday.

———. 1961b. *Encounters: Two Studies in the Sociology of Interaction*. Indianapolis: Bobbs Merrill.

———. 1964. *Stigma: Notes on the Management of Spoiled Identity*. Englewood Cliffs, NJ: Prentice Hall.

———. 1967. *Interaction Ritual: Essays on Face to Face Behavior*. Garden City, NY: Anchor.

———. 1986. *Frame Analysis: An Essay on the Organization of Experience*. Boston: Northeastern University Press.

Gold, Harry. 2002. *Urban Life and Society*. Upper Saddle River, NJ: Prentice Hall.

Goldenberg, Sheldon. 1992. *Thinking Methodologically*. New York: HarperCollins.

Goldthorpe, J.E. 1987. *Family Life in Western Societies: A Historical Sociology of Family Relationships in Britain and North America*. Cambridge: Cambridge University Press.

Goldthorpe, J.H., David Lockwood, Frank Bechhofer, and Jennifer Platt. 1969. *The Affluent Worker in the Class Structure*. Cambridge: Cambridge University Press.

Gomme, Ian McDermid. 2002. *The Shadow Line: Deviance and Crime in Canada*. Toronto: Nelson.

Goode, William J. 1960. "A Theory of Role Strain." *American Sociological Review*, 25: 483–96.

Gordon, Philip H., and Sophie Meunier. 2001. "Globalization and French Cultural Identity." *French Politics, Culture and Society*, 19: 22–41.

Gordon, Robert M., and Jacquelyn Nelson. 2000. "Crime, Ethnicity, and Immigration." In *Crime in Canadian Society*, 6th edn, edited by Robert A. Silverman, James J. Teevan, and Vincent F. Sacco. Toronto: Harcourt Brace.

Gorz, Andre. 1999. *Reclaiming Work: Beyond the Wage-Based Society*. Translated by Chris Turner. Cambridge: Polity.

Gottdiener, Mark, and Ray Hutchison. 2000. *The New Urban Sociology*. 2nd edn. Toronto: McGraw-Hill.

Gottfredson Michael, and Travis Hirschi. 1990. *A General Theory of Crime*. Stanford, Calif.: Stanford University Press.

GPI Atlantic. n.d. "The Economic Value of Housework and Child Care." Available at <www.gpiatlantic.org/ab_housework.shtml>, accessed 27 May 2003.

Grabb, Edward G. 2002. *Theories of Social Inequality*. 4th edn. Toronto: Harcourt.

Grafton, R. Quentin, Robert W. Lynch, and Harry W. Nelson. 1998. "British Columbia's Stumpage System: Economic and Trade Policy Implications." *Canadian Public Policy*, 24 (suppl.): S41–50.

Graham, Hilary. 1984. *Women, Health and the Family*. Brighton, UK: Wheatsheaf.

Gramsci, Antonio. 1992. *Prison Notebooks*. Vol. 1. Translated by Joseph A. Buttigieg and Antonio Callari. New York: Columbia University Press.

Granovetter, Mark S. 1974. *Getting a Job: A Study of Contacts and Careers*. Cambridge, Mass.: Harvard University Press.

———. 1982. "Alienation Reconsidered: The Strength of Weak Ties." *Connections*, 5, no. 2: 4–16.

Grant, Karen. 1998. "It's All in Your Genes." In *Critical Thinking About Canadian Social Issues*, edited by Wayne Antony and Les Samuelson, 200–17. Halifax: Fernwood.

Gray, Gary, and Neil Guppy. 2003. *Successful Surveys: Research Methods and Practice*. 3rd edn. Toronto: Nelson Thomson.

Gray, Herman. 1995. *Watching Race: Television and the Struggle for "Blackness."* Minneapolis: University of Minnesota Press.

Graydon, Shari. 2001. "The Portrayal of Women in the Media: The Good, the Bad, and the Beautiful." In *Communication in Canadian Society*, 5th edn, edited by C. McKie and B, Singer, 179–195. Toronto: Thompson.

Grbich, Carolyn. 1992. "Societal Response to Familial Role Change in Australia: Marginalisation or Social Change." *Journal of Comparative Family Studies*, 23, no. 1: 79–94.

Green, Leonard. 2000. "Attention-Deficit/Hyperactivity Disorder: Constructing Deviance, Constructing Order." In *New Perspectives on Deviance: The Construction of Deviance in Everyday Life*, edited by Lori G. Beaman, 263–82. Toronto: Prentice-Hall Allyn and Bacon.

Green, Melvyn. 1986. "A History of Canadian Narcotics Control: The Formative Years." In *The Social Dimensions of Law*, edited by Neil Boyd, 24–40. Scarborough, Ont.: Prentice-Hall.

Gregory, J.W., and V. Piché. 1983. "Inequality and Mortality: Demographic Hypotheses Regarding Advanced and Peripheral Capitalism." *International Journal of Health Services*, 13: 89–106.

Grewal, San. 2005. "The Audiences Are Bigger than the Stars." *Toronto Star*, 26 April.

Grimes, Michael D. 1991. *Class in Twentieth-Century American Sociology: An Analysis of Theories and Measurement Strategies*. New York: Praeger.

Grosjean, Michele, and Michele Lacoste. 1998. "L'oral et l'écrit dans les communications de travail ou les illusions du 'tout ecrit'." *Sociologie du travail*, 40: 439–61.

Gross, Edward, and Gregory P. Stone. 1981. "Embarrassment and the Analysis of Role Requirements." *American Journal of Sociology*, 70: 1–15.

Grossman, Dave. and DeGaetano, Gloria. 1999. *Stop Teaching Our Kids to Kill*. New York: Crown Publishing.

Guernsey, Judith Read, Ron Dewar, Swarna Weerasinghe, Susan Kirkland, and Paul J. Veugelers. 2000. "Incidence of Cancer in Sydney and Cape Breton County, Nova Scotia 1979–1997." *Canadian Journal of Public Health*, 91: 285–92.

Guillén, Mauro F. 2001. "Is Globalization Civilizing, Destructive or Feeble? A Critique of Five Key Debates in the Social Science Literature." *Annual Review of Sociology*, 27: 235–60.

Guindon, Hubert. 1967. "Two Cultures: An Essay on Nationalism, Class, and Ethnic Tension." In *Contemporary Canada*, edited by Richard Leach, 33–59. Durham, NC: Duke University Press.

———. 1968. "Social Unrest, Social Class and Quebec's Bureaucratic Revolution." In *Canadian Society: Sociological Perspectives*, edited by Bernard R. Blishen, Frank E. Jones, Kaspar D. Naegele, and John Porter, 702–10. Toronto: Macmillan.

———. 1983. "Quebec and the Canadian Question." In *An Introduction to Sociology*, edited by M. Michael Rosenberg, William B. Shaffir, Allan Turowetz, and Morton Weinfeld, 619–42. Toronto: Methuen.

Guppy, Neil, and Scott Davies. 1998. *Education in Canada: Recent Trends and Future Challenges*. Ottawa: Statistics Canada.

Gusfield, Joseph R. 1963. *Symbolic Crusade: Status Politics and the American Temperance Movement*. Urbana: University of Illinois Press.

———. 1981. *The Culture of Public Problems: Drinking-Driving and the Symbolic Order*. Chicago: University of Chicago Press.

———. 1989. "Constructing the Ownership of Social Problems: Fun and Profit in the Welfare State." *Social Problems*, 36: 431–41.

Haberland, Nicole, and Diana Measham, eds. 2002. *Responding to Cairo: Case Studies of Changing Practice in Reproductive Health and Family Planning*. New York: Population Council.

Habermas, Jürgen. 1975. *Legitimation Crisis*. Translated by Thomas McCarthy. Boston: Beacon.

———. 1984. *The Theory of Communicative Action*. 2 vols. Translated by Thomas McCarthy. Cambridge: Polity.

Hackett, Robert A., Richard Gruneau, Donald Gutstein, Timothy Gibson, and The News Watch Canada. 2000. *The Missing News: Filters and Blindspots in Canada's Press*. Aurora, Ont.: Canadian Centre for Policy Alternatives/Garamond.

Haddad, Tony, and Lawrence Lam. 1988. "Canadian Families—Men's Involvement in Family Work: A Case Study of Immigrant Men in Toronto." *International Journal of Comparative Sociology*, 29: 269–79.

Hagan, John, and Ruth D. Peterson, eds. 1995. *Crime and Inequality*. Stanford, Calif.: Stanford University Press.

Hales, Dianne. 2000. *Just Like a Woman: How Gender Science Is Redefining What Makes Us Female*. New York: Bantam.

Hall, Edward T. 1966. *The Hidden Dimension*. Garden City, NY: Doubleday.

Hall, Emmett. 1964–5. *Report of the Royal Commission on Health Services*. Ottawa: Queen's Printer.

Hall, Stuart. 1980. "Encoding/Decoding." In *Culture, Media, Language*, edited by Stuart Hall, Dorothy Hobson, Andrew Lowe, and Paul Willis, 128–38. London: Unwin Hyman.

Hamilton, Roberta. 1978. *The Liberation of Women*. London: Allen and Unwin.

Hanamoto, Darrell. 1995. *Monitored Peril: Asian Americans and the Politics of Representation*. Minneapolis: University of Minnesota Press.

Handel, Gerald, ed. 1988. *Childhood Socialization*. New York: Aldine de Gruyter.

Haney, Banks, and Zimbardo. 1973. "The Mind is a Formidable Jailer: A Pirandellion Prison." *The New York Times Magazine*, Section 6, 36.

Hardey, Michael. 2002. "The Story of My Illness: Personal Accounts of Illness on the Internet." *Health*, 6, no. 1: 31–46.

Hardoy, Jorge E., Diana Mitlin, and David Satterthwaite. 2001. *Environmental Problems in an Urbanizing World*. London: Earthscan.

Harris, Chauncy, and Edward L. Ullman. 1945. "The Nature of Cities." *Annals of the American Academy of Political and Social Science*, no. 242: 7–17.

Hartmann, Heidi. 1981. "The Unhappy Marriage of Marxism and Feminism: Towards a More Progressive Union." In *The Unhappy Marriage of Marxism and Feminism: A Debate on Class and Patriarchy*, edited by Lydia Sargent, 2–41. London: Pluto.

Hartnagel, Timothy F. 2000. "Correlates of Criminal Behaviour." In *Criminology: A Canadian Perspective*, edited by Rick Linden, 94–136. Toronto: Harcourt.

Harvey, David. 1989. *The Condition of Postmodernity: An Enquiry into the Origins of Cultural Change*. New York: Routledge.

Hassan, Robert. 2004. *Media, Politics, and the Networked Society*. Maidenhead, UK: Open University Press/McGraw-Hill Education.

Hawley, Amos A. 1950. *Human Ecology: A Theory of Community Structure*. New York: Ronald Press.

———. 1981. *Urban Society*. 2nd edn. New York: Wiley.

Health Reports. 2001. "Women's Health Needs." *Health Reports*, 12, no. 3: 34.

Heimer, Robert. 2002. *Social Problems: An Introduction to Critical Constructionism*. New York: Oxford University Press.

Held, David. 1980. *Introduction to Critical Theory: Horkheimer to Adorno*. Berkeley: University of California Press.

Helwig, David. 2000. "NWT Residents Are Accident Prone, Live Shorter Lives." *Canadian Medical Association Journal*, 162: 681–2.

Henry, Frances. 1994. *The Caribbean Diaspora in Toronto: Learning to Live with Racism*. Toronto: University of Toronto Press.

Henry, Frances, and Effie Ginzberg. 1985. *Who Gets the Work: A Test of Racial Discrimination in Employment*. Toronto: Urban Alliance on Race Relations and Social Planning Directorate.

————. 1990. "Racial Discrimination in Employment." In *Images of Canada: The Sociological Tradition*, edited by James Curtis and Lorne Tepperman, 302–9. Toronto: Prentice-Hall.

Henry, Frances, and Carol Tator. 2002. *Discourses of Domination: Racial Bias in the Canadian English-Speaking Press*. Toronto: University of Toronto Press.

Herek, Gregory M. 2002. "Gender Gaps in Public Opinion About Lesbians and Gay Men." *Public Opinion Quarterly*, 66: 40–66.

Herman, Ed, and Noam Chomsky. 1988. *Manufacturing Consent*. New York: Pantheon.

Hewitt, John P. 2000. *Self and Society: A Symbolic Interactionist Social Psychology*. 8th edn. Boston: Allyn and Bacon.

Hickman, B. 1988. "Men Wise Up to Bald Truth." *Australian*, 21 May: 4.

Hier, Sean P. 2002. "Raves, Risks and the Ecstasy Panic: A Case Study in the Subversive Nature of Moral Regulation." *Canadian Journal of Sociology*, 27: 33–52.

Hier, Sean, and Joshua Greenberg. 2002. "News Discourses and the Problematization of Chinese Migration to Canada." *Ethnic and Racial Studies*, 25: 138–62.

Higgins, Robert R. 1994. "Race, Pollution and the Mastery of Nature." *Environmental Ethics*, 16: 251–64.

Hilgartner, Stephen, and Charles Bosk. 1988. "The Rise and Fall of Social Problems: A Public Arenas Model." *American Journal of Sociology*, 94: 53–78.

Hirschi, Travis. 1969. *Causes of Delinquency*. Berkeley: University of California Press.

Hirschi, Travis, and Michael Gottfredson. 1985. "Age and Crime, Logic and Scholarship: Comment on Greenberg." *American Journal of Sociology*, 91: 22–7.

Hirst, Paul, and Grahame Thompson. 1996. *Globalization in Question: The International Economy and the Possibilities of Governance*. Cambridge, UK: Polity.

Hobbes, Thomas. [1651] 1968. *Leviathan*. Baltimore: Penguin.

Hochschild, Adam. 1998. *King Leopold's Ghost: A Story of Greed, Terror, and Heroism in Colonial Africa*. Boston: Houghton Mifflin.

Hochschild, Arlie. 1983. *The Managed Heart: Commercial-ization of Human Feeling*. Berkeley: University of California Press.

————. 1997. *The Time Bind: When Work Becomes Home and Home Becomes Work*. New York: Metropolitan Books.

————. 2001. "The Third Shift." In *Family Patterns, Gender Relations*, 2nd edn, edited by Bonnie J. Fox, 338–51. Toronto: Oxford University Press.

Hochschild, Arlie, with Anne Machung. 1989. *The Second Shift: Working Parents and the Revolution at Home*. New York: Viking.

Hodson, Randy. 2001. *Dignity at Work*. Cambridge: Cambridge University Press, 2001.

Hofrichter, Richard, ed. 1993. *Toxic Struggles: The Theory and Practice of Environmental Justice*. Philadelphia: New Society.

Holmes, Malcolm D., and Judith A. Antell. 2001. "The Social Construction of American Indian Drinking: Perceptions of American Indian and White Officials." *Sociological Quarterly*, 42: 151–73.

Holton, Robert J. 1998. *Globalization and the Nation-State*. New York: St Martin's.

Homans, George. 1951. "The Western Electric Researchers." In *Human Factors in Management*, edited by Schyler Dean Hoslett, 210–41. New York: Harper.

Hope, Steven, Chris Power, and Bryan Rodgers. 1998. "The Relationship Between Parental Separation in Childhood and Problem Drinking in Adulthood." *Addiction*, 93: 505–14.

Hoskins, Colin, Stuart McFadyen, and Adam Finn. 2004. *Media Economics: Applying Economics to New and Traditional Media*. Thousand Oaks, Calif.: Sage.

Hoyt, Homer. 1939. *The Structure and Growth of Residential Neighborhoods in American Cities*. Washington, DC: Federal Housing Administration.

Hughes, Diane, and Deborah Johnson. 2001. "Correlates in Children's Experiences of Parents' Racial Socialization Behaviors." *Journal of Marriage and Family*, 63: 981–96.

Hughes, Karen. 1999. *Gender and Self-Employment in Canada: Assessing Trends and Policy Implications*. Ottawa: Canadian Policy Research Networks.

Human Fertilisation and Embryology Authority (HFEA). 1997. *Sixth Annual Report*. United Kingdom: HFEA.

Human Resources Development Canada (HRDC). 2002. *Knowledge Matters: Skills and Learning for Canadians*. Hull, Que.: Human Resources Development Canada.

Human Resources Development Canada (HRDC) and Statistics Canada. 1998. *High School May Not Be Enough: An Analysis of Results from the School Leavers Follow-up Survey 1995*. Ottawa: Minister of Public Works and Government Services Canada.

Humphrey, Craig R., and Frederick R. Buttel. 1982. *Environment, Energy and Society*. Belmont, Calif.: Wadsworth.

Humphreys, Laud. 1970. *Tearoom Trade: Impersonal Sex in Public Places*. Chicago: Aldine.

Humphries, Karin H., and Eddy van Doorslaer. 2000. "Income-Related Health Inequality in Canada." *Social Science and Medicine*, 50: 663–71.

Hunter, Alfred A. 1981. *Class Tells: On Social Inequality in Canada*. Toronto: Butterworths.

Hunter, Alfred A., and Jean McKenzie Leiper. 1993. "On Formal Education, Skills and Earnings: The Role of Educational Certificates in Earnings Determination." *Canadian Journal of Sociology*, 18: 21–42.

Hunter, Floyd. 1953. *Community Power Structure: A Study of Decision Makers*. Chapel Hill: University of North Carolina Press.

Hurrelmann, Klaus, ed. 1989. *The Social World of Adolescents*. Berlin: Walter de Gruyter.

Illich, Ivan. 1976. *Limits to Medicine: Medical Nemesis: The Expropriation of Health*. Toronto: McClelland & Stewart.

Imershein, Allen W., and Carroll L. Estes. 1996. "From Health Services to Medical Markets: The Commodity Transformation of Medical Production and the Non-profit Sector." *International Journal of Health Services*, 26: 221–38.

Imig, Doug, and Sidney Tarrow. 2001. "Mapping the Europeanization of Contention: Evidence from a Quantitative Data Analysis." In *Contentious Europeans:*

*Protest and Politics in an Emerging Polity*, edited by Doug Imig and Sidney Tarrow, 27–49. New York: Rowman and Littlefield.

Income Security Advocacy Centre. 2002. "The Inquest into the Death of Kimberly Rogers." Available at <www.incomesecurity.org/index_html>.

Infantry, Ashante. 2005. "Studios Need to Do the Right Thing." *Toronto Star*, 6 March.

Inglehart, Ronald. 1977. *The Silent Revolution: Changing Values and Political Styles Among Western Publics*. Princeton, NJ: Princeton University Press.

———. 1990a. *Culture Shift in Advanced Industrial Society*. Princeton, NJ: Princeton University Press.

———. 1990b. "Values, Ideology, and Cognitive Mobilization in New Social Movements." In *Challenging the Political Order*, edited by R.J. Dalton and M. Kuechler, 23–42. New York: Oxford University Press.

International Labour Organization. n.d. *Multinational Corporations*. Available at <www.itcilo.it/english/actrav/telearn/global/ilo/multinat/multinat.htm>, accessed 27 May 2003.

Isajiw, Wsevolod W., Aysan Sev'er, and Leo Driedger. 1993. "Ethnic Identity and Social Mobility: A Test of the 'Drawback Model'." *Canadian Journal of Sociology*, 18: 177–96.

Jablin, Frederic M. 1984. "Assimilating New Members in Organizations." In *Communication Yearbook*, edited by R.N. Bostrom, 594–626. Newbury Park, Calif.: Sage.

Jackson, Andrew. 2005. *Work and Labour in Canada: Critical Issues*. Toronto: Canadian Scholars' Press.

Jackson, Andrew, and David Robinson. 2000. *Falling Behind: The State of Working Canada*, 2000. Ottawa: Canadian Centre for Policy Alternatives.

Jamieson, Lynn. 1998. *Intimacy: Personal Relationships in Modern Societies*. Cambridge: Polity.

Janigan, Mary. 2002. "Immigrants. How Many Is Too Many? Who Should Get In? Can We Tell Them Where to Live?" *Maclean's*, 16 December: 20–5.

Janis, Irving Lester. 1982. *Groupthink: Psychological Studies of Policy Decisions and Fiascoes*. 2nd edn. Boston: Houghton Mifflin.

Jenkins, J. Craig. 1983. "Resource Mobilization Theory and the Study of Social Movements." *Annual Review of Sociology*, 9: 527–53.

Jenkins, Philip. 1994. *Using Murder: The Social Construction of Serial Homicide*. New York: Aldine de Gruyter.

Jeter, Jon. 2002. "Zambia Reduced to a Flea-Market Economy: Cheap Foreign Imports Have Destroyed the Once Thriving Textile Industry." *Washington Post*, 22 April, A1.

Jette, Allan M., Sybil L. Crawford, and Sharon L. Tennstedt. 1996. "Toward Understanding Ethnic Differences in Late-Life Disability." *Research on Aging*, 18: 292–309.

Jiwani, Jasmin. 1992. "In the Outskirts of Empire: Women of Colour in Popular Film and Television." *Aquellarre*, Fall, 13–17.

Johnson, Chalmers, Laura D'Andrea Tyson, and John Zysman. 1990. *Politics and Productivity: How Japan's Development Strategy Works*. New York: Harper Business.

Johnson, Holly. 1990. "Wife Abuse." In *Canadian Social Trends*, edited by Craig McKie and Keith Thompson, 173–76. Toronto: Thompson Educational.

———. 1996. *Dangerous Domains: Violence Against Women in Canada*. Toronto: Nelson.

Johnson, Laura. 1986. *Working Families: Workplace Supports for Families*. Toronto: Working Families Project of the Social Planning Council of Metropolitan Toronto.

Johnson, Terence. 1972. *Professions and Power*. London: Macmillan, 1972.

Junger, Marianne, Peter van der Heijden, and Carl Keane. 2001. "Interrelated Harms: Examining the Association Between Victimization, Accidents and Criminal Behaviour." *Injury Control and Safety Promotion*, 8, no. 1: 13–28.

Kachur, Jerrold L., and Trevor W. Harrison. 1999. "Introduction: Public Education, Globalization, and Democracy: Whither Alberta?" In *Contested Classrooms: Education, Globalization, and Democracy in Alberta*, edited by Trevor W. Harrison and Jerrold L. Kachur, xiii–xxxv. Edmonton: University of Alberta Press and Parkland Institute.

Kadar, Marlene. 1988. "Sexual Harassment as a Form of Social Control." In *Gender and Society*, edited by Arlene Tigar McLaren, 337–46. Toronto: Copp Clark Pitman.

Kalin, Rudolf, and John W. Berry. 1994. "Ethnic and Multicultural Attitudes." In *Ethnicity and Culture in Canada: The Research Landscape*, edited by J.W. Berry and J.A. Laponce, 293–321. Toronto: University of Toronto Press.

Kanungo, Shivraj. 1998. "An Empirical Study of Organizational Culture and Network-Based Computer Use." *Computers in Human Behavior*, 14, no. 1: 79–91.

Karim, H. Karim. 1998. *From Ethnic Media to Global Media: Transnational Communication Networks among Diasporic Communities*. Ottawa: International Comparative Research Group, Strategic Research and Analysis, Canadian Heritage.

Kasper, Anne S., and Susan J. Ferguson, eds. 2000. *Breast Cancer: Society Shapes an Epidemic*. New York: St Martin's Press.

Kawachi, Ichiro, Bruce P. Kennedy, Vanita Gupta, and Deborah Prothrow-Stith. 1999. "Women's Status and the Health of Women and Men: A View from the States." *Social Science and Medicine*, 48: 21–32.

Kendall, Diana, Jane L. Murray, and Rick Linden. 2004. *Social Problems in a Diverse Society*. Scarborough, Ont.: Pearson.

Kent, Tom. 2003. "Ban Media Convergence, Make Papers Independent." *Canadian Speeches*, 18, no. 2: 24–27.

Kenway, Jane, and Helen Modra. 1992. "Feminist Pedagogy and Emancipatory Possibilities." In *Feminisms and Critical Pedagogy*, edited by Carmen Luke and Jennifer Gore, 138–66. London: Routledge.

Keyfitz, Nathan. 1993. "Are There Ecological Limits to Population?" *Proceedings of the National Academy of Sciences USA*, 90: 6895–9.

Kidd, Bruce. 1987. "Sports and Masculinity." In *Beyond Patriarchy*, edited by Michael Kaufman, 250–65. Toronto: Oxford University Press.

Kiernan, Kathleen. 1997. *The Legacy of Parental Divorce: Social, Economic, and Demographic Experiences in Adulthood.* London: Centre for Analysis of Social Exclusion.

Kilbourne, Jean. 2001. *Can't Buy My Love: How Advertising Changes the Way We Think and Feel.* New York: Simon & Schuster.

Kilgour, David. 1998. "From Informal Economy to Micro-enterprise: The Role of Microcredit." Address to Results/Résultats Canada convention, Ottawa, 24 October. Available at <www.david-kilgour.com/ssap/informal.htm>, accessed 4 July 2003.

Kilmarten, Christopher T. 1994. *The Masculine Self.* Toronto: Maxwell Macmillan.

Kindleberger, Charles P. 1986. *The World in Depression, 1929–1939.* Berkeley: University of California Press.

Kinney, David. 1993. "From Nerds to Normals: The Recovery of Identity Among Adolescents from Middle School to High School." *Sociology of Education,* 66: 21–40.

Kirk, Dudley. 1998. "Demographic Transition Theory." *Population Studies,* 50: 361–87.

Kitschelt, Herbert. 1993. "Social Movements, Political Parties, and Democratic Theory." *Annals of the American Academy of Political and Social Science,* 528 (July): 13–29.

———, ed. 1999. *Continuity and Change in Contemporary Capitalism.* Cambridge: Cambridge University Press.

Klein, David M., and James M. White. 1996. *Family Theories: An Introduction.* Thousand Oaks, Calif.: Sage.

Klein, Naomi. 1999. *No Logo: Taking Aim at the Brand Bullies.* New York: Picador.

Knight, Rolf. 1996. *Indians at Work: An Informal History of Native Labour in British Columbia, 1858–1930.* Vancouver: New Star.

Knighton, Tamara, and Sheba Mirza. 2002. "Postsecondary Participation: The Effects of Parents' Education and Household Income." *Education Quarterly Review,* 8, no. 3: 25–31.

Kohn, Melvin L. 1977. *Class and Conformity: A Study of Values, with a Reassessment,* 1977. 2nd edn. Chicago: University of Chicago Press.

Kopinak, Kathryn. 1988. "Women in Canadian Municipal Politics: Two Steps Forward, One Step Back." In *Gender and Society,* edited by Arlene Tigar McLaren, 372–89. Toronto: Copp Clark Pitman.

Kornhauser, Ruth R. 1978. *Social Sources of Delinquency: An Appraisal of Analytic Models.* Chicago: University of Chicago Press.

Kortenhaus, Carole, and Jack Demarest. 1993. "Gender Stereotyping in Children's Literature: An Update." *Sex Roles,* 28, nos 3/4: 219–33.

Krahn, Harvey J., and Graham S. Lowe. 1998. *Work, Industry, and Canadian Society.* 3rd edn. Toronto: Nelson.

Kriesel, Warren, Terrence J. Centner, and Andrew Keeler. 1996. "Neighborhood Exposure to Toxic Releases: Are There Racial Inequities?" *Growth and Change,* 27: 479–99.

Krosenbrink-Gelissen, Lilianne E. 1993. "The Canadian Constitution, the Charter, and Aboriginal Women's Rights: Conflicts and Dilemmas." *International Journal of Canadian Studies,* nos 7–8: 207–24.

Kwong, Jeff C., Irfan A. Dhalla, David L. Streiner, Ralph E. Baddour, Andrea E. Waddell, and Ian L. Johnson. 2002. "Effects of Rising Tuition Fees on Medical School Class Composition and Financial Outlook." *Canadian Medical Association Journal,* 166: 1023–8.

Lambert, Ronald D. 1971. *Sex Role Imagery in Children.* Ottawa: Royal Commission on the Status of Women.

Lambertus, Sandra. 2004. *Wartime Images, Peacetime Wounds: The Media and Gustafsen Lake Standoff.* Toronto: University of Toronto Press.

Landy, Sarah, and Kwok Kwan Tam. 1996. "Yes, Parenting Does Make a Difference to the Development of Children in Canada." In *Statistics Canada, Growing Up in Canada,* 103–11. Ottawa: Human Resources Development Canada and Statistics Canada.

LaPrairie, Carol. 2002. "Aboriginal Over-representation in the Criminal Justice System: A Tale of Nine Cities." *Canadian Journal of Criminology,* 44: 181–208.

Larsen, Nick. 2000. "Prostitution: Deviant Activity or Legitimate Occupation." In *New Perspectives on Deviance: The Construction of Deviance in Everyday Life,* edited by Lori G. Beaman, 50–67. Toronto: Prentice-Hall Allyn and Bacon.

Lasn, Kalle. 1999. *Culture Jam: The Uncooling of America.* New York: Eagle Press.

Laufer, William S., and Freda Adler. 1994. *The Legacy of Anomie Theory: Advances in Criminological Theory.* New Brunswick, NJ: Transaction.

Lautard, Hugh, and Neil Guppy. 1990. "The Vertical Mosaic Revisited: Occupational Differentials Among Canadian Ethnic Groups." In *Race and Ethnic Relations in Canada,* edited by Peter S. Li, 189–208. Toronto: Oxford University Press.

Lawr, Douglas, and Robert Gidney, eds. 1973. *Educating Canadians: A Documentary History of Public Education.* Toronto: Van Nostrand Reinhold.

LeBlanc, J. Clarence. 1994. *Educating Canadians for the New Economy.* Working paper prepared for the Canadian Institute for Research on Regional Development. Moncton, NB: Canadian Institute for Research on Regional Development.

Lemert, Edwin. 1951. *Social Pathology: A Systematic Approach to the Theory of Sociopathic Behavior.* New York: McGraw-Hill.

Leslie, Gerald, and Sheila K. Korman. 1989. *The Family in Social Context.* 7th edn. New York: Oxford University Press.

Levin, Benjamin, and J. Anthony Riffel. 1997. *Schools and the Changing World: Struggling Toward the Future.* London: Falmer.

Lewicki, Roy J., and Barbara Benedict Bunker. 1996. "Developing and Maintaining Trust in Work Relationships." In *Trust in Organizations: Frontiers of Theory and Research,* edited by Roderick M. Kramer and Tom R. Tyler, 114–39. Thousand Oaks, Calif.: Sage.

Li, Peter S. 1988. *The Chinese in Canada.* Toronto: Oxford University Press.

———. 2000. "Earning Disparities Between Immigrants and Native-Born Canadians." *Canadian Review of Sociology and Anthropology,* 37: 289–311.

Library of Parliament. 2002. "Women—Party Standings in the House of Commons: Current List." Available at <www.parl.gc.ca/information/about/people/house/StandingsHofCwm.asp>, accessed January 2003.

Lieberman, Seymour. 1956. "The Effects of Changes in Roles on the Attitudes of Role Occupants." *Human Relations*, 9: 385–402.

Lieberson, Stanley. 2000. *A Matter of Taste: How Names, Fashions, and Culture Change*. New Haven, Conn.: Yale University Press.

Liebow, Elliot. 1993. *Tell Them Who I Am: The Lives of Homeless Women*. New York: Free Press.

Lin, Zhengxi, Janice Yates, and Garnett Picot. 1999. *Rising Self-employment in the Midst of High Unemployment: An Empirical Analysis of Recent Developments in Canada*. Ottawa: Statistics Canada.

Lindert, Peter H., and Jeffrey G. Williamson. 2001. *Does Globalization Make the World More Unequal?* Cambridge, Mass.: National Bureau of Economic Research.

Linteau, Paul-André, René Durocher, and Jean-Claude Robert. 1983. *Quebec: A History 1867–1929*. Toronto: Lorimer.

Linton, Ralph. 1936. *The Study of Man: An Introduction*. New York: Appleton-Century-Crofts.

Lipman, Ellen L., David R. Offord, and Martin D. Dooley. 1996. "What Do We Know About Children from Single-Parent Families? Questions and Answers from the National Longitudinal Survey on Children." In *Growing Up in Canada*, 83–91. Ottawa: Human Resources Development Canada.

Little, Don. 1995. "Earnings and Labour Force Status of 1990 Graduates." *Education Quarterly Review*, 2, no. 3: 10–20.

Livingstone, D.W. 1999. *The Education–Jobs Gap: Underemployment or Economic Democracy*. Toronto: Garamond.

Lock, Margaret. 1998. "Menopause: Lessons from Anthropology." *Psychosomatic Medicine*, 60: 410–19.

Lofland, Lyn H. 1973. *A World of Strangers: Order and Action in Urban Public Space*. New York: Basic Books.

———. 1998. *The Public Realm: Exploring the City's Quintessential Social Territory*. New York: Aldine de Gruyter.

Looker, E. Dianne, and Graham S. Lowe. 2001. *Post-secondary Access and Student Financial Aid in Canada: Current Knowledge and Research Gaps*. Ottawa: Canadian Policy Research Networks. Available at <www.cprn.ca/en/doc.cfm?doc=192>, accessed 19 June 2003.

Looker, E. Dianne, and Victor Thiessen. 1999. "Images of Work: Women's Work, Men's Work, Housework." *Canadian Journal of Sociology*, 24: 225–54.

Lorber, Judith, and Susan Farrell. 1991. *The Social Construction of Gender*. London: Sage.

Lorimer, Rowland, and Mike Gasher. 2002. *Mass Communication in Canada*. Toronto: Oxford University Press.

Loseke, Donileen R. 1992. *The Battered Woman and Shelters: The Social Construction of Wife Abuse*. Albany: State University of New York Press.

———. 1999. *Thinking About Social Problems: An Introduction to Constructionist Perspectives*. New York: Aldine de Gruyter.

Losh-Hesselbart, Susan. 1987. "Development of Gender Roles." In *Handbook of Marriage and the Family*, edited by Marvin B. Sussman and Suzanne K. Steinmetz, 535–63. New York: Plenum.

Lowe, Graham S. 1987. *Women in the Administrative Revolution: The Feminization of Clerical Work*. Toronto: University of Toronto Press.

———. 1989. *Paid/Unpaid Work and Stress: New Directions in Research*. Ottawa: Canadian Advisory Council on the Status of Women.

———. 2000. *The Quality of Work: A People-Centred Agenda*. Toronto: Oxford University Press.

Lowe, Marion. 1983. "Sex Differences, Science and Society." In *The Technological Woman*, edited by Jan Zimmerman, 7–17. New York: Praeger.

Luckenbill, David F. 1977. "Criminal Homicide as a Situational Transaction." *Social Problems*, 25: 176–86.

Lukes, Steven. 1974. *Power: A Radical View*. London: Macmillan.

Lutz, Wolfgang, ed. 1994. *The Future Population of the World: What Can We Assume Today?* London: Earthscan.

Luxton, Meg. 1980. *More Than a Labour of Love*. Toronto: Women's Press.

———. 1983. "Two Hands for the Clock: Changing Patterns in the Gendered Division of Labour in the Home." *Studies in Political Economy*, 12: 27–44.

———. 2001. "Family Coping Strategies: Balancing Paid Employment and Domestic Labour." In *Family Patterns, Gender Relations*, 2nd edn, edited by Bonnie Fox, 318–37. Toronto: Oxford University Press.

Luxton, Meg, and June Corman. 2001. *Getting By in Hard Times: Gendered Labour at Home and on the Job*. Toronto: University of Toronto Press.

Lyman, P.. and H.R. Varian. 2003. "How Much Information? 2003." Available at http://www.sims.berkeley.edu/research/projects/how-much-info-2003/.

Lynch, Kathleen. 1989. *The Hidden Curriculum: Reproduction in Education*, A Reappraisal. London: Falmer.

Lynn, Stephen. 2002. *Zapata Lives! Histories and Cultural Politics in Southern Mexico*. Berkeley: University of California Press.

Maaka, Roger, and Augie Fleras. 2005. *The Politics of Indigeneity*. Dunedin, NZ: University of Otago Press.

McAdam, Doug. 1996. "Conceptual Origins, Current Problems, Future Directions." In *Comparative Perspectives on Social Movements*, edited by Doug McAdam, John McCarthy, and Mayer Zald, 23–40. New York: Cambridge University Press.

Macbeth, Tannis. 2001. "The Impact of Television: A Canadian Natural Experiment." In *Communications in Canadian Society*, 5th edn, edited by C. McKie and B. Singer, 196–214. Toronto: Thompson.

McCabe, Marita P., L. Ricciardelli, D. Mellor, and K. Ball. 2005. "Media Influences on Body Image and Disordered Eating among Indigenous Adolescent Australians." *Adolescence*, 40: 71–91.

McCarthy, John D. 1996. "Constraints and Opportunities in Adopting, Adapting, and Inventing." In *Comparative*

*Perspectives on Social Movements*, edited by Doug McAdam, John McCarthy, and Mayer Zald, 141–51. New York: Cambridge University Press.

McCarthy, Shawn. 2002. "Valenti Pitches to Film Makers." *Globe and Mail*, 8 February, A1.

McChesney, R.W. 1999. *Rich Media, Poor Democracy: Communication Politics in Dubious Times*. Urbana: University of Illinois Press.

Maccoby, Eleanor. 1992. "Trends in the Study of Socialization: Is There a Lewinian Heritage?" *Journal of Social Issues*, 48, no. 2: 171–86.

Maccoby, Eleanor, and Carole Jacklin. 1974. *The Psychology of Sex Differences*. Stanford, Calif.: Stanford University Press.

McDaniel, Susan. 1988. "Women's Roles, Reproduction and the New Reproductive Technologies: A New Stork Rising." In *Reconstructing the Canadian Family*, edited by Nancy Mandell and Ann Duffy, 175–206. Toronto: Butterworths.

MacDowell, Laurel Sefton, and Ian Radforth, eds. 1992. *Canadian Working Class History: Selected Readings*. Toronto: Canadian Scholars' Press.

Macfarlane, Alan. 1997. *The Savage Wars of Peace: England, Japan and the Malthusian Trap*. Oxford, UK: Blackwell.

McIntosh, Mary. 1978. "The State and the Oppression of Women." In *Feminism and Materialism*, edited by Annette Kuhn and Ann Marie Wolpe, 254–89. London: Routledge and Kegan Paul.

McIntyre, Amanda, and Michael Rosenberg. 2000. "Ethnic Women's Organizations in Montreal." Unpublished paper, Concordia University, Montreal.

McKeown, Thomas. 1976. *The Modern Rise of Population*. London: Edward Arnold.

Mackie, Marlene. 1983. *Exploring Gender Relations*. Toronto: Butterworths.

———. 1987. *Constructing Women and Men: Gender Socialization*. Toronto: Holt Rinehart and Winston.

———. 1996. *Gender Relations in Canada: Further Explorations*. Toronto: Harcourt Brace.

MacKinnon, Mark, and Keith Lacey. 2001. "Bleak House." *Globe and Mail*, 18 August, F1.

McLaren, Peter. 1998. *Life in Schools: An Introduction to Critical Pedagogy in the Foundations of Education*, 3rd edn. New York: Longman.

McLorg, Penelope A., and Diane E. Taub. 1987. "Anorexia Nervosa and Bulimia: The Development of Deviant Identities." *Deviant Behavior*, 8: 177–89.

MacMillan, Harriet L., Angus B. MacMillan, David R. Offord, and Jennifer L. Dingle. 1996. "Aboriginal Health." *Canadian Medical Association Journal*, 155: 1569–78.

Magnusson, Warren. 1990. "Critical Social Movements: De-centring the State." In *Canadian Politics: An Introduction to the Discipline*, edited by Alain G. Gagnon and James P. Bickerton, 525–41. Peterborough, Ont.: Broadview.

Mahtani, Minelle. 2002. "Representing Minorities. Canadian Media and Minority Identities." *Canadian Ethnic Studies*, 33, no. 3: 99–131.

Malthus, Thomas R. [1798] 1970. *An Essay on the Principle of Population*. Harmondsworth, UK: Penguin.

Mandell, Nancy. 2001. "Women, Families and Intimate Relations." In *Feminist Issues: Race, Class and Sexuality*, 3rd edn, edited by Nancy Mandell, 193–218. Toronto: Prentice-Hall.

Manzer, Jenny. 2001. "Clinical Guidelines Ignore Gender Differences." *Medical Post*, 37, no. 13: 2, 65.

Manzer, Ronald. 1994. *Public Schools and Political Ideas: Canadian Educational Policy in Historical Perspective*. Toronto: University of Toronto Press.

Mao, Y., J. Hu, A.M. Ugnat, and K. White. 2000. "Non-Hodgkin's Lymphoma and Occupational Exposure to Chemicals in Canada." *Annals of Oncology*, 11, suppl. 1: 69–73.

Maquiladora Solidarity Network. 2000. "Child Labour and the Rights of Youth." Available at <www.maquilasolidarity.org/resources/child/issuesheet.htm>, accessed 28 May 2003.

Marchak, Patricia. 1991. *The Integrated Circus: The New Right and the Restructuring of Global Markets*. Montreal: McGill-Queen's University Press.

Marcil-Gratton, Nicole. 1998. *Growing Up with Mom and Dad? The Intricate Family Life Courses of Canadian Children*. Ottawa: Statistics Canada.

Marr, William L. 1992. "Post-war Canadian Immigration Patterns." In *The Immigration Dilemma*, edited by Steven Globerman, 17–42. Vancouver: Fraser Institute.

Marsden, Peter V., Cynthia R. Cook, and Arne L. Kalleberg. 1996. "Bureaucratic Structures for Coordination and Control." In *Organizations in America: Analyzing Their Structures and Human Resource Practices*, edited by Arne L. Kalleberg, David Knoke, Peter V. Marsden, and Joe L. Spaeth, 69–86. Thousand Oaks, Calif.: Sage.

Marshall, Katherine. 1987. "Women in Male Dominated Professions." *Social Trends*, Winter: 7–11.

———. 1993. "Employed Parents and the Division of Labour." *Perspectives on Labour and Income*, 5, no. 3: 23–30.

———. 1994. "Balancing Work and Family Responsibilities." *Perspectives on Labour and Income*, 6, no. 1: 26–30.

———. 1998. "Stay-at-Home Dads." *Perspectives on Labour and Income*, 10, no. 1: 9–15.

Marshall, Sheree. 1995. "Ethnic Socialization of African American Children: Implications for Parenting, Identity Development, and Achievement." *Journal of Youth and Adolescence*, 24: 377–96.

Martin, Michele. 1997. *Communication and Mass Media: Culture, Domination, and Opposition*. Scarborough, Ont.: Prentice Hall.

Martin, Philip L. 2002. *Germany: Managing Migration in the 21st Century*. Unpublished paper, University of California–Davis, Comparative Immigration and Integration Program.

Marx, Karl. [1867] 1967. *Capital: A Critique of Political Economy*. New York: International Publishers.

———. 1956. *Selected Writings in Sociology and Social Philosophy*. Edited by T.B. Bottomore and Maximilien Rubel. Translated by T.B. Bottomore. New York: McGraw-Hill.

———. 1964. *The Economic and Philosophical Manuscripts of 1844*. Edited by Dirk J. Struik. Translated by Martin Milligan. New York: International Publishers.

Marx, Karl, and Friedrich Engels. [1845–6] 1970. *The German Ideology. Part I, with Selections from Parts 2 and 3*. Translated by C.J. Arthur. New York: International Publishers.

———. [1848] 1948. *Manifesto of the Communist Party*. New York: International Publishers.

———. [1848] 1983. "Manifesto of the Communist Party." In *The Portable Karl Marx*, edited by Eugene Kamenka, 197–324. New York: Penguin.

Maslovski, Mikhail. 1996. "Max Weber's Concept of Patrimonialism and the Soviet System." *Sociological Review*, 44: 294–308.

Mason, David. 1999. "The Continuing Significance of Race? Teaching Ethnic and Racial Studies in Sociology." In *Ethnic and Racial Studies Today*, edited by Martin Bulmer and John Solomos, 13–28. London: Routledge.

Matza, D., and Gresham Sykes. 1957. "Techniques of Neutralization: A Theory of Delinquency." *American Sociological Review*, 5: 1–12.

Maule, Christopher. 2003. "Grappling with Change." *Canadian Speeches*, 18, no. 2:40–42.

Maxim, Paul S., and Paul C. Whitehead. 1998. *Explaining Crime*, 4th edn. Newton, Mass.: Butterworth–Heinemann.

May, Harvey. 2004. *Broadcast in Colour: Cultural Diversity and Television Programming in Four Countries*. Brisbane, Australia: Australian Film Commission, Creative Industries Review and Application Centre.

Mead, George Herbert. 1934. *Mind, Self, and Society from the Standpoint of a Social Behaviorist*. Chicago: University of Chicago Press.

Mead, Margaret. 1935. *Sex and Temperament in Three Primitive Societies*. New York: Dell.

Meissner, Martin, Elizabeth Humphries, Scott Meis, and William Schell. 1975. "No Exit for Wives: Sexual Division of Labour and the Culmination of Household Demands." *Canadian Review of Sociology and Anthropology*, 12: 424–39.

Melucci, Alerbero. 1989. *Nomads of the Present: Social Movements and Individual Needs in Contemporary Society*. Philadelphia: Temple University Press.

Merten, Hans-Joachim. 1997. 'Lemercatoria: A Self-Applying System Beyond National Law?" In *Global Law Without a State*, edited by Gunther Teubner, 31–43. Aldershot, UK: Dartmouth.

Mertig, Angela, and Riley Dunlap. 2001. "Environmentalism, New Social Movement and the New Class: A Cross-national Investigation." *Rural Sociology*, 66, no. 1: 113–36.

Mertig, Angela, Riley Dunlap, and Denton Morrison. 2002. "The Environmental Movement in the United States." In *Handbook of Environmental Sociology*, edited by Riley Dunlap and William Michelson, 448–81. Westport, Conn.: Greenwood.

Merton, Robert K. 1957. *Social Theory and Social Structure*. New York: Free Press.

Messing, Karen. 1987. "The Scientific Mystique: Can a White Lab Coat Guarantee Purity in the Search for Knowledge About the Nature of Women?" In *Women and Men: Interdisciplinary Readings on Gender*, edited by Greta Hofmann Nemiroff, 103–16. Toronto: Fitzhenry and Whiteside.

———. 1998. *One-Eyed Science: Occupational Health and Women Workers*. Philadelphia: Temple University Press.

Messner, Steven, and Richard Rosenfeld. 1997. *Crime and the American Dream*, 2nd edn. Belmont, Calif.: Wadsworth.

Meston, Cindy M. 1990. "Ethnic, Gender, and Length-of-Residence Influences on Sexual Knowledge and Attitudes." *Journal of Sex Research*, May: 1–22.

Meyer, David, and Suzanne Staggenborg. 1996. "Movements, Countermovements and the Structure of Political Opportunity." *American Journal of Sociology*, 101: 1628–60.

Meyer, John W. 2000. "Globalization: Sources and Effects on National States and Societies." *International Sociology*, 15: 233–48.

Meyerson, Debra, Karl E. Weick, and Roderick M. Kramer. 1996. "Swift Trust and Temporary Groups." In *Trust in Organizations: Frontiers of Theory and Research*, edited by Roderick M. Kramer and Tom R. Tyler, 166–95. Thousand Oaks, Calif.: Sage.

Michels, Robert. 1962. *Political Parties*. New York: Free Press.

Michelson, William. 1976. *Man and His Urban Environment: A Sociological Approach*. Reading, MA: Addison-Wesley.

———. 1983. *From Sun to Sun: Daily Obligations and Community Structure in the Lives of Employed Women and Their Families*. Totowa, NJ: Rowman and Allanheld.

———. 1985. *From Sun to Sun: Daily Obligations and Community Structure*. Toronto: Rowman and Allanhead.

Micklin, Michael, ed. 1973. *Population, Environment and Social Organization: Current Issues in Human Ecology*. Hinsdale, Ill.: Dryden.

Miethe, Terance D., and Richard C. McCorkle. 1998. *Crime Profiles: The Anatomy of Dangerous Persons, Places, and Situations*. Los Angeles: Roxbury.

Milgram, Stanley. 1970. "The Experience of Living in Cities." *Science*, 167: 1461–8.

Milkman, Ruth. 1987. *Gender at Work: The Dynamics of Job Segregation by Sex During World War II*. Chicago: University of Illinois Press.

Miller, Gale, and James A. Holstein. 1993. *Constructionist Controversies: Issues in Social Problems Theory*. New York: Aldine de Gruyter.

Mills, C. Wright. 1956. *The Power Elite*. New York: Oxford University Press.

———. 1959. *The Sociological Imagination*. New York: Oxford University Press.

Mitchell, Ann. 1985. *Children in the Middle: Living Through Divorce*. London: Tavistock.

Mitchell, Elizabeth. [1915] 1981. *In Western Canada Before the War*. Saskatoon: Western Producer Prairie Books.

Mitchell, Robert Cameron, Angela G. Mertig, and Riley E. Dunlap. 1992. "Twenty Years of Environmental Mobilization: Trends Among National Environmental Organizations." In *American Environmentalism*, edited by

Riley Dunlap and Angela G. Mertig, 11–26. Philadelphia: Taylor and Francis.

Moir, Anne, and David Jessel. 1992. *Brain Sex: The Real Difference Between Men and Women*. London: Michael Joseph.

Mondschein, E.R., K.E. Adolph, and C.S. Tamis-LeMonda. 2000. "Gender Bias in Mothers' Expectations About Infant Crawling." *Journal of Experimental Child Psychology*, 77: 304–16.

Monière, Denis. 1981. *Ideologies in Quebec: The Historical Development*. Translated by Richard Howard. Toronto: University of Toronto Press.

Moodie, Susannah. [1852] 1995. *Roughing It in the Bush*. Toronto: McClelland & Stewart.

Moore, Barrington, Jr. 1969. *Social Origins of Dictatorship and Democracy*. London: Peregrine.

Morris, Marika, Jane Robinson, and Janet Simpson with Sherry Galey. 1999. *The Changing Nature of Home Care and Its Impact on Women's Vulnerability to Poverty*. Ottawa: Status of Women Canada.

Morrison, Denton, and Riley E. Dunlap. 1986. "Environmentalism and Elitism: A Conceptual and Empirical Analysis." *Environmental Management*, 10: 581–9.

Morton, Desmond. 1998. *Working People: An Illustrated History of the Canadian Labour Movement*, 4th edn. Montreal: McGill-Queen's University Press.

Moynihan, Ray, Iona Heath, and David Henry. 2002. "Selling Sickness: The Pharmaceutical Industry and Disease Mongering." *British Medical Journal*, 324: 886–91.

Muncie, John, and Margaret Weatherell. 1995. "Family Policy and Political Discourse." In *Understanding the Family*, edited by John Muncie, Margaret Weatherell, Rudi Dallos, and Allan Cochrane, 39–80. London: Sage.

Munro, Marcella. 1997. "Ontario's 'Days of Action' and Strategic Choices for the Left in Canada." *Studies in Political Economy*, 53: 125–40.

Murdie, Robert. 1969. *Factorial Ecology of Metropolitan Toronto*. Department of Geography Research Paper 116. Chicago: University of Chicago.

Murdock, George. 1949. *Social Structure*. New York: Macmillan.

Murphy, Elizabeth. 2000. "Risk, Responsibility and Rhetoric in Infant Feeding." *Journal of Contemporary Ethnography*, 29: 291–325.

Murray, Catherine. 2002. "Silent on the Set: Cultural Diversity and Race in Canadian TV Drama." Unpublished manuscript. School of Communication, Simon Fraser University, Vancouver, BC.

Mustard, Cameron A., Shelley Derkson, Jean-Marie Berthelot, Michael Wolfson, and Leslie L. Roos. 1997. "Age-Specific Education and Income Gradients in Morbidity and Mortality in a Canadian Province." *Social Science and Medicine*, 45: 383–97.

Mustard, Fraser. 1999. "Health Care and Social Cohesion." In *Market Limits in Health Reform: Public Success, Private Failure*, edited by Daniel Drache and Terry Sullivan, 329–50. London: Routledge.

Nabalamba, Alice. 2001. "Locating Risk: A Multivariate Analysis of the Spatial and Socio-demographic Characteristics of Pollution." Unpublished Ph.D. dissertation, University of Waterloo, Waterloo, Ont.

Naess, Arne. 1973. "The Shallow and the Deep, Long Range Ecology Movement." *Inquiry*, 16: 95–100.

Nakhaie, M. Reza, Robert A. Silverman, and Teresa C. LaGrange. 2000. "An Examination of Gender, Ethnicity, Class and Delinquency." *Canadian Journal of Sociology*, 25: 35–59.

Nanda, Serena. 1991. *Cultural Anthropology*. Belmont, Calif.: Wadsworth.

Nathe, Patricia. 1978. "The Flux, Flow, and Effluvia of Bohemia." *Urban Life*, 6: 387–416.

National Council of Welfare. 2002. *Poverty Profile 1999*. Ottawa: Minister of Public Works and Government Services.

National Longitudinal Survey of Children and Youth (NLSCY). 1996. *Growing Up in Canada*. Ottawa: Human Resources Development Canada and Statistics Canada.

National Research Council. Committee on Population and Working Group on Population Growth and Economic Development. 1986. *Population Growth and Economic Development: Policy Questions*. Washington, DC: National Academy Press.

Navarro, Véase Vicente. 1975. "The Industrialization of Fetishism or the Fetishism of Industrialization: A Critique of Ivan Illich." *Social Science and Medicine*, 9: 351–63.

———. 1999. *NWT Health Status Report*. Ottawa: Department of Health and Social Services, Statistics Canada.

Nedelmann, Birgitta. 1991. *Review of Ideology and the New Social Movements*, by Alan Scott. Contemporary Sociology, 20: 374–5.

Nelson, Adie. 2006. *Gender in Canada*, 3rd edn. Toronto: Pearson.

Nelson, Adie, and Barrie W. Robinson. 2002. *Gender in Canada*, 2nd edn. Toronto: Pearson Educational.

Nelson, Fiona. 1999. "Maternal Identities, Maternal Practices and the Culture(s) of Motherhood." Paper presented at the annual meeting of the Canadian Sociology and Anthropology Association.

Nesbitt-Larking, Paul. 2001. *Politics, Society, and the Media: Canadian Perspectives*. Peterborough, Ont.: Broadview.

Nett, Emily. 1981. "Canadian Families in Social-Historical Perspective." *Canadian Journal of Sociology*, 6: 239–60.

Newbold, K. Bruce. 1998. "Problems in Search of Solutions: Health and Canadian Aboriginals." *Journal of Community Health*, 23, no. 1: 59–73.

Nicholson, Linda, and Steven Seidman. 1995. *Introduction to Social Postmodernism: Beyond Identity Politics*, edited by Linda Nicholson and Steven Seidman. Cambridge: Cambridge University Press.

Nisbet, Robert A. 1959. "The Decline and Fall of Social Class." *Pacific Sociological Review*, 2: 11–17.

Notestein, Frank. 1945. "Population: The Long View." In *Food for the World*, edited by Theodore W. Schultz, 36–57. Chicago: University of Chicago Press.

Oakes, J.M. 1996. "A Longitudinal Analysis of Environmental Equity in Communities with Hazardous Waste Facilities." *Social Science Research*, 25: 125–48.

O'Brien, Mary. 1981. *The Politics of Reproduction*. London: Routledge & Kegan Paul.

Occhionero, Marisa Ferrari. 1996. "Rethinking Public Space and Power." *Revue internationale de sociologie/ International Review of Sociology*, 6 (n.s.): 453–64.

O'Connor, Julia S., Ann Shola Orloff, and Sheila Shaver. 1999. *States, Markets, Families: Gender Liberalism and Social Policy in Australia, Canada, Great Britain and the United States*. Cambridge: Cambridge University Press.

Offe, Claus. 1984. *Contradictions of the Welfare State*. Cambridge, Mass.: MIT Press.

Offer, Daniel, Eric Ostrov, Kenneth Howard, and Robert Atkinson. 1988. *The Teenage World: Adolescents' Self-Image in Ten Countries*. New York: Plenum.

O'Leary, K. Daniel, J. Barling, Ilena Arias, Alan Rosenbaum, J. Malone, and A. Tyree. 1989. "Prevalence and Stability of Physical Aggression Between Spouses: A Longitudinal Analysis." *Journal of Consulting and Clinical Psychology*, 57: 263–8.

Olewiler, Nancy. 1999. "National Tax Policy for an International Economy: Divergence in a Converging World?" In *Room to Manoeuvre? Globalization and Policy Convergence*, edited by Thomas J. Courchene, 345–72. Montreal: McGill-Queen's University Press.

Olsen, Denis. 1980. *The State Elite*. Toronto: McClelland & Stewart.

Olzak, Susan. 1983. "Contemporary Ethnic Mobilization." *Annual Review of Sociology*, 9: 355–74.

Omer, Bartov. 2005. *The "Jew" in Cinema: From the Golem to Don't Touch My Holocaust*. Bloomington: Indiana University Press.

Organization for Economic Co-operation and Development (OECD). 2001. *OECD Economic Outlook 70* (December, 2001). Paris: OECD.

O'Riordan, T. 1971. "The Third American Environmental Conservation Movement: New Implications for Public Policy." *Journal of American Studies*, 5: 155–71.

Osberg, Lars. 1992. "Canada's Economic Performance: Inequality, Poverty, and Growth." In *False Promises: The Failure of Conservative Economics*, edited by Robert C. Allen and Gideon Rosenbluth, 39–52. Vancouver: New Star.

Osborne, Ken. 1999. *Education: A Guide to the Canadian School Debate: Or, Who Wants What and Why?* Toronto: Penguin.

Overbeek, Johannes. 1974. *History of Population Theories*. Rotterdam, The Netherlands: Rotterdam University Press.

Pais, José Machado. 2000. "Transitions and Youth Cultures: Forms and Performances." *International Social Science Journal*, 52: 219–33.

Pakulski, Jan, and Malcolm Waters. 1996. *The Death of Class*. London: Sage.

Palmer, Howard H. 1991. *Ethnicity and Politics in Canada Since Confederation*. Ottawa: Canadian Historical Society.

Palys, Ted. n.d. "Russel Ogden v. SFU." Available at <http://www.sfu.ca/~palys/OgdenPge.htm>, accessed 15 July 2003.

Pampel, Fred C. 1998. *Aging, Social Inequality, and Public Policy*. Thousand Oaks, Calif.: Pine Forge.

Pandey, Sanjay K., and Stuart I. Bretschneider. 1997. "The Impact of Red Tape's Administrative Delay on Public Organizations' Interest in New Information Technologies." *Journal of Public Administration Research and Theory*, 7: 113–30.

Panitch, Leo, ed. 1977. *The Canadian State: Political Economy and Political Power*. Toronto: University of Toronto Press.

Park, Robert E. 1925. "The City: Suggestions for the Investigation of Human Behavior in the Urban Environment." In *The City*, edited by Robert E. Park, Ernest Burgess, and Roderick McKenzie, 1–46. Chicago: University of Chicago Press.

Park, Robert, and Ernest Burgess. 1921. *Introduction to the Science of Sociology*. Chicago: University of Chicago Press.

Park, Robert, and Roderick D. McKenzie, eds. 1925. *The City*. Chicago: University of Chicago Press.

Parsons, Talcott. 1949. *Essays in Sociological Theory*. New York: Free Press.

———. 1951. *The Social System*. Glencoe, Ill.: Free Press.

———. 1955. *Family, Socialization and Interaction Process*. New York: Free Press.

———. 1959. "The School Class as a Social System: Some of Its Functions in American Society." *Harvard Educational Review*, 29: 297–318.

Parsons, Talcott, and Robert F. Bales. 1955. *Family Socialization and Interaction Process*. New York: Free Press.

Pearce, Frank, and Laureen Snider, eds. 1995. *Corporate Crime: Contemporary Debates*. Toronto: University of Toronto Press.

Perlmutter, David D. 2000. *Policing the Media: Street Cops and Public Perception of Law Enforcement*. Thousand Oaks, Calif.: Sage.

Petersen, William. 1989. "Marxism and the Population Question: Theory and Practice." *Population and Development Review*, 14 (suppl.): 77–101.

Peterson, Richard A. 1994. "Culture Studies Through the Production Perspective: Progress and Prospects." In *The Sociology of Culture: Emerging Theoretical Perspectives*, edited by Diana Crane, 163–89. Oxford: Blackwell.

Petrovic, Edit. 2000. "Conceptualizing Gender, Race, and Ethnicity as a Field of Study." In *Perspectives on Ethnicity in Canada*, edited by Madeleine Kalbach and Warren Kalbach, 48–54. Toronto: Harcourt.

Pfohl, Stephen J. 1977. "The Discovery of Child Abuse." *Social Problems*, 24: 310–23.

Pfuhl, Erdwin H., and Stuart Henry. 1993. *The Deviance Process*, 3rd edn. New York: Aldine de Gruyter.

Picot, Garnett, and John Myles. 1995. *Social Transfers, Changing Family Structure, and Low Income Among Children*. Ottawa: Statistics Canada.

Piliavin, Erving, and S. Briar. 1964. "Police Encounters with Juveniles." *American Journal of Sociology*, 70: 206–14.

Pineo, Peter. 1977. "The Social Standing of Ethnic and Racial Groupings." *Canadian Review of Sociology and Anthropology*, 14: 147–57.

Plumwood, Val. 1992. "Feminism and Ecofeminism: Beyond the Dualistic Assumptions of Women, Men and Nature." *Ecologist*, 22, no. 1: 8–13.

Pollack, William. 1998. *Real Boys: Rescuing Our Sons from the Myths of Boyhood*. New York: Random House.

Pomerleau, Andrée, Daniel Bolduc, Gerard Malcuit, and Louise Cossess. 1990. "Pink or Blue: Environmental Gender Stereotypes in the First Two Years of Life." *Sex Roles*, 22: 359–67.

Population Reference Bureau. 2002. *World Population Data Sheet for 2002*. Washington, DC: Population Reference Bureau.

———. 2003. *World Population Data Sheet for 2003*. Washington, DC: Population Reference Bureau.

Porter, John. 1965. *The Vertical Mosaic: An Analysis of Social Class and Power in Canada*. Toronto: University of Toronto Press.

Portes, Alejandro. 1997. *Globalization from Below: The Rise of Transnational Communities*. Princeton, NJ: Centre for Migration and Development.

———. 1999. "Conclusion: Towards a New World: The Origins and Effects of Transnational Activities." *Ethnic and Racial Studies*, 22: 463–77.

Portes, Alejandro, Luis E. Guarnizo, and Patricia Landolt. 1999. "The Study of Transnationalism: Pitfalls and Promise of an Emergent Research Field." *Ethnic and Racial Studies*, 22: 217–37.

Posner, Judith. 1987. "The Objectified Male: The New Male Image in Advertising." In *Women and Men: Interdisciplinary Readings on Gender*, edited by Greta Hofmann Nemiroff, 180–8. Markham, Ont.: Fitzhenry and Whiteside.

Potter, W. James. 2005. *Media Literacy*. 3rd edn. Thousand Oaks, CA: Sage.

Potuchek, Jean L. 1997. *Who Supports the Family: Gender and Breadwinning in Dual-Earner Marriages*. Stanford, Calif.: Stanford University Press.

Poulantzas, Nicos. 1975. *Classes in Contemporary Capitalism*. Translated by David Fernbach. London: New Left Books.

———. 1978. *State, Power, Socialism*. Translated by Patrick Camiller. London: New Left Books.

Preston, Samuel H. 1986. "Mortality and Development Revisited." *United Nations Population Bulletin*, 18: 34–40.

Pringle, Rosemary. 1988. *Secretaries Talk: Sexuality, Power and Work*. London: Verso.

Prus, Robert. 1987. "Generic Social Processes: Maximizing Conceptual Development in Ethnographic Research." *Journal of Contemporary Ethnography*, 16: 250–93.

Pryor, Edward. 1984. "Canadian Husband–Wife Families: Labour Force Participation and Income Trends, 1971–1981." *Labour Force*, May: 93–109.

Pryor, Jan, and Bryan Rodgers. 2001. *Children in Changing Families: Life After Parental Separation*. Oxford: Blackwell.

Psychology Today. 2000. "Makeup vs. Math." *Psychology Today*, November/December: 18.

Quadagno, Jill. 1990. "Race, Class, and Gender in the US Welfare State." *American Sociological Review*, 55: 25–7.

Raadschelders, Jos C.N. 1997. "Size and Organizational Differentiation in Historical Perspective." *Journal of Public Administration Research and Theory*, 7: 419–41.

Ralston, Helen. 2000. "Redefinition of South Asian Women." In *Race and Racism: Canada's Challenge*, edited by Leo Driedger and Shiva S. Halli, 204–34. Ottawa: Carleton University Press.

Ram, Bali. 1990. *New Trends in the Family: Demographic Facts and Figures*. Ottawa: Statistics Canada.

Ramcharan, Subhas. 1982. *Racism: Nonwhites in Canada*. Toronto: Butterworths.

Ramirez, Francisco O. 1981. "Comparative Social Movements." *International Journal of Comparative Sociology*, 22: 3–21.

Ramsay, Patricia. 1991. *Making Friends in School: Promoting Peer Relationships in Early Childhood*. New York: Teachers College Press, Columbia University.

Raphael, Dennis. 2001. "From Increasing Poverty to Societal Disintegration: The Effects of Economic Inequality on the Health of Individuals and Communities." In *Unhealthy Times: The Political Economy of Health Care*, edited by Pat Armstrong, Hugh Armstrong, and David Coburn, 223–46. Toronto: Oxford University Press.

Reinarman, Craig. 1996. "The Social Construction of an Alcohol Problem." In *Constructing Crime: Perspectives on Making News and Social Problems*, edited by Gary W. Potter and Victor E. Kappeler, 193–220. Prospect Heights, Ill.: Waveland.

Reiss, Albert J., Jr. 1959. "Rural–Urban and Status Differences in Interpersonal Contacts." *American Journal of Sociology*, 65: 182–95.

Reiter, Ester. 1991. *Making Fast Food: From the Frying Pan into the Fire*. Montreal: McGill-Queen's University Press.

———. 1996. *Making Fast Food: From the Frying Pan into the Fryer*, 2nd edn. Montreal: McGill-Queen's University Press.

Reitz, Jeffrey G. 1980. *The Survival of Ethnic Groups*. Toronto: McGraw-Hill Ryerson.

———. 1998. *The Warmth of the Welcome: The Social Causes of Economic Success for Immigrants in Different Nations and Cities*. Boulder, Colo.: Westview.

Rex, John. 1987. "The Role of Class Analysis in the Study of Race Relations: A Weberian Perspective." In *Theories of Race and Ethnic Relations*, edited by John Reand David Mason, 64–83. Cambridge: Cambridge University Press.

Rice, Suzanne. 1996. "The Evolution of the Concept of Sexual Harassment." *Initiatives*, 57, no. 2: 1–14.

Richardson, Laurel. 1988. *The Dynamics of Sex and Gender*. New York: Harper and Row.

Rifkin, Jeremy. 1995. *The End of Work: The Decline of the Global Labour Force and the Dawn of the Post-market Era*. New York: Putnam.

Riggins, Stephen, ed. 1992. *Ethnic Minority Media: An International Perspective*. Newbury Park, Calif.: Sage.

Rinehart, James. 2001. *The Tyranny of Work: Alienation and the Labour Process*. 4th edn. Toronto: Harcourt.

Rinehart, James, Christopher Huxley, and David Robertson. 1994. "Worker Commitment and Labour Management Relations Under Lean Production at CAMI." *Industrial Relations*, 49: 750–75.

Ritzer, George. 2000. *The McDonaldization of Society*. 3rd edn. Thousand Oaks, Calif.: Pine Forge.

Robert, Maryse. 2000. *Negotiating NAFTA: Explaining the Outcome in Culture, Textiles, Autos, and Pharmaceuticals*. Toronto: University of Toronto Press.

Robertson, Ann. 2001. "Biotechnology, Political Rationality and Discourses on Health Risk." *Health*, 5: 293–310.

Robertson, David, James Rinehart, Chris Huxley, Jeff Wareham, Herman Rosenfeld, A. McGough, and Steven Benedict. 1993. *The CAMI Report: Lean Production in a Unionized Auto Plant*. North York, Ont.: CAW Research, 1993.

Robinson, B.W., and E.D. Salamon. 1987. "Gender Role Socialization: A Review of the Literature." In *Gender Roles: Doing What Comes Naturally?* edited by E.D. Salamon and B.W. Robinson, 123–42. Toronto: Methuen.

Robinson, Tracy L. 2001. "White Mothers of Non-white Children." *Journal of Humanistic Counseling, Education and Development*, 40, no. 2: 171–85.

Rodgers, Bryan, and Jan Pryor. 1998. *Divorce and Separation: The Outcomes for Children*. York, UK: Joseph Rowntree Foundation.

Rodrik, Dani. 1997. *Has Globalization Gone Too Far?* Washington, DC: Institute for International Economics.

Rose, Steven, Leon J. Kamin, and R.C. Lewontin. 1984. *Not in Our Genes: Biology, Ideology, and Human Nature*. New York: Penguin.

Rose, Vicki. 1974. "Rape as a Social Problem: A Byproduct of the Feminist Movement." *Social Problems*, 25: 75–89.

Rosenberg, M. Michael, and Jack Jedwab. 1992. "Institutional Completeness, Ethnic Organizational Style and the Role of the State: The Jewish, Italian and Greek Communities of Montreal." *Canadian Review of Sociology and Anthropology*, 29: 266–87.

Rosenthal, Carolyn J. 1985. "Kinkeeping in the Familial Division of Labour." *Journal of Marriage and the Family*, 47: 965–74.

Ross, David P., and Paul Roberts. 1999. *Income and Child Well-Being: A New Perspective on the Poverty Debate*. Ottawa: Canadian Council on Social Development.

Ross, David P., E. Richard Shillington, and Clarence Lochhead. 1994. *The Canadian Fact Book on Poverty 1994*. Ottawa: Canadian Council on Social Development.

Rossi, Alice. 1984. "Gender and Parenthood." *American Sociological Review*, 49: 1–18.

Rotermann, Michelle. 2001. "Wired Young Canadians." *Canadian Social Trends*, Winter, 4–8.

Rothermund, Dietmar. 1993. *An Economic History of India: From Pre-colonial Times to 1991*, 2nd edn. London: Routledge.

Royal Commission on Aboriginal Peoples. 1996. *Report of the Royal Commission on Aboriginal Peoples. Vol. 3: Gathering Strength*. Ottawa: The Commission.

Royal Commission on Bilingualism and Biculturalism. 1970. *Report of the Royal Commission on Bilingualism and Biculturalism. Vol. 4. The Cultural Contribution of the Other Ethnic Groups*. Ottawa: Queen's Printer.

Ruble, Diane N., and Carol Lynn Martin. 1998. "Gender Development." In *Handbook of Child Psychology*, 5th edn, edited by William Damon, 933–1016. New York: Wiley.

Ryan, John, and William M. Wentworth. 1999. *Media and Society: The Production of Culture in the Mass Media*. Toronto: Allyn & Bacon.

Sacco, Vincent F. 1992. "An Introduction to the Study of Deviance and Control." In *Deviance: Conformity and Control in Canadian Society,* edited by Vincent F. Sacco, 1–48. Scarborough, Ont.: Prentice-Hall.

Sachs, Wolfgang. 1991. "Environment and Development: The Story of a Dangerous Liaison." *Ecologist*, 21: 252–7.

Sadovnick, Alan R., ed. 1995. *Knowledge and Pedagogy: The Sociology of Basil Bernstein*. Norwood, NJ: Ablex.

Said, Edward W. 1978. *Orientalism*. London: Routledge & Kegan Paul.

Salazar, Lilia P., Shirin M. Schuldermann, Eduard H. Schuldermann, and Cam-Loi Huynh. 2001. "Canadian Filipino Adolescents Report on Parental Socialization for School Involvement." *Canadian Ethnic Studies*, 33, no. 2: 52–76.

Salem, Rob. 2005. "Watching TV Makes Me Smarter than You." *Toronto Star*, 28 April.

Samson, Jane, ed. 2001. *The British Empire*. New York: Oxford University Press.

Sartorius, N. 2001. "The Economic and Social Burden of Depression." *Journal of Clinical Psychiatry*, 62 (suppl. 15): 8–11.

Sassen, Saskia. 1991. *The Global City: New York, London, Tokyo*. Princeton, NJ: Princeton University Press.

———. 1996. *Losing Control? Sovereignty in an Age of Globalization*. New York: Columbia University Press.

———. 2002. "Introduction: Locating Cities on Global Circuits." In *Global Networks: Linked Cities*, edited by Saskia Sassen, 1–36. New York: Routledge.

Sasson, Theodore. 1995. *Crime Talk: How Citizens Construct a Social Problem*. Hawthorne, NY: Aldine de Gruyter.

Scarce, Rik. 1990. *Eco-warriors: Understanding the Radical Environmental Movement*. Chicago: Noble.

Schecter, Tanya. 1998. *Race, Class, Women and the State: The Case of Domestic Labour*. Montreal: Black Rose.

Schissel, Bernard, and Terry Wotherspoon. 2003. *The Legacy of School for Aboriginal People: Education, Oppression, and Emancipation*. Toronto: Oxford University Press.

Schnaiberg, Allan. 1975. "Social Synthesis of the Societal–Environmental Dialectic: The Role of Distributional Impacts." *Social Science Quarterly*, 56: 5–20.

Schnore, Leo F. 1958. "Social Morphology and Human Ecology." *American Journal of Sociology*, 63: 620–34.

Schonberg, Harold C. 1977. *The Lives of the Great Composers*. 3rd edn. New York: Norton.

Schur, Edwin. 1979. *Interpreting Deviance: A Sociological Introduction*. New York: Harper and Row.

Segrave, Kerry. 1998. *American Television Abroad: Hollywood's Attempt to Dominate World Television*. Jefferson, NC: McFarland.

Seiber, Timothy, and Andrew Gordon. 1981. *Children and Their Organizations*. Boston: G.K. Hall.

Seltzer, Judith, and Debra Kalmuss. 1988. "Socialization and Stress Explanations for Spouse Abuse." *Social Forces*, 67: 473–91.

Sennett, Richard. 1998. *The Corrosion of Character: The Personal Consequences of Work in the New Capitalism*. New York: Norton.

Shaw, Susan. 1988. "Gender Difference in the Definition and Perception of Household Labour." *Family Relations*, 37: 333–7.

Shelton, Beth Anne, and Juanita Firestone. 1989. "Household Labor Time and the Gender Gap in Earnings." *Gender and Society*, 3, no. 1: 105–12.

Shively, JoEllen. 1992. "Cowboys and Indians: Perceptions of Western Films Among American Indians and Anglos." *American Sociological Review*, 57: 725–34.

Sieber, Sam. 1981. *Fatal Remedies: The Ironies of Social Intervention*. New York: Plenum.

Siegel, Lloyd, and Arthur Zitrin. 1978. "Transsexuals in the New York City Welfare Population: The Function of Illusion in Transsexuality." *Archives of Sexual Behavior*, 7: 285–90.

Silva, Elizabeth B., and Carol Smart, eds. 1999. *The New Family?* London: Sage.

Silverstone, Roger, and Myria Georgiou. 2005. "Editorial Introduction: Media and Minorities in a Multicultural Europe." *Journal of Ethnic and Migration Studies*, 31: 433–41.

Simmel, Georg. 1950. "The Metropolis and Mental Life." In *The Sociology of Georg Simmel*, translated by Kurt Wolff, 400–27. New York: Free Press.

——. 1957. "Fashion." *American Journal of Sociology*, 62: 541–58.

Simmons, J.L. 1969. *Deviants*. Berkeley, Calif.: Glendessary Press.

Simon, David R., and Frank E. Hagan. 1999. *White Collar Deviance*. Boston: Allyn and Bacon.

Simon, Julian, ed. 1995. *The State of Humanity*. Cambridge, Mass.: Blackwell.

——. 1996. *The Ultimate Resource 2*. Princeton, NJ: Princeton University Press.

Sinclair, Peter R. 1982. "Towards a Class Analysis of Contemporary Socialist Agriculture." *Sociologia Ruralis*, 22: 122–39.

Sinclair, Peter, and Lawrence Felt. 1992. "Separate Worlds: Gender and Domestic Labour in an Isolated Fishing Region." *Canadian Review of Sociology and Anthropology*, 29: 55–71.

Singer, Dorothy, and Jerome Singer. 2001. *Handbook of Children and the Media*. Thousand Oaks, Calif.: Sage.

Sjoberg, Gideon. 1960. *The Preindustrial City: Past and Present*. New York: Free Press.

Skidelsky, Robert. 2000. *John Maynard Keynes: Fighting for Britain, 1937–1946*. London: Macmillan.

Skill Development Leave Task Force. 1983. *Learning a Living in Canada: Report to the Minister of Employment and Immigration Canada*. Ottawa: Employment and Immigration Canada.

Sklair, Leslie. 1994. "Global Sociology and Global Environmental Change." In *Social Theory and the Global Environment*, edited by Michael Redclift and Ted Benton, 205–27. New York: Routledge.

Skocpol, Theda. 1979. *States and Social Revolutions: A Comparative Analysis of France, Russia, and China*. Cambridge: Cambridge University Press.

Slaughter, Matthew J., and Phillip Swagel. 1997. *Does Globalization Lower Wages and Export Jobs?* International Monetary Fund Economic Issues 11. Washington, DC: International Monetary Fund.

Smelser, Neil J. 1963. *Theory of Collective Behavior*. New York: Free Press.

Smelser, Neil J., William Julius Wilson, and Faith Mitchell. 2001. *America Becoming: Racial Trends and Their Consequences*. Washington, DC: National Research Council Press.

Smith, Adam. [1776] 1976. *An Inquiry into the Nature and Causes of the Wealth of Nations*. Edited by W.B. Todd. Oxford: Oxford University Press.

Smith, Dorothy. 1975. "Ideological Structures and How Women Are Excluded." *Canadian Review of Sociology and Anthropology*, 12: 353–69.

——. 1999. *Writing the Social: Critique, Theory, and Investigations*. Toronto: University of Toronto Press.

Smith, Michael R. 1999. "What Is the Effect of Technological Change on Earnings Inequality?" *International Journal of Sociology and Social Policy*, 19: 24–59.

——. 2001a. "La mondialisation à-t-elle un effet important sur les marchés du travail des pays riches?" In *Une société monde? Les dynamiques de la mondialisation*, edited by Daniel Mercure, 201–14. Quebec City: Presses de l'Université Laval.

——. 2001b. "What Have the FTA and the NAFTA Done to the Canadian Labor Market?" *Forum for Social Economics*, 30: 25–50.

Smith, Philip. 2001. *Cultural Theory: An Introduction*. Oxford: Blackwell.

Smith, Raymond T. 1996. *The Matrifocal Family: Power, Pluralism and Politics*. New York: Routledge.

Snow, David A., E. Burke Rochford, Jr, Steven K. Worden, and Robert D. Benford. 1986. "Frame Alignment Processes, Mobilization, and Movement Participation." *American Sociological Review*, 51: 464–81.

Sontag, Susan. 1978. *Illness as Metaphor*. New York: Farrar, Straus & Giroux.

Spector, Malcolm, and John I. Kitsuse. 1977. *Constructing Social Problems*. Menlo Park, Calif.: Cummings.

Spitzer, Steven. 1975. "Toward a Marxian Theory of Deviance." *Social Problems*, 22: 638–51.

Stack, John F., Jr. 1986. "Ethnic Mobilization in World Politics: The Primordial Perspective." In *The Primordial Challenge: Ethnicity in the Contemporary World*, edited by John F. Stack, Jr, 1–11. New York: Greenwood.

Starowicz, Mark. 2003. "Why CBC Needs Stronger Support." *Canadian Speeches*, 18, no. 2: 26–29.

Stasiulis, Daiva. 1980. "The Political Structuring of Ethnic Community Action: A Reformulation." *Canadian Ethnic Studies*, 12: 19–44.

———. 1990. "Theorizing Connections: Gender, Race, Ethnicity, and Class." In *Race and Ethnic Relations in Canada*, edited by Peter S. Li, 269–305. Toronto: Oxford University Press.

———. 1999. "Feminist Intersectional Theorizing." In *Race and Ethnic Relations in Canada*, 2nd edn, edited by Peter S. Li, 347–97. Toronto: Oxford University Press.

Statistics Canada. 1973. *Education in Canada 1973*. Ottawa: Statistics Canada.

———. 1992. *Census Metropolitan Areas and Census Agglomerations: Population and Dwelling Counts*. Ottawa: Statistics Canada.

———. 1996. *Canada Year Book 1997*. Ottawa: Statistics Canada.

———. 1998a. *Characteristics of Dual-Earner Families 1996*. Ottawa: Statistics Canada.

———. 1998b. "1996 Census: Education, Mobility and Migration." *The Daily*, 14 April.

———. 2000. *Women in Canada*. Ottawa: Statistics Canada.

———. 2001a. *Canada Year Book 2001*. Ottawa: Statistics Canada.

———. 2001b. *The Changing Profile of Canada's Labour Force*. Ottawa: Statistics Canada.

———. 2001c. "Internet Use on the Cusp of the 21st Century." *Canadian Social Trends*, Winter: 2–3.

———. 2001d. "Television Viewing." *The Daily*, 23 Oct.

———. 2002a. "Advance Statistics/Education at a Glance." *Education Quarterly Review*, 8, no. 3: 41–53.

———. 2002b. "Fact Sheet on Unionization." *Perspectives on Labour and Income*, 13, no. 3: 1–25.

———. 2002c. "Perspectives on Labour and Income: Fact-Sheet on Unionization." Ottawa: Statistics Canada.

———. 2003a. *Canada's Ethnocultural Portrait: The Changing Mosaic*. Ottawa: Statistics Canada.

———. 2003b. "Population 15 Years and over by Hours Spent on Unpaid Housework, 1996 Census." Available at <http://www.statcan.ca.80/english/Pdgb/famil56_96a.htm>, accessed 5 August 2003.

———. 2004. *Women in Canada: Work Chapter Updates*. Ottawa: Ministry of Industry.

Statistics Canada and Council of Ministers of Education Canada (CMEC). 2000. *Education Indicators in Canada: Report of the Pan-Canadian Education Indicators Program 1999*. Available at <www.cmec.ca/stats/pceip/1999/Indicatorsite/index.html>, accessed 19 June 2003.

Statistics Canada and Human Resources Development Canada (HRDC). 2001. *A Report on Adult Education and Training in Canada: Learning a Living*. Ottawa: Statistics Canada and HRDC.

Status of Women Canada. 1986. *Report of the Task Force on Child Care*. Ottawa: Status of Women Canada.

Steffensmeier, Renee. 1982. "A Role Model of the Transition to Parenthood." *Journal of Marriage and the Family*, 44: 319–34.

Stern, Nicholas. 2002. "Keynote Address: A Strategy for Development." In *Annual World Bank Conference on Development Economics 2001/2002*, edited by Boris Pleskovic and Nicholas Stern, 11–35. Washington, DC: World Bank; New York: Oxford University Press.

Stevans, Lonnie K. 1998. "Assessing the Effect of the Occupational Crowding of Immigrants on the Real Wages of African American Workers." *Review of Black Political Economy*, 26: 37–46.

Stevenson, Kathryn. 1999. "Family Characteristics of Problem Kids." *Canadian Social Trends*, 55, Winter: 2–6.

Stone, Gregory P. 1981. "Appearance and the Self: A Slightly Revised Version." In *Social Psychology Through Symbolic Interaction*, edited by Gregory P. Stone and Harvey A. Farberman, 187–202. New York: Wiley.

Storey, Robert. 2002. "From Capitalism to Socialism." Unpublished paper. McMaster University, Hamilton, Ont..

Strange, Susan. 1996. *The Retreat of the State*. Cambridge: Cambridge University Press.

Strauss, Murray A., and Richard J. Gelles. 1990. *Physical Violence in American Families: Risk Factors and Adaptations to Violence in 8,145 Families*. New Brunswick, NJ: Transaction.

Sugiman, Pamela. 1994. *Labour's Dilemma: The Gender Politics of Auto Workers in Canada, 1937–1979*. Toronto: University of Toronto Press.

———. 2001. "Privilege and Oppression: The Configuration of Race, Gender, and Class in Southern Ontario Auto Plants, 1939 to 1949." *Labour/Le Travail*, 47 (Spring): 83–113.

Suranovic, Steven M. 1997. "Why Economists Should Study Fairness." *Challenge*, 40: 109–24.

Surette, Ray. 1998. *Media, Crime, and Criminal Justice: Images and Realities*, 2nd edn. Toronto: Wadsworth.

Sutherland, Edwin. 1947. *Principles of Criminology*, 4th edn. Chicago: Lippincott.

Sydie, Rosalind. 1987. "Sociology and Gender." In *An Introduction to Sociology*, edited by M. Michael Rosenberg, William B. Shaffir, Allan Turowetz, and Morton Weinfeld. Toronto: Methuen.

Szasz, Andrew. 1994. *Ecopopulism: Toxic Waste and the Movement for Environmental Justice*. Minneapolis: University of Minneapolis Press.

Tannenbaum, Frank. 1938. *Crime and the Community*. Boston: Ginn and Company.

Tanner, Julian. 2001. *Teenage Troubles: Youth and Deviance in Canada*. 2nd edn. Toronto: Nelson.

Tannock, Stuart. 2001. *Youth at Work: The Unionized Fast-Food and Grocery Workplace*. Philadelphia: Temple University Press.

Tapscott, Don. 1998. *Growing Up Digital: The Rise of the Net Generation*. New York: McGraw-Hill.

Taras, David. 2001. *Power and Betrayal in the Canadian Media*. Peterborough, Ont.: Broadview.

Tardy, Rebecca. 2000. "But I Am a Good Mom: The Social Construction of Motherhood Through Health-Care Conversations." *Journal of Contemporary Ethnography*, 29: 433–73.

Tarrow, Sidney. 1988. "National Politics and Collective Action: Recent Theory and Research in Western Europe and the United States." *Annual Review of Sociology*, 14: 421–40.

———. 1998. *Power in Movements: Social Movements and Contentious Politics*. 2nd edn. New York: Cambridge University Press.

Task Force. 2003. *Cultural Diversity on Television*. Report commissioned by the Canadian Association of Broadcasters. Toronto: Solutions Research Group.

Taylor, Bron. 1991. "The Religion and Politics of Earth First!" *Ecologist*, 21: 258–66.

Taylor, Frederick W. 1911. *Principles of Scientific Management*. New York: Harper.

Teitelbaum, Michael S. 1975. "Relevance of Demographic Transition Theory for Developing Countries." *Science*, 2 May: 420–5.

Ten Bos, Réné. 1997. "Essai: Business Ethics and Bauman Ethics." *Organization Studies*, 18: 997–1014.

Theodorson, George A. 1961. *Studies in Human Ecology*. New York: Harper and Row.

———. 1982. *Urban Patterns: Studies in Human Ecology*. University Park: University of Pennsylvania Press.

Thio, Alex. 1998. *Deviant Behavior*. New York: Longman.

Thomas, Derrick. 2001. "Evolving Family Living Arrangements of Canada's Immigrants." *Canadian Social Trends*, Summer: 16–22.

Thomas, W.I., and D.S. Thomas. 1928. *The Child in America*. New York: Knopf.

Thompson, Kevin, and Leslie Heinberg. 1999. "The Media's Influence on Body Image Disturbance and Eating Disorders: We've Reviled Them, Now Can We Rehabilitate Them?" *Journal of Social Issues*, 55: 339–53.

Thompson, Warren S. 1929. "Population." *American Journal of Sociology*, 34: 959–75.

———. 1944. *Plenty of People*. Lancaster, Penn.: Jacques Cattel.

Thomson, Elizabeth, Sara McLanahan, and Roberta Curtin. 1992. "Family Structure, Gender and Parental Socialization." *Journal of Marriage and the Family*, 54: 368–78.

Thorne, Barry. 1982. "Feminist Rethinking of the Family: An Overview." In *Rethinking the Family: Some Feminist Questions*, edited by Barry Thorne with Marilyn Yalom, 1–24. New York: Longman.

Thorns, David C. 2002. *The Transformation of Cities: Urban Theory and Urban Life*. New York: Palgrave Macmillan.

Tilly, Charles. 1978. *From Mobilization to Revolution*. Reading, MA: Addison-Wesley.

———. 1998. *Durable Inequality*. Berkeley: University of California Press.

Tokar, Brian. 1988. "Exploring the New Ecologies." *Alternatives*, 15, no. 4: 31–43.

Tomic, Patricia, and Ricardo Trumper. 1992. "Canada and the Streaming of Immigrants: A Personal Account of the Chilean Case." In *Deconstructing a Nation: Immigration, Multiculturalism, and Racism in '90s Canada*, edited by Vic Satzewich, 163–81. Halifax, NS: Fernwood.

Tönnies, Ferdinand. [1887] 1957. *Community and Society (Gemeinschaft und Gesellschaft)*. New York: Harper and Row.

Torres, Carlos Alberto. 1998. *Democracy, Education, and Multiculturalism: Dilemmas of Citizenship in a Global World*. Lanham, Md: Rowman and Littlefield.

Touraine, Alain. 1981. *The Voice and the Eye: An Analysis of Social Movements*. Cambridge: Cambridge University Press.

Travers, Jim. 2000. "Journalism That Inflames but Doesn't Inform." *Canadian Speeches*, 18, no. 2: 42–43.

Tremblay, Manon. 1998. "Do Female MPs Substantively Represent Women? A Study of Legislative Behaviour in Canada's 35th Parliament." *Canadian Journal of Political Science*, 31: 435–65.

Tremblay, Richard E., Bernard Boulerice, Philip Harden, Pierre McDuff, Daniel Perusse, Robert Pihl, and Mark Zoccolillo. 1996. "Do Children in Canada Become More Aggressive as They Approach Adolescence?" In Statistics Canada, *Growing Up in Canada*, 127–38. Ottawa: HRDC and Statistics Canada.

Tremblay, Sylvain. 1999. "Illicit Drugs and Crime in Canada." In Canadian Centre for Justice Statistics, *The Juristat Reader: A Statistical Overview of the Canadian Justice System*, 253–65. Toronto: Thompson.

Troyer, Ronald, and Gerald Markle. 1983. *Cigarettes: The Battle over Smoking*. New Brunswick, NJ: Rutgers University Press.

Tuggle, Justin L., and Malcolm D. Holmes. 1997. "Blowing Smoke: Status Politics and the Shasta County Smoking Ban." *Deviant Behavior*, 18: 77–93.

Turk, Austin T. 1976. "Law as a Weapon in Social Conflict." *Social Problems*, 23: 276–92.

Turner, Bryan S. 1988. *Status*. Minneapolis: University of Minnesota Press.

Turner, Jay R., and William R. Avison. 2003. "Status Variations in Stress Exposure: Implications for the Interpretation of Prior Research." *Journal of Health and Social Behaviour*. 44, no. 4: 488–505.

Turner, Ralph. 1962. "Role-Taking: Process Versus Conformity." In *Human Behavior and Social Processes*, edited by Arnold Rose, 20–40. Boston: Houghton Mifflin.

Tylor, Edward. 1871. *Primitive Culture: Researches into the Development of Mythology, Philosophy, Religion, Language, Art and Custom*. London: John Murray.

United Nations. 2003. *World Population Prospects: The 2002 Revision*. Highlights. New York: UN Department of Economic and Social Affairs Population Division.

United Nations Centre for Human Settlements (HABITAT). 2001. *Cities in a Globalizing World*. London: Earthscan.

United Nations Population Division. 2002. *International Migration Report 2002*. New York: United Nations.

United States. Bureau of Census. 1999. *World Population Profile: 1998*. Report WP/98. Washington, DC: US Government Printing Office.

Urmetzer, Peter, and Neil Guppy. 1999. "Changing Income Inequality in Canada." In *Social Inequality in Canada: Patterns, Problems, and Policies*, edited by James E. Curtis, Edward G. Grabb, and Neil L. Guppy, 56–65. Scarborough, Ont.: Prentice-Hall Allyn and Bacon.

Ursel, Jane. 1992. *Private Lives, Public Policy: 100 Years of State Intervention in the Family*. Toronto: Women's Press.

Valaskakis, Gail Guthrie. 2005. *Indian Country: Essays on Contemporary Native Culture.* Waterloo, Ont.: Wilfrid Laurier University Press.

Van den Berghe, Pierre L. 1987. *The Ethnic Phenomenon.* New York: Praeger.

van Wormer, Katherine Stuart, and Clemens Bartollas. 2000. *Women and the Criminal Justice System.* Boston: Allyn and Bacon.

Vanier Institute of the Family. 2000. *Profiling Canada's Families II.* Ottawa: Vanier Institute of the Family.

Veenstra, Gerry. 2001. "Social Capital and Health." *Canadian Journal of Policy Research,* 2: 1672–81.

Vold, George B. 1958. *Theoretical Criminology.* New York: Oxford University Press.

Vold, George B., Thomas J. Bernard, and Jeffrey B. Snipes. 2002. *Theoretical Criminology,* 5th edn. New York: Oxford University Press.

Vosko, Leah. 2000. *Temporary Work: The Gendered Rise of a Precarious Employment Relationship.* Toronto: University of Toronto Press.

Wagner, David. 1997. *The New Temperance: The American Obsession with Sin and Vice.* Boulder, Colo.: Westview.

Waksler, Frances. 1991. *Studying the Social Worlds of Children: Sociological Readings.* London: Falmer.

Walkom, Thomas. 1997. "The Harris Government: Restoration or Revolution?" In *The Government and Politics of Ontario,* 5th edn, edited by Graham White, 402–17. Toronto: University of Toronto Press.

Waller, Willard. [1932] 1965. *The Sociology of Teaching.* New York: Wiley.

Walzer, Michael. 1983. *Spheres of Justice: A Defense of Pluralism and Equality.* New York: Basic Books.

Waring, Marilyn. 1996. *Three Masquerades: Essays on Equality, Work and Human Rights.* Toronto: University of Toronto Press.

Warren, Karen. 1990. "The Power and Promise of Ecological Feminism." *Environmental Ethics,* 12, no. 2: 125–46.

Watson, William. 1999. "Globalization and the Meaning of Canadian Life." In *Room to Manoeuvre? Globalization and Policy Convergence,* edited by Thomas J. Courchene, 259–70. Montreal: McGill-Queen's University Press.

Weber, Max. [1904] 1958. *The Protestant Ethic and The Spirit of Capitalism.* Translated by Talcott Parsons. New York: Scribner.

———. [1908] 1978. *Economy and Society.* Translated by Ephraim Fischoff. Berkeley: University of California Press.

———. [1922] 1946. From *Max Weber: Essays in Sociology.* Translated and edited by H.H. Gerth and C. Wright Mills. New York: Oxford University Press.

———. [1922] 1958. *Essays in Sociology.* Translated by H.H. Gerth and C. Wright Mills. New York: Oxford University Press.

Weeks, Jeffrey, Catherine Donovan, and Brian Heaphy. 1998. "Everyday Experiments: Narratives of Non-heterosexual Relationships." In *The New Family?* edited by Elizabeth B. Silva and Carol Smart, 83–99. London: Sage.

Weiner, Gaby. 1994. *Feminisms in Education: An Introduction.* Buckingham, UK: Open University Press.

Weinfeld, Morton. 1981. "The Development of Affirmative Action in Canada." *Canadian Ethnic Studies,* 13, no. 2: 23–39.

———. 1983. "The Ethnic Sub-economy: Explication and Analysis of a Case Study of the Jews of Montreal." *Contemporary Jewry,* 6: 6–25.

Wernick, Andrew. 1987. "From Voyeur to Narcissist: Imaging Men in Contemporary Advertising." In *Beyond Patriarchy,* edited by Michael Kaufman, 277–97. Toronto: Oxford University Press.

Wertham, Frederic. 1954. *Seduction of the Innocent.* New York: Rinehart.

West, G. Page, III, and G. Dale Meyer. 1997. "Communicated Knowledge as a Learning Foundation." *International Journal of Organizational Analysis,* 5: 25–58.

Westhues, Kenneth. 1982. *First Sociology.* New York: McGraw-Hill.

White, David Manning. 1950. "The 'Gatekeeper': A Case Study in the Selection of News." *Journalism Quarterly,* 27: 383–90.

Whyte, William Foote. 1943. *Street Corner Society: The Social Structure of an Italian Slum.* Chicago: University of Chicago Press.

Wickberg, Edgar. 1982. *From China to Canada: A History of Chinese Communities in Canada.* Toronto: McClelland & Stewart.

Wiley, Norbert F. 1967. "The Ethnic Mobility Trap and Stratification Theory." *Social Problems,* 15: 147–59.

Wilkins, Russell, Owen Adams, and Anna Brancker. 1989. "Change in Mortality by Income in Urban Canada from 1971 to 1986." *Health Reports,* 1: 137–74.

Wilkinson, Derek. 1992. "Change in Household Division of Labour Following Unemployment in Elliot Lake." Paper presented to Learned Societies, Charlottetown, PEI.

Williams, David R., and Chiquita Collins. 1995. "U.S. Socioeconomic and Racial Differences in Health: Patterns and Explanations." *Annual Review of Sociology,* 21: 349–86.

Williams, Frank P., III, and Marilyn D. McShane, eds. 1994. *Criminological Theory.* 2nd edn. Englewood Cliffs, NJ: Prentice-Hall.

Willis, Paul. 1977. *Learning to Labour: How Working Class Kids Get Working Class Jobs.* Farnborough, UK: Saxon House.

Wilson, Clint C., II, F. Gutierrez, and Lena M. Chao. 2003. *Racism, Sexism, and the Media: The Rise of Class Communication in Multicultural America.* 3rd edn. Thousand Oaks, Calif.: Sage.

Wilson, Susannah J. 1991. *Women, Families, and Work.* 3rd edn. Toronto: McGraw-Hill Ryerson.

———. 2001. "Intimacy and Commitment in Family Formation." In *Families: Changing Trends in Canada,* 4th edn, edited by Maureen Baker, 93–114. Toronto: McGraw-Hill Ryerson.

Wimberley, Dale W. 1990. "Investment Dependence and Alternative Explanations of Third World Mortality." *American Sociological Review,* 55: 75–91.

Winter, James. 2001. *Media Think.* Montreal: Black Rose.

Wirth, Louis. 1938. "Urbanism as a Way of Life." *American Journal of Sociology,* 44: 1–24.

Witz, Anne. 1992. *Professions and Patriarchy*. London: Routledge.

Wolf, Naomi. 1991. *The Beauty Myth: How Image of Beauty Are Used Against Women*. New York: Anchor.

Wolfe, David A., and Meric S. Gertler. 2001. *The New Economy: An Overview*. Discussion paper produced for the Social Sciences and Humanities Research Council of Canada.

Wolfgang, Marvin, and Franco Ferracuti. 1967. *The Subculture of Violence: Towards an Integrated Theory in Criminology*. Beverly Hills, Calif.: Sage.

Wolfson, Michael C., and Brian B. Murphy. 1998. "New Views on Inequality and Trends in Canada and the United States." *Monthly Labor Review*, April: 3–23.

Wollstonecraft, Mary. [1792] 1986. *Vindication of the Rights of Women*. Middlesex, UK: Penguin.

Wood, Adrian. 1994. *North–South Trade, Employment and Inequality*. Oxford, UK: Clarendon.

Wood, Chris, with Rima Kar. 2000. "Why Do Men Do It?" *Maclean's*, 7 August: 5–7.

Woods, Peter. 1979. *The Divided School*. London: Routledge and Kegan Paul.

Woolmington, Eric. 1985. "Small May Be Inevitable." *Australian Geographical Studies*, 23 (October): 195–207.

World Commission on Environment and Development. 1987. *Our Common Future*. New York: Oxford University Press.

World Health Organization (WHO). 2003. "WHO Definition of Health." Available at <www.who.int/about/definition/en/>, accessed 19 June 2003.

Wortley, Scott. 1999. "A Northern Taboo: Research on Race, Crime and Criminal Justice in Canada." *Canadian Journal of Criminology*, 41: 261–74.

Wotherspoon, Terry. 1995. "The Incorporation of Public School Teachers into the Industrial Order: British Columbia in the First Half of the Twentieth Century." *Studies in Political Economy*, 46: 119–51.

———. 1998. *The Sociology of Education in Canada: Critical Perspectives*. Toronto: Oxford University Press.

———. 2000. "Transforming Canada's Education System: The Impact on Educational Inequalities, Opportunities, and Benefits." In *Social Issues and Contradictions in Canadian Society*, edited by B. Singh Bolaria, 250–72. Toronto: Harcourt Brace.

Wotherspoon, Terry, and Vic Satzewich. 1993. *First Nations: Race, Class and Gender Relations*. Toronto: Nelson.

Wright, Erik Olin. 1985. *Classes*. London: Verso.

———. 1997. *Class Counts: Comparative Studies in Class Analysis*. Cambridge: Cambridge University Press.

———. 1999. "Foundations of Class Analysis: A Marxist Perspective." Paper presented at the annual meeting of the American Sociological Association.

Wrong, Dennis. 1961. "The Oversocialized Concept of Man in Modern Sociology." American Sociological Review, 26: 183–93.

Yalnizyan, Armine. 1998. *The Growing Gap: A Report on the Growing Inequality Between Rich and Poor in Canada*. Toronto: Centre for Social Justice.

Yancey, William L., Eugene P. Ericksen, and Richard N. Juliani. 1976. "Emergent Ethnicity: A Review and Reformulation." *American Sociological Review*, 41: 391–403.

Zang, Xiaowei. 1998. "Elite Transformation and Recruitment in Post-Mao China." *Journal of Political and Military Sociology*, 26, no. 1: 39–57.

Zeitlin, I.M. 1990. *Ideology and the Development of Sociological Theory*, 4th edn. Englewood Cliffs, NJ: Prentice-Hall.

Zimbardo, Philip G. 1972. "Pathology of Imprisonment." *Society*, 9: 4–8.

Zingrone, Frank. 2001. *The Media Symplex: At the Edge of Meaning in an Age of Chaos*. Toronto: Stoddart.

Zola, Irving Kenneth. 1972. "Medicine as an Institution of Social Control." *Sociological Review*, 20: 487–504.

Zucker, Lynne G., Michael R. Darby, Marilynn B. Brewer, and Yusheng Peng. 1996. "Collaboration Structure and Information Dilemmas in Biotechnology." In *Trust in Organizations: Frontiers of Theory and Research*, edited Roderick M. Kramer and Tom R. Tyler, 90–113. Thousand Oaks, Calif.: Sage.

# Glossary

**Agents of socialization**  Those groups in a child's environment that have the greatest effect on his or her socialization.

**Alienation**  A concept derived from Marx's analysis of the position of workers under capitalism, it refers to the separation of workers from the products of their labour, from the control of the work process, from owners, managers, and other workers, and even from themselves.

**Allopathic medicine**  Conventional medicine that treats by opposing, whether the germs, the bacteria, or other pathology.

**Anticipatory socialization**  Explicit or implicit learning, in preparation for a future role; in Merton's definition, the acquisition of values and orientations found in statuses and groups in which one is not yet engaged but that one is likely to enter.

**Authority**  Power considered legitimate by those subject to it.

**Baby boom, baby bust**  The dramatic rise in the birth rate in Canada following the Second World War and lasting until well into the 1960s is called the baby boom. The continuing decline in fertility following the end of the baby boom in the industrialized world is called the baby bust.

**Beliefs**  Any statement or part of a statement that describes an aspect of collective reality. Beliefs are ideas and explanations of what is commonly accepted as the truth. Beliefs may also be normative, saying what ought—or ought not—to be done.

**Bilateral descent pattern**  A system under which a newly married couple is considered part of both the bride's and the groom's kin groups.

**Biological determinism**  The view that nature dominates nurture.

**Bourgeoisie**  Owners of the means of production; the ruling class.

**Breakdown approach**  An approach to social movements that assumes that rapid, thorough, or uneven change in social institutions weakens social bonds and encourages the formation of groups advocating radical change.

**Bride price**  Money or property provided by a groom's parents to a bride's parents for permission for the groom to marry the bride.

**Broadcasting**  Over-the-air transmission of radio or television signals from a central source.

**Bureaucracy**  A type of formal organization, found in government and private industry and in capitalist and socialist societies alike, that has the following six characteristics: a division of labour, a hierarchy of positions, a formal system of rules, a separation of the person from the office, hiring and promotion based on technical merit, and the protection of careers. Administrative efficiency is achieved by depersonalized treatment and mass processing of cases, as dictated by regulations and filed information.

**Capital-intensive production**  All production involves both labour and capital, but the proportions of the two can vary considerably across different goods and services. In dollar terms, the inputs of capital into the production of aluminum are enormous (equipment, plant, electricity, bauxite) but the labour inputs are modest. This is a capital-intensive industry. In contrast, hairdressers use negligible amounts of capital equipment (a chair, scissors, a mirror). The bulk of the cost of that activity is labour. This is a labour-intensive industry.

**Capitalism**  An economic system characterized by a relationship of unequal economic exchange between capitalists (employers) and workers. Because they do not own the means of production, workers must sell their labour to employers in exchange for a wage or salary. Capitalism is a market-based system driven by the pursuit of profit for personal gain.

**Census**  A complete count of the population at one point in time, usually taken by a country every 5 or 10 years. The census is distinguished from the vital statistics system, a continuous registration system of births, deaths, marriages, and divorces.

**Census family**  Statistics Canada's definition of the family; includes married couples and cohabiting couples who have lived together for longer than one year, with or without never-married children, as well as single parents living with never-married children.

**Census metropolitan area (CMA)**  Large urban agglomeration, with a population in the urban core of at least 100,000 according to the previous Canadian census, that most often includes adjacent urban and rural areas that are socially and economically integrated with the urban core.

**Charismatic authority**  Power considered legitimate because those subject to it believe in the exceptional qualities of an individual person, who appears exemplary or heroic and able to solve what others cannot.

**Charter groups**  Canadians of British and French origin are known as charter groups because they have a special status entrenched in the Canadian Constitution and have effectively determined the dominant cultural characteristics of Canada. Each of these groups has special rights and privileges, especially in terms of the languages used in the legislature, the courts, and education.

**Claims-making**  The social constructionist process by which groups assert grievances about the troublesome character of people or their behaviour.

**Class**  The theoretical division of society into stratified groups based on such factors as income, education, socio-economic status, and relation to the means of production that reflects inequality because of the uneven distribution of material resources.

**Collective conscience, collective consciousness**  Durkheim's term for the collective intellectual property of a culture; something that we can all share in and contribute to but that no one person can know or possess. The cognitive-moral system of shared symbols, beliefs, and sentiments of a social group. Individuals think and feel what they learn and internalize as members of a collective. The content of the collective consciousness is determined by the structural organization of the society in question.

**Collective effervescence**   The experience of psychological excitement and empowerment that often happens to individuals caught up in large crowd activities such as political rallies, sporting events, or rock concerts.

**Common-sense knowledge**   Facts of life accepted without being fully researched and understood.

**Communication**   Purposeful exchange of information between two or more parties; a process involving an exchange of meaningful information between sender and receiver and back again. A social view of communication inquires into the meanings and impacts of the content and form of communication, a technical view into the mechanisms and means of communicating.

**Community**   Tangible interpersonal contact patterns.

**Concept**   An abstract idea that cannot be tested directly. Concepts can refer to anything, but in social research they usually refer to characteristics of individuals, groups, or artifacts, or to social processes. Some common sociological concepts include religiosity (strength of religious conviction), social class, and alienation.

**Conflict theory**   A theoretical paradigm that emphasizes conflict and change as the regular and permanent features of society, because society is made up of various groups that wield varying amounts of power.

**Contested site**   The idea that social spaces in a changing and diverse society are increasingly battlegrounds involving a struggle between different groups for control of agendas.

**Control theory**   A category of explanation that maintains that people engage in deviant behaviour when the various controls that might be expected to prohibit them from doing so are weak or absent.

**Convergence**   The merging ("converging") of conventional media with digital media to create new and more powerful patterns of communication.

**Cultural capital**   A term coined by Pierre Bourdieu for the cultural and linguistic competence, such as prestigious knowledge, tastes, preferences, and educational expertise and credentials, that individuals possess and that influences the likelihood of their educational and occupational success.

**Cultural diffusion**   The process whereby the beliefs and customary behaviours of one society spread to, and are adopted within, another society.

**Cultural support theory**   A category of explanation that argues that people become and remain deviant because the cultural environments in which they find themselves teach deviance and define such behaviour as appropriate.

**Culture**   At its broadest, the sum total of the human-produced environment (the objects, artifacts, ideas, beliefs, and values that make up the symbolic and learned aspects of human society) as separate from the natural environment; more often refers to norms, values, beliefs, ideas, and meanings; an assumption that different societies are distinguished by their shared beliefs and customary behaviours; the products and services delivered by a number of industries—theatre, music, film, publishing, and so on.

**Decoding**   See **Encoding and decoding**.

**Demographic transition**   The process by which a country moves from high birth and death rates to low birth and death rates. The shift in fertility rates is often referred to as the fertility transition, while the complementary change in death rates is referred to as the mortality transition. The epidemiological transition theory is a complementary theory to demographic transition theory.

**Developed countries**   The most industrialized countries of the world. According to the United Nations, these are the countries in Europe and in North America, as well as Australia, New Zealand, and Japan.

**Developing countries**   All the countries not in the developed world. A subdivision of developing countries is the least developed countries, defined by the United Nations as countries with annual incomes of less than $9,000 (US). See also **Third World**.

**Deviance**   Behaviours and conditions of people that are subject to social control.

**Dialogical**   A two-way and open-ended process of communication (a "dialogue" rather than a "monologue").

**Discourse**   A way of talking about and conceptualizing an issue, presented through ideas, concepts, and vocabulary that recur in texts; distinctive ways of thinking and talking about aspects of the social world.

**Discrimination**   An action whereby a person is treated differently, usually unfairly, because of his or her membership in a particular group or category.

**Disease, illness, and sickness**   Distinguished from one another in the sociology of health, illness, and medicine. Disease is the disorder that is diagnosed by the physician. Illness is the personal experience of the person who acknowledges that he or she does not feel well. Sickness is the social action taken by a person as a result of illness or disease.

**Double standard**   Expecting or requiring different behaviour from women and men, boys and girls.

**Dowry**   Money or property provided by a bride's family upon her marriage to help obtain a suitable husband and to be used by her in case of divorce or widowhood.

**Education**   The process by which human beings learn and develop capacities through understanding of their social and natural environments, which takes place in both formal and informal settings.

**Encoding and decoding**   The inclusion and subsequent interpretation of cues, meanings, and codes in cultural productions.

**Environmental justice**   The branch of environmentalism that focuses on the inequitable distribution of environmental risks affecting the poor and racial minorities.

**Ethnic group**   People sharing a common ethnic identity who are potentially capable of organizing and acting on their ethnic interests.

**Ethnicity** Sets of social distinctions by which groups differentiate themselves from one another on the basis of presumed biological ties. Members of such groups have a sense of themselves as a common "people" separate and distinct from others.

**Eurocentrism** A tendency to see the world from a "Western" point of view as natural, normal, and superior, while dismissing alternative points of view as inferior and irrelevant

**Exploitation** At the heart of Marxist sociology, the situation under capitalism in which the bourgeoisie takes advantage of the proletariat. Class-based exploitation occurs when the bourgeoisie appropriates the labour effort of the proletariat to create its own material advantage.

**Extended family** Several generations sharing a residence and co-operating economically.

**False consciousness** Condition in which the working class does not recognize its exploitation and oppression under capitalism because they have become inured to the dominant ideology.

**Feminism** A theoretical paradigm that focuses on causes and consequences of inequality between men and women, especially patriarchy and sexism.

**Finance capital** In contrast to physical capital, instruments that can be used to purchase physical capital—bank loans, equity (voting shares in a company), fixed interest bonds, and so on; the monetary expression of physical capital.

**First Nations** "Indians" in Canadian law; together with Métis and Inuit, they constitute Canada's Aboriginal peoples.

**Flexible specialization** Another component of the new flexible approach to management; involves multiskilling, job rotation, the organization of workers into teams, and concentrated yet decentralized decision-making power within work organizations.

**Formal organization** A deliberately formed social group in which people, resources, and technologies are consciously co-ordinated through formalized roles, statuses, and relationships to achieve a division of labour intended to attain a specific set of objectives.

**Gender** Socially recognized distinctions of masculinity and femininity.

**Gender stereotyping** A belief about differences in the natural capabilities and attributes of women and men.

**Generalized other** In Mead's theory, the "internalized audience" with which we, as "minded selves," dialogue or converse during the reflective prelude to action. It represents the collective attitudes and sentiments of our society or group.

**Global cities** Cities favoured under globalization that are at high levels of technology, finance, and international transportation, serving as the focal points for multinational corporations but not for local manufacturing.

**Globalization** Worldwide control and co-ordination of economic (and cultural) production and distribution by large private-sector interests not constrained by local or national boundaries.

**Globalization of work** The relocation of production and consumption beyond national borders to various parts of the globe. It is done in the interest of increasing profits by decreasing labour costs and maximizing employer control of the larger work process.

**Hawthorne effect** The finding that when people know they are subjects of an important experiment and receive a large amount of special attention, they tend to behave the way they think the researchers expect them to.

**Hegemony** The process of achieving conformity and control by way of consensus rather than by coercion (changing people's attitudes without their awareness that attitudes are changing).

**Hidden curriculum** The understandings that students develop as a result of the institutional requirements and day-to-day realities they encounter in their schooling; typically refers to norms, such as competition, individualism, and obedience, as well as to a sense of one's place in school and social hierarchies.

**Hot money** Liquid assets that can be turned into cash quickly and with negligible cost. They can, consequently, be moved between investment locations—including countries—rapidly and easily.

**Household** Term used by Statistics Canada to refer to people sharing a dwelling, whether or not they are related by blood, adoption, or marriage.

**Human ecology** The science of ecology, as applied to sociological analyses. See also **Ecology**.

**Human relations school** An approach within organizational theory that focuses on relationships in informal groups and assumes that happy group relationships produce job satisfaction, which, in turn, produces high productivity.

**Identity** The way in which we see ourselves and how others see us. How we view ourselves is a product of our history and of our interpretation of others' reactions to us. How others view us is termed "placement" and is other people's reactions to our projections of ourselves, which, in turn, is termed "announcement."

**Identity-based approach** An approach to social movements that assumes that dominant interpretations of reality preserve class, gender, racial, and other inequalities. The central task of social movements is to challenge and reformulate the dominant culture by reshaping identities.

**Ideology** A system of beliefs, ideas, and norms, reflecting the interests and experiences of a group, class, or subculture, that legitimizes or justifies the existing unequal distribution of power and privilege; ways of seeing and of understanding the world and its actors. Ideologies function by making the social appear natural or functional rather than constructed for partisan interests and advantage.

**Illness** See **Disease, illness, and sickness**.

**Impression management** Goffman's term for the "dramatic moves" individuals make in trying to advance "definitions of the situation" favourable to their interests and self-image. It is achieved by carefully manipulating the elements of appearance, manner, and setting.

**Inclusiveness** The idea of making institutions more "diversity-friendly" by improving access and retention, removing discriminatory barriers, and transforming rules, procedures, and rewards.

**Informal economy** A wide range of legal and illegal economic activities that are not officially reported to the government.

**Informal organization** Complex personal and informal networks that develop among people within a bureaucracy who interact on the job.

**Institutional completeness** A measure of the degree to which a community offers a range of services to its members.

**Institutional discrimination** Discrimination that is built into how an institution is structured or how it operates.

**Labour power** Marx argued that labour is work and labour power is the capacity to work. The only real power that the proletariat has under capitalism is the power to choose whether to work.

**Life expectancy at birth** The average number of years left to live for a newborn in a given period. Life expectancy is distinct from life span, which is the oldest age humans can attain.

**Lifelong learning** The ongoing requirements for people to acquire new knowledge and capacities through learning that occurs in various levels and kinds of formal education as well as in other learning contexts; associated with increasing emphasis on the new economy and the continuing transitions that individuals undergo throughout their lives.

**Looking-glass self** In Cooley's symbolic interactionist approach, the idea that self-concept is based on a person's perceptions of the opinions that others hold about him or her.

**Macro** See **Micro, macro**.

**Macrosociology** The study of social institutions and large social groups; the study of the processes that depict societies as a whole and of the social structural aspects of a given society.

**Marxism** Based on the work of Karl Marx, the historical materialist school of thought that posits a structural explanation for historical change, namely, that the economic base of society determines change in all other realms.

**Mass communication** A process by which messages are encoded, transmitted, and decoded as well as transformed by this three-stage process.

**Mass media** The centralized production and technology-mediated distribution of information and entertainment.

**Master status** A status characteristic that overrides other status characteristics. When a person is assigned a label of "deviant" (for example, "murderer," "drug addict," "cheater"), that label is usually read by others as signifying the most essential aspects of the individual's character.

**Matrifocal** A family system in which life is organized around the women, who earn most of the money and hold the family together (often in the absence of husbands/fathers).

**Matrilineal descent** The tracing of relationships and inheritance through the female line.

**Means of production** Wealth-generating property such as land, factories, and machinery.

**Media** Intervening agencies for the transmission of communication.

**Media effects** The influence that media messages have on individual thought and behaviour.

**Media impacts** The process by which media generate public debates about what is right, normal, and acceptable in society.

**Medicalization** The tendency for more and more of life to be defined as relevant to medical diagnosis and treatment.

**Melting pot** An American ideology that assumes that immigrants should discard all of the traditions and distinctions they brought to the United States with them, such as their ethnic language or national identity, and become nothing but "Americans."

**Metropolitan area** With respect to everyday behaviour and economic activity, the unified entity formed on a de facto basis by a large city and its suburbs. See also **Census metropolitan area (CMA)**.

**Micro, macro** Used analytically to distinguish small-scale, face-to-face interaction settings (micro) from institutional arrangements such as the economy or state and from large-scale collective processes like revolutions and religious movements (macro).

**Microsociology** The analysis of small groups and of the face-to-face interactions that occur within these groups in everyday life.

**Mind** In Mead's theory, a "social emergent" created through symbolic interaction, consisting of the ability to think, to carry on an internal conversation. Mind is made possible through the internalization of language.

**Mode of production** Marx's concept referring to the economic structure of society, consisting of the forces and relations of production. It is the "base" that conditions the "superstructure" of politics, law, religion, art, and so on.

**Modified extended family** Several generations not sharing a residence but living near each other and maintaining close social and economic contact.

**Morbidity rate** The sickness rate per a specified number of people over a specified period of time.

**Mortality rate** The death rate per a specified number of people over a specified period of time.

**Multiculturalism** Official multiculturalism is a government policy to promote tolerance among cultural groups and to assist ethnic groups in preserving the values and traditions important to them.

**Multinational corporations** Companies that have significant production facilities in more than one national jurisdiction. Those that become detached from any particular country, with loyalty to no country, are sometimes labelled transnational corporations.

**Negotiation** A discussion intended to produce an agreement.

**Neighbourhood** A recognizable physical area within a city, with or without formal boundaries.

**New economy** A term used to highlight the shift in emphasis from industrial production within specific industries, firms, and nations to economic activities driven by information and high-level technologies, global competition, international networks, and knowledge-based advancement.

**Non-standard work** Jobs characterized by an increasingly tenuous or precarious relationship between employer and employee, including part-time employment, temporary employment, contract work, multiple job holding, and self-employment; also termed contingent work and casual work.

**Norms** The rules and expectations of appropriate behaviour under various social circumstances. Norms create social consequences that have the effect of regulating appearance and behaviour.

**Nuclear family** A husband, wife, and their children, sharing a common residence and co-operating economically.

**Numerical flexibility** Part of a new general managerial approach that rests on flexibility in employment; involves shrinking or eliminating the core workforce (in continuous, full-time positions) and replacing them with workers in non-standard employment.

**Ontology** Inquiry that deals with the fundamental nature of things—of reality or existence—and that specifies the essential properties or characteristics of phenomena.

**Operationalization** The translation of abstract theories and concepts into observable hypotheses and variables. Once our abstract ideas are operationalized, we can test them in a study.

**Organization** A group of people participating in a division of labour that is co-ordinated by communication and leadership to achieve a common goal or goals; includes both spontaneous and formal organizations.

**Paradigm** A set of assumptions used to view society and people's behaviour. A paradigm serves as a model for which questions sociologists should ask and how they should interpret the answers.

**Parties** Voluntary associations that organize for the collective pursuit of interests such as political parties or lobbying groups; common in Weberian scholarship.

**Patriarchy** A society or form of social organization oriented towards men and dominated by men, which has empowered men to control and limit female possibilities. For example, patriarchal families are families in which authority resides with males.

**Patrilineal descent** The tracing of relationships and inheritance through the male line.

**Pedagogy** Processes associated with the organization and practice of teaching; more generally, various kinds of interactions (and how these are understood and organized) in teaching/learning situations.

**Political conflict perspective** A resource mobilization approach that focuses on how groups (typically classes) promote collective interests.

**Political institutions** Established rules and procedures for the conduct of political affairs.

**Political party** An organization dedicated to winning political power by controlling government.

**Political process approach** An approach that assumes that political constraints and opportunities influence the rise and fall of social movements, as well as their institutional organization.

**Politics** The process in which individuals and groups act to promote their interests, often in conflict with others.

**Polyandry** The practice of being legally married to more than one husband at a time.

**Polygamy** The practice of being legally married to more than one spouse at a time.

**Polygyny** The practice of being legally married to more than one wife at a time.

**Population momentum** The tendency for population to keep growing even when the fertility rate drops to just the replacement level of 2.1 children per woman, as a consequence of a high proportion of persons in the child-bearing ages.

**Power** In Marxist sociology, a social relationship that has a material base. Those who own the means of production have the power to exploit workers through the appropriation of their labour efforts. In Weberian sociology, *power* is more broadly defined and can reflect an individual's or group's capacity to exert their will over others.

**Prejudice** An attitude in which individuals are prejudged on the basis of stereotyped characteristics assumed to be common to all members of the individual's group.

**Primary socialization** The most intense socialization, which occurs from birth to adolescence and takes place in or is strongly influenced by the family.

**Privatization** The movement away from a completely universally available and state-funded medical system to one that includes profit-making components.

**Progressive conservation** The movement originating in the nineteenth century that sought to check environmental destruction caused by unbridled economic growth and that resulted in the founding of such modern environmental organizations as the Audubon Society and the Sierra Club.

**Proletariat** People who sell their labour power to capitalists in return for a wage; the working class.

**Protestant ethic thesis** Weber's argument that aspects of the Protestant religion originally imbued people with a sense of dedication to their work that helped lay the foundations for capitalism.

**PYLL** "Potential years of life lost"; refers to premature mortality, taking into account the average age of death from a particular cause.

**Race** A group defined on the basis of perceived physical differences, such as skin colour.

**Race to the bottom** The outcome produced by competitive tax-cutting motivated by the desire to attract (and keep) investors.

**Racism** A belief that groups that differ in physical appearance also differ in personality characteristics, intelligence, honesty, reliability, willingness to abide by the law, and so on. Racism also implies a belief that these differences make one group superior to another.

**Rationalization** In Weber's view, the movement away from mystical and religious interpretations of the world to the development of human thought and belief based on the systematic accumulation of evidence; associated with the emergence of impersonal authority.

**Rational-legal authority**  Power considered legitimate because those subject to it believe commands are based on formally established rules, procedures, and certified expertise.

**Relative deprivation theory**  A breakdown approach that claims that radical social movements result from people's subjective feelings of fear and frustration.

**Resocialization**  The process of learning new roles in response to changes in life circumstances.

**Resource mobilization approach**  An approach that assumes that social movements are quite similar to other organizations.

**Risk society**  A theory of the new modernity that argues that perception of risk is modernity's defining feature, creating uncertainty and compelling individuals to seek new strategic allegiances.

**Role expectations**  The expected characteristics and social behaviours of an individual in a particular position in society.

**Role-making**  The continual improvising and revising of our actions as others' reactions to them change and are imputed.

**Roles**  The specific duties and obligations expected of one who occupies a specific status.

**Schooling**  Processes that take place within formal educational institutions.

**Scientific management**  A managerial method that rests on breaking up work processes into their smallest constituent parts in an effort to maximize efficiency in productivity, resulting in the separation of mental from manual labour and in the deskilling of workers; assumes that workers are motivated by economic rewards alone and that specialists know more than workers about how a task can most effectively be performed; also known as Taylorism.

**Secondary socialization**  The ongoing lifelong process of socialization, based on the accumulated learning of childhood and adolescence.

**Self**  In Mead's theory, an emergent entity with a capacity to be both a subject and an object, as reflected upon in one's own mind. In Goffman's dramaturgical theory, the self is more a shifting "dramatic effect," a staged product of the scenes one performs in.

**Serial monogamy**  A pattern of marriage, divorce, and remarriage, resulting in having more than one spouse over a lifetime, but only one at a time.

**Service economy**  The economic sector in which most Canadians are currently employed. In comparison to primary industry (which involves the extraction of natural resources) and manufacturing (which involves processing raw materials into usable goods and services), the service economy is based on the provision of services (as opposed to a tangible product) ranging widely from advertising and retailing to entertainment to generating and distributing information. Also called the tertiary sector.

**Sex**  The biological differences between females and males, determined at conception.

**Sexual harassment**  Unwanted attention linked to the gender of the person receiving that attention.

**Sickness**  See **Disease, illness, and sickness**.

**Situated identity**  According to symbolic interactionist theory, social life is in a constant process of change, imposing, in turn, changes in, and new forms of, identity announcement and identity placement. A particular announcement–placement identity at any point in time is referred to as a situated identity.

**Situated transaction**  A process of social interaction that lasts as long as the individuals find themselves in each other's company. As applied to the study of deviance, the concept of the situated transaction helps us to understand how deviant acts are social and not just individual products.

**Social capital**  A concept widely thought to have been developed by American sociologist James Coleman in 1988, but discussed by Pierre Bourdieu in a similar way in the early 1980s; reflects the power derived from ties to social networks.

**Social constructionism**  The sociological theory that argues that social problems and issues are less objective conditions than they are collective social definitions based on how they are framed and interpreted; the belief that there is nothing natural or normal about the social world we live in, but rather that people create and recreate definitions of what is accepted and "normal" through meaningful activity.

**Social control**  The various and myriad ways in which members of social groups express their disapproval of people and behaviours. These include name-calling, ridicule, ostracism, incarceration, and even killing.

**Social environment**  The people and relationships that surround us.

**Social group**  A number of individuals, defined by formal or informal criteria of membership, who share a feeling of unity or are bound together in stable patterns of interaction; two or more individuals who have a specific common identity and who interact in a reciprocal social relationship.

**Social institution**  A stable, well-acknowledged pattern of social relationships that endures over time, including the family, the economy, education, politics, religion, the mass media, medicine, and science and technology. Social institutions are the result of an enduring set of ideas about how to accomplish various goals generally recognized as important in a society.

**Social interaction**  The process by which people act and react in relationships with others.

**Socialization**  The process by which people learn to become members of society. See also primary socialization; secondary socialization.

**Social movements**  The co-ordinated, voluntary actions of non-elites (those people with no control over major resources) for the manifest purpose of changing the distribution of social goods.

**Social networks**  Based on kinship, friendship, or economic ties, these may include social transactions (shared recreation, communication, gift exchanges, mutual assistance) and shared tastes and values.

**Social relationships**  Interactions of people in a society. Because people share culture and a sense of collective existence, these interactions will to some extent be recurrent and predictable.

**Social reproduction** A range of unpaid activities that help to reproduce workforces daily and over generations; typically, though not exclusively, performed by women in the family household.

**Social revolution** A rapid, fundamental transformation of a society's state and class structures, often accomplished through violent means.

**Social structure** Patterns of behaviour or social relationships developed and accepted through time in a given group, organization, or society.

**Society** The largest collection of social relationships in which people live their lives. There are some very encompassing international relationships among nations, too (such as the European Common Market or the North American Free Trade Agreement), but these cover only a narrow range of types of activities (for example, economic relationships).

**Sociological imagination** Mills's conception for the understanding of how personal experiences and troubles are interrelated with others' experiences and troubles as public or societal problems.

**Sociology** The systematic study of social behaviours in human societies.

**Solidarity** The quality of an integrated and well-functioning society that is brought into harmony through an adaptive cultural foundation.

**Spontaneous organization** An organization that arises quickly to meet a single goal and then disbands when that goal is achieved or perceived to be beyond reach, or when the organization becomes absorbed by a formal organization.

**the State** Procedures and organizations concerned with creating, administering, and enforcing rules or decisions for conduct within a given territory.

**Status** A socially defined position that a person holds in a given social group or organization, to which are attached certain rights, duties, and obligations. Note that status is a relational term, as each status exists only through its relation to one or more other statuses filled by other people.

**Status degradation ceremony** The rituals by which the formal transition is made from non-deviant to deviant status. Examples include the criminal trial and the psychiatric hearing.

**Status groups** Organized groups comprising people who have similar social status situations. These groups organize to maintain or expand their social privileges by excluding outsiders from their ranks and by trying to gain status recognition from other groups.

**Strain theory** A category of explanation that seeks to understand how deviant behaviour results as people attempt to solve problems that the social structure presents to them.

**Structural analysis or approach** An approach within organizational theory in the Weberian tradition; focuses on the structural characteristics of organizations and their effect on the people within them; in the context of urban studies, the analysis of the functions cities

perform, the size and shape of their governments, and who has what bearing on decisions and outcomes involving cities.

**Structural discrimination** See **Institutional discrimination**.

**Structural functionalism** A theoretical paradigm that emphasizes the way each part of a society functions to fulfill the needs of society as a whole.

**Structure** The "concrete" elements of society that are embodied and enacted by things and people, in opposition to the cultural elements of society.

**Subculture** A subset of cultural traits of the larger society that also includes distinctive values, beliefs, norms, style of dress, and behaviour.

**Sustainable development** The principle that economic growth and environmental conservation are compatible goals.

**Symbolic interactionism** The study of the processes by which individuals interpret and respond to the actions of one another.

**Symbolic markers** Cultural manifestations of identity, such as language, nationality, or skin colour, that groups use either to generate a common identity or to differentiate themselves from others.

**Symbols** The heart of cultural systems, for with them we construct thought, ideas, and other ways of representing reality to others and to ourselves; gestures, artifacts, or language that represents something else.

**Systemic discrimination** Discrimination that is built into the very fabric of Canadian life, as in the case of institutional self-segregation.

**Systemic theory** A breakdown approach, advanced by Neil Smelser, that views society as a set of interrelated elements that work together to maintain stability.

**Systems theory** An approach within organizational theory that sees organizations as open systems and that views organizations and their goals as shaped by the interests of their participants and their environments.

**Theory** An integrated set of concepts and statements that specify relations of ordered dependence and causal connection between phenomena. At the most general level, theories are perspectives, or ways of seeing, that conceptualize and highlight certain patterns and relations among complex realities. Theories are not tested directly. They may also be simple or complex: the more complex a theory, the more difficult it is to operationalize and test it.

**Totalitarianism** Form of the state that involves intervening in and controlling all aspects of both public and private life.

**Traditional authority** Power considered legitimate because those subject to it believe that is the way things have always been done.

**Transitions** The pathways that people follow from family life, into and out of education, and into various jobs or other social situations throughout their life course.

**Unemployment rate** People are considered to be unemployed only if they do not have a job and are actively looking for a job. The unemployment rate, expressed as a percentage, is the number of people who meet those two conditions divided by the labour force (which includes both the employed and unemployed). Those who do not have a job and are not looking for one are considered to be not in the labour force.

**Urbanism**  Behaviour patterns associated with cities.

**Urbanization**  The nature, extent, and distribution of cities in the larger society or nation.

**Utilitarian perspective**  A resource mobilization approach that focuses on how individuals promote self-interest.

**Values**  Shared ideas about how something is ranked in terms of its relative social desirability, worth, or goodness; what a group or society views as right and wrong, good and bad, desirable and undesirable.

**Vertical mosaic**  A view of Canadian society as constituting an ethnically divided stratification system, with the charter groups at the top, Native people at the bottom, and other ethnic immigrant groups fitting in depending on their entrance status.

# Contributors

**Cheryl Albas** is part-time associate professor at the University of Manitoba. She has an ongoing interest in higher education as it relates to university student life, where she is researching study types. Another area of interest is families and how the physical structure of households influences family interaction. In addition, she is involved in a long-term study of non-tenured faculty and the dynamics of knowledge production in university-based professional education. Her publications have appeared in *Handbook of Symbolic Interactionism* (2003) and the *Canadian Review of Sociology and Anthropology*.

**Daniel Albas** is professor of sociology at the University of Manitoba. His areas of interest include social psychology and non-verbal communication. He is currently studying university student study types and issues relative to academic integrity. His published works have appeared in a wide variety of national and international journals, including *Journal of Cross-Cultural Psychology*, *Sociological Quarterly*, *Symbolic Interaction*, and the *Canadian Review of Sociology and Anthropology*, and in *Handbook of Symbolic Interactionism* (2003).

**Bruce Arai** is associate professor of sociology at Wilfrid Laurier University. His research interests are in the areas of economic sociology, environmental sociology, and the sociology of education. Recent publications have appeared in *Education Policy Analysis Archives*, the *Canadian Journal of Education*, the *Canadian Review of Sociology and Anthropology*, and *Organization and Environment*.

**Pat Armstrong** is co-author of such books on health care as *Vital Signs: Nursing in Transition* (1990), *Take Care: Warning Signals for Canada's Health System* (1994), *Wasting Away: The Undermining of Canadian Health Care* (1996), *Universal Health Care: What the United States Can Learn from Canada* (1998), and *Heal Thyself: Managing Health Care Reform* (2000). She has also published on a wide variety of issues related to women's work and to social policy. She currently holds a CHSRF/CIHR Chair in Health Services, is a partner in the National Network on Environments and Women's Health, and chairs a working group on health reform. Her current research compares care management in Canada and the United States. She is involved as well with projects on nursing retention, quality indicators, gender-sensitive evidence, and the health-care labour force.

**Maureen Baker** is professor of sociology at the University of Auckland in New Zealand. She has previously taught in several Canadian universities, including the University of Toronto and McGill University, as well as in Australia. From 1984 to 1990, she worked as a senior researcher in Ottawa for the Canadian Parliament, specializing in policy issues relating to families, women, and children. Professor Baker is the author or editor of 13 books and over 60 articles on family trends, aging, adolescent women, cross-national family policies, women and work, and comparative restructuring. She has lived and worked in New Zealand since January 1998.

**Shyon Baumann** is assistant professor of sociology at the University of Toronto at Mississauga. He works in the areas of the sociology of art, culture, and the media. His current projects include an analysis of the intersection of racial and gender stereotypes in advertising. In addition, he has published articles on the history of the American film industry and tensions there between art and entertainment, and he is now working on a book on this topic.

**Joseph M. Bryant** teaches in the Department for the Study of Religion and in the Department of Sociology at the University of Toronto. His main areas of interest are historical sociology and the sociology of culture. He is the author of *Moral Codes and Social Structure in Ancient Greece* (1996), and his articles on sociological theory, ancient Greek social thought, and the rise of Christianity have appeared in a variety of journals, including the *Canadian Journal of Sociology*, the *British Journal of Sociology*, *History of Political Thought*, and *Archives européennes de sociologie*. He is currently working on a book entitled *Principles of Historical Social Science: A Primer on Theory and Method*.

**Juanne Nancarrow Clarke**, a medical sociologist at Wilfrid Laurier University, is the author of *Health, Illness and Medicine in Canada* (4th edn, 2004). One of her areas of research interest is the social construction of illness in the mass print media. Her current studies concern mass print media presentations of diseases such as cancer, heart disease, and AIDS and their portrayal in magazines and newspapers directed to audiences that differ in gender, social class, ethnicity, and age. Her daughter Lauren was diagnosed with leukemia in 1995, and subsequent to that Clarke has done research on parents whose children have cancer and has written a book, with her daughter, called *Finding Strength: A Mother and Daughter's Story of Childhood Cancer* (1999).

**James Curtis** was professor in the departments of Sociology and of Health Studies and Gerontology at the University of Waterloo, where he taught introductory sociology for many years until his death in 2005. Among other professional activities, he served as editor of the *Canadian Review of Sociology and Anthropology* and was a member of Statistics Canada's Advisory Committee on Social Conditions. He received the Outstanding Contributions Award from the Canadian Sociology and Anthropology Association for his overall research contributions to sociology. His publications included collaborations on sociology textbooks in the areas of introductory sociology, social problems, Canadian society, sociology of knowledge, social inequality, and physical activity and sport.

**Augie Fleras** is associate professor of sociology at the University of Waterloo. He is the author of numerous books, including *Social Problems in Canada* (Thompson: 3rd edn) and *Unequal Relations* (Thompson: 3rd edn; with Jean Elliott) and *Recalling Aotearoa* (Thompson, with Paul Spoonley).

**Randle Hart** is a doctoral candidate in the Department of Sociology at the University of Toronto. His co-authored articles on aging, immigration, cohabitation and marriage, and health have appeared in the *Journal of Marriage and the Family*, the *Journal of Family Issues*, *Social Biology*, *Research on Aging*, and the *International Journal of Sociology*.

**Julie Ann McMullin** is associate professor in the Department of Sociology at the University of Western Ontario. Her research explores how class, age, gender, ethnicity, and race structure inequality in paid work and families. She is also the author of *Understanding Inequality: Class, Age, Gender, Ethnicity, and Race in Canada* (2003).

**William Michelson** is S.D. Clark Professor of Sociology at the University of Toronto. His long-standing research interests focus on how people's everyday contexts, such as housing and urban infrastructure, bear on their lives and life chances. His publications include *Man and His Urban Environment: A Sociological Approach* (2nd edn, 1976), *Environmental Choice, Human Behavior, and Residential Satisfaction* (1977), *From Sun to Sun: Daily Obligations and Community Structure in the Lives of Employed Women* (1985), and the *Handbook of Environmental Sociology* (2002, co-edited by Riley Dunlap). In 1994, he was elected to the Royal Society of Canada.

**Richard John (Jack) Richardson**, now deceased, made a tremendous contribution to Canadian sociology. He received his BA with high distinction (double gold medallist) from the University of Toronto in 1978, his MA in sociology the following year, and his PhD in sociology, also at the University of Toronto, in 1984. From 1985, Dr Richardson was assistant professor at McMaster University in the Department of Sociology. Throughout his distinguished career, he won many awards; taught countless undergraduate classes in Canadian studies, organized behaviour, work and occupations, and research methods; and led many graduate-level courses in organizational sociology and comparative social systems. His main areas of interest were economic sociology, socio-economic change and development, social organization, formal organization, inter-corporate relations, and Canadian society. His publications include *The Social World* (1986), co-edited with Lorne Tepperman, and, the following year, *An Introduction to the Social World*, also co-edited with Lorne Tepperman. Dr Richardson also contributed to many books, including Robert Brym's *The Structure of the Canadian Capitalist Class* (1985), and to many journals, such as the *Canadian Journal of Sociology* and the *Canadian Review of Sociology and Anthropology*.

**Michael Rosenberg** has been a member of the Sociology Department at Dawson College from 1974 to 1997 and adjunct assistant professor at Concordia University since 1997. Dr Rosenberg has co-authored and edited several books, including *Social Deviance: An Integrated Approach* (1993) and *Quebec Society: Critical Issues* (1997). His previous research was on ethnicity and school system structure, and his current research is on the organizational capacity of ethnocultural minority groups in Montreal.

**Vincent Sacco** is professor in and former chair of the Department of Sociology, Queen's University. Prior to coming to Queen's, he was a member of the faculty of the School of Criminology at Simon Fraser University. His research interests relate to the causes of criminal victimization and media images of crime and deviance. His recent publications include co-authored books, such as *Crime Victims in Context* (1998) and *Advances in Criminological Theory* (2001), and articles in the *International Journal of Law and Psychiatry* and *Criminologie*.

**Peter R. Sinclair** is University Research Professor at Memorial University of Newfoundland. His current research is in global commodity systems and local restructuring, information technology occupations, timber dependency in rural Alabama and western Newfoundland, and interdisciplinary ecosystems theory. He is author of *From Traps to Draggers: Domestic Commodity Production in Northwest Newfoundland, 1850–1982* (1985) and *State Intervention and the Newfoundland Fisheries* (1987), as well as co-author of many books, including *When the Fish Are Gone: Ecological Disaster and Fishers of Northwest Newfoundland* (1997). Over 100 of his refereed articles, book chapters, and book reviews have been published since 1970.

**Michael Smith** is professor of sociology at McGill University. He has published extensively on a range of issues that fall, broadly, under the heading of economic sociology. His recent publications dealing with issues of globalization include "La mondialisation: à-t-elle un effet important sur le marché du travail dans les pays riches?" in *Une société monde? Les dynamiques sociales de la mondialisation* (2001) and "What Did the FTA and the NAFTA Do to the Canadian Labor Market?" in *Forum for Social Economics*.

**Pamela Sugiman** is associate professor in the Department of Sociology at McMaster University, where she teaches Introduction to Sociology and courses in gender relations. In the Arts and Science Programme at McMaster, she teaches in the area of diversity and multiculturalism. She is the author of *Labour's Dilemma: The Gender Politics of Auto Workers in Canada, 1937–1979* (1994) and of articles in several journals, including *Labour/Le Travail* and *Studies in Political Economy*. She is currently researching the internment experiences of Japanese-Canadian Nisei women during the Second World War.

**Lorne Tepperman**, professor of sociology at the University of Toronto, has, for three decades, advised both public and private organizations as an applied sociologist. His co-authored and co-edited books on women's work and family lives—*Lives of Their Own: The Individualization of Adult Women's Lives* (1993), *Next of Kin: An International Reader on Changing Families* (1993), *The Futures of the Family* (1995), and *Close Relations: An Introduction to the Sociology of*

*Families* (2000)—use Canadian and cross-national data to examine recent changes and project them into the future. His most recent work includes a co-authored book, *Social Problems: A Canadian Perspective* (2003), with James Curtis. He recently received the Outstanding Contributions Award from the Canadian Sociology and Anthropology Association for his overall research contributions to sociology.

**Frank Trovato** is professor of sociology at the University of Alberta, where he teaches introductory and advanced courses in demography and population studies. His publications include numerous articles in professional journals and three edited books. His research deals with topics spanning diverse aspects of demography and sociology: fertility, nuptiality, internal migration, immigrant health and mortality, sex and marital status differentials in mortality, and the social demography of racial, immigrant, and ethnic groups. Professor Trovato is president of the Canadian Population Society, the professional association of Canadian demographers outside of Quebec. He also reviews extensively for journals in the areas of population and general sociology, has served on the editorial boards of *Social Forces* and *Sociological Perspectives*, and is a former editor of *Canadian Studies in Population*.

**John Veugelers** is associate professor in the Department of Sociology at the University of Toronto. His previous research has focused on immigration politics and right-wing extremism in Canada and Europe, with recent articles appearing in *Current Sociology*, *Sociological Quarterly*, and the *Canadian Review of Sociology and Anthropology*. Under a project funded by the Social Sciences and Humanities Research Council of Canada, he is currently studying the politics of French repatriates from colonial North Africa. He was the recipient of an Outstanding Teaching Award from the University of Toronto in 2001.

**G. Keith Warriner** is associate professor and chair of the Department of Sociology, University of Waterloo. Dr

Warriner's major research interests concern natural resources and environmental sociology, as well as research methods and statistics. His studies have examined energy conservation, the west coast commercial fishing industry, adaptation to change by Ontario tobacco farmers, public participation in environmental decision-making, and grassroots environmental protest. His recent publications have investigated issues of environmental justice, urban dispersion and the housing preferences of city-dwellers, and bias contained in the measurement of socio-economic status by surveys.

**Sue Wilson** teaches in the School of Nutrition and is the associate dean of the Faculty of Community Services at Ryerson University. Her research interests include women's work, women's health, women at mid-life, students with dependant care responsibilities, the long-term effects of job loss, and breast cancer and spirituality. She has published a number of textbooks, including *Women, Work and Families* (4th edn, 1996), and several co-authored introductory and family sociology texts.

**Terry Wotherspoon** is professor of sociology and head of the Department of Sociology at the University of Saskatchewan, where he has worked since 1986. In addition to several years of teaching experience at elementary, secondary, and post-secondary levels, he has engaged in research and published widely on issues related to education, social policy, indigenous peoples, and social inequality in Canada. Among his many publications, he is co-author or co-editor of *First Nations: Race, Class and Gender Relations* (1993), *Multicultural Education in a Changing Global Economy: Canada and the Netherlands* (1995), and *The Legacy of School for Aboriginal People: Education, Oppression, and Emancipation* (2003). His book *The Sociology of Education in Canada: Critical Perspectives* (1998) received a book award from the Canadian Association for Foundations of Education. In 2002, his work was honoured by the Canadian Education Association with the presentation of a Whitworth Award for Educational Research.

# List of Tables, Figures, and Boxes

## Boxes

# Author Index

# Subject Index

Aalborg project, 312
Aboriginal people: confrontation with,
　195, 328; culture of, 54; education
　and, 256–7; gender and, 155, 181;
　health of, 228; politics and, 189;
　work and, 278–80
abuse, wife, 215–17
accounts, 91–2
adolescents: socialization and, 69–72,
　78–80; work and, 273, 281
advertising, 292, 293; men and, 155
aesthetics: culture and, 49–51
age: deviance and, 122; population and,
　233
aggression: socialization and, 69–70
AIDS; see HIV/AIDS
alienation, 17, 100–3, 270–1; class and,
　146–7; role and, 88
analysis: content, 27–8; secondary data,
　26–8
anomie, 17
art: culture and, 49–51
associations, voluntary, 323; see also
　organizations
audiences: mass media and, 294
authority: charismatic, 311–12; class
　and, 134–5, 141; families and, 204;
　rational-legal, 312–13; traditional,
　311; types of, 311–13
autonomy: political economy and,
　218–19

baby boom, 240
banking model, 249
behaviourism, 64
beliefs, 8–9; culture and, 37
bilingualism, 178, 179, 186–8
biological determinism, 21, 74, 153
body image: media and, 305
bohemians, 96–7
bourgeoisie, 43, 133–4, 143, 262
Bové, José, 364
breakdown approach, 324–5
Bretton Woods agreement, 365, 366,
　370
British: as charter group, 174, 176,
　178–9, 181–2
broadcasting, public, 295–6; see also
　mass media communication
bureaucracies, 14, 93, 99–109, 312–13;
　characteristics of, 100–1; function
　of, 103–8; informal organizations in,
　102–3; outside world and, 107–8
bureaucratic personality, 101–2

CAM (complementary and alternative
　medicines), 221
Canada Health Act, 230

capital: cultural, 50, 148–9; finance,
　367; social 148, social health and,
　227–8
capital-intensive industries, 368
capitalism, 12, 13, 43, 133–5, 261,
　262–4, 266–9; bureaucracies and,
　100; corporate, 263–4; culture and,
　378; education and, 245; family,
　263; gender and, 138–9; global,
　265–6; health and, 222, 232, 234;
　monopoly, 263–4; welfare, 264
careers, 85–6; deviant, 127–8;
　interruptions in, 168, 169
caregiving: gender and, 165–6
categories, 93–4; deviant, 123–8; ethnic,
　176
census, 201, 348
census metropolitan area, 352
central business district (CBD), 352–3
change: climate, 30; cultural, 40–1,
　51–4, 56–7; economic, 52; "for sake
　of change", 52–4; social, 28–31;
　technological, 52
children: care of, 168, 212–13; divorce
　and, 213–15; immigrant, 67;
　socialization of, 60–82; work and,
　265
China: Nike in, 267; politics in,
　313–14
Chinese: treatment of, 191–2
chromosomes, 154–5
cities: ecology of, 351–3; first, 345–7;
　global, 347–8, 376–8; immigration
　and, 184–6; theories of, 348–51
claims: deviance and, 124–6
class, 131–51; in Canada, 143–50;
　capitalist, 262–3; capitalist-executive,
　142, 143; conflict theory and,
　133–8; "death" of, 150; definition
　of, 140–2; deviance and, 116–17,
　122–3; inequality and, 142–50;
　Marxism and, 11, 133–5;
　measurement of, 140–2; media and,
　304–6; middle, 137–8, 146–50; new
　middle, 142–4, 146; old middle,
　142–4, 146; socialization and, 60,
　76–7; structural functionalism and,
　140–2; symbolic interactionism and,
　140; upper, 137; Weber and, 14,
　135–7; working, 137–8, 142–4,
　146–50, 262–3
class locations, 141–2
class situation, 135
class theories, 177
cliques, 96–9
collective agreement, 283
collective consciousness, 15, 50
collective effervescence, 16

colonialism, internal, 177–8
common-sense knowledge, 5–6
communication, 20, 46; globalization
　and, 379–80; see also mass media
　communication
communism, 264–5, 313
communities, 94–5; ethnic, 176;
　partial, 176, 179
"community", urbanism and, 353
complementary and alternative
　medicines, (CAM), 221
concentric ring pattern, 352–3
conflict theory, 15, 18–19; class and,
　132–8; deviance and, 125–6;
　education and, 245–7; health and,
　222–3; media and, 296–7
connection, direct/indirect, 94
constraints: trade agreements and,
　370–1
control: class and, 134–5; technical,
　270; work and, 269–71
control theory, 118–19
convergence: cultural, 378–81;
　economic, 373–5; media, 290
Co-operative Commonwealth
　Federation (CCF), 331
corporation, 263; multinational, 265,
　366
counter-movement, 323–4
credentials, immigrants and, 190, 195
crime: mass media and, 289, 298–9;
　see also deviance
cultural studies tradition, 44–5, 46
cultural support theory, 118
culture, 7, 8–10, 36–58; American, 56;
　"autonomy of", 46; Canadian,
　54–6; elements of, 38; globalization
　and, 364; high, 48, 49–50;
　homogenization of, 265, 378–81;
　meaning of, 37–42, 56–7; national,
　38–9; organizational, 105; place and
　time and, 38–41; popular, 48,
　49–50, 56; social theory and, 42–6;
　as symbolic, 41–2

data, existing, 26–8
death: causes of, 222–3, 225–6
decoding, 44
democracy, 313–14, 315–20; Canadian,
　320–22; direct, 315; participatory,
　327
democratization, 316
demographic transition theory, 340–2
demography, 339–45
descent, family, 204
deskilling, 146–7
determinism: biological, 21, 74, 153;
　urbanism and, 349